THE ENCYCLOPEDIA OF
ANCIENT CIVILIZATIONS

1997 Library Reference Edition published by Sharpe Reference
Sharpe Reference is an imprint of M.E. Sharpe, INC.

M.E. Sharpe INC
80 Business Park Drive
Armonk, NY 10504

AN ANDROMEDA BOOK

Produced and prepared by
Andromeda Oxford Ltd
11–15 The Vineyard
Abingdon
Oxfordshire OX14 3PX

© Andromeda Oxford Ltd 1997

Originated in Singapore
Printed in Italy

**Library of Congress
Cataloging-in-Publication Data**
The Encyclopedia of ancient civilizations
of the Near East and Mediterranean /
John Haywood, editor. p.   cm.
Includes bibliographic references and index.
Summary: Focuses on the civilizations of the ancient
Near East and Egypt, as well as Greece and Rome.
ISBN 1-56324-799-2
1. Middle East–Civilization–To 622–
Encyclopedias, Juvenile.
2. Mediterranean Region–Civilization–
Encyclopedias, Juvenile.
[1. Civilization, Ancient–Encyclopedias.]
I. Haywood, John, 1956-.
DS57. E47 1997
939'.4–dc21   97–13611
CIP
AC

Managing editor Susan Kennedy
Cartographic editor Richard Watts
Art editor Chris Munday

Picture manager Claire Turner
Cartographer Nathalie Johns
Editorial assistance Marian Dreier
Typesetter Brian Blackmore
Production Maria Harper
Index John Baines

THE ENCYCLOPEDIA OF
ANCIENT CIVILIZATIONS

—— *of the* ——

NEAR EAST AND MEDITERRANEAN

JOHN HAYWOOD

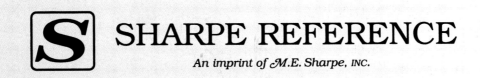

SHARPE REFERENCE

An imprint of M.E. Sharpe, INC.

CONTENTS

8   *Chronological tables*

12   *Introduction*

Part One   THE ANCIENT NEAR EAST AND EGYPT

16   The Neolithic in the Near East 12000–4000 BC

24   From City States to Kingdoms 4000–1600 BC

48   Kingdoms of Ancient Egypt 3000–332 BC

72   The Great Empires 1600–331 BC

Part Two   THE GREEK WORLD

108   The Bronze Age Aegean 2000–800 BC

120   Birth of the City States 800–500 BC

142   The Classical Age 500–356 BC

172   The Hellenistic Age 356–30 BC

Part Three   THE ROMAN WORLD

194   Early Rome & the Conquest of Italy 1000–272 BC

208   The Rise of Rome 272–30 BC

234   The Imperial Peace 44 BC–AD 284

266   The Christian Empire AD 284–610

290   *Glossary*

294   *Lists of Rulers*

297   *Acknowledgments and Further Reading*

298   *Index*

SITE FEATURES

18 Jericho

22 Chatal Huyuk

26 Uruk

30 Ur

56 Thebes

60 El-'Amarna

86 Kalhu

94 Babylon

102 Persepolis

110 Knossos

114 Mycenae

122 Paestum

126 Corinth

128 Olympia

131 Sparta

138 Athens

152 Delphi

181 Alexandria

189 Ay Khanoum

200 Archaic Rome

220 Republican Rome

236 Pompeii

258 Imperial Rome

262 Palmyra

271 Split

273 Constantinople

274 Ephesus

278 Early Christian Rome

284 Leptis Magna

FEATURES

42 Ziggurats

44 Early Technology

46 The Origins of Writing

64 Pyramids: 1

66 Pyramids: 2

68 Warfare in Ancient Egypt

70 Egyptian Religion

93 Science of the Near East

104 Warfare in the Ancient Near East

125 Gods and Goddesses of Olympos

134 Archaic Art

136 Sport in the Greek World

146 The Greek Soldier

150 Greek Medicine

158 Decorative Pottery

162 The Greek Theater

174 The Royal Tombs of Macedon

196 The Etruscans

214 Roman Religion

224 Roman Roads

232 Parthians and Sasanians

240 Roman Gaul

246 The Imperial Army

254 Roman Technology

268 Frontiers of the Empire

MAPS AND PLANS

16	The Birth of Farming
18	Jericho
20	The Spread of Farming Settlements
22	Chatal Huyuk
24	The First Cities
26	Uruk
29	The Conquests of the Kings of Agade
31	Ur
32	The Empire of the 3rd Dynasty of Ur
35	The Indus Valley Civilization
36	Rivalry between City States 1990–1936 BC, 1910 BC, 1879 BC, 1802 BC
39	The Kingdom of Shamshi-Adad
40	The Kingdom of Hammurabi
43	The Ziggurats of Mesopotamia
49	Predynastic and Early Dynastic Egypt
51	Old Kingdom Egypt
52	The Middle Kingdom and Second Intermediate Period
55	The Empire of the New Kingdom
57	Thebes
58	The Levant of the Amarna Letters
61	El-'Amarna
63	Civil War and the Nubian Conquest
66	The Pyramids of Egypt
69	The Battle of Qadesh
73	The Empire of Mittani
74	The Hittite Empire
75	Hattusas
76	The Kassite Kingdom of Babylon
78	The Middle Assyrian Kingdom
79	The Kingdom of David
79	The Kingdom of Solomon
81	The Trading Empire of the Phoenicians
82	Assyrian Revival in the 9th Century
84	The Kingdom of Urartu
87	Kalhu
89	The Assyrian Empire in the Late 8th Century
90	The End of the Assyrian Empire
91	Nineveh
94	Babylon
96	The Conquests of Cyrus
98	The Empire of Darius the Great
108	The Mycenaean World
109	Minoan Crete
110	Knossos
113	The Mycenaean Kingdoms of Greece
114	Mycenae
117	The Dark Age in the Aegean
119	Dialects of the Aegean
120	Greek Colonization
123	Paestum
126	Corinth
127	The Age of Tyrannies
128	Olympia
130	Spartan Expansion
131	Sparta
133	6th-Century Athens
137	Olympic Footrace Winners
138	Athens
142	The Silver Mines of Laurion
143	The Rise of the Persian Empire
144	Persian Campaigns against Greece
144	The Persian Wars: Battle Plans
148	The Known World of the Greeks
150	Sanctuaries of Asklepios
153	Delphi
154	The Classical Greek Legacy
156	The Athenian Empire 460–446 BC
157	The Peloponnesian War
157	Pylos and Sphakteria 425 BC

157	The Siege of Syracuse 415–413 BC	*222*	The Social War 91–89 BC
163	The Distribution of Greek Theaters	*225*	The Roman Roads of Italy
166	Poets and Philosophers of the Greek World	*227*	Colonization in Italy, 1st Century BC
169	The Second Athenian League	*228*	Campaigns of Julius Caesar
172	The Expansion of Macedon	*233*	The Parthian and Sasanian Empires
176	The March of the Ten Thousand	*235*	The Empire of Augustus
180	The Conquests of Alexander the Great	*237*	The Eruption of Vesuvius
181	Alexandria	*241*	Roman Gaul
182	The Migrations of the Celts	*242*	The Wars of Succession 68–69 BC
184	The Successor Kingdoms 303 BC	*245*	The Roman Empire to AD 106
185	The Successor Kingdoms 240 BC, 188 BC	*249*	The Jewish World to AD 300
186	The Successor Kingdoms 129 BC	*251*	Trade in the Roman Empire
187	Egypt under the Ptolemies	*252*	Silk and Spice Routes
189	Ay Khanoum	*253*	Languages, Urbanization and Agriculture
191	The Successor Kingdoms 90 BC, 63 BC	*258*	Imperial Rome
194	The Languages of Pre-Roman Italy	*260*	The Germanic Migrations
195	Bronze and Iron Age Sites in Italy	*263*	Palmyra
197	Etruscan Cities of the 6th Century BC	*264*	The 3rd-Century Invasions
198	Sites in Latium Vetus	*265*	The Saxon Shore Defenses
200	Archaic Rome	*266*	Diocletian's Reorganization of the Empire
202	The Early Growth of Rome		
203	The Celts in Northern Italy	*268*	Hadrian's Wall
205	The Conquest and Colonization of Italy 334–241 BC	*268*	The Rhine-Danube *limes*
		269	The Syrian *limes*
205	Central Italy in 338 BC	*273*	Constantinople
206	The Growth of Roman Power in Italy 302 BC, 290 BC	*275*	Ephesus
		276	Distribution of Christian Churches c. 325
207	The Growth of Roman Power in Italy 241 BC	*277*	Julian's Mesopotamian Campaign AD 363
		279	Early Christian Rome
208	The First Punic War 264–241 BC	*280*	Monasticism 300–500
211	The Second Punic War 218–202 BC	*282*	The First Wave of Invasions
213	Colonization 2nd Century BC	*283*	Pressure on the Empire Increases
215	Cult Centers of Southern Italy	*284*	Leptis Magna
216	The Expansion of Roman Power 201–70 BC	*286*	The End of the Western Empire
219	Land Reforms of the Gracchi	*287*	The Barbarian Kingdoms c. 526
220	Republican Rome	*289*	The Empire of Justinian

	10,000 BC	5000 BC	3000 BC	2500 BC	2000 BC	1750 BC	1500 BC

MESOPOTAMIA & THE NEAR EAST

Political

- **c.9000** Walled settlement built at Jericho
- **c.3500** City states develop in Sumer
- **2334–2279** Sargon of Agade conquers Mesopotamia
- **2112–2095** Ur-Nammu founds 3rd Dynasty of Ur
- **c.1813–1781** Ashur becomes a great power under Shamshi-Adad
- **1792–1750** Babylon dominates Mesopotamia under Hammurabi
- **c.1550–1400** Mitta is dominant state in Near East
- **c.1344–132** Suppilulian establishes Hittite emp
- **1595** Babylon sacked by Hittites

Cultural

- **c.10,000** Natufian hunter–gatherers harvest wild cereals
- **c.9300** First farmers
- **c.7000** Earliest use of pottery
- **c.6200** Earliest copper smelting in Anotolia
- **c.5500** Development of irrigation
- **c.4500** Plow and sailing ships in use
- **3800** Arsenical bronze in use
- **c.3400** Writing in use in Mesopotamia
- **c.3000** Development of cuneiform script
- **c.3000** Tin bronze in use
- **c.2350** Urukagina, king of Lagash, issues earliest known law code
- **c.2100** First ziggurats built in Sumer
- **c.1600** Canaanites invent first alphabetic script
- **c.1600** Earliest glass
- **c.1700** Horse-drawn war chariots in use
- **c.1500** Ironworking in Near East

EGYPT

Political

- **c.3000** Early Dynastic period
- **2649–2134** Old Kingdom period
- **c.3000** Unification of Egypt by Narmer
- **c.3500** Desertification of the Sahara begins
- **c.3500** First towns develop in Egypt
- **2134–2040** First Intermediate period. Egypt splits into two kingdoms
- **2040–1640** Middle Kingdom period
- **1878–1841** Reign of Senwosret III. Middle Kingdom at its peak
- **1640–1550** Second Intermediate period. Hyksos rule Lower Egypt
- **1550–1070** New Kingdom period
- **1504–1492** Tuthmosis III conquers Nubia and the Levant

Cultural

- **c.6000** Farming begins in the Nile Valley
- **7000–6000** Cattle herding and cereal cultivation in the eastern Sahara
- **c.3000** Development of hieroglyphic script
- **c.3500** Copper working in Egypt
- **c.4000** Sailing ships in use on the Nile
- **c.2630** First pyramid built at Saqqara ("Step Pyramid")
- **c.2550** Great Pyramid at Giza built
- **c.2150** Period of low Nile floods brings succession of famines
- **c.2000** Classical period of Ancient Egyptian literature
- **c.1800** Bronze working introduced in Egypt
- **c.1470** Queen Hatshepsut se trading expedi to East Africa

GREECE & THE EASTERN MEDITERRANEAN

Political

- **c.2000** Emergence of Minoan palace civilization on Crete
- **c.1600** Emergence of Mycenaean civilization in Greece
- **c.1700** Knossos becomes dominant center of palace culture on Crete
- **c.1450** Mycenaeans conquer Crete and colonize coast of Anato
- **c.1628** Eruption of Thera destroys Minoan town of Akro

Cultural

- **c.6500** Farming begins in Greece and the Balkans
- **c.6200** Farming spreads to Italy
- **c.4500** Copper smelting in the Balkans. Plow introduced to Europe
- **c.3000** Bronze in use throughout the Aegean region
- **c.2000** Development of Minoan hieroglyphic script
- **c.1700** Development of Minoan "Linear A" script
- **c.1450** Development Mycenaean "Linear B" scr
- **16th century** Richly furnished shaft burials at Mycenae

- **1243–1207** Assyrian expansion under Tukulti-ninurta I
- **c.1000** Aramaean nomad invasions: decline of Assyria and Babylon
- **824** Internal disputes following death of Shalmaneser III cause temporary Assyrian decline
- **680–627** Assyrian empire reaches greatest extent under Esarhaddon and Ashurbanipal
- **559–530** Rise of Persia under Cyrus the Great

- **c.1200** Unknown invaders destroy Hittite empire
- **934–912** Reign of Ashur-dan II: Assyrian recovery begins
- **744–727** Tiglath-pileser III reforms administration of army of Assyrian empire
- **547** Cyrus conquers Lydia

- **c.1220–1100** Hebrews settle in Canaan
- **c.1000** King David captures Jerusalem
- **928** After the death of Solomon, the kingdom of the Hebrews divides into Israel and Judah
- **c.763–734** Kingdom of Urartu at its peak during reign of Sarduri II
- **612** Babylonians and Medes overthrow Assyrian empire
- **539** Cyrus conquers Babylonian empire

- **c.1200–1000** New waves of migration initiate cultural dark age
- **c.700** Signs of the zodiac identified by Babylonian astrologers
- **630–553** Life of Zoroaster, Persian prophet, founder of Zoroastrianism

- **9th century** First use of cavalry
- **c.700** First coinage in use in Lydia (Anatolia)
- **c.600** "Babylonian" captivity of Hebrews: books of Old Testament approach their present form

- **673** Babylonian astrologers accurately predict solar eclipse

- **1070–712** Third Intermediate period: royal power in decline
- **712–332** Late Period

- **290–1224** Ramses II builds temples at Abu Simbel
- **924** Shoshenq I ravages Israel and Judah
- **712–671** Nubian dynasty rules Egypt
- **525** Persians under Cambyses conquer Egypt

- **1285** Battle of Qadesh: Ramses II narrowly avoids defeat by the Hittites
- **835–783** Dynastic disputes during the reign of Shoshenq III cause the Egyptian state to fragment
- **671–651** Assyrians occupy Egypt

- **c1180** Ramses III defeats the "Sea Peoples" in the delta

- **8th century** Ironworking introduced to Egypt
- **c.600** Necho II builds a canal linking the Nile with the Red Sea

- **53–1335** Akhenaten omotes cult of the Aten as te religion

- **c.1200** Mycenae, Pylos and other centers destroyed by invaders
- **c.800–500** Main period of Greek colonization overseas
- **c.657** Kypselos becomes
- **499** Ionian Greeks rebel against Persian rule

- **c.900** founding of Sparta
- **814** Traditional date of founding of Carthage by the Phoenicians
- **594** Solon reforms the Athenian constitution

- **1184** Traditional date for the sack of Troy
- **546** Peisistratos becomes tyrant in Athens

- **753** Traditional date of Rome's founding by Romulus

- **c.1100** Dorians invade Greece
- **509–507** Athens becomes a democracy

- **730–710** Spartans conquer Messenia

- **c.1200–800** The Aegean dark age. Towns and villages are abandoned and knowledge of writing disappears
- **c.800** Greeks adopt the Phoenician alphabet and introduce vowel signs
- **8th century** Homer composes the *Iliad* and the *Odyssey*
- **c.550** Thespis writes the first dramas

- **c.530** Pythagoras of Samos, early Greek philosopher, scientist and mathematician

- **776** Earliest recorded Olympic games
- **620–621** Earliest Athenian law code issued by Drakon

- **c.750** Beginning of the Hallstatt ("Celtic") Iron Age in central Europe
- **c.600** Coinage in use in Greece

- **c.1000** Iron in widespread use in Greece

THE ROMAN WORLD

Political

- **509** Roman monarchy overthrown and republic established
- **494** Roman people form an assembly (the *concilium plebis*) to represent their interests
- **396** Capture of Etruscan city of Veii begins Roman conquest of Italy
- **390** Gauls sack Rome
- **343–290** Wars between Rome and Samnites, inhabitants of central south Italy
- **272** Capture of Tarentum completes Roman conquest of central and south Italy
- **264–241** Rome wins 1st Punic war against Carthage
- **225–192** Rome conquers Cisalpine Gaul (northern Italy)
- **218–202** Rome wins 2nd Punic war against Carthage
- **91–98** The Social war: Rome's Italian allies fight for citizenship
- **133** Tribune Gaius Gracchus attempts land reform
- **107–100** Marius reforms army
- **149–146** Final defeat and destruction of Carthage
- **58–52** Julius Caesar conquers Gaul
- **48** Caesar defeats Pompey
- **44** Murder of Julius Caesar leads to civil war
- **31** Octavian's victory at Actium ends civil war
- **27** Augustus (Octavian) "restores" republic: imperial rule begins

Cultural

- **c.450** The Laws of the Twelve Tables: earliest Roman law code
- **c.400** Gauls settle in the Po valley, eclipsing Etruscan civilization
- **378** City walls built around Rome
- **312** The Via Appia, the first Roman road, built between Rome and Capua
- **250–184** Plautus, comic playwright
- **c.200** Greek influence on Roman civilization becomes marked
- **196** First triumphal arch built in Rome
- **148** First Greek-style marble temple built in Rome
- **106–43** Cicero, lawyer, statesman and writer
- **70–19** Virgil, poet: author of the *Aeneid*
- **c.59 BC–AD 17** Livy, historian of Rome
- **55** Pompey builds the first theater in Rome
- **51** Caesar publishes the *Gallic War*
- **43 BC–AD 17** Ovid, poet

EGYPT AND THE NEAR EAST

Political

- **401** Cyrus the Younger recruits 10,000 Greek mercenaries to fight for him in Persia
- **334–328** Persian empire conquered by Alexander the Great
- **332** Egypt conquered by Alexander
- **312** Babylon captured by Seleukos, who founds Seleukid kingdom
- **304–31** Egypt ruled by Ptolemies
- **239** Independent Hellenistic kingdom of Bactria established
- **238** Arsaces I wins Parthian independence
- **190** Seleukid king Antiochos III defeated by Romans at Magnesia
- **166–160** Judas Maccabeus leads Jewish rebellion against Seleukid rule
- **141** Parthia conquers Mesopotamia
- **c.135** Kushan nomads destroy Bactrian kingdom
- **83** Fall of the Seleukid kingdom
- **53** Parthians defeat Roman army at Carrhae
- **30** Egypt annexed by Rome on death of Cleopatra VII

Cultural

- **410** Earliest surviving horoscope from Babylon
- **332** Alexander founds Alexandria in Egypt
- **300** Museum at Alexandria founded by Ptolemy
- **280** The Pharos, the greatest lighthouse of antiquity, built at Alexandria
- **c.105** College of technology founded at Alexandria
- **c.50** Glassblowing technique invented in Phoenicia
- **c.6 BC–AD 30** Life of Jesus of Nazareth

THE GREEK WORLD

Political

- **490** Athenians defeat Persian army at Marathon
- **480–479** Persian invasion of Xerxes retreats after Greek victories at Salamis and Plataea
- **431–404** Peloponnesian war between Sparta and Athens
- **371** Thebans break Spartan power at battle of Leuktra
- **359–336** Under Philip II, Macedon becomes dominant power in Greece
- **336–323** Reign of Alexander the Great
- **279–278** Celts invade Greece and Anatolia
- **214–205** First Macedonian war leads to Roman intervention in Greece
- **168** Romans abolish Macedonian monarchy after battle of Pydna
- **146** Romans destroy Corinth and make Greece the Roman province of Achaea

Cultural

- **525–456** Aeschylus, tragic dramatist
- **497–406** Sophocles, tragic dramatist
- **484–425** Herodotus, historian
- **469–399** Socrates, philosopher
- **445–385** Aristophanes, comic dramatist
- **c.429–347** Plato, philosopher and founder of the Academy at Athens
- **447–432** Parthenon constructed
- **384–322** Aristotle, philosopher
- **336–263** Zeno, founder of Stoicism
- **c.325–300** Pytheas of Massilia circumnavigates Britain
- **280–212** Archimedes, mathematician
- **270–294** Erastosthenes, astronomer and geographer
- **280** Colossos of Rhodes built
- **c.140** Statue of Venus de Milo

Political Events

- **9** Roman attempt to conquer Germany is defeated
- **14** Death of Augustus, accession of Tiberius
- **32** Food shortages in Rome lead to rioting
- **43** Claudius begins the conquest of Britain
- **64** Nero initiates first persecution of Christians
- **68–9** Civil war breaks out on death of Nero: "Year of Four Emperors"
- **106** Trajan conquers Dacia
- **114–117** Trajan conquers Armenia and Mesopotamia
- **122–3** Hadrian builds a defensive wall across northern Britain

- **167** Marcomanni (German invaders) sack Aquileia.
- **165–7** Plague rages throughout empire
- **193–7** Civil war follows murder of Commodus
- **212** Caracalla grants Roman citizenship to all free inhabitants of the empire
- **235–284** Period of extreme political instability and civil war: 26 emperors in 49 years
- **c.250** Debasement of coinage causes acute inflation
- **272** Rebel Queen Zenobia of Palmyra defeated by Rome
- **284–305** Diocletian's reforms restore political stability
- **301** Diocletian issues price edict in attempt to end inflation
- **303–11** Last major persecution of Christians
- **313** After victory at the Milvian Bridge, Constantine is sole ruler in West

- **376** Valens allows Visigoths to settle in the empire as protection from the Huns
- **378** Visigoths rebel and kill Valens at battle of Adrianople
- **395** Permanent division of empire into eastern and western parts
- **406** Vandals, Sueves and Alans invade Gaul
- **410** Visigoths under Alaric sack Rome. Britain becomes independent
- **439** Vandals capture Carthage
- **476** End of Roman empire in the west. Barbarian general Odoacer proclaimed king of Italy
- **489–93** Theodoric, king of Ostrogoths, conquers Italy
- **533–4** Justinian's forces retake Carthage from the Vandals
- **536–62** Justinian's forces conquer Ostrogothic kingdom of Italy
- **568–82** Lombards invade and occupy much of Italy

- **610–641** Reforms of emperor Heraclius mark end of Eastern Roman empire and beginning of Byzantine empire

Cultural Events

- **c.1–50** Alexandrian merchants make direct trading voyages to India
- **1st century** Mithraism spreads to Roman empire from Persia
- **c.27** fl. Vitruvius, architect
- **42–46** St Paul's missionary journeys help spread Christianity
- **c.55–116** Tacitus, historian
- **75–161** Suetonius, historian
- **79** Pliny the Elder killed while investigating eruption of Vesuvius. Destruction of Pompeii
- **113** Trajan's column erected in Rome
- **125–148** fl. Ptolemy of Alexandria, astronomer and geographer

- **130–200** Galen, physician
- **c174–80** Emperor Marcus Aurelius writes *Meditations*
- **c.200** Empire's road system completed
- **205–69** Plotinus, Neoplatonic philosopher
- **260–340** Eusebius of Caesarea, historian of the early church

- **324** Constantine founds Constantinople as new capital
- **354–430** Augustine, theologian, author of the *City of God*
- **361–3** Julian attempts to revive paganism in empire
- **391** Theodosius outlaws paganism and abolishes the Olympic Games
- **c313** Edict of Milan grants toleration to Christians
- **313–22** First Christian basilica built at Rome

- **c.480–522** Boethius, last significant philosopher of the Classical tradition
- **499–566** Procopius, historian of Justinian's wars.
- **529–34** Justinian orders new codification of Roman law
- **529** Justinian closes the Platonic Academy at Athens

Political

- **18** Parthians invade India

- **197** Ctesiphon, the Parthian capital, sacked by the Romans
- **c.200** German tribes begin to form powerful confederations
- **224–6** Persian Sasanian dynasty overthrow the Parthians
- **260** Sasanian king Shapur I defeats Roman army at Edessa and captures emperor Valerian

- **c.372** Huns defeat the Ostrogothic king Ermanaric
- **484** Huns kill Sasanian king Peroz

- **607–627** Sasanian empire defeated in war with Eastern Roman/Byzantine empire
- **634–652** Arabs overrun Sasanian empire

Cultural

- **217–77** Life of Mani, founder of Manichaeanism
- **c.220–40** Zoroastrianism established as state religion in Persia
- **c.300** Armenia is first state to adopt Christianity as official religion

- **c.400** Christianity introduced to Ireland
- **5th century** Windmill invented in Persia
- **c.450** Anglo-Saxon migrations to Britain begin

- **c.570–632** Life of Muhammad

INTRODUCTION

IT IS GENERALLY AGREED THAT THE EMERGENCE OF CIVILIZATION *has been one of the most important developments in human history. But what do archeologists and ancient historians mean by "civilization"? There is no universally accepted definition, but most experts would argue that the following characteristics are all signs that high levels of social and economic complexity and of material and technological achievement have been reached: fulltime specialization of labor; the collection and redistribution of surplus food and other products; a class structure; state organization; monumental public works; long-distance trade; standardized monumental artwork; writing; knowledge of arithmetic, geometry and astronomy.*

Though civilizations have developed independently in many parts of the world, and at many different times, the first societies to display all these characteristics emerged in the ancient Near East (the region of southwest Asia encompassed by the Mediterranean Sea in the west, the Anatolian peninsula in the north, the Zagros mountains in the east and the Arabian desert in the south, the heartland of which is the fertile floodplain of the Euphrates and Tigris rivers), the Nile valley, and the eastern Mediterranean between c.3500 and 2000 BC.

The history of the ancient civilizations of the Near East and the Mediterranean extends over more than 4000 years. Their endurance dwarfs that of our own industrial civilization, which is little more than 200 years old. The story is not one of continuous progress: there were many "dark ages" when civilizations fell and written records became scarce or non-existent. But always much was preserved to be handed on to succeeding civilizations.

The first civilizations – in Mesopotamia, Egypt, the Indus valley and Crete – developed more or less in isolation from each other. Ideas traveled slowly, and each had little in common with the others, though they exercised a strong influence – through trade, culture and war – on their pre-civilized neighbors, spurring their own development toward state organization and cultural attainment. From the second millennium BC on, increasing trade, migration, and the rise of great conquerors forced the ancient civilizations into ever closer contact with one another. The creation of the Persian empire in the 6th century BC brought together elements of

all the major civilizations of the time in a single state, promoting a greater cultural mixing than ever before. After the Persian empire was conquered by Alexander the Great, a Macedonian Greek, in 331 BC, a Greek could find himself equally at home in Spain, Egypt or central Asia. The Roman empire, heir to the cultural traditions of the Greek world, imposed a greater degree of uniformity than ever before. By the beginning of the Christian era the Mediterranean and the Near East were dominated by just two traditions of civilization, the Greco-Roman and the Persian.

The decline of the ancient world was a complex process, lasting more than three centuries and involving the rise of new cultural and political forces. The triumph of Christianity in the 4th century had begun to transform the Roman empire socially and culturally even before barbarian invaders overran its western provinces in the 5th century. The Greek-speaking eastern Roman empire developed its own Christian "Byzantine" civilization, while the barbarian west became a cultural and economic backwater for hundreds of years. Finally, in the early 7th century, the Arabs, newly converted to Islam, swept away the entire Persian empire and conquered the Middle East, North Africa and Spain in only a few decades. Their vigorous new civilization took hold from the Indus valley to the Atlantic Ocean.

These new civilizations, however, looked back to the ancient world for inspiration: both the "western" and Islamic civilizations are built on foundations laid down by the ancient civilizations. Nearly 1500 years after they came to an end, they continue to exert a powerful influence. Monotheism, democracy, republicanism, alphabetic writing, the 24-hour day and the 7-day week are only a few ideas of the ancient world that still shape our lives today.

JOHN HAYWOOD

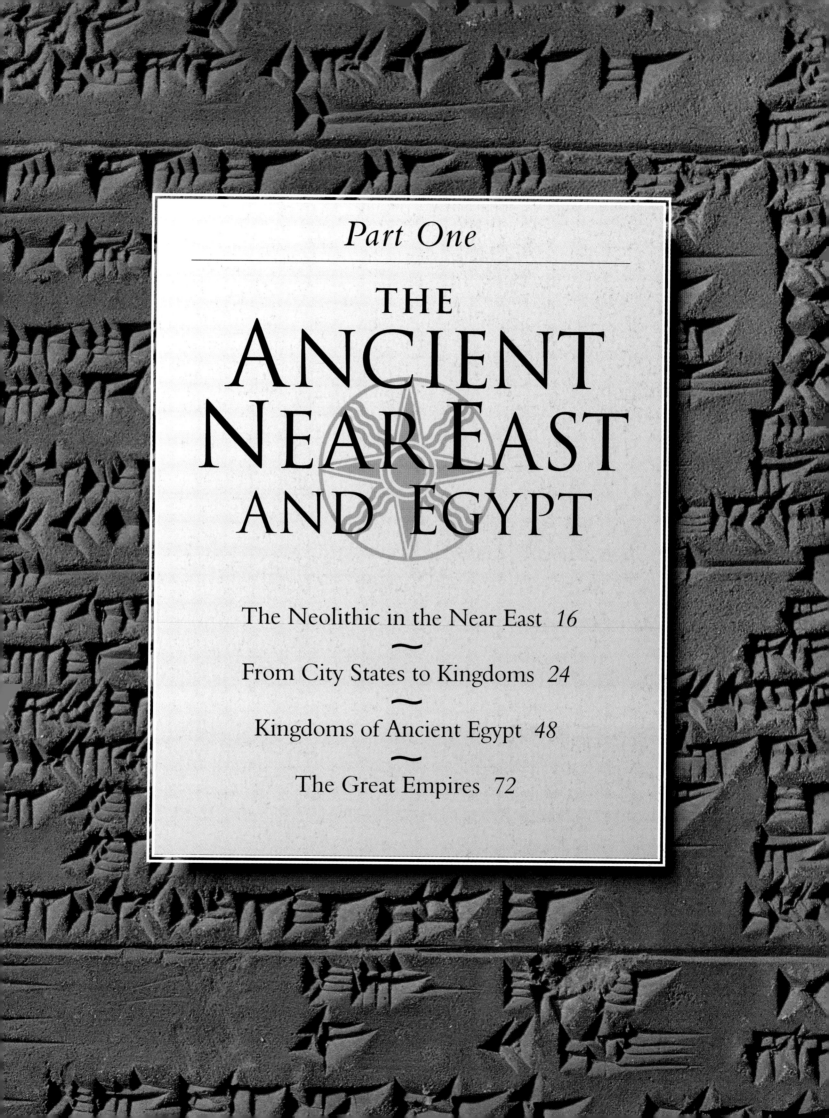

Part One

THE
ANCIENT
NEAR EAST
AND EGYPT

The Neolithic in the Near East *16*

~

From City States to Kingdoms *24*

~

Kingdoms of Ancient Egypt *48*

~

The Great Empires *72*

The Neolithic in the Near East

12000 – 4000 BC

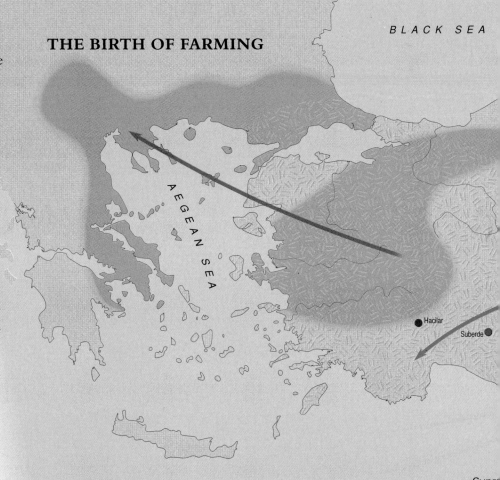

THE BIRTH OF FARMING

The basis of the early civilizations of the Near East – as of all human civilizations before the Industrial Revolution – was farming. The Fertile Crescent, a region of good soils and light but reliable rainfall, extends in an arc from Israel through Lebanon, Syria and southern Turkey to the foothills of Iraq's Zagros mountains near the Persian Gulf. It was here that the shift from a nomadic hunting–gathering existence to a reliance on farming for food first took place. During the late Ice Age the climate of this region was milder and wetter than it is today and wild cereals such as barley, einkorn and emmer wheat flourished, together with pulses, almond, oak and pistachio trees. These provided an abundant supply of food for the local hunter–gatherer peoples of the late Paleolithic (Epipaleolithic) or Old Stone Age. The most important of such groups were the Natufians of the Levant who around 10,500 BC began to adopt a more settled way of life, living in villages of wooden huts built on stone foundations, and migrating at certain times of the year to seasonal camps. They hunted gazelle, but their staple food was wild cereals which they harvested with stone reaping knives.

During the 9th millennium BC the climate became drier and the natural range of wild cereals began to shrink. To secure their food supply, the Natufians planted the seeds of wild cereals close to their settlements. Around 8000 BC they learned to breed wild cereals selectively for characteristics (such as bigger heads) that increased their yield and made them easier to harvest. Within a few centuries domesticated strains of barley, einkorn and emmer wheat had appeared. These transitional (or "Proto-Neolithic") farmers continued to obtain a great part of their food supply by hunting and gathering from the wild, but as the population rose their dependence on farming increased. By around 7500 communities with a full farming economy had developed, marking the beginning of what archeologists term the Neolithic or New Stone Age.

The Natufians were not alone in finding ways to control the natural food supply. In parts of southern Anatolia and the Zagros mountains hunter–gatherers intensified their management of flocks of wild sheep and goats. Examination of animal bones found on a settlement at Zawi Chemi Shanidar (c. 9000 BC) show that the inhabitants killed and ate mainly immature sheep. If these animals had been obtained by hunting alone, there would have been a more random distribution of ages, and it therefore seems likely that sheep were kept in pens and selectively culled. Wild cereals were also cultivated at Zawi Chemi Shanidar. Since these early farmers did not use pottery, this period of the Neolithic is known as the Aceramic or prepottery Neolithic. Pottery first began to be made around 7000. Its usefulness in

16

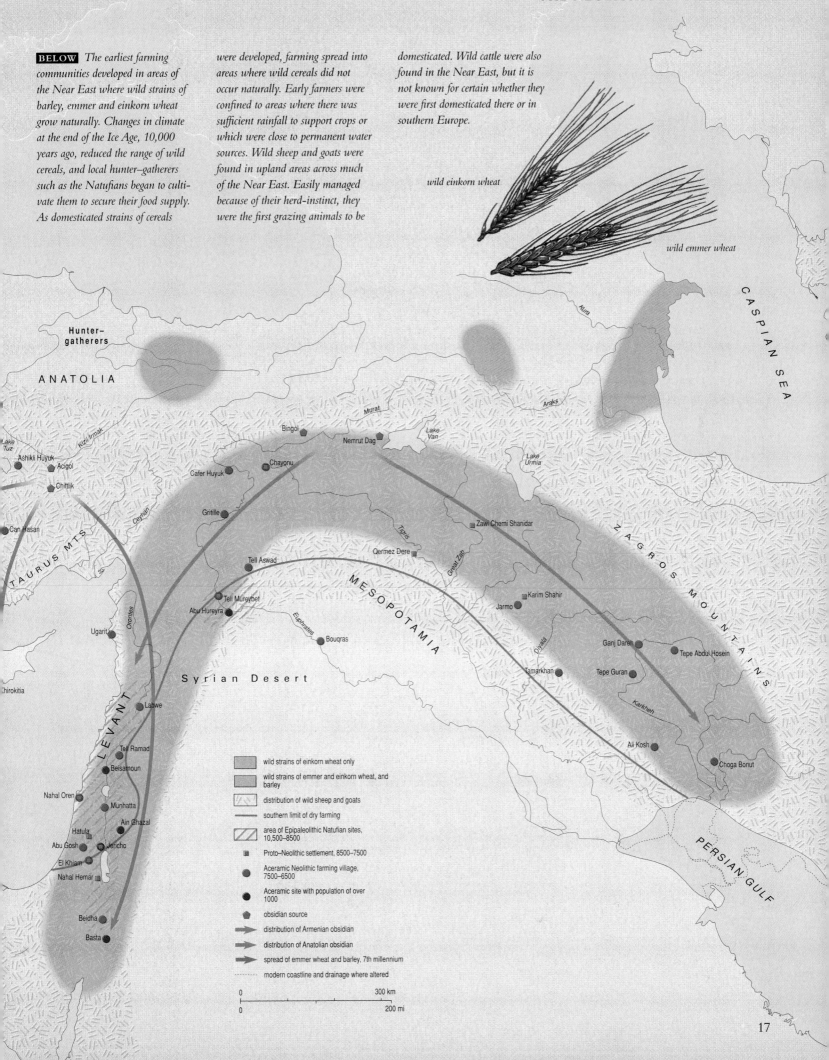

BELOW *The earliest farming communities developed in areas of the Near East where wild strains of barley, emmer and einkorn wheat grow naturally. Changes in climate at the end of the Ice Age, 10,000 years ago, reduced the range of wild cereals, and local hunter–gatherers such as the Natufians began to cultivate them to secure their food supply. As domesticated strains of cereals were developed, farming spread into areas where wild cereals did not occur naturally. Early farmers were confined to areas where there was sufficient rainfall to support crops or which were close to permanent water sources. Wild sheep and goats were found in upland areas across much of the Near East. Easily managed because of their herd-instinct, they were the first grazing animals to be domesticated. Wild cattle were also found in the Near East, but it is not known for certain whether they were first domesticated there or in southern Europe.*

wild einkorn wheat

wild emmer wheat

CASPIAN SEA

Hunter-gatherers

ANATOLIA

Lake Tuz

Ashikli Huyuk
Acigol
Chiftlik

Can Hasan

Kizil Irmak

Murat

Bingol

Nemrut Dag

Lake Van

Lake Urmia

Araks

Kura

Chayonu

Cafer Huyuk

Gritille

Ceyhan

TAURUS MTS

Tigris

Zawi Chemi Shanidar

ZAGROS MOUNTAINS

Tell Aswad

Qermez Dere

Great Zab

MESOPOTAMIA

Tell Mureybet

Abu Hureyra

Karim Shahir

Jarmo

Orontes

Ugarit

Euphrates

Bouqras

Diyala

Ganj Dareh

Tepe Abdul Hosein

Tamarkhan

Tepe Guran

Syrian Desert

Chirokitia

LEVANT

Labwe

Karkheh

Ali Kosh

Choga Bonut

Tell Ramad
Beisamoun

Nahal Oren
Munhatta
Ain Ghazal

Hatula
Abu Gosh
Jericho
El Khiam
Nahal Hemar

PERSIAN GULF

Beidha

Basta

	wild strains of einkorn wheat only
	wild strains of emmer and einkorn wheat, and barley
	distribution of wild sheep and goats
	southern limit of dry farming
	area of Epipaleolithic Natufian sites, 10,500–8500
	Proto–Neolithic settlement, 8500–7500
	Aceramic Neolithic farming village, 7500–6500
	Aceramic site with population of over 1000
	obsidian source
	distribution of Armenian obsidian
	distribution of Anatolian obsidian
	spread of emmer wheat and barley, 7th millennium
	modern coastline and drainage where altered

0   300 km
0   200 mi

17

JERICHO

By the time that Jericho first enters the historical record as the city whose walls were tumbled by the sound of the Israelites' trumpets, around 1250 BC, the settlement was already almost 7000 years old. The site of ancient Jericho, now known as Tell al-Sultan, lies 656 feet (200 m) below sea level in the blisteringly hot valley of the Dead Sea. A permanent spring led Natufian hunter–gatherers to camp here in the 10th millennium BC. The site was permanently occupied in the Proto-Neolithic period and by 8000 a settlement of some 1500 people had grown up. Jericho's permanent water supply may have excited the envy of its neighbors as it was strongly fortified with masonry walls and a tower. Domesticated barley and emmer wheat, pulses and figs were cultivated but wild animals – gazelle, wild sheep and goats – were also important sources of food. These early farmers lived in huts of sun-dried mudbricks. This is the earliest known use of what was to become the most important building material of the Near East. Mudbrick was easy to produce and when a house fell into disrepair it was simply knocked down and replaced by a new one. Over the centuries, successive rebuildings on the same site produced a high mound of debris. These settlement mounds, called a *tell* in Arabic (Turkish *huyuk*, Persian *tepe*), are the most characteristic archeological sites of the Near East. Excavation of the layers of debris, and the finds within them, provides evidence of successive periods of occupation. Deposits at Jericho are particularly thick as the site was almost continually occupied until the late 1st millennium BC. Settlement then shifted to a larger site nearby.

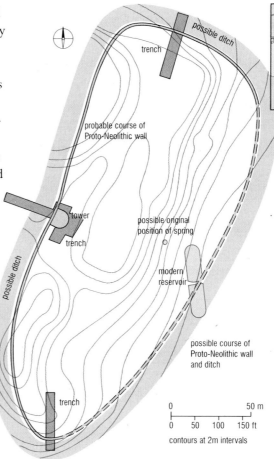

probable course of Proto-Neolithic wall

trench

possible ditch

tower

trench

possible ditch

possible original position of spring

modern reservoir

possible course of Proto-Neolithic wall and ditch

trench

Jericho

```
0                    50 m
0    50   100   150 ft
contours at 2m intervals
```

LEFT In the Proto-Neolithic period Jericho was surrounded by a masonry wall and rock-cut ditch. Jericho is quite considerably the largest known Near East settlement at this period – covering an area of approximately 7 acres (3 hectares), it contained a community of around 1500 people who lived in circular huts built of sun-dried mud bricks. Several later building phases have been identified at the earliest habitation site at Jericho, which developed into an important city in the Bronze Age.

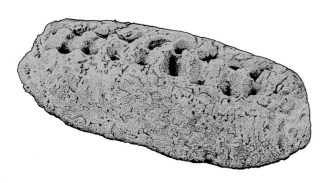

LEFT Mudbricks are made from mud tempered with straw to stop them from cracking when they are dried by the heat of the sun. This brick from Jericho belongs to the Aceramic period before 7000. The brickmaker has pressed his thumbs into the top to make a herringbone pattern as a key to hold the mud mortar.

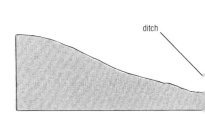

ditch

LEFT This stone mortar and pestle from Proto-Neolithic Jericho would have been used for food preparation or for grinding pigments. Stone vessels like this have been a part of everyday village life in the Near East from the Natufian period to modern Islamic times. Early stone and bone tools included pins, hooks, needles, awls and arrowheads. Wooden implements, basketry and textiles would have been widely used but few have survived.

LEFT AND BELOW *The most remarkable feature of Proto-Neolithic Jericho is a stone tower attached to the inside of the city walls. The tower is 33 feet (10 m) in diameter and still survives to a height of over 26 feet (8 m). It had a door and an internal staircase of 22 steps, each made from a single block of stone. Whether it was used as a watchtower or had another, possibly ritual, function is unknown. Jericho's walls were rebuilt and extended several times before the site was abandoned in the 1st millennium BC.*

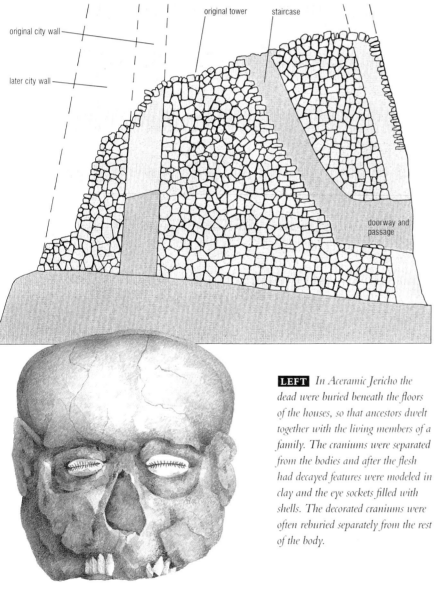

original city wall

later city wall

original tower

staircase

doorway and passage

LEFT *In Aceramic Jericho the dead were buried beneath the floors of the houses, so that ancestors dwelt together with the living members of a family. The craniums were separated from the bodies and after the flesh had decayed features were modeled in clay and the eye sockets filled with shells. The decorated craniums were often reburied separately from the rest of the body.*

providing vessels for cooking and storage ensured that its use was widespread among the peoples of the Fertile Crescent by 6500. By this time bread wheat had been developed, flax – the raw material of linen cloth – was being grown, and pigs and cattle had been domesticated.

As nomadic hunter–gatherers settled down to become farmers, communities gradually became less self-sufficient. Long-distance trade, particularly in salt and high-quality toolmaking stone such as obsidian (volcanic glass), became more important. Obsidian from Anatolia has been found in early Neolithic sites almost as far south as the Red Sea, while obsidian from Lake Van reached the Mediterranean and the Persian Gulf.

SETTLEMENT OF THE MESOPOTAMIAN PLAIN

In 6500 the densest concentrations of farming settlements were still to be found in areas of reliable rainfall in the uplands of the Levant, southern Anatolia and the Zagros mountains. Though some large settlements, such as Jericho (see opposite) and Chatal Huyuk (see page 22), developed in these areas, it was on the fertile but almost rainless Mesopotamian plain to the east and south that the first towns developed. With the development of irrigation techniques, farmers began to move from the upland fringes onto to the plain itself. Archeologists have identified a series of cultures, each with its own distinctive pottery style, that trace this expansion, which took about a thousand years. The first was the Hassuna culture (6500–6000), centered on northern Mesopotamia, mostly within the dry farming zone. The Hassuna people grew emmer, einkorn and barley, bred sheep, goats, pigs and cattle, and also hunted a little. There is evidence of copper and lead smelting, and the Hassunans were the earliest group to produce painted pottery and fire it in purpose-built kilns. Stamp seals, later used widely in Mesopotamia to indicate ownership, were also first used in the Hassuna culture.

In about 6000 the Hassuna culture was replaced by the Halaf. A storehouse excavated at Arpachiyeh in northern Mesopotamia contained a concentration of fine pottery, jewelry, sculpture and flint and obsidian tools – probable evidence that the Halaf people were ruled by chiefs who controlled the community's trade contacts and amassed considerable personal wealth. The influence of the Halaf culture was confined almost entirely to the dry farming zone but this was not

THE SPREAD OF FARMING SETTLEMENTS

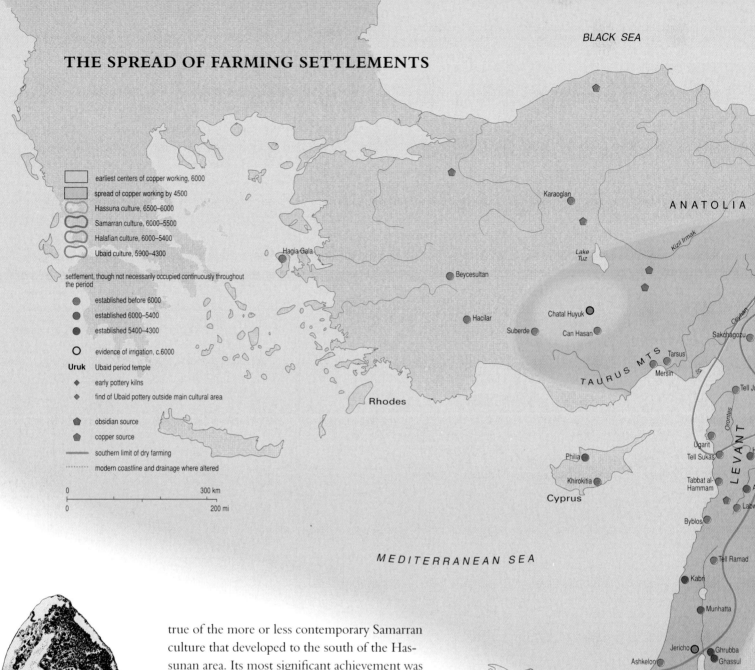

earliest centers of copper working, 6000

spread of copper working by 4500

Hassuna culture, 6500–6000

Samarran culture, 6000–5500

Halafian culture, 6000–5400

Ubaid culture, 5900–4300

settlement, though not necessarily occupied continuously throughout the period

- established before 6000
- established 6000–5400
- established 5400–4300

○ evidence of irrigation, c.6000

Uruk Ubaid period temple

◆ early pottery kilns

◆ find of Ubaid pottery outside main cultural area

⬠ obsidian source

⬠ copper source

—— southern limit of dry farming

- - - - modern coastline and drainage where altered

```
0            300 km
0        200 mi
```

BLACK SEA

ANATOLIA

Karaoglan

Lake Tuz

Kizil Irmak

Hagia Gala

Beycesultan

Hacilar

Chatal Huyuk ○

Suberde   Can Hasan

TAURUS MTS   Tarsus

Mersin

Sakchagozu

Rhodes

Orontes

LEVANT

Ugarit

Philia   Tell Sukas

Khirokitia   Tabbat al-Hammam

Cyprus   Byblos

MEDITERRANEAN SEA   Tell Ramad

Kabri

Munhatta

Jericho ○   Ghrubba

Ashkelon   Ghassul

Tell Ju

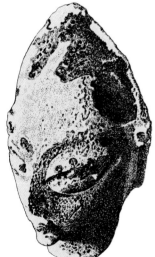

ABOVE *The head of a pottery female figurine of the Samarran culture (6000–5500). The hairstyle, a long plait wound over the top of the head, is similar to those of the later Sumerian civilization.*

true of the more or less contemporary Samarran culture that developed to the south of the Hassunan area. Its most significant achievement was the development of large-scale irrigation techniques such as canal building. These boosted yields within the dry farming zone but more importantly allowed Samarran farmers to begin to settle on the arid plains of central Mesopotamia.

The earliest farming culture of the floodplains of the Tigris and Euphrates rivers in southern Mesopotamia was the Ubaid (c. 5900–4300). In its early stages it shows many similarities with the Samarran culture to the north, from which it may have been derived. Southern Mesopotamia already had a sparse population that depended mainly on fishing, hunting and herding but the introduction of irrigation techniques from the north unlocked the vast potential of southern Mesopotamia's rich alluvial soils. Population densities rose rapidly and many new farming villages were founded. Most Ubaid settlements grew up near the Euphrates,

which was more suitable for irrigation schemes than the faster flowing Tigris. Agricultural productivity received another boost in the 5th millennium with the invention of the plow.

The Ubaid culture laid the foundations of the later Sumerian civilization of southern Mesopotamia. By the 5th millennium settlements were developing into small towns with populations of between 4000 and 5000. A simple shrine established at Eridu, the culture's best-known site, in early Ubaid times already had the distinctive features of later Mesopotamian temples: an ornamental facade, an offering table and an altar for

BELOW *The earliest centers of metalworking were in the highlands of Anatolia and the Zagros mountains where native copper (naturally occurring copper metal) was used to make small tools and ornaments as early as 7000 BC. The smelting of copper ores began at sites such as Chatal Huyuk around 6200 and* *had become widespread by 4500. Pottery came into use between 7000 and 6500. The development of irrigation techniques enabled farmers to move out of the dry farming zone onto the fertile but arid Mesopotamian plain by about 5500. By the end of the Ubaid period (c.4000) small towns were beginning to develop.*

Lake Van

Tepecik
Norshuntepe
Arslantepe
Tiki Tepe
Lake Urmia
Yanik Tepe
Tepe Seavan
Turlu
rcemish
Chagar Bazar
Tell Halaf
Tell Abu Dhahir
Hajii Firuz
Hasanlu
Banahilk
Tigris
Great Zab
Tell Hamman al-Turkman
Yarim Tepe
Tepe Gawra
Nineveh
Shusharra
Kul Tepe
Tell Azzo
Arpachiyeh
Tell Zaidan
Hassuna
Abu Hureyra
Euphrates
Jarmo
Diyala
Tell Umm Dabaghiyeh
Choga Maran
GodinTepe
Bouqras
MESOPOTAMIA
Tell Madhhur
Tepe Sarab
Tepe Giyan
Samarra
Baghouz
Tell al-Sawwan
Tell Abadeh
Choga Mami
Tepe Guran
Syrian Desert
Karkheh
Ali Kosh
Boneh Fazili
Choga Mish
Tell Uqair
Susa
Nippur
Lagash (Girsu)
Uruk
Tell Awayli
Hajji Muhammad
Ur
Tell al-Ubaid
Eridu
Tepe Sialk

ZAGROS MOUNTAINS

ABOVE *Distinctive regional styles of pottery help archeologists reconstruct trade contacts and trace the spread of cultural influences. This pot, which is in Late Ubaid style, is from Arpachiyeh in northern Mesopotamia. Pottery of the Late Ubaid period is very widespread: examples have been found at sites as far apart as the Iranian plateau, Bahrain and the Mediterranean coast.*

the statue of the god. This temple was rebuilt a number of times. By the end of the Ubaid period it had become a multi-roomed complex built on top of a platform 3 feet (1 m) high. Over the centuries these platforms grew still taller and by about 2100 had evolved into ziggurats (see pages 42–43). Eridu seems to have been a religious center for the surrounding farming villages which it may have controlled through the spiritual power of a priesthood or by management of irrigation or trade. Southern Mesopotamia lacked basic materials such as timber, stone and metals for building, sculpture and toolmaking, as well as semi precious stones, and trade links were important. These helped to spread the influence of the Ubaid culture and by 5400 it had replaced the Halaf culture in northern Mesopotamia, while Ubaid pottery manufactured around Ur has been found throughout the Persian Gulf region. An important innovation of the Ubaid culture was an accounting system based on

PERSIAN GULF

clay tokens, a precursor of the first writing system. Though some form of social organization would have been needed to construct and manage irrigation works and to build temples, burial practices suggest that society in the Ubaid period was basically egalitarian. At its close (c.4300) the population of southern Mesopotamia was still growing. The succeeding Uruk period saw the development of a society that was far more complex and hierarchical.

21

CHATAL HUYUK

Most early farming villages had no more than a few hundred inhabitants. Their simple subsistence economies were based on cereal farming and herding sheep, goats or cattle. A remarkable exception to this rule was Chatal Huyuk, a town in southern Anatolia which grew up about 6500 BC. Excavation of part of the site took place in the early 1960s. The state of preservation was excellent and even some highly perishable materials such as textiles had survived. The settlement was made up of densely packed single storey houses built of timber and mudbrick. Each house accommodated a single family and the town's population is estimated to have been around 6000, making it the largest Neolithic settlement yet found. Skeletal evidence shows that the inhabitants were well built and had an average life expectancy of about 40 years. Two factors probably affected Chatal Huyuk's development into a town: domination of the trade in obsidian from nearby volcanoes, and improved agricultural yields resulting from the introduction of simple irrigation techniques. Despite this, hunting remained an important source of supplementary food: deer, gazelle and turtles were regularly eaten. Chatal Huyuk had rich artistic traditions of wall painting and sculpture. Many

RIGHT *Chatal Huyuk was a town without streets: the tightly-packed houses shared their walls with their neighbors. A typical house plan consisted of a square living room with a hearth and oven and narrow storerooms. Access to the houses was via a hole in the roof which also served to let smoke escape: there were no intercommunicating doors or windows. The few open spaces in the town – the "courts" – were created by abandoned houses that had fallen down. They were used as garbage dumps by the other inhabitants.*

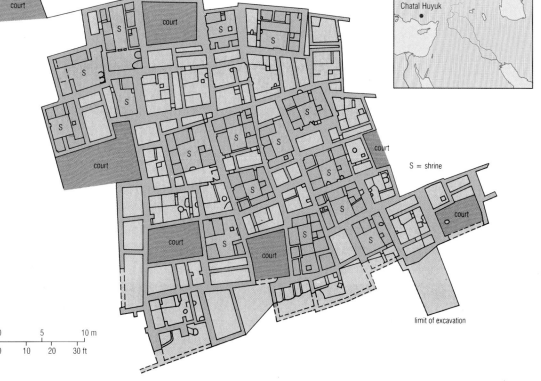

Chatal Huyuk

S = shrine

limit of excavation

| 0 | | 5 | | 10 m |
| 0 | 10 | 20 | | 30 ft |

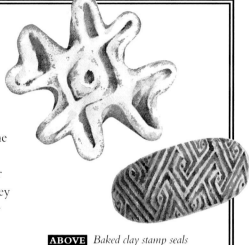

other crafts were practiced including weaving, basketry, leather, wood and copper working (it is the earliest site where evidence of copper smelting has been found), fine stone tool manufacture and pottery. Though its exact nature is not understood, religion was evidently a major social force: shrines were elaborately decorated, and they were so numerous that there was almost one to every house. Though its achievements were impressive, Chatal Huyuk did not develop into a full civilization. The local environment was not capable of sustaining long-term urban growth and the site was abandoned after about 800 years, probably because soils had become exhausted by overuse. The population presumably dispersed into the small villages that were typical of the rest of Neolithic Anatolia.

ABOVE *Baked clay stamp seals were found as offerings in some adult male graves. No impressions made by these seals have been found, and they were probably used to stamp patterns on materials such as textiles or skins, which have not survived.*

ABOVE *Baked clay or stone figurines of fat pregnant females were found in the shrines at Chatal Huyuk. They have been identified as birth goddesses.*

BELOW *Reconstruction of a shrine or mortuary. The walls were decorated with painted plaster and with bulls' skulls and horns which perhaps represented a male deity. Men were buried under the low platform to the right, women and children under the others. Around half the buildings excavated at Chatal Huyuk have been identified as shrines.*

ABOVE *This reconstruction of a wall painting from a shrine at Chatal Huyuk shows hunters armed with bows closing in on a wild bull.*

BELOW *A reconstruction of part of the settlement. The houses were built in terraces, getting higher toward the center of the town.*

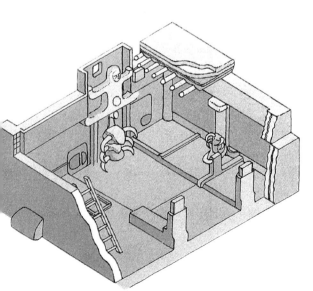

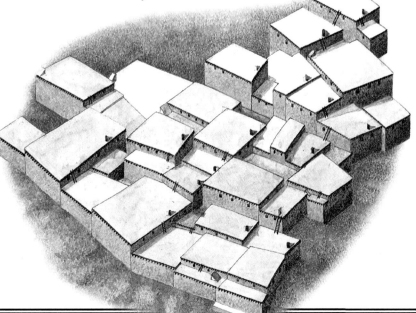

From City States to Kingdoms

4000 – 1600 BC

The development of the first cities and states took place in southern Mesopotamia during the Uruk period (c. 4300–3100). A complex combination of factors lay behind this social and economic revolution, and it seems likely that rising population and agricultural yields, competition for resources, increasing social differentiation, the need for coordinating bodies to organize more and more complex irrigation and flood defense schemes, and the growth of organized religion all played their part. The first cities had populations of between 5000 and 8000, though the largest, Uruk (see pages 26–27), had over 10,000. Urban growth continued in the subsequent Jemdet Nasr (3100–1900 BC) and Early Dynastic (2900–2334 BC) periods. By 2700 Uruk's population had risen to approximately 50,000. But the early Mesopotamian cities were vulnerable to sudden floods and shifts of river courses: their populations could fluctuate considerably and some, such as Eridu, were even completely abandoned for short periods.

Though most urban-dwellers were farmers who traveled each day to their fields, these cities were the first to have the resources to support large numbers of people in fulltime specialist occupations such as scribes, metalworkers, stonemasons, sculptors, potters, weavers, bakers and brewers. Temple complexes dominated the cities. Here food surpluses from the countryside and craft products were stored for redistribution or to be traded abroad. Timber, gold, silver, tin, copper and precious stones made their way to the cities of Mesopotamia from central Asia, Afghanistan, the Persian Gulf and Egypt, and trade helped to spread the influence of Mesopotamian civilization throughout the Near East. By about 3400 BC a system of pictographic writing had been developed to aid record keeping (see page 46). At the end of the Uruk period bronze – an alloy of tin (or sometimes arsenic) and copper – came into use. Bronze is much harder and keeps its edge better than pure copper, and from now on metal tools and weapons gradually began to supplant those of stone, despite their greater cost.

THE FIRST CITIES

The first cities grew up on the flood plain of the Tigris and Euphrates rivers in the 4th millennium BC. They served as collection and redistribution centers for the agricultural surplus grown on the plain's fertile alluvial soils and they developed as independent states, each one dominating the countryside immediately surrounding it. In the 3rd millennium BC competition between these city states appears to have become increasingly fierce, as recorded in the Sumerian King List.

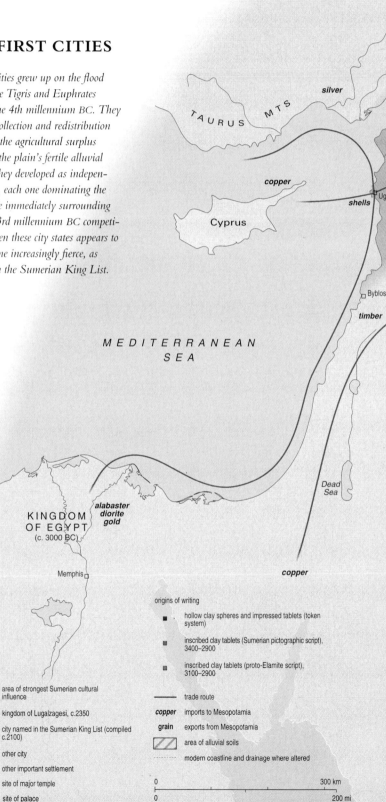

origins of writing

■ hollow clay spheres and impressed tablets (token system)

■ inscribed clay tablets (Sumerian pictographic script), 3400–2900

■ inscribed clay tablets (proto-Elamite script), 3100–2900

▨ area of strongest Sumerian cultural influence

◯ kingdom of Lugalzagesi, c.2350

● city named in the Sumerian King List (compiled c.2100)

● other city

□ other important settlement

Mari site of major temple

Kish site of palace

—— trade route

copper imports to Mesopotamia

grain exports from Mesopotamia

▨ area of alluvial soils

- - - modern coastline and drainage where altered

0 _____ 300 km
0 _____ 200 mi

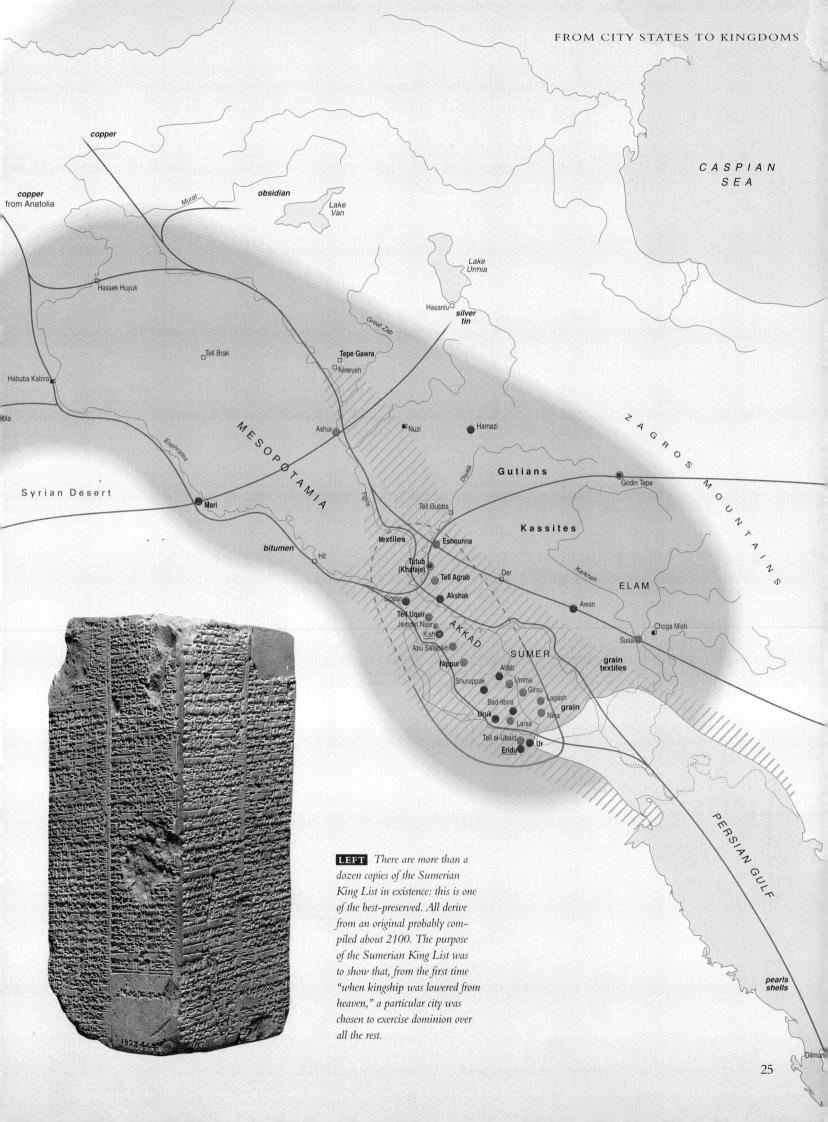

CASPIAN
SEA

copper

copper
from Anatolia

obsidian

Lake
Van

Murat

Lake
Urmia

Hasanlu □ silver
tin

Hassek Huyuk

Great Zab

Habuba Kabira

Tell Brak

Tepe Gawra
□ Nineveh

bla

Ashur

M E S O P O T A M I A

Nuzi

Hamazi

Euphrates

Z A G R O S   M O U N T A I N S

Syrian Desert

Mari

Tigris

Diyala

Gutians

Godin Tepe

Tell Gubba

Kassites

bitumen

Hit

textiles

Eshnunna

Der

Karkheh

ELAM

Tutub
(Khafaje)

Tell Agrab

Awan

Sippar

Akshak

Choga Mish

Tell Uqair
Jemdet Nasr
Kish

A K K A D

Susa

Abu Salabikh

S U M E R

grain
textiles

Nippur

Adab

Shuruppak

Umma

Bad-tibira

Girsu

Lagash

Uruk

Nina

grain

Larsa

Tell al-Ubaid

Ur

Eridu

PERSIAN
GULF

LEFT *There are more than a
dozen copies of the Sumerian
King List in existence: this is one
of the best-preserved. All derive
from an original probably compiled about 2100. The purpose
of the Sumerian King List was
to show that, from the first time
"when kingship was lowered from
heaven," a particular city was
chosen to exercise dominion over
all the rest.*

pearls
shells

Dilmun

URUK

The site of the ancient settlement of Uruk (modern Warka) is today largely buried by desert sands. It had already been occupied for more than a thousand years when, in the Uruk period to which it gives its name (4300–3100 BC), it began to grow rapidly in size. By about 3400 Uruk was twice as large as any other settlement in the region, with a population of perhaps 10,000. The city had two major temple complexes, Kullaba, dedicated to the sky god An, and Eanna, dedicated to the love goddess Inanna. Clay tablets inscribed with a pictographic script discovered in the Eanna complex are the earliest known evidence of writing. Uruk reached its peak in the 3rd millennium BC, when its population was about 50,000, but began to decline thereafter, possibly because the surrounding farmlands had begun to lose fertility. Uruk features prominently in Sumerian mythology – a clear indication of its formative role in the development of the civilization. The myth "Inanna and Enki: the transfer of the arts of civilization from Eridu to Uruk" symbolizes Uruk's emergence as Sumer's leading city and religious center, and Uruk's early kings such as Gilgamesh and Dumuzi became the deified legendary heroes of epic tales.

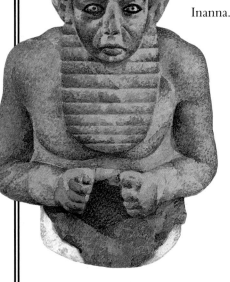

ABOVE *This statuette of an unknown ruler of Uruk dates from the late 4th millennium BC. Such figures were placed in temples as a sign of the ruler's devotion to the gods.*

RIGHT *In the 3rd millennium BC Uruk covered an area of 988 acres (400 hectares) and had a population of c. 50,000: the city walls were 6 miles (10 km) long. According to the Epic of Gilgamesh, one-third of the city consisted of temples, one-third of houses and one-third of gardens. Excavations have been concentrated on Kullaba and Eanna, the two temple districts of the city, and little is known about the residential districts. Uruk remained an important religious center until its abandonment early in the Christian era.*

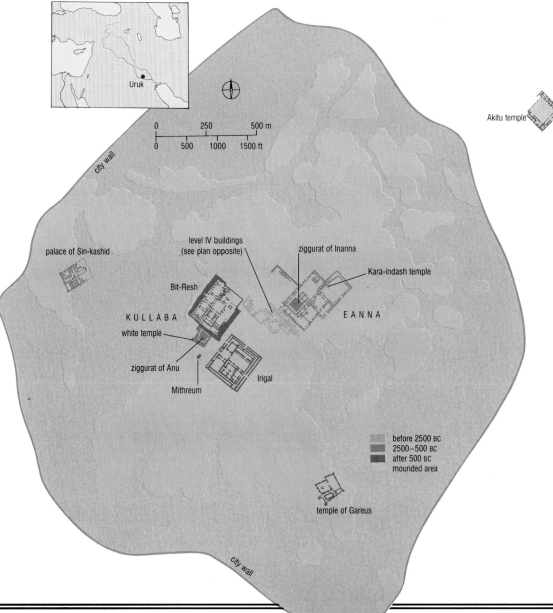

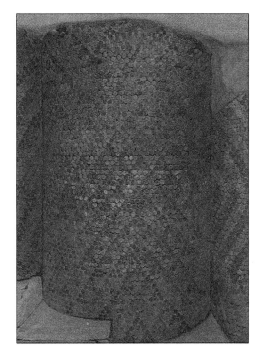

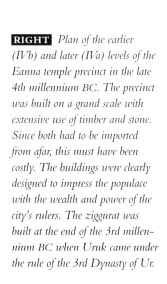

LEFT AND ABOVE *The Warka vase (c. 3000) was one of a pair found in the temple treasury at Uruk. It is carved with scenes of offerings being presented to the goddess Inanna, who is shown with the ruler in the scene on the vase's top register. Such scenes are common in*

Sumerian art. They indicate the importance of temples as centers for the collection and redistribution of agricultural surpluses. Inanna, the goddess of love and war, became known to the Akkadians as Ishtar. Elsewhere in the Near East she was later worshiped as Astarte.

ABOVE *Reconstruction of columns decorated with "clay cone mosaic" at the entrance to the Eanna temple complex (late 4th millennium BC). The geometric patterns were made by setting hundreds of painted baked-clay or stone cones (right) in plaster. The patterns are similar to those used on woven matting.*

RIGHT *Plan of the earlier (IVb) and later (IVa) levels of the Eanna temple precinct in the late 4th millennium BC. The precinct was built on a grand scale with extensive use of timber and stone. Since both had to be imported from afar, this must have been costly. The buildings were clearly designed to impress the populace with the wealth and power of the city's rulers. The ziggurat was built at the end of the 3rd millennium BC when Uruk came under the rule of the 3rd Dynasty of Ur.*

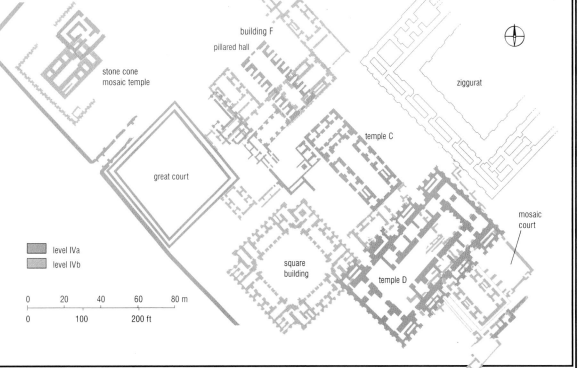

building F
pillared hall
stone cone mosaic temple
ziggurat
temple C
great court
level IVa
level IVb
square building
temple D
mosaic court

0   20   40   60   80 m
0   100   200 ft

This head, found in the area of the Ishtar Temple at Nineveh, was for long thought to be that of Sargon I (2334–2279), the founder of the Agade dynasty, who is the first great conqueror known to history. Scholars now believe that it is more likely to represent his grandson Naram-Sin (2254–2218). The head is of copper and was cast using the lost wax method (see page 45).

Cylinder seals, usually made of stone but sometimes of glass, pottery, bone, ivory or metal, were incised with designs which, when rolled onto wet clay, produced a continuous impression in relief. The earliest date from the 4th millennium BC and come from Uruk. They remained in use for the next 3000 years as a convenient way of marking patches of wet clay used to seal storeroom doors, boxes and jars, and as "envelopes" for the clay tablets used for cuneiform writing. They frequently depict religious and mythological scenes and are often inscribed with charms, prayers and the personal names and genealogies of their owners.
RIGHT: Usually about ³⁄₄ in (2.5 cm) high and ¹⁄₃ in (1.5 cm) in diameter, the seals doubled as talismans and items of jewelry, worn on a pin or string or mounted on a swivel, like this green jasper seal from Syria (18th century BC). Shown to its right are two chalcedony seals from Assyria (8th century BC).
RIGHT: impressions of cylinder seals of (left to right): Uruk period, c.3300; Late Uruk period; Akkadian c.2250; Kassite c.1300; Middle Assyrian c.1300.

Because they were dominated by temple complexes, it was for long held that the cities of Mesopotamia were ruled by priesthoods during the Uruk period. However, it seems unlikely that any clear distinction was made between the secular and the religious at this time, and it is now more commonly argued that the temples were used by emerging elites to help underpin their pre-eminent position in society.

THE EARLY DYNASTIC PERIOD

In the Early Dynastic period (2900–2334) competition between the Mesopotamian city states became intense as the population density on the plains reached saturation point. Massive defensive walls were built around the cities, production of bronze weapons increased and war became a favorite subject of official art with rulers often being shown trampling on their enemies. Royal dynasties and traditions of kingship developed. Rulers of the city states used three titles, *en* (lord), *ensi* (governor) and *lugal* (big man). The distinctions between the titles are not clear. The *en* may originally have been priests, but as all Sumerian rulers had religious duties, this is not certain. The first *lugal* may have been war leaders, elected in times of emergency, such as during conflicts with other city states. Later they succeeded in making their power permanent. To show that their rule had divine approval, rulers built palaces next to the temple precincts where they lived in opulence. In death they were given extravagant burials: the

rich tombs of the Royal Cemetery at Ur (see pages 30–31) contained numerous gold artifacts and jewelry of superb workmanship. Mention is made in the records of slaves (probably prisoners-of-war) for the first time.

At the end of the Early Dynastic period we find the name Sumer being given to the southernmost part of the Euphrates–Tigris floodplain bordering on the Persian Gulf. Roughly to the north of the city of Nippur lay Akkad. At this time most of the population in the south seem to have spoken Sumerian, a language that has no known close relatives, while in the north most spoke Akkadian, a Semitic language from which Babylonian and Assyrian are descended, and related to Hebrew and Arabic. But Sumer and Akkad were not separate kingdoms or countries in any modern sense, rather a collection of city states, each with its own ruler, and there was close contact and rivalry

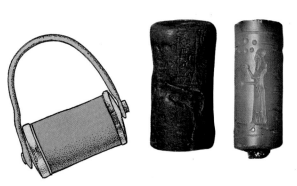

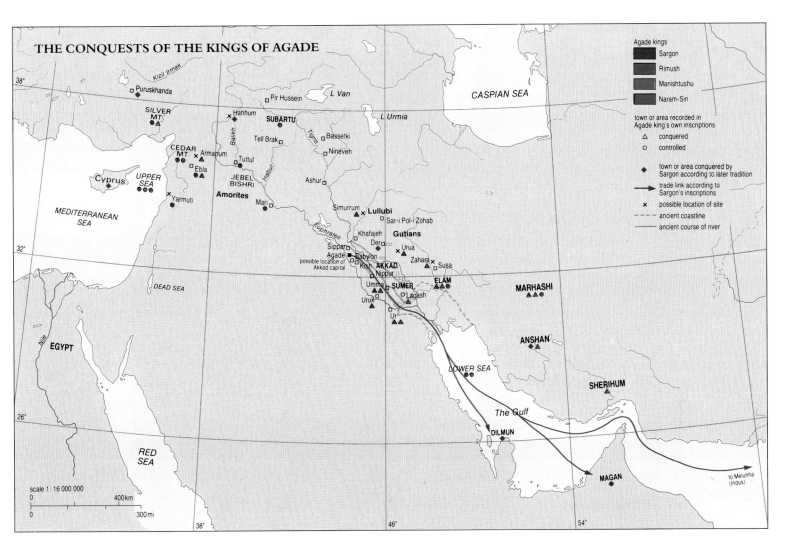

THE CONQUESTS OF THE KINGS OF AGADE

between the cities of Sumer and Akkad through-out the Early Dynastic period.

The later Early Dynastic saw writing applied to purposes other than administration. Rulers such as Urukagina of Lagash (c. 2350) issued written leg-islation and reforms to establish their authority. Rulers also began to record their achievements on cuneiform tablets, votive vases and monuments. This makes it possible to construct at least an out-line of the turbulent political history of the Early Dynastic period. The Sumerian King List records the dynasties of Sumer from earliest times. The oldest surviving copy dates from the beginning of the 2nd millennium BC. It names nearly a dozen Sumerian city states in the Early Dynastic period.

Many smaller cities had already lost their indepen-dence: Girsu and Nina, for instance, were ruled by Lagash.

At the start of the Early Dynastic period the region was dominated by rivalry between the city states of Kish, Uruk and Ur. Outside invasions, first from Elam and then from Hamazi, a king-dom in the Zagros mountains, brought this phase to an end. Around 2500 king Mesilim of Kish seems to have had nominal overlordship of Sumer. This continued for about 100 years until Kish was defeated by king Eannatum of Lagash who also fought successful wars against Akshak, Mari and Elam. Lagash was itself conquered in about 2350 by Lugalzagesi of Umma, thereby

ABOVE *The kings of Agade (2334–2279) were the first to establish their rule over all Sumer and Akkad; their inscriptions claim that they controlled cities as far away as the Mediterranean and later traditions credit Sargon with conquests around the Persian Gulf and even on Cyprus. Agade itself, the dynasty's capital, is thought to have been a little to the north of Babylon.*

UR

Founded early in the Ubaid period, Ur had become an important city by the Early Dynastic period. It was Mesopotamia's main port and through it passed trade from as far afield as India. The wealth of the Early Dynastic rulers of Ur was revealed by the discovery of the Royal Cemetery, in use from about 2600 to 2400. Seventeen tombs, furnished with spectacular gold and silver work, jewelry, musical instruments and other high-quality craft objects, have been excavated. Some of the tombs contained evidence of human sacrifices: in one, 74 retainers had been drugged before being killed. Under the kings of the 3rd Dynasty, Ur-Nammu, Shulgi and Amar-Sin (2112–2004), Ur became the capital of an empire that dominated Mesopotamia, and the city was completely rebuilt in suitably imperial style. After the fall of the 3rd Dynasty Ur continued as an important religious center but never recovered its political importance, except for a brief moment in the 18th century when it was ruled by the Sealand Dynasty. Ur was finally abandoned in the 4th century BC, perhaps because of changes in the course of the Euphrates.

ABOVE *The partially restored remains of the ziggurat of the Moon god Nanna dominate the ruins of Ur. Begun by Ur-Nammu (r. 2112–2095), the ziggurat was completed by his son Shulgi (r. 2094–2047). When complete it probably had three stages; only the lower stage has been rebuilt.*

LEFT *This statue of a ram standing on its hind legs behind a golden plant is one of two found in the Great Death Pit of the Royal Cemetery of Ur. The face and legs are made of gold, the horns, eyes and fleece over the shoulders of lapis lazuli. The rest of the fleece is made of white shell.*

Shrine of Nanna

Court of Nanna

Ziggurat

E-temen-ni-gur of Ur-Nammu

E-dub-lal-mah

E-nun-mah

Giparu of Amar-Sin

enclosure wall of Nebuchadnezzar II

E-hursag of Ur-Nammu and Shulgi

0   50 m
0   150 ft

2600–2400 BC
2112–2004 BC
604–562 BC

enclosure wall

Tombs of Shulgi and Amar-Sin

Royal Tombs

Ur

BELOW *A helmet made of electrum (an alloy of gold and silver) from the tomb of king Meskalamdug in the Royal Cemetery. It originally had a cloth lining attached to the holes along its lower edge and was for show only.*

ABOVE *Ur was dominated by the sacred precinct built by the kings of the 3rd Dynasty. As well as the temple and ziggurat of Nanna, the precinct contained the Giparu (residence) of the chief priestess. The E-nun-mah may have been a treasury and temple, and the E-hursag a royal palace. In the 6th century BC a new wall was built around the precinct, which also contained the Royal Cemetery.*

RIGHT *The so-called Standard of Ur from the Royal Cemetery was probably a sounding box for a musical instrument. It is decorated with shell set in bitumen. The scenes show a military campaign and, here, a victory banquet with men carrying goods and leading animals, possibly plundered from the enemy.*

31

bringing to an end a long-standing rivalry between the two city states. Lugalzagesi went on to carve out a considerable kingdom for himself in Sumer and Akkad. His rule marked the last chapter in the Early Dynastic period of independent city states.

THE EMPIRE OF AGADE

Lugalzagesi's kingdom lasted only about 16 years before being overthrown in 2334 by a far greater conqueror, Sargon of Agade (c. 2334–2279). According to one of several later legends, Sargon was the illegitimate child of a high-priestess. As a baby he was placed in a basket, like Moses, and floated down the Euphrates. Rescued by a servant, he was trained as a gardener but through the favor of the goddess Ishtar was raised to kingship. An earlier story tells a more credible tale. The son of a humble date grower, Sargon became a servant of king Urzababa of Agade. He rose in the service to become the king's cupbearer and when the gods decreed the downfall of Urzababa, Sargon some-how succeeded him. Sargon is the form of his name that comes down to us from the Bible. In Akkadian it is Sharrum-kin, meaning "legitimate king," a strong hint that he may indeed have been a usurper.

Sargon recorded the achievements of his reign in an inscription on a monument which he had placed in the temple of Enlil at Nippur. This monument, which probably depicted Sargon with his armies and defeated enemies, was destroyed in antiquity but a meticulous copy of the text, made about 1800 BC, has survived. It tells how Sargon conquered Uruk, then the greatest power in Mesopotamia, and led its king Lugalzagesi in a wooden collar into captivity at Nippur. Sargon then went on to build an empire that included all the lands between the "Upper Sea" (the Mediter-ranean) and the "Lower Sea" (the Persian Gulf). Other surviving inscriptions confirm Sargon's wide-ranging conquests. He made the city of Agade his capital: later traditions say he also founded it. The city has so far not been located but probably lay between Kish and Babylon.

Until recently, Sargon's reign was seen as marking a decisive break in Mesopotamian history. Following his conquest of Sumer, he appointed Akkadian governors to many cities and made his own daughter Enheduanna high priestess of the temple of the moon god Nanna at Ur. These developments were thought to have begun the extinction of the Sumerian language and of the Sumerians as a distinct people. It is now clear,

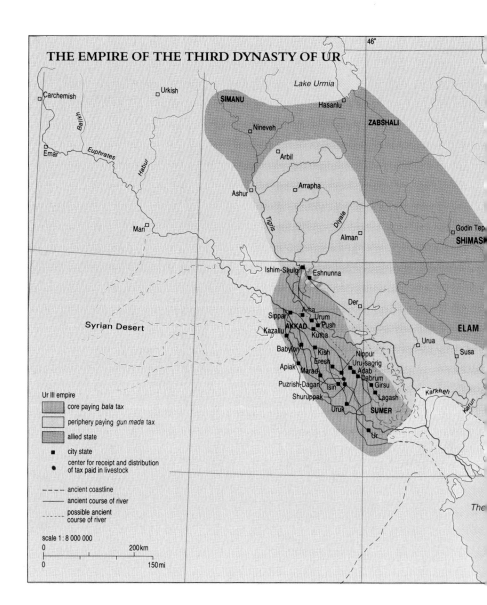

however, that Akkadian influence had been increasing in the south for centuries and that Sumerian was already declining as a spoken lan-guage. By 1800 it survived only as an administra-tive and literary language.

Rebellions broke out throughout the empire after Sargon's death but they were put down by his son Rimush (r. 2278–2270). Rimush was murdered by his servants in a palace conspiracy and was succeeded by his brother Manishtushu (r. 2269–2255), another able soldier. In one inscription he claimed to have conquered the dis-tant regions of Anshan and Sherihun (to the east of the Persian Gulf). In case future generations should find this unbelievable he swore "these are no lies. It is absolutely true!"

The empire of Agade reached its peak in the reign of his son Naram-Sin (r. 2254–2218). Whereas earlier Mesopotamian kings had claimed to rule as agents of the gods, Naram-Sin declared himself to be a god and adopted the title "king of

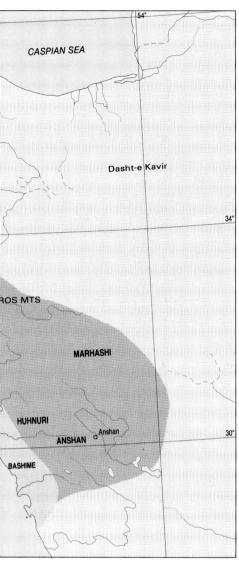

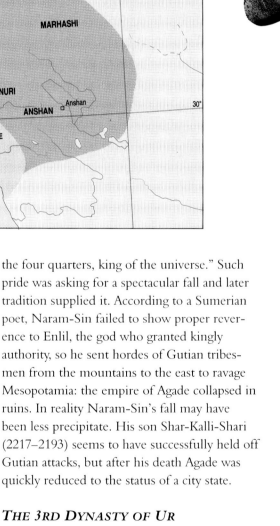

LEFT *Statue of Gudea, ensi of Lagash (c. 2100). Gudea was probably a contemporary of Utuhegal of Uruk who brought his people peace and prosperity in a troubled period of Mesopotamian history. He rebuilt 15 temples in Girsu, which became the administrative center of the state of Lagash. The extent of Gudea's kingdom is unknown but he claimed to have defeated the Elamites and may have exercised some influence in Ur.*

FAR LEFT *The 23 city states of Sumer and Akkad that formed the core of the empire of the 3rd Dynasty of Ur (2112–2004) were ruled by civil and military governors who paid a monthly bala tax to the king. To the north and east was a military zone comprising over 90 settlements, most of which have not been identified. Though under direct rule, royal control was not so secure in this area and its military officers paid only an annual livestock tax, the gun mada. In a zone beyond this, the 3rd Dynasty exerted influence over local states through treaties and marriage alliances.*

the four quarters, king of the universe." Such pride was asking for a spectacular fall and later tradition supplied it. According to a Sumerian poet, Naram-Sin failed to show proper reverence to Enlil, the god who granted kingly authority, so he sent hordes of Gutian tribesmen from the mountains to the east to ravage Mesopotamia: the empire of Agade collapsed in ruins. In reality Naram-Sin's fall may have been less precipitate. His son Shar-Kalli-Shari (2217–2193) seems to have successfully held off Gutian attacks, but after his death Agade was quickly reduced to the status of a city state.

THE 3RD DYNASTY OF UR

The fall of the empire of Agade was followed by a period of political anarchy in Sumer and Akkad: "Who was king? Who was not king?" asked the author of the Sumerian King List. Utuhegal of Uruk (r. 2119–2113) claimed to have ended the Gutian threat to Mesopotamia but was over-

thrown by the man he had appointed as governor of Ur, Ur-Nammu (r. 2112–2095). The founder of the 3rd Dynasty of Ur, Ur-Nammu was a competent soldier – one of his first actions was the conquest of the powerful city of Lagash, a Gutian ally. But his reign was not marked by the martial spirit that was so typical of the Agade dynasty. Though he created a sphere of influence that included the whole of Sumer and Akkad, diplomacy, alliances and religious influence played a greater part in this undertaking than force of arms.

It was left to Ur-Nammu's son Shulgi (r. 2094–2047) to turn influence into imperial control. Shulgi built a unified administrative structure for Sumer and Akkad. Provinces were created, each with a provincial city center, and placed under the rule of an *ensi* (governor) who was probably recruited from the local elite. Beside them were the *shagin* (military commanders) who, to make as certain of their loyalty as possible, were usually related to the king by birth or marriage. It is possible that they were answerable directly to the king so that they could act to check the activities of an over-ambitious provincial governor. The plains to the north and east that Shulgi conquered as far as the foothills of the Zagros mountains proved difficult to pacify completely and remained under the military rule of *sukkalmah*, officials who exercised vice-regal powers. To help unite the empire, roads were improved and hostels built along them where travelers could find secure lodgings at night.

Shulgi emulated the imperial style of Naram-Sin, having himself declared a god in his own lifetime. He introduced a complex tax system with centrally located collection and redistribution centers into which the provinces paid their dues and on which the government drew to supply rations to temple staff, officials and soldiers. Dues were also sometimes paid to the state in the form of labor. A large civil service was required to administer this system, and the 3rd Dynasty state appears to have suffered the familiar ills of all bureaucracies: clay tablets have been found on which the death of a single sheep is recorded in triplicate. Shulgi was an active legislator and it is now believed that he promulgated the law-code formerly attributed to Ur-Nammu. In prescribing, for the first time, fixed penalties for fixed offenses it was similar in form to the famous code of the Babylonian king Hammurabi (r. 1792–1750).

The empire of the 3rd Dynasty of Ur maintained its borders until the reign of Shulgi's grandson Ibbi-Sin (2028–2004). In the third year of his reign, Ibbi-Sin lost control of Susa, the Elamite capital, and for the rest of his reign had to face increasingly serious invasions from Elam. From the west the Amorites, nomads from the Arabian desert, invaded and settled in Mesopotamia: some even became rulers of Mesopotamian cities. In 2017, Ishbi-Erra, one of Ibbi-Sin's most trusted governors, seized power at Isin where he founded an independent dynasty.

The end came in 2004 when the Elamites sacked Ur after a long siege. A poem, *The Lamentation over the Destruction of Ur*, written within a generation of the event, graphically describes the city's, and Ibbi-Sin's, downfall. The people and the garrison were reduced to a desperate state by starvation, so weak they could hardly hold their weapons. Ibbi-Sin retreated into gloomy isolation within his palace. The Elamites finally stormed the city, destroying its temples and slaughtering and enslaving many of its people; Ibbi-Sin was captured and placed in chains. "Elam, like a swelling flood wave, left only the spirits of the dead" lamented the poet. Much of the city was abandoned and its streets became overgrown.

THE INDUS VALLEY CIVILIZATION

Documents belonging to the Agade empire and 3rd Dynasty of Ur refer to trade between Mesopotamia and "Meluhha." This has been plausibly identified as the Indus valley civilization – the first civilization of south Asia that emerged about 2600 BC. In terms of the area it occupied, the Indus civilization was the greatest of the Bronze Age civilizations.

The first known farming communities in south Asia are found at sites such as Mehrgarh in the mountains of Baluchistan between 7000 and 6000 BC. Settlement spread from the uplands into the

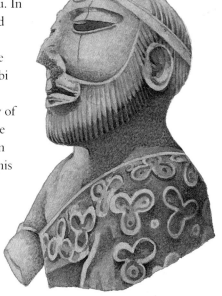

LEFT *This small steatite bust from the Indus valley settlement of Mohenjo-Daro has been called the "Priest King" partly because of the man's solemn and authoritative expression, partly because the head fillet, arm ring, trefoil patterned robe and exposed right shoulder were signs of holiness in later Indian civilizations.*

RIGHT *The Indus valley civilization flourished between 2500 and 1800. The two largest cities of the civilization, Mohenjo-Daro and Harappa, had populations of 40,000 or more but most other settlements had less than 5000 inhabitants. Similarities in the planning of Mohenjo-Daro and Harappa have led to suggestions that they were twin capitals of a large state but nothing is known for certain about the civilization's political organization.*

Shahr-i-Sokhta

Bampur

Shahi-Tum

Sutkagen Dor   Sotk

ARABIAN SE

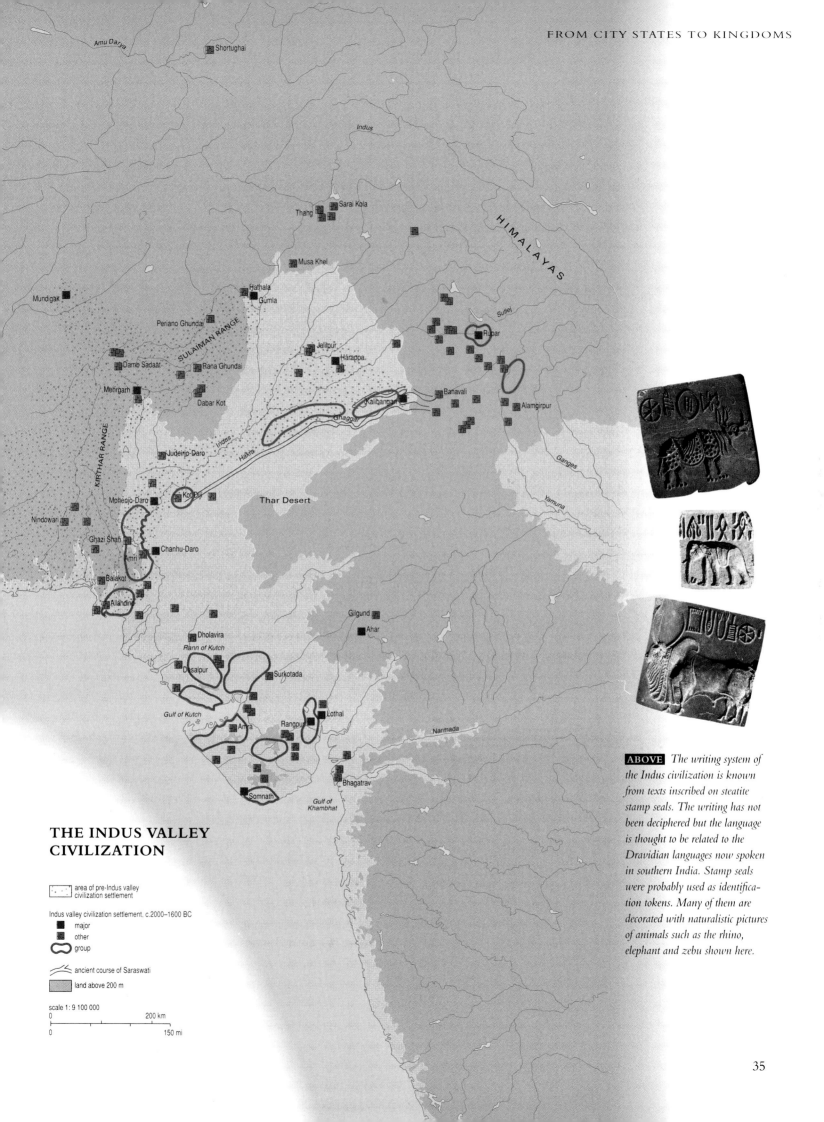

Amu Darya

Shortughai

Indus

Thang Sarai Kola

H I M A L A Y A S

Musa Khel

Mundigak

Hathala
Gumla

Periano Ghundai

SULAIMAN RANGE

Rupar

Suttej

Damb Sadaat

Rana Ghundai

Jalilpur

Harappa

Banavali

Metirgarh

Dabar Kot

Kalibangan

Alamgirpur

Ghaggar

Indus

Hakra

KIRTHAR RANGE

Judeirjo-Daro

Ganges

Kot Diji

Thar Desert

Yamuna

Mohenjo-Daro

Nindowari

Ghazi Shah

Chanhu-Daro

Amri

Balakot

Allahdino

Gilgund

Ahar

Dholavira

Rann of Kutch

Desalpur

Surkotada

Gulf of Kutch

Lothal

Amra

Rangpur

Narmada

Bhagatrav

Somnath

Gulf of
Khambhat

THE INDUS VALLEY
CIVILIZATION

⋯ area of pre-Indus valley
civilization settlement

Indus valley civilization settlement, c.2000–1600 BC

■ major

▪ other

⬭ group

∿ ancient course of Saraswati

land above 200 m

scale 1: 9 100 000

0   200 km

0   150 mi

ABOVE *The writing system of
the Indus civilization is known
from texts inscribed on steatite
stamp seals. The writing has not
been deciphered but the language
is thought to be related to the
Dravidian languages now spoken
in southern India. Stamp seals
were probably used as identification tokens. Many of them are
decorated with naturalistic pictures
of animals such as the rhino,
elephant and zebu shown here.*

RIVALRY BETWEEN CITY STATES

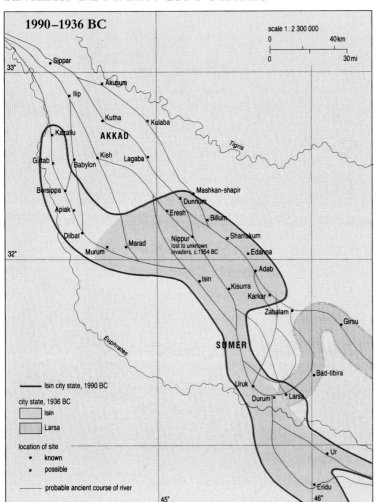

1990–1936 BC scale 1 : 2 300 000

Isin city state, 1990 BC

city state, 1936 BC
- Isin
- Larsa

location of site
- • known
- × possible

— probable ancient course of river

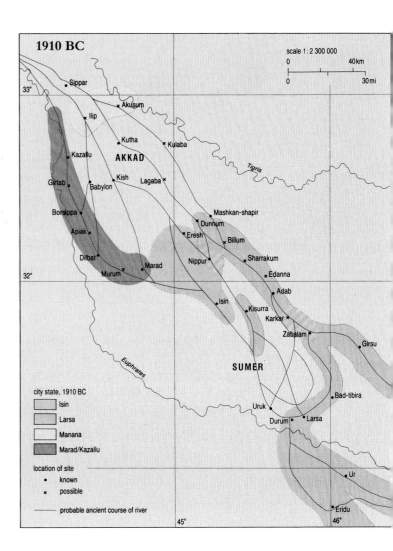

1910 BC scale 1 : 2 300 000

city state, 1910 BC
- Isin
- Larsa
- Manana
- Marad/Kazallu

location of site
- • known
- × possible

— probable ancient course of river

Indus valley during the 4th millennium BC. As in Mesopotamia, irrigation of the river plain's arid but fertile soils brought high yields. It was soon populated with farming villages and small towns, some of which, like Kot Diji, possessed fortifications and flood defenses, planned streets and evidence of copper working. There was considerable interaction between the valley settlements and those in the highlands. Highland peoples took their flocks to overwinter in the valley and traded metals, semiprecious stones and timber for grain and other foodstuffs.

The early farming communities of the Indus valley showed no signs of social ranking. In about 2600, however, a rapid transition to a hierarchical society seems to have taken place. The reasons for this are unclear, but it may have resulted from the establishment of trading contacts with Mesopotamia. Towns grew up in the Indus valley as a result of this trade. The metals and other products of the highlands were gathered in the towns and reexported to Mesopotamia. The trade was large in scale – one shipment of 13,007 lb (5,900 kg) of

copper is recorded in a Mesopotamian source.

Most of the cities and towns in the Indus valley were small. Two, however – Mohenjo-Daro and Harappa – had populations of between 30,000 and 40,000, placing them among the largest Bronze Age cities anywhere. They were so much larger than any others in the Indus valley, and so similar in plan, that it seems possible that they were twin capitals of a single state. Both had impressive mudbrick city walls, a citadel with public buildings and granaries, and streets laid out on a grid pattern with efficient underground drainage and sewerage systems. Houses were built to standard plans and different social classes and occupations were assigned different quarters of the city. The Indus civilization was literate but its pictographic script has not been deciphered. As a result, the identity of the Indus people remains a mystery but it is thought that they may have been related to the modern Dravidian-speaking peoples of southern India.

By 1800 BC the Indus cities were in decline. A century later they had been abandoned; writing

ABOVE *After the fall of the 3rd Dynasty of Ur, there was fierce rivalry between the city states of Mesopotamia. At first Isin, and then Larsa, both in Sumer, had greatest control, but by 1802 Babylon in Akkad was gaining the upper hand. The status of those cities not shown within the shaded areas on the maps is unknown: they may or may not have been independent.*

RIGHT *This bronze figure is of Warad-Sin, king of Larsa (r. 1834–1823) and comes from Girsu. He is carrying a basket of earth on his head for the ritual molding of the first brick. The Larsa dynasty, which was not of Sumerian origin, restored many ancient temples, no doubt to associate it with Sumerian tradition.*

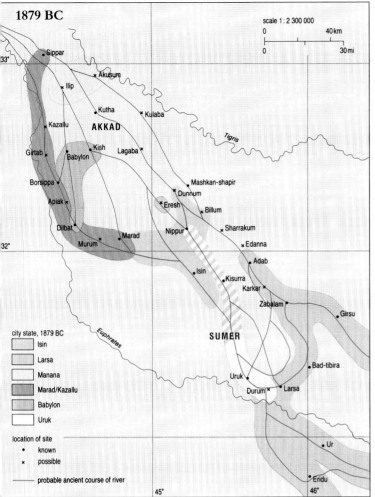

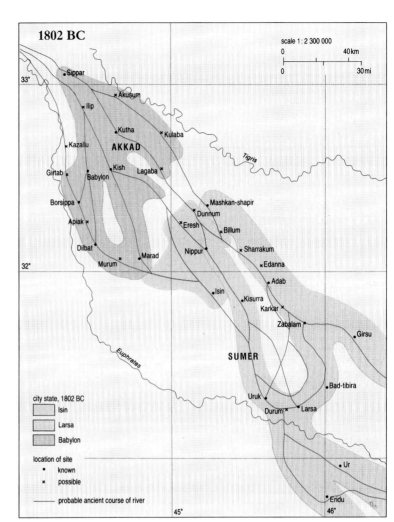

fell out of use. No entirely convincing explanation has been found to account for this collapse of urban civilization. However, as life in the countryside continued unchanged for several centuries more, it seems unlikely that it came about as a result of outside invasion. Sometime around 1500 BC the Aryans, a seminomadic pastoralist people from Central Asia, migrated into the Indian subcontinent and occupied the territory once covered by the Indus civilization. Some aspects of its culture were absorbed by the Aryans but all memory of the civilization itself was lost. It remained undiscovered until the early 1920s when excavations started at Mohenjo-Daro and Harappa.

SUMERIAN DECLINE

The half-millennium between the fall of the 3rd Dynasty of Ur (2004 BC) and that of the 1st Dynasty of Babylon (1595 BC) is known as the Old Babylonian period. It witnessed the decline of Sumerian civilization and the emergence of Babylon as the leading political power and cultural center of Mesopotamia.

The most powerful of the states to emerge from the collapse of the 3rd Dynasty of Ur and the breakup of its empire was Isin. After taking control of the city from Ibbi-Sin, Ishbi-Erra (r. 2017–1985) gradually extended his authority over almost all of Sumer, filling the power vacuum created by the decline of Ur. In 1995 he took Ur itself after expelling the Elamites. Ishbi-Erra and his successors preserved Sumerian traditions and ruled in the style of the 3rd Dynasty kings, though they failed to restore the centralized institutions of the 3rd Dynasty state.

Isin's domination was ended by an ambitious Amorite called Gungunum (r. 1932–1906) who came to power in the nearby city of Larsa and took Ur soon after. Since Ur was the major seaport of Mesopotamia, this meant that Isin no longer controlled the valuable Persian Gulf trade routes. Isin's power was further weakened in the reigns of Gungunum's successors, Abisare (r. 1905–1895) and Sumuel (r. 1894–1866), who built canals to divert the city's water supply. Similar tactics have continued to be used in the region

37

right up to the present day: Saddam Hussein's forces diverted rivers to drain the marshland refuges of Shiite rebels in southern Iraq following the Gulf War in AD 1991.

Isin was finally conquered by Larsa during the reign of Rim-Sin (r. 1822–1763), the last noteworthy Sumerian ruler. For about 30 years Rim-Sin dominated Sumer, adopting, like Ishbe-Erra before him, the style of the 3rd Dynasty rulers though his empire was even less centralized than his predecessor's. In 1763 Rim-Sin was defeated by Hammurabi (r. 1792–1750), the able and energetic king of the previously unimportant Akkadian city of Babylon, and his empire collapsed.

SHAMSHI-ADAD THE CONQUEROR

The beginning of the 2nd millennium BC saw the emergence of a number of powerful city states in northern Mesopotamia – Eshnunna, Mari, Yamhad (modern Aleppo) and Ashur, the city that gave its name to the later Assyrian state. Ashur, first mentioned in written sources in the Agade period, had become an important trading city with a network of merchant colonies throughout Anatolia by the 19th century BC. About 1813 Shamshi-Adad, an Amorite chieftain (r.c. 1813–1781), became king of Ashur and used it as a power base to conquer most of northern Mesopotamia. He ruled with the assistance of his two sons. The elder and more capable, Ishme-Dagan, was installed at the key fortress of Ekallatum, the younger, Yasmah-Addu, at Mari, a wealthy city on the Euphrates.

Letters between the three of them, found preserved in the palace archives at Mari, paint a vivid picture of court life and diplomacy in Shamshi-Adad's kingdom. He had little faith in his younger son and often wrote to berate him for his indifferent attitude to administrative matters.

Are you still a child? he asked on one occasion, *Have you no beard on your chin? Even in the prime of life you haven't organized a proper household. Ever since Usur-awassu died, who has been running your household? Promise me that you will appoint an official within two or three days, so that the post will not just vanish. I can't understand why you didn't appoint a man to that post the day it fell vacant.*

After receiving a particularly stinging rebuke from his father, Yasmah-Addu replied petulantly

Now how can I be like a child and incapable of directing affairs when Daddy promoted me? How can it be, that although I have grown up with Daddy ever since I was little, now some servant or other has succeeded in ousting me from Daddy's affections? So now I am coming to Daddy right now, to have it out with Daddy about my unhappiness.

Yasmah-Addu's incompetence made him a liability at times and one occasion his father had to dispatch 16,000 troops to support him. Ishme-Dagan sent his brother regular reports of his military achievements, making him feel even more inadequate and resentful. He enjoyed a more congenial correspondence with Aplahanda the ruler of Carchemish, with whom he shared a taste for fine wine. In one letter Aplahanda invites Yasmah-Addu to write to him if ever he lacked good wine to drink: clearly Yasmah-Addu did, as Aplahanda wrote again to say that he was sending fifty jars of the best wine from his private supplies.

On Shamshi-Adad's death in 1781 his kingdom was divided between his sons. Predictably, Yasmah-Addu was quickly overthrown and Zimri-Lim (r. 1779–1757), an exiled member the old ruling family of Mari, took over. Not so predictable was the fate of Ishme-Dagan who inherited his father's throne. On his accession, Ishme-Dagan boasted that he held the halters of the kings of Elam and Eshnunna but early success had made him over-confident. Weakened by attacks from these supposedly subservient states, he soon lost most of his father's kingdom including its capital at Shubat-Enlil. Reduced to ruling the Assyrian heartland of Ashur and Nineveh, Ishme-Dagan survived as a minor ruler until about 1740.

THE RISE OF BABYLON

In about 1894 BC an able Amorite dynasty established itself at the minor Akkadian city of Babylon. Over the next century the Babylonian kings gradually extended their influence so that by the time Hammurabi came to the throne in 1792 Babylon controlled most of Akkad. Hammurabi was probably a vassal of Shamshi-Adad. According to the year-names of his reign (the Mesopotamian system of dating which referred to events that had occurred in the previous year) he conquered Isin and Uruk in 1787, but in the first half of his reign he is said mostly to have built temples and canals.

In 1762 Hammurabi claimed to have defeated a coalition of Elam, Subartu, Gutium, Eshnunna and Malgium and the following year overcame Rim-Sin of Larsa in alliance with Mari and Eshnunna, going on to annex all of Sumer. Subsequently he turned against his former allies. Mari was destroyed in 1757 and Eshnunna conquered in 1755, by diverting its water supply. Hammurabi's

ABOVE *A life-size statue of Isht-up-ilum, who was governor of Mari around 2100. It was found in the throne room of the palace destroyed by Hammurabi about 450 years later, tumbled down a flight of stairs.*

RIGHT *The site of Mari on the Euphrates river. An important city state on the west bank of the Euphrates, Mari grew wealthy from tolls on the trade passing along the river. It was conquered at the end of the 19th century by Shamshi-Adad, who installed his younger son Yasmah-Addu there as king. After Shamshi-Adad's death Mari regained its independence under Zimri-Lin (r. 1779-1757), who rebuilt the palace. In 1757 the city was attacked and destroyed by Hammurabi, king of Babylon, and the site was abandoned. More than 20,000 clay tablets have been excavated from the palace archives at Mari. They provide a remarkably detailed picture of Mesopotamian administration in the 19th and 18th centuries BC.*

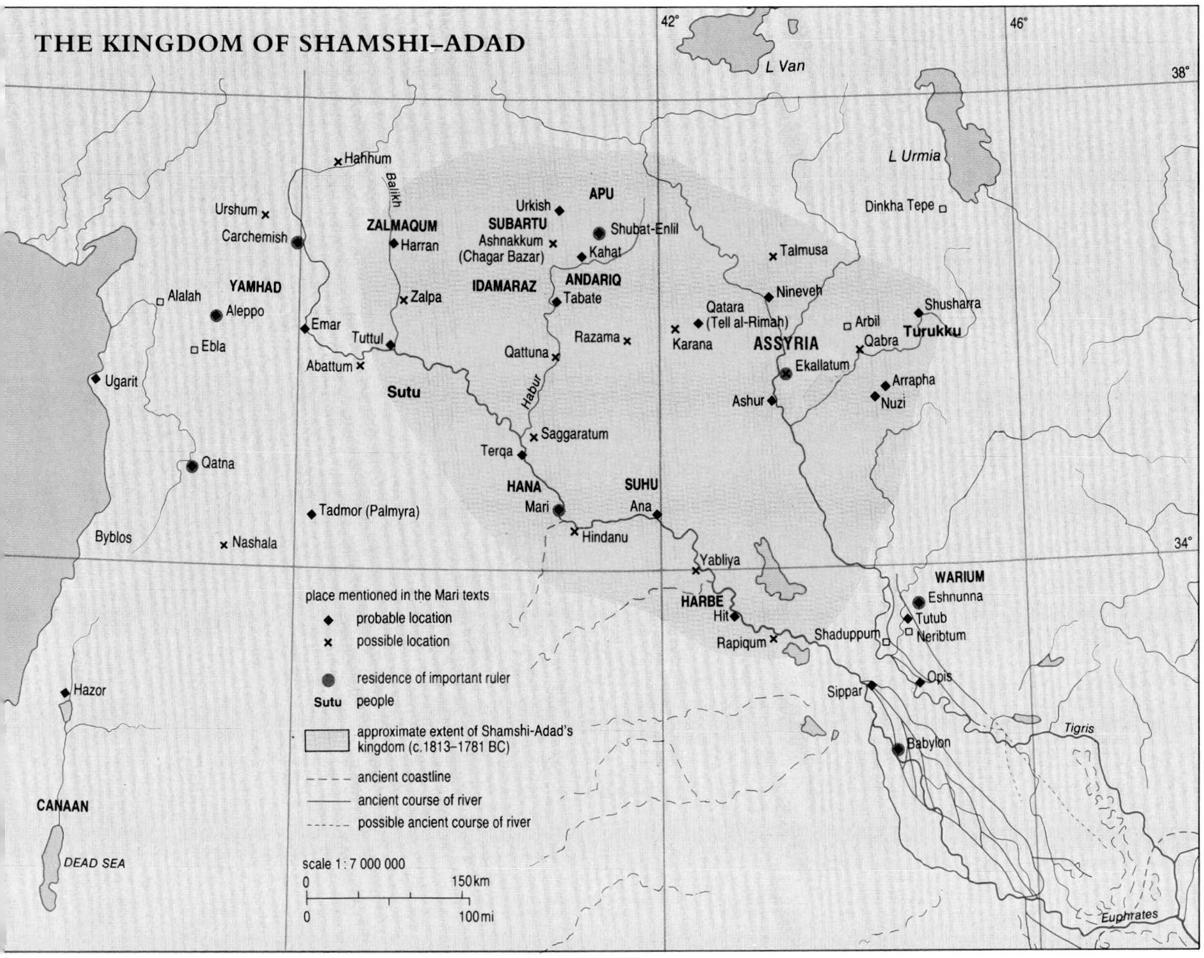
THE KINGDOM OF SHAMSHI-ADAD
42°
46°
38°
34°
L Van
L Urmia
Dinkha Tepe
Harhum
Balikh
Urshum
Carchemish
ZALMAQUM
Harran
SUBARTU
Urkish
APU
Shubat-Enlil
Ashnakkum
(Chagar Bazar)
Kahat
IDAMARAZ
ANDARIQ
Tabate
Zalpa
Talmusa
Nineveh
Qatara
(Tell al-Rimah)
Karana
ASSYRIA
Arbil
Qabra
Turukku
Shusharra
Ekallatum
Arrapha
Nuzi
Ashur
Alalah
YAMHAD
Aleppo
Ebla
Emar
Tuttul
Abattum
Razama
Qattuna
Habur
Ugarit
Sutu
Saggaratum
Terqa
Qatna
HANA
Mari
SUHU
Ana
Hindanu
Tadmor (Palmyra)
Byblos
Nashala
Yabliya
HARBE
Hit
Rapiqum
Shaduppum
Neribtum
WARIUM
Eshnunna
Tutub
Opis
Sippar
Babylon
Tigris
Euphrates
Hazor
CANAAN
DEAD SEA
place mentioned in the Mari texts
probable location
possible location
residence of important ruler
Sutu people
approximate extent of Shamshi-Adad's kingdom (c.1813–1781 BC)
ancient coastline
ancient course of river
possible ancient course of river
scale 1 : 7 000 000
0
150km
0
100mi

LEFT *From nothing, Shamshi-Adad (c. 1813–1781) created a kingdom that included most of northern Mesopotamia. Ashur, Nineveh and the capital Shubat-Enlil were under his direct rule. The fortress-city of Ekallatum was ruled by his heir Ishme-Dagan and the wealthy city of Mari by his younger son Yasmah-Addu. Smaller centers such as Karana were left under local rulers who became his vassals. The tablets found at Mari record more than 400 place-names, but only a fraction can be identified with confidence.*

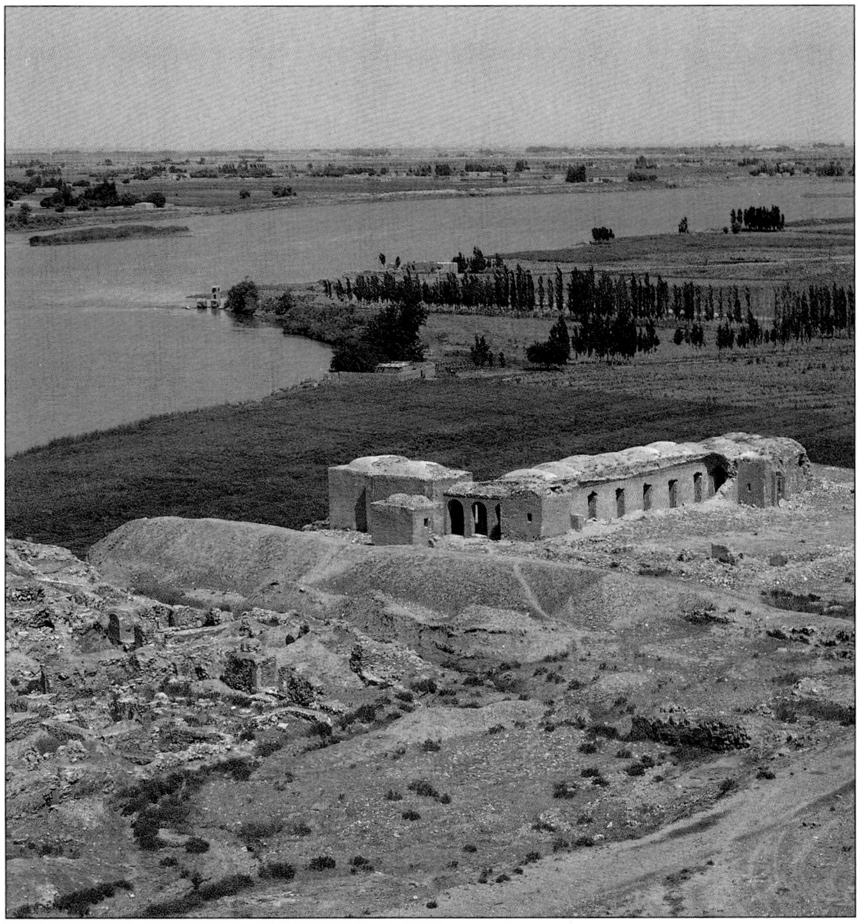

influence, though not his direct control, may even have extended as far north as Assyria as he claimed to have restored temples at Nineveh and Ashur. In Mesopotamian tradition, restoring a city's temples was an important way of demonstrating overlordship. Under Hammurabi Babylon became the leading religious and cultural center of Mesopotamia, a position it retained even when its political fortunes declined after his death in 1750.

Hammurabi's Law Code

Today Hammurabi is chiefly remembered for his law code. Following in a tradition of legislation established in Sumerian times, Hammurabi defined its purpose as "to cause justice to prevail in the land, to destroy the wicked and the evil, that the strong may not oppress the weak." However, in its heavy reliance on brutal retaliatory punishments involving the mutilation or death of the guilty party or members of his family, the code departs radically from Sumerian customs:

> *If a freeman has put out the eye of the son of a freeman, they shall put out his eye....If a builder has built a house for a freeman and has not made his work sound, so that the house he has made falls down and causes the death of the owner of the house, that builder*

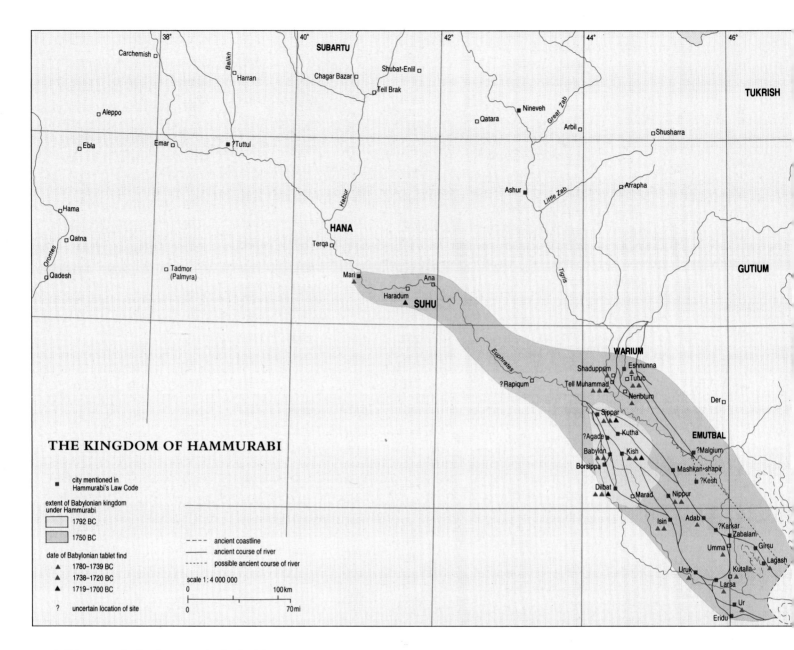

THE KINGDOM OF HAMMURABI

■ city mentioned in
    Hammurabi's Law Code

extent of Babylonian kingdom
under Hammurabi

☐ 1792 BC

▨ 1750 BC

date of Babylonian tablet find

▲ 1780–1739 BC

▲ 1738–1720 BC

▲ 1719–1700 BC

? uncertain location of site

– – – ancient coastline

——— ancient course of river

- - - - possible ancient course of river

scale 1 : 4 000 000

0   100km

0   70mi

shall be put to death. If it causes the death of the son of the owner of the house, they shall kill the son of that builder.

The 282 sections of the code deal with commercial, family and property law, slavery, fees, prices and wages. They do not, however, constitute a complete legal system. Though the code instructs plaintiffs to consult it, it is likely that Hammurabi caused it to be set up on a stone monument, or stele, mainly for the benefit of the gods, so that they might see what a just ruler he was. His code presents an idealized view of Babylonian society. At its head was the king and below him three classes: the *awilum* or freeman; the *mushkennum*, a property-less dependent of the state; and the *wardum* or slave. The class structure was not static. Slaves could own and accumulate property and buy their freedom, while freemen could be forced into slavery as a result of debt.

And in their relation to the king, all men and women were slaves.

Babylonian power went into decline under Hammurabi's son, Samsu-iluna (r. 1749–1712). In 1742 he faced a rebellion by Rim-Sin II of Larsa which took five years to defeat and caused great economic damage to the south. By the end of Samsu-iluna's reign, control of the south, and with it the important Persian Gulf trade routes, had passed from Babylon to the shadowy "Sealand" dynasty. In the 17th century BC new and threatening powers began to gather on the northern borders of Mesopotamia. Most dangerous were the Hurrians – a tribal people from Armenia who overran Assyria in about 1680 – and the Hittites, who invaded Anatolia from Thrace about 1800 BC and had emerged as a powerful kingdom there by 1650. Some fifty years later, in 1595, the Hittite king Mursilis led a campaign

ABOVE *In the second half of his reign, Hammurabi (r. 1792–1750), king of Babylon, won control over much of Mesopotamia, ending the independence of many cities. In his Law Code he claimed to have restored many temples including those of Ashur, Nineveh and Tuttul.*

RIGHT *This basalt stele inscribed with the text of of Hammurabi's famous Law Code is surmounted by a relief showing the Babylonian king standing before the sun-god Shamash, Lord of Justice. The stele was found at Susa where it was taken as booty by the Elamites after sacking Babylon in c.1159.*

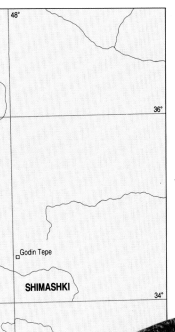

down the Euphrates and sacked Babylon, bringing an end to Hammurabi's dynasty and ushering in a dark age that lasted almost two centuries.

INHERENT WEAKNESSES

The most obvious characteristic of the early Mesopotamian empires was their instability. The ancient Mesopotamians themselves recognized the pattern of rapid rise and fall. With the favor of the gods, they believed, one city or dynasty might for a time be permitted to dominate the others but when the gods decreed, it would be cast down and replaced by another. The success of an early Mesopotamian state was very dependent on the abilities of its ruler. Military craft counted for much. A successful warrior king, such as Shamshi-Adad, could expect to form alliances with other rulers who would be willing to accept vassal status in return for protection or a share in the booty of successful campaigns. For this reason a good soldier could quickly build up an empire through conquest and diplomacy. A letter of Zimri-Lim of Mari written about 1770 shows how necessary such alliances were:

> There is no king who can be mighty alone. Ten or fifteen kings follow Hammurabi, the man (i.e. king) of Babylon; as many follow Rim-Sin, the man of Larsa, as many follow Ibal-pi-El, the man of Eshnunna, and as many follow Amut-pi-El, the man of Qatna, and twenty kings follow Yarim-Lim, the man of Yamhad.

However, if luck turned against a ruler, or his successor lacked his abilities, these allies usually turned out to be fair weather friends only.

The administrative structures of early Mesopotamian states – essentially still city governments – were weak. Without the king's constant attention to detail they could easily break down, as happened with the indolent Yasmah-Addu of Mari. Conquered city-states might be garrisoned but they could not generally be brought under direct rule. Instead governors were recruited from the local elite and given the duty of tax collection. The imperial power might appoint an advisor to keep a supervisory eye on the native governor but there was no question of imposing a completely alien administration. This system worked well as long as the imperial power was militarily strong and was able to deter rebellion. However, in times of weakness, dynastic confusion or other misfortune, the native governors could simply stop forwarding the taxes they raised, call on traditional local loyalties and declare independence.

All rulers, whatever their abilities, faced the problem that Mesopotamia lacked defensible frontiers. This meant that it was always vulnerable to invasion and infiltration by nomads from the Syrian desert to the west or tribes from the Zagros mountains to the east. The inhabitants of these regions were eager for a share in the wealth and fertility of the plains themselves and therefore, though they might overthrow states, they did not seek to destroy Mesopotamian civilization itself. Those, like the Kassites and Amorites, who did succeed in settling on the plains, quickly adopted Mesopotamian customs and became fully assimilated with the native population.

ZIGGURATS

Ziggurats – the most distinctive monuments of ancient Mesopotamia – developed out of the ancient Sumerian custom of raising temples on platforms. Three, and eventually as many as eight, platforms were built on top of one another to lift the temple high above the ground. The first ziggurats proper were built by Ur-Nammu (2112–2095), founder of the 3rd Dynasty of Ur, at Ur, Eridu, Nippur and Uruk. They all followed the same rectangular plan with the upper stages being reached by three staircases meeting at right-angles. This was also the plan for the most famous of all ziggurats – that of the god Marduk at Babylon, built in the 18th century BC. Known as Etemananki ("the house that is the foundation of heaven and earth"), this has passed into western mythology as the Tower of Babel. It was eight stages tall and had benches halfway up on which worshipers could rest during the steep ascent. The Babylonians believed that Marduk slept on a couch in the temple on its summit. This was left unoccupied at night except by a priestess whom the god was believed to have chosen as a consort for himself.

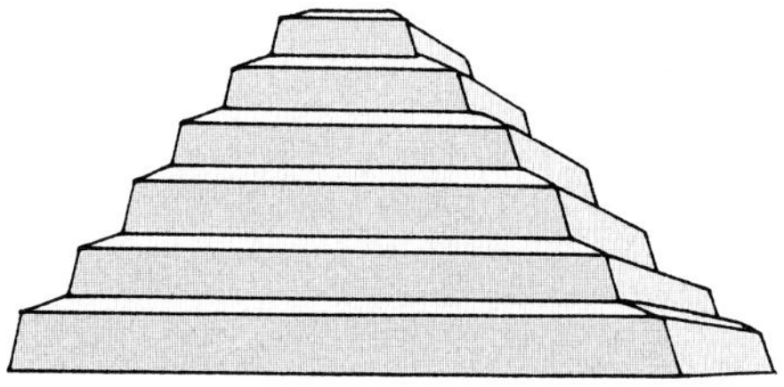

Egyptian stepped pyramid

Mesoamerican temple pyramid

LEFT *Ziggurats were similar in shape to the stepped pyramids of Egypt like the one at Saqqara (top).* But there were important differences. Pyramids were monumental tombs with tomb chambers hidden in the center and no structures on top. Ziggurats were imposing platforms for the temples built on their summits. In this respect they resemble the Mesoamerican pyramids such as the one at Chichen Itza (below).

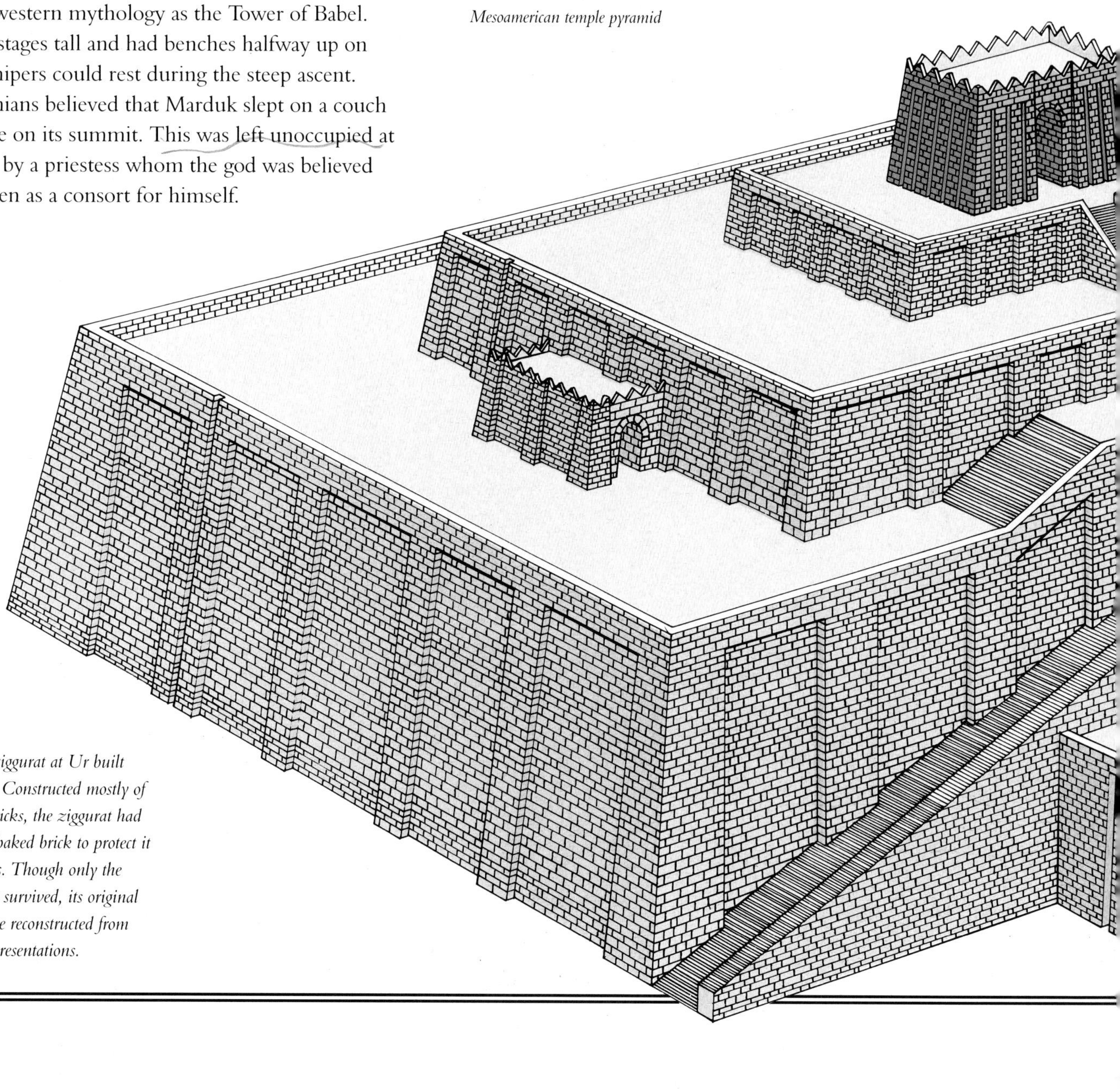

RIGHT *The ziggurat at Ur built by Ur-Nammu. Constructed mostly of sun-dried mudbricks, the ziggurat had a thick facing of baked brick to protect it from the elements. Though only the lower stages have survived, its original appearance can be reconstructed from contemporary representations.*

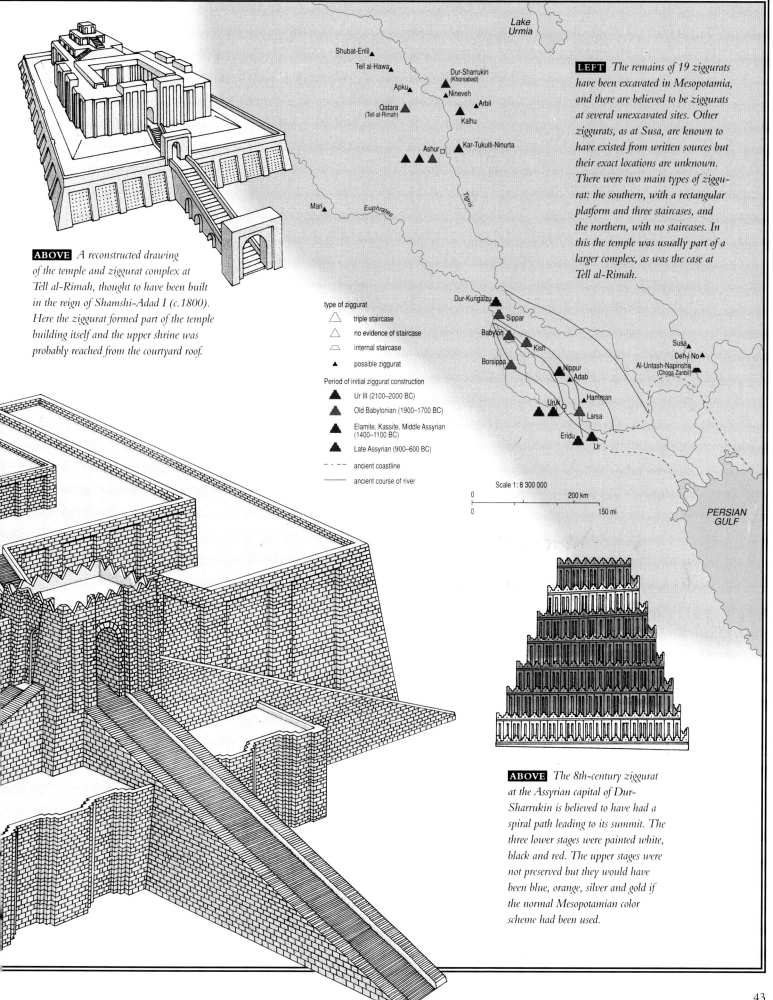

ABOVE *A reconstructed drawing of the temple and ziggurat complex at Tell al-Rimah, thought to have been built in the reign of Shamshi-Adad I (c.1800). Here the ziggurat formed part of the temple building itself and the upper shrine was probably reached from the courtyard roof.*

LEFT *The remains of 19 ziggurats have been excavated in Mesopotamia, and there are believed to be ziggurats at several unexcavated sites. Other ziggurats, as at Susa, are known to have existed from written sources but their exact locations are unknown. There were two main types of ziggurat: the southern, with a rectangular platform and three staircases, and the northern, with no staircases. In this the temple was usually part of a larger complex, as was the case at Tell al-Rimah.*

Lake Urmia

Shubat-Enlil
Tell al-Hawa
Apku
Qatara (Tell al-Rimah)
Dur-Sharrukin (Khorsabad)
Nineveh
Arbil
Kalhu
Ashur
Kar-Tukulti-Ninurta
Mari
Euphrates
Tigris

type of ziggurat
△ triple staircase
△ no evidence of staircase
⬱ internal staircase
▲ possible ziggurat

Period of initial ziggurat construction
▲ Ur III (2100–2000 BC)
▲ Old Babylonian (1900–1700 BC)
▲ Elamite, Kassite, Middle Assyrian (1400–1100 BC)
▲ Late Assyrian (900–600 BC)
--- ancient coastline
— ancient course of river

Dur-Kurigalzu
Sippar
Babylon
Kish
Borsippa
Nippur
Adab
Uruk
Hamman
Larsa
Eridu
Ur
Susa
Deh-i No
Al-Untash-Napirisha (Choga Zanbil)

Scale 1: 8 300 000
0 — 200 km
0 — 150 mi

PERSIAN GULF

ABOVE *The 8th-century ziggurat at the Assyrian capital of Dur-Sharrukin is believed to have had a spiral path leading to its summit. The three lower stages were painted white, black and red. The upper stages were not preserved but they would have been blue, orange, silver and gold if the normal Mesopotamian color scheme had been used.*

EARLY TECHNOLOGY

The transition to a settled way of life about 7500 had very great significance for technological development, freeing it from the limitations imposed by the need for nomadic or seminomadic hunting–gathering groups to have only artifacts that were easily portable – simple stone axes, weapons, scrapers and cutting tools, fishing hooks and harpoons, wooden implements, fiber ropes and baskets. In the next four thousand years or so a wide range of technologies was developed until, by about 3500, the peoples of the Near East possessed almost all the technical skills that formed the basis of civilized life before the Industrial Revolution: building construction, wheeled vehicles, shipbuilding, metalworking, carpentry, pottery, spinning and weaving, together with food processing techniques such as baking and brewing.

The two most important technological developments in the ancient Near East were the discovery of the means of capturing and storing river floodwaters to irrigate fields and the invention of the plow to prepare the ground for sowing. These allowed the full agricultural potential of the fertile soils of the arid Mesopotamian floodplains to be realized. Though sails were used on ships to harness the wind, the main source of energy in the ancient Mesopotamian civilizations – indeed, in all ancient civilizations – was the organized muscle power of men and animals. It was this that built the ziggurats. It was not until the Middle Ages that wind and water were harnessed on a large scale to power industrial activities.

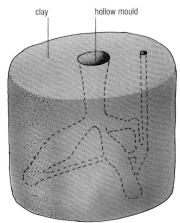

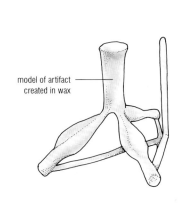

model of artifact created in wax

clay

hollow mould

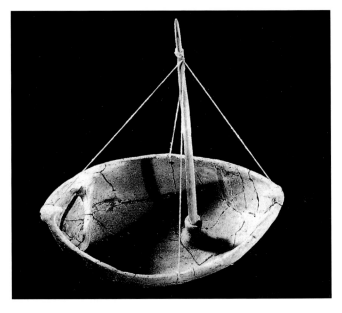

ABOVE *A baked clay model of a boat from an Ubaid period grave at Eridu, c.4000. The model has a socket for a mast and holes for rigging (reconstructed here). Ubaid pottery was widely traded around the Persian Gulf, suggesting that seafaring was already well advanced.*

LEFT *The lines of ancient irrigation canals scar the plains of southern Mesopotamia. These canals were designed to avoid silting up too quickly, and some are still in use today. As irrigation water evaporated from the surface of the land, mineral salts built up in the soil, leading to a gradual loss of fertility. Many believe it was this that brought about the eventual decline of Mesopotamian civilization.*

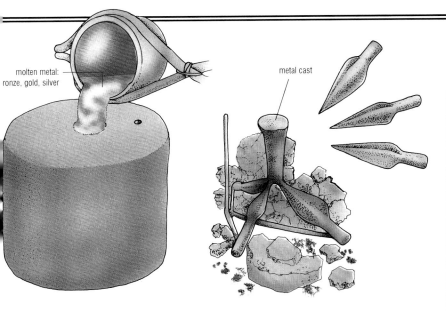

molten metal: ronze, gold, silver

metal cast

ABOVE *The lost wax method of casting in bronze, silver and gold was invented in the Near East in the 4th millennium BC. A model of the object to be cast was made in wax and covered in clay to make a mold. When this was heated the wax melted and and was poured away. Molten metal was then poured into the mold. Once the metal had cooled and hardened the mold was broken open to release the cast object. Objects were made out of native (i.e. natural) metallic copper in the Aceramic Neolithic period and by about 6200*

copper was being smelted from ore. Metal tools only began to replace stone in everyday use in the 4th millennium BC after it was discovered that copper could be hardened by alloying it with arsenic or tin to make bronze. Iron was first smelted in the 2nd millennium but only came into widespread use after 1000. Because it was cheaper and harder it soon replaced bronze in everyday use.

ABOVE *The invention of glass about 1600 was one of the greatest achievements of Mesopotamian craftsmen. This 14th-century glass vessel from Tell al-Rimah imitates the shape of contemporary pottery vessels. The vessel was molded on a core. Rods of colored glass were let into the still molten surface of the vessel and then drawn up and down to create the pattern.*

LEFT *A baked clay model of a four-wheeled war chariot from northern Syria, 19th century BC. Wheeled vehicles were probably invented in the Near East in the 4th millennium BC, the idea possibly developing out of the potter's wheel. From there the wheel spread to Europe, North Africa, southern and central Asia.*

The earliest known examples of writing, on clay tablets found in the Sumerian city of Uruk, date from around 3300 BC. They use simple pictographic signs. Since more than 700 signs are known at this date, development of the system must have begun much earlier. The more easily written, stylized cuneiform script evolved during the 3rd millennium BC. The signs were made by pressing a reed stylus onto wet clay, leaving a series of wedgelike marks (*cuneus* is the Latin for wedge), and were gradually refined to represent phonetic values. Cuneiform was adapted successfully to many other Near Eastern languages including Akkadian, Assyrian and Babylonian. Around 2400 writing began to be used for purposes other than accounting – to record law codes, letters, chronicles, religious texts and for literary composition. Cuneiform script included hundreds of different signs and scribes took several years to master it. Literacy was the preserve of a tiny minority and letters began with the formula "Say to…" since they would have to be read aloud by a trained scribe.

LEFT *A hollow clay sphere and tokens from Susa, Iran. The surface has impressed marks recording the tokens sealed inside the sphere; others have scratched signs on the surface. This system of accounting was widely used in the Near East as a precursor to writing.*

RIGHT *Documents were inscribed on wet clay tablets which were then allowed to dry. To prevent forgery, tablets were sometimes sealed inside clay envelopes that had the same text written on the outside as on the tablet. This example is from Alalah, Syria (c. 1800).*

LEFT *Sumerian pictographic tablets usually record the transfer of goods. This example from Kish (c. 3000) lists various commodities including beer, bread and livestock. The circular, crescent and D-shaped signs represent numbers. The pictograph for "eat" (a head combined with a bowl) can be be seen in the lower lefthand corner (see below). The tablet would have been read in columns from right to left.*

RIGHT *Fully developed cuneiform script carved on a relief sculpture from the 9th-century Assyrian palace at Kalhu. By this time the symbols have become highly stylized and abstract, and bear little resemblance to the original pictographs. Cuneiform script was read across from left to right.*

DEVELOPMENT OF THE CUNEIFORM SCRIPT

The meanings of most Sumerian pictographs were fairly obvious. Sometimes they were by association – a leg meant "stand" or "walk", a bowl "food". The signs were gradually simplified so they could be inscribed with a rectangular ended reed stylus, but most can be traced back to identifiable pictures. Some of the words and phonetic values represented by the signs changed with the passage of time.

PICTOGRAPHIC SIGN c.3100 BC									
INTERPRETATION	star	?sun over horizon	?stream	ear of barley	bull's head	bowl	head and bowl	lower leg	?shrouded body
CUNEIFORM SIGN c.2400 BC									
CUNEIFORM SIGN c.700 BC (turned through 90°)									
PHONETIC VALUE*	dingir, an	u_4, ud	a	še	gu_4	nig_2, ninda	ku_2	du, gin, gub	lu_2
MEANING	god, sky	day, sun	water, seed, son	barley	ox	food, bread	to eat	to walk, to stand	man

*Some signs have more than one phonetic value and some sounds more than one sign. U_4 means the fourth sign with the phonetic value u.

Kingdoms of Ancient Egypt

3000–332 BC

To the ancient Egyptians the Nile was simply the "Great River." Its rhythms dominated their lives; their civilization could not have existed without it. Recognition of this absolute dependence led the Greek historian Herodotus, writing in the 5th century BC, to describe Egypt as "the gift of the Nile." From the first cataract, the rapids that conventionally marked the boundary of ancient Egypt with Nubia to the south, the Nile flowed for 500 miles (800 km) through a narrow, fertile valley. Until it broadens out into the delta, its floodplain is nowhere more than a few miles, and often only a few hundred yards, wide. It was probably the most favorable area for agriculture anywhere in the ancient world. The river flooded annually in August, after the summer rains had fallen in the East African highlands. As the waters subsided in the fall they left the fields moist and fertilized with fresh silt ready for sowing. Crops grew through the warm winter and were harvested in the spring before the next cycle of flooding began. In marked contrast with Mesopotamia, where the rivers flooded in spring after the start of the growing season and changed their courses violently and unpredictably, the Nile floodplain was a stable, if confined, environment. The complex irrigation systems and flood defenses used in Mesopotamia were largely unnecessary here, though canals and dykes helped spread the flood waters and extend the cultivable area to the edges of the valley. Cultivation of the delta would have posed a greater problem, but drainage of its swamps and lagoons seems to have begun quite early. The Faiyum, a lakeside oasis west of the Nile valley, was also an important area of settlement. The lake was much larger then than it is now, and major drainage works were undertaken by the 12th Dynasty kings.

High yields of grain were possible year after year by the farmers of ancient Egypt. Their surpluses were collected as taxes and taken to state storehouses for redistribution to administrators, craftsmen and priests, for trade or to build up

food reserves against the famine that inevitably followed if the annual flood failed, as it sometimes did. The very dependability of its environment gave ancient Egyptian civilization an appearance of serenity that emerges through its art and sculpture. Its main themes were religion and country life, while the official statues of its kings watched over the state with calm and benign expressions.

On the broad plains of Mesopotamia, farmers lived in cities and traveled out daily to work in the surrounding fields. In the long, narrow Nile valley, such an arrangement would have meant most cultivators having to walk great distances to their fields. Egypt consequently developed a more dispersed settlement pattern than Mesopotamia, becoming a land of villages and small towns rather than cities. Its towns were administrative and religious centers, not the major population centers of the Mesopotamian civilizations.

The Nile was Egypt's main highway. The prevailing winds blow north to south up the valley,

LEFT *A slate palette made to commemorate the victories of king Narmer over Lower Egypt and border tribes around 3000 BC. On this side Narmer, wearing the white crown of Upper Egypt and attended by his sandal bearer, prepares to execute a defeated foeman. Before him is a falcon, the symbol of Horus, a god closely associated with royal power. On the reverse side, Narmer wears the red crown of Lower Egypt as he surveys a battlefield and is also shown, in the guise of a bull, breaking into a walled town.*

RIGHT *In the late prehistoric period (the Predynastic, c. 6000–3000 BC) a number of regional, small-scale farming cultures developed in the Nile valley and delta. The latest was the Naqada culture of Upper Egypt, which emerged about 4000. By 3300 it had spread over the entire Nile valley and into the delta, and significant population centers had developed. This period saw the beginnings of state organization in Egypt, during which differences with the Nubian cultures to the south became more pronounced. Eventually the political border with Nubia settled at the first cataract, though Egyptian influence continued to extend beyond it. The development of writing and the emergence of a unified Egyptian kingdom under historically attested royal dynasties about 3000 marks the beginning of the Early Dynastic period. There is evidence for trade with settlements in the Levant, and some outside cultural influences may have been transmitted along this route.*

PREDYNASTIC AND EARLY DYNASTIC EGYPT

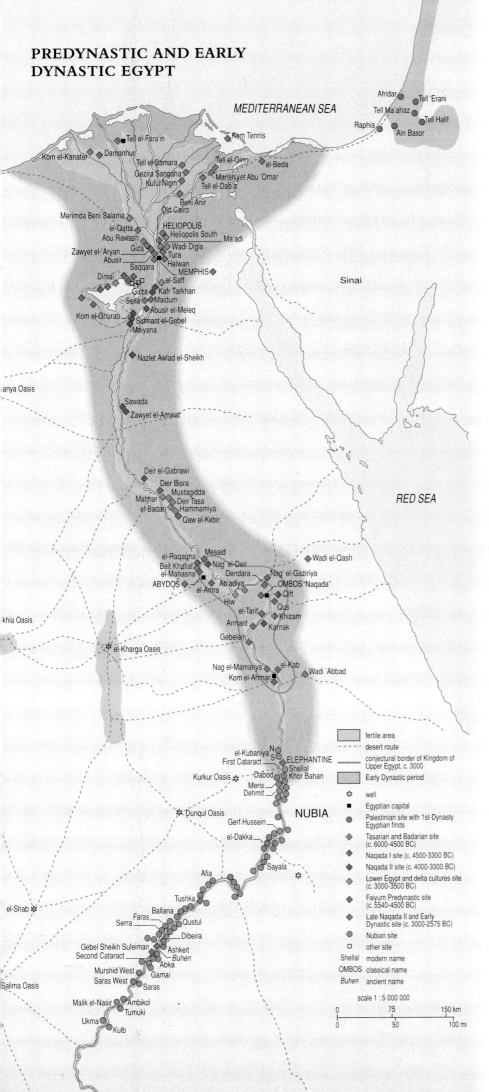

MEDITERRANEAN SEA

RED SEA

Sinai

NUBIA

fertile area

- - - desert route

conjectural border of Kingdom of Upper Egypt, c. 3000

Early Dynastic period

✳ well

■ Egyptian capital

● Palestinian site with 1st-Dynasty Egyptian finds

◆ Tasarian and Badarian site (c. 6000–4500 BC)

◆ Naqada I site (c. 4500–3300 BC)

◆ Naqada II site (c. 4000–3300 BC)

◆ Lower Egypt and delta cultures site (c. 3000–3500 BC)

◆ Faiyum Predynastic site (c. 5540–4500 BC)

◆ Late Naqada II and Early Dynastic site (c. 3000–2575 BC)

● Nubian site

□ other site

Shellal   modern name

OMBOS   classical name

Buhen   ancient name

scale 1 : 5 000 000

| 0 | 75 | 150 km |
| 0 | 50 | 100 mi |

enabling ships to travel upstream under sail and make return journeys downstream with the flow. As few settlements lay far from the river it was relatively easy to transport heavy loads of grain or building stone over long distances by boat. On either side of the narrow valley was the desert. This provided rough grazing for nomadic pastoralists and was the source of important raw materials: stone for building, sculpture and tool-making, emeralds, copper, tin and gold. Oases such as the el-Kharga were pockets of sedentary agriculture and were linked with the Nile valley by desert trade routes. The desert was a major factor in determining the unique character of Egyptian civilization. By isolating it from the influence of other civilizations and protecting it from invaders (the Egyptian kingdom was more than 1300 years old before it was first conquered by invaders from outside), the desert was largely responsible for ensuring its remarkable continuity over a span of more than 3000 years.

THE PREDYNASTIC AND EARLY DYNASTIC PERIODS

There is considerable uncertainty about the date that human settlement began in Egypt. Present evidence suggests that farmers moved into the Nile valley only after 6000 BC, but it is possible that earlier sites lie deeply buried under silt from the Nile floods. The North African climate at this time was wetter than it is today and the Sahara was mostly dry grassland, sparsely settled by pastoral and cereal farmers. In the 4th millennium BC climatic conditions changed and the Sahara began to turn into desert, forcing its farming communities to seek refuge in the Nile valley. This rapid population growth saw a number of different regional cultures developing. Chiefdoms and towns emerged. These chiefdoms had little room for expansion in the narrow confines of the valley and competition between them was probably intense. According to later written traditions, they were amalgamated into two kingdoms, Upper (southern) Egypt and Lower (northern) Egypt. The ruler regarded as the first king of both was Narmer, a king of Upper Egypt who conquered Lower Egypt about 3000 BC.

Important changes were taking place at this time, marking the beginning of the Early Dynastic period (c. 3000–2649). Writing was just coming into use – some of the earliest examples appear on the stone palettes that Narmer had carved to commemorate his victory over Lower Egypt. It was

RIGHT *The 4th Dynasty ruler Menkaure (2490–2472) flanked by the mother goddess Hathor (the wife of Horus) on his left and a personification of the seventh nome (province) of Upper Egypt on his right. Menkaure's pyramid is the last built and the smallest of the three Great Pyramids at Giza.*

BELOW *This statue of king Khephren (2520–2494) and the falcon god Horus is from the valley temple of Khephren's pyramid at Giza. Horus's wings are wrapped around the nape of Khephren's neck, symbolizing the god's protection of the king. The most famous representation of Khephren is as the face of the Great Sphinx – the huge statue with a human head and lion's body that guards the approach to his pyramid at Giza.*

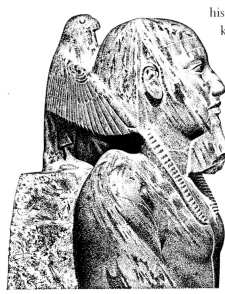

used mainly for administrative purposes and it was from the early records of year names that the dynastic lists of the kings of Egypt were later compiled. Another significant development was the founding of Memphis, strategically located where the Nile valley widened into the delta, as a new political capital: it remained the favored place for coronations throughout ancient Egyptian history. It is clear that the principle of theocratic kingship which formed the basis of the ancient Egyptian state was already well established by the beginning of the Early Dynastic period. Narmer's palettes, for example, show that the king was regarded as an incarnation of the falcon-headed sky god Horus, son of the sun god Ra. To the ancient Egyptians, the annual Nile flood was a gift from the gods and the king drew his authority from the power he claimed to control it. If the flood failed, the king's authority could be called into question and his dynasty might even be overthrown. As the king was believed to be of divine descent, he was held to be immortal. After death the king's soul

rejoined the gods and his tomb became a holy site where he was worshiped. Royal tombs were built under a mudbrick platform called a mastaba which were sometimes designed to look like palaces and were furnished with rich grave goods. At first kings and queens were accompanied in death by sacrificed retainers but this had ceased by about 2700.

THE OLD KINGDOM (2649–2134)

The development of theocratic kingship, writing and a civil service made possible an enormous increase in the power of the monarchy during the period of the Old Kingdom. This is generally reckoned to have begun with the accession of Zanakht (2649–2630), the first king of the 3rd Dynasty, but is sometimes dated from the beginning of the 4th Dynasty (2575). Written records from the Old Kingdom are still fairly sparse: as in Mesopotamia, it would be centuries before writing would be used to record history or for literary composition. Through most of the Old Kingdom period Egyptian power was confined to the delta and the Nile valley north of the first cataract, but there were times when Egyptian influence extended into Nubia as far south as the second cataract.

Old Kingdom Egypt was governed by an efficient central and local bureaucracy. The kingdom was treated as the personal property of the king and the central bureaucracy was simply an extension of the royal household. The highest official, whose title is conventionally translated as vizier, supervised the day-to-day administration of justice and taxation. Below him were chancellors, controllers of stores and other officials supported by a staff of scribes, trained in mathematics, measurement and astronomy as well as writing, who kept the records and made the calculations on which the administrative system depended. The earliest Egyptian writing system had used hieroglyphs, pictographs developed from the symbolic motifs used to decorate pottery in the Predynastic period. During the Old Kingdom period a new script, known as hieratic, was developed for administrative purposes. Hieratic characters were simpler and more flexible than hieroglyphs and were designed to be written quickly on papyrus (a paper made from the pith of the papyrus reed). For the purposes of local government, Egypt was divided into administrative provinces called nomes (from the Greek *nomos*; the ancient Egyptian term was *sepat*) under governors or nomarchs. These were selected from the royal or noble families, and had their own staff of administrators and scribes. One

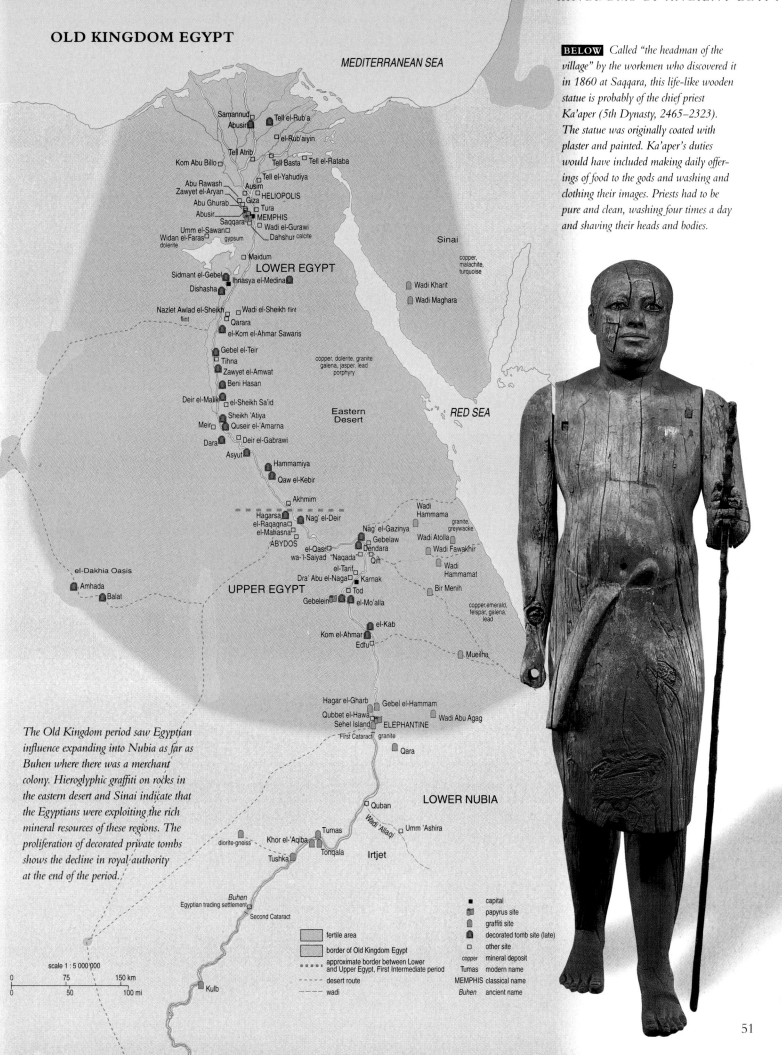

OLD KINGDOM EGYPT

MEDITERRANEAN SEA

Samannud
Abusir
Tell el-Rub'a
el-Rub'aiyin
Tell Atrib
Tell Basta
Tell el-Rataba
Kom Abu Billo
Tell el-Yahudiya
Abu Rawash
Ausim
Zawyet el-Aryan
HELIOPOLIS
Abu Ghurab
Giza
Tura
Abusir
MEMPHIS
Saqqara
Wadi el-Gurawi
Umm el-Sawan
Dahshur calcite
Widan el-Faras
gypsum
dolerite
Maidum

Sinai

copper,
malachite,
turquoise

LOWER EGYPT

Sidmant el-Gebel
Ihnasya el-Medina
Dishasha
Wadi Kharit
Wadi Maghara

Nazlet Awlad el-Sheikh
Wadi el-Sheikh flint
flint
Qarara
el-Kom el-Ahmar Sawaris

Gebel el-Teir
Tihna
Zawyet el-Amwat
Beni Hasan
Deir el-Malik
el-Sheikh Sa'id
Sheikh 'Atiya
Meir
Quseir el-'Amarna
Dara
Deir el-Gabrawi
Asyut
Hammamiya
Qaw el-Kebir

copper, dolerite, granite
galena, jasper, lead
porphyry

**Eastern
Desert**

RED SEA

Akhmim

Wadi
Hammama
Hagarsa
el-Raqagna
el-Mahasna
Nag' el-Deir
ABYDOS
Nag' el-Gazinya
Gebelaw
Dendara
el-Qasr
wa-'l-Saiyad "Naqada"
Qift
el-Tarif
Dra' Abu el-Naga
Karnak
granite,
greywacke
Wadi Atolla
Wadi Fawakhir
Wadi
Hammamat

UPPER EGYPT
Tod
Gebelein
el-Mo'alla
Bir Menih

el-Kab
copper, emerald,
felspar, galena,
lead
Kom el-Ahmar
Edfu
Mueilha

el-Dakhla Oasis
Amhada
Balat

Hagar el-Gharb
Gebel el-Hammam
Qubbet el-Hawa
Sehel Island
ELEPHANTINE
Wadi Abu Agag
First Cataract granite
Qara

The Old Kingdom period saw Egyptian
influence expanding into Nubia as far as
Buhen where there was a merchant
colony. Hieroglyphic graffiti on rocks in
the eastern desert and Sinai indicate that
the Egyptians were exploiting the rich
mineral resources of these regions. The
proliferation of decorated private tombs
shows the decline in royal authority
at the end of the period.

Quban
LOWER NUBIA
Wadi 'Allaqi
Umm 'Ashira
Tumas
diorite-gneiss
Khor el-'Aqiba
Tonqala
Irtjet
Tushka

Buhen
Egyptian trading settlement
Second Cataract

scale 1 : 5 000 000
0   75   150 km
0   50   100 mi

fertile area
border of Old Kingdom Egypt
approximate border between Lower
and Upper Egypt, First Intermediate period
desert route
wadi

■ capital
papyrus site
graffiti site
decorated tomb site (late)
□ other site
copper   mineral deposit
Tumas   modern name
MEMPHIS   classical name
Buhen   ancient name

Kulb

BELOW *Called "the headman of the
village" by the workmen who discovered it
in 1860 at Saqqara, this life-like wooden
statue is probably of the chief priest
Ka'aper (5th Dynasty, 2465–2323).
The statue was originally coated with
plaster and painted. Ka'aper's duties
would have included making daily offerings of food to the gods and washing and
clothing their images. Priests had to be
pure and clean, washing four times a day
and shaving their heads and bodies.*

of the major responsibilities of the nomarchs was the organization of irrigation works and the restoration of boundaries and landmarks washed away by the Nile floods.

The pyramids (see pages 64–67) are impressive evidence of the absolute power wielded by the rulers of the Old Kingdom over their subjects, and of their ability to marshal the resources of their kingdom. The first pyramid was built at Saqqara as a tomb for king Djoser (2630–2611) by the civil servant Imhotep, the first architect whose name is known to history and who later became deified. Pyramid building reached its peak with the Great Pyramid at Giza, 478 feet (147 m) high, built for king Cheops (Khufu, 2551–2528), and the only slightly smaller pyramid of his son Khephren (2520–2494). It was believed that only the king, as the son of Ra, was guaranteed an afterlife, but he could allow his loyal subjects to join him. In this way the pyramids helped to weld the people of Egypt into a community of interest, as everyone who contributed towards their construction gained the reassurance of life after death. In time, however, these great pyramids proved a strain on the resources of the kingdom: the pyramids of the Middle Kingdom rulers were much smaller and less elaborately built.

During the 5th Dynasty (2465–2323) the monarchy was weakened by granting out lands as rewards and favors to the nobility. The provincial governorships became hereditary positions that gradually drifted out of the the control of the king. The proliferation of lavish noble tombs dating to the late Old Kingdom is evidence of this decentralization of authority. The Old Kingdom was finally finished off by a succession of low Nile floods that occurred about 2150. Carved reliefs of emaciated people and animals demonstrate

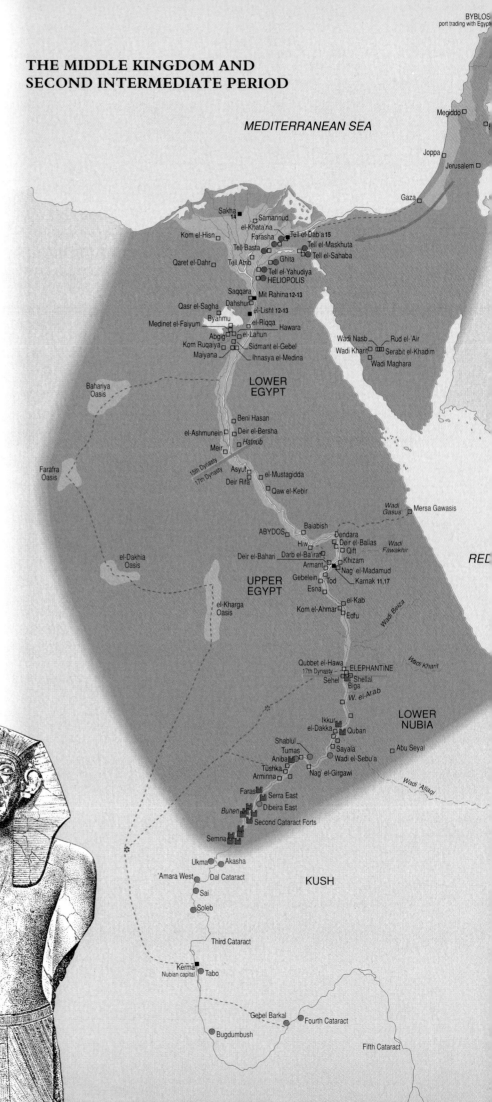

RIGHT *Senwosret III (c. 1878 –1841) was the greatest king of the Middle Kingdom period. He extended Egyptian control of Nubia as far south as Semna where, in later times, he was worshiped as a god. A campaign into Palestine during his reign began a period of Egyptian influence there. Senwosret is shown here with a careworn face, symbolizing the burdens of kingship.*

THE MIDDLE KINGDOM AND SECOND INTERMEDIATE PERIOD

	fertile area
	maximum extent of Middle Kingdom influence
→	direction of Hyksos migration
—	frontier 15th (Hyksos)/ 17th (native) dynasty
- - - -	desert route
– – – –	wadi
✿	well
■12	Egyptian capital with dynasty number
□	Egyptian site
🏛	Egyptian fort
●	Nubian site
●	Palestinian culture find
Timna	modern name
SIMYRA	classical name
Buhen	ancient name

scale 1 : 7 000 000

0   100   200 km
0   50   100 mi

the famine and starvation that followed. The monarchy's self-evident failure to bring about the return of the annual floods destroyed what was left of its authority, and pyramid building came to an end. The state eventually collapsed and for the next century Egypt was divided between rival dynasties in Upper and Lower Egypt, a period that is known to historians as the First Intermediate period (2134–2040).

THE MIDDLE KINGDOM *(2040–c.1640)*

In 2040 Egypt was reunified under Mentuhotpe (2061–2010) of the Theban dynasty of Upper Egypt. This marks the beginning of the Middle Kingdom (2040–1640). During the previous period, belief in the divine nature of the king had declined. Egyptians no longer believed that he alone was guaranteed an afterlife. Worship of the life-giving vegetation god Osiris had become popular, and through him even the humblest could aspire to an afterlife in the "Field of Reeds," a lush paradise that lay below the western horizon.

A considerable body of literature, including books of teachings and prophecy, moral tales and hymns to kings has survived and is regarded as the classical literature of ancient Egypt. It shows how the rulers of the early Middle Kingdom deliberately set about enhancing the prestige of monarchy to rebuild their authority. Royal statuary was similarly used to convey an image of the king as the "good shepherd" who takes upon himself the cares of his people. As already noted, when pyramid building returned, it was on a far more modest scale than in the Old Kingdom. By the end of the 20th century BC these measures had been successful: royal authority and political stability

had been restored and the power of the provincial governors was reduced.

Egypt's neighbors were now becoming organized in chiefdoms and small kingdoms and it became necessary for the Middle Kingdom rulers to pursue a more aggressive foreign policy than their Old Kingdom predecessors. Senwosret I (1971–1926) conquered Lower Nubia, with its extensive gold deposits, and established a new Egyptian frontier at the second cataract. This was garrisoned by his 12th Dynasty successors and protected with sophisticated fortifications. Egyptian influence spread northeast into the Levant during the reign of Senwosret III (1878–1841). Local rulers were forced to become vassals of Egypt but the area was not occupied or subjected to provincial government. In the course of the 18th century BC the bureaucracy began to grow out of control and for much of the time the effective rulers of Egypt were the viziers. During the next century there was considerable peaceful immigration from Palestine into the delta. Most of these immigrants were absorbed into the lower classes of Egyptian society but one, Khendjer, became king in about 1745.

Around 1640 the Middle Kingdom collapsed. A period of division followed, known as the Second Intermediate period (1640–1532). Exploiting Egypt's weakness, the Hyksos, a Semitic people from Palestine, invaded and quickly conquered Lower Egypt, establishing a dynasty (the 15th) at Avaris (modern Tell el-Dab'a) in the delta. Upper Egypt remained independent under the native 17th Dynasty based at Thebes (see pages 56–57) but control over Lower Nubia was lost to the Upper Nubian kingdom of Kush.

Middle Kingdom Egypt – reliant still on essentially Neolithic technology – had lagged behind its Mediterranean and Near Eastern neighbors in many important respects. Now the Hyksos rulers of the delta brought it more directly into contact with Near Eastern influences than ever before in its history. Wheeled vehicles and bronze tools and weapons came into use in Egypt for the first time. Warfare changed dramatically with the introduction of war chariots and new weapons such as the composite bow and scimitar (see pages 68–69). The Hyksos also introduced new fashions in dress, new musical instruments, new crops and domestic animals (including the horse). Some old customs, such as pyramid building, fell into disuse and were finally abandoned.

THE NEW KINGDOM: EGYPT'S IMPERIAL AGE

In many other respects, however, the Hyksos adopted Egyptian customs and there was no break in the continuity of Egyptian civilization. But for all their efforts to conform with Egyptian tradition, the Hyksos remained outsiders. Under the Theban king Seqenenre II (d.c. 1555) a long struggle began to expel the Hyksos from the delta, finally completed by Ahmose (1550–1525) in 1532. Ahmose's victory marks the beginning of the New Kingdom. The Hyksos' invasions had shown that Egypt's northeastern border was no longer secure. The New Kingdom rulers, assisted by the new methods of warfare acquired from the Hyksos dynasty, now embarked on a policy of

ABOVE *Hunting was a popular sport for New Kingdom nobles such as Nebamun, shown here in a painting from his tomb wild-fowling in a reed boat with his wife and daughter. In his hand is a throwing stick, not unlike a boomerang. Scenes and models of the good life were used to decorate and furnish tombs in the belief that they could be activated and turned into reality in the afterlife.*

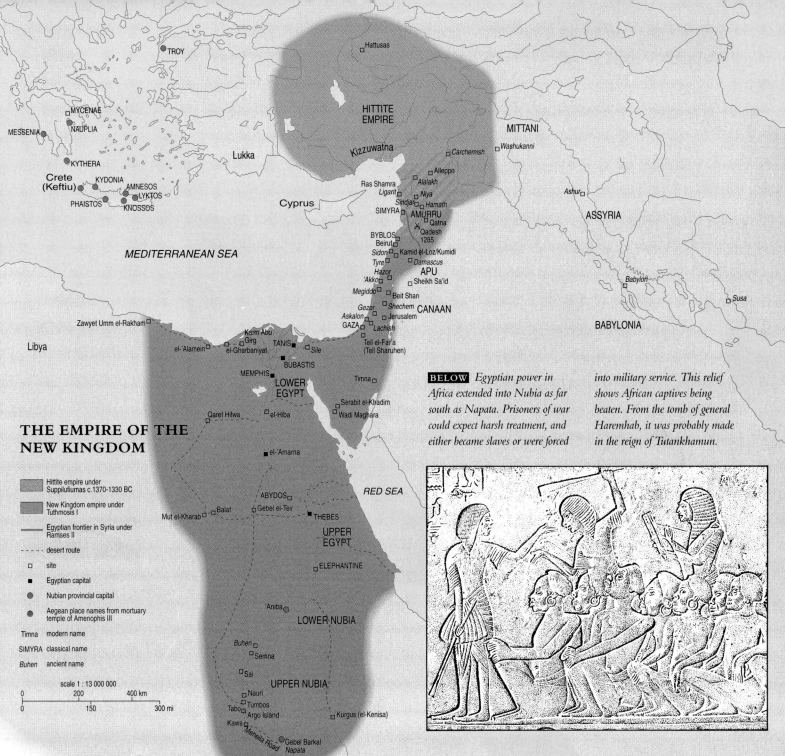

THE EMPIRE OF THE NEW KINGDOM

Map labels:

TROY
MYCENAE
NAUPLIA
MESSENIA
KYTHERA
Crete (Keftiu)
KYDONIA
AMNESOS
LYKTOS
PHAISTOS
KNOSSOS
Lukka
HITTITE EMPIRE
Hattusas
Kizzuwatna
MITTANI
Carchemish
Washukanni
Alleppo
Alalakh
Ras Shamra
Niya
Ligarit
Sindjar
Hamath
SIMYRA
AMURRU
Qatna
Qadesh 1285
Ashur
ASSYRIA
Cyprus
MEDITERRANEAN SEA
BYBLOS
Beirut
Sidon
Kamid el-Loz/Kumidi
Tyre
Damascus
Hazor
APU
'Akko
Sheikh Sa'id
Megiddo
Beit Shan
Gezer
Shechem
CANAAN
Askalon
Jerusalem
GAZA
Lachish
Tell el-Far'a (Tell Sharuhen)
Babylon
Susa
BABYLONIA
Zawyet Umm el-Rakham
Libya
el-'Alamein
Karm Abu
Girg
TANIS
Sile
el-Gharbaniyat
BUBASTIS
MEMPHIS
LOWER EGYPT
Timna
Serabit el-Khadim
Qaret Hilwa
el-Hiba
Wadi Maghara
el-'Amarna
RED SEA
ABYDOS
Balat
Gebel el-Teir
Mut el-Kharab
THEBES
UPPER EGYPT
ELEPHANTINE
'Aniba
LOWER NUBIA
Buhen
Semna
Sai
UPPER NUBIA
Nauri
Tumbos
Tabo
Argo Island
Kurgus (el-Kenisa)
Kawa
Meheila Road
Gebel Barkal
Napata

Legend:

- Hittite empire under Suppilufiumas c.1370-1330 BC
- New Kingdom empire under Tuthmosis I
- Egyptian frontier in Syria under Ramses II
- desert route
- □ site
- ■ Egyptian capital
- ● Nubian provincial capital
- ● Aegean place names from mortuary temple of Amenophis III

Timna — modern name
SIMYRA — classical name
Buhen — ancient name

scale 1 : 13 000 000

0 200 400 km
0 150 300 mi

BELOW *Egyptian power in Africa extended into Nubia as far south as Napata. Prisoners of war could expect harsh treatment, and either became slaves or were forced into military service. This relief shows African captives being beaten. From the tomb of general Haremhab, it was probably made in the reign of Tutankhamun.*

ABOVE *Under Tuthmosis I (r. 1504–1492) Egyptian rule in the Levant reached as far as the Euphrates but was pushed back under his successors. Opposition came at first from Mittani and then from the Hittite empire. Ramses II tried to restore Egypt's former position at the battle of Qadesh. A list of place-names from Greece and Crete in the mortuary chapel of Amenophis III shows there were trade links with the Aegean at this time.*

expansion and conquest which made Egypt the greatest power in the Near East. It was at this time that the Egyptian kings began to be known by the title of pharaoh (literally "great palace.")

The New Kingdom reached its greatest extent under the warrior king Tuthmosis I (1504–1492) who conquered the entire Levant and established a frontier on the upper Euphrates. Almost all important excavated sites of this period in Palestine have destruction layers that can probably be attributed to the Egyptian conquest. To the south, Lower Nubia was reconquered and the kingdom of Kush overrun to beyond the fourth cataract.

The primary motives for expansion into the Levant were to prevent a repetition of the Hyksos invasions and to establish a buffer zone against the powerful northern Mesopotamian empire of Mittani. Local rulers were left in control but were supervised by Egyptian officials, and key cities were garrisoned. In the Levant, the Egyptians had to deal both with local rebellions and with the intervention of foreign powers such as the Hittite empire and had a constant struggle to maintain control. By contrast, the motive for conquering Nubia was to exploit its rich gold deposits and control its trade routes to tropical Africa – the source of ebony, ivory and slaves. Nubia therefore was subjected to full colonial government under a viceroy directly responsible to the king.

THEBES

RIGHT *The main residential area of Thebes lay on the east bank between the temples of Karnak and Luxor. On the west bank, besides the royal burial sites, was a village for the craftsmen working on the tombs, the palace of Amenophis III (1391–1353) and several temple complexes.*

Previously only a minor provincial town, Thebes rose to prominence in the First Intermediate period when the kings of the 11th Dynasty (2134–1991) chose it as their capital. Even after the 12th Dynasty kings moved the capital north to Itjtawy, Thebes continued as the administrative center of Upper Egypt. It reached the peak of its splendor in the New Kingdom when Egypt was ruled again from Thebes. The city lay close to the rich mineral reserves of the eastern desert and was well-placed to benefit from the trade in gold and other valuable commodities from Nubia and beyond. Its temples became the most powerful and wealthiest in Egypt. Its isolation from the main power centers of the delta made it a natural center for local particularism in times of political weakness. For most of the Third Intermediate period the wealthy high-priests of the temple of Amun at Karnak ruled Upper Egypt from Thebes in virtual independence.

Thebes was divided in two by the river Nile. Dominating the city on the east bank was the vast temple complex at Karnak – ancient Egyptian Ipet-isut, meaning "The Most

ABOVE *The Valley of the Kings contains the tombs of the kings of the 18th to 20th Dynasties. With the sole exception of Tutankhamun's, all were looted of their rich burial furnishings in* antiquity. *This frieze, which shows the king offering wine to Horus and standing in adoration before the goddess Hathor, is from the tomb of Haremhab (1319–1307).*

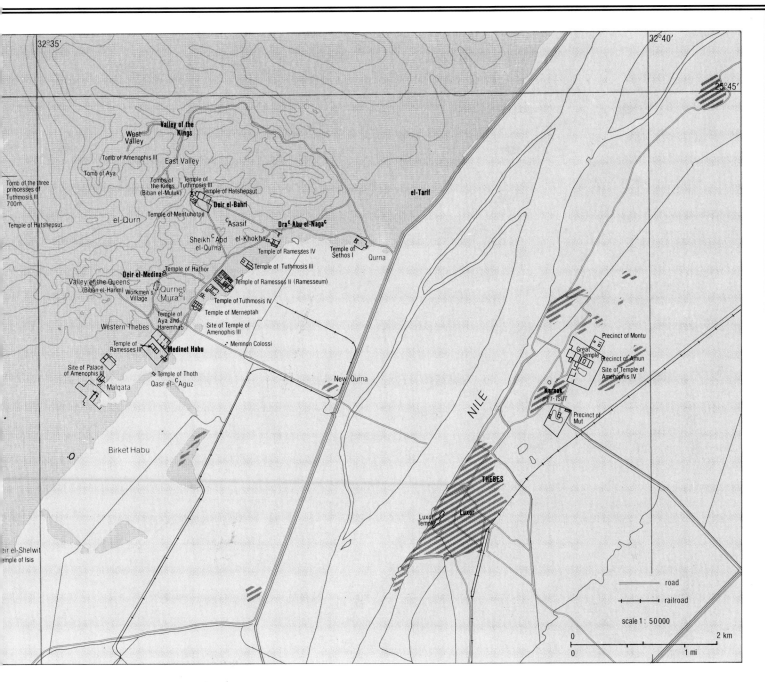

LEFT *The sanctuary of the Great Temple of Amun at Karnak. Before entering the sanctuary, priests bathed ritually in the sacred lake (in the foreground). Ceremonies were regularly performed during which the barks of the three gods worshiped at Karnak – Amun, Mut and Montu – were ritually sailed on the lake.*

Select of Places." This dates from the early Middle Kingdom when the Theban god Amun first became important. Continually expanded and rebuilt over the next 2000 years, it eventually covered nearly 250 acres (100 hectares). Two other Theban gods, Montu and Mut, had shrines at Karnak, while the temple of Luxor, also connected with the worship of·Amun, lay to the south. On the western bank were the royal burial sites of the Valley of the Kings and the Valley of the Queens, with their associated cult temples.

THE HERETIC PHARAOH

One of the few sharp breaks in the cultural continuity of Egyptian civilization occurred during the reign of Amenophis IV (1353–1335), one of Egypt's most remarkable, though not most successful, rulers. Amenophis was a radical religious reformer who attempted to replace Egypt's traditional polytheism with the monotheistic cult of the Aten or sun disk. In the fifth year of his reign Amenophis changed his name to Akhenaten ("He Who is Pleasing to the Aten") and founded a new capital which he called Akhetaten ("Horizon of the Aten"), known today as El-'Amarna (see pages 60–61). The priesthoods of the traditional gods were abolished and their property was confiscated by the crown.

Akhenaten's monotheism was not entirely unprecedented in ancient Egyptian religion. Already hymns to Amun, a Theban sun-god equated to Ra, addressed him in terms of universal power, but there remained room for the traditional gods who were seen as complementary manifestations of Amun-Ra. In Akhenaten's religion, Aten was the only god and showed himself to mankind as the sun disk. He was the creator of all things, the giver of life, and his temples were open to the sky so that worshipers could see the manifestation of the Aten. There were no mysteries, no secret rites, no priesthood: the king was the sole intermediary between the Aten and humanity. Striking similarities between the Aten hymns and

THE LEVANT OF THE AMARNA LETTERS

city mentioned in the Amarna letters
● with ruler
● other
× city with Egyptian governor

scale 1 : 2 600 000
0 — 100 km
0 — 70 mi

The sickly pharaoh Amenophis III (r. 1391–1353) presided over a period of peace and prosperity. Many of the Amarna letters were written during his reign.

Ugarit

Tunip

Arvad   Qatna

Simurru   AMURRU

Arqite   Qadesh
Ardata
Ammiya

Batroun   Labwe

Byblos

Hashabu

Beirut   Hasi

Sidon   Kumidu   APU

Unidentified cities with rulers mentioned in the Amarna letters:

Arashni
Barga
Bit-Tenni
Enishasi
Gintiashna
Gintikirmal
Guddashuna
Halunnu
Mushihuna
Naziba
Ruhizzi
Shaskhini
Tubu
Tunanad
Tushultu

Tyre   Usu   Dan

Hazor

Acco

Hannaton   Ashtaroth
Achshaph   Kenath
Shimron   Yenoam
                        Bozrah
Megiddo   Shunem
Taanach
Gina   Beth-Shan
Gath-Padalla   Pella
                Zaphon
Shechem

Gath-Rimmon
Jaffa   Shiloh   CANAAN

Gezer   Aijalon   Jericho
Ashdod   Ekron
          Jerusalem
Ashkelon
          Keilah

Gaza   Lachish

Sharuhen   *DEAD SEA*

Yurza

Zoar

There were three Egyptian provinces in the Levant: Amurru, Apu and Canaan. Local vassal-kings were responsible to the Egyptian governor of each province. Over half the cities mentioned in the Amarna letters have been identified but the rest are still unknown.
LEFT: A cuneiform clay tablet from the Amarna archive in which the ruler of Amurru tries to explain why he refused to receive the pharaoh's envoys.

Psalm 104 of the Bible have raised the possibility of a link between Atenism and the religion of the Hebrews and both may have developed out of a wider ferment of religious ideas in the Near East at this period.

What did Akhenaten hope to gain from his religious revolution? One explanation is that he saw Atenism as a way to increase royal authority by neutralizing the politically powerful priest-hoods of the traditional cults. However, there was little popular enthusiasm for the new religion – even the workmen building Akhetaten stuck to the traditional gods – and by attacking the priest-hoods Akhenaten earned the resentment of many within the ruling class. Atenism seem to have become established only among the immediate court circle. A strong reaction followed Akhenaten's death, and his religion was abandoned along with his capital. His successor Tutankhaten, a sickly son by a minor wife, was persuaded to change his name to Tutankhamun, and Akhenaten's name was erased from monuments.

None the less, Akhenaten's reign has left an enduring and, to historians of the ancient Near East, invaluable legacy. In the late 19th century, excavation of the abandoned palace "record office" at his capital of Akhetaten revealed an archive of over 350 letters written in cuneiform on clay tablets relating to matters of diplomacy during the reigns of Amenophis III and Akhenaten. Over 300 of the letters, the majority, are from vassal rulers in Palestine and the Levant. The region was divided into three provinces, each with an Egyptian governor: Amurru in southern Syria, Apu (roughly equivalent to modern Lebanon) and Canaan (approximating to modern Israel). As vassals of the pharaohs, the local rulers of Ashkelon, Lachish, Jerusalem, Megiddo, Tyre, Sidon, Beirut, Damascus, Qadesh, Byblos, Ugarit and other cities were responsible to these governors, but in practice they enjoyed much latitude. Their letters greet the pharaoh in obsequious phrases such as "the king, my lord, my sun god, I prostrate myself at the feet of my lord, my sun god, seven times and seven times." They include protestations of loyalty, complaints against neighboring city states and requests for military assistance against the nomadic tribes of the Syrian desert.

The rulers of powerful independent states such as Assyria, Mittani and Babylon addressed the pharaoh as an equal: "brother." They were clearly anxious to establish good relations with Egypt, if only because the pharaoh was known to send his friends and allies lavish gifts of gold. Products of Egyptian craftsmanship, such as the suite of ebony furniture, sheathed in gold and inlaid with ivory, that Amenophis III sent the Babylonian king for his new palace, were also highly desirable.

Many of the Amarna letters are concerned with the sealing of alliances by marriage. A major duty of envoys was to check that the brides in such arrangements were being treated properly – a good indicator of the true value put on relations with her home country. The envoys of a friendly power could expect to be accommodated in some luxury, but if relations were strained or hostile they might be kept waiting a long time for an audience as a calculated insult to the king they represented. Envoys often traveled with merchant caravans. If the merchants were plundered, the ruler in whose territory it happened was held responsible. A Babylonian envoy whose caravan was violently robbed in Canaan by agents of the Egyptian vassal king of Akko demanded that the pharaoh recover his money and execute the perpetrators, hinting that if he did not do so, diplomatic relations might be broken off.

RAMSES II

In the period of political instability that followed Akhenaten's failed religious revolution Egypt lost control of the Levant to the Hittites and the Canaanites. The advent of the 19th Dynasty in 1307 brought about the beginning of a recovery. Under Sethos I (r. 1306–1290) Egyptian rule was restored as far north as the river Orontes. Seeing an opportunity to reestablish the frontier at the Euphrates, the young pharaoh Ramses II (r. 1290–1224) led an army into Syria in 1285. According to detailed Egyptian accounts of the campaign, Ramses won a great victory over the Hittite king Muwattalis at Qadesh on the Orontes (see page 69), but he failed to secure any long-term advantage, and Hittite dominion was extended south of the Orontes to Damascus. Subsequent campaigns by Ramses deprived the Hittites of some of their gains and in about 1268 the two powers reached a peace settlement.

RIGHT *Sarcophagus of the boy-king Tutankhamun. During his brief reign real power was exercised by the high-priest Aya and the general Haremhab, who restored the traditional worship of the gods. When Tutankhamun's tomb in the Valley of the Kings was discovered still intact in the 1920s, it revealed an unrivaled wealth of treasures.*

EL-'AMARNA

El-'Amarna, ancient Akhetaten ("The Horizon of the Aten" or the Sun Disk), was founded by Akhenaten about 1348 as a capital and center for his new state religion, the cult of the Aten. The city was laid out on a virgin site, untainted by the presence of the old gods whose worship Akhenaten was attempting to abolish, and remote from the influence of their priesthoods. It lies in a bay in the cliffs on the east bank of the Nile about halfway between Memphis and Thebes. It is not known why Akhenaten chose this site for his new capital, but it has been suggested that the lie of the landscape may have resembled the hieroglyph for "horizon."

The Great Temple of the Aten and the Great Palace lay at the city's center, with private houses, workshops and sculptors' studios clustered round about. At its northern edge was the North Palace, perhaps another royal residence, and at the southern edge a lake and garden complex called the *Maru-Aten*, dedicated to pleasure and prayer. The officials of Akhetaten had their tombs cut in the cliffs surrounding the city, while Akhenaten chose a site for his family tomb in a ravine about 6 miles (10 km) away. The fields that provided the city with food were on the opposite bank of the river.

Estimates of Akhetaten's population vary from between 20,000 and 30,000 to over 50,000. But the city had a life of only 15 years – it was abandoned soon after Akhenaten's death, during the reaction against his religious reforms. The temple of the Aten was leveled and most of the stone later removed to be reused on other sites. The tombs were desecrated and Akhenaten's name erased from inscriptions. The city was soon buried by drifting sands and the site was never reoccupied. Because of this, it has escaped the destruction that would have resulted had it been continuously occupied, and Akhetaten is one of the few ancient Egyptian cities to have been extensively excavated. Though little remains of any buildings, many superb works of art executed in the distinctive official style of Akhenaten's reign have been found during excavations at el-'Amarna.

ABOVE *In his official art, Akhenaten is represented with a distorted body and a strikingly elongated face and head. Some experts have suggested that he was physically deformed, possibly as the result of a disease of the endocrine system; others that this was done in order to portray kingship as something lying quite outside ordinary human experience.*

LEFT *Fragment of a red quartzite female statue from el-'Amarna, probably of Akhenaten's queen Nefertiti. It is one of the most sensual studies of the female body in ancient Egyptian art.*

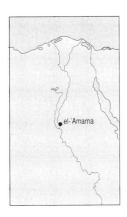

el-'Amarna

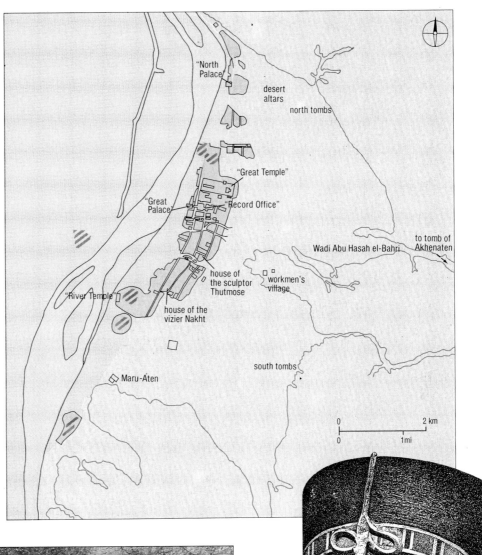

"North Palace"

desert altars

north tombs

"Great Temple"

"Great Palace"

"Record Office"

Wadi Abu Hasah el-Bahri

to tomb of Akhenaten

house of the sculptor Thutmose

workmen's village

house of the vizier Nakht

south tombs

"River Temple"

Maru-Aten

0   2 km
0   1mi

RIGHT *The administrative core of Akhenaten's state capital consisted of the Great Temple of the Aten with the Great Palace close by containing the State Apartments, a complex of courts and columned halls including the Coronation Hall, harem and servants' quarters. Akhenaten himself lived in private quarters connected to the Great Palace by a bridge. The Amarna letters – diplomatic exchanges with neighboring rulers written on cuneiform clay tablets – were found in the Record Office.*

BELOW *Detail of a painting from the king's private residence, showing two of Akhenaten's daughters. Freed from the constraints of traditional forms, artists working at el-'Amarna produced works of great informality and naturalism.*

RIGHT *This painted limestone bust of queen Nefertiti shows her wearing her characteristic crown with the* ureaus *(the rearing cobra symbol of kingship). It was found with many other pieces that were left in the studio of the sculptor Thutmose when the city was abandoned. The name of the sculptor is known from inscriptions found in the ruins.*

During his long reign Ramses II built more temples and erected more huge statues of himself than any other Egyptian ruler. He also had his name carved on many older monuments and was worshiped as a god in his own lifetime. Perhaps his most famous and impressive monuments are the rock-cut temples at Abu Simbel. He founded a new royal capital at Pi-Ri'amseses ("the house of Ramses") at an unknown site in the delta, which was by now the economic powerhouse of Egypt. Ramses' high-profile exercises in self-glorification left Egypt impoverished but made his name synonymous with kingship for generations. Even today he is still commonly called "the Great."

DECLINE OF THE NEW KINGDOM

At the end of the 13th and beginning of the 12th century BC Egypt and the Eastern Mediterranean were disrupted by waves of migrations. An attempt by tribes from Libya to settle in the rich farmlands of the delta about 1219 was decisively repulsed by the Egyptians. A generation later came an invasion by the Sea Peoples, a mysterious coalition whose identity has led to much speculation: they probably included Aegean, Levantine, Libyan and perhaps even western Mediterranean peoples. The Sea Peoples were finally driven off from Egypt in 1180 by Ramses III (r. 1194–1163) after a decisive naval battle in the delta. Some of the survivors, the "Peleset" (better known from the Bible as the Philistines), settled on the coast of Canaan around Gaza and subsequently gave their name to Palestine.

One of the most important developments of the New Kingdom was the granting of large tracts of land to the temples. These gifts were made on such a lavish scale that by the 11th century BC a third of all land in Egypt was in the hands of the temples. The holdings of the temple of Amun at Karnak (Thebes) were so large that it effectively controlled the whole of Upper Egypt. The priesthood had become hereditary and so was largely out the king's direct control. This so weakened both the authority and the wealth of the monarchy that it was unable to hold onto its possessions in Nubia and the Near East. In the 19th year of the reign of Ramses XI (r. 1100–1070) a general called Herihor became high-priest at Thebes. For the next 130 years he and his descendants ruled Upper Egypt in virtual independence. The effective division of the kingdom initiated the Third Intermediate period (1070–712), a complex time of weak monarchies and decentralized power.

The decline of Egyptian prestige is well illustrated by the story of Wenamun, a temple official sent by Herihor to the Phoenician port of Byblos to buy timber to repair the sacred bark of Amun. Wenamun's money was stolen on the way and he was forced to rob some Tjeker sailors to finance the rest of his journey. At Byblos he cut a poor figure for, as the city's governor scornfully remarked, Egyptian missions in the past had arrived with shiploads of gifts whilst Wenamun had not even come in an Egyptian ship. The Phoenicians demanded payment in advance, so Wenamun was detained in humiliating circumstances while the money was sent from Egypt. Finally the timber was delivered but before Wenamun could leave Byblos, the Tjeker sailors he had robbed appeared on the scene to demand his arrest. He escaped but was shipwrecked on Cyprus and taken prisoner by a local queen. The rest of the story is lost but we can guess that Wenamun overcame all difficulties and returned safely to Egypt with his timber.

Shoshenq I (r. 945–924) temporarily halted the decline of royal power by taking advantage of the extinction of Herihor's line to install his son as high-priest at Thebes. He restored Egyptian prestige and influence with a successful campaign in Palestine in 925, which culminated in the plundering of Solomon's temple in Jerusalem. Civil war broke out during the reign of Takelot II (860–835 BC), and in the reign of his successor Shoshenq III (835–783) dynastic disputes led to the collapse and fragmentation of the state. By the 8th century BC Egypt had come to be ruled by half a dozen rival kings.

NUBIAN CONQUEST

For over 200 years after it had become independent, Nubia vanishes into obscurity. By the early 8th century BC a powerful kingdom had arisen there, centered on Napata, the former Egyptian provincial capital of Upper Nubia. By this time Nubia had been exposed to strong Egyptian cultural influences for well over a thousand years, and Nubian religion and funerary practices, art, architecture and ideals of kingship were thoroughly Egyptian in character. In 770 BC a Nubian king Kashta (r. 770–750) was accepted as ruler at Thebes: it is possible that he was called in by the

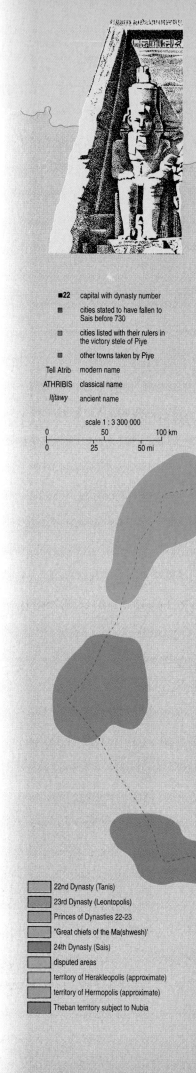

■22   capital with dynasty number

■   cities stated to have fallen to Sais before 730

■   cities listed with their rulers in the victory stele of Piye

■   other towns taken by Piye

Tell Atrib   modern name

ATHRIBIS   classical name

Itjtawy   ancient name

scale 1 : 3 300 000

0   50   100 km

0   25   50 mi

22nd Dynasty (Tanis)

23rd Dynasty (Leontopolis)

Princes of Dynasties 22-23

'Great chiefs of the Ma(shwesh)'

24th Dynasty (Sais)

disputed areas

territory of Herakleopolis (approximate)

territory of Hermopolis (approximate)

Theban territory subject to Nubia

CIVIL WAR AND THE NUBIAN CONQUEST

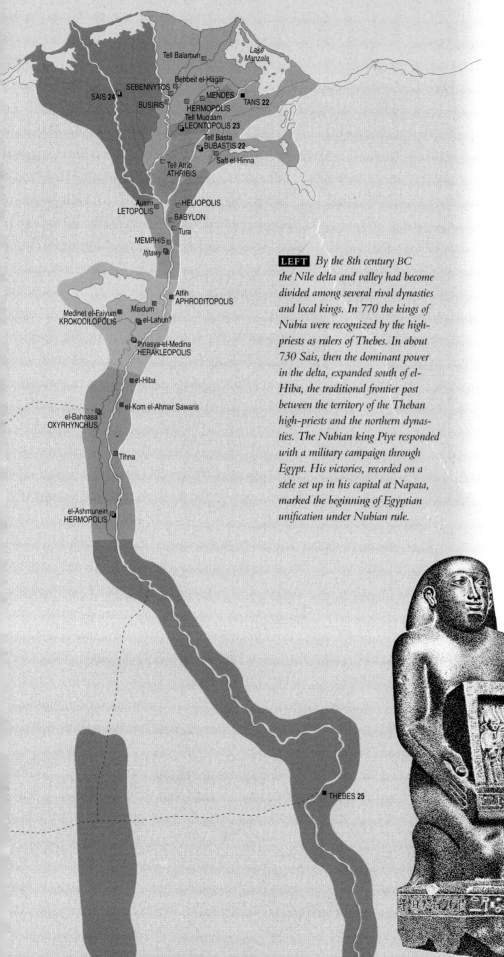

LEFT *By the 8th century BC the Nile delta and valley had become divided among several rival dynasties and local kings. In 770 the kings of Nubia were recognized by the high-priests as rulers of Thebes. In about 730 Sais, then the dominant power in the delta, expanded south of el-Hiba, the traditional frontier post between the territory of the Theban high-priests and the northern dynasties. The Nubian king Piye responded with a military campaign through Egypt. His victories, recorded on a stele set up in his capital at Napata, marked the beginning of Egyptian unification under Nubian rule.*

high-priests who were fearful of the growing chaos in Egypt. Around 730, Tefnakhte of Sais in the western delta began to extend his power southward into the Nile valley, provoking king Piye (r. 750–712), the son and successor of Kashta, into a campaign to bring the local rulers of Egypt into submission.

Piye was succeeded by his son Shabaka (r. 712–698) whose reign marks the beginning of the Late Period (712–332). Though the Assyrian king Sennacherib, campaigning in Palestine in 701 BC, famously compared Egypt to a "broken reed" (2 Kings 18: 22), the Nubian kings managed to keep Assyrian ambitions at bay for the next thirty years. Between 674 and 667, however, the Assyrians succeeded in conquering Egypt and expeled the Nubians. Assyrian rule ended about 653 and Egypt enjoyed a precarious period of freedom until it was conquered by the Persian king Cambyses in 525. With the exception of sixty years of native rule that lasted from 404 to 343, Egypt remained under Persian rule until 332 when it was conquered by Alexander the Great. From then on Egypt fell permanently under outside rule, first that of the Greek Ptolemaic dynasty, then that of the Roman emperors.

Traditions of loyalty to the centralized state were so strong that it was easy for foreign rulers to take control of Egypt simply by adopting the conventional forms of kingship. For this reason the Roman emperor Trajan (AD 98–117) is portrayed on a relief at the temple of Hathor at Dendara in much the same style, dress and pose as Narmer was on his palettes carved more than 3000 years earlier. The culture of ancient Egypt eventually died out in the 4th century AD. By then most Egyptians had converted to Christianity and the ancient civilization simply disappeared along with the religious outlook that had sustained it for so long.

LEFT *The Third Prophet of Montu, Pakhelkhons, kneels with a shrine containing a statuette of the fertility god Osiris. Montu was the local god of Thebes, and this statue dates from the Third Intermediate period when Thebes, with the high-priest of Amun at its head, enjoyed importance as the capital of Upper Egypt.*

PYRAMIDS: 1

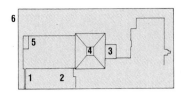

The pyramids, the most famous monuments of the ancient world, were built between 2630 and 1640 as vast royal tombs. The pyramid was constructed before the king's death. Once his body had been interred in the prepared burial chamber, the entrance passage was sealed off and concealed. Despite these precautions, most of the pyramids were robbed in antiquity. The walls of the burial chamber were inscribed with texts and spells intended to ensure that the king's spirit joined the gods, and it was richly furnished with funerary goods and possessions for the afterlife. Pyramids were associated with the cult of Ra, and their flared shape may have symbolized the rays of the sun, along which the deceased king could ascend to heaven: the ancient Egyptian word for pyramid was *mer*, or "Place of Ascension." Contrary to popular belief, the pyramids were not built by teams of slaves but by skilled craftsmen. During the flood season, when no work could be done on the land, peasant farmers were drafted to provide additional labor.

THE TRUE PYRAMID

4) true pyramid

6) enclosure wall

5) subsidiary pyramid

6 4 3 2 1
   5

THE STEP PYRAMID

6) enclosure wall

5) south tomb

staged enlargements

descending shaft

burial chamber

mastaba

ABOVE AND RIGHT *The earliest pyramid was built at Saqqara for king Djoser about 2630. It was originally a flat-topped mastaba or platform tomb and the structure was progressively*

BELOW *The transition from step pyramid to true pyramid was made in the reign of Snofru (2575–2551). This reconstruction of the pyramid of king Sahure (2458–2446) at Abusir shows a new element in pyramid*

building, namely the construction of a causeway linking the mortuary temple with a valley temple on the banks of the Nile, where there was a landing stage for river arrivals. The burial chamber itself was reached by a descending passage from the pyramid's north face. Pyramid complexes often included subsidiary pyramids for the burial of queens.

3) mortuary temple

4) step pyramid

3) mortuary temple

1) entrance complex

2) *sed*-festival complex

heightened by the addition of six stepped platforms. Beside it was a mortuary temple in which food and prayers were offered for the well-being of the dead king, and both structures were contained within an enclosure wall. A unique feature of Djoser's pyramid is the sed-festival complex where the king could celebrate the sed, a ritual race to show he still possessed the vigor to rule, in death as in life.*

BUILDING METHODS

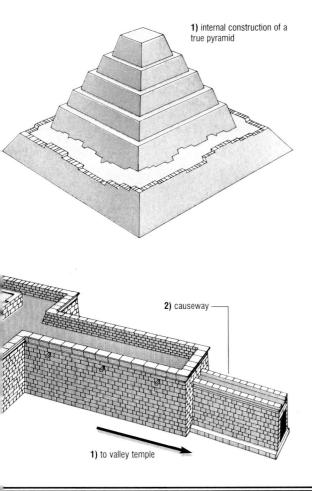

1) internal construction of a true pyramid

2) causeway

1) to valley temple

LEFT AND BELOW *In the Old Kingdom, most true pyramids were built by first constructing a step pyramid (**1**). This gave the pyramid a firm base. Packing blocks were then used to fill in the steps and a casing of fine quality limestone completed the transformation into a true pyramid. The more modest pyramids of the Middle Kingdom were built around a cheap mud-brick core: most have long since collapsed. It is still far from certain how the heavy stone building blocks were moved into place. The Egyptians at this time did not have wheeled vehicles, nor is there any evidence that they used cranes or other lifting devices. Most probably, the* blocks were dragged on sledges up ramps of mudbricks. To maintain a constant gradient as the pyramid grew in height, the length of the ramp and the width of its base had to be constantly increased (**2a**), requiring the use of enormous quantities of materials. Smaller ramps would have been needed to raise the blocks when building a step pyramid (**2b**).*

2b) construction ramps

2a) construction ramps

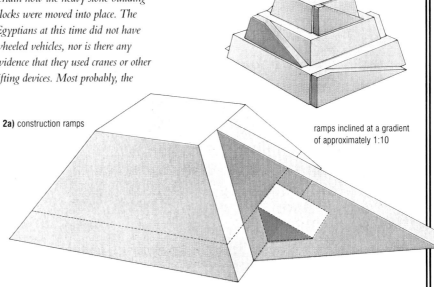

ramps inclined at a gradient of approximately 1:10

PYRAMIDS: 2

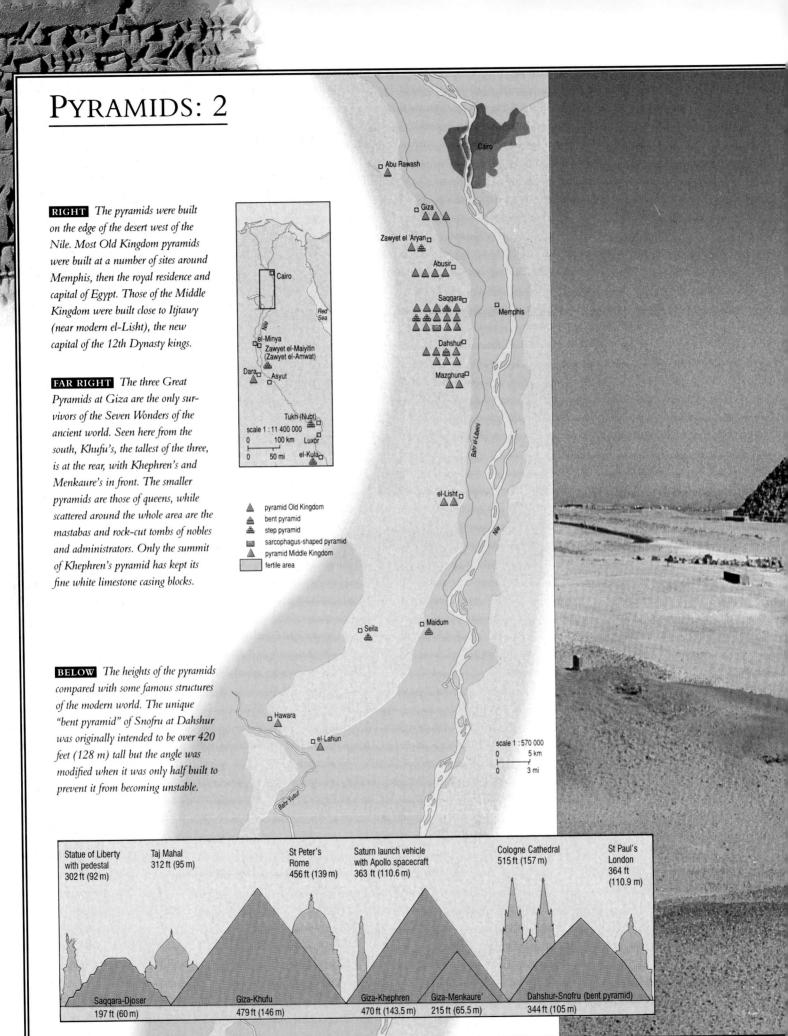

RIGHT *The pyramids were built on the edge of the desert west of the Nile. Most Old Kingdom pyramids were built at a number of sites around Memphis, then the royal residence and capital of Egypt. Those of the Middle Kingdom were built close to Itjtawy (near modern el-Lisht), the new capital of the 12th Dynasty kings.*

FAR RIGHT *The three Great Pyramids at Giza are the only survivors of the Seven Wonders of the ancient world. Seen here from the south, Khufu's, the tallest of the three, is at the rear, with Khephren's and Menkaure's in front. The smaller pyramids are those of queens, while scattered around the whole area are the mastabas and rock-cut tombs of nobles and administrators. Only the summit of Khephren's pyramid has kept its fine white limestone casing blocks.*

BELOW *The heights of the pyramids compared with some famous structures of the modern world. The unique "bent pyramid" of Snofru at Dahshur was originally intended to be over 420 feet (128 m) tall but the angle was modified when it was only half built to prevent it from becoming unstable.*

scale 1 : 11 400 000

0   100 km

0   50 mi

▲ pyramid Old Kingdom
▲ bent pyramid
▣ step pyramid
▨ sarcophagus-shaped pyramid
▲ pyramid Middle Kingdom
▢ fertile area

scale 1 : 570 000

0   5 km

0   3 mi

Cairo
Abu Rawash
Giza
Zawyet el 'Aryan
Abusir
Saqqara
Memphis
Dahshur
Mazghuna
Bahr el-Libeini
Nile
el-Lisht
Seila
Maidum
Hawara
el-Lahun
Bahr Yusuf

Red Sea
Nile
el-Minya
Zawyet el-Maiyitin (Zawyet el-Amwat)
Dara
Asyut
Tukh (Nubt)
Luxor
el-Kula

Statue of Liberty with pedestal
302 ft (92 m)

Taj Mahal
312 ft (95 m)

St Peter's Rome
456 ft (139 m)

Saturn launch vehicle with Apollo spacecraft
363 ft (110.6 m)

Cologne Cathedral
515 ft (157 m)

St Paul's London
364 ft (110.9 m)

Saqqara-Djoser
197 ft (60 m)

Giza-Khufu
479 ft (146 m)

Giza-Khephren
470 ft (143.5 m)

Giza-Menkaure´
215 ft (65.5 m)

Dahshur-Snofru (bent pyramid)
344 ft (105 m)

WARFARE IN ANCIENT EGYPT

Because of its isolation and relative security from invasion, Egypt was long in developing a strong military tradition. During the Old and Middle Kingdoms its main opponents were desert nomads and tribal farmers, who were no match for Egypt's small but effectively organized standing army. At this early date weapons were of stone and copper. The introduction of the horse, lightweight chariot, bronze weapons and the composite bow by the Hyksos in about 1600 transformed Egypt's armies, making them the equal, in technology and tactics, of the military powers of the Near East. Egypt's wealth and highly centralized government made possible the maintenance of large standing armies which could be kept for long periods in the field hundreds of miles from home. The armies were organized under a hierarchy of professional officers into "divisions," "brigades" and "companies" – the smallest unit composed of 250 men led by a standard bearer. The pharaohs frequently campaigned in person, even leading troops into battle. After the end of the New Kingdom, Egypt's military power declined as it failed to keep up with the tactical and technological advances of its Near Eastern neighbors. The Late Period pharaohs relied on foreign mercenaries.

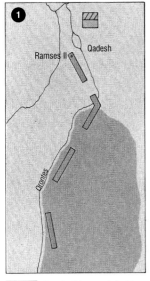

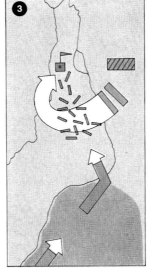

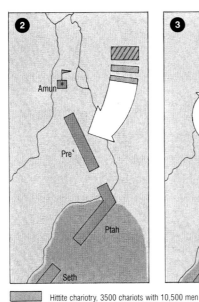

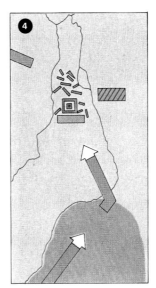

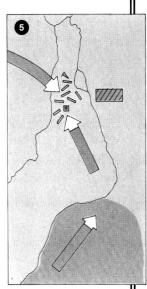

Egyptian infantry and chariotry, total 20,000 men

Egyptian camp

Hittite chariotry, 3500 chariots with 10,500 men

Hittite infantry, 8000 men

LEFT *This group of 40 painted wooden soldiers carrying bows, spears and hide shields comes from the tomb of Mesehti, a Middle Kingdom official, at Asyut. The simple, lightweight equipment used by early Egyptian armies shows they lacked any serious military threat.*

ABOVE AND BELOW LEFT

The earliest battle in history that can be reconstructed in detail took place between the Egyptians and Hittites at Qadesh in Syria in 1285. **(1)** *Ramses II's army consisted of four divisions (Amun, led by Ramses himself, Pre', Ptah and Seth) and a smaller unit operating independently (off map). The Egyptians advanced confidently, unaware that the Hittite army lay in wait beyond Qadesh.* **(2)** *Amun division had reached Qadesh and made camp when the Hittite chariots launched a devastating surprise attack on Pre' division.* **(3)** *Ptah division was too distant to give support and Pre' was scattered. The survivors fled to Ramses' camp which was surrounded by the Hittite chariots* **(4)**. *Amun division suffered heavy casualties as the royal guard launched desperate charges to break out. The Hittite king Muwattalis sent in his reserve chariots to finish off Amun* **(5)** *but Ramses' charges had bought enough time for Ptah to arrive and drive off the Hittite chariots, incurring heavy losses, before their infantry could advance. Ramses claimed a great victory and caused it to be commemorated by inscriptions and relief carvings on several temples in Egypt (below left). Subsequent events show that he exaggerated the scale of his success.*

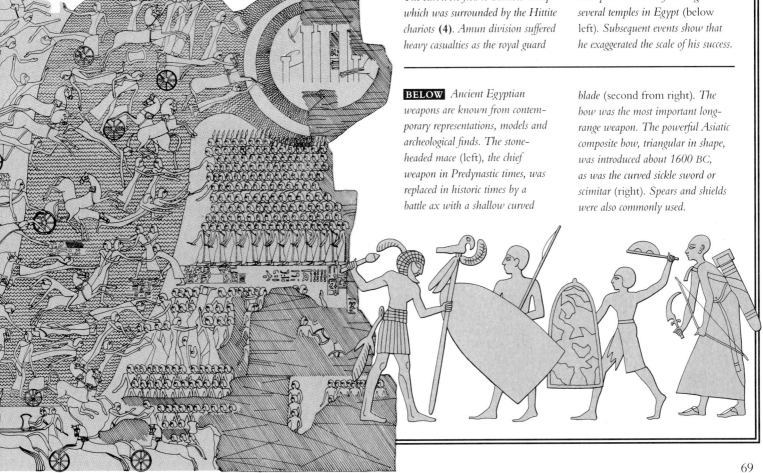

BELOW *Ancient Egyptian weapons are known from contemporary representations, models and archeological finds. The stoneheaded mace (left), the chief weapon in Predynastic times, was replaced in historic times by a battle ax with a shallow curved blade (second from right). The bow was the most important longrange weapon. The powerful Asiatic composite bow, triangular in shape, was introduced about 1600 BC, as was the curved sickle sword or scimitar (right). Spears and shields were also commonly used.*

EGYPTIAN RELIGION

Religion pervaded all aspects of ancient Egyptian life: because the king was the chief intermediary between humanity and the gods there was no clear distinction between secular and spiritual matters. A great deal is known from inscriptions in temples and tombs about official state religion and about the practices accompanying death and burial. We have considerably less information about everyday religious beliefs and customs.

Official worship was conducted in temples. These were treated as the palaces of the resident god or gods. The holiest part of a temple was the sanctuary or shrine containing the cult statue of the god worshiped there. The statue was tended daily by the chief priest much as the king was tended by his servants: it was washed, dressed, perfumed and "fed" with offerings of food. These rituals were hidden from the eyes of ordinary people. Even during festivals when the cult statues were carried outside so that the gods could "speak" to the people, they were kept hidden from sight within a shrine that was carried on a symbolic bark. Sometimes cult statues went on journeys. During the annual "Festival of the Good Meetings" the goddess Hathor was taken from her temple at Dendara to visit her husband Horus at his temple at Edfu, some 80 miles (130 km) away.

Egyptian religion had no systematic theology and no two surviving versions of its myths are alike. Most gods were associated with some particular aspect of life, such as Ra with the sun, Ptah with crafts or Taweret with pregnant women, but they could all take on most aspects of divinity. To the Greeks and Romans the most striking characteristic of Egyptian religion was the worship of animals, the most famous being the Apis or bull sacred to Ptah. Sacred animals were mummified on their deaths: mummified cats, ibises, dogs, rams, baboons, snakes and even fish have been found. During the Late Period there was a proliferation of animal cults. This seems to have been accompanied by a corresponding decline in belief in the survival of the individual after death.

THE GODS OF ANCIENT EGYPT

1   2   3   4   5   6   7

BELOW *The Egyptians portrayed their gods in human and semi-human form, though they did not believe that this represented what they actually looked like. From early times numerous "local" gods were associated with particular places or towns, whose fate they shared. In time, some became part of the pantheon of "state" gods whose cults were recognized throughout Egypt. Others were "universal" gods, whose worship was not associated with any particular center. From left to right below:*

1) *Horus, sky god closely associated with kingship. Main cult center: Heliopolis.*

2) *Seth, brother and enemy of Horus, he signified disorder and violence. Popular in the eastern delta.*

3) *Thoth, ibis-headed and often shown with moon crescent, the god of writing, counting and wisdom. Main cult center: el-Ashmunein.*

4) *Khnum, ram-headed creator god who shaped men on his potter's wheel. Also associated with the Nile flood. Main cult center: Elephantine.*

5) *Hathor, goddess of women, pleasure, love and fertility; also sky and tree goddess. Main cult centers: Heliopolis, Memphis and several more.*

6) *Sobek, crocodile-headed god of the Faiyum region.*

7) *Ra the sun-god shown bearing a sun disk on his head. Main cult center: Heliopolis.*

8) *Amun, sun-god who became linked to Ra. Main cult center: Thebes.*

9) *Anubis, dog-headed god of mummification. Universal god.*

10) *Osiris, the god of vegetation and ruler of the underworld, carrying a scepter and flail. Universal god.*

11) *Isis, wife of Osiris, mistress of magic. Her worship became widespread outside Egypt in Roman times. Universal goddess.*

BELOW *The ancient Egyptians practiced mummification, the artificial preservation of the bodies of people and animals, believing that this ensured they would continue to exist after death. Processes of mummification varied but all involved removing the internal organs. The body was then dehydrated using a natural chemical called natron and the body cavities packed with fragrant substances such as myrrh and cinnamon, and with resin-soaked linen and*

sawdust. After it had been wrapped in bandages, and amulets and jewelry set between each layer, it was put in a highly decorated, human-shaped coffin, which was itself often placed inside one or more sarcophagi of wood or stone. The craft of mummification reached its peak in the New Kingdom but declined thereafter. The scientific examination of mummies has much to tell us about the health, diet and actual facial appearance of the ancient Egyptians.

Painted and gilded funeral mask covering the mummy of a New Kingdom noblewoman.

8   9   10   11

The Great Empires

1600 – 330 BC

The Hittites, who sacked Babylon in 1595 BC and brought about the end of Hammurabi's dynasty, appear to have moved from their original homeland in southeastern Europe into the land of Hatti (from which they took their name) in central Anatolia about 2000. For several centuries the Hittites remained just one of several minor powers in Anatolia. While they retained their Indo-European language and imposed it on the indigenous Hattian people, they came, in time, to adopt the religious, literary and artistic traditions of their Near Eastern neighbors. The first Hittite king of whom anything is known is Hattusilis I (r.c. 1650–1620). Inscriptions erected at the time claim him to have been an energetic campaigner who enriched the temples of the Hittite capital Hattusas (modern-day Boghazkoy in Turkey) with the deported slaves, plunder and tribute of conquered states and compared him favorably with the great conqueror Sargon of Agade. For all this, Hattusilis was killed in the course of a disastrous attack on Aleppo (then called Halab). It was to avenge this defeat that his son Mursilis (c. 1620–1590) conquered Aleppo and then led a daring expedition down the Euphrates to bring about the downfall of Babylon. Such rapid expansion seems to have caused internal strains and when Mursilis was assassinated, the Hittite state collapsed into a century of chaos and decline. Its frontiers were attacked by the Hurrians, a mountain people who had settled in northern Mesopotamia early in the previous century, and by the Kaskas, a tribal people from northern Anatolia who had gained control of Hattusas by the middle of the 14th century.

THE EMPIRE OF MITTANI

In the course of the next century the Hurrians took advantage of the Hittites' factional weakness to establish the kingdom of Mittani in northern Mesopotamia and Syria. Little is known about its history, and archeologists have had to depend on the archives of neighboring states, particularly

Egypt, and on chance finds from within the boundaries of the empire, for what information they have. Mittanian influence spread westward into the Levant where it began to come into conflict with the 18th Dynasty kings of Egypt who also had ambitions to rule there. Under Tuthmosis I (r. 1504–1492) Egypt took control of the entire Levant and established a frontier on the river Euphrates. But it was unable to maintain this forward position for long and by about 1480 the important cities of Aleppo and Alalah were under Mittanian control. The power of Mittani reached its peak during the reign of Saushtatar (late 15th century BC). He claimed to control the rich port of Ugarit – long an Egyptian trading satellite – as well as Kizzuwatna (Cilicia) and Assyria.

The Hittites enjoyed a brief period of recovery under Tudhaliya I (1420–1400) who skillfully exploited the conflicts between Mittani and Egypt to increase his own power. As a result, Mittani

LEFT *Statue of king Idrimi of Alalah, found in the city's temple. Idrimi is seated on a throne on a raised basalt base. A long autobiographical inscription covering his body states that he was a younger son of the royal house of Aleppo who rebelled against the Mittani and spent years of exile among the desert nomads before becoming king of Alalah. He sent tribute to king Parrattarna of Mittani and as a vassal was allowed considerable freedom of action, for example to make treaties with other states.*

RIGHT *The Hurrian empire of Mittani was the dominating power of the Near East during the dark age of the 14th and 15th centuries BC. Little is known of its history. Such records as there are come from the fringes of the empire – the cities of Alalah in the west and Nuzi in the east – and from neighboring states such as Egypt and the Hittite empire. The heartland of the empire was on the upper Habur river but the site of its capital, Washukanni, has not so far been located. Suggestions that it was at Tell al-Fakhariyeh in Syria, which has yet to be excavated, are by no means certain.*

sought rapprochement with Egypt. The pharaoh Tuthmosis IV (r. 1401–1391) married the sister of king Artatama I, and twice in the reign of the sickly pharaoh Amenophis III (1391–1353) Mittanian kings sent the statue of the goddess Ishtar from Nineveh to Egypt to help effect a cure. King Tushratta was anxious to put his relations with the pharaoh Akhenaten (r. 1353–1335) on an even warmer footing. In a letter from the Amarna archive, he tells Akhenaten that while the pharaoh's grandfather and father had both had to ask his predecessors repeatedly for a Mittanian bride, he was prepared to send his own daughter at the first time of asking. Later Tushratta requested that Akhenaten send him a statue of his daughter cast in gold so that he would not miss her so much. Tushratta's eagerness for an Egyptian alliance was no doubt prompted by concern at the resurgent power of the Hittites and also of the Mittanian vassal-state of Assyria which, quite suddenly, after four centuries of obscurity following the break-up of Shamshi-Adad's empire (c. 1780), was becoming an aggressive expansionist power under Ashur-uballit I (1363–1328).

THE HITTITE EMPIRE

Mittani was now dangerously exposed to its enemies. When Tushratta was murdered during factional fighting Mittani divided into rival parties, one apparently supported by the Hittites, the other by Assyria. Even before he came to the throne, the great Hittite king Suppiluliumas (r. 1344–1322) had shown his abilities by recovering Hattusas from the Kaskas and restoring Hittite hegemony over the Anatolian plateau. Akhenaten's preoccupation with religious reform disinclined him from foreign adventures, and Mittani's dynastic chaos gave Suppiluliumas the opportunity to establish the Hittites as the Near East's major power. In about 1340 he sacked Washukanni. A second campaign in about 1328 (or 1323) secured the western half of the Mittanian kingdom in his hands, but his attempts to set up a buffer state against Assyria in eastern Mittani, with a puppet king in Washukanni, were ultimately unsuccessful, and Assyria took over the Mittanian lands west of the Euphrates. In the political uncertainty following Akhenaten's reign the Egyptians lost control of their provinces in the Levant, giving the Hittites

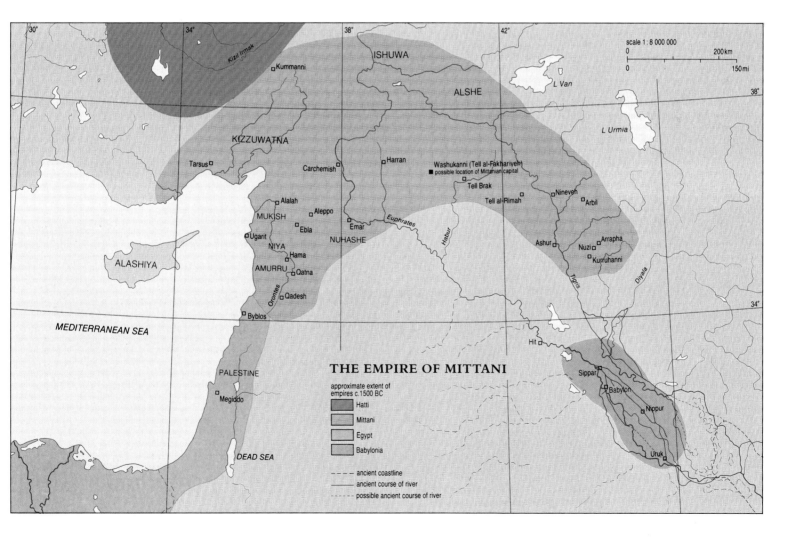

THE EMPIRE OF MITTANI

approximate extent of empires c. 1500 BC

- Hatti
- Mittani
- Egypt
- Babylonia

- - - - ancient coastline
———— ancient course of river
– – – – possible ancient course of river

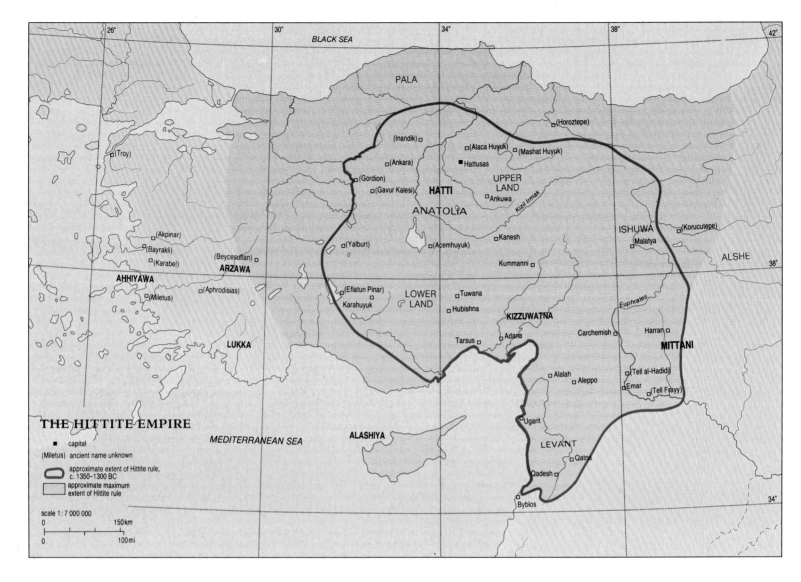

the commanding position in the region that Mittani had held in the 15th century.

In 1307 a new dynasty came to power in Egypt, eager to prove its mettle by reestablishing its authority in the Levant. By 1290 the Egyptians had recovered Canaan and in 1285 Ramses II (1290–1224) launched a major invasion of Hittite territory, probably intending to restore the frontier Tuthmosis I had established on the Euphrates. However, the Hittite king Muwatallis II (1295–1271) was prepared for him, and when the two armies met at Qadesh, Ramses only narrowly avoided a catastrophic defeat. The Egyptians withdrew and Hittite control was extended as far south as Damascus. Relations remained hostile until 1258 when Ramses and Hattusilis II (Muwatallis' successor) became allies.

The terms of the Hittite–Egyptian alliance were written on tablets of silver. These have been lost but copies of the treaty have been found on cuneiform tablets in Hattusas and in hieroglyphic inscriptions at Karnak and Thebes in Egypt. The treaty bound the two kings and their successors in perpetual friendship and guaranteed each other military support in the event of invasion by a third party. It went on to establish practical measures to reduce tensions in the Levant, such as agreeing to extradite fugitives and to help suppress rebellious vassals. The circumstances of the treaty are reminiscent of the earlier Egyptian–Mittanian alliance: the Hittites were now becoming alarmed by the renewed growth of Assyrian power under a succession of able warrior kings. The greatest of these were Shalmaneser (1273–1244) and Tukulti-Ninurta I (1243–1207). Tukulti-Ninurta extended the borders of the Assyrian empire to the western Euphrates and claimed that on one campaign he even crossed the Euphrates to take 28,800 Hittite prisoners. He attacked the Kassite kingdom of Babylonia and for a time his rule reached as far as the Persian Gulf. But military losses at the end of his reign made him unpopular in Assyria and the Middle Assyrian empire went into decline after he was murdered by his discontented nobles.

ABOVE *In the later 14th century BC the Hittites under Suppiluliumas I and his successors dominated the Anatolian plateau and benefited from the decline of Mittani to extend their influence into the northern Levant. As yet, relatively few of the empire's main centers have been identified and its western borders are still uncertain. The empire collapsed suddenly about 1200, probably as a result of invasion by migrants from west of the Black Sea.*

BELOW *Hattusas, now called Boghazkoy, lies in the mountains of central Turkey about 90 miles (145 km) east of Ankara. The site was first occupied at the end of the 3rd millennium BC and later became an important trading center. In about 1650 it became the capital of the emerging Hittite empire. The city was extended and fortified under Suppiluliumas I (c. 1344) but was violently destroyed and abandoned in about 1200. This view looks across the ruins of Temple III (see plan) toward the royal palace and citadel.*

RIGHT *The oldest part of Hattusas was the Lower Town which developed on a spur between two gorges. The chief building here was the Great Temple of the weather-god of Hatti. The royal palace was sited in the citadel on the commanding rocky hill of Buyukkale. A little distance to the northeast is the rock-cut temple of Yazilikaya, decorated with relief carvings of over 100 Hittite gods. Later the city spread onto the plateau to the south. The site was reoccupied in the 7th century BC when it was known as Pteria.*

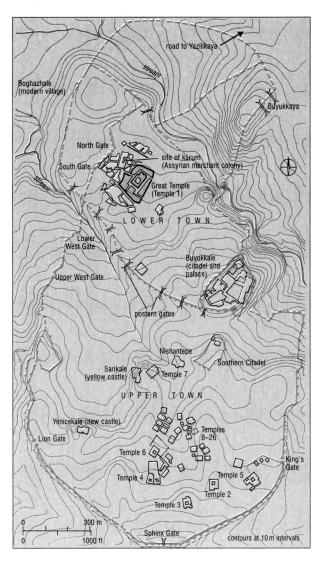

KASSITE BABYLONIA

For nearly 200 years after its sacking by the Hittites, Babylon vanished into obscurity. When the historical record begins again in about 1415, the city was ruled by a Kassite dynasty. Little is known about the origins of the Kassites. They are first mentioned in records from the reign of the Old Babylonian king Samsu-iluna (1749–1712), when they were primarily agricultural workers and mercenaries. How they came to power in Babylon, probably about 1570, is unknown. Fewer than a hundred words of their language are known – the inscriptions of Kassite kings are written in Sumerian, other documents in Babylonian – and their gods were an eclectic mixture from across the Near East. Apart from the rulers themselves, very few Kassites lived in Babylon itself: their heartland appears to have been to the northeast on the Diyala river and they may have come originally from the Zagros mountains. The Kassites preserved a clan-based tribal organization and never became fully integrated into Babylonian society.

Despite this, the Kassite dynasty's legitimacy was almost universally accepted by their Babylonian subjects. Under the Kassites the cities of southern Mesopotamia were finally welded into a single political entity. Even when they had controlled large empires, earlier Mesopotamian kings had seen themselves first and foremost as city rulers. Hammurabi had been "king of Babylon" even though he ruled most of southern Mesopotamia. Kassite kings, however, styled themselves "kings of Babylonia": rulers of a territorial state.

Kassite Babylonia's relations with its neighbors were troubled. The Assyrians were sometimes allies, sometimes overlords, but at least they respected Babylon's culture and history. This was not the case with Babylonia's eastern neighbor, the ancient kingdom of Elam. The Elamites had been settled on the plains of what is now southwestern Iran since prehistoric times and spoke a language unrelated to any other now known. Around 2500 they began to develop into a state. Though they were profoundly influenced by the Mesopotamian civilizations, their relations with them were frequently hostile. Elam was often forced to pay tribute to Mesopotamian rulers and, in turn, the Elamites raided Mesopotamia whenever the opportunity arose. Nothing certain is known of Elam's relations with Kassite Babylonia until Susa, the Elamite capital, was plundered by Kurigalzu II (r. 1332–1308) in about 1317. Elam recovered its strength under Untashnapirisha (c. 1260–1235), and after that, war between the two states was frequent and merciless.

The Kassite dynasty's warmest relations were with the Egyptian pharaohs with whom they corresponded regularly and exchanged brides and precious gifts. The Egyptians sent gold, so much of it that for a time it replaced silver as the main medium of exchange in Babylonia. In return the Kassites supplied the Egyptians with lapis lazuli, which they imported from Afghanistan, and chariots with trained teams of horses. One historian has described the last as the ancient equivalent of making a present of a fully equipped jet-fighter.

The Kassite dynasty fell in 1154 following a particularly devastating Elamite invasion, but Babylonia soon recovered under the native 2nd Dynasty of Isin. The next time that Elam threatened Babylonia, Nebuchadnezzar I (r. 1125–1104) led a forced march of over 155 miles (250 km) to Susa. The Babylonian army suffered agonies in the intense summer heat. The road "burnt like fire, the water gave out, the horses died of exhaustion and the legs of the men lost their power" says one of Nebuchadnezzar's inscriptions, but the Elamites were taken by surprise. Nebuchadnezzar's victory was so complete that the Elamites disappeared from history for the next 300 years.

A NEW DARK AGE

Between 1200 and 1000 new waves of migrations threw the Near East into another dark age. Shortly after 1205 Hittite inscriptions suddenly ceased and their kingdom simply vanished without trace. Written sources give no indication of impending catastrophe but excavations have shown that Hattusas was violently destroyed in about 1200. The identity of the attackers is not known for certain: the best guess is that they were Phrygians. another Indo-European people who had crossed the Bosporus from Thrace to enter northern Anatolia. At about the same time several cities in Syria and the Levant were violently destroyed, including Alalah, Carchemish and Ugarit, probably by the same Sea Peoples who attacked Egypt. One group

associated with the Sea Peoples, the Peleset or Philistines, settled in the area of Gaza and began to expand inland. The nomadic Aramaeans and Hebrews also moved into the Levant. The indigenous Canaanite peoples were unable to resist these invasions and by 1000 BC, almost all had been conquered and assimilated by the newcomers. Only on the coast of modern Syria and Lebanon did a Canaanite people – the Phoenicians – maintain their independence and cultural identity.

At the end of the 12th century, Assyria was attacked by a confederation of Mushki (probably Mysians, related to the Phrygians) and native Anatolian peoples, including the Kaskas and Hurrians. Fortunately for the Assyrians, an able warrior king, Tiglath-pileser I (1115–1076), had just come to the throne. His prompt counterattack in 1115 forced the invaders to retreat into Anatolia but he was less successful in halting the advance of Aramaean nomads from the Arabian desert, despite campaigning vigorously against them. His successors proved even less effective and by 1000 Assyria had been reduced to its heartland around the cities of Ashur and Nineveh.

Like Assyria, Babylonia found itself without an effective strategy to deal with migrations of Aramaeans in the north and Chaldeans in the south. Babylon itself held out, but was isolated in a countryside dominated by bands of nomads. Traditional religious festivals had to be canceled

ABOVE *This limestone relief, probably of the god himself, was found in the well of the temple of Ashur in the Assyrian capital. The Assyrian kings derived their authority from being the priests of Ashur, the city's patron god.*

BELOW *The Kassites seem to have been most densely settled around the Diyala river in the northeast of Babylonia. Among the most distinctive monuments of the Kassite kings are the kudurrus, carved stones decorated with religious symbols which commemorated royal grants of land. The largest number have been found at Susa, where they were taken as plunder by the Elamites in 1154.*

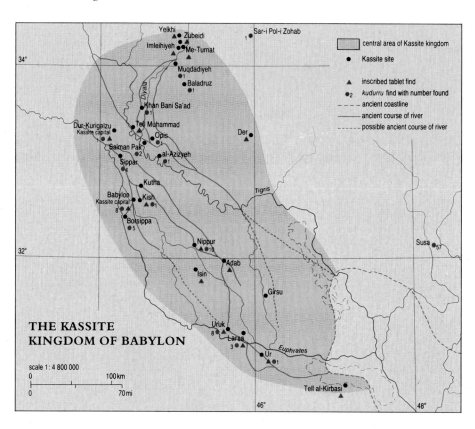

THE KASSITE KINGDOM OF BABYLON

BELOW *Early travelers from Europe thought that the twisted remains of the ziggurat of Dur-Kurigalzu were the ruins of the tower of Babel. In fact the ziggurat was built in the 14th century BC by the Kassite king Kurigalzu as part of a new capital city. The layers of reed bonding that were inserted between every seventh course of brick can be seen clearly as horizontal lines on the ruined ziggurat. The lower stage is a restoration.*

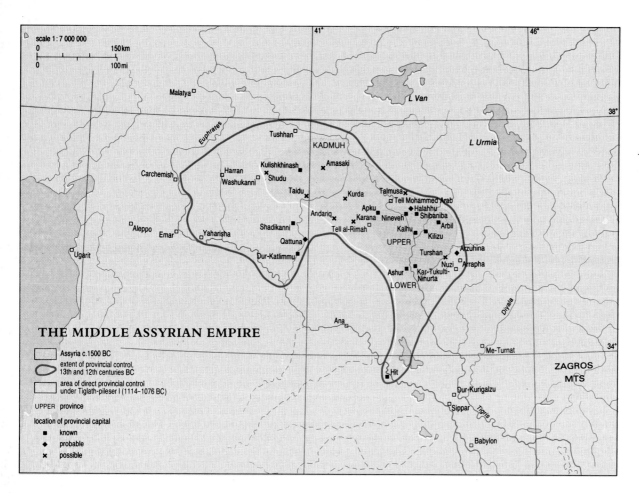

THE MIDDLE ASSYRIAN EMPIRE

scale 1:7 000 000

Assyria c.1500 BC

extent of provincial control, 13th and 12th centuries BC

area of direct provincial control under Tiglath-pileser I (1114–1076 BC)

UPPER province

location of provincial capital

■ known
◆ probable
✕ possible

LEFT *By mid 13th century the Middle Assyrian empire had expanded from around Ashur and Nineveh as far as the western Euphrates. It later declined but its fortunes were revived by Tiglath-pileser I (1114–1076). The area under direct control during his reign is known from a list of offerings made by the provinces to the Ashur temple. His successors were unable to halt the advance of nomadic invaders and by 1000 the empire was reduced to its original heartland once again.*

RIGHT *King David (c. 1006–965) unified the Hebrew tribes, making Jerusalem his capital. An important factor in his success was the decline of Egyptian power at the end of the New Kingdom. David's rule caused tensions in a Hebrew society that was unused to centralized control and he had to put down two major rebellions, including one led by his own son.*

BELOW *A limestone statue of a Moabite king of the 9th–10th century BC. Moab was one of the neighboring states conquered by king David but it later regained its independence.*

because it was unsafe to travel. It may seem surprising that powerful militaristic states like Assyria and Babylonia were so easily overwhelmed by the nomads. However, the fragmented tribal and clan-based social structures of the desert nomads made it very difficult for either state to subdue them effectively. There was no central authority to destroy or negotiate with. The nomads did not inhabit cities that could be taken or grow crops that could be burned. The powerful Assyrian and Babylonian armies simply had no target to aim at.

THE HEBREW KINGDOMS

Though they could in no way compare with them in territory, power, and longevity, the kingdoms founded by the Hebrews in the Levant are at least as significant in world history as the great empires of Egypt and the Near East. The period of independent monarchy was a formative time for Judaism, giving the Jewish people the sense of historical destiny that enabled them to preserve their religion and identity through centuries of foreign rule, exile and worldwide dispersal. Without the survival of Judaism neither Christianity nor Islam would have developed in their present form.

The Hebrews arrived in Palestine in the 12th century BC and settled in scattered tribal units

under chieftains (the "judges" of the Old Testament Book of Judges). However, they were unable to occupy all of Palestine. There remained many independent Canaanite enclaves and Hebrew expansion to the southwest was blocked by the Philistines. Most of the Canaanite enclaves were mopped up in the 11th century but at the same time the Hebrews began to lose ground to the Philistines.

The need to organize effectively against the Philistines led the Hebrew tribes to combine under a monarchy. According to the Bible the first king of the Hebrews was Saul (c. 1020–c.1006) but it was his successor David (c. 1006–965) who was responsible for consolidating the monarchy and creating the first Hebrew state. David was an able soldier who conquered the Philistines, Ammonites, Moabites and Edomites and forced several of the Aramaean tribes of the Levant to accept his overlordship. These were great achievements for any ruler, but David was aided by the temporary impotence of Egypt, Assyria and Babylonia, who might otherwise have intervened. It was also to his advantage that the Aramaeans of the Levant (who had moved into the area after the fall of the Hittite empire) had settled in urban communities by 1000 and so were vulnerable to

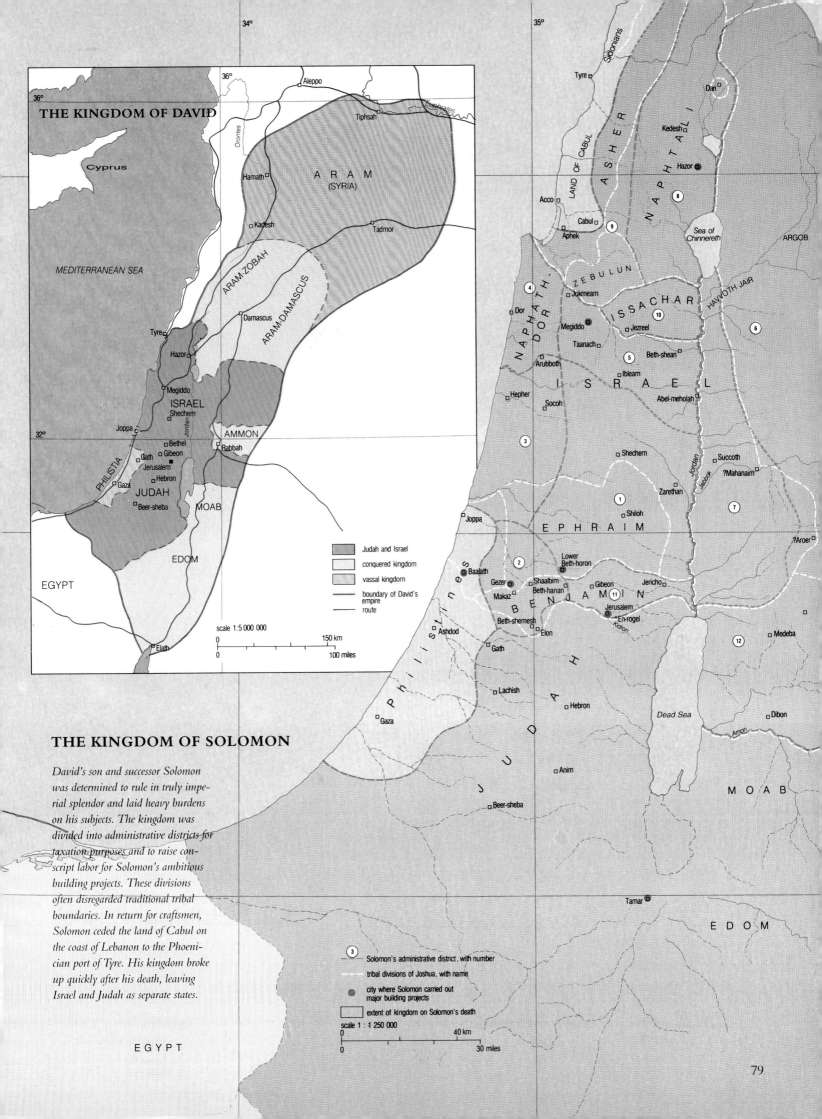

THE KINGDOM OF DAVID

Cyprus

MEDITERRANEAN SEA

ARAM (SYRIA)

Aleppo
Tiphsah
Euphrates
Hamath
Kadesh
Tadmor
ARAM-ZOBAH
Damascus
ARAM-DAMASCUS
Tyre
Hazor
Megiddo
ISRAEL
Shechem
Joppa
Bethel
Gibeon
Gath
Jerusalem
Rabbah
AMMON
Hebron
PHILISTIA
Gaza
JUDAH
Beer-sheba
MOAB
EDOM
EGYPT
Elath
Orontes
Jordan

Judah and Israel
conquered kingdom
vassal kingdom
boundary of David's empire
route

scale 1:5 000 000

0 — 150 km
0 — 100 miles

THE KINGDOM OF SOLOMON

David's son and successor Solomon was determined to rule in truly imperial splendor and laid heavy burdens on his subjects. The kingdom was divided into administrative districts for taxation purposes and to raise conscript labor for Solomon's ambitious building projects. These divisions often disregarded traditional tribal boundaries. In return for craftsmen, Solomon ceded the land of Cabul on the coast of Lebanon to the Phoenician port of Tyre. His kingdom broke up quickly after his death, leaving Israel and Judah as separate states.

③ Solomon's administrative district, with number
⟍⟍⟍ tribal divisions of Joshua, with name
● city where Solomon carried out major building projects
☐ extent of kingdom on Solomon's death

scale 1 : 1 250 000

0 — 40 km
0 — 30 miles

Tyre
Sidonians
Dan
Kedesh
ASHER
NAPHTALI
LAND OF CABUL
Hazor
⑧
Acco
Cabul
⑨
Aphek
Sea of Chinnereth
ARGOB
NAPHTALI-DOR
ZEBULUN
HAVVOTH JAIR
Dor
④
Jokmeam
ISSACHAR
⑩
⑥
Megiddo
Jezreel
Taanach
Beth-shean
⑤
Arubboth
Ibleam
ISRAEL
Hepher
Socoh
Abel-meholah
Shechem
Succoth
③
Jordan
Jabbok
?Mahanaim
①
Zarethan
⑦
Shiloh
EPHRAIM
Joppa
?Aroer
②
Lower Beth-horon
Baalath
Gezer
Shaalbim
Gibeon
Jericho
Makaz
Beth-hanan
⑪
Jerusalem
Philistines
Beth-shemesh
BENJAMIN
En-rogel
Kidron
Elon
Medeba
Ashdod
⑫
Gath
JUDAH
Dead Sea
Dibon
Lachish
Hebron
Arnon
Gaza
Anim
MOAB
Beer-sheba
Tamar
EDOM
EGYPT

79

attack. In about 1000 David captured Jerusalem from the Canaanite Jebusites. By making it his capital, David ensured its lasting importance as a religious center.

David was succeeded by his son Solomon (965–928). Solomon's reign was largely peaceful but maintaining his splendid court life and ambitious building projects, including the temple at Jerusalem, proved burdensome. Some Hebrews were used as forced labor and territory was even ceded to Phoenician Tyre in return for supplying craftsmen and materials. Solomon's successor Rehoboam (928–911) dealt tactlessly with the economic complaints of the northern tribes and the kingdom split in two to form Israel and Judah, and most of the non-Hebrew provinces fell away.

Disunity was a luxury the Hebrews could ill afford with the revival of Egyptian and Assyrian power in the late 10th century. In 924 the pharaoh Shoshenq I (945–924) led a campaign through the land of the Philistines and into Judah and Israel, sacking many cities and imposing tribute. In the 9th century Israel became a tributary of Assyria and Judah followed in the next century. After the fall of the Assyrian empire in 605 both came under Babylonian rule. In 597 a rebellion in Judah was swiftly crushed by Nebuchadnezzar. Jerusalem was taken, the temple plundered and many of its citizens were deported to Babylonia. Ten years later another unsuccessful rebellion was followed by more deportations: many other Hebrews fled into exile in Egypt. The Babylonian captivity was a surprisingly

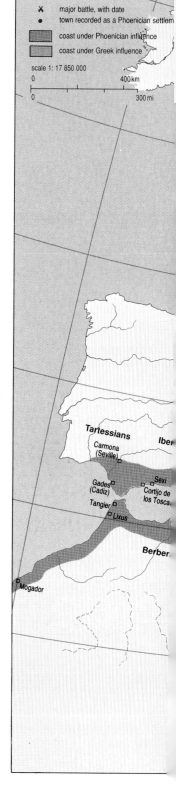

PROTO-CANAANITE	EARLY LETTER NAMES AND MEANINGS		PHOENICIAN	EARLY GREEK	EARLY MONUMENTAL LATIN	MODERN ENGLISH CAPITALS
	alp	oxhead				A
	bêt	house				B
	gaml	throwstick				C
	digg	fish				D
	hô(?)	man calling				E
	wô (waw)	mace				F
	zê(n)	?				
	ḥê(t)	fence?				H
	ṭê(t)	spindle?				
	yad	arm				I
	kapp	palm				K
	lamd	ox-goad				L
	mêm	water				M
	naḥš	snake				N
	cên	eye				O
	pi't	corner?				P
	sa(d)	plant				
	qu(p)	?				Q
	ra'š	head of man				R
	tann	composite bow				S
	tô (taw)	owner's mark				T

RIGHT *During the 1st millennium BC the Phoenicians and the Greeks established competing spheres of influence. The Greeks controlled trade in the Black Sea, the Aegean and the northern Mediterranean while the Phoenician colonies were concentrated in Sicily and Sardinia and along the North African and Spanish coasts, strategically placed to dominate the western Mediterranean and the exit to the Atlantic Ocean.*

LEFT *Development of the alphabet. The Mesopotamian cuneiform script included hundreds of different signs for syllables and words which scribes took many years to learn to write. The development of the phonetic alphabet, with fewer than 30 signs, made writing into a skill that was easily learned. The phonetic alphabet was invented by the Canaanites before 1600 BC. Canaanite letters were based on Egyptian hieroglyphs but, instead of complete words, they stood for consonants. The Aramaeans adapted this alphabet to Aramaic and in this form it spread to the rest of the Near East, replacing cuneiform in everyday use by about 400 BC. The Phoenicians introduced the alphabet to the Greeks who improved it by using some letters to represent vowel sounds instead of consonants.*

RIGHT *A 4th-century coin from Byblos showing a Phoenician galley above a sea monster. The cities of the Phoenician homeland lost their independence to Assyria in the 7th century, and by the time this coin was struck Phoenician ships were serving the Persian empire.*

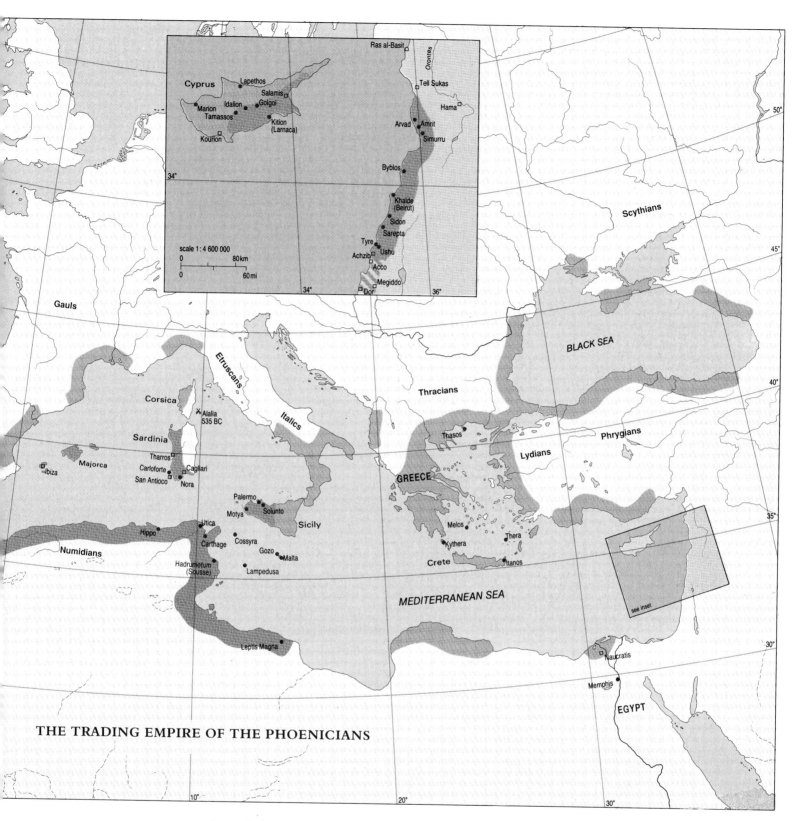

Cyprus

Ras al-Basit
Tell Sukas
Hama
Arvad
Amrit
Simurru
Byblos
Khalde (Beirut)
Sidon
Sarepta
Tyre
Ushu
Achzib
Acco
Megiddo
Dor

Lapethos
Salamis
Golgoi
Idalion
Marion
Tamassos
Kition (Larnaca)
Kourion

scale 1:4 600 000
0   80km
0   60mi

Gauls

Etruscans

Corsica

Alalia
535 BC

Sardinia

Italics

Tharros
Ibiza
Majorca
Carloforte
Cagliari
San Antioco
Nora

Palermo
Motya
Solunto
Sicily

Utica
Hippo
Carthage
Cossyra
Gozo
Malta
Hadrumetum (Sousse)
Lampedusa

Numidians

Leptis Magna

Thasos

GREECE

Thracians

Lydians

Phrygians

BLACK SEA

Scythians

Melos
Thera
Kythera
Crete
Itanos

see inset

MEDITERRANEAN SEA

Naucratis
Memphis

EGYPT

THE TRADING EMPIRE OF THE PHOENICIANS

creative period in Jewish history. Exile caused a great deal of religious reflection and it was at this time that much of the Old Testament came to be written down in something close to its present form. When Cyrus the Great destroyed the Babylonian empire in 539, he gave the Hebrews leave to return home but thousands chose to remain where they were. Many others stayed in Egypt. It was the beginning of the Jewish Diaspora.

PHOENICIAN EXPANSION

The Phoenician homeland was on the coast of modern Lebanon and Syria where some of the best natural harbors in the eastern Mediterranean are to be found. Small ports had grown up as early as the 3rd millennium BC, trading cedar wood, purple dye (obtained from the murex shellfish), ivory and other commodities with Egypt and Mesopotamia. The leading Phoenician ports – Tyre, Sidon, Beirut,

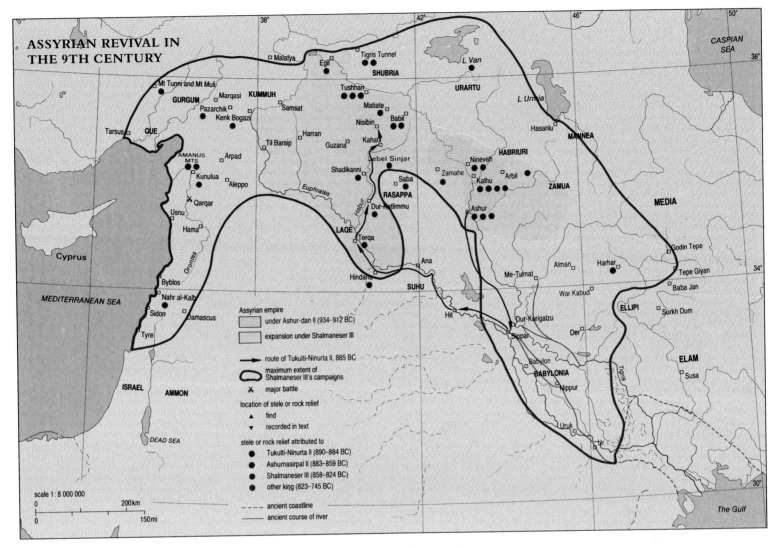

ASSYRIAN REVIVAL IN THE 9TH CENTURY

Assyrian empire
☐ under Ashur-dan II (934–912 BC)
☐ expansion under Shalmaneser III

→ route of Tukulti-Ninurta II, 885 BC

⬭ maximum extent of Shalmaneser III's campaigns

✕ major battle

location of stele or rock relief
▲ find
▼ recorded in text

stele or rock relief attributed to
● Tukulti-Ninurta II (890–884 BC)
● Ashurnasirpal II (883–859 BC)
● Shalmaneser III (858–824 BC)
● other king (823–745 BC)

- - - ancient coastline
—— ancient course of river

scale 1 : 8 000 000
0   200km
0   150mi

Byblos, Arvad and Ugarit – had developed into independent city states by about 1500. The Phoenician cities never exercised control far inland and for the greater part of their history they were vassals of one or other of the region's great powers. In the earliest records they were ruled by hereditary kings, such as Solomon's ally Hiram of Tyre, but by the 6th century BC these rulers had been replaced by elected officials.

During the 1st millennium BC, Phoenician merchant seafarers began to establish an overseas trading empire. A colony was founded at Kition on Cyprus in about 1000. Cyprus was an important source of copper and had had close trade links with Phoenicia for centuries before this. The main period of Phoenician overseas expansion lasted from the late 9th century to the mid 7th century. The main concentrations of Phoenician colonies were in Tunisia, Sicily and Sardinia, which gave them control over the main approaches to the western Mediterranean. By the 8th century Phoenician trade routes extended through the Strait of Gibraltar and some way along the Atlantic

coasts of Spain and Morocco. At first the Phoenicians maintained only seasonal trading posts in this area but permanent colonies, such as Tingis (Tangier) and Gades (Cadiz), were established in the 7th century. It was through these colonies that the late Bronze Age and early Iron Age peoples of western Europe first felt the influence of the civilizations of the eastern Mediterranean and Near East. The Phoenician colonies remained subject to their parent cities. When the Phoenician homeland was conquered by the Assyrians in the 7th century, Carthage, strategically situated on the Tunisian coast, took control of the Phoenician empire in the western Mediterranean. It remained a major power until its defeat by Rome in 202 BC.

THE ASSYRIAN REVIVAL

By the 10th century the Aramaeans were beginning to settle in city states across a wide area of the Levant and northern Mesopotamia. The process was also being repeated among the Chaldeans in southern Mesopotamia. Both adopted Mesopotamian culture but the Aramaeans, at least, did not

ABOVE *The process of Assyrian recovery was begun by Ashur-dan II in the late 10th century, but it was his successors in the 9th century, particularly Ashurnasirpal II and Shalmaneser III, who made Assyria the dominant power in the Near East.*

RIGHT *Shalmaneser III's military campaigns are commemorated on bronze reliefs from the great gates of Balawat (Imgur-Enlil), his palace near Kalhu. (Top to bottom): war chariots in action against the Chaldeans in Babylonia; local rulers from the upper reaches of the Tigris prostrate themselves before Shalmaneser; a sacrifice in the mountains northwest of Assyria (priests studied the entrails of sacrificed animals for signs of the future); Phoenicians from Tyre bring boatloads of tribute to Shalmaneser.*

lose their identity, and the Aramaic language and alphabet had became the most widely used in the Near East by about 500 BC. Mesopotamia did not experience any further immigrations during this period, but in the north, Anatolia and Iran saw the arrival of several waves of Indo-Iranian peoples from the Eurasian steppes, including the Medes and the Persians who had founded powerful kingdoms by the 6th century.

Once they had abandoned nomadism, the Aramaeans and Chaldeans lost most of their military advantages over the old Near Eastern powers, and these now began to recover lost ground. Of the three empires – the Hittite, Assyrian and Babylonian – that had dominated the Near East before 1200, it was the Hittites who made the least impressive recovery. With their heartland lost to the Phrygians, the Neo-Hittites (as they are known to historians) formed a number of small states in southern Anatolia, the most successful of which were Carchemish, Kummukhu (Commagene) and Khilakku (Cilicia). The Neo-Hittites were conquered by Assyria in the 8th century after which they disappear as a separate culture.

The Assyrian heartland around Ashur and Nineveh, which had survived the Aramaean invasions relatively unscathed, formed a strong base for recovery. The pattern established by the earlier Mesopotamian empires, of expansion under able warrior kings, followed by contraction under weak ones, was continued in the new Assyrian empire. The Assyrian revival was begun by Ashur-dan II (934–912). His first priority was to secure the borders of the Assyrian heartland. Once this was achieved he embarked on an ambitious program to restore the Assyrian economy. Cities were rebuilt, refugees resettled in new housing, and a major effort was made to increase the area of land under cultivation. He boasted, "I hitched up more plows in the districts of my lands and thereby laid by more grain than ever before". Ashur-dan also began to construct a system of supply bases to allow for the rapid movement and efficient provisioning of troops, thereby laying the foundation of Assyria's formidable military machine. His successor Adad-nirari II (911–891) went on to recover much of the empire of the Middle Assyrian period and Assyria grew wealthy on the huge quantities of booty and captives won by these reconquests. Adad-nirari's son Tukulti-ninurta II (890–884) consolidated the achievements of the previous two reigns. He has left a detailed account of an expedition he made in 884, traveling south along the

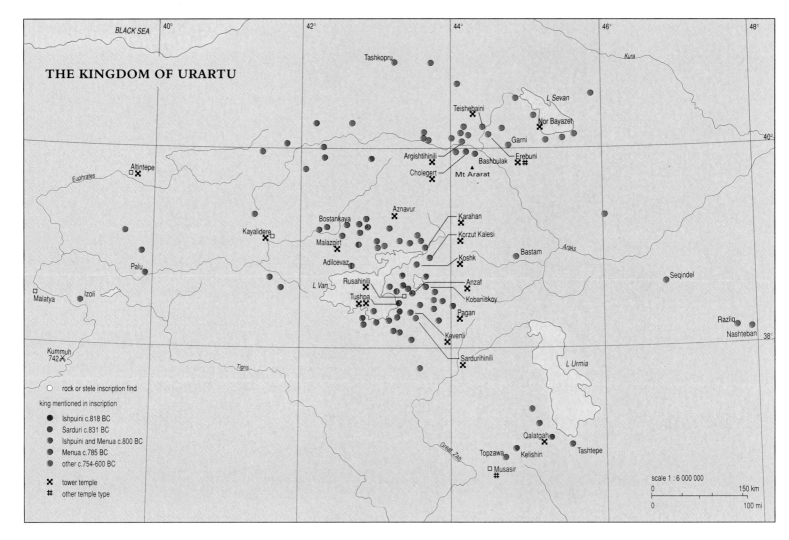

THE KINGDOM OF URARTU

BLACK SEA

Tashkopru

Teishebaini

L Sevan

Nor Bayazet

Garni

Argishtihinili
Bashbulak
Erebuni
Cholegert
Mt Ararat

Altintepe

Euphrates

Aznavur
Karahan

Bostankaya
Korzut Kalesi

Kayalidere
Malazgirt
Koshk
Bastam

Adilcevaz
Araks

Palu
Anzaf
Seqindel

L Van
Rusahinili
Kobaniskoy
Izoli
Tushpa

Malatya
Pagan
Razliq
Nashteban

Kevenli

Kummuh
742
Sardurihinili
L Urmia

Tigris

Qalatqah

Great Zab
Topzawa   Kelishin   Tashtepe

Musasir

○ rock or stele inscription find

king mentioned in inscription

● Ishpuini c.818 BC
● Sarduri c.831 BC
● Ishpuini and Menua c.800 BC
● Menua c.785 BC
● other c.754–600 BC

✕ tower temple
other temple type

scale 1 : 6 000 000

0   150 km
0   100 mi

ABOVE *The Urartians occupied the mountainous country that forms the borderlands of modern Turkey, Armenia, Iran and Iraq. The distribution of the monumental rock-cut inscriptions of its kings indicates that in the 9th century BC Urartian control was restricted to the area around the capital, Tushpa. By the middle of the 8th century, benefiting from Assyrian weakness, the kingdom of Urartu extended from Lake Urmia in the south to Lake Sevan in the north, and from Nashteban in the east to the Euphrates in the west. Characteristic of the Urartians' distinctive culture are the tower temples of their mountain citadels.*

Tigris to visit his Babylonian allies, and then west and north along the Euphrates and Habur to Nisibin, gathering tribute from subject states. The lack of opposition to his progress shows how far Assyria had come in 50 years.

Expansion continued under Ashurnasirpal II (883–859), who carried out successful campaigns in Syria and the Levant. In 877 he reached the Mediterranean and – as the inscription has it – washed his weapons in the sea. The small Neo-Hittite, Aramaean and Phoenician states proved no match for the might of Assyria, but they were not subjected to direct rule. In a pattern that would remain typical of Assyrian aggression, the local rulers became dependent vassals. As long as they continued to send suitable tribute they were left unscathed, but any failure to continue payment was treated as rebellion and punished with overwhelming force. The king would then appoint a local vassal ruler, or the state was annexed and placed under a governor. Particularly troublesome populations might be deported wholesale: between 881 and 815, 193,000 people were deported from the Levant to Assyria where they

could be supervised. Ashurnasirpal was responsible for moving the Assyrian capital from Ashur to Kalhu (known as Calah in the Bible), which he rebuilt in magnificent style (see pages 86–87).

The Assyrian empire was only as strong as its rulers. Constant vigilance was needed to prevent or punish rebellions. At the beginning of his reign Shalmaneser III (858–824) faced a rebellion by Ahuni, the Aramaean ruler of Til Barsip. It took four years to suppress. He was then opposed by a coalition of Levantine states, including Damascus, Israel, Byblos and Arvad, which tried to halt the expansion of Assyrian power in the region. The coalition met Shalmaneser in battle at Quarqar on the Orontes in 853, and though Shalmaneser claimed complete victory, Assyrian power in the Levant suffered a setback. Damascus was still holding out as late as 838, sometime after the other members of the coalition had been cowed into submission.

The Assyrians admired Babylonian culture, and relations between the two states had been close since about 911 when they became allies. Shalmaneser gave military support to the Babylonians against the Chaldean nomads and also provided assistance against internal enemies. In official Assyrian art the king was always shown as superior to everyone else, but Shalmaneser uniquely allowed the Babylonian king Marduk-zakir-shumi to be portrayed as his equal.

URARTU

Shalmaneser III also led five major campaigns against the kingdom of Urartu in the Anatolian highlands. Urartu first entered the historical record in the 14th century BC, when the Assyrian kings campaigned against the region's many local rulers. The difficult mountain terrain made it impossible for the Assyrians to dominate the area permanently, and the main aim of their campaigns was to overthrow troublesome rulers and install pro-Assyrian rulers in their place. As a result of repeated Assyrian aggression, fortified cities and centralized political structures began to develop in the region of Lake Van, and by the 9th century Urartu had emerged as a strong unified kingdom. From the time of Sarduri I (c. 832) the Urartian capital was at Tushpa on Lake Van. This, the heartland of Urartu, was the target of Shalmaneser's campaigns. The Assyrian armies threw everything they could into their assault, crossing formidable natural obstacles, destroying crops and burning

fortresses and cities, but they were unable to curb the kingdom's power, and for the next century Urartu would remain a dangerous rival.

Early Urartian kings borrowed their titles from Assyria and wrote their inscriptions in the Assyrian language. Later they used their own language, which was related to Hurrian. Relatively few Urartian documents have been discovered, so most of our knowledge of the kingdom's history comes from unsympathetic Assyrian sources. The most common surviving Urartian sites are heavily fortified mountaintop settlements. Distinctive thick-walled tower temples, most of them dedicated to the war god Haldi, have been identified at many of these sites. The Urartians were skilled at working in bronze and iron. Their country, watered by mountain springs, possessed fertile soils and good grazing, and their kings actively promoted agriculture and the building of irrigation canals and storehouses.

After the death of Shalmaneser III, Assyria, weakened by internal problems, went into decline. Its borders remained much the same, but provincial governors usurped royal prerogatives and ruled in virtual independence. Relieved of the threat of Assyrian invasion, Urartu was able to expand unhindered. By the reign of Ishpuini I (c. 825–c. 810) the Urartians had secured their southern border against Assyria and had gained control of Musasir, only 50 miles (80 km) northeast of Nineveh. Inscriptions by king Menua (c. 810–c. 785) have been found on the Araks river, over 125 miles (200 km) north of Tushpa, and at Tashtepe on Lake Urmia, 280 miles (450 km) to the southeast. Under his successor Argishti I (c. 785–763), control was extended northeast as far as Lake Sevan. Sarduri II (c. 763–c. 734) campaigned west of the Euphrates to take control of Malatya and Kummuh.

ASSYRIAN EXPANSION

Assyrian weakness was brought to an end by Tiglath-pileser III (744–727). Though one of Assyria's greatest kings, his origins are obscure. Assyrian kings traditionally justified their claims to the throne through divine favor and descent from the previous king. Tiglath-pileser's inscriptions, however, make little reference to his family background, and this has led some historians to conclude that he must have been a usurper. A fine soldier and an imaginative and able administrator, Tiglath-pileser quickly reestablished Assyria as the leading power of the Near East.

BELOW *Archeological finds from citadels and tombs have shown that the Urartians were expert metalworkers, particularly in bronze. Though influenced by Assyrian art, Urartian metalworking had its own distinct style. This solid bronze figurine of a winged centaur-ox comes from the area of Lake Van. Originally its face, divine horns and wings were inlaid and it was covered with gold leaf. It is thought to have been part of a gilded throne.*

KALHU

Tell Nimrud was first excavated in 1845 by the pioneering Victorian archeologist Austen Henry Layard. He thought he had found the remains of Nineveh, but cuneiform inscriptions from the site later showed that he had discovered Kalhu, the 9th-century capital of the Assyrian empire established by Ashurnasirpal II (883–859) who dug canals to irrigate the surrounding farmlands and provide drinking water for the inhabitants. The city was enclosed within a 5-mile (8-km) long wall. Among the dramatic finds unearthed by Layard were the colossal stone lions and winged bulls that guarded the doorways of Ashurnasirpal's magnificent Northwest Palace. Its walls were lined with relief carvings of Assyrian gods and the king's successes in war and hunting, and it lay within the citadel, which was built on an ancient settlement mound dominating the city. In the northwest part of the citadel were the ziggurat and temples of Ishtar, Ninurta and Kidmuru. To the south of the ziggurat was Ashurnasirpal's palace, and further south were the palaces built by Ashurnasirpal's successors. The citadel also contained an arsenal where booty from successful campaigns was stored. Kalhu was destroyed in 612 when the Assyrian empire was overthrown by the Babylonians and their Median allies.

ABOVE *A relief carving from the throne room of the Northwest Palace. Ashurnasirpal II is shown twice, on each side of a sacred tree. The god in the winged disk above the tree is either the sun god Shamash or Ashur, the supreme god of the Assyrians. The scene was carved twice: once at the main entrance to the throne room from the outer courtyard and once behind the throne at the east end of the room.*

LEFT *A gold wristlet inlaid with precious stones, part of a rich collection of grave goods found in the recently discovered tombs of queens at the Northwest Palace. Similar wristlets are shown on reliefs on the palace walls where they are worn by members of the royal family (see above) and by divine beings.*

Kalhu (Nimrud)

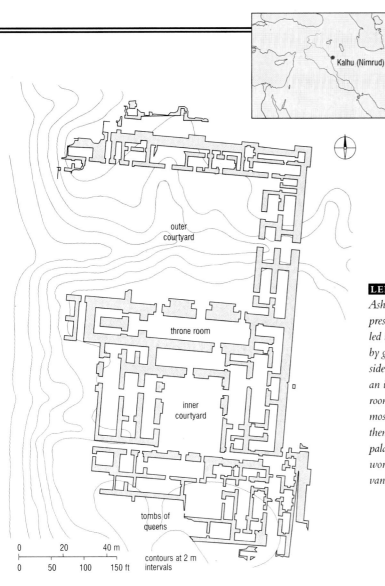

outer courtyard

throne room

inner courtyard

tombs of queens

| 0 | 20 | 40 m |

contours at 2 m intervals

| 0 | 50 | 100 | 150 ft |

LEFT The main entrance of Ashurnasirpal II's palace, the best preserved of the buildings at Kalhu, led into an outer courtyard flanked by government offices. On the south side was the main throne room with an inner courtyard beyond. The rooms surrounding this court were mostly decorated with religious themes. The southern part of the palace housed kitchens, workshops and servants' quarters.

ABOVE Thousands of carved ivory figurines have been found at Kalhu. Many of them, including this winged sphinx, came from the bottom of a well in the Northwest Palace where they may have been thrown for safe keeping before the city was sacked in 612. Carved ivory like this piece was imported from Phoenicia where the art flourished.

LEFT A painting of the throne room by A. H. Layard, the original excavator of the site. Though some details are now considered to be incorrect, the overall impression is accurate. Rain being infrequent in Mesopotamia, light was admitted through a hole in the roof.

RIGHT A colossal statue of a human-headed winged bull from an entrance in the inner courtyard of the Northwest Palace. The bull was carved with five legs because it was designed to be viewed either from the front or from the side. It is 10 feet 9 inches (3.28 m) high. Sculptures of human-headed winged lions stood guard over entrances in other parts of the palace.

Early in his reign, Tiglath-pileser campaigned successfully in Babylonia, taking Sippar and Dur-Kurigalzu and receiving the remnants of the offerings from the temples of Babylon, Borsippa and Kutha – normally the privilege of the king of Babylon. A eunuch was appointed governor of Babylonia but, though Tiglath-pileser assumed the ancient title "King of Sumer and Akkad," he allowed the king of Babylon, Nabu-nasir (747–734), to retain his throne. In 742 Tiglath-pileser defeated a coalition of Anatolian states under the leadership of king Sarduri II of Urartu at Kummuh. He pursued Sarduri as far as Tushpa but was unable to capture the city. Urartu remained a major independent power, though Kummuh and Malatya were lost to Assyria.

For most of the remainder of his reign, Tiglath-pileser concentrated his campaigns in the west. By the time of his death the list of Assyrian tributary regions in the Levant included the Aramaean and Neo-Hittite states of Syria, the Phoenician coastal cities, Israel, Judah, Gaza, Ammon, Moab and Edom, as well as many nomadic Arabian tribes. Assyrian overlordship was sometimes welcomed. An inscription of Bar-rakib, the ruler of Sam'al (in southern Turkey), gratefully described how his father had "grasped the hem of Tiglath-pileser" and how he and his father "ran at the chariot wheel of the king of Assyria," thereby bringing prosperity to his kingdom.

In 732 the native dynasty of Babylon was overthrown and a Chaldean chieftain called Nabu-mukin-zeri (731–729) seized the throne. This Chaldean coup led Tiglath-pileser to intensify his involvement in Babylonian internal affairs. After two years of campaigning, the Chaldeans submitted to the Assyrian king. Tiglath-pileser chose neither to appoint a vassal ruler nor to reduce Babylon to a mere province, but instead assumed the Babylonian throne himself.

TIGLATH-PILESER'S REFORMS

Tiglath-pileser's military and political achievements were based on a fundamental restructuring of Assyria's military and administrative machinery. An intelligence system and a professional standing army were established. The infantry were recruited chiefly from the Aramaeans, but the chariotry and cavalry were largely Assyrian. The elite chariot forces were placed under the control of the chief eunuch – since eunuchs could have no dynastic ambitions they were expected to be more loyal to the king than the nobility. Hereditary provincial governors in the Assyrian heartlands were replaced by eunuchs and a hierarchy of officials under direct royal control. Traveling inspectors were sent out to examine the performance of local officials. A post system was introduced and officials were ordered to report regularly to the capital. Staging posts were set up at intervals along the main roads to improve communications. Representatives were appointed to the courts of vassal states to safeguard Assyrian interests.

By bringing the administrative system under tighter royal control, Tiglath-pileser was able to expand the provincial system. His predecessors had traditionally regarded the Euphrates as the western limit of direct rule but Tiglath-pileser successfully pursued a policy of annexing vassal states in this region and imposing full provincial government on them if they showed themselves at all likely to rebel. As a result, a larger area than ever before was subjected to direct Assyrian rule. Under Tiglath-pileser's successors even loyal vassal states, such as Sam'al, were annexed and converted into provinces of the empire. Large-scale deportations and resettlements of peoples were carried out with the aim of curbing nationalistic tendencies and undermining local loyalties. Tiglath-pileser is recorded as having deported 155,000 Chaldeans and 65,000 Medes, most of whom were settled in Assyria as farmers.

ABOVE *A relief carving of Tiglath-pileser III from the central palace at Kahlu. Tiglath-pileser ended nearly a century of stagnation in Assyria to make it once again the leading power in the Near East.*

RIGHT *Assyrian foreign policy changed under Tiglath-pileser III and Sargon II in the late 8th century. Large areas that had formerly been subjected only to indirect control were annexed and placed under provincial governors. The expansion of the empire was achieved by constant campaigning, recorded in the royal annals. These include a detailed description of Sargon's eighth campaign when he defeated the Urartians.*

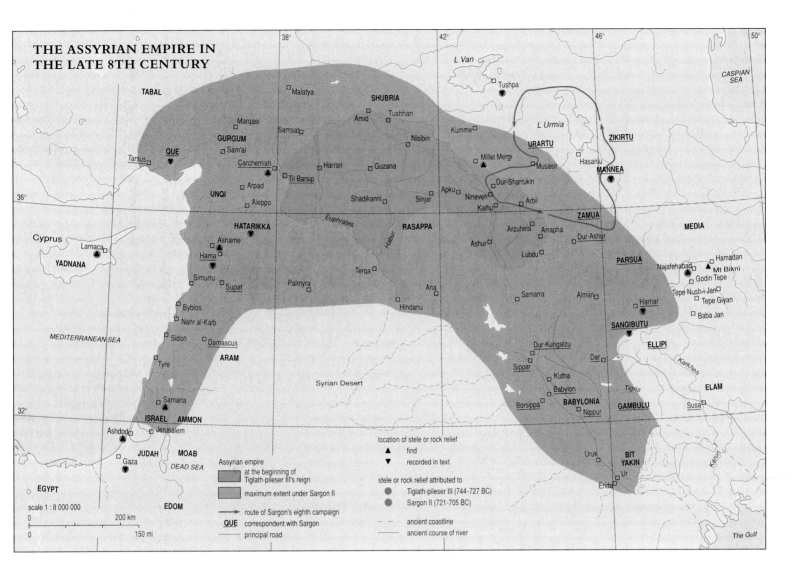

THE ASSYRIAN EMPIRE IN THE LATE 8TH CENTURY

TABAL
Malatya
SHUBRIA
Tushpa
L Van
CASPIAN SEA

Marqasi
Amid
Tushhan
Kumme
L Urmia
ZIKIRTU

GURGUM
Samsat
Nisibin
URARTU

Sam'al
Carchemish
Harran
Guzana
Millet Mergi
Musasir
Hasanlu
MANNEA

Tarsus
QUE
Til Barsip
Shadikanni
Sinjar
Apku
Dur-Sharrukin
Arbil

UNQI
Arpad
Nineveh
Kalhu
ZAMUA
MEDIA

Aleppo
Euphrates
RASAPPA
Arzuhina
Arrapha
Dur-Ashur

Cyprus
HATARIKKA
Ashur
Lubdu
PARSUA
Hamadan

Larnaca
Ashame
Habur
Najafehabad
Mt Bikni

YADNANA
Hama
Terqa
Samarra
Alman
Godin Tepe

Simurru
Palmyra
Ana
Harhar
Tepe Nush-i Jan

Supat
Hindanu
Tepe Giyan

Byblos
SANGIBUTU
Baba Jan

Nahr al-Kalb
Dur-Kurigalzu
ELLIPI

MEDITERRANEAN SEA
Sidon
Damascus
Der
Karkheh

Tyre
ARAM
Sippar
Kutha
ELAM

Samaria
Syrian Desert
Borsippa
Babylon
GAMBULU
Susa

ISRAEL
AMMON
BABYLONIA
Nippur

Ashdod
Jerusalem
location of stele or rock relief
▲ find
▼ recorded in text

JUDAH
MOAB
DEAD SEA
Assyrian empire
Uruk
BIT YAKIN

Gaza
at the beginning of Tiglath-pileser III's reign
stele or rock relief attributed to
● Tiglath-pileser III (744–727 BC)
Ur

EGYPT
maximum extent under Sargon II
● Sargon II (721–705 BC)
Erida

scale 1 : 8 000 000
route of Sargon's eighth campaign
ancient coastline

EDOM
QUE correspondent with Sargon
ancient course of river

200 km
150 mi
principal road
The Gulf

LEFT *A relief from the North Palace at Nineveh shows the 7th-century Assyrian king Ashurbanipal and his queen Ashur-sharrat feasting in a garden. The head of the Elamite king Teumman, sent to Assyria after his defeat and death at the battle of Til-Tuba in 653, hangs in a tree to the left. Ashurbanipal's reign ended in chaos after his brother Shamash-shum-ukin, the dependent king of Babylon, rebelled against him.*

IMPERIAL PRIME

Tiglath-pileser's son and successor Shalmaneser V (726–722) made himself unpopular in Ashur by attempting to impose forced labor. A rebellion broke out, as a result of which Shalmaneser was overthrown and replaced by Sargon II (721–705), probably another of Tiglath-pileser's sons. The rebellion in Assyria sparked off further uprisings throughout the empire. The most serious of these was in Babylonia where Marduk-apla-iddina II (721–710), a Chaldean chief, seized the throne. Sargon acted quickly but was defeated by the Elamites, called in by the Babylonians as allies, at Der in 721. It took ten years and several hard-fought campaigns before Marduk-apla-iddina was forced into exile in Elam and Sargon could assume the kingship of Babylon. Sargon also faced rebellions in the west by the vassal rulers of Hama, Arpad, Simurru, Damascus and Samaria but these were easily suppressed and the rebel states annexed. When the Egyptians supported Gaza in rebellion, Sargon imposed Assyrian rule right up to the borders of Egypt.

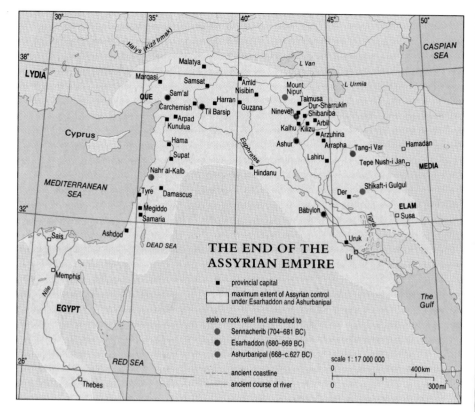

THE END OF THE
ASSYRIAN EMPIRE

■ provincial capital

□ maximum extent of Assyrian control
under Esarhaddon and Ashurbanipal

stele or rock relief find attributed to

● Sennacherib (704–681 BC)

● Esarhaddon (680–669 BC)

● Ashurbanipal (668–c.627 BC)

scale 1:17 000 000

--- ancient coastline

— ancient course of river

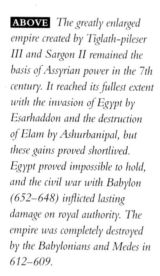

ABOVE *The greatly enlarged
empire created by Tiglath-pileser
III and Sargon II remained the
basis of Assyrian power in the 7th
century. It reached its fullest extent
with the invasion of Egypt by
Esarhaddon and the destruction
of Elam by Ashurbanipal, but
these gains proved shortlived.
Egypt proved impossible to hold,
and the civil war with Babylon
(652–648) inflicted lasting
damage on royal authority. The
empire was completely destroyed
by the Babylonians and Medes in
612–609.*

With his hold on the empire secured, Sargon
turned his attention to Urartu which had recovered from its defeat by Tiglath-pileser III and was
once again threatening Assyria's northern borders.
In 716 the Urartians overthrew the king of Mannea and installed their own vassal king. Sargon
considered Mannea – an important source of
horses for the Assyrian army – to be within his
sphere of influence. In 716 he invaded its borders,
captured the Urartians' vassal king, had him flayed
alive and appointed his pro-Assyrian brother king
in his place. Urartu retaliated by seizing 22 Man-
nean fortresses.

In 714 Sargon launched a well-planned campaign to end Urartian interference in Mannea
once and for all. The army was accompanied by
engineers who built roads where necessary
through the difficult terrain of the Zagros mountains. Somewhere near the southwest corner of
Lake Urmia Sargon defeated the Urartian king
Rusa I and went on to ravage the country between
there and Lake Van almost unopposed. The Assyrian campaign ended in the destruction of Musasir,
the site of the main shrine of Urartu's chief god
Haldi and the coronation place of its kings. The
kingdom of Urartu survived Sargon's attack but its
power was broken and it was unable to resist the
nomadic Cimmerians who invaded from the
steppes shortly afterward. The last reference to the
kingdom dates to 643: what happened to it after

that is unknown. However, Urartu did not vanish
quite without trace as it has given its name to
Mount Ararat in eastern Turkey, the legendary
landing place of Noah's ark.

Another threat to Assyria's northern border
came from king Midas of the Anatolian kingdom
of Phrygia. Early in Sargon's reign Midas supported rebellious Assyrian vassals in northern Syria
but Assyrian retaliation was fierce and prompt and
he was persuaded to become an ally in 709.
According to later tradition, Midas committed
suicide in about 695 after Phrygia was overrun by
the Cimmerians. Excavations of a large burial
mound – believed to be that of Midas himself – at
Gordion, the Phrygian capital, have yielded some
of the earliest known artifacts of brass, an alloy of
copper and zinc. Its golden-yellow color may have
given rise to the legend of Midas's "golden touch,"
for which he is chiefly remembered today.

The Phrygian alliance greatly strengthened
Assyrian power in northern Syria. With no possibility of outside support, the local rulers had little
choice but to submit and, as a letter from Sargon
to one of his governors said, "polish the sandals of
the Assyrian governor with their beards." As the

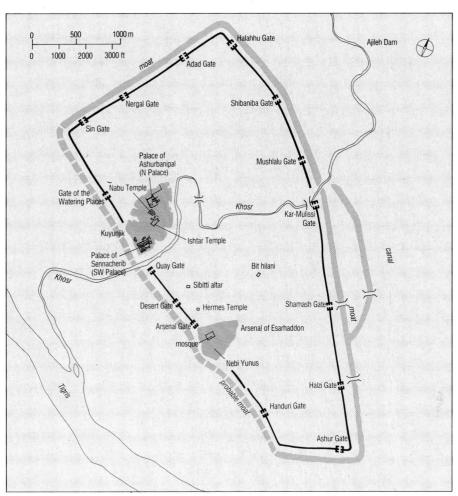

ABOVE *Looking west along the restored outer northern wall of Nineveh, the capital city of the last great kings of Assyria. King Sennacherib, who built it at the end of the 8th century, called it "the wall that terrifies the enemy." It ran for over 7 miles (12 km) around the city, had 15 gates and was defended by a crenellated parapet and interval towers.*

ABOVE RIGHT *Nineveh was already an ancient city, famous for its shrine to the war goddess Ishtar, when Sennacherib chose it as his capital. He greatly enlarged it and built an elaborate system of canals and dams to supply the population with water. His palace, which he called the "Palace without a Rival," was decorated with relief carvings celebrating his campaigns. The North Palace was built by his grandson Ashurbanipal.*

governor in question was a beardless eunuch, this was a prospect he may well have relished.

ZENITH AND COLLAPSE

Sargon had brought Assyria to the peak of its power but his reign ended in disaster. Leading a campaign in Tabal in Anatolia he was killed in battle: his body was not recovered. On the advice of oracles, Sargon's son and heir Sennacherib (704–681) abandoned his father's newly built capital city of Dur-Sharrukin ("Fort Sargon") for nearby Nineveh in order to distance himself from his father's ill fate. Sennacherib's palace at Nineveh was decorated with relief carvings of military victories which give the impression that he enjoyed a triumphant reign. In reality, it was very troubled, having to withstand major rebellions in Palestine and Babylonia and invasions from Elam and Egypt. Sennacherib dealt with opposition energetically and ruthlessly, culminating in the destruction of Babylon in 689.

Egypt's Nubian rulers interfered so persistently in Palestine that Sennacherib's son Esarhaddon (680–669) undertook an invasion of Egypt in the first year of his reign. Initial success was followed

by rebellion, and by the time of Esarhaddon's death, Egypt was again under the control of its Nubian kings. Esarhaddon had restored the Babylonian monarchy and the arrangements he had made for the succession went ahead smoothly, the Assyrian throne passing to his son Ashurbanipal (668–c. 627); another son Shamash-shum-ukin became king of Babylon. In 667 Ashurbanipal sent an army to reconquer Egypt and by 663 the Nubians had once again been expelled, this time for good. Egypt was placed under the rule of Psammetichus I (664–610) who, because he was already in Assyrian service, was confidently expected to be a loyal vassal pharaoh.

The Assyrian empire was now at its zenith. But it was becoming dangerously over-extended. In 652 Shamash-shum-ukin, tired of Ashurbanipal's constant intervention in Babylonian affairs, rebelled. He was supported by the Elamites, who were eager to avenge a defeat by Assyria the previous year, and the Arabs. Encouraged by the civil war, Psammetichus, who had never proved as pro-Assyrian as had been hoped, threw off Assyrian overlordship and expelled the Assyrian garrisons from Egypt. Ashurbanipal did not regain control of Babylon until 648: when he did, his reprisals against the rebels were terrible. Turning his full fury on the Elamites, in 647 he sacked and looted Susa. Elam collapsed, never to recover. The later years of Ashurbanipal's reign were marked by growing internal disorder. A measure of Assyrian weakness is that a rebellion in Judah in 629 was allowed to go unpunished.

Following Ashurbanipal's death, a Chaldean noble called Nabopolassar (626–605) seized the Babylonian throne. Ten years of bitter fighting followed but in the end the Assyrians were driven out of Babylonia. In 615 Nabopolassar took the offensive and, supported by the Medes, overran Nineveh in 612, putting it to the torch. Assyrian defenders held out at Harran in Syria until 609, but after that all resistance ended. Nabopolassar described his victory over the hated enemy in graphic terms:

> I slaughtered the land of Assyria, I turned the hostile land into heaps of ruins. The Assyrian, who since distant days had ruled over all the peoples, and with his heavy yoke, and brought injury to the people of the land, I turned his feet away from Babylonia, I threw off his yoke.

The pharaoh Necho II (610–595) seized the opportunity offered by the dramatic collapse of Assyrian power to reoccupy Palestine but was defeated by the Babylonian crown prince Nebuchadnezzar at Carchemish in 605. The Babylonians followed up their victory by occupying virtually all of the territory previously held by Assyria.

THE NEO-BABYLONIAN EMPIRE

A year later Nebuchadnezzar succeeded to the throne of Babylon. He spent the early part of his reign (604–562) putting down rebellions in Judah, Phoenicia, Elam and Babylonia. In 601 he invaded Egypt but met with such stiff resistance in battle that he was forced to retreat. Describing the action, Nebuchadnezzar wrote "in open battle they smote each other and inflicted a major defeat on each other." Nebuchadnezzar used traditional Assyrian methods to govern his troublesome provinces, including the mass-deportation of rebellious populations such as the Jews. He devoted a great part of his empire's resources to the rebuilding of Babylon (see pages 94–95).

Nebuchadnezzar's dynasty barely outlived him. In 556 his successor was overthrown in a palace coup which placed an official called Nabonidus (555–539) on the Babylonian throne. Nabonidus was a devotee of the moon god Sin and the favor

he showed to the god's shrine at Harran made him unpopular in the Babylonian heartland. Nor was his position helped by the runaway inflation that was the legacy of Nebuchadnezzar's expensive wars and building projects. For ten years of his reign Nabonidus went into a self-imposed exile at Taima in the Arabian desert, apparently in response to an omen. Though he left his son Bel-shar-usur (or Belshazzar, as he is called in the Bible) in charge, the king's absence meant that the Babylonian New Year festival could not be celebrated. This lasted eleven days and the king had an essential role in the ceremonies. He was required to prostrate himself before the priests of Marduk, the chief Babylonian god, and swear that he had not neglected the wellbeing of Babylon. If he shed tears, it was considered to be a good omen for the land.

When Nabonidus at last returned to Babylon sometime between 544 and 540 he found that a new power had emerged on Babylonia's eastern and northern flanks to threaten the security of his kingdom. This was the Persian empire of Cyrus the Great, whose recent conquests of the Medes and Lydians had made him the most powerful ruler in the Near East. In 539 Cyrus invaded Babylon. It surrendered without a fight, bringing to a quiet end an imperial tradition that was almost 2000 years old. Mesopotamian civilization survived for some centuries more, but gradually declined under Persian and Hellenistic influences and had died out by the Christian era.

THE ACHAEMENID EMPIRE OF PERSIA

The Persians who took Babylon in 539 were comparative newcomers to the Near East. Nomads of Indo-Iranian descent, they had followed their close relations, the Medes, from the steppes of Central Asia to Iran in the 8th century BC. While the Medes remained on the Iranian plateau, the Persians migrated further south to settle east of the ancient state of Elam. The founder of the Persian monarchy was said to be Achaemenes, from whom the ruling dynasty gets its name, but it is uncertain when he ruled. The first opportunity for Persian expansion came when Ashurbanipal destroyed the Elamite kingdom in 648. Though the Assyrians occupied Susa, the Elamite capital, the kingdom's eastern territories were seized by the Persians. Despite this, Persia remained a minor kingdom, overshadowed by, and often subject to, the powerful kingdom of the Medes to the north. Only in the reign of Cyrus the Great (c. 559–530) did it make its dramatic rise to empire.

SCIENCE OF THE NEAR EAST

By the 1st millennium BC, mathematics in Mesopotamia was well advanced. Counting was done in sixties. Sixty has many divisors, making calculations relatively simple, and surviving texts show knowledge of square roots, squares, reciprocals, cubes, logarithms and linear and quadratic equations. Astrology was also an important science. Unusual celestial events were interpreted as omens and systematic records kept. By 700 BC the signs of the zodiac had been identified and by 500 astrologers were able to predict with great accuracy the movements of the sun, moon, planets and stars, and the occurrence of eclipses. Medicine was also practiced, and hundreds of different diseases were recognized.

BELOW *This detail from an obelisk at Kalhu shows tribute being weighed before Ashurnasirpal II. Mesopotamian weights were based on the sexagesimal system. There were 60 shekels to 1 mina (1 mina = c. 1.1 lb, 0.5 kg) and 60 minas to 1 talent. There may have been different weight standards in different cities. The five bronze lions (at bottom) belong to a set of 17 bronze weights found at Kalhu, weighing from 44 lb (20 kg) down to 1.7 oz (50 g). They were made in the reign of king Sennacherib (704–681).*

ABOVE *This clay tablet is known as the "Babylonian Map of the World" (c. 500 BC). The circle represents the ocean and in its center is depicted the known world of Babylonia, Assyria, Urartu and Susa, drawn with west at the top. Vertical lines probably represent the Euphrates river. Beyond the ocean are fabulous realms which are described in the text at the top of the map. The earliest known map, of an estate, was made by the Sumerians about 2200 BC.*

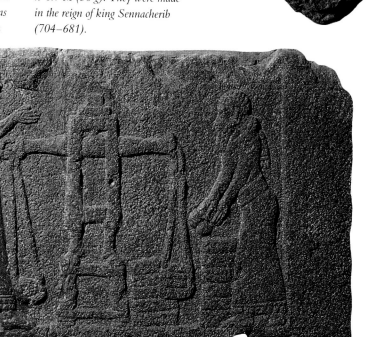

BABYLON

One of the most famous cities of the ancient world, Babylon has, thanks to the Bible, become a byword for vice, luxury, splendor and tyranny. The city, whose name means "Gate of the Gods," was the cult center of the creator god Marduk. During the 18th century BC it became the political, cultural and religious capital of southern Mesopotamia under Hammurabi. Long-standing rivalry between Babylon and Assyria culminated in the destruction of the city in 689 BC by the Assyrian king Sennacherib. After the fall of the Assyrian empire, Nabopolassar (625–605) and his son Nebuchadnezzar II (604–562) rebuilt Babylon on a grand scale, adorning it with magnificent buildings. The famous Hanging Gardens of Babylon were part of Nebuchadnezzar's palace. Other structures included the ziggurat of Marduk known as the Etemenanki ("The House that is the Foundation of Heaven and Earth") and the Esagila temple with its 22-ton golden statue of Marduk. After its conquest by Alexander the Great in 331, Babylon was supplanted by the nearby Greek city of Seleucia.

LEFT *Babylon in the 7th century BC. The city was divided by the Euphrates into two parts, linked by a bridge supported on stone boat-shaped piers. The eastern city, which contained the royal palaces, temples and ziggurat, was heavily defended by a double wall and moat.*

ABOVE *A reconstruction of the Ishtar Gate, looking south along the Procession Street with the ziggurat of the city god Marduk in the right background. The gate was decorated with relief figures of bulls and dragons made in glazed brick. On the right, inside the walls, is the Southern Palace of Nebuchadnezzar II, the northeast corner of which has been identified as the Hanging Gardens, one of the Seven Wonders of the ancient world.*

ABOVE *A large number of antiquities, including this late 3rd millennium diorite statue of a god or deified king from Mari, were found in a "museum" in the Northern Palace. There were also inscriptions of the 3rd Dynasty of Ur and a basalt stele of a Hittite weathergod. A large number of clay tablets point to the existence of a royal library. The museum was maintained at least into Persian times as it contained a stele of Darius I.*

RIGHT *Babylonian craftsmen were famed for their decorative use of glazed brick. This reconstructed panel, 40 feet (12 m) high, was part of the facade of the throne room in the Southern Palace.*

Western Outwork

0   50   100 m
0   100   200   300 ft

Ishtar Gate

?Hanging Gardens

Annex Court

Western Court

Principal Court

Central Court

Eastern Court

throne room

Procession Street

LEFT *The Southern Palace was built around five courtyards with reception rooms on the south side. Its creator Nebuchadnezzar II called it "the marvel of mankind, the center of the land, the shining residence, the dwelling of majesty." It was very probably the scene of Belshazzar's feast when the writing on the wall appeared, an event famously described in the Bible. The palace was later used by the kings of Persia and it was here that Alexander the Great died.*

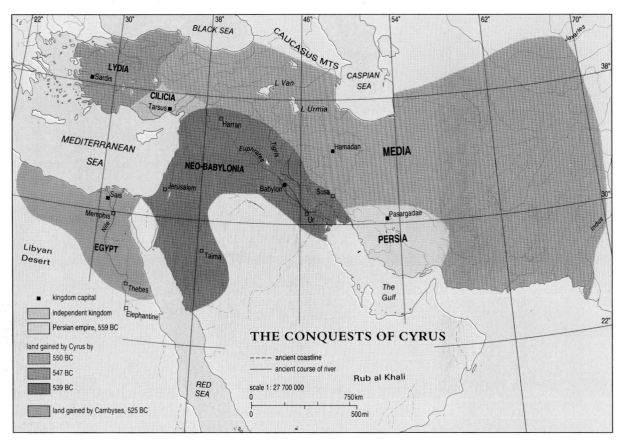

THE CONQUESTS OF CYRUS

- - - - ancient coastline
—— ancient course of river

scale 1: 27 700 000

■ kingdom capital
□ independent kingdom
□ Persian empire, 559 BC
land gained by Cyrus by
550 BC
547 BC
539 BC
land gained by Cambyses, 525 BC

LEFT *When Cyrus became king (c. 559), the Persians were vassals of the Medes. By the time of his death in 530, Persian rule extended over the Medes, Lydians and Babylonians. Egypt, the last of the great Near Eastern powers, would be conquered within a few years by his son Cambyses. Cyrus was killed on campaign near the Jaxartes river in the northeast corner of his empire. Whether he himself conquered the eastern territories of his empire, or whether he inherited them from the Medes, remains uncertain.*

RIGHT *Cyrus's tomb at Pasargadae, the Persian capital, is a simple gabled building set on a stepped platform. An inscription on the tomb read "O man, I am Cyrus, who founded the empire of the Persians and was king of Asia. Grudge me not therefore this monument."*

ABOVE *This carved relief decorated a gatehouse building at Pasargadae. An inscription, "I, Cyrus, an Achaemenid," was carved in three languages. The figure wears an Egyptian head-dress and an Elamite garment and bears the four-fold wings of Assyria. This eclecticism was typical of Achaemenid art, which borrowed styles and motifs from all over the Persian empire.*

In about 550 Cyrus appears to have led a Persian uprising against the Median king Astyages, his nominal overlord. Astyages invaded Persia, but he was an unpopular ruler and, on meeting Cyrus in battle at Pasargadae, was deserted by his own men and captured. Cyrus followed up this easy victory by taking the Median capital of Hamadan. His almost bloodless capture of the kingdom of the Medes, which extended from Anatolia onto the Iranian plateau, put vast resources of wealth and manpower at Cyrus's disposal.

The rapid growth of Persian power alarmed Croesus (c. 560–546), the king of Lydia, an Anatolian kingdom to the west of Media which had grown rich through gold and trade. The Lydians are credited with introducing the first official government coinage, and the name of Croesus – who extended Lydian authority over the Greek cities of the coast of Anatolia – is still synonymous with proverbial wealth. The Greek historian Herodotus tells us that Croesus, unsure what to do in the face of the Persian threat, sought the advice of the oracle at Delphi in Greece. The oracle gave him the type of ambiguous answer for which it was notorious: if he attacked Persia, Croesus was told, he would destroy a great empire. Believing the empire in question to be Persia, he crossed the Halys river on Lydia's eastern border into Persian

territory and fought a fierce but indecisive battle with Cyrus near Pteria (ancient Hattusas). With winter coming on, Croesus then withdrew to his capital of Sardis and disbanded his army, intending to campaign again next spring. Cyrus, however, had nothing against winter campaigns and arrived unexpectedly outside the walls of Sardis. Unprepared for a siege, the city fell to the Persian army after only 14 days.

The empire that was destroyed was Croesus' own. Delegating the conquest of the rest of Lydia and the Greek cities to his generals, Cyrus marched east to push the frontiers of his empire far across the Iranian plateau toward Afghanistan and the river Indus. In 539 he crowned his career by conquering the Babylonian empire. Babylonia was seething with discontent over Nabonidus's absence from Babylon and his religious unorthodoxy. The Persian invasion force met with little more than token resistance. Cyrus presented himself as a servant of Marduk and restorer of the orthodox religion. In this way, he was even welcomed in Babylon.

In little more than a decade, and with remarkably little hard campaigning, Cyrus had built the largest empire the world had yet seen. Clearly the close relationship between the Medes and Persians aided Cyrus in what had more of the character of

a dynastic takeover than a conquest, but it does not explain the ease with which the states of Mesopotamia were conquered. The answer is to be found in the centuries of imperial government which had mixed peoples and cultures in the Assyrian and Babylonian empires, weakened local and national identities and accustomed people to rule from outside. As a result, there was little spirit of resistance among the peoples of Mesopotamia to what amounted in practice to no more than the succession of a new imperial dynasty. Cyrus was as much a diplomat as a soldier and the consolidation of his empire owed a great deal to his tolerance and moderation. Defeated rulers such as Croesus and the Babylonian king Nabonidus were treated generously, demands for tribute were modest, no attempt was made to interfere with local customs, and laws and local institutions of government were left intact.

THE GREEK CAMPAIGNS OF DARIUS AND XERXES

Cyrus was killed in 530 on campaign in Central Asia, possibly against the Sakas, Indo-Iranian nomads related to the Scythians. He was succeeded by his able son Cambyses (529–522) who added Egypt and Libya to the Persian empire before dying in mysterious circumstances, possibly murdered by his brother Smerdis. Darius (521–486), a member of a junior Achaemenid house, soon disposed of Smerdis to take power himself. He quickly suppressed rebellions throughout the empire and within a year was secure enough to campaign against the Scythians living in the area around the Caspian Sea. In 518 he extended Persian control as far as, and possibly a little beyond, the Indus, before turning his attention, a few years later, to the western limits of his empire.

Darius crossed into Europe in 513 to conquer

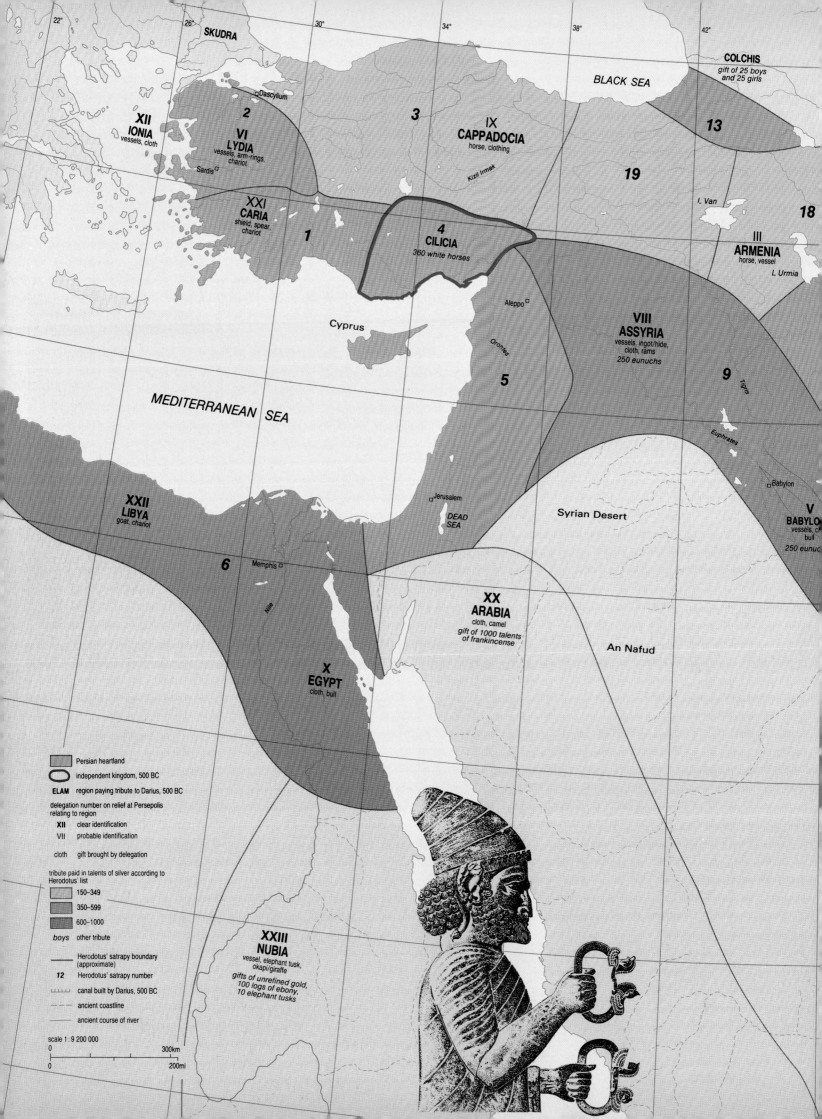

SKUDRA

COLCHIS
gift of 25 boys
and 25 girls

BLACK SEA

**XII
IONIA**
vessels, cloth

2

Dascylium

**VI
LYDIA**
vessels, arm-rings,
chariot

Sardis □

3

**IX
CAPPADOCIA**
horse, clothing

Kizil Irmak

13

19

I. Van

18

**XXI
CARIA**
shield, spear,
chariot

1

**4
CILICIA**
360 white horses

**III
ARMENIA**
horse, vessel

L Urmia

Cyprus

Aleppo □

Orontes

**VIII
ASSYRIA**
vessels, ingot/hide,
cloth, rams
250 eunuchs

9

Tigris

5

MEDITERRANEAN SEA

Euphrates

□ Babylon

Jerusalem □

DEAD
SEA

Syrian Desert

**V
BABYLO**
vessels, c
bull

250 eunuc

**XXII
LIBYA**
goat, chariot

6

Memphis □

Nile

**XX
ARABIA**
cloth, camel
gift of 1000 talents
of frankincense

An Nafud

**X
EGYPT**
cloth, bull

**XXIII
NUBIA**
vessel, elephant tusk,
okapi/giraffe

gifts of unrefined gold,
100 logs of ebony,
10 elephant tusks

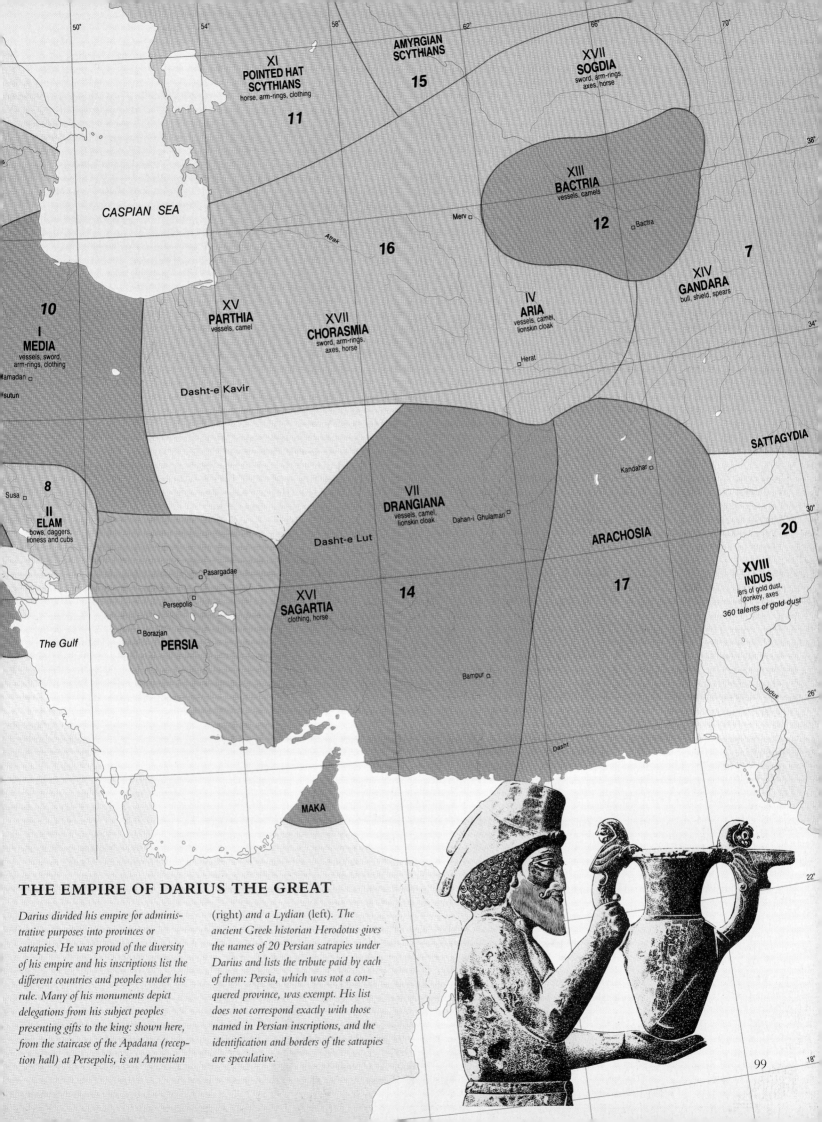

50° 54° 58° 62° 66° 70°

AMYRGIAN SCYTHIANS

XI POINTED HAT SCYTHIANS
horse, arm-rings, clothing

15

11

XVII SOGDIA
sword, arm-rings, axes, horse

38°

CASPIAN SEA

XIII BACTRIA
vessels, camels

Merv □

12

□ Bactra

Atrak

16

7

10

I MEDIA
vessels, sword, arm-rings, clothing

Hamadan □

Bisutun □

XV PARTHIA
vessels, camel

XVII CHORASMIA
sword, arm-rings, axes, horse

Herat □

IV ARIA
vessels, camel, lionskin cloak

XIV GANDARA
bull, shield, spears

34°

Dasht-e Kavir

SATTAGYDIA

Kandahar □

8

Susa □

II ELAM
bows, daggers, lioness and cubs

VII DRANGIANA
vessels, camel, lionskin cloak

Dahan-i Ghulaman □

ARACHOSIA

30°

Dasht-e Lut

Pasargadae □

Persepolis □

Borazjan □

XVI SAGARTIA
clothing, horse

14

17

20

XVIII INDUS
jars of gold dust, donkey, axes
360 talents of gold dust

PERSIA

The Gulf

Bampur □

26°

Dasht

MAKA

Indus

22°

THE EMPIRE OF DARIUS THE GREAT

Darius divided his empire for administrative purposes into provinces or satrapies. He was proud of the diversity of his empire and his inscriptions list the different countries and peoples under his rule. Many of his monuments depict delegations from his subject peoples presenting gifts to the king: shown here, from the staircase of the Apadana (reception hall) at Persepolis, is an Armenian (right) and a Lydian (left). The ancient Greek historian Herodotus gives the names of 20 Persian satrapies under Darius and lists the tribute paid by each of them: Persia, which was not a conquered province, was exempt. His list does not correspond exactly with those named in Persian inscriptions, and the identification and borders of the satrapies are speculative.

18°

99

and occupy parts of Thrace, but his expedition failed in its main objective of subduing a branch of the Scythians settled around the mouth of the Danube on the Black Sea. This encouraged the Greek colonies of Asia Minor and the Aegean to rebel against Persian rule in 499. The rebellion was put down in 494, and Darius dispatched an expedition to punish the mainland Greeks for their part in supporting the uprising. Defeat at the hands of the Athenian army at the battle of Marathon in 491 persuaded Darius that the only way to prevent further trouble from the Greeks was to conquer the mainland outright.

Darius died before his plans for an invasion were complete and it was left to his son Xerxes (485–465) to carry them out. According to some reports, the Persian army that marched into Greece in 480 was 200,000 strong and was supported by a fleet of around 1000 ships. Xerxes expected an easy victory but the very size of the Persian forces created enormous problems of supply and control. His fleet was decisively defeated by the Athenians off the island of Salamis and the following year the Spartans won a victory over his army at Plataea, a defeat that brought the expansion of the Persian empire to an end.

THE ADMINISTRATION OF THE PERSIAN EMPIRE

While Cyrus had been content to govern the conquered provinces of his empire through existing institutions, Darius reorganized the Persian empire into about 20 provinces (satrapies) which he placed under governors (satraps), who were normally relatives or close friends of the king. The system of taxation and tribute was regularized and fixed tributes, based on the wealth of each province, were introduced to guard against extortion by the satraps. Usually tribute was set at about half the level of what each province was thought able to pay. A further check was placed on the power of the satraps by appointing local garrison commanders who remained directly responsible to the king.

The official capital of the empire under Cyrus had been Pasargadae, with Hamadan, the former Median capital, effectively the administrative capital. Darius moved the administrative capital to Susa and founded a new official capital at Persepolis (see pages 102–103), a few miles to the southwest of Pasargadae. The king was frequently on the move around his empire. To ensure good communications at all times with his satraps, the old Assyrian imperial post system was expanded and the roads

improved. The main trunk road of the empire was the 1600-mile (2575-km) long Royal Road that linked Susa with Sardis on the Aegean Sea. Along the route were 111 relay stations where overnight accommodation and fresh horses were provided. The journey normally took 90 days but the fastest couriers could cover it in a week. Similar roads probably linked Memphis, in Egypt, and Bactra, in the foothills of the Hindu Kush, with Susa. Under Darius the imperial administration continued to use various local languages transcribed into cuneiform script and written on clay tablets for recording purposes, but his successors abandoned this cumbersome system in favor of writing on parchment in the Aramaic language and alphabet,

ABOVE *This glazed brick relief panel from the palace of Darius at Susa shows a horned winged lion with eagle's feet. Darius gathered raw materials and craftsmen from all over the Achaemenid empire: bricks and brickmakers from Babylonia, gold from Bactria and Cappadocia, goldworkers from Egypt and Media, stonecarvers from Ionia and Lydia, lapis lazuli from Sogdia, ivory from Indus and Nubia, timber from the Levant and Gandara, woodworkers from Egypt and Lydia – a remarkable demonstration of the wealth of resources at his disposal.*

states and in no way threatened the survival of the empire. Xerxes died in 465 in suspicious circumstances. His eldest son Darius was accused, probably unjustly, of murdering him and was killed by his brother Artaxerxes I who succeeded as king (464–425). In 448 Artaxerxes recognized the independence of the Ionian Greeks, bringing the desultory war to an end. However, by backing Sparta against Athens in the Peloponnesian War, Persia regained control of Ionia in 404. This success was offset by the loss of Egypt, which rebelled successfully against Persian rule in 404 and was not reconquered until 343.

In the late 5th century palace and harem intrigues began to plague the Achaemenid dynasty. Artaxerxes was succeeded by three of his sons in quick succession, the first two having been murdered after reigns of only a few months. The third, Darius II (423–405), secured his position only by a massacre of potential opponents. On his death, the throne was disputed between his sons Artaxerxes II (404–359) and Cyrus, satrap of Sardis, who recruited an army of 13,000 Greek mercenaries to fight for him. The Greeks advanced as far as Cunaxa, near Babylon, where Cyrus was killed. The Greek force, itself undefeated, refused to surrender and made its way from the heart of the Persian empire back to the Black Sea where it sailed for Greece. It was opposed only by local forces, in itself an indication of Persia's military weakness. Xenophon, one of the commanders of the Greeks, observed in his account of the expedition (which is known as the March of the Ten Thousand) that "whereas the king's empire was strong in that it covered a vast territory with large numbers of people, it also was weak because of the need to travel great distances and the wide distribution of its forces, making it vulnerable to a swift attack."

by now in widespread use. The Persian empire was a thoroughly cosmopolitan state that succeeded in uniting elements of all the major Eurasian civilizations of its time, except the Chinese. By throwing together peoples from so many different civilizations the empire promoted the diffusion and mixing of cultures on a scale never before possible.

THE DECLINE OF ACHAEMENID PERSIA

Despite the decisive defeat of Xerxes' Greek expedition, the Achaemenid empire remained the largest, richest and most powerful state in the Near East. Though Athens continued the war against Persia in defense of the Ionian Greeks, it did so without the support of the other Greek city

The Greeks, however, were too embroiled in their own interminable wars to take advantage of this situation. Their quarrels were brought to an end by Philip II of Macedon (359–336) who imposed strong rule on his own unstable kingdom and then went on to annex neighboring Thrace and Thessaly. After defeating an Athenian alliance in 338, he imposed unity on the Greeks and was planning an invasion of Persia when he was murdered. It was left to his 20-year-old son Alexander to carry out the plan. It took him only eight years of tireless campaigning to conquer the entire Achaemenid empire and, in so doing, to bring the history of the ancient Near East to a close.

PERSEPOLIS

Persepolis ("City of Persia") was the chief royal residence and ceremonial capital of the Achaemenid dynasty of Persia. Founded by Darius I (521–486), it was added to by his son Xerxes (485–465) and grandson Artaxerxes (464–425). Famed throughout the ancient world for its opulent splendor, Persepolis was plundered and burned by Alexander the Great in 330 BC. The magnificent palace complex was contained within a heavily fortified citadel built on a massive limestone platform. As the citadel lacked water, sanitation and kitchens, the palace was probably used for ceremonial purposes only. As well as the Apadana, a vast pillared audience hall, and the "Hall of 100 Columns," the throne room, it housed many impressive ceremonial gates and stairways, private royal quarters, a harem, stables and a labyrinthine treasury. It was built in a mixture of styles – Assyrian, Babylonian, Median, Lydian, Greek and Egyptian – that reflected the great cultural diversity of the Achaemenid empire.

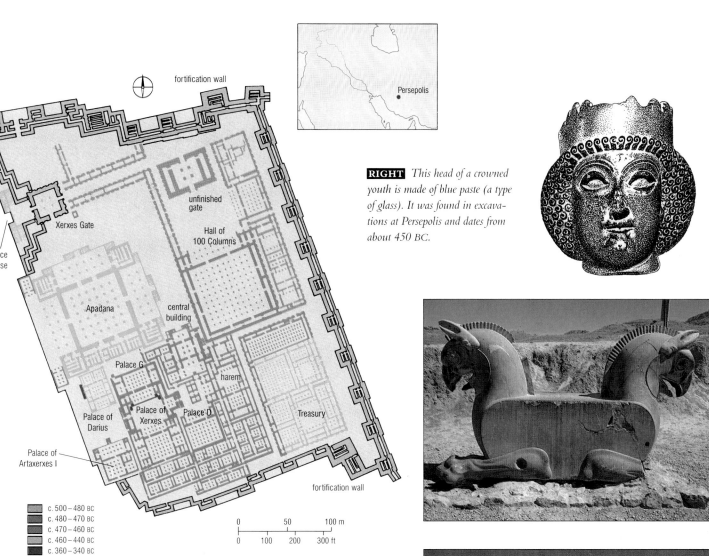

fortification wall

Persepolis

Xerxes Gate

unfinished
gate

Hall of
100 Columns

entrance
staircase

Apadana

central
building

Palace G

harem

Palace of
Xerxes

Palace D

Treasury

Palace of
Darius

Palace of
Artaxerxes I

fortification wall

- c. 500 – 480 BC
- c. 480 – 470 BC
- c. 470 – 460 BC
- c. 460 – 440 BC
- c. 360 – 340 BC

0   50   100 m
0   100   200   300 ft

RIGHT *This head of a crowned youth is made of blue paste (a type of glass). It was found in excavations at Persepolis and dates from about 450 BC.*

ABOVE *Plan of the citadel at Persepolis. Most of the site was built in the 5th century when the Achaemenid empire was at its peak, though some small additions were made later. The citadel was used only for ceremonial occasions: the kings' permanent dwellings were probably on the surrounding plain.*

LEFT *The Apadana, the royal reception hall. All of the palace's major buildings made use of slender stone columns, up to 65 feet (20 m) tall, with ornate capitals to support wooden roof beams. Many remain standing while the massive fortifications, built of mudbrick, have crumbled to dust. The style and workmanship of the columns shows that they were made by Greek or Lydian craftsmen.*

ABOVE RIGHT *A double griffon capital found near the Xerxes Gate. Columned halls were characteristic of Persian architecture and capitals decorated with bulls, human-headed bulls and lions were common. The roof beams rested between the carved heads.*

RIGHT *A carving of Darius I from a relief on the Apadana staircase that shows members of the court, soldiers of the Immortals' Regiment and subjects from the provinces presenting gifts to the king. The inspiration for the relief is probably Assyrian. A similar relief, 200 years earlier in date, has been found at the Assyrian palace at Kar-Shalmaneser (Til Barsip) on the Euphrates. In line with its function as a royal ceremonial center, the king is the focus of most of the decoration at Persepolis.*

WARFARE IN THE ANCIENT NEAR EAST

BELOW *A relief of cavalry in battle from Kalhu. Soldiers rode in pairs so that one could control both horses while the other used his bow. They rode bareback at this period: saddles came into use in the Near East only in the 7th century BC.*

ABOVE *Scenes from the siege of Lachish in Palestine in 701, taken from reliefs at Nineveh. On the left an Assyrian spearman covers an archer with his shield while an Assyrian siege engine is shown battering at the city walls.*

The warrior kings of the late Assyrian and Babylonian empires, and their Persian successors, practiced a tradition of warfare that stretched back to the earliest Mesopotamian city states when competition for land and water was fierce. Cylinder seals from Uruk and Susa, dating to the late 4th millennium, depict scenes of fighting and the taking of prisoners. As metalworking came into use in the 3rd millennium copper and bronze axes and daggers were specially developed for warfare. Successful war leaders celebrated their military triumphs on stone monuments: the earliest clear evidence of battle tactics comes from carvings on the "Vulture Stele" from Lagash (c. 2450), which shows a phalanx of spearmen advancing with their shields locked together.

Military success or failure depended on the ability to raise large armies and move them around the countryside, on mobility in battle, and on the use of siege tactics. By the early 2nd millennium siege warfare had been developed to a fine art. The battering ram was a particularly effective weapon against city walls made of friable mudbrick: siege towers and scaling ladders were also used. In exceptional circumstances armies of 20,000–60,000 soldiers could be raised but armies of a few thousand were more typical. The most important advance in battle

tactics came with the introduction of light, speedy war-chariots, made possible by the development of wood-bending techniques. These same techniques produced the composite bow, a formidable hard-hitting, long-range weapon. Bronze scale-armor came into use, together with bronze swords. Around 1000 BC they began to be replaced by harder edged iron weapons, and mounted cavalry gradually supplanted chariots in battle.

As their armies grew into efficient war machines, the Near Eastern empires flourished as militaristic states. Marauding armies destroyed crops and buildings and carried off livestock and people. Civilians were the main sufferers in siege warfare; the best they could look forward to if their cities were taken by storm was slavery. Captured soldiers who were not killed out of hand were enslaved, deported, or forced to join the victor's army.

ABOVE *Much of our information about Assyrian war tactics comes from the reliefs of victories that decorated the walls of royal palaces. This relief of the Lachish campaign of 701 shows Assyrian troops advancing in two ranks through wooded country, followed by scouts and a messenger.*

LEFT *Assyrian soldiers are seen slaughtering enemy soldiers fleeing from a battle. Prisoners were not always killed, but captured rebels could expect little mercy. Assyrian reliefs show them being impaled or flayed alive.*

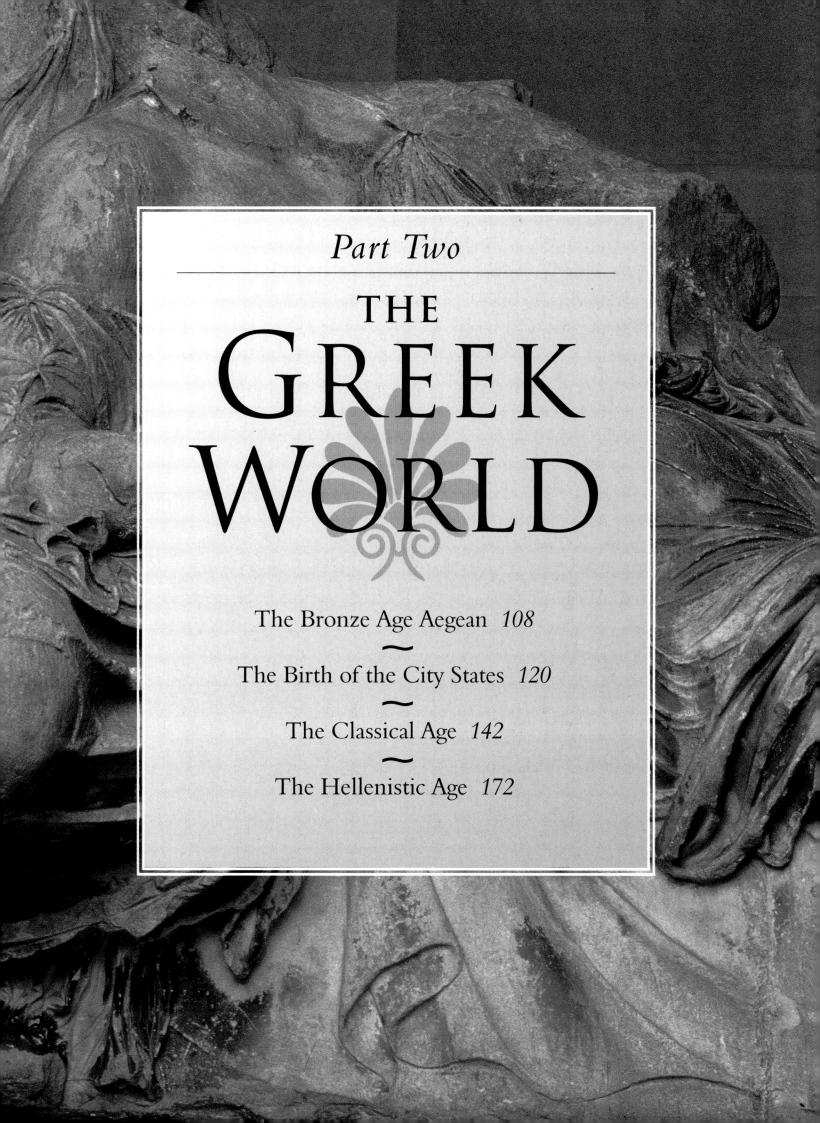

Part Two

THE GREEK WORLD

The Bronze Age Aegean *108*

~

The Birth of the City States *120*

~

The Classical Age *142*

~

The Hellenistic Age *172*

The Bronze Age Aegean

2000–800 BC

ntil the late 19th century the origins of civilization in Europe were obscure. Most historians believed that it had developed earliest in Greece but reliable historical records only went back to the 7th or 8th centuries BC, several centuries after the start of the Iron Age. Yet Greek myths, legends and Homer's epic poem of the Greek war against Troy (the *Iliad*) told of an earlier heroic civilization when iron was unknown and weapons were made of bronze. Was there any truth in them? The Greeks of the Classical Age had thought so, but most 19th century historians were skeptical. Then, in 1870, the German amateur archeologist Heinrich Schliemann discovered

in Turkey the site of the city of Troy. Schliemann's techniques were crude by modern standards, but his excavations clearly demonstrated that the site had been occupied in the Bronze Age. A few years later Schliemann excavated at Mycenae (see pages 114–115), the hilltop citadel on the Greek mainland that was the legendary seat of Agamemnon, the leader of the Greeks who attacked Troy. Spectacular finds confirmed Homer's description of Mycenae as being "rich in gold." In 1900, the English archeologist Arthur Evans began excavating at Knossos on the island of Crete (see pages 110–111). He discovered the remains of a palace civilization considerably older than the one

RIGHT *The walls of Minoan buildings were decorated with frescoes painted in naturalistic style. This fisherman with his catch was found in a house at Akrotiri on Thera, where frescoes have been preserved in remarkable condition because the town was buried by ash from a volcanic eruption in about 1628 BC. The inhabitants appear to have evacuated the town in good time, taking most of their belongings with them, as no bodies and few artifacts were found during excavations.*

LEFT *The Mycenaeans, the first Greeks known to history, flourished 1600–1100 BC. The distribution of major sites shows that the Mycenaean heartland was in the south and east of mainland Greece, but their influence extended to Crete, Rhodes, the coast of Asia Minor and Cyprus. Mycenaean kings controlled far-flung trading networks, extending to Italy, the Levant and Egypt. Excavation of a Mycenaean ship wrecked off the coast of Turkey in the 14th century BC revealed that it was carrying luxury goods from all around the Mediterranean.*

FAR RIGHT *Europe's first civilization, the Minoan, developed on Crete about 2000 BC. Great palaces at Knossos, Phaistos, Mallia and Khania were probably the capitals of small kingdoms which fought each other for supremacy. Around 1700 Knossos emerged as the dominant center. Bronze Age cult figures of goddesses and other ritual objects have been found in several cave and mountaintop shrines.*

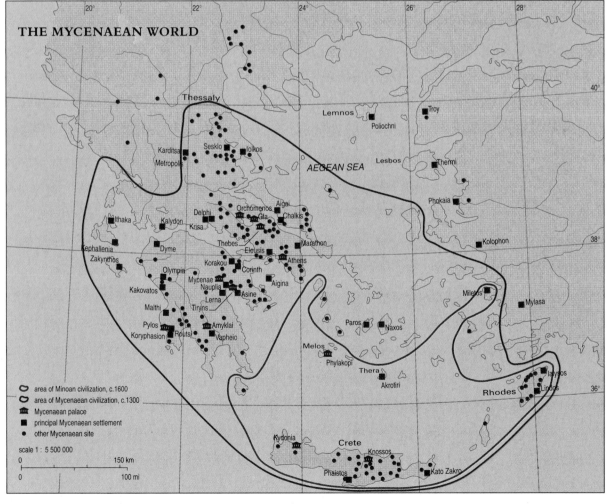

THE MYCENAEAN WORLD

Thessaly

Lemnos
Poliochni

Troy

Karditsa
Sesklo   Iolkos
Metropolis

Lesbos   Thermi

AEGEAN SEA

Ithaka   Kalydon   Delphi   Orchomenos   Aigai
Krisa   Gla   Chalkis

Phokaia

Kephallenia   Dyme   Thebes   Eleusis   Marathon
Zakynthos   Korakou   Athens

Kolophon

Olympia   Corinth
Mycenae   Aigina
Kakovatos   Nauplia
Lerna   Asine
Malthi   Tiryns

Miletos
Mylasa

Pylos   Amyklai
Koryphasion   Routsi   Vapheio

Paros   Naxos

Melos

Phylakopi

Thera   Ialysos
Akrotiri   Lindos
Rhodes

Kydonia   Crete
Knossos
Phaistos   Kato Zakro

⌒ area of Minoan civilization, c.1600
⌒ area of Mycenaean civilization, c.1300
🏛 Mycenaean palace
■ principal Mycenaean settlement
● other Mycenaean site

scale 1 : 5 500 000
0   150 km
0   100 mi

that Schliemann had uncovered at Mycenae, which flourished from about 1600 to 1100 BC. Knossos was the traditional site of the palace of the semi-legendary king Minos of Crete, and so this civilization came to be known as the Minoan.

THE MINOANS

The origins of Minoan civilization are found in the 3rd millennium BC, when bronze was coming into use among the peoples living around the Aegean. Whether its use developed locally on Crete, or whether it was introduced by immigrants from overseas, is not known, though similarities in burial customs, dress and art styles point to some connections between Crete and Libya in the early Bronze Age. Unlike Egypt and Mesopotamia, Crete has no major rivers and few large areas of fertile land so at first glance it looks an unpromising location for early civilization. However, the Minoans were able to develop a system of intensive agriculture based on wheat, olives and vines. The last two grew well on the island's rough, scrubby hillsides and produced two valuable and easily stored commodities, olive oil and wine, which could be profitably traded over long distances. The limited areas of good farmland could therefore be used exclusively for growing wheat. Large flocks of sheep were kept on Crete's

MINOAN CRETE

Khania
Mt Dreparion
Tylissos
Amnissos
Nirou Chani
Mallia
Milatos
Knossos
Kamares
Karphi
Pseira
Palaikastro
Petsopha
Mt Jurkas
Vathypetro
Dictaean cave
Idaean cave
Gortyn
Gournia
Praisos
Kato Zakro
Hagia Triada
Vasiliki
Myrtos
Phaistos
Messara
Hierapytna

mountain shrine
sacred cave
Minoan palace
principal Minoan settlement

scale 1 : 2 000 000

0 — 60 km
0 — 40 mi

KNOSSOS

Knossos, on the north coast of Crete, is the greatest of the Minoan palaces. It was its discovery and excavation by Arthur Evans (who partially restored some of its buildings) that first brought the Minoan civilization to world attention at the beginning of the 20th century. Excavation has continued there ever since, adding new information, and debate, about this complex site. The palace, built on a habitation mound already thousands of years old, dates from about 1900 BC. Its multi-storied buildings were laid out around a central court and housed lavishly decorated state rooms, an extensive range of grain and oil magazines, workshops, shrines and archives. There was a sophisticated sewerage and drainage system. The richness of the finds, including pottery, jewelry and metalwork of very high quality, indicate the wealth of the Minoan palace culture. The palace was damaged by earthquakes and war several times, but was always repaired and rebuilt to the same magnificent standards. Around 1450 BC it was taken over by Mycenaeans from the Greek mainland who occupied it until its destruction by fire and final abandonment between 1400 and 1200 BC.

LEFT *The palace at Knossos was built on several floors around a central open courtyard and included a maze of workshops and storerooms (magazines). This complex layout may be the root of the legend of king Minos's labyrinth. The royal apartments, including the king's hall or megaron,* were in the southeast of the building.

RIGHT *A view of the south wing of the palace, partly restored by Arthur Evans. The stone bull's horns (left of center), known as "horns of consecration", are a common Minoan religious symbol.*

northeast house

sacred way

west court

magazines

staircase to piano nobile

throne room

central court

pillar crypts

grand staircase

royal apartments

south propylaeum

king's megaron

covered stairway to south entrance

southeast house

south house

Athens

Knossos

0   25 m
0   80 ft

BELOW *This highly decorative fresco from the east wing of the palace shows athletes leaping over a bull's horns. Whether bull-leaping was part of a religious ritual or was merely a* dangerous sport is unknown. According to later Greek legend, Knossos was the home of the Minotaur, half human and half bull, that dwelt in king Minos's labyrinth.

ABOVE *A clay tablet inscribed with Linear B script, part of an archive that was preserved by being baked in the fire that destroyed the palace of Knossos. The tablets, in an early form of Greek, give great insight into the life of the palace after the Mycenaean takeover. Sheep and wool were the main source of wealth. Hundreds of workers and craftsmen were employed: shepherds, huntsmen, woodcutters, masons, shipbuilders, metalworkers.*

BELOW *This painted ivory figurine from the palace at Knossos (1600–1550) is holding snakes in either hand and has a cat on her head. She has been given the name of the "snake-goddess", but it is possible that she represents a priestess. Minoan palaces and houses contained cult rooms and small shrines.*

LEFT *This magnificent Mycenaean age gold cup (c. 1500 BC)
comes from a domed tomb at
Vápheio in the southern Peloponnese. It depicts a wild bull, which
has already killed two of its
attempted captors, being trapped
with nets and ropes, and is an
example of the quality of craft-
manship at the disposal of the
Mycenaean warrior aristocracy.*

BELOW *This simple clay figure
of a nursing mother comes from
Crete. A mother goddess cult was
shared by many of the late Bronze
Age peoples of the Aegean, including the Minoans and Mycenaeans,
and goes back beyond them (as in
the geometric Cycladic figurines of
the 3rd millennium BC).*

extensive mountain pastures and these formed the
basis of a textile industry that exported cloth to
Egypt. The Minoans were also expert potters and
metalworkers whose products were in demand
throughout the Eastern Mediterranean.

By about 2000 BC Minoan society had developed from one of small, fragmented clan-based
chiefdoms into one centered on four great palaces
at Knossos, Phaistos, Mallia and Khania, which
were probably the capitals of small kingdoms.
There were also a number of smaller palaces,
possibly subordinate centers. All the palaces had
great storehouses (magazines) with containers for
storing grain, oil and other produce. Produce collected in taxes or as tribute from the surrounding
countryside was gathered at the palaces to be
issued as rations to support administrators and
craftsmen working there and in the surrounding
towns. Imports, such as ingots of copper, were
also stored at the palaces: control over the distribution of such important commodities would have
given the rulers great power. To keep track of
these stores the Minoans adopted a system of
writing based on hieroglyphs. Records were kept
on unbaked clay tablets, few of which have survived. Around 1700 the hieroglyphic script was
superseded by a system based on syllabic symbols,
which is known as Linear A. Neither of these

scripts, which hold the key to discovering the
identity of the Minoans, has been deciphered.
However, study of the oldest Cretan placenames
suggests that the Minoans did not speak an Indo-
European language. This leads historians to
deduce they were not Greeks, but nothing else is
known for certain about their origins.

Around 1700 most of the Cretan palaces were
destroyed by fire. As there is no evidence that
Crete was invaded at this time, such widespread
destruction was probably the result of warfare
between the palace states. All the palaces were
subsequently rebuilt, but only Knossos regained
its former splendor. It seems to have taken control
of the whole island, reducing the other palace
states to the status of tributaries. Minoan civilization entered its greatest period of artistic achievement, producing wall paintings and pottery of
superb quality.

A period of overseas expansion began. The
Minoans had been established on the island of
Kythera since about 2000. Now colonies appeared
on Thera, Melos, Rhodes and Kea and, in about
1550, at Avaris in the Nile delta. Later Greek
traditions held that king Minos had personal
command of great fleets of ships to suppress the
pirates that preyed on Cretan trade in the Aegean.
The Minoans also began to exert a strong cultural

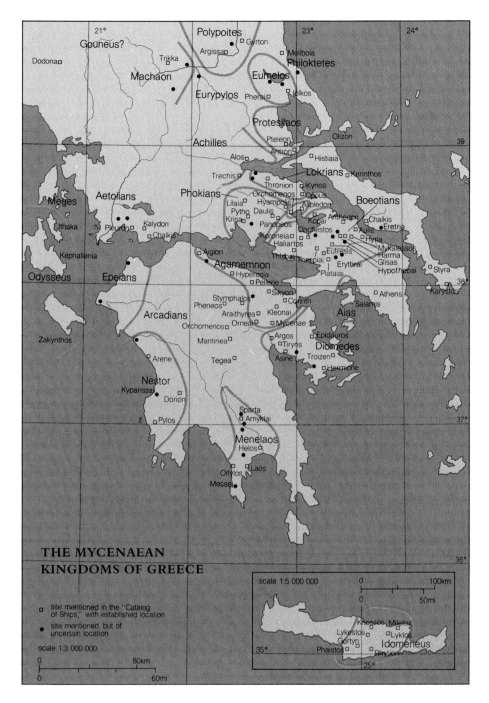

THE MYCENAEAN
KINGDOMS OF GREECE

□ site mentioned in the "Catalog
   of Ships," with established location

● site mentioned, but of
   uncertain location

scale 1:3 000 000

0   80km
0   60mi

scale 1:5 000 000

0   100km
0   50mi

ABOVE *Book Two of Homer's*
Iliad contains the "Catalog of
Ships", a detailed survey of the
places ruled by the heroes of the
Trojan War. The historical accu-
racy of the catalog has been much
debated but it possibly records the
political geography of mainland
Greece in Mycenaean times.
According to the catalog Greece
was divided into small indepen-
dent kingdoms, each of which sent
contingents to join the Greek
attack on Troy under the leader-
ship of Agamemnon. This map
shows the conjectural areas of the
kingdoms, together with the sites
mentioned in the catalog.

influence in mainland Greece. The legend of Theseus, the Athenian hero who volunteered to go to
Crete as part of the annual tribute of youths laid
on Athens by king Minos, suggests that some areas
of the mainland may have been politically subject
to Crete in this period.

Theseus is said to have killed a beast, half-
human and half-bull, in the Labyrinth at Knossos.
We know that bulls played an important part in
Minoan culture. Wall paintings in the palace at
Knossos show youths leaping over the backs of
bulls in what appears to be a ritual game, and
stone bull's horns were important religious symbols. Another major figure in Minoan religion was
a mother goddess whose cult spread to mainland
Greece where she became identified as Artemis,
the goddess of the Moon, the hunt and nature.

Though the palaces had cult rooms, the Minoans
did not build temples to their gods. Caves and
mountain tops were the most important ritual
sites. Minoan religion had its darker side; the
remains of child sacrifices have been found at
Knossos and a few other sites.

Around 1628 BC the neighboring volcanic
island of Thera was blown apart during a massive
eruption that completely destroyed the Minoan
settlements there. Excavations carried out at
Akrotiri in the 1960s and 1970s have uncovered a
Minoan city buried beneath layers of lava and ash.
Palace buildings on Crete collapsed under the
fallout of ash and in the earthquakes that followed
the eruption, but the damage was repaired and life
seems to have continued as before. In about 1450
BC, however, almost all the island's known
palaces, towns and country houses were damaged
or destroyed by fire and many were abandoned for
ever. Only at Knossos was the damage limited, and
new burial customs, more warlike forms of art,
and a new script were introduced at about this
time. The evidence suggests that a foreign ruling
dynasty had taken over at Knossos, probably as the
result of invasion and conquest, bringing an end
to the Minoan civilization.

THE MYCENAEANS

The new rulers installed at Knossos were Mycenaeans from the Greek mainland. We know this
because of an archive of clay tablets discovered at
Knossos inscribed with a script known to scholars
as Linear B. Inscriptions in Linear B have been
found only at Knossos in Crete, and at Mycenaean
settlements on the Greek mainland. It seems to
have been adapted from the Linear A script (suggesting that the Mycenaeans borrowed the idea of
writing from the Minoans), but unlike Linear A,
it has been deciphered and shown to be an early
form of Greek. Greek is an Indo-European language, and the Mycenaeans were probably
descended from peoples who entered Greece from
the Balkans around 2000 BC. It is clear from the
inscriptions on Linear B tablets that the Mycenaeans already worshiped some of the Greek gods
of the Classical period, including Zeus, Athene,
Apollo and Poseidon.

The Mycenaeans were much more warlike
than the Minoans. The earliest evidence of the
emergence of a Mycenaean civilization comes
from a series of richly furnished shaft graves at
Mycenae, dating to between 1650 and 1550,
which reveal a wealthy warrior society. Mycenaean

MYCENAE

The Mycenaean civilization of Bronze Age mainland Greece takes its name from Mycenae, the hilltop citadel that dominates the passes leading from the isthmus of Corinth into the Peloponnese. Homer names Mycenae as the home of Agamemnon, the great king who led the Greeks during the Trojan War, and modern archeology has confirmed its status as an important center during the late Bronze Age. Nearly all the visible remains of the Bronze Age settlement, including the hilltop palace, the granary and the massive walls with their famous Lion Gate, date from the 13th century BC, at the end of its period of greatness, when the Mycenaean settlements of mainland Greece were beginning to be threatened by unidentified invaders. However, rich artifacts discovered in a series of royal shaft-burials show that Mycenae was already a wealthy center in the 16th

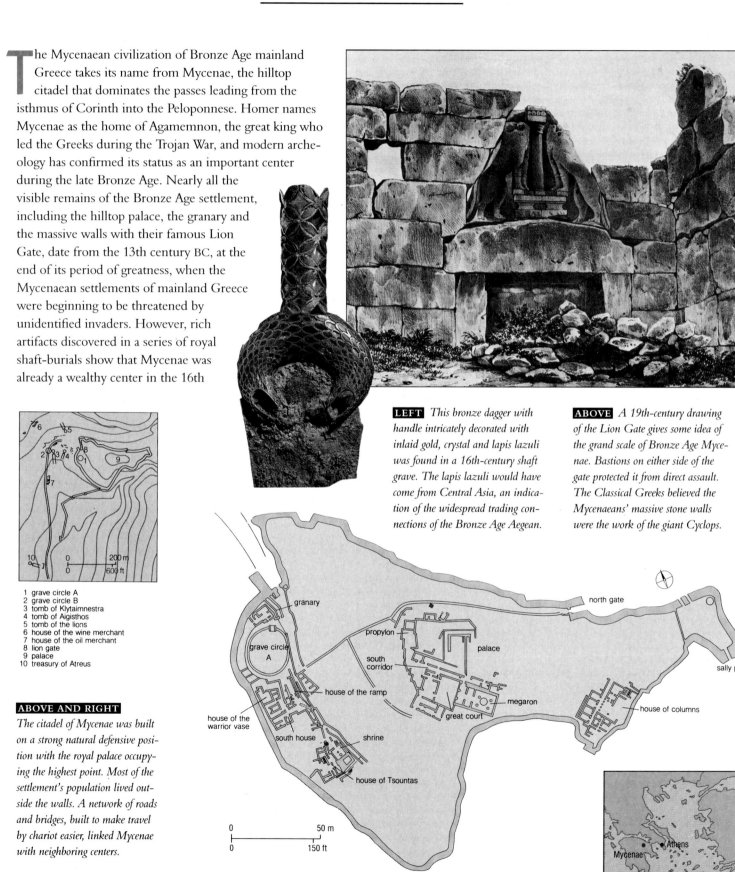

LEFT *This bronze dagger with handle intricately decorated with inlaid gold, crystal and lapis lazuli was found in a 16th-century shaft grave. The lapis lazuli would have come from Central Asia, an indication of the widespread trading connections of the Bronze Age Aegean.*

ABOVE *A 19th-century drawing of the Lion Gate gives some idea of the grand scale of Bronze Age Mycenae. Bastions on either side of the gate protected it from direct assault. The Classical Greeks believed the Mycenaeans' massive stone walls were the work of the giant Cyclops.*

1 grave circle A
2 grave circle B
3 tomb of Klytaimnestra
4 tomb of Aigisthos
5 tomb of the lions
6 house of the wine merchant
7 house of the oil merchant
8 lion gate
9 palace
10 treasury of Atreus

ABOVE AND RIGHT
The citadel of Mycenae was built on a strong natural defensive position with the royal palace occupying the highest point. Most of the settlement's population lived outside the walls. A network of roads and bridges, built to make travel by chariot easier, linked Mycenae with neighboring centers.

granary
north gate
propylon
palace
grave circle A
south corridor
house of the ramp
megaron
house of columns
house of the warrior vase
great court
sally po
south house
shrine
house of Tsountas

Athens
Mycenae

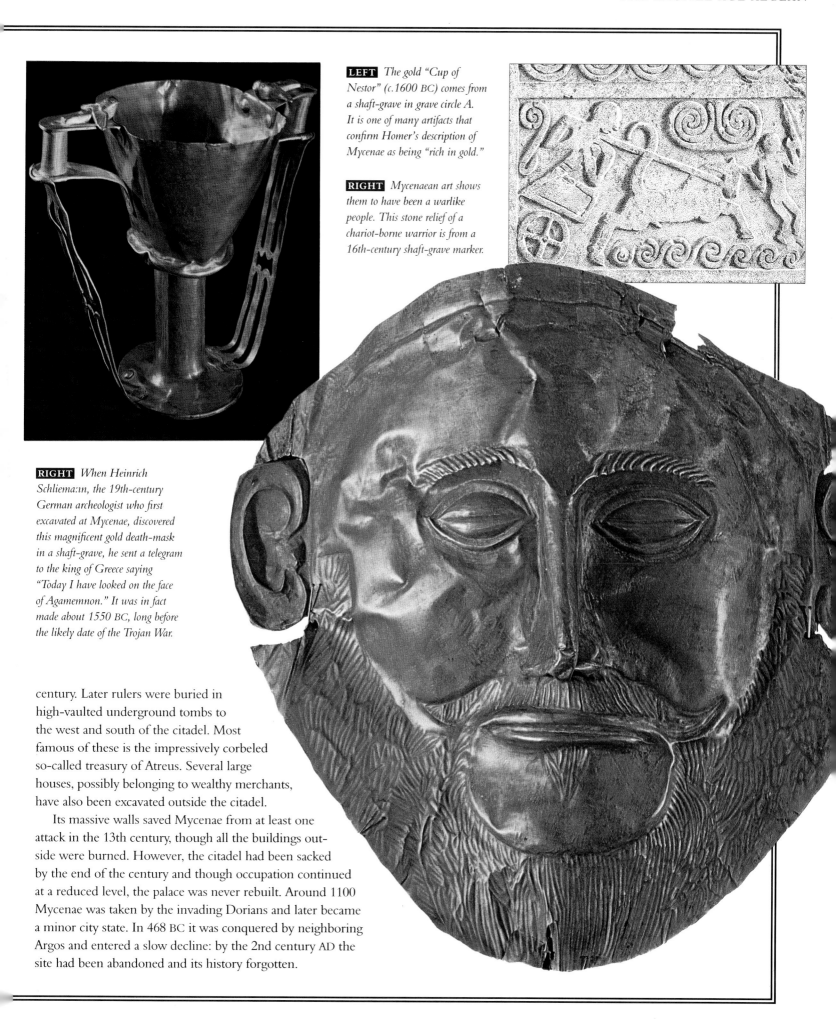

LEFT The gold "Cup of Nestor" (c.1600 BC) comes from a shaft-grave in grave circle A. It is one of many artifacts that confirm Homer's description of Mycenae as being "rich in gold."

RIGHT Mycenaean art shows them to have been a warlike people. This stone relief of a chariot-borne warrior is from a 16th-century shaft-grave marker.

RIGHT When Heinrich Schliema:in, the 19th-century German archeologist who first excavated at Mycenae, discovered this magnificent gold death-mask in a shaft-grave, he sent a telegram to the king of Greece saying "Today I have looked on the face of Agamemnon." It was in fact made about 1550 BC, long before the likely date of the Trojan War.

century. Later rulers were buried in high-vaulted underground tombs to the west and south of the citadel. Most famous of these is the impressively corbeled so-called treasury of Atreus. Several large houses, possibly belonging to wealthy merchants, have also been excavated outside the citadel.

Its massive walls saved Mycenae from at least one attack in the 13th century, though all the buildings outside were burned. However, the citadel had been sacked by the end of the century and though occupation continued at a reduced level, the palace was never rebuilt. Around 1100 Mycenae was taken by the invading Dorians and later became a minor city state. In 468 BC it was conquered by neighboring Argos and entered a slow decline: by the 2nd century AD the site had been abandoned and its history forgotten.

ABOVE One of the wealthiest Mycenaean settlements was at Pylos in the remote southwest corner of the Peloponnese. The site of the Bronze Age citadel, popularly known as Nestor's palace, has been extensively excavated. It stood high on a rocky outcrop above Navarino bay (the coastline itself has altered greatly over the course of time). The palace fell to unknown invaders (probably the mysterious Sea Peoples) at the end of the 13th century. Archeologists have unearthed an archive of Linear B clay tablets recording the frantic, but ultimately futile, efforts that were made to organize an effective defense.

RIGHT Mycenaean civilization collapsed after the 13th-century invasions. In the dark age that followed, the Dorians entered the Greek mainland from the Balkans (c. 1100), probably bringing with them the use of iron. Overseas trade and town life came to end and did not begin to recover until the 9th century when Phoenician traders from the Levant renewed contact with Euboea, bringing gold jewelry that has been found at Lefkandi. The period saw large-scale Greek migration to Ionia on the Anatolian coast. The most characteristic artifacts of the period are pots decorated with geometrical patterns. These were made by all the Greek-speaking communities, except those on Lesbos and in Aeolis.

warriors used horse-drawn chariots as battlefield transport but usually fought on foot with spear, sword and dagger. They carried large "figure-of-eight" shaped ox-hide shields and wore distinctive boar's tooth-covered helmets. During the 15th century Mycenaean rulers began to build high-vaulted *tholos* (beehive shaped tombs) consisting of a burial chamber and a larger chamber, where it is thought rituals relating to a cult of kingship were performed. From the 14th century, and particularly in the 13th century, they built defensive walls around their settlements made of massive stone blocks, like those still standing at Tiryns.

Each Mycenaean stronghold was an independent center of local power that dominated the surrounding countryside. It was ruled over by a petty king or *wanax* with the support of a warrior aristocracy known as the *lawagetas*. The kings controlled large numbers of craftsmen – the ruler of Pylos employed about 400 bronzesmiths, for example – and large numbers of mainly female slaves. Mycenaean palaces were smaller than those on Crete. We know little about the relationships between the Mycenaean rulers but the "Catalog of Ships" preserved in the *Iliad* lists about twenty petty kingdoms that theoretically acknowledged the leadership of Mycenae.

Around 1450 BC the Mycenaeans expanded into the Cycladic islands of the Aegean and south and east to Crete and Cyprus. They even gained a foothold in Asia Minor at Miletos, where they built a fortified settlement. Mycenaean merchant ships sailed throughout the Eastern Mediterranean and as far west as Malta, Sicily and Italy in search

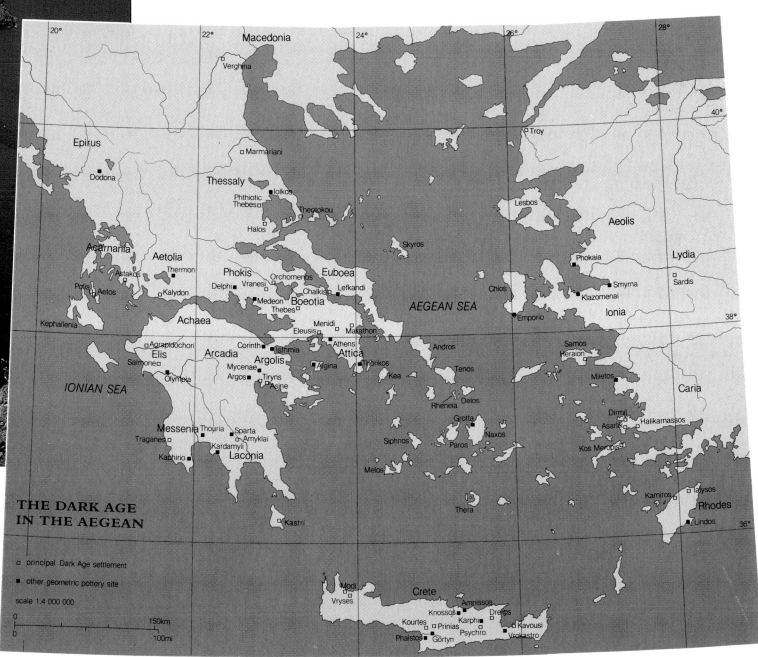

THE DARK AGE IN THE AEGEAN

□ principal Dark Age settlement

■ other geometric pottery site

scale 1:4 000 000

RIGHT *Homer's is the single voice that speaks to us from the Greek dark age. He drew on a variety of oral traditions to compose his epic poems, the* Iliad *and the* Odyssey, *which were not written down until long after his death in the 8th century BC. He was by far the most important influence on ancient Greek literature. This bust is from late Classical times when he was traditionally portrayed with a suffering face in token of his too clear understanding of the tragedy of human life.*

RIGHT *An illustration of the Trojan horse from a pot made about 675 BC, about 50 years after Homer's lifetime. This legend of the Trojan War tells how the Greeks made a show of abandoning their 10-year siege of Troy, leaving behind a huge wooden figure of a horse. The Trojans thought this was a tribute left by the defeated Greeks and carried the horse inside their walls, unaware that a detachment of Greek soldiers was hiding inside it. That night as the Trojans slept, the soldiers let themselves out of the horse and opened the city gates to the rest of the Greek army which had secretly returned.*

of luxuries. A 14th-century Mycenaean shipwreck, discovered at Kas off the Turkish coast, was carrying a cargo of pottery and copper ingots from Cyprus, tin from Anatolia, amphorae of terebrinth resin, glass and ivory from the Levant, ebony, weapons and jewelry from Egypt and ostrich eggs from Libya.

Records from Egypt of about 1400 refer to raids by a people called *Akhaiwashi,* while slightly later documents of the Hittite empire of Asia Minor mention attacks from *Ahhiyava.* Both may be derivatives of *Akhaivoi* (Achaeans), the name Homer gives to the Greeks who besieged Troy. Did the Trojan War take place during this period of Mycenaean expansion? The historical Troy was never as magnificent as Homer's descriptions of it, but it was well fortified and its commanding position at the entrance to the Hellespont gave it control of the trade route to the Black Sea, making it a likely target for attack by an aggressive trading power like Mycenae. Excavations have shown that Troy was destroyed twice in the 13th century BC – not very distant from the date, 1184 BC, that later Greek historians gave to the sack of Troy. But by the 13th century the Mycenaeans were themselves being overwhelmed by a new wave of invaders from the north. Many settlements, including Mycenae, Tiryns and Athens, strengthened their defenses at this time and a wall was built across the isthmus of Corinth to try and keep invaders out of the Peloponnese. By the end of the century,

however, all the major Mycenaean sites in the Aegean had been sacked. Late 13th-century tablets from the palace at Pylos record the settlement's frantic last days. Orders were issued to the coastguards, suggesting that an attack was expected from the sea. Bronze ornaments were collected to be recast as weapons, extra taxes were levied and human sacrifices performed in a desperate attempt to win over the gods. None of these measures, however, prevented Pylos's total destruction and subsequent near-abandonment.

THE AEGEAN DARK AGE

Mycenaean civilization never recovered from the onslaught of these invaders. Historians believe them likely to have been the mysterious Sea Peoples who caused so much disruption in the Near East at this time. Many small towns and villages were abandoned for easily defended hill-top refuges. Occupation continued at a few centers such as Mycenae, Tiryns and Lefkandi on the island of Euboea, but with far fewer inhabitants

and at a much lower material level than before. Pylos was reduced to 10 percent of its population before the invasion, and this decline was reflected everywhere. Knowledge of writing disappeared for the next four centuries.

Historians are unable to reconstruct the events of the Greek dark age, but at its end Greece and the Aegean coast of Asia Minor were home to several Greek-speaking peoples, the most important of whom were the Dorians and the Ionians. The Dorians migrated from the Balkans in about 1100 to fill the power vacuum left by the collapse of the Mycenaeans and quickly took over much of mainland Greece, Crete and Rhodes. They probably introduced the use of iron about this time. Used at first only to edge bronze blades, it was another three centuries before it became the principal metal for weapons and tools. The Ionians were descended from the Mycenaeans who had managed to hold out against the Dorian invaders in Attica (the area around Athens) and Euboea. Over the next 300 years there was considerable emigration from here to the Aegean coast of Asia Minor, known to the Greeks as

Ionia. Ionian Greek, the dialect spoken by Homer, eventually came to form the basis of Classical Greek.

Homer composed his epic poems in the 8th century BC, drawing on oral traditions dating back hundreds of years. The events on which the *Iliad* and the *Odyssey* are based happened in Mycenaean times, but the values, beliefs and social structures that motivate Homer's heroes belong to late dark age society, which was simpler than that of Mycenaean times. The dark age Greeks lived in tribal communities under hereditary chiefs, or petty kings, who combined the roles of war leader and chief priest and ruled with a council of elders and warriors. The king and the warrior aristocracy lived off private estates worked by slaves and hired laborers. Rivalry between neighboring kings sometimes found expression in war but more often in lavish shows of hospitality and feasting. Honor was a man's most important possession, and skill in battle and the hunt his most valued qualities. Barbaric and warlike though this society was, magnanimity and compassion were also admired, especially in the powerful.

RIGHT *At the end of the dark age, Greece was divided into several dialect regions. The Arcadian dialect, spoken in the central Peloponnese, was probably the closest to that spoken in Mycenaean times. In a few places pre-Greek languages, such as Lemnian and Eteocretan, continued to be spoken into Classical times.*

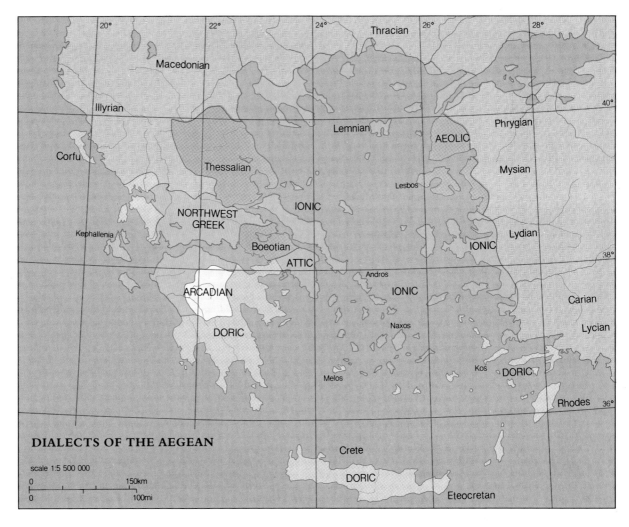

DIALECTS OF THE AEGEAN

scale 1:5 500 000

Birth of the City States

800 – 500 BC

GREEK COLONIZATION

LIGURIA

Agatha
Massalia
Emporion
Corsica — Alalia
Gravisca

ETRUSCAN CITY - STATES
Po
Spina

Kymai — Neapolis
Pithekoussai
Poseidonia
Eléa
Pyxoùs
Skidros

Tartessos — *Guadalquivir*
Hemeroskopeion

Sardinia — Tharros
Caralis
Sulcis
Nora

MEDITERRANEAN SEA

Gadir
Malaca
Mainake?
Sexi

Matauros — Hipi / M
Lipara
Sicily Zakale
Panormos Soloeis
Motya Mylai
Himera Katana
Selinus N
Minoa Leontinoi M
Akragas H
Gela Akrai
Kamarina Ka

Lixus

Utica
Carthage

Mogador
Phoenician trading post

Hadrumetum

Melite

Leptis Magna
Kinyps

TRIPOLITANIA

D uring the 10th century BC a certain amount of stability seems to have returned to Greece and town life began slowly to revive. Most towns grew up around an acropolis, a fortified hilltop citadel that served as a refuge for the people of the city and the surrounding countryside in times of war. This development seems to have started among the Ionian Greeks of Anatolia, perhaps because they were coming under threat from their neighbors, but town life had become firmly re-established in mainland Greece by the 8th century. Greek towns and cities were independent states, at this stage usually ruled by hereditary kings or aristocratic oligarchies. The city state or *polis* (from which our word politics comes) would form the basic political unit of Greece until the 4th century BC.

GREEK EXPANSION

These conditions of comparative peace and stability, together with improved agricultural techniques, meant that the population of Greece began to rise in the 9th century. By the 8th century it was climbing fast: in the 100 years after 800 BC, the population of Attica (the region around

Athens) increased sixfold. Population growth brought increased prosperity, and the 9th-century Greeks began to take a larger share in the trade of the Mediterranean. This had been stimulated into new growth by the Near East's recovery, under Assyrian leadership, from the dark age that had followed the nomadic invasions of the 12th and 11th centuries. The founding of trading colonies at favorable overseas locations enabled the Greek city states to benefit from the economic recovery. At the same time it offered them a solution to the problem of severe agricultural land shortage, resulting from rapid population growth, by providing settlements for their surplus populations.

Once again, the impetus came from the Ionian Greeks. The earliest known Greek colony was founded in the 9th century by colonists from Euboea at Al Mina, at the mouth of the Orontes river in Syria, to take advantage of the booming trade of the Near East. Al Mina was not an exclusively Greek settlement – pottery remains suggest they made up only about half the population – and it was probably only a trading post. The Ionians continued to take the lead when the founding of overseas colonies gathered pace in the 8th century.

■	Etruscan city-states c. 500 BC
■	Greek homeland in 11th-10th centuries
●	Mycenaean settlements of late 13th century
●	Greek settlements of 11th-10th centuries
●	9th-century colonies
●	8th-century colonies
●	7th-century colonies
●	6th-century colonies
■	Dorian colony
□	Ionian colony
●	Aeolian colony
●	Achaean colony
●	Achaean/Troizenian colony
●	Lokrian colony
●	East Greek colony
◆	Greek trading post
●	Phoenician colony
◆	Phoenician trading post
○	temporary settlement

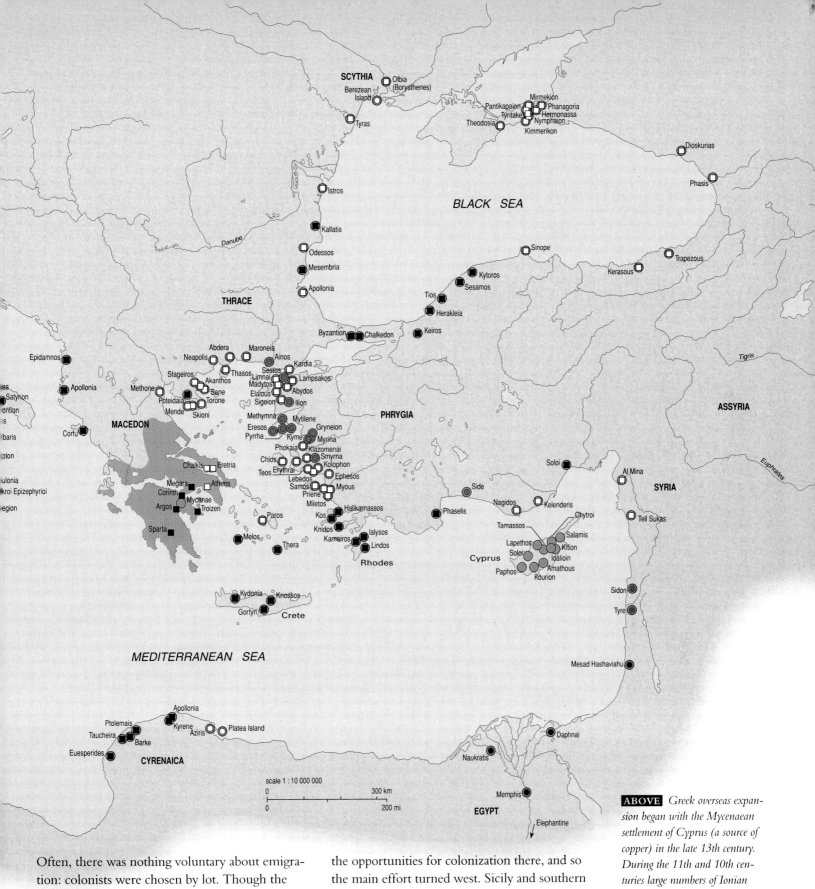

SCYTHIA
Olbia (Borysthenes)
Berezean Island
Tyras
Mirmekion
Pantikapaion · Phanagoria
Tyritake · Hermonassa
Theodosia · Nymphaion
Kimmerikon
Dioskurias
Phasis

BLACK SEA

Istros
Kallatis
Odessos
Mesembria
Apollonia
THRACE
Sinope
Trapezous
Kerasous
Kytoros
Sesamos
Tios
Herakleia
Keiros
Byzantion Chalkedon

Tigris

Abdera Maroneia
Neapolis
Stageiros
Akanthos
Sane
Poteidaia Torone
Mende Skioni
Methone
Thasos
Ainos Kardia
Sestos
Limnai Lampsakos
Madytos Abydos
Elaious
Sigeion Ilion
Methymna
Eresos Mytilene
Pyrrha Gryneion
Kyme Myrina
Phokaia Klazomenai
Chios Smyrna
Teos Erythrai Kolophon
Lebedos Ephesos
Samos Myous
Priene
Miletos
Halikarnassos
Kos
Knidos
Kameiros Ialysos
Lindos
Rhodes

PHRYGIA

ASSYRIA

Soloi
Al Mina
SYRIA
Tell Sukas

Side
Nagidos Kelenderis
Phaselis
Tamassos Chytroi
Lapethos Salamis
Soloi Kition
Cyprus Idalioin
Paphos Amathous
Kourion

Euphrates

Sidon
Tyre

Mesad Hashaviahu

MACEDON
Epidamnos
Apollonia
Corfu
Chalkis Eretria
Megara Athens
Corinth
Mycenae Troizen
Argos
Sparta
Paros
Melos
Thera

Satyrion
ontion
baris
oton
ulonia
kroi Epizephyrioi
egion

Kydonia Knossos
Gortyn
Crete

MEDITERRANEAN SEA

Apollonia
Ptolemais Kyrene
Taucheira Aziris Platea Island
Barke
Euesperides
CYRENAICA

scale 1 : 10 000 000
0   300 km
0   200 mi

Daphnai

Naukratis

Memphis
EGYPT
Elephantine

Often, there was nothing voluntary about emigration: colonists were chosen by lot. Though the colonies usually maintained close links with their mother cities, they were founded from the outset as independent city states. Successful trading colonies were founded on the coasts of Thrace and Macedon and, across the Aegean, along the coast of Anatolia and on its offshore islands (an area that came to called Ionia). But the presence of the Phoenician ports and of other powerful trading states in the eastern Mediterranean limited the opportunities for colonization there, and so the main effort turned west. Sicily and southern Italy proved particularly attractive because there were many good harbors to promote trade, together with fertile agricultural land to support the colonists. The Dorian Greeks were also active in Sicily and Italy. Their colonies included Syracuse, which would become one of the most important of all Greek cities in the 5th century BC. Relations with the native Sicel and Italic peoples were poor, with the Greeks taking over

ABOVE *Greek overseas expansion began with the Mycenaean settlement of Cyprus (a source of copper) in the late 13th century. During the 11th and 10th centuries large numbers of Ionian Greeks fled from the troubles of mainland dark age Greece to settle around the Aegean. The 9th to the 6th centuries saw an explosion of Greek colonizing activity extending from the Black Sea to the coast of Spain. It was largely driven by trade, but also provided a means of solving the problem of population growth at home.*

PAESTUM

Paestum, ancient Poseidonia, is one of the best preserved Greek colonies in Italy. A little way to the south of Naples, it was founded in the mid 7th century by the older Achaean colony of Sybaris. From its position on the Gulf of Taranto, Sybaris was keen to challenge the dominance of trade that the Euboean colony of Cumae (Kymai), north of Naples, enjoyed with the Etruscans. Paestum was defended by a wall 16 feet (5 m) thick and 3 miles (5 km) long; much of it is still standing. Its finest monuments are the three temples built in the 6th and 5th centuries. Paestum was taken over by the local Lucanians, who lived there side by side with the Greeks, in the 5th century. Though the Greeks lamented the decline in the city's cultural life, a fine style of painting was practiced there in this period. Paestum was conquered by the Romans in the 3rd century. It was flooded by the sea during the Middle Ages and abandoned, but further earth movements since then have raised the ruins above sea level again.

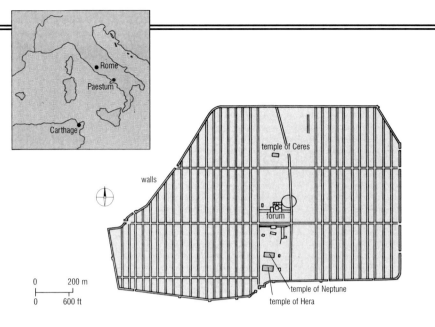

0   600 ft

LEFT *The "temple of Neptune" was built in the mid 5th century in Doric style. During the Middle Ages the temple was partially submerged by seawater. The ruins became fashionable with foreign visitors to Naples in the 18th century, helping to reawaken interest in Greek architecture.*

ABOVE *Paestum was built on a level platform close to the sea and laid out in a simple grid pattern. Its most important monuments are the three fine temples built between the 6th and 5th centuries. The central forum, with a Roman temple of peace, occupies the site of the earlier Greek agora.*

ABOVE *View looking north over the center of Paestum. In the foreground is the 6th-century temple of Hera, the goddess of fertility. The "temple of Neptune" beyond lies within the same sanctuary and was probably also dedicated to Hera. The third of Paestum's Greek temples, known as the temple of Ceres but actually dedicated to Athene, can be seen in the far distance.*

the best land, but the Greeks were generally able to hold their own against weak opposition until the 3rd century BC, when they were conquered by the Romans, by then in sole control of Italy.

In the 7th century BC both the Dorians and Ionians began to found colonies around the Black Sea coasts. The main attraction here was access to the rich grain lands of the Scythian steppes. Greek wine, oil, pottery and luxury goods were traded for grain to feed the growing cities of the homeland. At the end of the 7th century, Egypt's pharaoh Amasis allowed the Ionians to found a colony at Naukratis in the Nile delta. The Greeks provided the best troops for the pharaohs' armies and exerted considerable political influence in Egypt. They in turn were strongly influenced by Egyptian art and architecture.

Colonization in the southern Mediterranean was restricted by the established dominance of the Phoenician colony of Carthage, but in the 6th century the Ionians established colonies on the coasts of Corsica, Gaul and Spain. Trading posts were also founded in the Etruscan territories of northern Italy. Through them, Greek civilization began to exert a strong influence on the Etruscans, but relations were often strained because they were in competition for trade north of the Alps. The foundation of Massalia (Marseille) was a serious blow to the Etruscans as it drew trade, particularly that in tin from Britain, away from the trans-Alpine routes. Massalia lost some of its importance in the 5th century when the Carthaginians established direct sea routes through the Pillars of Hercules to Britain, capturing most of the tin trade for themselves.

By the end of the 6th century, Greek expansion was drawing to a close, and in some places the Greeks had even lost ground. In 539 a combined Etruscan-Carthaginian fleet had defeated the Greeks at Alalia and expelled them from Corsica. The Carthaginians controlled the western tip of Sicily, and in 515 they destroyed a Spartan colony at Kinyps in Tripolitania (Libya). The western Mediterranean was now effectively closed off to the Greeks but despite these reverses they were firmly established as the most widespread people in the Mediterranean. Greek culture would be the strongest external influence on the developing civilizations of the west for centuries. Except in Italy, Greek expansion was achieved with remarkably little opposition from native peoples, perhaps because they benefited from the colonies almost as much as the Greeks did themselves.

CULTURAL CHANGE

The expansion and trading activities of the Greeks brought them into close contact with the old civilizations of the Near East and Egypt, helping to produce the cultural and social changes that marked the transition from the Greek dark age to the Archaic period (800–480 BC). During the 8th century, the Homeric warriors' feast was replaced by the more sophisticated table manners of the east, where rich diners reclined on couches. Egyptian architectural and sculptural styles, Babylonian mathematics and astronomy, and the Phoenician alphabet were adopted and modified. It was the Greek genius to use their cultural borrowings as the basis of new and ultimately far greater achievements. This is well seen with the alphabet. The Greeks of the dark age were illiterate, all knowledge of the Mycenaean Linear B script having vanished. As government and commerce became more complex, writing had to be reinvented. Through their commercial dealings with the Phoenicians, the Greeks became acquainted with their alphabet. The Phoenician alphabet had symbols only for consonants. When they adopted it for their own purposes in about 800, the Greeks added vowels. This created a much more flexible alphabet that allowed literacy to spread quickly and widely through Greek society. This high level of literacy would be a major factor in the remarkable cultural achievements of the Archaic and Classical ages.

One of the first uses to which writing was put was to record law codes. These were often inscribed publicly and the earliest known codes date from the 7th century. The Greeks believed that the origins of law were human, not divine. They recognized that judgements in similar cases should be consistent. Laws were therefore written down and encoded in order to provide consistent rules to limit the discretion and power of judges and safeguard against arbitrary judgements.

In the 8th century the Ionians, Dorians and other Greek peoples still spoke different dialects and were conscious of their separate origins; indeed, the Dorians were still regarded as intruders. Most Greeks were loyal first and foremost to their cities but they were also aware of sharing a common cultural identity with other Greeks. This was mainly expressed through religious festivals held at common shrines. Most famous of these were the games held in honor of Zeus at Olympia (see pages 128–129). The holding of national or Panhellenic festivals led the city states to establish basic rules of interstate conduct, including the maintenance of truces, during major games and safe conduct for heralds and messengers (see pages 136–137).

The Greek cities were fiercely competitive and disputes over spheres of influence led to frequent wars. To judge from Homer, the outcome of battles in dark age Greece was often settled by set-piece duels between aristocratic champion warriors, such as the contest between Hector and Achilles in the *Iliad*. The prosperous city states of the 8th century could support larger and better equipped armies than the petty dark age kingdoms. This led to the emergence of a new kind of Greek warrior, the hoplite (see pages 146–147).

ABOVE *The earliest Greek law codes were inscribed on tablets that were set into the walls of public buildings. A remarkable survival from Gortyn in southern Crete is a 5th-century copy of the city's Archaic law code, drawn up in the 7th century: it is the best preserved and longest of early Greek inscriptions. Like other Greek city states, Gortyn had a clear division of classes: the free, those without political rights, household slaves, serfs and slave laborers.*

GODS AND GODDESSES OF OLYMPOS

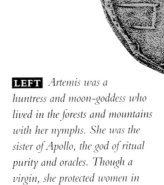

The Greeks worshiped dozens of gods, many of whom had only local or domestic significance. Each city state had its own patron god or gods. The most important of the gods were those believed to dwell on Mount Olympos in northeast Greece. Though there were 12 Olympian gods, they were not always or everywhere held to be the same ones. High in the pantheon were the supreme sky-god Zeus and his consort Hera, Aphrodite the goddess of love, Hermes the messenger, Athene the goddess of wisdom, and the corn goddess Demeter. The Olympian gods had diverse origins. Zeus has affinities with other Indo-European deities – the Latin word *deus* (god) has the same linguistic root. Aphrodite has links with the Sumerian Inanna (the Astarte of the Near East) and her cult probably reached Greece via Cyprus. Hera may originally have been a Minoan mother-goddess.

LEFT *Artemis was a huntress and moon-goddess who lived in the forests and mountains with her nymphs. She was the sister of Apollo, the god of ritual purity and oracles. Though a virgin, she protected women in childbirth.*

ABOVE *Poseidon, armed with a trident, was the god of the sea, earthquakes and horses. He was one of the oldest Greek gods, known from Mycenaean times.*

ABOVE *Hermes was the messenger of the gods, who guided dead souls to the underworld, and the god of travelers, herdsmen and shepherds. He is usually shown carrying a herald's rod, as here.*

RIGHT *The supreme god, Zeus was the master of the sky, storms and thunderbolts. He was a violent god with a harsh sense of justice – attributes that are apparent in this stern bronze head.*

Armed with shield and iron-tipped spear, the hoplite was a footsoldier. He was trained to fight as part of a phalanx, a tight formation of spearsmen that created a wall against frontal attack. The city states were well-matched militarily, and it was rare for one to gain more than a temporary advantage over its rivals. Though wars between the Greeks themselves were often indecisive, the phalanx gave the Greeks a clear advantage over their neighbors. This lasted until the 3rd century BC, when the Romans developed the more versatile legion as a fighting unit. The 8th century also saw the use of the first specialized warships, the ram-equipped galleys that dominated naval warfare for the next 1000 years.

THE TYRANTS

Now that armies were recruited more widely from the free citizens, political power began to ebb away from the old military classes, the aristocracy and the monarchy. Between the mid 7th century and the early 5th century, popular leaders known as tyrants, supported by the hoplite armies and other free citizens, swept away the old aristocratic and monarchical order in many Greek city states. In others the fear of tyranny alone led to the extension of political rights. The term tyrant (*tyrannos*) simply described a ruler who had gained power by his own efforts rather than inherited it; the association of tyranny with autocracy and oppression came later. Some tyrants were in fact model rulers and most were lavish patrons of the arts. The prototype tyrant was Pheidon, an energetic and autocratic king who ruled the city state of Argos in about 660 and issued the first coinage of mainland Greece. He found an imitator in Kypselos, a popular leader who seized power in Corinth in about 657. Kypselos and his successors brought commercial success to the city, and it became wealthy enough to found several overseas colonies. Tyrants had also seized power in Sikyon, Mytilene, Megara and Miletos by the end of the 7th century.

Tyrannies generally continued for no more than two or three generations. The founder of a tyranny was usually an aristocrat who broke with his class and appealed to the people for political support. Greece's new prosperity was not shared by all and the growing inequalities of wealth inevitably created social tensions. The aristocrats were unpopular with the newly rich for their

CORINTH

Strategically situated on the isthmus that joins the Peloponnese to the rest of Greece and with excellent sea communications to east and west, Corinth was already an important trading center at the end of the dark age. It flourished under the Kypselid tyranny (c. 657–585), becoming a major center of pottery manufacture. By the 5th century Athens had replaced it in commercial importance but Corinth continued to enjoy a reputation for wealth and luxury.

BELOW *Little survives of the Greek city of Corinth, destroyed by the Romans after a rebellion in 146 BC. Most of the monuments visible today are from Roman Corinth, refounded on the same site in 44 BC.*

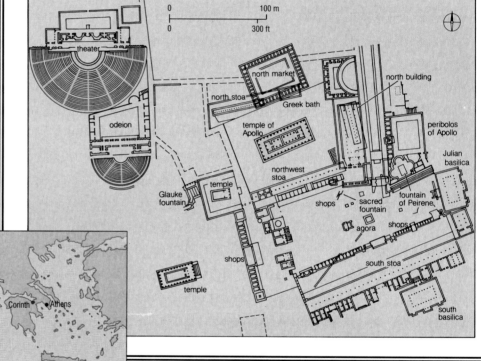

monopoly of public office and with the poor for the crippling interest they charged on debts: defaulters could be enslaved. Moreover, as the overseas colonies were ruled without aristocracies, their political power came to be questioned at home. Tyrants frequently confiscated land from the members of the old regime and redistributed it among the citizens. Debts were written off. To begin with at least, tyrannies were genuinely popular anti-aristocratic governments. But popular support could ebb as fast as it flowed and tyranny proved to a be a highly unstable form of government. As the people gained political confidence, tyrants found that their authority and popularity were undermined. Their only way of holding on to power was to become more and more authoritarian. The tyrant consequently became an object

RIGHT *From the mid 7th century tyrants replaced the aristocratic oligarchies of many city states in mainland Greece and the Aegean. Tyrants courted popularity by redistributing land from the supporters of the old regimes to the poor but their dynasties were usually shortlived, coming to depend on violence to keep themselves in power. Tyrannies were still flourishing in Sicily as late as the early 5th century BC.*

ABOVE *A striking reminder of ancient Corinth are these monolithic Doric columns. They are part of the 6th-century BC temple of Apollo, one of the oldest in Greece. Excavation of the site discovered fragments of painted wall plaster of 7th-century date, indicating that the temple replaced an earlier building.*

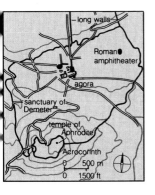

LEFT *Like many of the city states that developed at the end of the dark age, Corinth grew up in the shelter of a strong fortress. This stood on the rocky, virtually impregnable hill of the Acrocorinth, visible in the background of the picture above.*

of hatred, and the citizens and the aristocracy were prepared to settle their differences to work together for his overthrow.

THE RISE OF SPARTA

Sparta, a conservative city state that never experienced tyranny and retained a monarchical constitution (albeit a very peculiar one), played a leading role in developing the new hoplite tactics. The Spartans were one of several Dorian peoples who settled in Laconia, in the central Peloponnese, sometime before 1000 BC. The city and state of Sparta (see page 131) arose from an amalgamation of four villages and it is likely that this gave rise to its unique form of monarchy – there were two kings from two royal families. By the 8th century Sparta had conquered the whole of Laconia. Its Dorian neighbors, the *perioikoi*, were forced to perform military service but otherwise enjoyed a privileged position. The original Achaean inhabitants of the region became serfs, called helots.

The rise of Sparta began with the conquest of Messenia, to the west of Laconia, in the late 8th century. Messenia was divided up equally among the Spartan citizens: the Messenians themselves were retained on the land as helots, paying half their produce to their Spartan masters. As a result Sparta had no need to engage in the colonizing activities of so many other Greek city states. Sparta's only important overseas colony, Tarentum (modern Taranto, Italy) was founded about 706 by citizens who, because they were of mixed Spartan/non-Spartan parentage, had been excluded from a share of the spoils of Messenia. The war

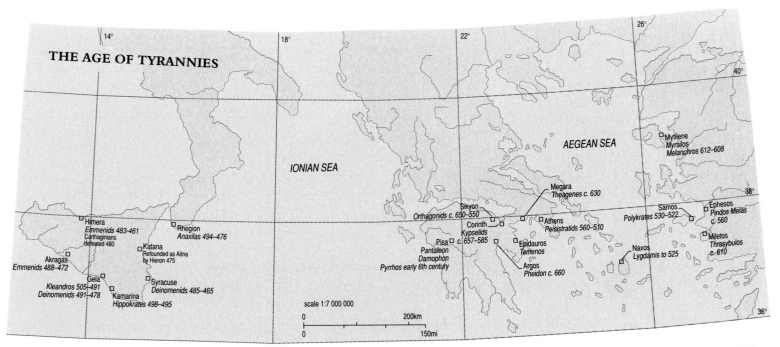

THE AGE OF TYRANNIES

IONIAN SEA

AEGEAN SEA

Mytilene
Myrsilos
Melanchros 612–608

Megara
Theagenes c. 630

Sikyon
Orthagonids c. 650–550
Corinth
Kypselids
c. 657–585
Athens
Peisistratids 560–510

Samos
Polykrates 530–522

Ephesos
Pindos Melas
c. 560

Himera
Emmenids 483–461
Carthaginians
defeated 480

Rhegion
Anaxilas 494–476

Katana
Refounded as Aitna
by Hieron 475

Pisa c.
Pantaleon
Damophon
Pyrrhos early 6th century

Epidauros
Temenos

Naxos
Lygdamis to 525

Miletos
Thrasybulos
c. 610

Akragas
Emmenids 488–472

Gela
Kleandros 505–491
Deinomenids 491–478

Kamarina
Hippokrates 498–495

Syracuse
Deinomenids 485–465

Argos
Pheidon c. 660

scale 1:7 000 000

0   200km

0   150mi

OLYMPIA

Olympia was a sanctuary dedicated to Zeus at the meeting point of the rivers Kladeos and Alfios in the western Peloponnese. It was named for the Olympian gods, and the hill that overlooked the site was sacred to Kronos, the father of Zeus. The athletic festival that made Olympia famous had its origins in the Greek dark age or earlier. The first recorded festival was held in 776, but it only achieved truly Panhellenic importance in the following century. By the 6th century BC Olympia had become immensely wealthy, enriched by the stream of offerings that poured in to the sanctuary of Zeus from across the Greek world.

The festival was held every four years. Two days before the start the athletes who had gathered at the nearby city of Elis processed to the sanctuary. For the five days of the festival Olympia swarmed with spectators; the stadium could seat 40,000. The festival was an all-male event; women were not even allowed to watch. At the end of the games, the victors went in procession to the magnificent temple of Zeus to receive their olive wreaths. Nearby was an altar, where 100 oxen were sacrificed to Zeus. The ashes were mixed into a paste and added to the altar that grew higher with each successive festival.

ABOVE *These ruined columns were part of the temple of Zeus, lying as they fell when tumbled by the earthquake that destroyed Olympia in the 6th century AD. The games themselves were abolished in AD 393 by the Christian Roman emperor Theodosius because of their pagan associations.*

BELOW *This small bronze figure is one of countless votive offerings found at Olympia.*

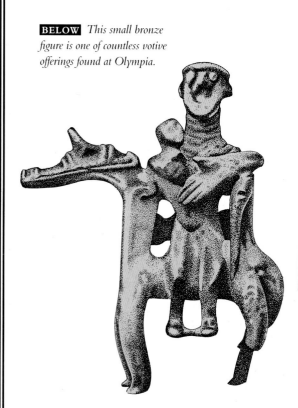

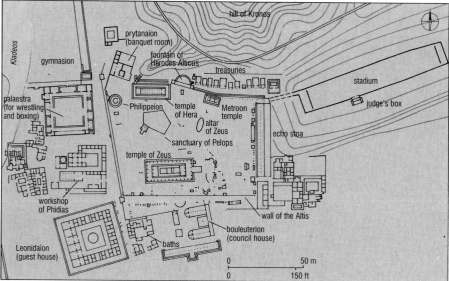

ABOVE *The sacred precinct of Zeus, originally a sacred grove called Altis, was later enclosed within a wall. The altar of Zeus lay roughly at the center. The earliest buildings (7th and 6th century BC) were the* stadium, the treasuries beneath the hill of Kronos and the temple of Hera. Originally this was dedicated to Zeus as well, until his own magnificent temple was erected in the 5th century.

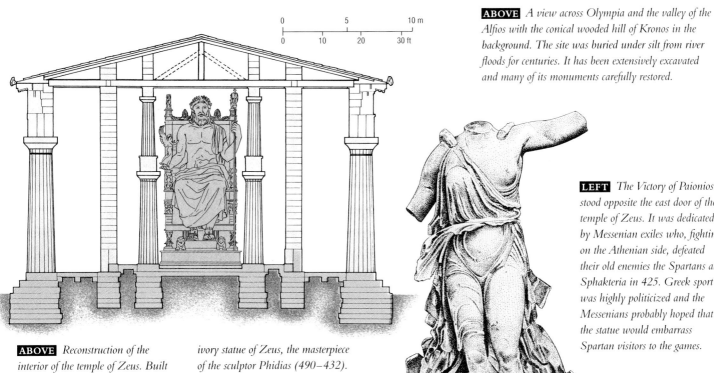

0   5   10 m
0   10   20   30 ft

LEFT *The Victory of Paionios stood opposite the east door of the temple of Zeus. It was dedicated by Messenian exiles who, fighting on the Athenian side, defeated their old enemies the Spartans at Sphakteria in 425. Greek sport was highly politicized and the Messenians probably hoped that the statue would embarrass Spartan visitors to the games.*

ABOVE *Reconstruction of the interior of the temple of Zeus. Built between 470 and 456, it was the largest Doric building on mainland Greece at that time. Seated in the sanctuary was a colossal gold and ivory statue of Zeus, the masterpiece of the sculptor Phidias (490–432). Excavations of Phidias' workshop at Olympia have shown that the statue was not made until 20 to 30 years after the temple was completed.*

129

against Messenia is thought to have been fought using pre-hoplite tactics. The change to the new tactics probably came about after a serious defeat at the hands of Argos in 669. A few years later a Messenian rebellion (c. 660) was put down only with great difficulty.

This rebellion shook the Spartans. They were outnumbered by their Messenian subjects by about 7:1. Future security could only be guaranteed if the Spartans kept themselves in a state of permanent battle-readiness. To this end Sparta developed a constitution that turned it into a hoplite state. Tradition records that the founder of the Spartan constitution was Lykourgos, a shadowy figure about whom nothing is known for certain: some modern historians even consider him to be legendary. Under the constitution the Spartan kings held limited but important powers, including the right to declare war and lead the Spartan armies. The philosopher Aristotle would later describe the Spartan kingship as essentially "a hereditary generalship for life." In other respects the monarchy was limited by the council of elders and the citizen assembly (comprising the entire hoplite body) and, uniquely in Greece, by five annually elected ephors, or supervisors, who had wide-ranging legal powers.

Male children were separated from their families at the age of seven to begin the austere *agoge*, or state-organized upbringing. Education was almost entirely physical, consisting of gymnastics and training in warfare. Luxuries, including shoes, were forbidden and the supply of food was deliberately inadequate so that boys would be forced to use their initiative to find or steal extra rations. Both bullying and homosexual relationships were officially encouraged. Murdering a helot was an acceptable way for a young man to demonstrate his virility. At the age of 20, those who had completed the *agoge* were eligible to become full citizens and join a combined dining-mess and military training unit called a *syssitia*. Though they could now marry, men had to continue living in the *syssitia* until the age of 30. They could then set up their own households but were still expected to eat daily in the *syssitia*, which remained the focal point of all social life. This common upbringing produced a conformist, disciplined, cohesive society in which distinctions of birth counted for little. As a result Spartans came to describe themselves as *homoioi*, "the men who are equal". The philosophers Plato and Aristotle regarded Sparta as being almost the ideal state. Its main limitation,

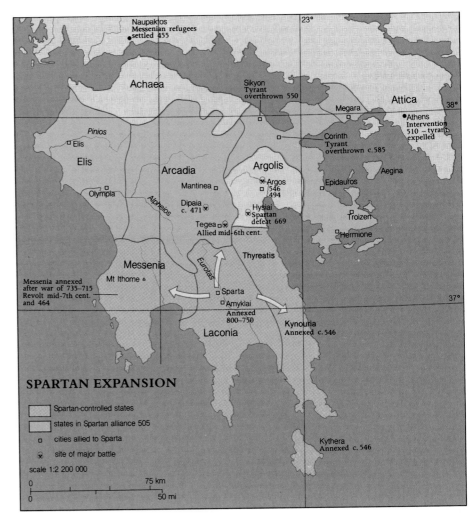

SPARTAN EXPANSION

- Spartan-controlled states
- states in Spartan alliance 505
- □ cities allied to Sparta
- ⊗ site of major battle

scale 1:2 200 000

0   75 km
0   50 mi

in their opinion, was that its aim was to make its citizens brave, rather than wise.

As the Spartans turned themselves into a military elite, all productive activities were left to the *perioikoi* and the helots. Coinage was not used – iron bars were the medium of exchange – and trade had little importance. Because the state had taken over much of the role of the family, Spartan women enjoyed greater freedoms than other Greek women. The women of Sparta even practiced gymnastics naked, like the men, something that other Greeks found extremely shocking.

Spartan territorial expansion resumed in the mid 6th century with the annexation of Kynouria to the east of Laconia. A major victory over its old enemy Argos in 546 established Spartan dominance of the Peloponnese. Sparta increased its influence by forging defensive alliances with other Peloponnesian states and by successfully intervening against tyrant dynasties at Sikyon, Corinth, Samos, Naxos and Athens. Many of these tyrants were pro-Persian but to what extent Spartan actions were motivated by a fear of Persian expansion is uncertain. However, when Xerxes invaded

ABOVE *By the mid 8th century Sparta was the dominant power in Laconia. It took control of Messenia c. 715 after a 20-year struggle, but territorial expansion slowed down in the 7th century following defeat by Argos and a serious Messenian rebellion. In the 6th century Sparta came to dominate the Peloponnese through a series of annexations, won at the point of a spear, and a system of defensive alliances. It used its military strength to intervene against a number of tyrannies including the Peisistratids in Athens.*

SPARTA

The city state of Sparta occupied an area of low hills in the center of the fertile plain of the river Eurotas. Rugged mountains surrounded it on all sides, and the city was protected by its remote situation as well as its formidable military reputation: it remained without a defensive wall until Spartan power went into terminal decline in the 3rd century BC. Art flourished in Sparta during the early Archaic period (two fine examples are shown on pages 134–135), but the growth of militarism from the mid 7th century BC onward stifled creativity. In the 6th and 5th centuries, when Sparta was at the height of its power, it produced nothing to compare with the brilliant sculpture and architecture of Athens and other Greek cities. Not surprisingly, the finest works of Spartan art relate to war; its only notable literary figure, Tyrtaeus (7th century BC), was a poet whose works extolled the glories of dying for the fatherland. On the banks of the Eurotas was the sanctuary of Artemis Orthia, which dated back to the 10th century. Here Spartan boys were flogged until unconscious as part of their initiation into manhood. This ceremony became a popular tourist attraction after Sparta had been incorporated into the Roman empire.

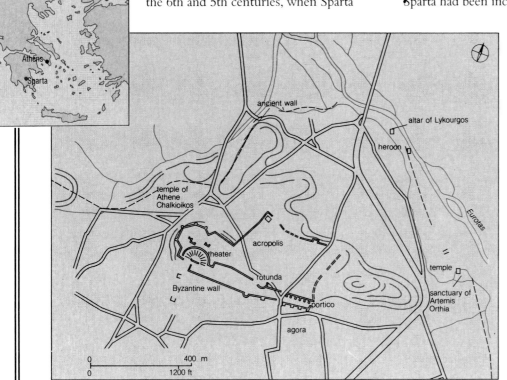

LEFT *Very little can be seen today of the ancient city of Sparta, though excavations have revealed the sites of several monuments. Most impressive are the remains of the theater at the foot of the acropolis, uncovered in the 18th century by a team of soldiers led by the Russian general Orloff. The second largest theater in the Greek world, it was built in the 2nd century BC when the city was under Roman administration.*

RIGHT *This bronze warrior figure forcefully expresses the martial spirit of Sparta and the high value that was placed on strength and courage.*

Greece in 480, Sparta and its Peloponnesian allies formed the backbone of the Greek armies.

EARLY ATHENS

While Sparta was Greece's leading military power at the time of the Persian wars, its leading naval power was Athens, which had a fine natural harbor at Peiraeus. Protected from attack by an encircling ring of mountains, Athens (see pages 138–141) was never conquered by the invading Dorians. By about 700 Athens still preserved a tribal and clan-based society but had ceased to be a monarchy. The religious, military and judicial functions of the king had been taken over by nine magistrates known as archons. When they left office the archons became members for life of the council of elders. This met on the Areopagus hill below the Acropolis and made all important political decisions. The citizen assembly elected the archons, but as eligibility was determined by birth, most Athenians were excluded and membership of the Areopagus council was largely aristocratic.

In the 7th century Athens experienced the same social tensions that had led to the establishment of tyrannies at Corinth and elsewhere. In 632 Kylon attempted to establish a tyranny with military support from his father-in-law who was tyrant of Megara. The Athenians rallied to support the archons and he failed. However, the attempted coup seems to have alarmed the aristocracy. In

621–620 the earliest known Athenian law code was written by Drakon, probably in order to help tighten the aristocracy's grip on power. The code was harsh, characterized by heavy fines and frequent use of the death penalty: we derive from it the word "draconian."

SOLON'S CONSTITUTION

Drakon's code did not end the social divisions of Athens. These were exacerbated by an economic crisis that forced many Athenians to mortgage land in return for food and seed corn. In 594 the lawgiver Solon (c. 639–c. 559) was elected archon and, to stave off tyranny, was granted absolute authority to draw up a new constitution. Before his appointment Solon had used poetry to express his political beliefs, setting himself up as the spokesman of the oppressed against the wealthy:

> *The leaders of the people have an evil mind, they are ripe*
> *to suffer many griefs for their great arrogance;*
> *for they know not how to restrain their greed,*
> *nor to conduct decently their present joys of feasting.*
> (trans. Oswyn Murray)

Solon believed that social justice was the essential prerequisite of a well-ordered society and his reforms attempted to do justice to the claims of all classes. He tackled the debt crisis by abolishing debt slavery, repatriating debtors who had been sold abroad and canceling outstanding debts. The aristocracy's automatic monopoly of power was ended by making wealth, not birth, the qualification for public office. The population was divided into four classes whose political rights were graduated according to their wealth. The richest class were the 500-measure men (those whose income was above 500 measures of corn a year). Next were the *hippeis*, men wealthy enough to equip themselves as cavalry soldiers. The third class were the hoplites, mainly small farmers, and the poorest were the landless laborers, the *thetes*.

As the two richest classes were dominated by the aristocracy, and because the highest officials could only be elected from these classes, this reform made little immediate difference to the aristocracy's domination of Athenian society. To undermine its entrenched position on the Areopagus council, Solon introduced a popular assembly of 400 members, elected by the four tribes of Athens, with authority to decide the legislation to be voted on by the popular assembly. The Areopagus council, however, retained the authority to veto any legislation that was against the constitution.

Solon also introduced a wide range of economic reforms designed to increase Athens' self-sufficiency in food and to boost trade and crafts. By 550 Attica had supplanted Corinth as the leading center of Greek pottery production. There were some marginal land reforms but Solon disappointed his supporters by failing to redistribute land from the rich to the poor. Neither were the aristocracy overjoyed by his cancellation of debts, the manipulation of which allowed them to force peasant farmers into dependent relationships, and his attacks on their political privileges. To escape the controversy he had caused, Solon went into voluntary exile as soon as he left office.

THE TYRANNY OF PEISISTRATOS

Solon's constitution laid the foundations for Athens' most important political legacy to the world: the development of democracy at the end of the 6th century. In the short term, however, it was a failure. Because of the new methods of warfare, the political importance of the hoplite class began to increase while that of the *hippeis*, who no longer had an important role to play in warfare, began to decline. Demands for a democratic constitution and redistribution of land grew more insistent. As its position became weaker, competition for power among the aristocracy increased and Athens was riven by faction and class conflict for the next fifty years.

In 546 Peisistratos (c. 605–527) made himself tyrant at the third attempt. Unlike many tyrants,

BELOW *Kleisthenes' reforms at the end of the 6th century gave Athenians important democratic rights. Every citizen could vote in the monthly citizen assemblies. Bronze wheels were used as voting counters: some of the wheels, such as those shown here, had solid axles; others were hollow. By holding the axle between his fingertips, the voter could conceal which way he was casting his vote.*

RIGHT *Kleisthenes' reforms also allowed Athenians to vote to exile troublesome citizens for ten years by scratching their names on pieces of broken pottery called* ostraka *(giving us the word "ostracize.") These* ostraka *bear the names of three prominent 5th-century Athenians: Kimon, Aristides and Themistocles.*

BELOW *By the beginning of the 8th century Athens controlled the surrounding area of Attica. Though the Atticans prided themselves on their common Ionian ancestry and continuity from Mycenaean times, until the reforms of Kleisthenes united the state it was wracked with local rivalries. Athens was often at war with its neighbors and added Salamis and Oropos to its territory in the 6th century. Lacking good farmland, Athens had to rely on food imports. Its rise to power in the 5th century was made possible mainly by its rich silver mines at Laurion.*

he had no popular following and he used his great wealth to recruit a mercenary army to help him gain power. Peisistratos chose his moment well; tyrant-hating Sparta, which might have been expected to intervene, was preoccupied with its war against Argos, and he won an easy victory over the Athenians. Peisistratos turned out to be an able and energetic ruler who quickly won widespread popular support for his reforms and for his conduct of a successful foreign policy that increased Athenian influence in the Aegean.

Among his reforms was a property tax to subsidize poorer farmers. Traveling judges improved the administration of justice in the countryside. Roads, public buildings, including the first temples on the Acropolis, and sculptures provided

work for laborers, craftsmen and artists. A new drama festival to the wine god Dionysos laid the foundations for the great achievements of Athenian dramatists in the next century (see pages 162–165), and Peisistratos was probably also responsible for establishing a fixed text for the works of Homer. He encouraged the development of silver mines at Laurion, establishing the basis of Athens' future wealth, and began exploiting the marble quarries on Mount Pentelikon that later supplied stone for the building of the Parthenon. Later generations remembered Peisistratos' tyranny as a golden age of peace and prosperity.

Peisistratos was succeeded by his sons Hippias and Hipparchus who continued his policies. Hipparchus was assassinated in 514 by members of a rival aristocratic family and the following year the exiled Alkmaionid family attempted to invade Attica. As generous patrons of the shrine, the Alkmaionids enjoyed the support of the priesthood of the oracle of Delphi (see page 152–153), which began to urge Sparta to overthrow the tyranny. In the face of this challenge Hippias' rule became more harsh, and to counter the threat of Spartan intervention he courted Persian support. His popularity waned and in 511–510 a Spartan invasion forced Hippias to seek exile with the Persians.

ATHENIAN DEMOCRACY

The Spartan intervention was engineered by Kleisthenes, a member of the exiled Alkmaionid family. His call to reorganize Athenian society as a democracy earned him the opposition of some aristocratic families, who wanted a restoration of the old order, but won him popular support. Attica's distinct geographical regions bred local rivalries and identities that aristocrats and tyrants had traditionally exploited for their own ends. Kleisthenes' reforms set out to abolish the territorially based tribal system that supported the power of the aristocracy.

Kleisthenes divided Attica into three regions – the interior, the coast and the city with its hinterland. The number of tribes was increased from four to ten, and each was given a division of land, or *trittye*, in all three regions. This had the effect of breaking up the traditional social structure and, by mixing peoples from different areas, fostering a common identity. Within each *trittye*, the basic unit of local government was the *deme* (village), of which there were around 170. The new tribes became the basis of military organization, the men of each tribe forming a separate regiment under an

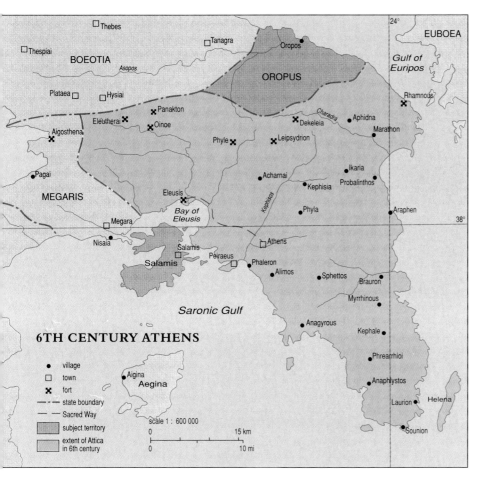

6TH CENTURY ATHENS

- • village
- ☐ town
- ✕ fort
- –·–·– state boundary
- – – Sacred Way
- subject territory
- extent of Attica in 6th century

scale 1 : 600 000

0   15 km
0   10 mi

elected commander. Each tribe now elected 50 representatives to a council of 500. This was divided into ten committees responsible for the day-to-day running of the state. Any citizen of the hoplite class or above who was 30 or older was eligible to run for office and men of quite humble origins were soon being elected. All citizens could vote at the monthly meetings of the citizen assembly which met on the Pnyx. Every major decision of state, including declarations of war, was subject to majority voting.

Democracy did not end aristocratic influence or prestige. Aristocrats were nearly always elected to the office of archon, or chief magistrate. And as membership of the Areopagus council, which could still veto unconstitutional legislation, was restricted to ex-archons, the latter body remained a bastion of aristocratic power. However, as the result of another of Kleisthenes' reforms, an over-ambitious aristocrat ran the risk of being voted into exile by his fellow citizens. This system, known as ostracism from the potsherds (ostraka) on which the votes were recorded, was a useful safeguard against tyranny.

Democracy as an ideal has as much power today as it did in ancient Athens. But an Athenian would not regard democracy in its modern form as true democracy. Unlike ancient Athens, no modern state has direct citizen rule but is instead ruled indirectly through elected representatives. Of course, the Athenian electorate was more narrowly based than any modern democracy's, since only freeborn males over 20 could become full citizens and vote. All women, foreigners and slaves – the majority of the population – were excluded. An Athenian man would not have seen this as being in any way undemocratic. It would no more have occurred to him to allow slaves voting rights than it did to the framers of the American constitution: slaves were simply considered as property. Nor would he have seen it as undemocratic to prevent women from voting. Ancient Greek men believed women to be less rational creatures than themselves, who were therefore incapable of voting wisely.

Kleisthenes' reforms were not passed without a struggle. When aristocratic diehards called in a Spartan army to help overthrow his measures, the Athenians confined the invading force on the Acropolis. But by the end of the 6th century, the new democratic system was in place. Athens, more united than it had ever been before, was about to embark on the most brilliant period of its history.

ARCHAIC ART

ABOVE A black-figure Athenian amphora of the late 6th century BC which shows Achilles leaping ashore from his ship at Troy. Many vases of this date are decorated with mythological or legendary scenes. The black-figure decorative style, with its bold silhouettes and incised detail, was influenced by the Orientalizing style introduced from the Near East in the 7th century BC (see also pages 156–157).

LEFT A bronze sculpture of a Spartan warrior (c. 500 BC). The grim realism of the figure is unusual for the period. The sculptor has taken particular delight in modeling the folds of the warrior's cloak.

Archaic style is the term used for the art of the late 7th and 6th centuries in Greece, characterized by a new use of naturalism. This came to full maturity in the Classical period that succeeded it. It is best seen in the statues of *kouroi* (youths; singular *kouros*) and *korai* (maidens; singular *kore*). These upright figure sculptures of wood, bronze and stone were erected as memorials to the dead or given as offerings to the gods. The earliest, from the late 7th century, are stiff and formal and betray the strong Egyptian influence on early Greek art. In the course of time, facial expressions became more naturalistic, musculature more supple and poses less stiff. *Kouroi* are commonly depicted naked in Archaic art but the *korai* wear finely draped robes. Female nudity in art did not become acceptable until the 4th century BC, reflecting the values of male-dominated Greek society, which accorded men superiority in physical beauty as well as intellect and strength.

BELOW *A miniature glass wine jar or amphora of the 7th century BC, perhaps a grave offering. Glass was an expensive luxury in the Archaic period and was used mainly for perfume bottles and trinkets such as this. Glassmakers are known to have been working at this date in Cyprus and Rhodes, and perhaps elsewhere in the Greek world.*

RIGHT *The front and rear view of a* kore, *a female statue that was presented as an offering on the Acropolis in the late 6th century BC. It was smashed by the Persians when they sacked Athens in 480. Her dress, hair and face are finely sculpted.*

BELOW *This bronze krater (a mixing bowl for wine and water) is considered one of the master-pieces of Archaic art. It stands 5 feet (1.64 m) high, weighs 458 lb (208 kg) and holds 264 gallons (1200 litres). Men at arms and chariots process around the neck and it has Gorgon's-head handles. It was made by a Spartan craftsman, possibly working in Italy. It was found with other Greek artifacts in the grave of a Celtic princess at Mont Lassois on the river Seine.*

SPORT IN THE GREEK WORLD

The Greeks believed passionately in the value of sport. As the development of the hoplite phalanx reduced the opportunity for one-to-one deeds of valor on the battlefield, competitive sport became the most important way by which a man could demonstrate his physical prowess. Training was constant and intensive. Success in the great athletic festivals brought prestige to the athlete and his family and – as the games became highly politicized events – to his city state. The most important of the athletic festivals was held every four years at Olympia. The earliest games attracted only local competitors and consisted of a single footrace. As the appeal of the games widened the number of events was expanded, and by 632 BC they included several footraces, horse racing, chariot racing, boxing, wrestling and the pentathlon (running, jumping, discus, javelin and wrestling).

Hostilities were suspended during the major athletic festivals but this did not mean they promoted peace. For the Greeks, sport was all too often a continuation of war by other means. However, cheating and breaches of the rules were severely punished. The games were theoretically open to all free men but in practice only those with the leisure to train could compete. Most athletes were therefore aristocrats and the glory they brought to the state helped maintain the prestige of their class. Though victory at the Olympic games was the pinnacle of athletic achievement, success at other festivals such as the Isthmian games also assured national status. Prizes were always modest but great athletes could expect to be treated as heroes, the equivalent of today's sporting superstars. Some winners even became semideified and the statues erected to celebrate their victories were believed to have miracle-working properties.

BELOW *Horse races were popular and spectacular events at the Olympic and other festivals. But the jockeys, who rode bareback and without stirrups, did not enjoy the prestige of other athletes – a winning horse was far more likely to be commemorated than its rider. This vigorous sculpture, celebrating a famous victory, was made in the 4th century BC.*

LEFT *This painting from a vase shows a young man exercising with halteres, specially shaped stone weights that were used as balancing aids in a jumping contest. Wrestling, in which the aim was to unbalance an opponent and throw him to the ground, and boxing, using hard leather gloves, were also popular sports.*

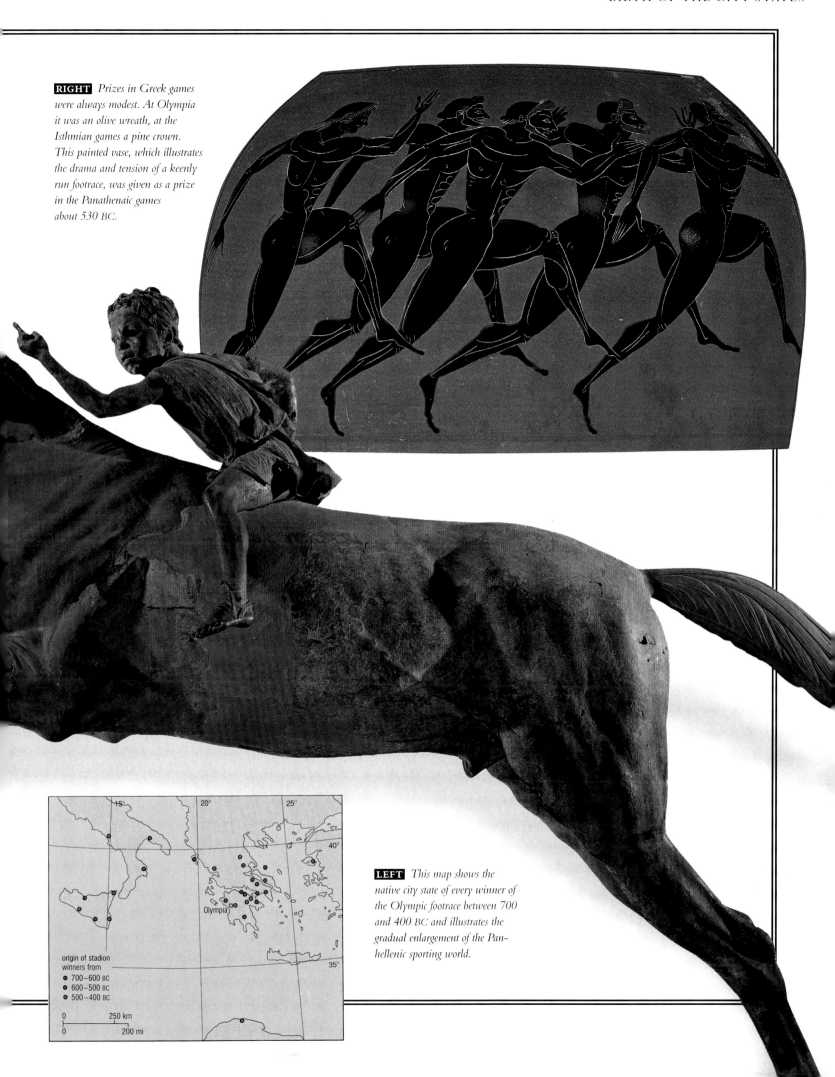

RIGHT *Prizes in Greek games were always modest. At Olympia it was an olive wreath, at the Isthmian games a pine crown. This painted vase, which illustrates the drama and tension of a keenly run footrace, was given as a prize in the Panathenaic games about 530 BC.*

LEFT *This map shows the native city state of every winner of the Olympic footrace between 700 and 400 BC and illustrates the gradual enlargement of the Pan-hellenic sporting world.*

Olympia

origin of stadion
winners from
● 700–600 BC
● 600–500 BC
● 500–400 BC

0   250 km
0   200 mi

ATHENS

There is evidence of occupation at Athens as early as 3000 BC. The craggy hill of the Acropolis was the site of a fortress and chief sanctuary, and a massive wall was added during the Mycenaean age (c. 1300 BC). Athens escaped the Dorian invasions and, in the succeeding dark age, it was able to bring the whole of Attica, including the influential cult center of Eleusis, under its control. Its port at Peiraeus became an important point of departure from the mainland to the Greek cities of Ionia. Even so, the city of Athens had few major buildings in the 6th century BC. The temple of Olympian Zeus, southeast of the Acropolis, was started by the Peisistratids (546–510) but was left unfinished after their fall until the 2nd century AD. Athens' most magnificent phase of construction dates from the 5th century BC, when the city – sacked by the Persians in 480 – was rebuilt by Kimon and Pericles. It was enclosed by defensive walls and the 7-mile (11-km) "Long Walls" were built to link the city with Peiraeus. During the Classical age, when Athens was at the height of its wealth and the head of a powerful empire, it was the leading cultural and artistic center of the Mediterranean world. The greatest figures in the history of western thought – men such as Socrates, Plato and Aristotle – all taught there. It was later overshadowed by Alexandria and Rome, but even at the end of the Roman period remained a famous center of philosophical thought and teaching. Some of Athens' most impressive monuments were built by the emperor Hadrian in the 2nd century AD.

ABOVE *The elegant temple of Wingless Victory overlooks the entrance to the Acropolis. Designed by the architect Kallikrates in the Ionic style, it was built in 427–424 BC. It stands on the site of an earlier altar to Athene Victory and is thought to be a monument to Athens' victories in the Persian wars.*

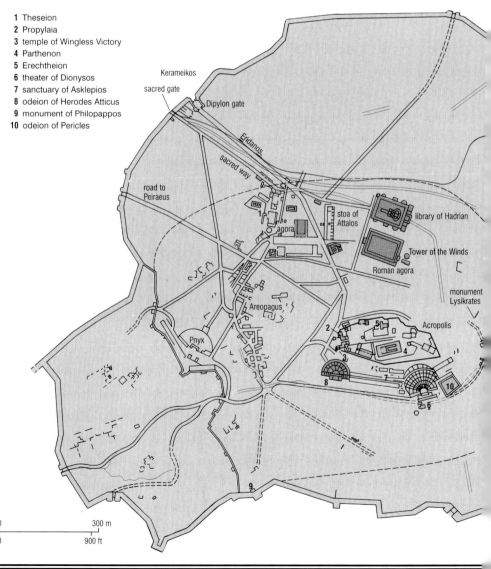

1 Theseion
2 Propylaia
3 temple of Wingless Victory
4 Parthenon
5 Erechtheion
6 theater of Dionysos
7 sanctuary of Asklepios
8 odeion of Herodes Atticus
9 monument of Philopappos
10 odeion of Pericles

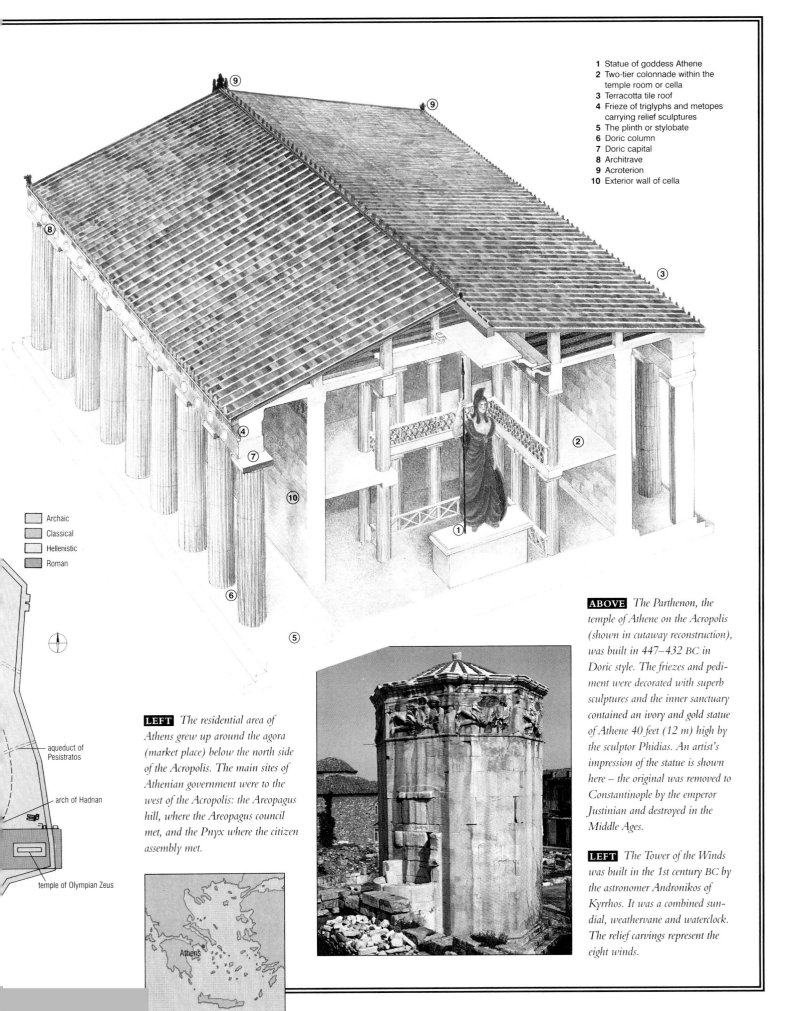

1 Statue of goddess Athene
2 Two-tier colonnade within the temple room or cella
3 Terracotta tile roof
4 Frieze of triglyphs and metopes carrying relief sculptures
5 The plinth or stylobate
6 Doric column
7 Doric capital
8 Architrave
9 Acroterion
10 Exterior wall of cella

Archaic
Classical
Hellenistic
Roman

aqueduct of Pesistratos

arch of Hadrian

temple of Olympian Zeus

ABOVE *The Parthenon, the temple of Athene on the Acropolis (shown in cutaway reconstruction), was built in 447–432 BC in Doric style. The friezes and pediment were decorated with superb sculptures and the inner sanctuary contained an ivory and gold statue of Athene 40 feet (12 m) high by the sculptor Phidias. An artist's impression of the statue is shown here – the original was removed to Constantinople by the emperor Justinian and destroyed in the Middle Ages.*

LEFT *The residential area of Athens grew up around the agora (market place) below the north side of the Acropolis. The main sites of Athenian government were to the west of the Acropolis: the Areopagus hill, where the Areopagus council met, and the Pnyx where the citizen assembly met.*

LEFT *The Tower of the Winds was built in the 1st century BC by the astronomer Andronikos of Kyrrhos. It was a combined sundial, weathervane and waterclock. The relief carvings represent the eight winds.*

Athens

THE ACROPOLIS

Seen here from the southwest, the Parthenon rises above the massive encircling wall of the Acropolis, some parts of which date back to Mycenaean times. The major monuments on the Acropolis belong to Athens' period of greatest power and prosperity in the 5th century. The complex of buildings to the left is the Propylaia, the main entrance to the sanctuary, with the temple of Wingless Victory just to its front on the right. The ruins in the foreground are those of the odeion (or theater) of Herodes Atticus (AD 160), one of the last public buildings to be erected in ancient Athens. Under the medieval dukes of Athens, a Florentine dynasty, the Propylaia was turned into a fortified castle with a Tuscan tower. The Parthenon has been both a church and a mosque. It was serving as a Turkish ammunition store when it was hit by Venetian cannon in 1687, causing major structural damage. In 1801 most of the sculptured reliefs were removed by Lord Elgin, then British ambassador in Constantinople, and are now in the British Museum in London.

The Classical Age
500–356 BC

The growth of the Persian empire in the second half of the 6th century BC presented the Greeks with the greatest challenge they had yet faced. The history of this momentous clash of civilizations was recorded in considerable detail in the 5th century by Herodotus, the first major Greek prose writer, in what is regarded as the first work of modern history. Herodotus was not content, as earlier writers had been, merely to chronicle events; he wanted also to investigate and understand their causes. He described his work as *historia*, meaning rational enquiry or research.

Persian involvement in Greek affairs began almost as an afterthought. In 547 Cyrus the Great captured Sardis, the capital of the wealthy Anatolian kingdom of Lydia. Before marching east into Central Asia he delegated the task of completing the conquest of Lydia to his generals. As part of their mopping-up operations, the Persians conquered the Ionian Greek cities of the coast of Anatolia. These had been loosely subject to Lydia for many years and the Persians met little resistance. Persian rule was not particularly onerous or oppressive; the cities retained their own governments but under tyrants appointed by the satrap (governor) of Sardis. Provided they delivered a usually modest tribute and supplied troops or ships when required, the satrap did not interfere in the running of the cities. Despite this, Persian rule was resented. The disruption of traditional trade routes caused by the Persian incursion into the Mediterranean was not to the Ionians' advantage. Nor were they immune to developments in mainland Greece where the mood was turning against tyrannical rule. Many Ionians fled to the mainland or to Italy to escape Persian domination.

The Persians took a further step into the Greek world in 512, when king Darius invaded Europe through Thrace. His goal was the gold mines in the region north of the Danube controlled by the Scythians, but his expedition proved to be an embarrassing failure. The highly mobile Scythians outmaneuvered the lumbering Persian army and

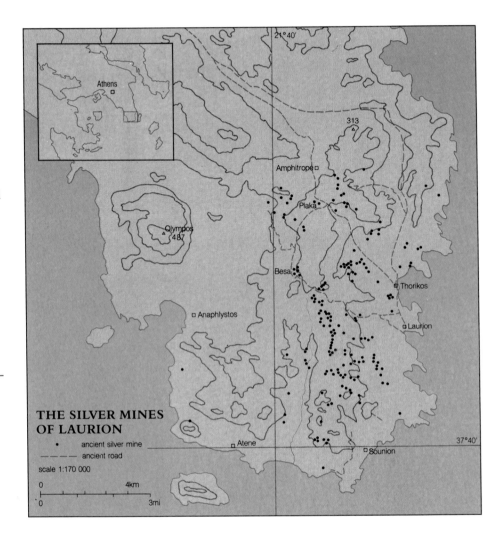

THE SILVER MINES OF LAURION

- ancient silver mine
- - - - ancient road

scale 1:170 000

0   4km

0   3mi

almost succeeded in trapping it. Darius retreated to Asia to nurse his wounded pride but left an army behind to conquer Thrace and its Greek coastal cities as a face-saving exercise.

THE IONIAN REVOLT

There is no evidence that the Persians were considering the conquest of Greece at this stage. Nevertheless, the mainland Greek city states could not be certain of Persian intentions. As they watched Persian power grow, they wavered between appeasement and opposition. Only Sparta remained consistently anti-Persian. The defining moment came in 499 BC when the Ionian Greeks

ABOVE *The silver mines at Laurion in Attica belonged to the Athenian state. The discovery of rich veins of ore in 483 financed the building of the fleet that helped defeat the Persians. Concessions were leased to individual citizens for a modest fee but, in practice, they were only available to those rich enough to afford the large numbers of slaves needed to work the mines. There were 20,000 to 30,000 slaves at Laurion, almost as many as the entire free citizen population of Athens.*

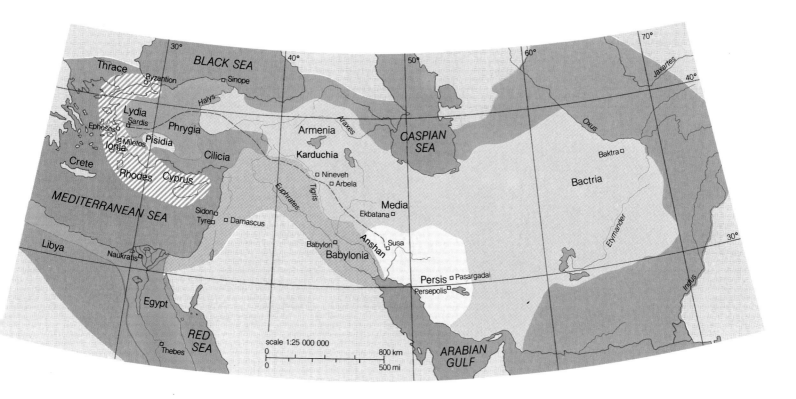

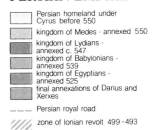

rebelled against Persian rule. The rebellion had its origins in an interstate rivalry that was typical of the Greeks. Aristagoras, the tyrant of Miletos, the southernmost of the Ionian cities, convinced his Persian masters that he should lead an expedition against Naxos, the Miletans' long-term trading rival. It ended in humiliating failure and Aristagoras' sudden disgrace. Facing the prospect of exile, and being the kind of man who believes that attack is the best form of defense, he took the Persians completely by surprise by all at once surrendering his tyranny and proclaiming equal rights for all the citizens of Miletos.

The rebellion spread quickly. The other cities of Ionia expelled their tyrants and appealed to the mainland for help. Sparta, at war with Argos, declined. However, Athens and the Euboean city of Eretria sent small fleets and in 498 joined in an attack on Sardis. As the city burned, revolt broke out among the Greek cities of Cyprus and the Hellespont. The Persian counterattack was slow in coming, but was overwhelming when it did. Miletos was taken in 494, ending all further resistance. Punitive reprisals inevitably followed, but were soon abandoned in favor of a conciliatory policy. Darius even allowed the Ionian cities to adopt democratic constitutions. There now had to be a reckoning with the mainland Greeks, and Darius did not want rebellious subjects at his back.

The involvement of Athens and Eretria in the Ionian revolt was ill-judged. Too little help had

been sent to the Ionian rebels to give them any chance of success, but mainland interference in the internal affairs of the Persian empire was a provocation that Darius could not ignore. According to Herodotos, the king was so incensed that he instructed one of his servants to say to him three times daily before dinner: "Master, remember the Athenians." In view of the Ionian Greeks' unimpressive military performance and the internal divisions of the mainland Greeks, it looked as if a punitive expedition would be a straightforward affair. In 492 Darius sent another force into Europe under his son-in-law Mardonios. Thrace and Macedon quickly submitted to the Persian army, but further progress was prevented when the Persian fleet, which Mardonios himself was commanding, was wrecked rounding Mount Athos. For the time being Athens and Eretria had escaped Persian retribution.

THE BATTLE OF MARATHON

In 490 Darius prepared a third expedition into Europe. He sent envoys to the Greek city states to demand offerings of earth and water in token of their submission. Most complied, but the Athenians and Spartans executed the envoys, an act of sacrilege that made war inevitable. Instead of taking the long overland route through Anatolia and Thrace, the Persian commander Datis struck directly across the Aegean with a fleet of 300 warships. With him was the exiled Athenian tyrant

THE RISE OF THE PERSIAN EMPIRE

- Persian homeland under Cyrus before 550
- kingdom of Medes · annexed 550
- kingdom of Lydians · annexed c. 547
- kingdom of Babylonians · annexed 539
- kingdom of Egyptians · annexed 525
- final annexations of Darius and Xerxes
- – – – Persian royal road
- ⁄⁄⁄ zone of Ionian revolt 499–493

ABOVE *In less than 50 years Persia rose from minor kingdom to world empire, dominating the entire Near East. The Greeks of Ionia and Cyprus were swallowed up by this empire in the 540s but though the Greeks of Thrace followed them in 512, there is no evidence that the Persians were contemplating the conquest of all of Greece. Athenian and Eretrian support for a rebellion by the Ionian Greeks finally convinced Darius that only this would ensure the security of the empire.*

Hippias who was to be restored to power as a Persian puppet ruler after Athens had fallen.

At first Datis' surprise tactics worked well. After taking Naxos and Eretria the Persian fleet sailed to the mainland to land unopposed at Marathon, 26 miles (42 km) north of Athens. The Athenians sent a runner to summon the Spartans, but they were celebrating a religious festival and said they would set out only when it was over. Meanwhile, 9000 hoplites of the Athenian citizen militia, with 1000 men from Plataea (Plataiai), faced the Persians alone at Marathon. They were outnumbered two to one: the Persians had both cavalry and archers, the Athenians had none. If caught in the open, the Athenian phalanx (see pages 146–147) could be broken up by archery and then ridden down by the Persian cavalry. Conscious of their weakness, most of the Athenian generals wanted to wait for the Spartan army. However, Miltiades, who had served with the Persians in Thrace, won assent for his plan to make an attack if a favorable opportunity arose.

It came at early dawn when scouts reported that the Persian cavalry had withdrawn during the night, probably to water their horses. Miltiades saw his chance and attacked. The two armies were a mile (1.6 km) apart, but the Athenians, wearing full armor, approached the Persian line at a run to minimize their exposure to the enemy archers. The best Persian forces were placed in the center

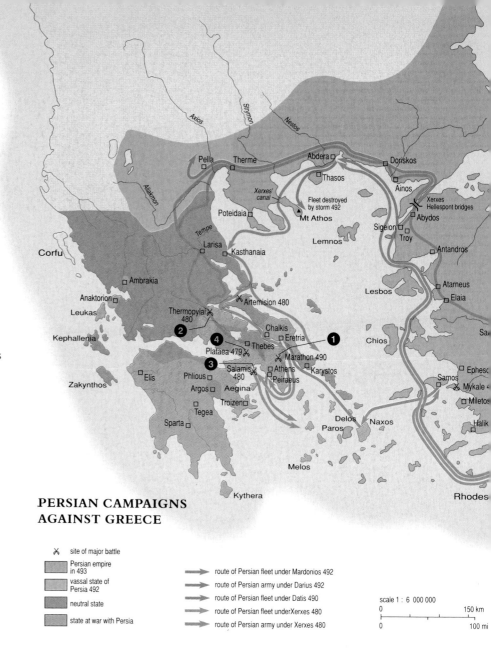

PERSIAN CAMPAIGNS AGAINST GREECE

✗ site of major battle

Persian empire in 493

vassal state of Persia 492

neutral state

state at war with Persia

→ route of Persian fleet under Mardonios 492

→ route of Persian army under Darius 492

→ route of Persian fleet under Datis 490

→ route of Persian fleet under Xerxes 480

→ route of Persian army under Xerxes 480

scale 1 : 6 000 000

0   150 km
0   100 mi

THE PERSIAN WARS – BATTLE PLANS

Greek forces
Persian forces
main road (passable by cart)
track
modern road
VRANA   modern name
Athens   ancient name

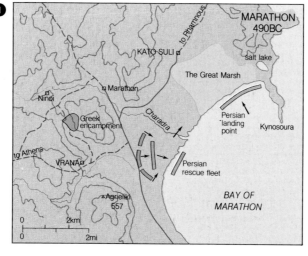

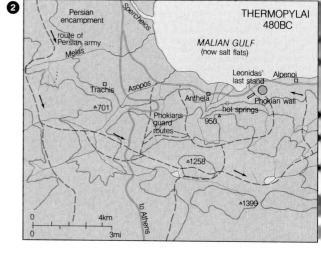

ABOVE (1) *The Greeks built a camp in the hills above the Marathon plain to prevent the Persians from exploiting their cavalry forces. When the cavalry were sent away for water, the Greeks attacked. The Persian flanks broke under the impact of the Greek phalanx and the center was enveloped.*

(2) *At Thermopylai the pass between the mountains and the sea narrows to a few yards. The Greeks made a stand here but the Persians found a route through the mountains and outflanked them. A heroic rearguard action by Sparta's king Leonidas bought time for the bulk of the Greek forces to escape.*

(3) *The island of Salamis lies in the Saronic Gulf off the coast of Attica. Wrongly believing that the Athenian fleet was escaping, the much larger Persian fleet pursued it into the narrow strait between Salamis and the main-land. Here the Persians were ambushed and comprehensively defeated.*

(4) *The battle of Plataea was preceded by days of complex maneuvering. Battle was joined when the Greeks executed a disorderly withdrawal. The Persian infantry was preparing to attack when an unexpected and well-timed counter-attack by Pausanias threw them into confusion and routed them.*

of the line and only they had the courage to stand their ground against the massed spears of the Athenian phalanx. As the men on the flanks broke ranks and fled to their ships, those in the center were surrounded and slaughtered. The Persians lost 6400 men, the Athenians only 192.

Datis still had a considerable force at his disposal and he set sail, hoping to launch a surprise attack on Athens. The Athenians, however, guessed his intentions. They returned to Athens by forced march and were waiting for Datis on the shore when he arrived later the same day. After allowing his oarsmen a short rest, Datis turned his fleet for home. Athenian pride in their victory was unbounded. Monuments in bronze and marble were dedicated at Delphi, and poems, paintings and histories celebrated the battle. Those who had fought in it were known for the rest of their lives as the "men of Marathon." Even the Spartans, the military experts of the day, were impressed when they arrived on the scene a day late.

XERXES' GREAT EXPEDITION

Undiscouraged, Darius at once began to plan another expedition but died before the preparations were complete. Xerxes, his son and successor, had inherited numerous problems with his vast empire and had little enthusiasm for further campaigns in Europe. Mardonios, however, persuaded him that the Greeks must be punished.

Anxious to avoid his father's mistakes, Xerxes spent four years preparing his expedition. Troops gathered at Sardis from every part of the Achaemenid empire. Xerxes' army, estimated to have been 200,000 strong, was one of the largest forces ever assembled in antiquity. It was supported by a fleet of perhaps 1000 ships. Faced with this vast force, most of the northern Greek states, not surprisingly, opted for neutrality or (in a few cases) alliance with Persia. The southern Greek states, however, united under the leadership of Sparta and prepared to resist the Persians.

Accounts of the resulting war frequently liken it to David's stand against Goliath, but the odds against the Greeks were less uneven than appears at first sight. The size of the Persian army was in fact a serious handicap. It was difficult to supply and impossible to control effectively on a battlefield. The quality of its troops also varied enormously, as many were unenthusiastic conscripts and only around 10,000 consisted of well-armed elite troops. By contrast the Greeks, though greatly outnumbered, were heavily armed and armored. They were experienced, disciplined and highly motivated – citizens defending their states, homes and families. By now they also possessed a fleet capable of challenging Persian control of the sea. This they owed to the foresight of the Athenian archon Themistocles. When, in 483, the silver miners of Laurion discovered a particularly rich

LEFT *Mardonios' campaign of 492 had as its first target the reestablishment of Persian control in Thrace. Any plans to carry on to invade southern Greece and punish Athens and Eretria for their part in the Ionian rebellion were dashed when the supporting fleet was wrecked off Mount Athos. In 490 a fleet under Datis' command sailed directly to Athens, stopping off only at Naxos and Eretria. Xerxes' massive invasion force (480) was intended to conquer all of Greece. The supporting fleet needed to keep in close touch with the land army and Xerxes' preparations included the digging of a canal across the Athos peninsula to avoid the risk of a second shipwreck.*

BELOW *The trireme was the fighting ship of the Persian wars. It carried three banks of oarsmen to give it speed, and was equipped with a ram. It was usually beached at night as there was no space for sleeping quarters.*

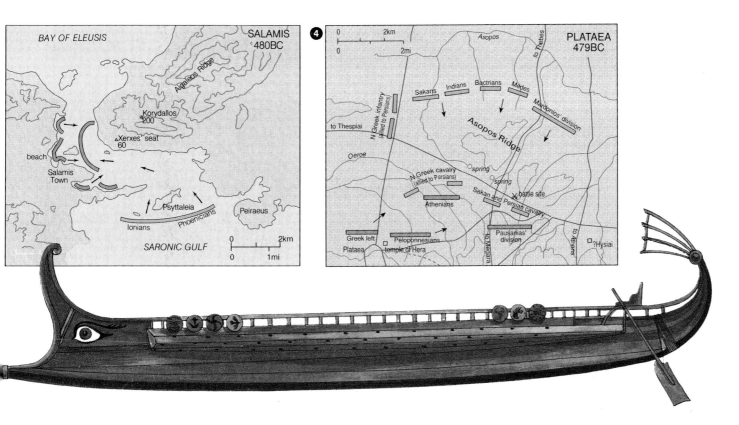

THE GREEK SOLDIER

Warfare was an everyday fact of life in ancient Greece. All able-bodied male citizens were charged with fighting for their city and had to provide their own arms and armor. Most Greek soldiers fought as hoplites, heavily armored infantrymen armed with long thrusting spears. Hoplites fought in tight formations, or phalanxes, which presented a wall of shields and a terrifying hedge of spear points to the enemy. There was no place for individual heroics: a hoplite could not fight effectively as a single unit and any action that threatened the integrity of the phalanx was frowned upon.

The object in battle was to cause the enemy phalanx to collapse. Phalanxes advanced at a run and the impact when they met was sometimes so great that the entire front ranks on both sides were brought crashing down. Each phalanx used its collective strength to try to push the other back. The crux of a battle usually came when one side began to lose its nerve and attempted to withdraw. If a rush for the rear broke out, the slaughter could be very one-sided as the pursuing victors aimed their spears at the exposed backs of their fleeing enemies.

RIGHT *There was considerable variety in the style of Greek helmets. The Corinthian helmet, which gave good protection at the cost of limited vision and hearing, was the most popular, remaining in use from the 8th to the 5th century. The Kegel was a cumbersome design that died out c. 700, but its Illyrian derivative remained in use until the 5th century. Helmets were made of bronze and had a padded shock-absorbent lining. They often carried flamboyant crests (below) which made the wearer look taller and more imposing.*

Kegel

Illyrian

early Corinthian

late Corinthian

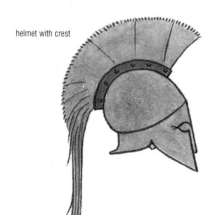

helmet with crest

146

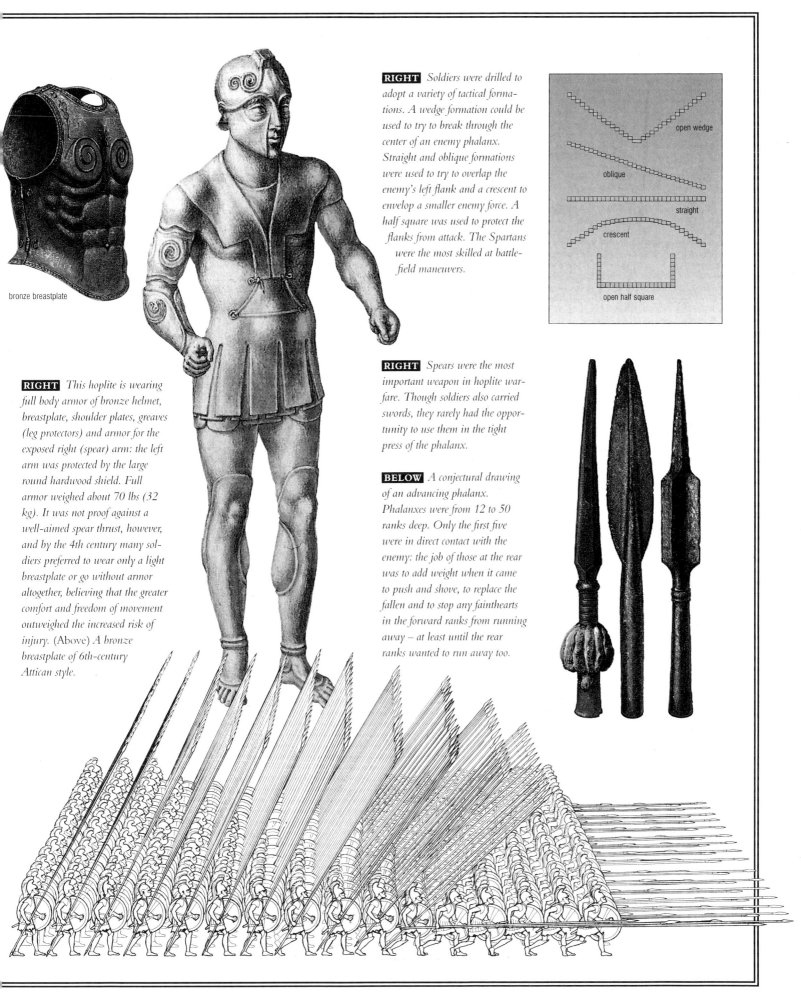

bronze breastplate

RIGHT Soldiers were drilled to adopt a variety of tactical formations. A wedge formation could be used to try to break through the center of an enemy phalanx. Straight and oblique formations were used to try to overlap the enemy's left flank and a crescent to envelop a smaller enemy force. A half square was used to protect the flanks from attack. The Spartans were the most skilled at battle-field maneuvers.

open wedge

oblique

straight

crescent

open half square

RIGHT This hoplite is wearing full body armor of bronze helmet, breastplate, shoulder plates, greaves (leg protectors) and armor for the exposed right (spear) arm: the left arm was protected by the large round hardwood shield. Full armor weighed about 70 lbs (32 kg). It was not proof against a well-aimed spear thrust, however, and by the 4th century many soldiers preferred to wear only a light breastplate or go without armor altogether, believing that the greater comfort and freedom of movement outweighed the increased risk of injury. (Above) A bronze breastplate of 6th-century Attican style.

RIGHT Spears were the most important weapon in hoplite warfare. Though soldiers also carried swords, they rarely had the opportunity to use them in the tight press of the phalanx.

BELOW A conjectural drawing of an advancing phalanx. Phalanxes were from 12 to 50 ranks deep. Only the first five were in direct contact with the enemy: the job of those at the rear was to add weight when it came to push and shove, to replace the fallen and to stop any fainthearts in the forward ranks from running away – at least until the rear ranks wanted to run away too.

Exploration, trade and colonization increased the Greeks' geographical knowledge. The world known to Homer was limited to the eastern Mediterranean, though the poetry of Hesiod (c. 700) mentions more distant peoples, including the Etruscans and Scythians. The Greeks were great explorers. As early as the 7th century BC, Aristeas of Prokonnesos wrote an account of a journey to the Issedones, near the Hindu Kush in central Asia. A further extension of geographical knowledge came after 546 when the Ionian Greeks were incorporated into the Persian empire. In the 4th century Massilian Pytheas explored the seas around Britain and Scandinavia, though his account was not widely believed at the time. The Greeks also benefited from reports of the journeys made by Phoenician sailors such as Hanno who visited the west African coast in the 6th century. The pharaoh Necho II (610–595) is supposed to have sent a Phoenician expedition down the east coast of Africa. It sailed into the Mediterranean three years later, having circumnavigated the continent. Herodotos gives an account of it in his History, *though he is uncertain whether to believe the story.*

Greek trading influence extended far around the Black Sea. The decorative motifs of this cap of state (c.400), from the Crimea, are Greek in origin. It was found in a grave together with an amphora and a Greek coin.

lode of ore, he had successfully persuaded the Athenians to invest the wealth in constructing a fleet of 200 triremes.

Xerxes led his army north from Sardis, crossing the Hellespont into Europe on a mile-long bridge of boats. The Persians spent the summer campaigning in northern Greece, adding the local harvest to their supplies before moving south in September. The Greeks sent an army of 10,000 north to the vale of Tempe in Thessaly but a retreat was made as soon as it became clear that their position could easily be outflanked. The narrow pass of Thermopylai 100 miles (160 km) to the south seemed a better position, and it was here that 7000 men under the Spartan king Leonidas made a stand. The battle raged for three days. At first the Persians made little progress, but on the second night they discovered a path through the mountains and outflanked the Greeks. With a force of 300 Spartans and 1400 allies, Leonidas fought to the death to buy time for the rest of the Greek army to escape. Their epitaph was written by the poet Simonides:

> *Tell them in Lakedaimon, passer-by,*
> *Obedient to their order, here we lie.*

After the defeat at Thermopylai, the Greek army retreated to the Isthmus of Corinth while the fleet departed to the island of Salamis off the coast of Attica. The bulk of the Athenian population sought safety on Salamis as well, so when the Persian army reached Athens, which they occupied and sacked, they found it empty except for a few diehards who held out on the Acropolis for a fortnight. The entire Peloponnese now seemed within the Persians' grasp. The Spartan defenses on the Isthmus could easily be bypassed by sea. But Themistocles, at the head of the Athenian fleet, managed to lure the Persian fleet into an ambush off Salamis, where it was almost completely destroyed. An eyewitness, the playwright Aeschylus (Aischylos), remembered that ships were overturned, while "piles of wreckage and dead men hid the sea from sight, corpses were awash on shores and reefs." Appalled and enraged, Xerxes watched the disaster from the shore. Since it was clear that Greece could not now be conquered in a single campaign, he returned to Asia with 60,000 men, leaving the remainder of his army under Mardonios to winter in Thessaly.

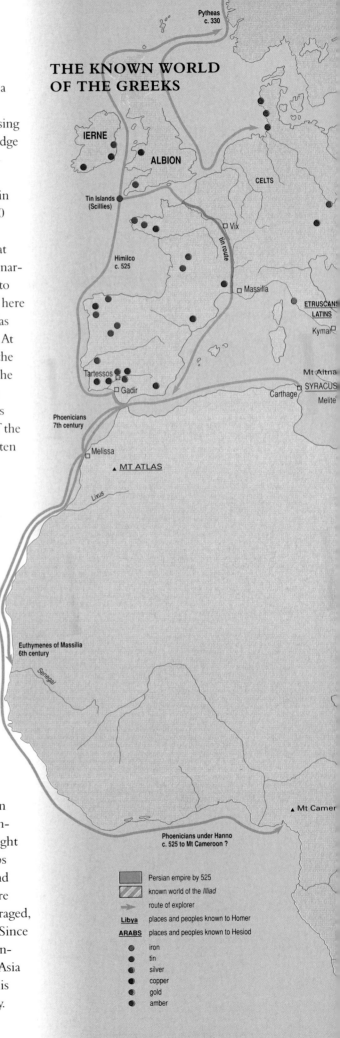

THE KNOWN WORLD OF THE GREEKS

Pytheas c. 330

IERNE

ALBION

CELTS

Tin Islands (Scillies)

Vix

Himilco c. 525

Massilia

ETRUSCANS LATINS

Kymai

Tartessos

Gadir

Mt Atna

SYRACUS

Carthage

Melite

Phoenicians 7th century

Melissa

▲ MT ATLAS

Lixus

Euthymenes of Massilia 6th century

Senegal

▲ Mt Camer

Phoenicians under Hanno c. 525 to Mt Cameroon ?

Persian empire by 525

known world of the *Illiad*

→ route of explorer

Libya places and peoples known to Homer

ARABS places and peoples known to Hesiod

● iron

● tin

● silver

● copper

● gold

● amber

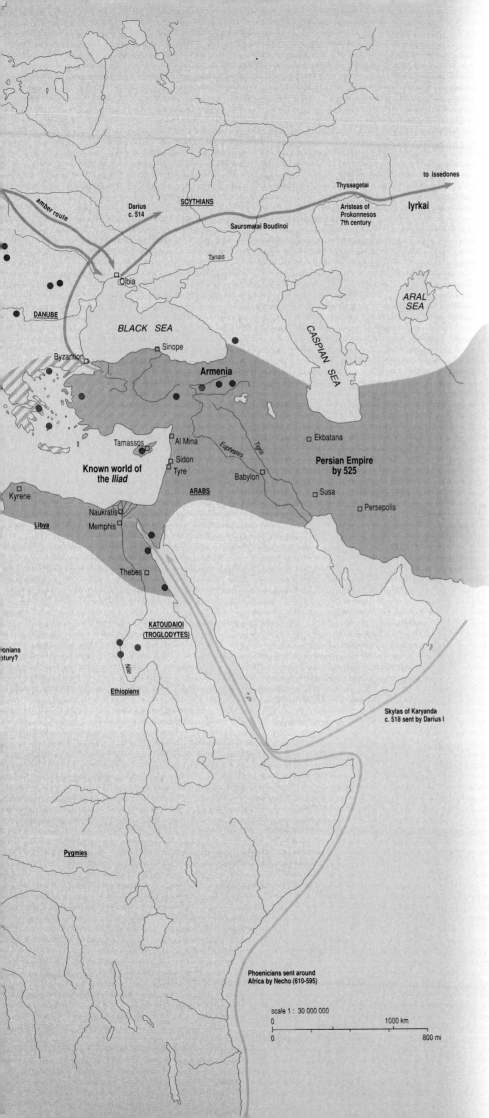

DECISIVE VICTORY

Mardonios tried to break up the Greek alliance by exploiting old rivalries and suspicions. Sparta feared that if its army were to leave the Isthmus and move north, its enemy Argos would take the opportunity to seize power in the Peloponnese. But without Spartan military intervention the northern Greek states could not hope to resist further Persian attacks. Thebes had gone over to the Persian side, and the Athenians indicated that they, too, would abandon the alliance if support was not forthcoming. Spurred on by the threat of the Athenian fleet falling into Persian hands, Sparta sent an army of 5000 hoplites, 5000 *perioikoi* and 20,000 helots north under the regent Pausanias in the summer of 479. They were joined by 8000 troops from Athens and another 10,000 from other allies. The armies met near Plataea within Theban territory, close to the border with Attica.

Here they faced each other for a fortnight, while either side hoped for a suitable opportunity to attack. Mardonios thought he saw his chance when the Spartans made an untidy withdrawal to a hilltop position after the Persians had cut off their water supply. Pausanias held his men back as they came under heavy fire from the Persian archers and waited for Mardonios to commit his troops to an attack. At this point Pausanias unexpectedly sent the Spartan phalanx charging downhill, throwing the Persians into confusion. Mardonios and the best of his troops were killed, the Thebans fought hard (their leaders were later executed as traitors to the Greek cause), but the rest of the Persian army fled. It was a decisive victory. The Greeks followed up their success by destroying the remnants of the Persian fleet at Mykale and wrecking the Hellespont bridge, already badly damaged by storms. No further Persian attempt was ever made to invade Greece.

THE LIBERATION OF THE IONIANS

The Persian war inspired many pious sentiments about the common identity of the Greeks, but the old rivalries resurfaced as soon as the immediate threat had passed. In 478 Sparta withdrew from the war against Persia. Most other members of the alliance did the same. Only Athens, now second in military strength and the leading naval power in Greece, felt confident enough to reject the Spartan lead and continue the war in Ionia, where the Persians remained unreconciled to the loss of the Greek cities. Athens, which had ancient ties with the Ionians and claimed to be the founder of

GREEK MEDICINE

Greek medicine began to develop as a scientific discipline in the 5th and 4th centuries BC. The earliest treatises on Greek medicine, dating to 430–330, are traditionally attributed to the physician Hippocrates (c. 460–377). Many of the principles outlined in these treatises – that medicine is a practical discipline based on observation and experience, that it is necessary to treat the patient as a whole, that the first duty of a physician is to his patient, not himself – remain basic to modern medical practice and ethics. However, the importance of scientific medicine should not be exaggerated: most Greeks still believed in magical and miraculous cures. The main centers of healing were the sanctuaries of Asklepios, the god of healing. In the 4th century BC they claimed better rates of cure than the "scientific" doctors.

BELOW *These bronze surgical instruments are from the Hellenistic age when physicians such as Herophilos of Chalkedon made great advances in anatomy and surgery by experimenting on, and probably dissecting, live convicts.*

RIGHT *A 4th-century relief showing a doctor working on a sleeping or drugged patient. Much healing work in the name of Asklepios was done at night: patients may have believed that the god himself came to cure them.*

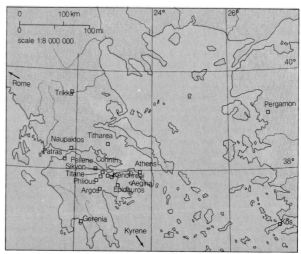

ABOVE AND RIGHT *The map shows the principal sanctuaries associated with Asklepios (Latin, Aesculapius) the god of healing. The son of Apollo, Asklepios was given a magic potion from the blood of the snake-haired Gorgon that enabled him to restore even the dead to life. Hades, ruler of the dead, complained to Zeus, who killed Asklepios. The statue (right) comes from Asklepios' sanctuary at Epidauros and was made during the Roman period.*

many of their cities, regarded itself as their natural protector. Support for the Ionians also presented the opportunity to build an independent political and commercial sphere of influence in the Aegean. But above all there was the burning desire for revenge against the enemy who had occupied and then sacked their city.

By 475 the last Persian garrisons had been cleared from Europe, opening the Bosporus once again to Greek ships. In 468 the Persians began to gather a fleet of 350 ships, together with a large army, at the mouth of the Eurymedon river in southern Anatolia, in readiness to attack the cities of Ionia. The Persians were still waiting for a contingent of 200 Phoenician ships to arrive when Kimon, the Athenian commander, launched a preemptive strike against them. Though his fleet was the smaller, consisting of about 200 Athenian and 100 allied triremes, the Persian ships retreated at its approach, so fearful was the reputation the Athenians had won for themselves at Salamis. Many Persian ships were beached by their crews, who then took to flight. Kimon forced a landing and defeated the Persian army that had lined up on the shore to meet him. The demoralization of the Persian forces was completed a few weeks later when the Athenians intercepted and destroyed the Phoenician fleet off Cyprus.

Though the independence of the Ionian Greeks was now secure, the war still dragged on. The Athenians were making preparations to liberate Cyprus when the expedition they were gathering was diverted to give support to an anti-Persian rebellion that had broken out in Egypt in 459. The opportunity to increase Athenian influence in grain-rich Egypt was irresistible but it was a disastrous move. In 454 the Athenian forces were trapped in the delta by the Persians and largely destroyed. However, a crushing defeat by the Athenians on Cyprus four years later finally persuaded the Persians to seek peace terms. Hostilities were formally ended in 448 by the treaty of Kallias (named after the chief Athenian negotiator). By the terms of the treaty, the Persians recognized Ionian independence and agreed not to send warships into the Aegean in return for Athenian acceptance of Persian rule in Cyprus and Egypt.

THE DELIAN LEAGUE

The Delian league, so called because its treasury was on Apollo's sacred island of Delos, had been formed by Athens and its Ionian allies in 477 to pursue their war aims against Persia. Its members swore oaths of permanent alliance and agreed to contribute either ships or money to it. Plans were agreed at an annual council attended by all the members on Delos. Athens was recognized as the league's leader, with the right of commanding its military forces and appointing its treasurers. The synod of allies, consisting of all the league's non-Athenian members, was theoretically equal in power to the Athenian state and no policy could be adopted without the agreement of both. In practice, however, Athens inevitably came to dominate the league, as no offensive action could be taken without its support and assent. When Naxos tried to leave the league in 469, the Athenian fleet was sent to enforce obedience. Four years later the Athenian seizure of a gold mine on Thasos provoked a rebellion, whereupon Athens confiscated the island's fleet and tore down its city walls. Other states, such as Karystos on Euboea, were forcibly enrolled in the league.

In 454, it became clear that Athens regarded the league as nothing less than its empire when the treasury was removed to the city from Delos, ostensibly for greater security after the loss of the Athenian army in Egypt. Another sign of Athens' growing imperialism was its policy of founding colonies (cleruchies) of Athenian citizens in the Aegean. The first, at Eion and Skyros, were on territory seized from the Persians and from pirates, but colonies were later established in states such as Naxos that had tried to secede from the league. Despite this, many members were grateful to Athens for the role it had played in the Persian wars and for introducing democracy, and their loyalty held. After the treaty of Kallias, the league became as much a commercial as a military organization, though still serving predominantly Athenian interests. Athenian coinage, weights and measures were introduced throughout the league.

THE BEGINNINGS OF ATHENIAN–SPARTAN RIVALRY

So long as it continued the war against Persia, Athens tried to maintain good relations with Sparta. A potential dispute over the refortification of Athens and Peiraeus in 478 was smoothed over by the diplomacy of Themistokles. But Athens was becoming a potential threat to Spartan leadership in Greece. An appeal from Thasos for aid against the Athenians in 463 found the Spartans ready to respond. Only an earthquake, followed by a major Messenian helot rebellion, prevented them from sending help. The disaster changed the

DELPHI

Delphi, a cult center since Mycenaean times, was famous throughout the Greek world as the home of the sacred oracle of the sun-god Apollo, the patron of prophecy, philosophy and the arts: it was sacred also to Dionysos and the nine Muses, the patron goddesses of music, poetry, drama, dance and history, and was the place where all creative forces met and from where all creative forms emerged. Apollo was believed to send messages to humans through a cleft in the rocks (the *omphalos*, or navel, held to be the center of the world). These sayings were interpreted by the oracle, a priestess known as the Pythia in honor of Apollo's slaying of a mythical beast called the Python. During the 8th century the city states began to seek the oracle's advice on colonizing ventures, and it grew in importance. Soon the oracle was being consulted on a wide range of personal and political problems. The oracle's replies were usually so ambiguous that it was difficult ever to prove them wrong, but this does not seem to have discouraged supplicants. The city states made rich offerings to Apollo to invoke his help, and during the internecine wars of the 5th and 4th centuries they vied with each other to erect monuments and statues within his sanctuary to celebrate their victories and enhance their reputations.

LEFT *The Greek states built treasuries at Delphi to house their offerings to Apollo. This frieze (c. 530), an outstanding example of Archaic art, is from the treasury of Siphnos, a Cycladic island that possessed rich gold and silver mines.*

FAR LEFT *The famous statue of a bronze charioteer is part of a far larger sculpture cast to celebrate a 5th-century victory in Delphi's Pythian games, one of Greece's four great athletic festivals.*

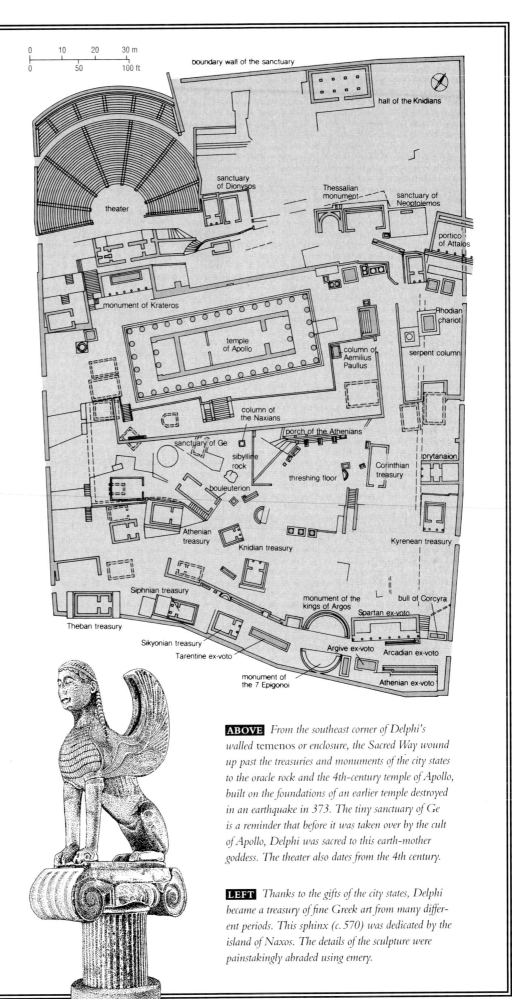

ABOVE Delphi stands on a remote site high on the slopes of Mount Parnassus north of the Gulf of Corinth. In ancient times access to Delphi was only possible by difficult mountain paths, yet it became the richest and greatest of all the sanctuaries of Apollo on mainland Greece. The standing columns in the foreground, which belong to the temple of Apollo, have been assembled from ancient column drums of different dates.

ABOVE From the southeast corner of Delphi's walled temenos or enclosure, the Sacred Way wound up past the treasuries and monuments of the city states to the oracle rock and the 4th-century temple of Apollo, built on the foundations of an earlier temple destroyed in an earthquake in 373. The tiny sanctuary of Ge is a reminder that before it was taken over by the cult of Apollo, Delphi was sacred to this earth-mother goddess. The theater also dates from the 4th century.

LEFT Thanks to the gifts of the city states, Delphi became a treasury of fine Greek art from many different periods. This sphinx (c. 570) was dedicated by the island of Naxos. The details of the sculpture were painstakingly abraded using emery.

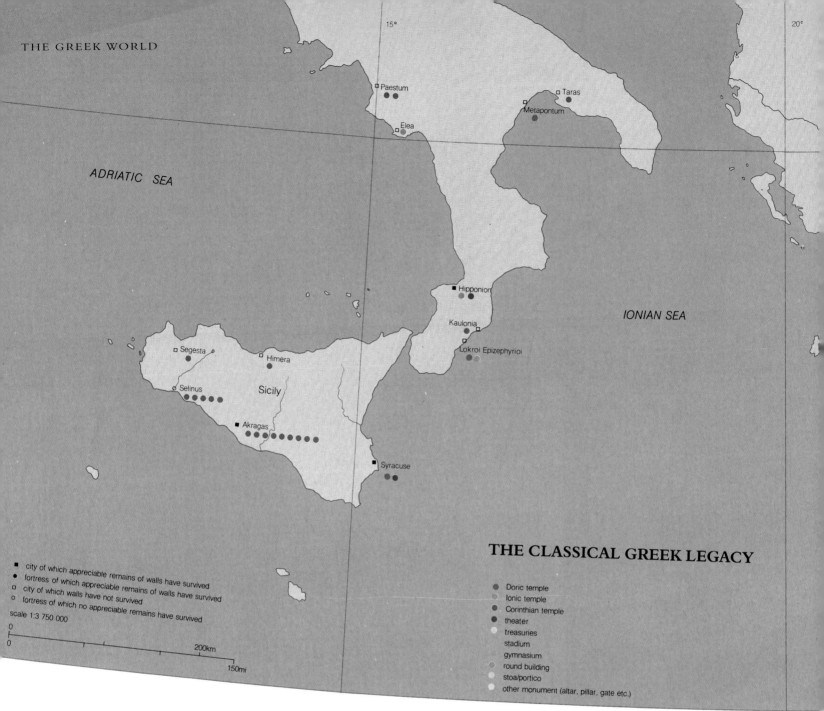

ADRIATIC SEA

IONIAN SEA

Paestum

Elea

Taras

Metapontum

Hipponion

Kaulonia

Lokroi Epizephyrioi

Segesta

Himera

Selinus

Sicily

Akragas

Syracuse

15°

20°

■ city of which appreciable remains of walls have survived
● fortress of which appreciable remains of walls have survived
□ city of which walls have not survived
○ fortress of which no appreciable remains have survived

scale 1:3 750 000

0
0
200km
150mi

THE CLASSICAL GREEK LEGACY

● Doric temple
● Ionic temple
● Corinthian temple
● theater
● treasuries
● stadium
● gymnasium
● round building
● stoa/portico
● other monument (altar, pillar, gate etc.)

balance of power in Greece. Laconia was overrun by helot rebels and Sparta was forced to ask for help from the other Greek powers. A powerful faction in Athens argued that Sparta should be abandoned to its fate, but Kimon won the debate and an army was dispatched to Sparta.

Within a year the Spartans had confined the rebels to a position on Mount Ithome in Messenia. Kimon led another force to help the Spartans storm their fortifications, but it was sent straight home again. News of a radical extension of democracy in Athens had broken and the Spartans feared that the Athenians might now side with the Messenian rebels. In 461 Kimon was ostracized for his role in the humiliating expedition and the pro-Spartan policy was abandoned for an alliance with Sparta's old enemy Argos. For the next century affairs in Greece would be dominated by the rivalry between Athens and Sparta.

THE DEMOCRATIC REVOLUTION

The constitution introduced by Kleisthenes in the 6th century had established only a limited form of democracy in Athens. Aristocrats were allowed to retain a powerful influence, and this had increased still further during the Persian wars when large numbers of citizens were absent for prolonged periods on military campaigns. Though elected, most generals were aristocrats and their successes in the wars reflected well on the aristocracy as a class. Generals tended to become political as well as military leaders. While public officers such as the archons had to step down after a year, generals could be re-elected year after year, making a military career attractive to a politically ambitious aristocrat. Yet, as many an Athenian general discovered, success on the battlefield was no protection

ABOVE *The distribution of major surviving monuments along the coast of Turkey and in southern Italy and Sicily as well as the Greek mainland and islands is an indication of the close cultural connections that linked all parts of the Classical Greek world.*

RIGHT *During the 5th century Akragas in Sicily benefited from the grain trade to become one of the largest and richest Greek cities. The temple of Concord, one of nine surviving Doric temples there, was built around the same time as the Parthenon and rivals it in the elegance of its proportions.*

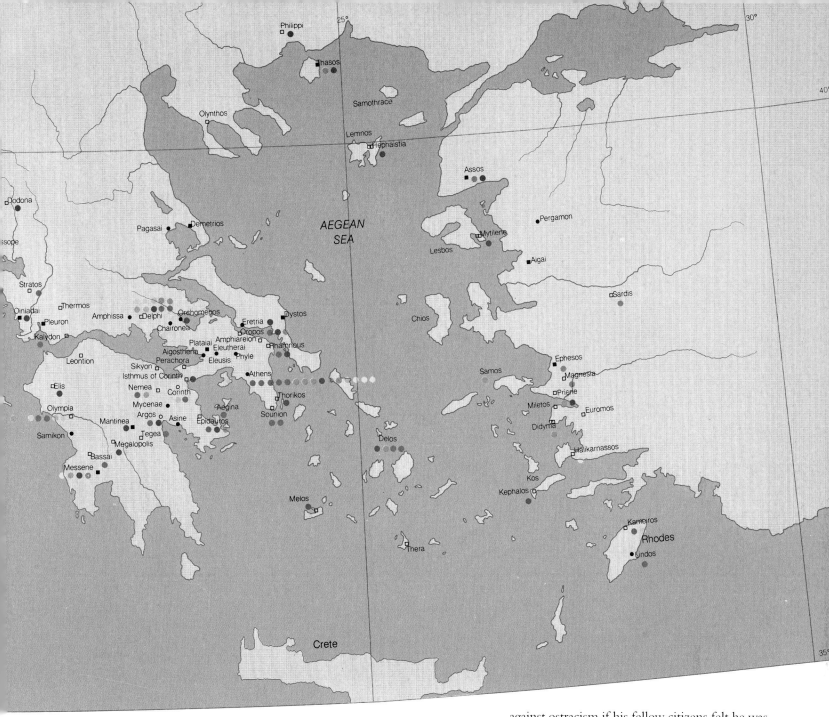

against ostracism if his fellow citizens felt he was becoming too self-important.

Pressure for further democratic reform had come about as a result of the growth of Athenian naval power. Only comfortably-off citizens could afford to equip themselves as hoplites, but no equipment was needed to be an oarsman. It was from the landless *thetes*, the largest and poorest class of citizen, that the crews for Athens' fleet of triremes were recruited. The manpower required by the fleet was enormous. Each trireme was crewed by about 170 men and they needed to be highly trained and well motivated. Their role in the defense of the state gave the *thetes* confidence and, as Athenian power depended more on its fleet than its army, they were quick to realize the new political importance of their class.

In 461 the democratic party in Athens, led by Ephialtes, seized upon the opportunity presented

by Kimon's absence in Messenia to effect a coup and carry out radical reforms. The Areopagus council was demoted to hearing cases of murder and sacrilege, and its powers transferred to the council of 500, the citizen assembly and the law-courts, giving them full control of the Athenian state. To counter aristocratic dominance of the judiciary, pay for jurors was introduced so that the less well-off could serve. There remained practical limits to Athenian democracy. About 30,000 citizens were eligible to attend the assembly, but its meeting place on the Pnyx hill could only accommodate about 6000 people (8000 after it was enlarged in 400 BC). Attendance at the citizen assembly was biased towards those who lived in the city and those who could afford to skip work for a day or two. However, this was remedied later in the century when those attending were paid. Despite the limitations placed on their class, Athenian politics continued to be dominated by aristocrats. But what counted now was not so much their connections and wealth as the persuasiveness of their oratory at the citizen assembly.

PERICLEAN ATHENS

When Ephialtes was killed in the disturbances that followed his coup Pericles, a member of the aristocratic Alkmaionid family, emerged as the leader of the democratic party. Pericles was a brilliant orator whose influence with the Athenian masses secured him re-election as general for an unprecedented 15 years in succession. His anti-Spartan and imperialist views dominated Athenian politics for the remainder of his life and beyond. In particular, he was responsible for tightening Athenian control of the Delian league and for a great program of public building.

For many years after the Persian war, the Athenians had left their city in ruins as a monument to its sufferings. But Pericles set out to rebuild it in deliberately imperial style. The finest monument of Periclean Athens is the Parthenon, the temple of Athene on the Acropolis, which displays the restraint and proportion of Classical Greek architecture at its finest. The elegant naturalism of the sculptural friezes of the Parthenon, by the Athenian sculptor Phidias, represent one of the high points of Classical Greek art. The pure white of the marble statues as they survive today give a misleading impression. In ancient times they were painted and would have looked rather gaudy to modern tastes.

THE PELOPONNESIAN WAR

Two years after Argos allied with Athens, a dispute with Corinth caused Megara to leave the Spartan-dominated Peloponnesian league and come over to Athens. Both these allies adopted democratic

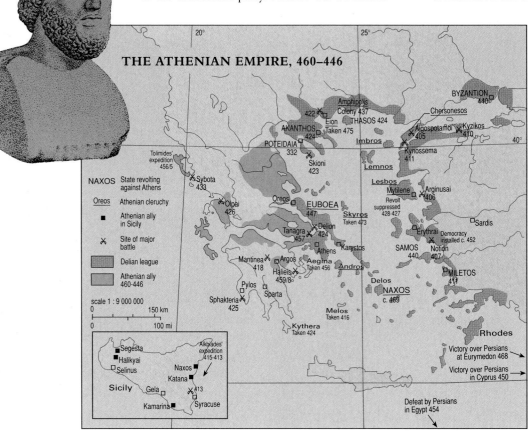

BELOW *Pericles (c. 495–429 BC) was the elected leader of Athens at the time of its greatest power. Though an aristocrat, he won the support of the Athenian masses by extending democracy and by the persuasive power of his brilliant oratory. Pericles' anti-Spartan and imperialist policies succeeded in increasing Athenian power and prestige in his lifetime, but they ultimately led to the ruin of Athens.*

THE ATHENIAN EMPIRE, 460–446

NAXOS State revolting against Athens
Oreos Athenian cleruchy
■ Athenian ally in Sicily
✗ Site of major battle
Delian league
Athenian ally 460–446

scale 1 : 9 000 000
0   150 km
0   100 mi

Tolimides' expedition 456/5
Sybota 433
Olpai 426
Oreos
EUBOEA 447
Tanagra 457
Delion 424
Mantinea 418
Argos
Athens
Aegina Taken 456
Halieis 459/8
Andros
Karystos
Pylos
Sparta
Sphakteria 425
Melos Taken 416
Kythera Taken 424
Naxos c. 469
Delos
SAMOS 440
Notion 407
MILETOS 411
Rhodes

Amphipolis Colony 437
422
Eion
THASOS 424
AKANTHOS 424
Taken 475
POTEIDAIA 332
Skioni 423
Imbros
Lemnos
Lesbos
Mytilene
Revolt suppressed 428–427
Arginusai 406
Erythrai
Democracy installed c. 452
Sardis
BYZANTION 440
Chersonesos
Aigospotamoi 405
Kyzikos 410
Kynossema 411
40°

Segesta
Halikyai
Selinus
Sicily
Gela
Kamarina
Naxos
Katana
413
Syracuse
Alkibiades' expedition 415–413

Victory over Persians at Eurymedon 468
Victory over Persians in Cyprus 450
Defeat by Persians in Egypt 454

20°   25°

LEFT *Sparta withdrew from the war against Persia in 478 BC but Athens carried on, forming an alliance of Aegean and Ionian states known as the Delian league. By the middle of the century, the league's treasury had been moved from Delos to Athens, and its other members complained that Athenians had begun to regard the league as their empire, talking about "rule" rather than "alliance". Cleruchies (colonies) were founded at many places around the Aegean. After the peace treaty with Persia in 448 BC, Athens tightened its control of the league but faced increasingly frequent rebellions.*

constitutions, heightening Spartan concerns over this extension of Athenian influence into the Peloponnese. Sparta still had the strongest army in Greece and was not going to surrender its traditional primacy to the Athenians without a fight. In 458 the Athenians destroyed the naval forces of Aegina and Corinth, finally provoking Sparta to war. To counter Athenian influence in the Peloponnese, the Spartans sent an expedition into Boeotia to strengthen Thebes. At the battle of Tanagra (457) Sparta and its Peloponnesian allies beat a slightly larger Athenian army, but the Spartans showed their traditional reluctance to move far outside the Peloponnese and the victory was not followed up. The Athenians had their revenge on Thebes later that year when they imposed a democratic constitution on it, and in 456 Aegina was forcibly enrolled in the Delian league.

This was as close as Athens was going to get to mastery in Greece. The city was still at war with Persia and the strain of fighting on two fronts was beginning to tell. Ironically, the peace treaty with Persia in 448 in some ways weakened the Athenian position. Without the fear of a return to Persian rule, many members of the Delian league felt less closely bound to Athens. Because it had no navy, Sparta concentrated its attack on the Athenian position in central Greece while attempting to foment rebellion among the members of the

Delian league. The Athenians successfully put down rebellions in Euboea and Thasos, but by 445 they had lost control of Megara and central Greece and agreed to a 30-years' peace that recognized Spartan dominance in the Peloponnese. Pericles accepted that Athens lacked the manpower to be both a great military and a great naval power. By adopting a defensive posture on land, he hoped to eliminate the cause of Sparta's hostility while using the fleet to control the Delian league and the Aegean trade routes.

The peace terms did nothing to dampen the mutual hostility of Sparta and Athens. In 435 Corcyra (Corfu) defeated Corinth, an ally of Sparta, in a minor conflict. Feeling sure that Corinth would

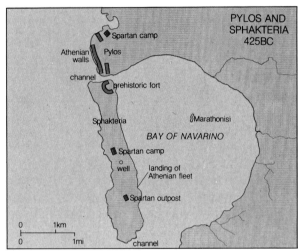

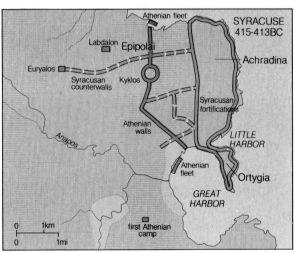

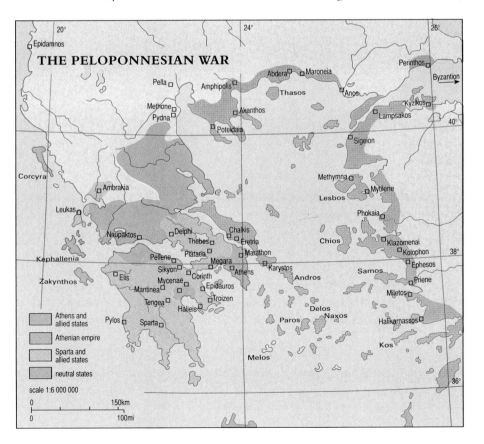

ABOVE (Top) *During the war with Sparta, Athens used its naval supremacy to raid around the coast of the Peloponnese. Pylos was captured from the Spartans in 425 BC and used as a base from which to foment unrest among the Messenians.* (Bottom) *The Athenians sought to deny their enemies access to Sicilian grain supplies by laying siege to Syracuse. Their failure to capture it proved a disastrous turning point in the war.*

DECORATIVE POTTERY

ABOVE *An 8th-century jug from Athens decorated with repeating zigzags, diamonds and triangles shows the formal patterning of the Geometrical style at its most intricate and fully developed.*

ABOVE RIGHT *This early Corinthian vase (7th century) is decorated in the Orientalizing style using the new black-figure technique. The animal frieze, with its exotic lions and the two-bodied panther-bird seen in the lower register, was a decorative motif introduced from the Near East. Under the Kypselids (657–585) Corinth became the leading center of pottery manufacture on the Greek mainland until it was superseded by Athens.*

At the beginning of the dark age Greek pottery was decorated with purely abstract patterns that were derived from earlier Mycenaean styles. During the 9th and 8th centuries, curvilinear patterns were replaced by rectilinear designs based on meanders, zigzags and swastikas (the Geometric style). Stylized human and animal figures, used rhythmically and repetitively as part of the design, begin to appear in this period. In the 7th century Near Eastern influences led to the development of the Orientalizing style that included animal friezes and vegetation as major decorative elements. This in turn inspired the "black-figure" technique, first put into practice at Corinth, where the figures are in black silhouette with incised details. The new technique allowed detailed action scenes to be created, so enabling artists to depict pictorial narratives of myths and other stories, and – in parallel with developments in other arts, especially Archaic sculpture – figures gradually became more naturalistic. Vase painting reached its highest attainment in Athens with the invention of the "red-figure" technique (c. 530). In this, the figures stand in a black background with details painted on. Vase-painting schools started by emigrant artists in Italy and Sicily were still flourishing in the 4th century. Red-figure decoration died out in the Hellenistic period, and with it vase painting as a major art.

ABOVE *Individual artists were famed for their skill at pottery decoration and founded workshops and painting schools. This wine cup (c. 540) was decorated by Exekias, the master Athenian painter, using the black-figure technique. The scene depicts the wine-god Dionysos. Captured by an Etruscan pirate ship, he has turned its crew into dolphins and caused its mast to sprout vines. Myths about Dionysos were popular subjects for drinking vessels.*

BELOW Red-figure painting, which was influenced by mural painting, was much more naturalistic than the black-figure technique. These two examples are from 5th-century Athens. (Top) This elegant vase shows Alkaios and Sappho, the lyric poets of 7th-century Lesbos. They are depicted here as aristocratic poets and singers, and the subject reflects contemporary Athenian interest in the art of song. (Bottom) Shallow wine cups were used at symposia or men's drinking parties. This detail from a wine cup shows one such party at which the seated guests have imbibed liberally. The naked flute girl entertaining them must have been a foreigner or a slave – Athenian women were never allowed to appear immodestly in public like this.

seek revenge, the Corcyrans allied with Athens in 433, causing the Spartans to fear Athenian ambitions in the Peloponnese once again. When Athens attacked the city of Potidaea, which had defected from the Delian league, Sparta demanded that Athens free all members of the league. A further provocation came when Athens placed its neighbor and rival Megara under economic blockade. In 431 the war broke out again, this time engulfing most of the Greek world. Thanks to the monumental *History of the Peloponnesian War* by Thucydides, we have a detailed description of this second phase of the conflict between Athens and Sparta. Thucydides was one of Athens' less successful generals – he was ostracized in 424 for his failings – but he was certainly its greatest historian, and was the first to use an understanding of human psychology to explain the causes of events.

The Spartans hoped they would be able to starve Athens into surrender by ravaging its agricultural hinterland in Attica. However, Pericles had planned for this contingency. A large cash surplus had been accumulated in the years prior to the resumption of the war and it was decided to abandon Attica, taking its population within the city walls. The city's wealth and naval command of the sea were harnessed to supply Athens from overseas and raid around the Peloponnesian coast. After Pericles' death in 429 (he fell victim to a plague that had broken out in the overcrowded city), the Athenian war effort was conducted with less skill. By 421 neither side had won a decisive

advantage and a 50-years' peace was made. However, its terms alienated Sparta's allies Corinth, Elis, Mantinea and Argos, and in 419 they came over to Athens' side. War broke out again unofficially, but this new alliance collapsed following a Spartan victory at Mantinea in 418.

The war entered a decisive phase in 416 when the Athenians, hoping to deprive their enemies of Sicilian grain supplies, sent a major expedition to besiege Syracuse. The expedition was a disaster from which Athens did not recover. In 414 Sparta

ABOVE *The sculptures of the Parthenon were designed by the sculptor Phidias and display all the confidence of 5th-century Athens. The frieze running right around the cella within the outer colonnade (see page 139) depicts a procession for the great Panathenaic festival. This slab from the south side shows youths near the head of the procession leading a heifer for the sacrifice.*

GREEK ARCHITECTURE

Architects of the Classical period used three architectural orders. The Doric, with its sturdy columns and simple undecorated capitals, was the most common order used on the Greek mainland and in Italy and Sicily. The Ionic order was developed in Ionia. Its columns were taller and *more slender than the Doric and the capitals were decorated with carved volutes (spirals). The Corinthian style developed from the Ionic. According to legend its ornate capitals were inspired by the sight of acanthus leaves growing from a basket set on a grave column.*

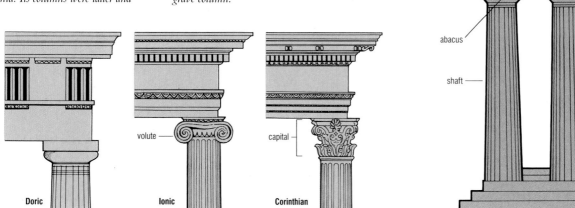

re-entered the war officially. It sent help to Syracuse and the Athenians were catastrophically defeated the following year, losing most of their 45,000-strong army. In the same year, Sparta garrisoned Decelea in Attica, forcing the closure of Athens' vital silver mines. Worse was to come in 412 when Persia, in return for a free hand in Ionia, paid for the construction of a Spartan fleet, tipping the balance of power decisively away from Athens. In 405 the Spartans won control of the Bosporus after defeating the Athenian fleet at Aegospotami. This had the effect of cutting Athens off from its essential imports of Black Sea grain and the next year the city surrendered. Its democratic constitution was briefly overthrown by a Spartan-supported aristocratic coup, the Delian league was disbanded, and the Ionian Greeks found themselves once again under Persian rule. But though the war broke the power of Athens, it did not leave Sparta strong enough to achieve the mastery of Greece that had eluded the Athenians. The war showed that no one Greek city state could achieve permanent dominance and unite Greece into a single state, as the city of Rome was later to do in Italy.

ATHENS AND THE GREEK CLASSICAL ACHIEVEMENT

Despite a background of almost unceasing war, Greek civilization flourished in the 5th century. It may even be that the challenge of the Persian invasion and competition between the city states

spurred intellectual achievement. Nowhere was this more so than in Athens, the unchallenged cultural leader of Greece at this time. Athens did not have a monopoly on creative genius, but it was only there that all the elements of Classical Greek civilization flourished together in the same place. Pericles, with very little exaggeration, described the city as "the school of Greece." Athens became a magnet for scholars, artists, craftsmen and the merely curious. Many were only temporary visitors attracted by the Dionysian drama festival or the athletic, poetic and musical competitions of the Panathenaic festival. Some came to study, others to teach. Though they could not qualify for citizenship, foreigners with useful skills were welcomed as permanent residents in Athens and made an important contribution to the city's prosperity. Over a third of the craftsmen who built the Parthenon were foreigners.

Athens' most important contribution to Greek – indeed to western – civilization was the invention of drama (see pages 162–163). Competitors in the Dionysian festival established by the tyrant Peisistratos in the 6th century were expected to produce four plays: a trilogy of tragic plays, which could be linked by a common theme, followed by a burlesque that featured satyrs, mythological creatures (part man, part goat) who had a ritualistic role in the Dionysian celebrations. These satyr plays would later develop as a separate genre – comedy. Only one example of a complete trilogy of tragic plays has survived, the *Oresteia* by Aeschylus (c. 525–456), the first great Athenian dramatist. In his dramatic works, Aeschylus develops the themes of vengeance, retribution and divine justice, playing on the ambiguities of Greek religion in which the gods hold humans answerable for their actions but do not make clear to them how they should act. By introducing a second actor into the drama, Aeschylus found a way of developing conflicts of character in his plays.

Aeschylus's younger contemporary Sophocles (496–406) increased the number of actors to three. The gods take more of a background role in his plays, but their influence is just as as pervasive. Sophocles' masterpiece is *Oedipus the King* (c. 429). Though Oedipus does everything in his power to escape a prophecy that he will kill his father and marry his mother, he cannot evade his destiny; that is his tragedy. It is immaterial to the gods that Oedipus, who was abandoned at birth, could not have recognized his father and mother; he has polluted himself and is mercilessly punished for it.

THE GREEK THEATER

Greek drama developed from the choral songs about the life and death of the god Dionysos performed at his festival in Athens. Around the mid 6th century the poet Thespis (from whose name the word "thespian" is derived) introduced a new musical form of religious performance in which he impersonated a single character and engaged in dialog with the chorus of singers and dancers. The new art form became known as tragedy (literally, "goat song" though no one is quite sure why). In 534 Peisistratos instituted a drama contest to be held during the Dionysian festival. The plays were performed in a natural amphitheater at the foot of the Acropolis close to the temple of Dionysos, with the audience seated on wooden benches overlooking a simple dancing circle or "orchestra." As the number of characters in the plays increased, and the role of the chorus declined, a stage house, the "skene," was built behind the orchestra facing the audience. Later the "proskenion," a raised stage, was added in front, reducing the size of the orchestra still further. Painted scenery and stage machinery for special effects also came into use. All Greek theaters followed this model.

LEFT *A 5th-century bronze votive mask based on the kind of mask that would be worn by an actor playing a tragic character. All actors wore masks. Their exaggerated expressions helped identify characters, as many people in the audience were seated a long way from the stage.*

BELOW *A composite and imaginary Greek provincial theater of 4th-century style. The skene hid the actors until they were ready to enter the stage through one of the three doors. Gods spoke from the balcony above while the chorus spoke from the orchestra. The stone thrones on the front row of seats were reserved for magistrates or important visitors. In later Greek theaters the skene and stage (proskenion) became more and more architecturally elaborate.*

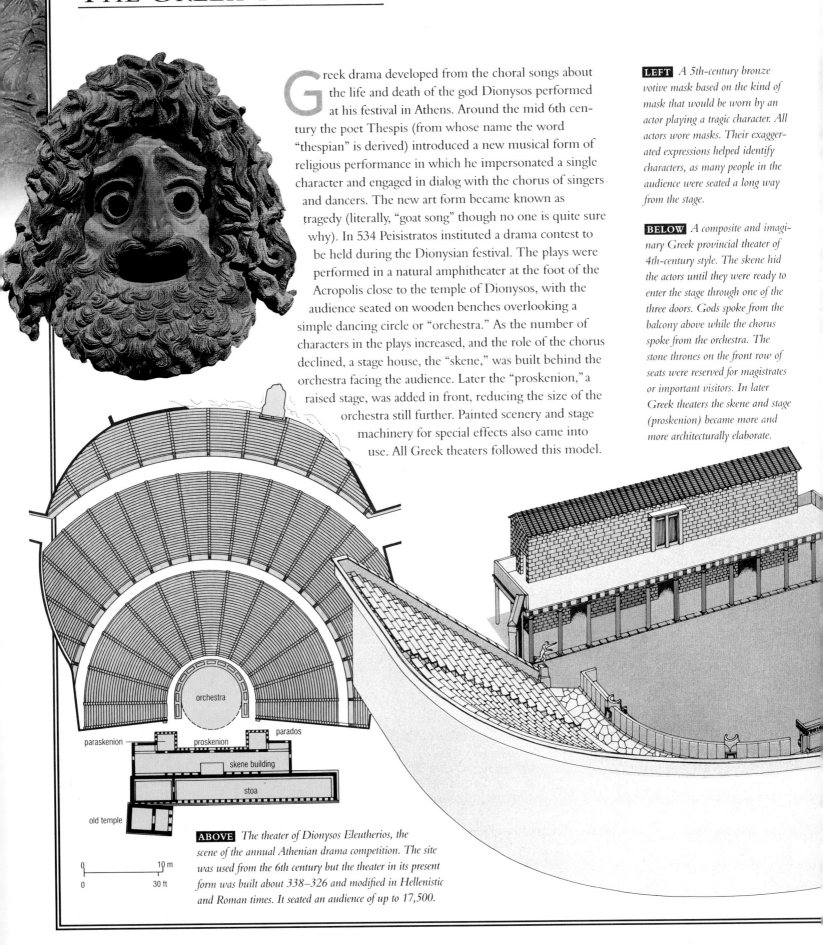

orchestra

paraskenion

proskenion

parados

skene building

stoa

old temple

0   10 m
0   30 ft

ABOVE *The theater of Dionysos Eleutherios, the scene of the annual Athenian drama competition. The site was used from the 6th century but the theater in its present form was built about 338–326 and modified in Hellenistic and Roman times. It seated an audience of up to 17,500.*

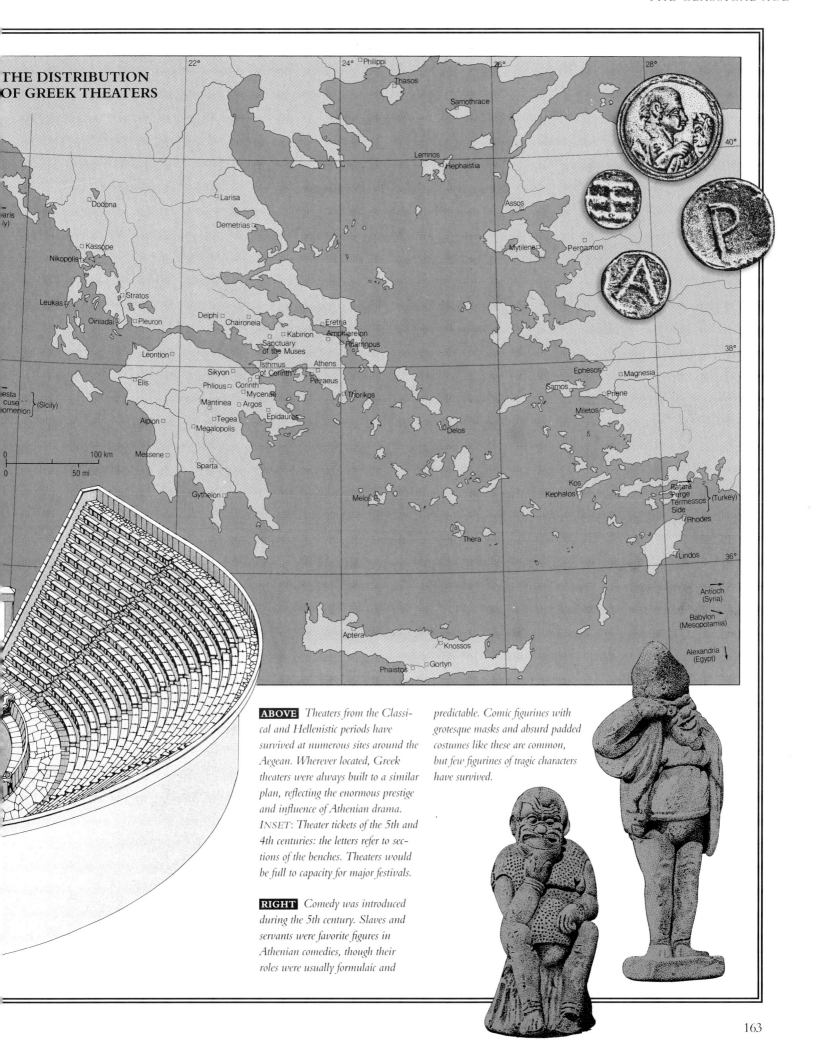

THE DISTRIBUTION OF GREEK THEATERS

22°   24° Philippi   26°   28°

Thasos

Samothrace

40°

Lemnos

Hephaistia

Assos

Dodona

Larisa

aris
ly)

Demetrias

Mytilene   Pergamon

Kassope

Nikopolis

Stratos

Leukas

Oiniadai   Pleuron

Delphi   Chaironeia

Eretria

Amphiareion

38°

Kabirion

Rhamnous

Sanctuary
of the Muses

Leontion

Isthmus
of Corinth

Athens

Ephesos   Magnesia

Sikyon

Peiraeus

Samos

Priene

Elis

Phlious   Corinth

Thorikos

Miletos

esta
cuse
omenion } (Sicily)

Mantinea   Argos

Mycenae

Aipion

Tegea

Epidauros

Delos

Megalopolis

0   100 km

Messene

0   50 mi

Sparta

Kos
Kephalos

Patara
Perge
Termessos } (Turkey)
Side

Gytheion

Meloś

Rhodes

Thera

Lindos   36°

Antioch
(Syria)

Babylon
(Mesopotamia)

Alexandria
(Egypt)

Aptera

Knossos

Phaistos   Gortyn

ABOVE Theaters from the Classical and Hellenistic periods have
survived at numerous sites around the
Aegean. Wherever located, Greek
theaters were always built to a similar
plan, reflecting the enormous prestige
and influence of Athenian drama.
INSET: Theater tickets of the 5th and
4th centuries: the letters refer to sections of the benches. Theaters would
be full to capacity for major festivals.

RIGHT Comedy was introduced
during the 5th century. Slaves and
servants were favorite figures in
Athenian comedies, though their
roles were usually formulaic and

predictable. Comic figurines with
grotesque masks and absurd padded
costumes like these are common,
but few figurines of tragic characters
have survived.

BELOW The theater at Dodona, the site of an ancient sanctuary of Zeus in northwest Greece, was built in Hellenistic times during the reign of Pyrrhus of Epirus (297–272). The cavea (the semicircle of stone benches for the audience), which was partly excavated into the side of the acropolis, originally seated over 14,000 spectators. The remains of the skene with its entrances for the actors can be clearly seen. The theater has recently been restored for use in drama festivals.

The last of the great Athenian tragic dramatists was Euripedes (484–406). In his plays, the human characters come finally to the fore, their actions dictated by their emotions and desires. Euripedes' plays, which were written in a time of almost constant warfare, frequently question the role of violence in human affairs.

In 486 a separate category for comedy was introduced into the Dionysian festival. Comedy served an important function in democratic Athens as it allowed anything and anyone to be mocked. The only surviving works of 5th-century Athenian comedy, known as Old Comedy, are by Aristophanes (c. 450–385). His works combine vicious satire, fantasy, sophisticated wit, sublime lyrics and extreme vulgarity. In Aristophanes' most famous play, *Lysistrata,* written in 411 when the Peloponnesian war was beginning to go badly for Athens, the war-weary women of Greece mount a sex strike until their men make peace. After Athens' defeat in 404 Old Comedy died out – its irreverent satire was not acceptable in a society that had lost much of its self-confidence. It was replaced by the New Comedy, exemplified in the work of Menander (342–292), whose plays have domestic settings and realistic characters.

A significant by-product of drama was the development of perspective painting, used as an optical illusion by Athenian stage scenery painters. The earliest known wall painting in a private house was commissioned by Pericles' nephew Alcibiades from a theatrical designer.

FROM SOCRATES TO ARISTOTLE

Athens certainly did not invent Greek philosophy – its earliest significant figures were all Ionians – but it did produce three of the most significant figures in the history of western thought, Socrates, Plato and Aristotle. It was the introduction of democracy that turned Athens into a major center for the study and teaching of philosophy. Now that skill in public speaking and debate was the key to success in politics, the demand for education increased greatly. It was met by the sophists, itinerant teachers who traveled from city to city teaching rhetoric and other subjects such as logic, astronomy, mathematics and music. While the sophists were often original thinkers, they were not primarily concerned with seeking objective truth which, for the most part, they did not believe existed. Some were openly skeptical about the existence of the gods: one of the most famous sophists, Protagoras of Abdera, declared that "man is the measure of all things." The ability of the sophists convincingly to argue a case from more than one viewpoint led many to regard them as intellectual tricksters and they were mercilessly lampooned in Aristophanes' comedy *The Clouds*.

The central character of *The Clouds* is Socrates (469–399), the first important Athenian philosopher. As Socrates did not teach for a living he was not, strictly speaking, a sophist. However, his ability to make those engaging in argument with him contradict themselves through his skillful and infuriating use of rational cross-questioning made

Heracleitus

Aeschylus

Herodotus

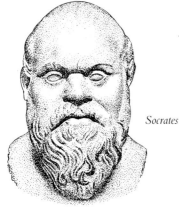

Socrates

NATIVE CITY STATES

ABDERA: Protagoras, Democritus
ATHENS: Euripides, Sophocles, Menander, Aristophanes, Aeschylus, Plato, Socrates, Epicurus, Thucydides, Solon
ASKRA: Hesiod
CHIOS: Homer
CYPRUS: Zeno
EPHESUS: Hipponax, Heracleitus, Kallinos
HALIKARNASSOS: Herodotus

KEA: Bacchylides, Simonides
KOLOPHON: Mimnermos, Xenophanes
MEGARA: Theognis
MILETOS: Anaximander, Anaximenes, Hekataios, Thales
MYTILENE: Alkaios, Sappho
PAROS: Archilochos
SAMOS: Pythagoras
SPARTA: Tyrtaios, Alkman
STAGEIRA: Aristotle
TEOS: Anacreon
THEBES: Pindar

RIGHT *Though no part of the Greek world had a monopoly on creativity, the dominance of Athens as a cultural center is clear. As well as its native geniuses, Athens played host to scholars from across the Greek world, including the poet Pindar and the philosophers Aristotle and Zeno, who went there to study and teach.*

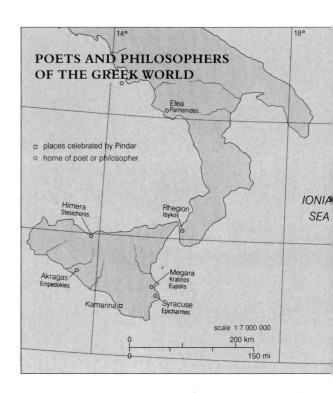

POETS AND PHILOSOPHERS OF THE GREEK WORLD

□ places celebrated by Pindar
○ home of poet or philosopher

Elea
Parmenides

Himera
Stesichoros

Rhegion
Ibykos

IONIAN SEA

Akragas
Empedokles

Megara
Kratinos
Eupolis

Kamarina

Syracuse
Epicharmos

scale 1:7 000 000

0   200 km
0   150 mi

him one in the public's eyes. Socrates himself wrote nothing; indeed he had some contempt for writing, regarding it as the means of trying to establish outside the mind what could in reality only exist within it. Most of what we know of Socrates' teachings comes from the writings of his pupil Plato. While pre-Socratic Greek philosophers were primarily concerned with metaphysical questions about the essential nature of the universe, Socrates was interested in the principles and values that affected what a person should do. He believed that there were objective concepts, such as "the good," "justice," "beauty," which could be understood by reason.

In the sorry aftermath of the Peloponnesian war the Athenians cast about for a scapegoat. That clever and irritating man Socrates was associated with several discredited aristocrats, such as the traitor Alkibiades, and he was charged with impiety and corrupting the youth of Athens. To judge from Plato's account of the trial, Socrates seems to have gone out of his way to antagonize the jury. He made no effort to disguise his intellectual elitism, provoking them to impose the death sentence rather than the lesser sentence of exile. Plato presents Socrates as a martyr for philosophy, a man who would not compromise his beliefs even to save his life but there is another tradition that holds that he in fact said very little at his trial.

Socrates' work was built on by Plato (c. 429–347) who sought to establish an absolute basis for knowledge with his doctrine of "Forms" in which

concepts such as bravery had a real existence as eternal entities. Plato had little time for democracy which he regarded as scarcely better than mob rule. Plato's best-known work *The Republic* outlines his version of the ideal state. This would be ruled by reason, rather than emotion and self-interest which Plato believed dominated democracy. But though he argued that the rule of reason was not tyranny, his was a vision of a totalitarian eugenic state ruled by an intellectual elite of "philosopher kings." Plato set out his thought in a very accessible way – a series of dramatic dialogs in which the discourse is placed in the mouths of characters, the central of whom is Plato's hero Socrates. Plato founded his own school, the Academy, in 388, thereby ensuring the continuing importance of Athens as a center for the study and teaching of philosophy.

Plato's thought was challenged by his student Aristotle (384–322). Born at Stageira in northern Greece, Aristotle came to Athens in 367 to study at the Academy: he stayed on to teach. In 343 he traveled to Macedon where he became tutor to the young Alexander the Great. Returning to Athens in 335 he founded the Lyceum, which taught a wider curriculum than the Academy. Plato had little interest in the physical world; for him, ultimate reality was the eternal world of Forms. But Aristotle did not believe that Forms had an independent existence: they were qualities of matter and soul. Thus he acknowledged that experience and observation of the physical world had a place in rational

Plato

Aristotle

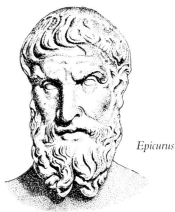

Epicurus

Zeno

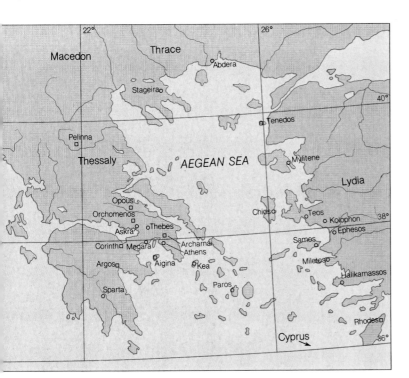

FAR LEFT AND RIGHT

Heracleitus of Ephesus (c. 540 – c. 480) was a philosopher who taught that fire was the basic element of the universe. Aeschylus (c. 525–456), the first of the great dramatic poets, won the Dionysian drama festival at Athens 13 times. Herodotus (c. 484–420) wrote the first great narrative history. The teachings of Socrates (469–399), who was sentenced to death for corrupting the youth of Athens, are known mostly from the writings of his friend and student Plato (c. 429–347), founder of the Athenian Academy. Aristotle (384–322) studied philosophy in Athens under Plato and later became tutor to Alexander the Great. Epicurus (c. 341–270) taught a materialist philosophy of moderate hedonism (Epicureanism). Zeno (335–263) was the founder of Stoicism, the philosophy of "the stiff upper lip."

enquiry. This has made Aristotle one of the key figures in the history of science. The scope of Aristotle's work was far wider than Plato's. As well as exploring the same ethical issues as Plato, Aristotle wrote extensively on the sciences of zoology, biology, chemistry, physics and astronomy and on the problems of change and causation, time and motion. His greatest achievement was his system of logic, which has not been superseded after 2000 years. But despite the part that Aristotle and his predecessors played in establishing philosophy as a branch of study, their ideas had little or no influence on the lives of ordinary people. They continued to believe in the old magic and cults of the gods as before.

SPARTAN DOMINATION

The Peloponnesian war confirmed Sparta as the dominant Greek state, but it was unable to consolidate its victory. Sparta's willingness to abandon the Ionian Greeks to the Persians in return for aid against Athens, and its support for Dionysios, tyrant of Syracuse, made a mockery of any claim it might have to be the champion of Greek freedom. Spartan policy at this time was in the hands of Lysander, an ambitious general who cultivated a remarkable personality cult: he was the first Greek to receive cultic honors, as a god or hero, in his own lifetime. It was an idea that was taken up, with more lasting effect, by Alexander the Great.

No one can have been greatly surprised when, after Lysander's death in 395, papers were found at his house indicating that he had planned to overthrow the monarchy. Lysander wanted Sparta to take over Athens' role as ruler of the Aegean but his arrogant approach destroyed what little pro-Spartan sentiment there was. Ten-man juntas, called dekarchies, were imposed on the Aegean states and they were forced to pay a heavy annual tribute for the upkeep of the Spartan fleet. This was as bad as Athenian rule. In 404 Athens itself was subjected to the rule of the "Thirty Tyrants", an anti-democratic aristocratic junta, but the regime lasted only a year before being overthrown with the help of Lysander's political enemies in Sparta. Lysander maintained close relations with the Persians, cultivating the friendship of Cyrus, the younger son of Darius II (423–405) and satrap of Sardis. However, this friendship was to cause the unraveling of Sparta's ambitions.

Darius was succeeded by his son Artaxerxes II (404–359). Cyrus was accused of plotting to overthrow his brother and in 402 he rebelled and

appealed to Sparta for support. Lysander helped Cyrus raise a force of Greek mercenaries and sent troops to Anatolia to tie down Persian forces in the area. Cyrus meanwhile marched east to meet his brother in battle at Cunaxa in Babylonia (401). Artaxerxes was defeated but Cyrus himself was killed. The Greek army of Ten Thousand, deserted by the Persians, subsequently fought its way back to the Black Sea (see page 176). The incident was a disaster for Sparta as it soured relations with Artaxerxes. As Lysander's influence declined, Sparta adopted an anti-Persian policy, backing the Ionians and rebel satraps and sending support to a rebellion in Egypt. In 396 a Spartan force under king Agesilaos invaded Anatolia with such success that the Persian general in charge of its defense was executed for incompetence.

Athens, Thebes, Corinth and Argos, for different reasons, had cause to resent the power of Sparta. These resentments were helped along by Persian money and in 395 the four states allied with Persia against Sparta in what is known as the Corinthian war (395–387). Lysander was killed in battle soon after the outbreak of hostilities, but Agesilaos hurried back from Anatolia and, at the battle of Koroneia (394), proved that the Spartan phalanx was still the best in Greece. At sea Sparta

(see page 176)

BELOW *The "Long Walls" provided a protected corridor between Athens and Peiraeus, its fortified harbor, enabling the city to be supplied from overseas if besieged. Completed in the mid 5th century BC, they were pulled down at the end of the Peloponnesian war and then rebuilt by Konon, with Persian subsidies, early in the 4th century.*

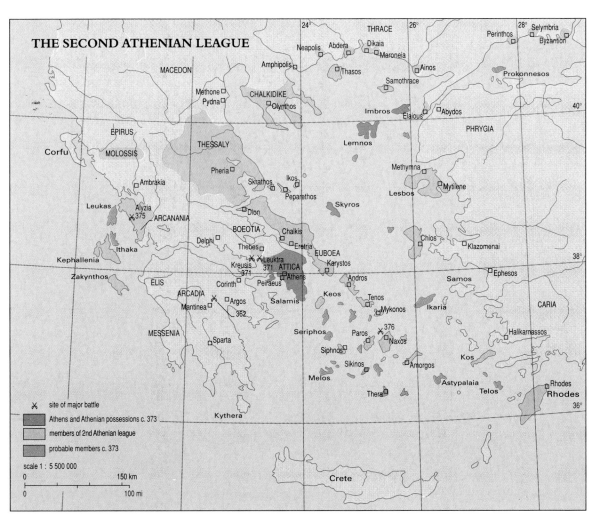

THE SECOND ATHENIAN LEAGUE

site of major battle

Athens and Athenian possessions c. 373

members of 2nd Athenian league

probable members c. 373

scale 1 : 5 500 000

0 — 150 km

0 — 100 mi

was less fortunate. Persia had rebuilt its fleet and placed it under the command of an Athenian general, Konon, who destroyed the Spartan navy at Knidos in the same year. With Persian subsidies, Athens rebuilt its walls and its fleet and then set about regaining its Aegean empire. The recovery of Athens alarmed Artaxerxes, who withdrew his support in 388. The war bogged down into stalemate until Persia changed sides and allied with Sparta in 387. Within six months Spartan dominance on land and sea had been restored and Artaxerxes was able to dictate his own peace terms, the so-called King's Peace. Sparta remained the strongest Greek state but Persia was the real winner of the war. By skillfully manipulating the balance of power, Artaxerxes had ended the Spartan threat without elevating any of its rivals. Persian control of Ionia and Cyprus was secured, and Persia was now the arbiter of Greece.

THE RISE OF THEBES

The fact that their victory in the Corinthian war was obtained through Persian support did nothing to diminish Spartan arrogance. The King's Peace had not satisfied Sparta's ambitions and it was

desperate to find some pretext to intervene against Thebes and Athens. This came in 382 when an elitist faction seized power in Thebes and abolished democracy, setting up its own government, or oligarchy. Sparta responded to its appeal for help by garrisoning the city and ending Theban independence. The cities of the Theban-led Boeotian league were also occupied. However, in 379 a rebellion broke out in Thebes and the Spartan garrison was forced to withdraw. At this point the Spartans foolishly provoked Athens into supporting Thebes' bid for independence by failing to punish a general who had violated Athenian territory. The Thebans avoided pitched battle against the Spartan army dispatched to Boeotia to deal with the rebels, but when it retired home the garrisons left behind were picked off one by one. By 374 the last of the Spartans had been expelled. Pro-Theban democracies were installed in all the cities, and the Boeotian league was reconstituted.

Meanwhile, Athens had been building a second Athenian league to pursue the war against Sparta. Memories of the Delian league still rankled and Athens had to promise not to interfere in the internal politics of member states or to impose tribute, but after the Athenians decisively defeated the Spartan fleet at Naxos in 376, most of the Aegean states joined up. Success went to the Athenians' heads: the leadership of Greece once more seemed to be in their grasp but their pretensions merely alienated Thebes. Besides, the Athenian treasury was almost empty. As a three-sided stalemate loomed, Artaxerxes intervened and proposed another King's Peace. It foundered because both Sparta and Athens, fearing the rising power of Thebes, wanted the Boeotian league disbanded. Epaminondas, a brilliant general who had emerged as the leader of Thebes, refused to comply. The Spartans invaded Boeotia but were crushingly defeated by Epaminondas' smaller army at Leuktra in 371. Over 2000 of the Spartan army were killed, at little cost to the Boeotians. Sparta's reputation for invincibility was shattered with a stroke.

As news of the disaster spread, democratic revolutions broke out in Mantinea, Corinth, Megara and other Peloponnesian cities where Sparta had imposed oligarchies. In 370–369 Epaminondas went on the offensive, invading the Peloponnese and liberating Messenia from Spartan rule. Able to muster a mere 800 citizen hoplites, Sparta was now reduced to a second-class power. But the collapse of Spartan power did not bring freedom to southern Greece. Corinth and Megara, on the strategically important Isthmus, became Theban client states and Epaminondas set up the Arcadian league in the Peloponnese to prevent a Spartan recovery there. Theban power was also extended into northern Greece following the defeat of the Thessalian tyrant Alexander of Pherai.

Theban domination of Greece was not to prove long lasting. In 362 Mantinea left the Arcadian league and appealed to Athens for help. Athens, still ambitious for leadership itself, now allied with Mantinea, Elis and Sparta against Thebes and its allies. Epaminondas invaded the Peloponnese and comprehensively defeated a combined Spartan and Athenian army at Mantinea but was himself killed during mopping up operations. Theban power abruptly collapsed: it had been dependent almost entirely on the genius of one man.

DECLINE OF THE CITY STATE

By the middle of the 4th century the Greek city states were close to exhaustion after a century of futile warfare. No state had managed to gain lasting supremacy over the others and the collapse in turn of Athenian, Spartan and Theban overrule had left the Greek world more fragmented than

RIGHT *The impressive inner walls of the fortified city of Aigosthena on the Gulf of Corinth are among the finest surviving examples of fortification building from 4th-century Greece. The inner wall protected the acropolis, the outer wall circled the entire city. Both were provided with bastion towers.*

ever. Perhaps the main reason why no state was able to achieve in Greece what Rome was able to do in Italy was the Greek attitude to citizenship. Citizenship was a jealously guarded privilege that could be acquired only by inheritance. In states such as Sparta and Athens (after 452) no one could inherit citizenship unless both parents were natives. Because of emigration, disenfranchisement as a result of impoverishment, casualties in war and the inevitable extinction of family lines, the number of citizens in the city states tended to decline. At the time of the Persian wars Sparta had been able to raise 8000 citizen hoplites; during the Corinthian war it could raise only 1200. The city states were increasingly compelled to rely on mercenaries – a solution they could not really afford. This is in contrast to the experience of the Roman republic which was highly successful at augmenting its citizen body and, therefore, the manpower eligible for military service. In Rome even a freed slave could become a citizen and defeated enemies could be turned into loyal allies by the granting of citizenship. In the Greek world, defeated enemies simply waited for the opportunity to rebel.

The rise of the mercenary brought other changes to Greek warfare. War had been a part-time business for citizen armies, confined to the summer months, but mercenaries could serve all year round. The new professional armies were less inhibited by the ancient conventions of Greek warfare. Epaminondas won his great victory at Leuktra by opening the attack with a specially strengthened left wing. This took the Spartans completely by surprise as the age-old custom was to place the best troops in the right wing and attack from there. The main object of summer campaigns had been to ravage the enemy's countryside and destroy the harvest. Now the need to reward mercenaries to maintain an army in the field meant that the cities as well were frequently plundered. Siege warfare grew considerably in importance and fortifications became more elaborate and widespread. No one in Greece understood the implications of the new warfare better than the ambitious king Philip of Macedon. His kingdom had always been a backwater of the Greek world. This was about to change.

The Hellenistic Age

356–30 BC

Before the late 5th century, BC Macedon, a mountainous country bordering the Aegean Sea to the north of Thessaly, played a peripheral role in Greek history. The kingdom was established by Perdiccas I in about 640. Though Perdiccas was supposedly a Dorian, Macedon had a mixed population of Greeks, Illyrians and Thracians. Its tribal organization made it weak and unstable and it was frequently threatened by its Thracian and other non-Greek neighbors. For a time, it was tributary to the Persian kings Darius I and Xerxes. The first steps toward centralization were made by Archelaos (r.413–399) who strengthened Macedon's military infrastructure by building roads, forts and supply depots. Pella became the administrative capital of the kingdom. Famous Greek artists such as the dramatist Euripedes were invited to the court. But the introduction of Greek influences (a process known as hellenization) affected only the principal towns and cities. Elsewhere, a tribal society still persisted. After Archelaos' death, Macedon suffered several Illyrian invasions, and it was further destabilized by the intrigues of Athens, Thebes and Thessaly.

In 359 Philip II (r.356–336) came to power as regent to his young nephew. Philip's reputation is overshadowed by that of his famous son Alexander the Great. Yet he was an excellent soldier and diplomat and a great ruler in his own right, who transformed Macedon from a backwater into a superpower capable of imposing unity on the fractious Greek city states. The key to Philip's success was his reorganization of the army in the 350s. Macedon was traditionally strong in the use of cavalry but had no experience of the infantry phalanx. Philip borrowed the idea from the Greeks but adapted it to fight in a looser order, making it more flexible and maneuverable than the traditional Greek phalanx. The main Macedonian weapon was the *sarissa*, an 18-foot (5.5-m) long spear, double the length of the Greek spear, that was used by both cavalry and foot soldiers. A Greek hoplite phalanx could not close with the

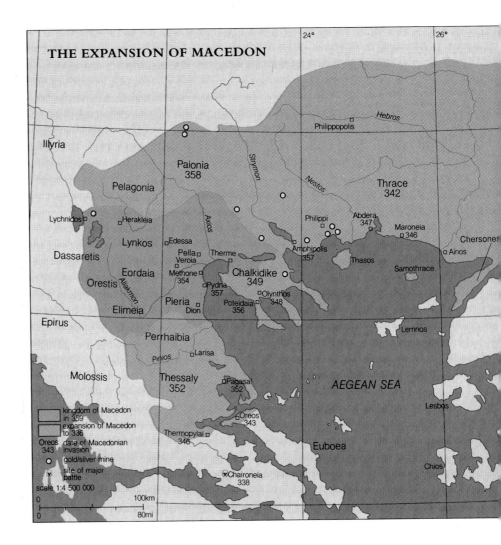

massed *sarissas* of a Macedonian phalanx, and it was easily broken up by those of the Macedonian cavalry. Because they fought at long range, Macedonian foot soldiers were able to dispense with most of the heavy, uncomfortable and expensive armor worn by a hoplite (see pages 146–147).

In his youth, Philip had been a hostage in Thebes and had studied the methods of the brilliant Theban general Epaminondas. This taught him the advantages of coordinating the use of infantry and cavalry, as well as the tactic of strengthening one wing employed so successfully by Epaminondas against the Spartans at Leuktra. For Epaminondas, the hoplite phalanx was, as it

ABOVE *The unstable kingdom of Macedon played only a minor role in Greek history until strong rule was imposed on it by Philip II, a talented and ruthless ruler who made the Macedonian army the finest in Greece. The Greek city states were unable to organize a common front to oppose Macedonian aggression, and after defeating a combined Theban and Athenian army at Chaironeia (338) Philip was ready to continue Macedonian expansion eastward into Asia.*

always had been, the battle-winning strength of the army. Philip, however, saw its main role as holding the enemy infantry until the cavalry could maneuver to deliver a decisive blow – a complete break with Greek tradition. Since Philip relied mostly on mercenary forces he was able to campaign all the year round. Cities were traditionally captured by blockade, a time-consuming tactic that failed more often than it succeeded. To take them quickly by storm, Philip developed siege engines such as catapults, which were capable of breaching walls.

On becoming regent Philip's most urgent task was to take control of Macedon and consolidate it against pressure from Illyria and Paionia in the north. This done he pushed eastward into Thrace, capturing the former Athenian colony of Amphipolis, whose gold mines paid for the expansion of the Macedonian army. By 356 he felt secure enough to declare himself king and continued to expand the boundaries of Macedon. Philip's territorial ambitions were taking shape as the Greek city states were expending the last of their strength in a series of minor wars. Athens bankrupted itself trying to hold the second Athenian league together in the Social War (357–355).

As this ended, a dispute over control of Delphi escalated into the Sacred War, which drew in most of the Greek city states, including Athens, Thebes and Sparta. This presented Philip with a heaven-sent opportunity. In 354 he captured Methone, two years later Thessaly fell, and in 349 the Chalkidike peninsula followed. Its principal city, Olynthos, was so comprehensively destroyed it was never re-occupied.

THE CONQUEST OF GREECE

The steady growth of Macedonian power created an atmosphere of panic and despair in Athens. The orator Demosthenes told the Athenians that "it was unworthy of you and the history of Athens and the achievements of your forefathers to let all the rest of Greece fall into slavery," but in reality it was not in the city's power to prevent it. In 340 Philip laid siege to Byzantion on the Bosporus, threatening Athens' vital grain imports from the Black Sea. Demosthenes convinced the Athenians that Philip was out to destroy their city and they voted to declare war. Demosthenes managed to win over Thebes and the Boeotian league to Athens' side in time to face Philip when he invaded Greece in 338. Philip crushed this alliance in a hard-fought battle at Chaironeia in Theban territory. As the two armies maneuvered, a gap opened in the Greek phalanx and Philip sent in his cavalry, breaking up the Greek army.

Thebes surrendered immediately and was harshly treated. The Athenians at first prepared to defend their city but when Philip offered generous terms they too gave in. Relieved and grateful that their worst fears would not be realized, they granted citizenship to Philip and his son Alexander. Philip now became the savior of Greece. The orator Isocrates urged him "to put an end to the madness and imperialism with which the Greeks have treated one another, reconcile and bring them into concord, and declare war on Persia."

All the mainland Greek states except Sparta, and many of the island states, were enrolled

LEFT *This ivory head, just over 1 inch (3 cm) high, belongs to a portrait statue of Philip II found in his tomb at Vergina (see pages 174–175). Examination of the remains of Philip's skull show that it was a good likeness. Though his reputation is overshadowed by that of his son Alexander, it was Philip who laid the foundations of future Macedonian greatness.*

THE ROYAL TOMBS OF MACEDON

Vergina, in northern Greece, was identified as the site of the Macedonian royal tombs in 1976. The tombs were buried under an enormous earth mound and had not been disturbed by grave robbers. They were found to contain a huge quantity of rich grave goods and were clearly connected with royal power and wealth: such burials had not been seen in Greece since Mycenaean times. Tomb II, the richest of the tombs, contained the cremated remains of a middle-aged man and a young woman surrounded by fine armor, luxurious tableware and rich ornaments including a golden diadem and ivory portraits. The tomb is almost certainly that of Philip II, father of Alexander the Great, who was murdered in 336, and his last wife Cleopatra, who was also murdered shortly after. The cremated remains of Philip's skull have been reconstructed: evidence of a serious injury to the right eye socket confirms a historical account that he was hit in the eye by an arrow at the siege of Methone in 355. Other tombs at Vergina were also richly furnished and decorated. One of them contains some of the finest Classical wall-paintings known from anywhere in the Greek world, including a dramatic scene of Persephone being carried off by Hades, ruler of the dead. The tombs leave no doubt that the kingdom of Macedon was thoroughly hellenized by the 4th century BC.

covering of earth

wooden beams

chamber of carefully carved stones

decorative entrance

antechamber

burial chamber

Therme
Vergina
Larisa
Athens

ABOVE *Part of the treasure from Philip's tomb photographed before it was touched or moved. Philip is known to have been slightly lame, and as one of the bronze greaves (leg guards) is 1 inch (3 cm) shorter than the other, this is further confirmation that the tomb is Philip's. The richly decorated golden quiver was probably for display rather than serious use.*

LEFT *Philip II was buried in a vaulted tomb with two chambers. The entire building was buried under a mound of earth to protect it from tomb robbers. This has helped to preserve the fine painted frieze of a lion hunt on the decorative facade.*

RIGHT *This fine silver jug discovered in Philip's tomb shows the elegance and decorative restraint that was typical of the art of Classical Greece.*

BELOW *The golden casket that held the cremated remains of Philip II measures only 13 by 16 inches (33 by 41 cm) but weighs 22 lbs (10 kg). The star on the lid was the symbol of the royal house of Macedon. Reconstruction of the fragments of skull confirmed historical accounts of injuries Philip received in battle.*

in a federal union, the Corinthian league, which entered into an alliance with Macedon. Philip was elected leader with full powers to command all Greek forces.

On completing his settlement of Greece, Philip did as he had been urged and announced a full-scale war of all Greece against Persia. Persian power appeared to be on the increase. In 343 Egypt's 50-year long rebellion had been decisively crushed and Persian control in Anatolia had been tightened. Nevertheless, Philip had good reason to be confident. Ever since the army of Ten Thousand had returned unscathed from the heart of the Persian empire after defeating Artaxerxes II some 70 years earlier, the Greeks had had nothing but contempt for the Persians. Only their unprofitable internecine wars had prevented them from following up this adventure with a full expedition against the Persian empire. The Persians had also been impressed by this feat of arms and Greek mercenaries were subsequently recruited in considerable numbers into the Persian army.

THE ACCESSION OF ALEXANDER

An advance guard was dispatched to Anatolia but Philip never fulfilled his dreams of invading Persia. In 336 he was assassinated at a wedding feast and his 20-year-old son Alexander succeeded to the throne. It seems unlikely that Alexander was a party to Philip's killing though his mother Olympias, whom Philip had recently divorced, appears to have been implicated in the plot. Alexander was one of the most charismatic figures of the ancient world: well educated – Aristotle was his tutor – imaginative and bold, even reckless, and violent. Supposedly descended from Heracles on his father's side and Achilles on his mother's, Alexander was driven from childhood by the urge to become a great hero and achieve divinity. He was already a promising soldier, having led the elite Companion cavalry at Chaironeia with some distinction. Philip had left Alexander a fine army and he soon showed that he knew how to use it.

Philip's death was welcomed by many in Greece: the Athenians who less than two years before had honored him with citizenship now voted a crown to his assassin. Demosthenes plotted against Alexander with the Macedonian general Attalos. The Thebans called for the disbanding of the Corinthian league. But Alexander gave his enemies no chance to organize themselves. Within weeks he was camped with his army outside the walls of Thebes and the Greeks fell back

THE MARCH OF THE TEN THOUSAND

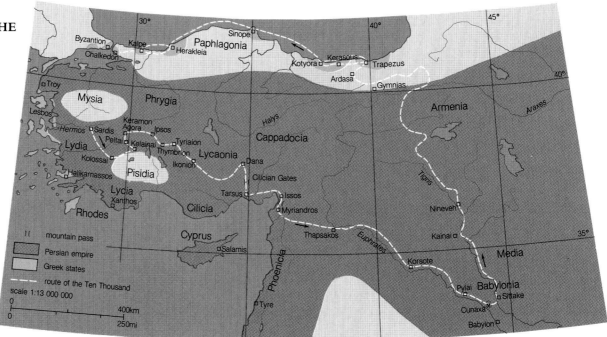

into line. Only Attalos was punished, he and all male members of his family being executed in accordance with the Macedonian law of treason. A successful campaign against the barbarians on the northern frontier of his kingdom soon showed that Alexander's military skills were at least equal to his father's.

While away on this campaign a rumor spread through Greece that Alexander was dead. Thebes openly rebelled and the Athenians sent envoys to ask for Persian help. But only 14 days later Alexander was again camped with an army outside Thebes. He waited three days to see if the citizens would surrender and when they did not he took the city by storm in less than a day. Six thousand Thebans were massacred and 30,000 men, women and children sold into slavery: the city was razed to the ground as a warning to others. The destruction of Thebes cowed the Greeks into submission but it also destroyed whatever slim chance there had been that the Corinthian League would lead the Greeks towards unity. It was now seen only as an instrument of Macedonian control.

ALEXANDER INVADES THE PERSIAN EMPIRE

By 334 Alexander's home base was secure and he was able to complete his father's planned invasion of Persia. A sizeable force of Macedonians was left behind in case the Persians tried to incite further rebellion in Greece. Alexander's army numbered around 37,000 men consisting of 5000 cavalry,

12,000 Macedonian foot soldiers, 12,000 Greek hoplites and 8000 ancillary troops (including javelin soldiers, slingers, surveyors, siege engineers, a secretariat and medical corps). A further 10,000 men from Philip's advance force joined the army in Anatolia. Though not large by Persian standards, this was a considerable force for the Greeks and, unlike the Persian armies, it was of a uniformly high quality. Alexander took only one month's supplies with him, counting on fast movement and quick victories to enable his army to live off the land. He had virtually bankrupted Macedon to raise the expedition and was relying on winning booty to pay his men. At sea, Alexander had a fleet of 160 Greek triremes, the small Macedonian navy and a host of supply ships to support his army.

Alexander's first stop in Anatolia was Troy. Here he performed a series of religious rituals, seeking in some way to associate himself with the Greek heroes of the Trojan war. Four days later Alexander's cavalry scouts made contact with a Persian army on the river Granicus (Turkish, Kocabas). A veteran Persian commander in the area, a Greek mercenary called Memnon of Rhodes, had sensibly advised a scorched earth policy to induce Alexander to withdraw. But the other Persian commanders were determined to fight. The two armies were of about equal strength and the Persians were superior in cavalry. In the ensuing battle, Alexander fought with reckless bravery and was lucky to escape with his life.

ABOVE *When Cyrus the Younger, satrap of Sardis, made a bid for the Persian throne against his brother Artaxerxes II in 401 BC, he recruited an army of 10,000 hoplites to support his Asian troops. At the battle of Cunaxa, the Greeks routed the entire left wing of Artaxerxes' army, suffering not a single casualty themselves. But when Cyrus was killed in a skirmish, the rest of his army melted away, leaving the Greeks to their fate. The Greek commanders were treacherously killed during negotiations with the Persians, but the army of "Ten Thousand", as it became known, elected new leaders and successfully fought its way back the 700 miles (1126 km) from Babylonia to the Greek city of Trapezus on the Black Sea. The march revealed the weakness of the Persian empire to the Greeks, but it survived another 70 years until Alexander the Great's invasion.*

However, the day was his. The Persians had drawn up their army badly and their cavalry and infantry were unable to support one another. Most of the Persian infantry were Greek mercenaries: Alexander refused to accept their offer to surrender and had them slaughtered as traitors.

Alexander's march down the Anatolian coast turned into a triumphal procession as the Greek cities were liberated one after another. The only serious resistance Alexander faced was at Miletos and Halikarnassos (Halicarnassus), where the Persian garrisons were supplied by the Persian fleet. Miletos was taken quickly by storm but Halikarnassos held out for 18 months. Before the year's end, Alexander was master of the western Anatolian satrapies of Phrygia, Lydia and Caria. So long as he was unopposed, Alexander was determined to win a reputation as a lenient conqueror. He therefore allowed no plundering and did not increase demands for tribute above what was already paid to the Persians. As far as possible he left Persian administrative structures intact.

THE CAMPAIGN AGAINST PHOENICIA AND EGYPT

While Persia retained control of the sea, there was always the danger that aid might be sent to Alexander's enemies in Greece. Alexander's own fleet was not strong enough to engage the Persians in battle so he decided to eliminate the Persian fleet by conquering its bases in Phoenicia and Egypt from the land. Accordingly in 333 he moved his army, strengthened by reinforcements from Macedon, from Anatolia to Tarsus in Cilicia. Meanwhile the Persian king Darius III (335–330) had begun to march west from Babylon with a massive army that included a force of about 30,000 Greek mercenaries.

It would have suited Darius best to have fought a battle on the broad Syrian plains where his strength of numbers could be used to some advantage. However, Alexander had now begun to march south along the Syrian coast. Modern historians regard this as a tactical mistake as it enabled Darius to cut his line of retreat by advancing to the coast at Issos on the Gulf of Iskenderun in southern Turkey. Ancient historians, perhaps with the benefit of hindsight, saw it as a masterful maneuver to lure Darius onto the narrow coastal plain where he could not deploy his huge army effectively. Whatever the truth, as soon as Alexander heard that Darius was behind him, he reversed his march and hurried back to confront the

Persian army on the Pinaros river near Issos.

Though Darius was taken by surprise, the outcome of the battle hung in the balance until a headlong charge by Alexander and the Companion cavalry forced the Persian king to flee for his life. Seeing their commander leaving the field, the rest of the Persian army panicked and fled. No reliable figures of Persian casualties exist, but they were certainly enormous – ancient sources say over 100,000. Macedonian losses were 4000 wounded but only 302 killed. Alexander's loot included Darius's baggage train and members of the royal family, including Darius's queen and his mother. To mark his victory, Alexander founded the first of many cities he would name Alexandria after himself (now called Iskenderun). Shocked by the scale of his defeat, Darius attempted to open negotiations but was rebuffed, Alexander demanding his submission before agreeing to talks.

Alexander was now free to resume his march south. He met no serious resistance until he reached the city of Tyre, which refused him entry. Built on an island about half a mile (750 m) offshore, Tyre was stoutly fortified and possessed a strong fleet. Alexander spent eight months building a causeway, which was 200 feet (60 m) wide, out from the mainland before he was able to take the city by storm. Tyrian resistance had been fierce and skillful throughout, and neither Alexander nor his men were in any mood to show mercy. Eight thousand Tyrians were killed and 30,000 sold into slavery. While Alexander was engaged in the siege,

ABOVE *This bronze statuette of Alexander the Great on horseback is a Roman copy of a Greek original. Alexander, one of the most charismatic and violent figures of the ancient world, was driven from an early age to emulate the heroes of Greek legend. Told by the desert oracle at Siwa that his true father was Zeus, by the end of his reign Alexander had probably come to believe that he was himself a god.*

OVERLEAF *Darius III flees in terror in his chariot from Alexander's headlong charge at the decisive battle of Gaugamela in 331 BC. A detail from the Alexander Mosaic found in the House of the Faun at Pompeii, thought to be a mosaic copy made in about 100 BC of a 4th-century painting by Philoxenos of Eretria.*

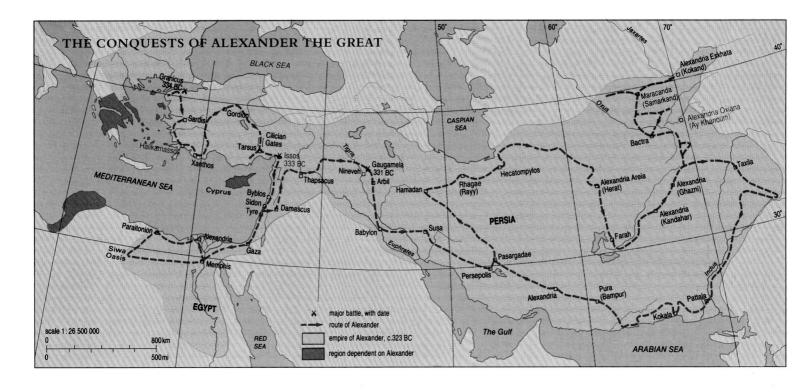

THE CONQUESTS OF ALEXANDER THE GREAT

ABOVE *When, in 343, Arta-xerxes III recovered Egypt after 60 years' independence, he restored the borders of the Persian empire close to what they had been under Darius I, 150 years earlier. Yet when Alexander the Great invaded in 334, the Persian empire collapsed in less than four years. Alexander spent a further six years pacifying the empire's eastern provinces and would have tried to conquer India if his army had not mutinied. Along his route Alexander founded cities that he named after himself or renamed existing cities in his honor.*

Darius offered to cede to him all of his lands west of the Euphrates. His generals thought it a good offer, but Alexander rejected it. Did these lands not belong to him already?

Except at Gaza, which fell after a short siege, Alexander met no further resistance as he continued south to Egypt. The newly appointed satrap of Egypt – his predecessor had been killed at Issos – had few troops at his disposal and surrendered the country to Alexander as soon as he arrived. The Egyptian people, who had rebelled so often against the Persians, welcomed him as a liberator. Alexander sacrificed to the Egyptian gods and at Memphis he was awarded the ancient titles: King of Upper and Lower Egypt, Son of the sun god Ra. From Memphis he sailed down the Nile and, on a spit of land between Lake Mareotis and the Mediterranean, laid out the boundaries of what would be the most successful of the new cities Alexander named after himself (see opposite).

CONQUEROR OF ASIA

The possibility of Persian interference in Greece had now been completely eliminated, leaving Alexander free to march into the heart of the Persian empire in 331 at the head of an army of 40,000 infantry and 7000 cavalry. Against him, Darius mustered a force of around 40,000 cavalry and 16,000 heavy infantry, supported by war elephants and chariots equipped with scythes. The armies met in the fall on a broad plain at Gaugamela in Assyria. At last Darius had a battlefield

suited to his large cavalry forces but once again Alexander completely outmaneuvered him. When a gap in the Persian line opened up, Alexander launched a direct assault on Darius's position, forcing him to flee the battlefield. Just as at Issos, the Persian army broke up in panic. Gaugamela proved to be the decisive battle: Darius was completely demoralized and Persian resistance now began to crumble. Alexander swiftly followed up his victory by capturing Babylon and the Persian treasury at Susa.

The following year Alexander destroyed the last sizeable Persian army at the Persian Gates pass in the Zagros mountains and swept on to capture the Persian capital at Persepolis. Alexander gave his men full license to loot the rich palaces, after which the city was put to the torch. Alexander later said he regretted this act of wanton destruction. Darius fled north and then east with Alexander in hot pursuit. When Alexander finally caught up with him, Darius was already dying of wounds inflicted by his despairing officials.

With Darius dead, Alexander's grip on his army began to weaken. His men considered the war to be over and asked to be sent home to enjoy the fruits of their success. Alexander persuaded them to fight on and complete the conquest of the Persian empire, but instead of sending back to Macedon for reinforcements he increasingly relied on local mercenaries. Alexander wanted to be accepted freely by the Persians as their king but by adopting Persian customs, taking a Persian bride and employing Persian personnel, he alienated many of his Macedonian commanders. He faced, or imagined he faced, plots against his life and had two of his finest commanders, Philotas and his father Parmenion, executed for treason.

It took Alexander three more years of tough campaigning in Sogdiana and Bactria (roughly equivalent to Bukhara, now part of Uzbekistan, and Afghanistan) to complete his conquest of the Persian empire. In 327 he crossed the river Indus into the Punjab and won his last major battle, against the kingdom of Poros at the river Hydaspes (Jhelum), a year later. Alexander wanted to press on into India and invade the Ganges plain but his soldiers had finally had enough and refused to go on. Instead Alexander marched down the Indus to the sea and turned west. After a grueling march through the

BELOW This coin of Alexander the Great shows him as Heracles: a portrait of Zeus appears on the reverse. Alexander's conquests netted a vast fortune in gold and silver, much of which he converted into coinage. The sudden influx of wealth into Greece caused inflation and quickly led to the rise of a class of new rich and the growth of social divisions.

deserts of southern Iran, he reached Babylon in 324 where, an overweight alcoholic aged 33, he died the following year.

When he was in Egypt in 333, Alexander had visited the oracle of Zeus Ammon at Siwa in the Libyan desert. The oracle told him that his true father was Zeus, confirming Alexander's belief, and that of many of his contemporaries, that his incredible achievements showed him to be no ordinary mortal. Though it distanced him from his commanders, Alexander from then on increasingly acted as if he were a demigod. Later in his reign he closely associated himself with the symbols of divinity. On coins he was shown holding the thunderbolt of Zeus and at feasts he appeared wearing the purple robes and ram's horns of Zeus Ammon. He ordered many Greek cities, including Athens, to accord him divine honors – an example that was lost neither on his Hellenistic successors nor, more than three centuries later, on the

ALEXANDRIA

Alexandria, founded by Alexander the Great in 332 BC, was the most enduring of the 13 or more cities that bore his name. Under the Ptolemies, the Hellenistic rulers of Egypt, it was the largest Greek-speaking city in the world, excelling even Athens as a cultural center. Its most famous monument was the Pharos, the biggest lighthouse in the ancient world and one of the Seven Wonders of the World. Built in 280 BC, it stood 400 feet (122 m) tall but was destroyed by an earthquake in the 14th century AD. Divers have discovered sculptures and fallen blocks from the Pharos in Alexandria's harbor. The city was also famed for its libraries, the Museum and the Serapeum (the temple of the Greco-Egyptian god Serapis), which were the largest in the world. Little remains to be seen of ancient Alexandria; it is buried beneath the thriving modern city. Recent diving expeditions, aided by satellite technology, have revealed the foundations of the Ptolemies' royal palaces submerged within the eastern harbor.

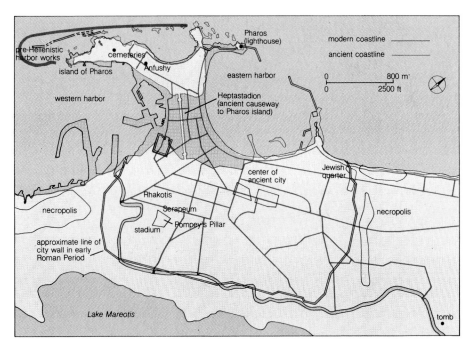

ABOVE The linking of the island of Pharos to the mainland with a causeway 1372 yards (1500 m) long created two of the finest harbors in the eastern Mediterranean, ensuring Alexandria's lasting commercial success.

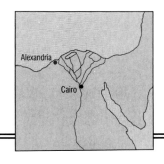

THE MIGRATIONS OF THE CELTS

RIGHT *Celts (Keltoi) was a general term used by the Greeks to describe the barbarian peoples to their north; the Romans described the same people as Gauls. Between the 6th and the 3rd centuries BC the Celts migrated from their homeland in central Europe into much of Europe. Rome was sacked in 390, Alexander the Great fought them on the Danube and in 279 they attacked Delphi. From the 3rd century onward, the Celts became increasingly squeezed between the expanding Roman empire and the westward migrations of the Germans. By the 2nd century AD, the only independent Celtic peoples were to be found in Ireland and the far north of Britain.*

BELOW *"The Dying Gaul," a Roman copy in marble of a bronze original erected by Attalos I of Pergamon to celebrate his victories over the Celtic Galatians in the mid 3rd century BC. Dramatic free-standing sculptures were typical of the Hellenistic age.*

Roman emperors. Alexander's last months were marked by a drift into arbitrary tyranny and madness amidst signs of increasing disaffection among his Macedonian subjects. At the time of his death he was preparing to conquer all of Arabia and had plans for a campaign in the western Mediterranean. There truly were no limits to the ambitions of this restless genius.

A general of exceptional ability, Alexander excelled not only on the conventional battlefield but also in irregular warfare. He was able to pacify the mountainous areas of Afghanistan which, in modern times, have proved stumbling blocks both to the armies of the British empire and the Soviet Union. But Alexander's achievements were not based on his military acumen alone. As with Cyrus the Great before him (who achieved almost as much in a longer time but at considerably less cost in human life), Alexander was aided by the long tradition of imperial rule in the Near East which had weakened local identities and loyalties.

The provinces of the Persian empire were used to foreign rule and, as Alexander respected local customs and did not make unreasonable demands for tribute, a change from Persian to Macedonian overlordship was for most of them a matter of indifference. Alexander's empire broke up within a few years of his death but this was for dynastic reasons. His immediate successors did not have to face any popular rebellions against their rule.

Alexander founded cities of Greek and Macedonian colonists throughout his empire and as the spate of colonization continued his successors founded or hellenized dozens more. These widely scattered cities became agents for an enormous expansion of Greek cultural influence: Greek became the common language of exchange from the Mediterranean to the Indus river. In the vast melting pot Alexander had created, aspects of Greek civilization were borrowed and adapted by Egyptian, Persian and other eastern cultures to create a new, Hellenistic civilization.

THE WARS OF THE DIADOCHI

Macedon suffered a great loss of loss of manpower through Alexander's conquests: most of the men who marched away as soldiers stayed on in the east as settlers. Alexander left as heirs a posthumous son and a mentally retarded brother, neither of whom was capable of ruling in his own right. The regent Perdiccas managed to keep the central administration of the empire going for a while, but he was murdered in 321. His successor Antipater (d. 319), governor of Macedon, could not prevent power being seized by the generals Alexander had left in charge of the provinces. A series of conflicts known as the wars of the Diadochi (successors) followed, and by 304 five separate kingdoms had arisen under Macedonian dynasties. Antipater's son Kassandros (Cassander), murdered both Alexander's brother and son to take control of Macedon, Lysimachos (Lysimachus) seized power in Thrace, Antigonos (Antigonus) in Anatolia, Seleukos (Seleucus) in Mesopotamia and the east, and Ptolemy in Egypt.

Of the five, only Antigonos hoped to recreate Alexander's empire. This united the other Diadochi against him. He was killed at Ipsos in Phrygia in 301, fighting the combined armies of Seleukos, Lysimachos and Kassandros, and his kingdom was divided up among the victors. Lysimachos got Anatolia; Seleukos, Syria and Cilicia; Ptolemy, who had been campaigning separately, Palestine and Cyprus. The battle of Ipsos did not bring an end to the struggles of the Diadochi. But it did ensure that the break up of Alexander's empire was now permanent.

During the chaos that followed his death, Alexander's empire had quickly started to fray at the edges. His conquest had been rapid and the rulers of the Persian satrapies of Bithynia, Paphlagonia, Cappadocia, Armenia and Atropatene had been allowed to retain their provinces after making only token submission. Alexander's early death prevented these provinces from being brought into full submission and during the wars of the Diadochi they became fully independent kingdoms. The Indus valley was also lost soon after Alexander's death. Preoccupied with the war against Antigonos, Seleukos ceded the Indian provinces to Chandragupta Maurya in 304 in return for a herd of 500 war elephants. Antigonos used them to good effect at the battle of Ipsos, and elephants subsequently became an important component of Hellenistic armies.

Greece now accounted for only a small part of the Hellenistic world. The cities of the Corinthian league rebelled against Macedonian control in 323, but were swiftly brought back into line. In Athens, Demosthenes committed suicide, and democracy was restricted to property-owning citizens. In 307 the Greeks attempted to defect to Antigonos, but after his defeat at Ipsos they were once again subjected to Macedonian control.

ABOVE (Top) *One of the five Diadochi, Ptolemy I (322–282) had risen through the ranks of Alexander's army to become a troop commander. On Alexander's death he became satrap of Egypt, which he turned into an independent kingdom. Like Alexander, Ptolemy was portrayed on his coins with divine attributes.* (Bottom) *Attalos I (241–197) made himself king of Pergamon, in Anatolia, after defeating the Celts of Galatia. Under the dynasty he founded Pergamon flourished as a wealthy imperial power. It gave rise to a new school of sculpture* (see opposite) *and its library was second only to that of Alexandria.*

THE CELTIC INVASIONS

The struggles of the Diadochi continued for another twenty years after the battle of Ipsos. When Kassandros died in 298 the Macedonian kingdom fell to Antigonos' son Demetrios (Demetrius) and was then annexed by Lysimachos, ruler of Thrace, in 285. Lysimachos himself was killed in battle against Seleukos at Korupedion in Anatolia (281). For a moment it looked as if Seleukos would reunite the greater part of Alexander's empire. But he was assassinated soon after by his unscrupulous protegé Ptolemy Keraunos, who proceeded to make himself king of Macedon and Thrace. In 279 Ptolemy's kingdom was invaded by the *Galatai*, Celtic barbarians from central Europe, who met and defeated the better-equipped Macedonian army in battle – the Celts' savage appearance and reckless courage seem to have won them the day. Ptolemy himself was killed.

A large Celtic force led by Brennus and Achichorius swept on through the Greek mainland. The Celts plundered widely in the countryside but, lacking arms and discipline, avoided fortified towns. They took the same route as the Persians two centuries earlier and outflanked a large army sent by an alliance of Greek cities to oppose them at Thermopylai before advancing on Delphi. Accounts are unclear whether the sanctuary was taken and looted before the constant harassment of the Greeks and unseasonably bad weather caused the Celts to retreat to Thrace. There the survivors founded a kingdom with its capital at Tulis which survived until 213. The routing of the Celts was the first military success the Greeks had enjoyed for almost a century and it did much for their self-confidence. Comparisons with the defeat of Xerxes rather exaggerated the threat but were pardonable under the circumstances.

Three Celtic tribes also crossed into Anatolia where they established themselves in the region that became known after them as Galatia. For 50 years they plundered the surrounding countryside until they were decisively beaten by Attalos of Pergamon in 230. Though Galatia itself quickly sank into obscurity, the Celtic language survived there until the 4th century AD.

THE ACHAEAN AND AETOLIAN LEAGUES

The Celtic invasions weakened Macedonian control, allowing the Greek cities to regain their independence. Two federal leagues of city states emerged as important political players, though significantly neither of them was created by a major city state of the Classical period. The Achaean league, founded in 280, was made up of the cities of Achaea (northern Peloponnese) and most other Peloponnesian states. Only Sparta, which remained independent, and Corinth, under Macedonian control, stayed outside. Member cities had voting rights proportionate to their populations and the league was led by two generals, elected annually. The Aetolian league, consisting of cities in central Greece at the western end of the Gulf of Corinth, had formed in the 4th century and played a major role in defeating the Celtic invasions. Both leagues conferred equal citizenship rights on all members.

In 276 Antigonos Gonatos became king of Macedon with the support of Antiochos I, Seleukos' successor in Mesopotamia and the east. He restored the kingdom's strength and sought to reestablish its dominance in Greece, if only to prevent it being taken over by any other power. Athens and Sparta had established close ties with Ptolemy II in Egypt, who sent naval and diplomatic support when Antigonos invaded Attica in 266 following an Athenian rebellion. However, a blockade of the city brought about Athens' submission in 261, restoring Macedonian supremacy in Greece. Antigonos did not seek to control the cities directly but ruled through tyrants who were dependent on him for support. The fall of the Macedonian stronghold of Corinth to the Achaean leader Aratos in 243 was followed by the overthrow of Antigonos' tyrants throughout the Peloponnese. In 239 the Achaeans allied with the Aetolian league and the Macedonian position in central Greece collapsed as well. By the reign of Antigonos Doson (229–221) Macedonian power looked all but finished. However, the victories of Kleomenes III of Sparta over the Achaeans in 227 brought about a remarkable reversal of fortune.

After its defeat by Thebes in the 4th century BC, Sparta had become a minor power, and the military system that had produced Sparta's near invincible hoplites was abandoned. Attempts by king Agis IV (244–241) to restore it and enroll new citizens failed because the rich would not agree to a cancellation of debts, the redistribution of land, and a return to traditional Spartan austerity. However, Agis' reforms were finally enacted by Kleomenes (r. 235–222). The new army he raised soon brought the Achaean league to the edge of collapse, causing Aratos to swallow his pride and enter into an alliance with his former

THE SUCCESSOR KINGDOMS

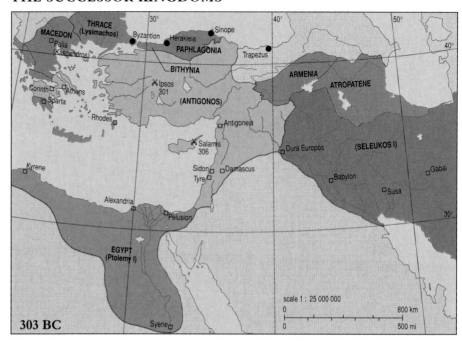

303 BC

scale 1 : 25 000 000

enemy, Antigonos Doson. A Macedonian victory over Kleomenes at Sellasia (222) laid the foundation for a new power structure in Greece – the Symmachy, a Hellenic league that embraced most of Greece except Aetolia. Though Antigonos was its leader, the Symmachy had no treasury. Its decisions had to be ratified by all its members. It was therefore a compromise between the Macedonian aim of control and the Greek ideal of liberty.

THE FALL OF MACEDON

In 220 the Romans, by now a rising power, seized control of a territory on the coast of Illyria. Essentially a defensive move to suppress piracy, it was resented by Philip V (221–179) of Macedon who saw this eastward expansion of Roman influence as a threat to Macedonian dominance in Greece. Rome was soon at war with Carthage for control of the western Mediterranean (the second Punic war 218–201) and in 215 Philip took the obvious move of allying with Carthage. By 205 it was clear that he had backed a loser and he made peace with Rome, but only at the cost of alienating the Achaeans who shared his fear of Roman expansion. Worse, the Romans had not forgiven Philip for his unprovoked aggression, and were merely biding their time until a suitable opportunity arose for revenge.

In 203 Philip, hoping to strengthen his position in the Aegean, formed an alliance with Antiochos III, ruler of the Seleukid empire in Syria and Mesopotamia, against Ptolemaic Egypt. Recognizing a potential threat to their independence, Pergamon and Rhodes sought, and won,

ABOVE *Alexander's failure to establish a dynasty proved fatal to the empire he had created. After his death generals in his army seized power in the provinces and the empire broke up into independent warring states. Only Antigonos aspired to maintain the unity of Alexander's empire but after his defeat at Ipsos in 301 his kingdom was divided between the other Diadochi.*

RIGHT *(Top) By 240 Lysimachos' Thracian kingdom had been overrun by Celtic invaders, while Macedon had fallen under the control of descendants of Antigonos. (Bottom) The balance of power was changed when Rome became involved in Greek affairs after the second Punic war. Roman victories at Kynoskephalai (197) and Magnesia (190) broke Macedonian dominance in Greece and drove the Seleukids out of Anatolia.*

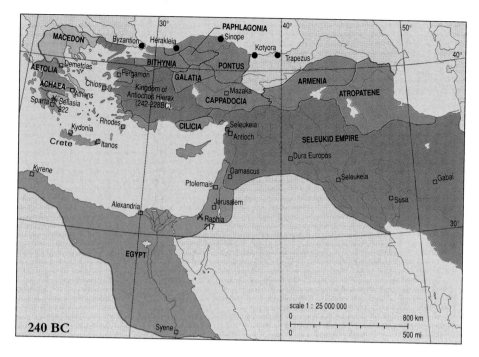

240 BC

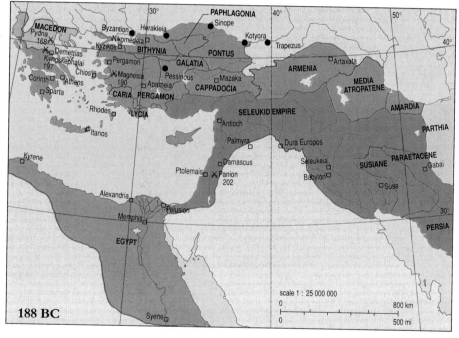

188 BC

Seleukid territory

Ptolemaic territory

Antigonid territory

Roman empire

Parthian empire

independent state

● city-state

✕ site of major battle

the Romans intervened. The Macedonian army was destroyed at the battle of Pydna (168). Perseus died in a Roman jail and Macedon was broken up into four separate republics. An attempt to restore the monarchy in 148 led to its formal annexation by Rome as the province of Macedonia. By this time the Romans had wearied of the constant disputes of the Greek city states. When Roman envoys were attacked at Corinth in 146, they decided to make an end of it once and for all. Corinth was utterly destroyed and its population massacred or sold into slavery. Democracy was abolished and local government by property qualification was established throughout Greece. The leagues of cities were disbanded. Taxes were imposed and Greeks were forbidden to acquire property outside Greece. It would be 2000 years before Greece was again independent.

THE SELEUKID KINGDOM

Seleukos' kingdom in Mesopotamia and the east emerged from the Diadochian wars as the largest of the Hellenistic successor states, but its very size and diversity made it a difficult inheritance for his heirs. The Seleukids had more than their fair share of succession disputes – all but one died by violence – while frequent wars with Ptolemaic Egypt sapped the kingdom's strength. By the mid 3rd century it had begun a long slow decline.

The first loss was the city of Pergamon in Anatolia. Its governor Eumenes rebelled with help from Ptolemaic Egypt and defeated, and probably killed, Seleukos' son Antiochos I in battle at Sardis (261). The final breach came when Eumenes' adopted son Attalos I (r. 241–197) declared himself king following a major victory over the Galatians. Neighboring Pontus and Cappadocia also became independent under hellenized native dynasties in the middle of the century. At the same time the Ptolemies won control of most of the Anatolian coastline, almost depriving the Seleukids of direct access to the Mediterranean. Another serious loss occurred in 239 when the Greeks of the remote central Asian province of Bactria rebelled and founded an independent kingdom under Diodotos. In 238 Arsaces I (c. 247–c. 211), the vassal ruler of Parthia (see pages 232–233), took encouragement from the success of the Bactrians and declared his independence too.

Under Antiochos III (223–187) the Seleukid kingdom began a spectacular recovery. His succession was at first undisputed, but after suffering a defeat by the Ptolemies at Raphia in 217 he

Roman protection. At the battle of Kynoskephalai (197) the Roman legion showed itself superior to the phalanx. Macedon was forced to become an ally of Rome, and the Greek cities were freed under Roman protection. The following year the Romans withdrew all their troops from Greece.

But things were not to prove that simple. The Romans found that they were continuously forced to settle quarrel after quarrel between the city states, for example in a war between Sparta and Achaea in 195. Philip's son Perseus (r. 181–168) made a last attempt to restore Macedonian power in Greece but was implicated in an attempt to assassinate Eumenes II of Pergamon. Once again

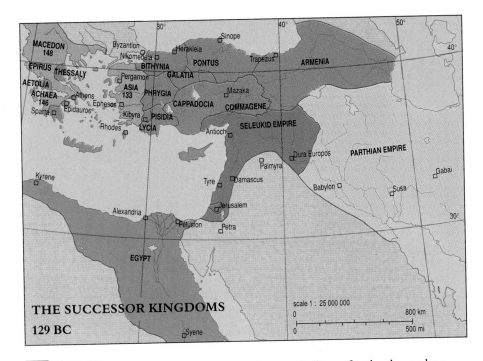

THE SUCCESSOR KINGDOMS
129 BC

scale 1 : 25 000 000

0 ——— 800 km
0 ——— 500 mi

■ Seleukid territory
■ Ptolemaic territory
■ Roman empire
■ Parthian empire
■ independent state

ABOVE *After defeating Macedon at Kynoskephalai (197), the Romans became the arbiters of Greece. The rivalries of the city states led to minor wars and the Macedonians would not accept subordinate status: the Romans imposed direct rule in 146. The Seleukid kingdom went into decline, losing its eastern provinces to the Parthians.*

ABOVE *Antiochos III "the Great" temporarily reversed the slow decline of the Seleukid kingdom with successful campaigns against the Parthians, Bactrians and Ptolemaic Egypt. Court flatterers compared him to Alexander.*

had to put down a challenge for the throne by a rebel general. By 212, however, he was secure enough to embark on a seven-year campaign in the east. Armenia was conquered and Parthia and Bactria contained, though at the price of recognizing their independence. A tribute of war elephants was exacted from the Indus valley. Court flatterers began to compare Antiochos to Alexander and bestowed on him the epithet "the Great." In 204, the 5-year-old Ptolemy V (r. 204–180) came to the Egyptian throne, giving Antiochos a golden opportunity to seize control of Palestine and the Ptolemaic possessions in Anatolia.

This was the peak of Antiochos' success. In 196, as the Romans were withdrawing from Greece, he crossed into Europe and annexed the coast of Thrace. To Antiochos this was a legitimate part of the Seleukid inheritance, but the Romans saw it as a bridgehead for further conquests in Europe. Neither side was eager for war and a stand-off ensued, during which each side proclaiming itself the protector of Greek liberty. However, the Seleukids' readiness to dilute their Macedonian blood by intermarrying with their Asian subjects meant that Antiochos seemed no more fitted for this role than the Romans.

The stalemate was ended in 192 when the Aetolians rashly tried to overthrow the settlement made in 197/196 by seizing the Thessalian city of Demetrias. Antiochos, somewhat half-heartedly, led a small army to support them but was easily defeated by the Romans at Thermopylai. The Romans followed up their success by invading, with their Greek and Pergamene allies, the

Seleukid empire in Anatolia, while Roman, Rhodian and Pergamene warships hunted down and destroyed Antiochos' fleet in the Aegean.

On a muddy battlefield at Magnesia, unable to put his armored cavalry, scythed chariots and elephants to effective use, Antiochos was crushingly defeated by the allied forces. He immediately sued for peace. The terms offered by the Romans were harsh. Antiochos was to surrender all of his territory in Anatolia west of the Taurus mountains along with his fleet, his elephants and a large sum of money and grain. The Romans kept no territory for themselves but shared it between their allies Pergamon and Rhodes. The provinces of Armenia and Atropatene quickly regained their independence and Antiochos himself was killed three years later while trying to recoup some of his financial losses by seizing a temple treasury.

Despite the disastrous end to Antiochos III's reign the Seleukid kingdom remained a powerful state: his son Antiochos IV Epiphanes (r. 175–163) was able to raise 25,000 soldiers of Greek and Macedonian descent alone. He capitalized on the weakness of the Ptolemies by invading Egypt in 170 and within two years had declared himself king. However, when an envoy arrived from Rome and demanded his withdrawal, Epiphanes immediately did so – he had spent time as a hostage in Rome and knew the Romans well enough not to trifle with them. He refounded Jerusalem as a Hellenistic city, provoking a Jewish revolt led by Judas Maccabaeus in 166 which led eventually to the creation of an independent Judaean kingdom in 142–141.

By this time the Seleukid kingdom had been reduced to little more than Syria. In mid century the Parthians under Mithradates I (170–138) conquered Persia and in 141 overran Mesopotamia, but they were prevented from following up their successes when Sakan nomads invaded their eastern provinces in the 130s. The main beneficiary of the collapse of Seleukid power was Armenia. Its king Tigranes I (c. 90–c. 55) conquered Syria in 83, only to be expelled in 66 by the Romans who established their frontier on the Euphrates facing the Parthians.

PTOLEMAIC EGYPT

Of Alexander's immediate successors only Ptolemy succeeded in dying in bed. His kingdom of Egypt enjoyed greater dynastic stability in its early days and endured longer than any of the other independent states of the Diadochi. This

EGYPT UNDER THE PTOLEMIES

RIGHT *Egypt under the Ptolemies was the most successful and long-lived of the Hellenistic kingdoms. In the 3rd century it dominated the eastern Mediterranean. The Ptolemies pursued traditional Egyptian foreign policies of expansion in Palestine and in Nubia, where they established a condominium, or joint rule, with the Egyptianized African kingdom of Meroë. Ptolemaic Egypt declined in the 2nd century but survived under Roman protection until 30 BC.*

BELOW *Granite statues of Ptolemy II Philadelphos (r. 285–246) and his queen Arsinoe. The style is wholly Egyptian: in order to appease their resentful Egyptian subjects the Ptolemies adopted the trappings and duties of traditional Egyptian kingship.*

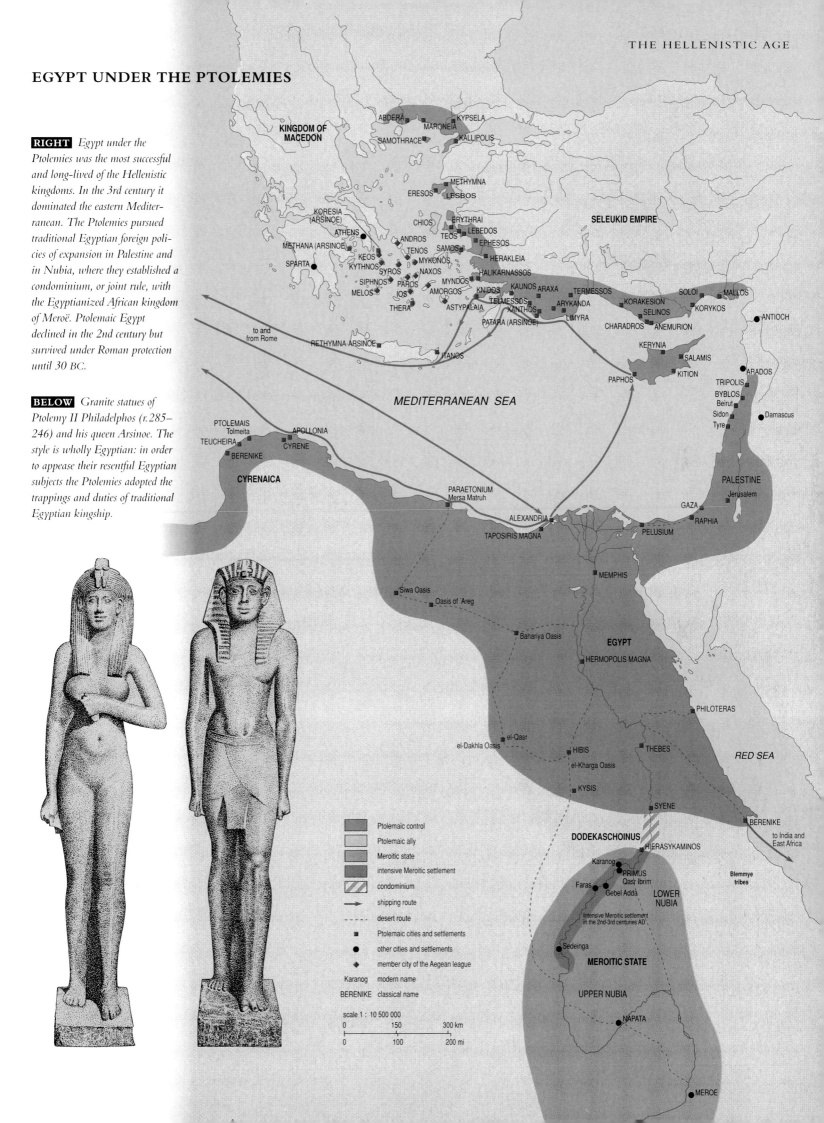

Key:
- Ptolemaic control
- Ptolemaic ally
- Meroitic state
- intensive Meroitic settlement
- condominium
- → shipping route
- --- desert route
- ■ Ptolemaic cities and settlements
- ● other cities and settlements
- ◆ member city of the Aegean league
- Karanog modern name
- BERENIKE classical name

scale 1 : 10 500 000
0 — 150 — 300 km
0 — 100 — 200 mi

was despite the fact that Egypt had a recent tradition of independence, having successfully thrown off Persian rule from 404 to 343, and its population was resentful of the Greeks and Macedonians who dominated the government and army under the Ptolemaic dynasty.

To placate the native Egyptians the Ptolemies adopted many of the trappings of the pharaohs and became patrons of the traditional religious cults. They also adopted the traditional Egyptian foreign policy of expanding into Palestine and Nubia. In an attempt to provide some common ground between the Egyptian and Greek populations the Ptolemies promoted the cult of Serapis, a deliberately invented god whose attributes appealed to both sections of the population. By the 2nd century BC some Egyptians had become hellenized while some Egyptian cults, such as that of the goddess Isis, found favor with Greeks. Egyptians began to play an important role in the army, though using Greek weapons and tactics. However, there was no real assimilation of the populations. There was also an important and influential Jewish community.

Alexandria, the capital of the Ptolemies (see page 181) became the largest and richest Greek city in the world. Rivaling Athens as a cultural center, it became supremely important in the study of the sciences. Ships from overseas were even searched for books to add to the city's vast libraries. The Ptolemaic kingdom was the major naval power of the eastern Mediterranean for most of the 3rd century and its fleets dominated the Aegean. The trireme was superseded by new generations of warships with five, six, seven and more banks of oars: the largest recorded was 423 feet (129 m) long, and carried 4000 oarsmen, 400 other crew and 2850 marines on deck.

The first signs of decline began to show during the reign of Ptolemy IV Philopater (r. 221–205). Philopater is credited with several dynastic murders, including that of his mother, and he outraged Greek opinion by marrying his sister (a custom that was regularly practiced by the later Ptolemies). Though he enjoyed some military success against Antiochos III, Philopater's reign was marked by rebellions in Upper Egypt and by

runaway inflation. The succession of his five-year old son Ptolemy V in 205 left the Seleukids under Antiochos III a free hand in Palestine.

Ptolemy V was succeeded by another child, his son Ptolemy VI Philometor (180–145). His aunt Cleopatra proved to be an efficient regent but her death in 176 left power in the hands of bureaucrats whose ambitions outstripped their abilities. They foolishly provoked a war with Antiochos IV and it was only the intervention of the Romans in 168 that saved Egypt for the Ptolemies. The remainder of Philometor's reign was marked by dynastic plotting and a continuing reliance on Roman support. The Ptolemaic dynasty continued under Roman protection until 30 BC when Egypt became a Roman province after the death of Cleopatra VII. Her affairs with Julius Caesar and Antony have made her the most famous ruler of the Ptolemaic dynasty. Ironically, she was the first of her line who was able to speak Egyptian.

BACTRIA

The most far-flung of the Hellenistic kingdoms was Bactria, deep in central Asia. The Bactrian Greeks prospered from their control of the major trans-Asian trade routes but their history is poorly recorded. Their coins, among the finest in the Hellenistic world, have given us the names of about 40 kings of whom almost nothing is known. However, finds from Ay Khanoum, the only Greek city in central Asia that has so far been excavated (see opposite), show that, despite their isolation, the Bactrian Greeks remained in contact with the mainstream of Greek culture.

It was an expansionist kingdom. By the early 2nd century control of the Indus valley had been won back from the weak descendants of Chandragupta Maurya and in the 180s Bactrian Greek rulers campaigned as far east as the Mauryan capital at Pataliputra on the lower Ganges, gaining temporary control of much of northern India. One of these rulers, Menander (c. 150 BC), engaged the Buddhist monk Nagasena in a famous dialog which is recorded in an important Buddhist text, the *Milindapanho*. Menander may even have been a Buddhist himself. His capital at Taxila in the Punjab was a remarkable cultural melting pot where artists and sculptors developed a fusion of Greek and Asian styles that influenced Buddhist art throughout Asia.

Bactria increasingly faced hostile attacks from the steppe nomads of Central Asia. In about 135 most of the kingdom was overrun by the Yue Qi

AY KHANOUM

LEFT *This silver disk shows the Anatolian goddess Cybele in completely hellenized form with a priest at a Persian-style fire altar – an example of cultural fusion.*

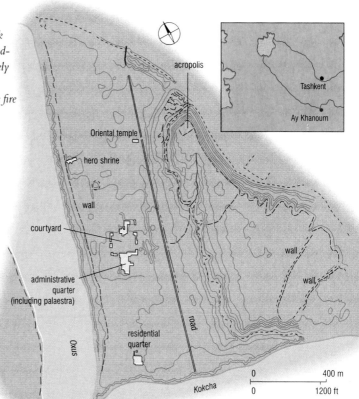

A y Khanoum, on the borders of Tajikistan and Afghanistan, is one of the most remote outposts of Greek civilization. It was probably originally called Alexandria Oxiana and was a typical Hellenistic city. Its monuments included a theater, library, extravagantly columned palace, fortified acropolis and city walls. Irrigated alluvial plains to the north supplied the city's food. Despite its remoteness, Ay Khanoum was not isolated from the cultural mainstream. It was visited by the philosopher Klearchos, one of Aristotle's pupils, and it contained a column inscribed with 140 moral maxims copied from a pillar at Delphi over 3000 miles (4828 km) away. The city was destroyed by nomads in the 1st century BC.

ABOVE *The site chosen for Ay Khanoum was at an easily defended position on the banks of an unfordable stretch of the Oxus (Amudar'ya) river. It was rediscovered and excavated in the 1960s.*

BELOW *The foot of a colossal male statue from the temple. The sandals bear the thunderbolt symbol, indicating that it was of Zeus himself or a ruler. It may be evidence of a religious cult of the ruler at Ay Khanoum.*

ABOVE *Among the buildings at Ay Khanoum were a palaestra, an enclosed sports training ground (seen here), and an equally fine gymnasium, or center for physical and* *intellectual education and socializing. These were the two most important social institutions of a Hellenistic city. The palaestra has yielded a fine marble head of the aging Heracles.*

nomads but some independent Greek principalities survived in the upper Indus valley. By the time they were finally extinguished, soon after the beginning of the Christian era, they were the last independent Hellenistic states anywhere in the ancient world.

HELLENISTIC CIVILIZATION

The collapse of the independent Hellenistic kingdoms did not bring an end to the rich civilization of the Hellenistic world, which continued to flourish and grow in the Roman empire. Similarly, the early art and architecture of the Parthian empire show a strong Hellenistic influence.

The Hellenistic world was dominated by monarchies. It is unlikely that any other form of government could have held together the huge ethnically diverse states created in the wake of Alexander's conquests. Compared to the city governments of Classical Greece, the Hellenistic kings had vast resources at their disposal and their courts became centers where they lavishly displayed their wealth with costly entertainments and magnificent art and architecture. The restraint that had characterized Classical art and architecture gave way to flamboyance, extravagance, complexity and size. For example, the Altar of Zeus at Pergamon (c.180) had a dramatic sculptural facade of gods battling giants. It was 328 feet (100 m) long and is virtually baroque in its decorative richness. Among the most striking monuments of the Hellenistic style are the richly carved temples and tombs of Petra, the ancient capital of the Arab kingdom of Nabataea (c.312–106 AD) in modern-day Jordan, for centuries the center of an important caravan trade. The wealth of the east, released by Alexander's conquests, produced a class of new rich who did not share the Classical distaste for ostentatious display but decorated their houses with murals, mosaics, sculptures and luxury objects of bronze and silver.

The sciences reached a level of sophistication in the Hellenistic world that was not equalled again until the Renaissance. The mathematician Euclid (c.300) wrote a handbook of geometry that remained the standard text into the modern era. Archimedes (287–212) was the first to calculate the true value of "pi" and pioneered the study of hydrostatics. In the 3rd century the astronomer Eratosthenes measured the circumference of the Earth to an accuracy within 186 miles (300 km) of the correct figure. Around 275 Aristarchos of Samos proposed that the Earth went around the

LEFT *Ptolemaic Egypt as seen through Roman eyes. This detail of the Nile mosaic from the sanctuary of Fortune at Praeneste in Italy (c. 80 BC) shows a warship and merchantman with scenes of everyday life and religious ritual. Its outward splendor, wealth and exotic culture belied the real weakness of the Ptolemaic kingdom, which by this time was a Roman protectorate.*

RIGHT *(Top) By the early 1st century BC the Seleukid kingdom had been reduced to no more than Syria. The last king of Pergamon (d. 133) had willed his kingdom to the Roman state, giving Rome a foothold in Asia. (Bottom) The Armenians who invaded Syria in 83, bringing about the final collapse of the Seleukid kingdom, were expelled by the Romans in 66. Rome extended its Asian frontier to the Euphrates, and by 63 BC, of the original kingdoms founded by the Diadochi, only Egypt was still independent.*

THE SUCCESSOR KINGDOMS

- Seleukid territory
- Ptolemaic territory
- Roman empire
- Parthian empire
- independent state

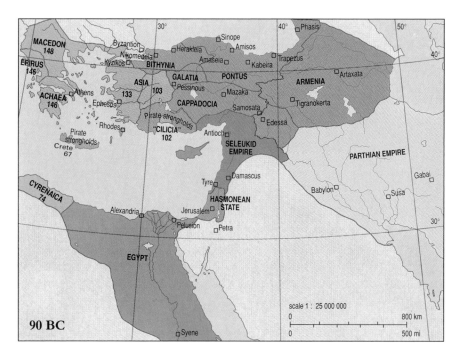

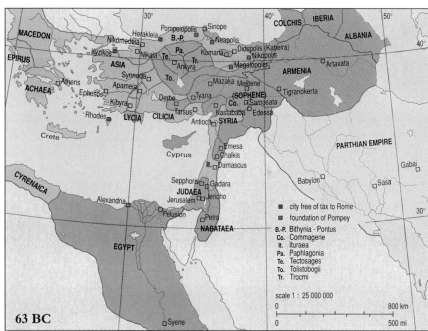

Sun. Since this did not seem to agree with observations of the motions of the heavens by the naked eye, astronomers continued to believe in an Earth-centered universe. As refined by Apollonios of Perge (c. 200 BC) and the Alexandrian astronomer Ptolemy (c. AD 127–145), this system held the field until the 17th century AD.

The Hellenistic age was a time of moral and spiritual uncertainty. Literal belief in the Olympian gods declined as people began to seek a more intimate religious experience. The mystery cults of Demeter and Dionysos were joined by new cults from overseas such as those of the mother-goddesses Cybele from Anatolia and Isis from Egypt.

These uncertainties were also reflected in philosophy. The Cynics rejected material possessions and social conventions: peace of mind did not lie in the pursuit of a successful public life. The Epicureans taught that the good life lay in moderate hedonism, friendship and rational thinking. The pantheistic creed of the Stoics held that humans shared in the divine intelligence that orders the universe and taught that both pleasure and pain should be regarded with equanimity, as both were inevitable. Stoicism became especially popular in Rome and influenced early Christianity. The most enduring work of Stoic philosophy is the *Meditations* of the Roman emperor Marcus Aurelius.

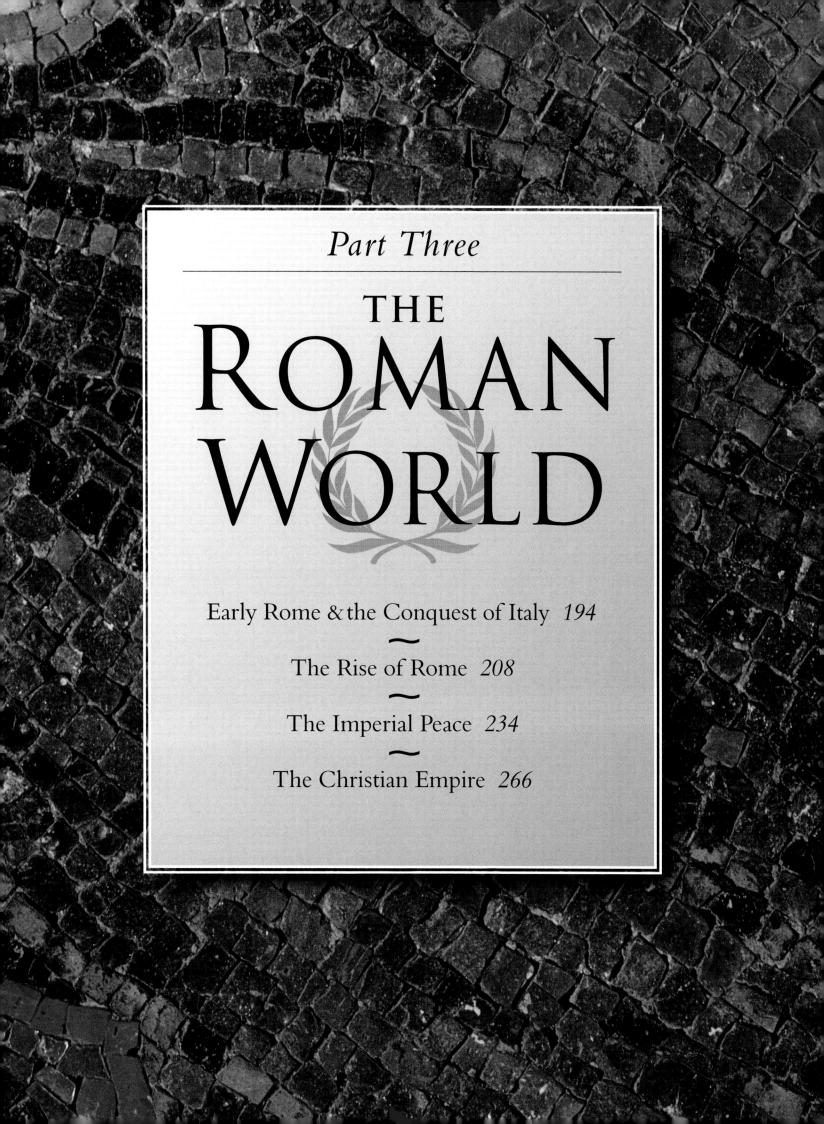

Part Three

THE ROMAN WORLD

Early Rome & the Conquest of Italy *194*

~

The Rise of Rome *208*

~

The Imperial Peace *234*

~

The Christian Empire *266*

Early Rome & the Conquest of Italy

1000–272 BC

BELOW *The linguistic diversity of pre-Roman Italy (c. 450–400 BC) is a sign of its complex settlement history. It was not until several centuries after the Roman conquest that Latin completely replaced the many local languages.*

THE LANGUAGES OF PRE-ROMAN ITALY
Raetic
12°
18°
46°
Celtic
Venetic
Etruscan
Padus
Ligurian
Celtic
Umbrian
East Italic
Etruscan
Sabine
Central Sabellic Languages
Faliscan
42°
Oscan
Latin
Messapic
Volscian
Etruscan
Greek
38°
Italic languages:
Latin
Faliscan
Osco-Umbrian
Venetic
East Italic
Other Indo-European languages:
Celtic
Messapic
Greek
Unclassifiable languages:
Ligurian
Etruscan
Raetic
scale 1:6 500 000
0
200km
0
150mi

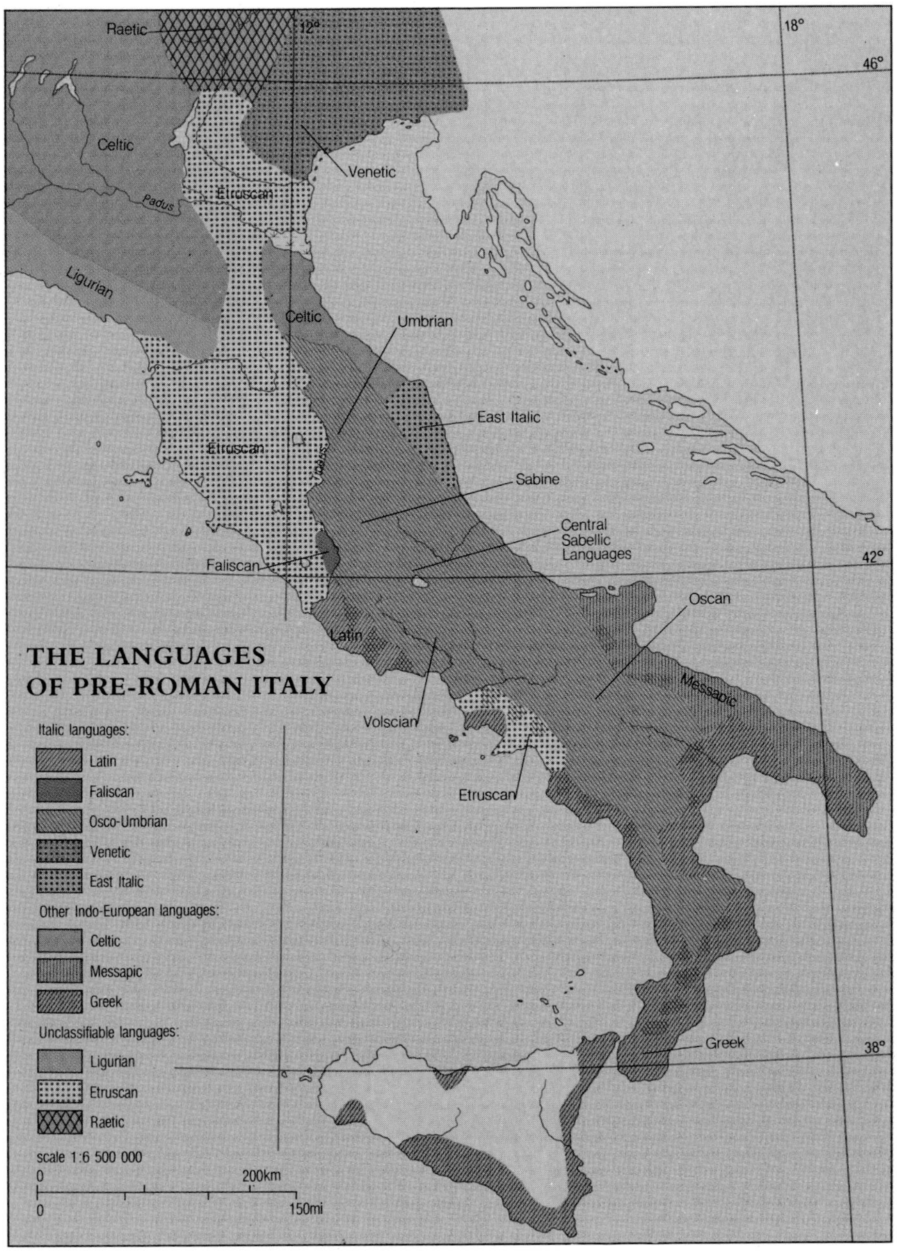

The origins of Rome are shrouded in myth. The first Roman to write about its history, Q. Fabius Pictor, lived around 200 BC when the city was already well over 500 years old, and the greatest historian of early Rome, Titus Livius (Livy), began his work in 29 BC when Rome was at the height of its power. They had few documents to work from and had to construct their narratives from myths, legends and family historical traditions: they also had a natural desire to provide Rome with a history commensurate with its present greatness. Modern historians do not give their accounts too much credence: it is more a case of deciding which traditions are pure invention and which contain at least a germ of truth. Fortunately, in the course of the 20th century, archeology has provided historians with more objective sources of evidence about early Rome.

EARLY ITALY

Before the rise of Rome Italy was a land of enormous ethnic, cultural and linguistic diversity. The two main ethnic groupings of the peninsula were the Etruscan and the Italic- speaking peoples. The Etruscans (see pages 196–197) remain something of an enigma. They spoke a language that is unrelated to any modern European language, and it is possible that they were descended from the aboriginal settlers of Italy. The archeological origins of the Etruscans are probably to be found in the Villanova culture, the first iron-using culture of Italy that flourished in Tuscany from about 1000 to 800 BC. By the 8th century the Etruscans had developed the first urban civilization of western Europe. They were active seafarers and traders and their contacts with the Greeks, from whom they adopted the alphabet, had great impact on their art and religion.

The other major group of peoples, the Italics, occupied the central part of the peninsula. They included the Latins, Sabines and Samnites and had probably migrated into Italy from central Europe during the 2nd millenium BC. At the start of the 7th century most of the Italic peoples were still tribally organized though city states were beginning to develop in Latium Vetus (Ancient Latium, the area of central Italy dominated by the Latins). One of these was Rome. Like the Etruscans, the Latins adopted alphabetic writing as a result of contacts with Greek colonists in Italy.

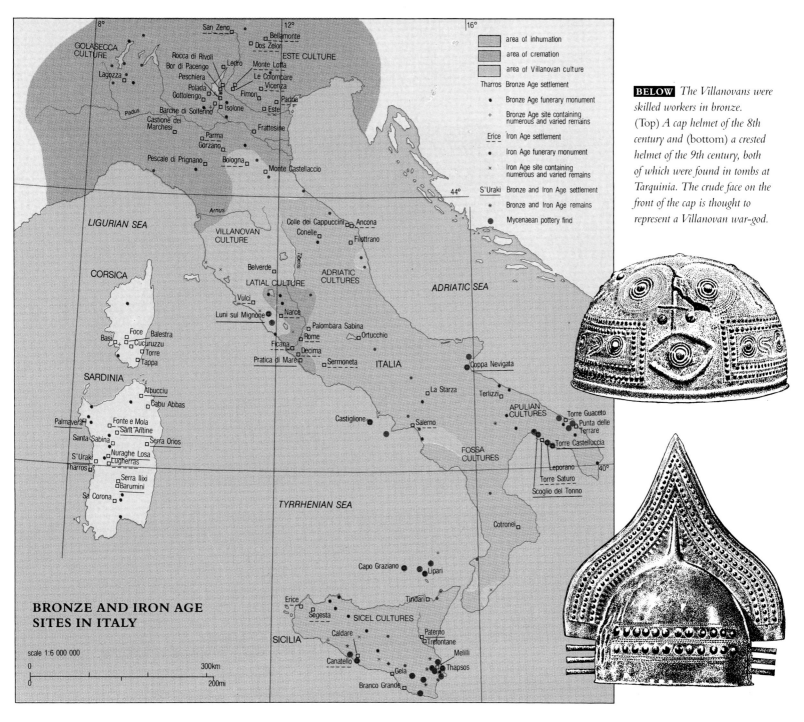

BRONZE AND IRON AGE
SITES IN ITALY

scale 1:6 000 000

| area of inhumation |
| area of cremation |
| area of Villanovan culture |

Tharros   Bronze Age settlement
•   Bronze Age funerary monument
+   Bronze Age site containing numerous and varied remains
Erice   Iron Age settlement
•   Iron Age funerary monument
×   Iron Age site containing numerous and varied remains
S'Uraki   Bronze and Iron Age settlement
*   Bronze and Iron Age remains
●   Mycenaean pottery find

BELOW *The Villanovans were skilled workers in bronze. (Top) A cap helmet of the 8th century and (bottom) a crested helmet of the 9th century, both of which were found in tombs at Tarquinia. The crude face on the front of the cap is thought to represent a Villanovan war-god.*

ABOVE *The culture of Bronze Age Italy, based largely on pastoralism, was relatively uniform, but with the introduction of iron working (c. 1000 BC) the number of settlements began to increase and regionally differentiated cultures emerged. Archeologists divide these into two groups according to the type of burial rite practiced. In the south and east inhumation (burial) prevailed, while in the north cremation was the rule. The Villanovan culture was the forerunner of the Etruscan civilization.*

THE ORIGINS OF ROME

According to later tradition, the Romans traced their ancestry back to the Trojan hero Aeneas who, with his son and father and a band of followers, had escaped the sack of Troy. His journeyings eventually brought him to Italy. He settled in Latium, married a local princess and founded a dynasty. Two of Aeneas' illegitimately born descendants, the twin brothers Romulus and Remus, were abandoned in infancy on the banks of the Tiber river. Their lives were saved when they were suckled by a she-wolf and they were eventually rescued by shepherds. Later, the brothers decided to found a city on the spot where they had been abandoned but they argued over who should rule it. Romulus killed Remus and named the city Rome after himself. Rome was soon at war with its neighbors, the Sabines. The Romans were short of marriageable women so Romulus invited the Sabines to a feast, whereupon the Roman men then seized all the Sabine women. The war that followed was stopped by the intervention of the Sabine women themselves, and a compromise was reached which placed Rome under the joint rule of Romulus and the Sabine leader Titus Tatius.

This story tells us more about the way later Romans saw themselves than it does about the origins of Rome. The Romans of historical times continuously assimilated new peoples and cultural

THE ETRUSCANS

ABOVE *Like many other Etruscan tombs, the tomb of the Leopards at Tarquinia (mid-5th century BC) is decorated with paintings showing a funeral banquet. The diners, and perhaps in some way also the deceased, were entertained by music and dancing.*

BELOW *The Etruscans are noted for the superb quality of their bronze sculptures. Shown here is a chimera (a Greek mythical beast with a lion's head, goat's body and serpent's tail). The legend of Bellerophon, slayer of the chimera, was popular with the Etruscans.*

The Etruscans are one of the mysterious peoples of history. Their literature, once extensive, has all been lost, their unique language is still not perfectly understood, and few of their cities have been excavated. They were mostly given a bad press by unsympathetic Greek and Roman historians.

The Etruscans' homeland, Etruria (roughly equivalent to modern Tuscany), had fertile soils and was rich in iron and copper ores which they skillfully exploited. The coastline possessed many natural harbors, and from early times they were active seafarers and traders. Roads, bridges, canals and city walls testify to their considerable engineering and architectural abilities. Etruscan cities were independent states ruled by kings but the twelve most important were loosely united in the Etruscan league. During the 8th century the Etruscans competed fiercely with the Greeks for control of trade in western and central Europe. Though relations between them were often hostile, the influence of Greek civilization is clearly evident on Etruscan art, writing and religion.

Most of our knowledge of Etruscan life comes from the tombs of the aristocracy. These were built in the style of houses and were richly furnished. They provide a vivid picture of a leisured lifestyle, but almost nothing is known of the rural serfs whose labor supported it.

RIGHT *Scores of artifacts have been excavated from Etruscan tombs. This bronze figure of a warrior comes from Cagli. It probably represents the war god Maris, the equivalent of the Roman god Mars. The figure originally held a shield and lance.*

ETRUSCAN CITIES OF THE 6TH CENTURY BC

CAPUA ancient name
Murlo modern name
scale 1:2 500 000

0 ——— 120km
0 ——— 80mi

TYRRHENIAN SEA

ABOVE *Portrait of Velia, a member of the aristocratic Veicha family: detail of a wall painting from the tomb of Orcus (c.400 BC) at Tarquinia. The style clearly reflects the influence of contemporary Greek art.*

BELOW *The Banditaccia necropolis near Cerveteri (Caere). The cemetery was laid out formally like a city in which the tombs represented houses. Circular in shape, they were carved directly out of the bedrock and covered with an earth mound. Each tomb accommodated several generations of the same aristocratic family.*

ABOVE *The Etruscan civilization grew up c.800 BC in the area bounded by the Tyrrhenian Sea in the west, the Arno river in the north and the Apennine mountains and Tiber river in the east and south. During the 6th century it spread north into the Po valley and south to the area around the Bay of Naples. The Etruscans' culture and identity survived for about another 200 years after they were conquered by the Romans early in the 3rd century.*

influences. They were not ashamed of being a mixture of peoples and races, or of deriving much of their culture from others. The fact that the Romans embodied and celebrated their mixed origins in their foundation myth shows that they rightly recognized that this was one of their strengths, though the main elements of the story are almost certainly pure invention. All the same, it is very probable that Rome developed through the fusion of several smaller communities, a process that may well be reflected in the story of the Sabine women.

THE ROMAN MONARCHY

Romulus may be a legendary figure but with his successor, the Sabine king Numa Pompilius, we almost certainly have a genuine historical figure. The histories portray Numa as a peaceable king but his successors appear to have been more war-like: Tullus Hostilius, a Latin, expanded Roman territory in Latium and Ancus Marcius, a Sabine, captured Ostia at the mouth of the Tiber. These early kings would have been little more than vil-lage chiefs but there are signs that late in the 7th century Rome began to grow into an urban center. Traditionally, it was Tarquin I (r.c. 616–579) who turned Rome into a city (see pages 200–201). An Etruscan who took advantage of Rome's openness to immigrants to seek a new life for himself, he succeeded in building up a network of supporters so that he was able to secure election as king on the death of Ancus Marcius.

Tarquin was murdered in a palace coup and the throne was seized by his son-in-law Servius Tullius (r.c. 578–535), who was probably a Latin. Servius is credited with altering the basis of Roman citizenship by reforming Rome's archaic tribal system to make residence rather than birth the basis of membership, thereby opening citizen-ship to immigrants. He created a new assembly, later known as the *comitia centuriata*. This placed the citizens in voting units called centuries and divided them into classes according to the amount of property they owned and the weapons and armor they could afford. It became the basis for creating a citizen army of about 6000 hoplite-style infantry and 600 cavalry. Servius further increased the citizen body by enfranchising the conquered Latins of the surrounding countryside. Thus began the policy of conquest and assimilation that continued throughout Rome's history.

Servius Tullius himself died violently in a coup led by Tarquin I's grandson Tarquin II, known as

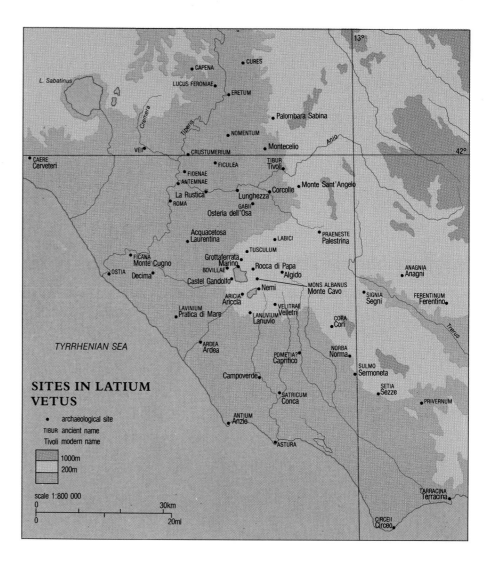

SITES IN LATIUM VETUS

• archaeological site
TIBUR ancient name
Tivoli modern name

1000m
200m

scale 1:800 000
30km
20mi

Tarquin the Proud (r.c. 535–509), who was to be the last king of Rome. He alienated the aristocracy by refusing to rule with the advice of the Senate (the assembly of the leading citizens appointed to advise the king). Livy tells us it was the rape of Lucretia, a Roman noblewoman, by Tarquin's son Sextus that drove a group of aristocrats to over-throw the Tarquins in 509 BC. The late monarchy was a critical period in Rome's development. By 509 Rome was by far the largest city in Latium with a population of between 20,000 and 40,000 and it controlled more than twice the territory of Tibur, its closest rival. Rome was also larger than any Etruscan city, though still considerably smaller than many of the Greek cities in the south of the peninsula, such as Tarentum and Agrigentum.

THE FOUNDATION OF THE ROMAN REPUBLIC

Later Romans regarded the overthrow of the monarchy as the decisive moment of their history, the beginning of their rise to greatness. It was traditionally represented as a liberation from

ABOVE *Most of the communities in Latium Vetus, including Rome itself, seem to have originated as small hut villages on low hills over-looking the fertile plains of central Italy's west coast. The so-called "Latial culture" developed in several phases between c. 1000 and c. 580 BC. In the early phases the settle-ments were simply hamlets of thatched huts but from the 8th cen-tury onward they grew in size and sophistication, developing trade contacts and craft specializations. In the final phases there is clear evidence for the development of the fortified urban centers that make their appearance in the historical sources as the towns of the Latin league.*

oppression, but in fact it was only the aristocracy who benefited. The rule of the last three kings of Rome is comparable to that of the contemporary tyrants of the Greek world: like them, they had based their positions on popular support and challenged the power and privileges of the aristocracy. Leadership now passed to the male heads of the small group of patrician families who were supposedly descended from the senators appointed by Romulus. They were determined not to lose the monopoly of power they now enjoyed as a class. In order to prevent any individual or family from assuming single control of the state, a collegiate magistracy was established in which two men, the consuls, shared regal powers. So that neither could emerge as a tyrant, each had the power to veto the decisions of the other. It was a unique institution in the ancient world.

The consuls were elected annually by the *comitia centuriata* which also had the right to vote on but not debate and make policy. This was the exclusive preserve of the Senate, which was dominated by the patricians who sat in it by hereditary right. Under the monarchy plebeians (citizens who lacked noble birth) had been "conscripted" to the Senate. This continued in the early republic but as an act of favor merely, not by right, and plebeians therefore had little influence on policy. Voting in the *comitia centuriata* was by class and was structured – rigged might be a more accurate description – to ensure that the richer classes could outvote the numerically larger poorer classes. In order to prevent anyone from consolidating a hold on power, consuls were not allowed to run for reelection to a second consecutive term in office.

Further elective magistracies were created in the first century of the republic. Quaestors were elected to supervise financial matters and censors to revise the register of citizens. In dire emergencies the consuls were empowered to appoint a dictator who could wield absolute power but for a period of six months only: this was later to prove a dangerously attractive office. Magistrates were unpaid which meant that in practice their offices were only open to the rich and the vast majority

ARCHAIC ROME

Cremation graves dating from the 10th to the 8th centuries BC, excavated on the site of the Roman Forum, suggest that it may have served as a burial ground for farmers living on the surrounding hills. Traces of the simple huts of an 8th- century Iron Age farming settlement provide the first evidence of habitation on the Palatine hill, which was traditionally regarded as the site of the city founded by Romulus in 753 BC. The transformation from village to city appears to have begun in the mid 7th century. According to Livy, it was Tarquin I (616–579 BC) who was responsible for carrying this out by draining the Forum (then a marsh) and laying it out as public square with shops and monumental buildings. His successor Servius Tullius is said to have enlarged the city and built a circuit of defensive walls. Traces of these walls have proved elusive (the so-called Servian wall was built in 378 BC), but the archeological evidence confirms a picture of steadily increasing urbanization during the late monarchy. The first stone houses, some of them large and luxurious, belong to this period. Temples and palaces, together with inscriptions, sculptures, roof tiles and drains, make their appearance. Large amounts of imported pottery attest to expanding trade links. When Rome became a republic in 509 BC it was already one of the largest and wealthiest cities in Italy.

BELOW *The "Capitoline Wolf," made around 500 BC, is a masterpiece of archaic bronze sculpture. The figures of the twins were added in the Renaissance but are believed to have replaced lost originals. If this is so, the sculpture shows that the legend of Romulus and Remus being suckled by a she-wolf was already well established at the end of the regal period. The name of Romulus would have been chosen to explain the city's name, a quite common device in foundation myths.*

hut urn from a
cremation burial

Iron Age hut –
8th century BC

ABOVE *The earliest occupants of Rome cremated their dead and placed their ashes in urns. These were often shaped like thatched huts and clearly represent dwellings. The foundations of oval and rectangular huts have been excavated on the Palatine hill.*

RIGHT *Rome was a natural site for settlement. Its hilltops were easily defended and it overlooked an important crossing of the Tiber, making it a natural center for trade. It had easy access to the sea yet was far enough inland to escape pirate raids.*

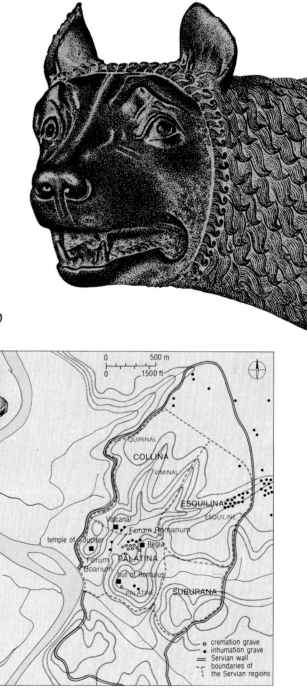

QUIRINAL
COLLINA
VIMINAL
ESQUILINA
ESQUILINE
Volcanal
Forum Romanum
temple of Jupiter
Regia
Forum Boarium
PALATINA
hut of Romulus
SUBURANA
PALATINE

○ cremation grave
● inhumation grave
═ Servian wall
boundaries of
the Servian regions

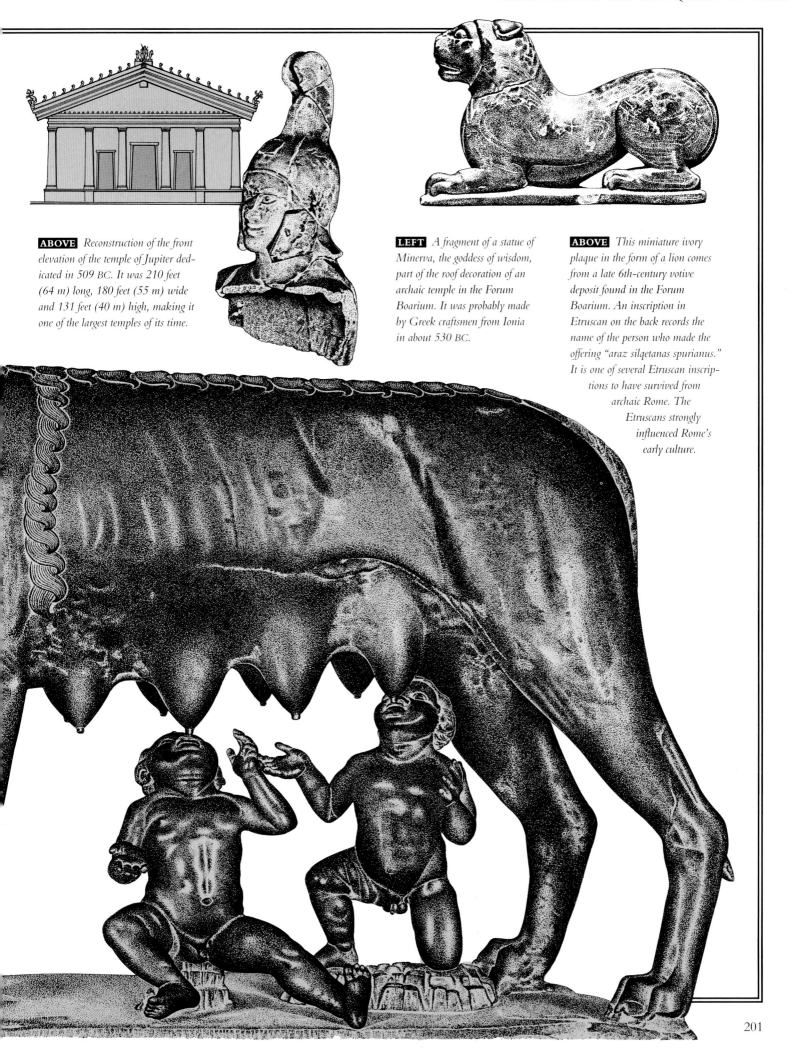

ABOVE *Reconstruction of the front elevation of the temple of Jupiter dedicated in 509 BC. It was 210 feet (64 m) long, 180 feet (55 m) wide and 131 feet (40 m) high, making it one of the largest temples of its time.*

LEFT *A fragment of a statue of Minerva, the goddess of wisdom, part of the roof decoration of an archaic temple in the Forum Boarium. It was probably made by Greek craftsmen from Ionia in about 530 BC.*

ABOVE *This miniature ivory plaque in the form of a lion comes from a late 6th-century votive deposit found in the Forum Boarium. An inscription in Etruscan on the back records the name of the person who made the offering "araz silqetanas spurianus." It is one of several Etruscan inscriptions to have survived from archaic Rome. The Etruscans strongly influenced Rome's early culture.*

201

were filled by members of the patrician families. The patricians were intensely competitive and used their wealth to recruit bands of dependents or clients to support their political ambitions. Arrayed against them were the plebeians (plebs), the mass of the citizens. They included both rich and poor – wealthy men whose lack of noble blood effectively excluded them from political power as well as struggling peasant farmers threatened with debt-bondage – who had a common interest in opposing the patricians' dominance.

THE RISE OF THE PLEBS

The first two centuries of the republic's history were dominated by the struggle for power between the patrician class and the plebs. In 494, the plebs formed their own assembly, the *concilium plebis* (popular assembly), and elected their own officers, the tribunes. To protect them from attack by the patricians, the plebs declared the tribunes to be sacred and invoked curses on any who should harm them. This personal inviolability gave the tribunes considerable power and influence and they became effective advocates for individual citizens against arbitrary decisions by magistrates. The plebs' ultimate weapon was "secession," a form of mass civil disobedience that was used at least five times between 494 and 287. Their first success came between 451 and 449 when they forced the publication of a written law code, the "Twelve Tables," which was to become the foundation of Roman law. The Twelve Tables accorded all citizens equal rights in law but it was left to the individual to take his opponent to court and execute judgment himself. For poorer citizens who lacked a rich and powerful patron this would have been nearly impossible.

The plebs' most frequent complaints were against the practice of debt-bondage. It was a lucky peasant farmer who could avoid going into debt at some time: interest rates were very high and the borrower was expected to offer his labor as security for the loan. The system was easily abused by the rich and defaulters could find themselves virtually enslaved. After serious civil disturbances in the 370s measures were taken to alleviate debt and in 326 debt-bondage was finally abolished. By this time the policy of distributing newly conquered lands had led to a rise in plebeian prosperity. The number of magistracies was increased and power-sharing was introduced to open them up to plebeian candidacy. After 342 one consul was always a pleb and from 367 onward the

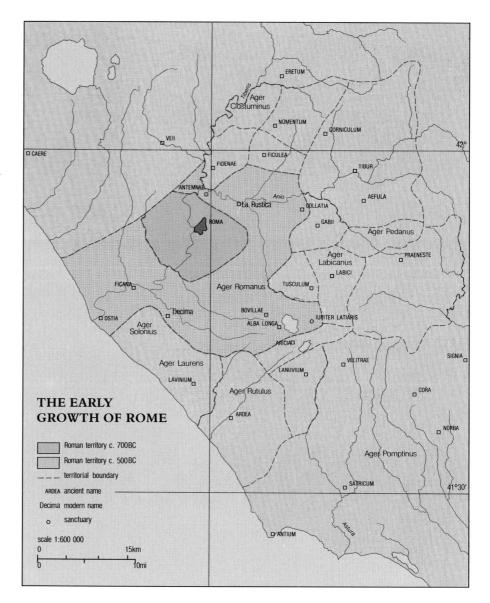

THE EARLY GROWTH OF ROME

Roman territory c. 700 BC
Roman territory c. 500 BC
– – – territorial boundary
ARDEA ancient name
Decima modern name
o sanctuary

scale 1:600 000

0   15km
0   10mi

censors were instructed to give preference to ex-magistrates when selecting senators, thereby ensuring that the number of plebs in the Senate increased. Plebs who held the senior magistracies (consulship, praetorship and dictatorship) became part of a new hereditary aristocracy, the *nobiles* or nobles. In 287 decisions of the popular assembly, known as plebiscites, were recognized as having the full force of law.

The main beneficiaries of these developments were the richer plebs who could afford to compete for political office. The patrician families lost their monopoly of power (though remaining prestigious) and the aristocracy became a more open class while continuing to dominate the Senate. The only effective challenge to the Senate's authority came when ambitious tribunes passed legislation through the popular assembly. But this rarely happened in practice because most tribunes were themselves wealthy and used the office as a

ABOVE *By the end of the period of monarchy (509 BC) Rome had gradually asserted its authority over its neighbors to control an estimated territory of 317 square miles (822 sq km), amounting to a third of Latium: next in importance were Tibur and Praeneste (the boundaries as shown are conjectural). The text of a treaty with Carthage, known from a document preserved by the Greek historian Polybius (c. 200–118 BC) and almost certainly authentic, which dates from the first year of the republic, explicitly recognizes Roman supremacy in Latium. Rome's control over its neighbors, however, was not secure until the later 4th century.*

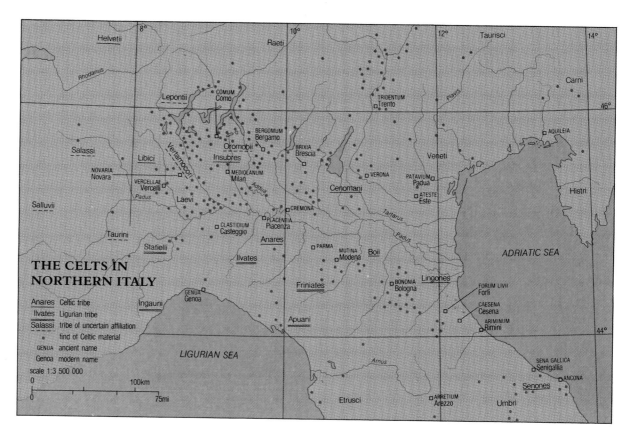

THE CELTS IN
NORTHERN ITALY

Anares   Celtic tribe
Ilvates   Ligurian tribe
Salassi   tribe of uncertain affiliation
•   find of Celtic material
GENUA   ancient name
Genoa   modern name
scale 1:3 500 000

RIGHT *Celtic tribes migrated across the Alps and settled in large numbers in the Po valley in the 5th century BC, displacing the Etruscan population of that region. Archeological evidence indicates that these settlers retained close cultural contacts with the Celts north of the Alps but also adopted many aspects of Etruscan material culture and customs, including urban living. The pressure of the Celtic invasions sent the Etruscan civilization into long-term decline. The Celts were known to the Romans as Gauls and the main area of Celtic settlement was given the name of Cisalpine Gaul (Gaul-this-side-of-the-Alps).*

RIGHT *Large sections still survive in Rome of the republican city wall, built in 378, after the sack of the city by the Gauls, but traditionally and wrongly associated with the early king of Rome, Servius Tullius. When complete the walls extended for 6 miles (10 km). The arches were added later, probably during the civil wars of the 1st century BC.*

FAR RIGHT *One of the first laws passed by the republican government was the* provocatio, *the right of appeal to the people. It was considered to be a fundamental privilege of Roman citizenship and safeguard against arbitrary judgments. This coin of the 2nd century BC shows* provocatio *in action and carries the inscription "provoco" – "I appeal."*

first step toward a magistracy. They therefore had no interest in challenging the system and Rome remained essentially an aristocratic oligarchic state. Despite this, the combination of collective policy-making, public consultation and social mobility achieved in the republican constitution helped create a community of interest between classes. This had the important effect of providing Rome with the strong and stable government that served it well during the centuries of its rise to the status of a great power.

ROME AND ITS NEIGHBORS

An immediate effect of the overthrow of the monarchy was to deprive Rome of the strong military leadership the kings had provided. Neighboring towns in Latium combined against Rome to take advantage of this sudden weakness but were narrowly defeated in battle at Lake Regillus (499). Both during and after the war, colonies of Roman citizens were founded on territory that was captured from the Latin towns. This policy of colonizing newly acquired land continued into imperial times. It served a double purpose, helping Rome to consolidate its hold on new conquests and offering a solution to social problems in the city itself by providing land and opportunities for its poorer citizens.

Shortly after the conclusion of the Latin war, hill-tribes from the Apennine mountains – the Aequi, Volsci and Sabines – began to move into Latium. In 494 Rome and the other Latin towns united against them in a defensive league that Rome dominated. By the end of the century the league had won the initiative, leaving Rome a free hand to deal with the Etruscan city of Veii. Some 10 miles (16 km) to the north of Rome, Veii was a rival for control of the Tiber valley and through-out the 5th century clashes between the two were frequent. According to Roman tradition, which was clearly influenced by Greek legends of the Trojan War, the final siege of Veii lasted ten years (405–396). The fall of the city doubled in size Rome's territorial area but the Romans were not able immediately to capitalize on their success.

Earlier in the 5th century large numbers of Celts, who were known to the Romans as Gauls, had begun to move across the Alps to settle in the Po valley, a region that came to be known as Cisalpine Gaul (Gaul-this-side-of-the-Alps). They now began to launch plundering raids across the Apennine mountains and in 390, after destroying a Roman army, they went on to sack Rome. A garrison held out on the Capitol hill for several months until a payment of gold persuaded the Gauls to leave. Several more raids followed but the Romans soon got the measure of the Gauls and each new incursion was more easily defeated than the last. The Etruscans, by contrast, were permanently weakened by the invasions of the Gauls. In the long term this helped the Romans to unify Italy, but the Gauls had given them a bad fright and the Romans never felt entirely secure until Cisalpine Gaul had been brought firmly under their control nearly 200 years later after the power of the Gauls was broken at the battle of Telamon (225).

Rome, meanwhile, recovered quickly from the immediate threat of Gallic invasion. By 340 its domination of Latium caused many of its Latin allies to rebel in a war that Rome won, with Samnite help, in 338. The settlement provided the pattern for future Roman expansion in Italy. The

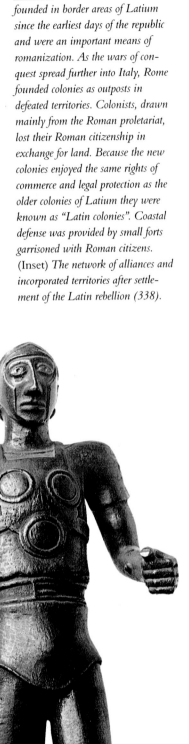

RIGHT *Colonies had been founded in border areas of Latium since the earliest days of the republic and were an important means of romanization. As the wars of conquest spread further into Italy, Rome founded colonies as outposts in defeated territories. Colonists, drawn mainly from the Roman proletariat, lost their Roman citizenship in exchange for land. Because the new colonies enjoyed the same rights of commerce and legal protection as the older colonies of Latium they were known as "Latin colonies". Coastal defense was provided by small forts garrisoned with Roman citizens. (Inset) The network of alliances and incorporated territories after settlement of the Latin rebellion (338).*

ABOVE *A hunting scene from a 4th-century Lucanian tomb painting found near Paestum in southern Italy. The Lucanians were an Italic people, closely related to the Samnites. During the 4th century they moved out of the mountains of the interior into the coastal plain, overwhelming many of the Greek cities of the Tyrrhenian coast, including Paestum. The Lucanians were overcome by the Romans during the last phase of their conquest of Italy in the early 3rd century.*

RIGHT *Bronze statuette of a Samnite heavy infantryman, 6th or 5th century BC. He is armed much like a Greek hoplite of the same period with greaves, breast-plate and helmet. His shield, spear and helmet crest have been lost.*

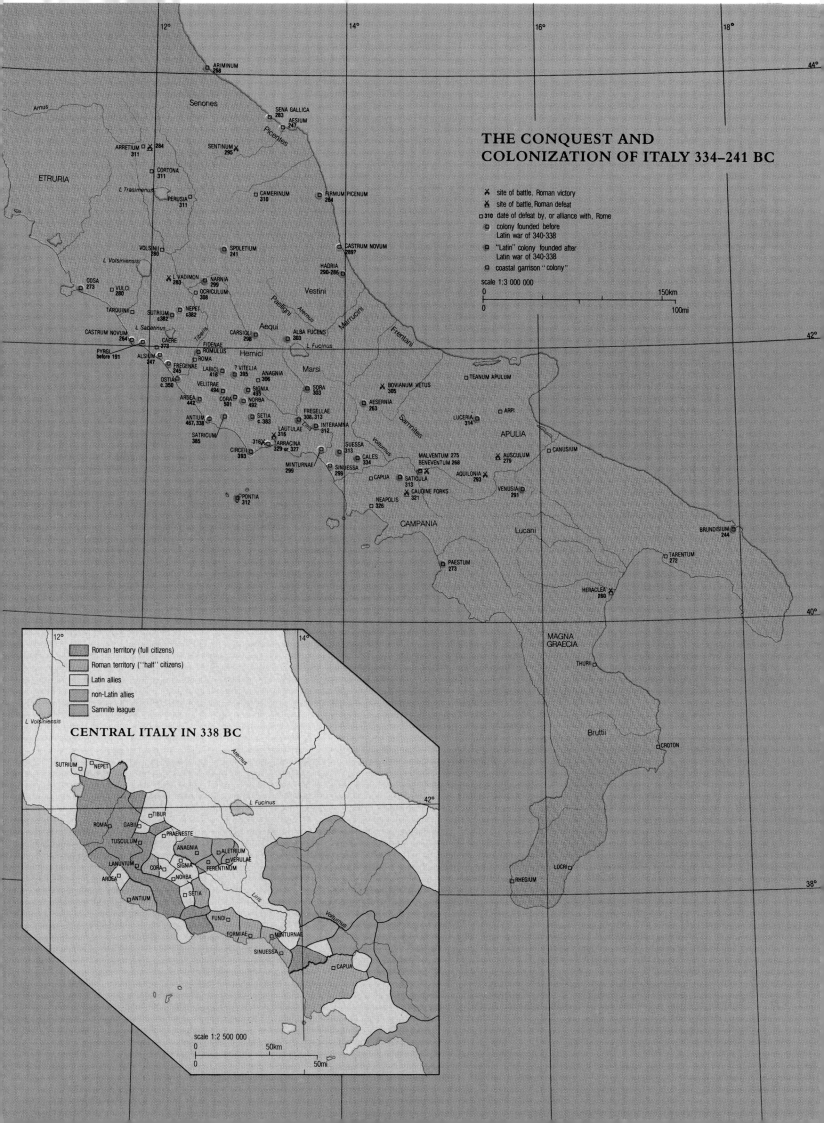

THE CONQUEST AND
COLONIZATION OF ITALY 334–241 BC

✕ site of battle, Roman victory

✕ site of battle, Roman defeat

▢ 310 date of defeat by, or alliance with, Rome

▢ colony founded before
Latin war of 340-338

▢ "Latin" colony founded after
Latin war of 340-338

▢ coastal garrison "colony"

scale 1:3 000 000

0   150km

0   100mi

44°

42°

40°

38°

12°

14°

16°

18°

ARIMINUM 268

SENA GALLICA 283

AESIUM 247

Senones

Picentes

Arnus

ETRURIA

L. Trasimenus

ARRETIUM 311 ✕ 284

CORTONA 311

SENTINUM 295 ✕

CAMERINUM 310

FIRMUM PICENUM 264

PERUSIA 311

VOLSINII 280

SPOLETIUM 241

CASTRUM NOVUM 289?

L. Volsiniensis

HADRIA 290-286

COSA 273

VULCI 280

L. VADIMON 283 ✕

NARNIA 299

OCRICULUM 308

Vestini

Paeligni

Aternus

Marrucini

Frentani

TARQUINII

SUTRIUM c382

NEPET c382

CARSIOLI 298

ALBA FUCENS 303

Aequi

L. Fucinus

CASTRUM NOVUM 264

L. Sabatinus

CAERE 273

FIDENAE

ROMULUS

FREGENAE 245

ROMA

Hernici

Marsi

BOVIANUM VETUS 305 ✕

TEANUM APULUM

PYRGI before 191

ALSIUM 247

LABICI 418

?VITELIA 395

ANAGNIA 306

SORA 303

AESERNIA 263

OSTIA c.350

VELITRAE 494

SIGNIA 495

ARPI

ARDEA 442

CORA 501

NORBA 492

FREGELLAE 308,313

INTERAMNA 312

Samnites

LUCERIA 314

APULIA

ANTIUM 467,338

SETIA c.383

LAUTULAE 316 ✕

SATRICUM 385

TARRACINA 329 or 327

CIRCEII 393

316 ✕

SUESSA 313

MALVENTUM 275
BENEVENTUM 268

AUSCULUM 279 ✕

CANUSIUM

MINTURNAE 299

CALES 334

SINUESSA 299

SATICULA 313 ✕

AQUILONIA 293 ✕

CAPUA

CAUDINE FORKS 321 ✕

VENUSIA 291

PONTIA 312

NEAPOLIS 326

CAMPANIA

Lucani

BRUNDISIUM 244

PAESTUM 273

TARENTUM 272

HERACLEA 280 ✕

MAGNA GRAECIA

THURII

Bruttii

CROTON

LOCRI

RHEGIUM

Inset map

12°

14°

42°

Roman territory (full citizens)

Roman territory ("half" citizens)

Latin allies

non-Latin allies

Samnite league

CENTRAL ITALY IN 338 BC

L. Volsiniensis

Aternus

L. Fucinus

Liris

Voltumus

SUTRIUM

NEPET

TIBUR

ROMA

GABII

PRAENESTE

TUSCULUM

ANAGNIA

ALETRIUM

VERULAE

LANUVIUM

CORA

SIGNIA

FERENTINUM

NORBA

ARDEA

ANTIUM

SETIA

FUNDI

FORMIAE

MINTURNAE

SINUESSA

CAPUA

scale 1:2 500 000

0   50km

0   50mi

THE GROWTH OF ROMAN POWER IN ITALY 302–241 BC

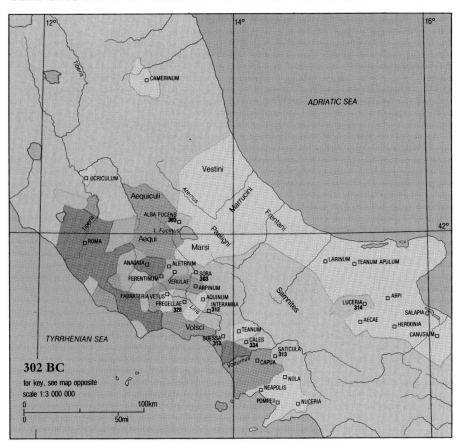

302 BC
for key, see map opposite
scale 1:3 000 000
0   100km
0   50mi

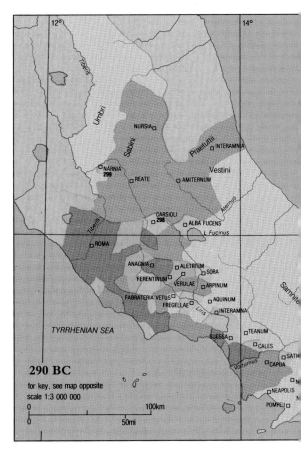

290 BC
for key, see map opposite
scale 1:3 000 000
0   100km
0   50mi

Latin cities were incorporated into the Roman
state and their inhabitants given Roman citizenship. The non-Latin communities that had joined
the revolt were given the status of *municipia*. The
inhabitants of a *municipium* kept their own local
government and were made half-citizens. This
gave them most of the rights and obligations of
Roman citizens, including military service, but not
that of voting in the assemblies. In time, as they
became more romanized, half-citizens could
become full Roman citizens, as happened to the
Sabines in 268. In addition, colonies of Roman
citizens were founded as military outposts in
strategic locations in conquered territories.

THE CONQUEST OF ITALY

Over the next 70 years almost the whole of penin-
sular Italy was brought under Roman control.
Whether the Romans held any long-term imperialist ambitions is open to doubt: many of the wars
of conquest began simply as attempts to secure
established borders against troublesome neighbors.
However, they were fought with the full support
of Rome's citizen body. For the common soldiers,
conquest brought the chance of plunder and land,
for their commanders it brought prestige and
political influence. Rome's most determined

opponents were their former allies, the Samnites.
The Romans had already fought a minor war
against them in 343– 341 but the second and
third Samnite wars (327–304; 298–290 BC) were
far more serious conflicts that eventually drew
in the Sabines, Umbrians, Etruscans and Gauls.
The Romans quickly learned that the Greek-style
hoplite phalanx was not well suited to fighting in
rough country. They replaced it with a more

ABOVE *During the wars of conquest (338–264 BC), the Romans
built up a complex system of
alliances and dependencies throughout the peninsula. A defeated state
forced into an alliance was compelled to contribute troops for
Roman armies; other territories were
incorporated into the Roman state
and given rights of citizenship.
Some were granted full Roman
citizenship but most of the newer
incorporated territories received
"half-citizenship" which meant they
carried out the obligations of Roman
citizens, including paying tax and
performing military service, but were
not allowed to vote or hold office.
All communities of half-citizens had
been upgraded to full citizenship by
the end of the 2nd century BC.*

LEFT *King Pyrrhus of Epirus
(319–272) invaded Italy in 280 at
the head of a well trained army. But
despite his skill as a general, he was
fought to a standstill by the Romans.*

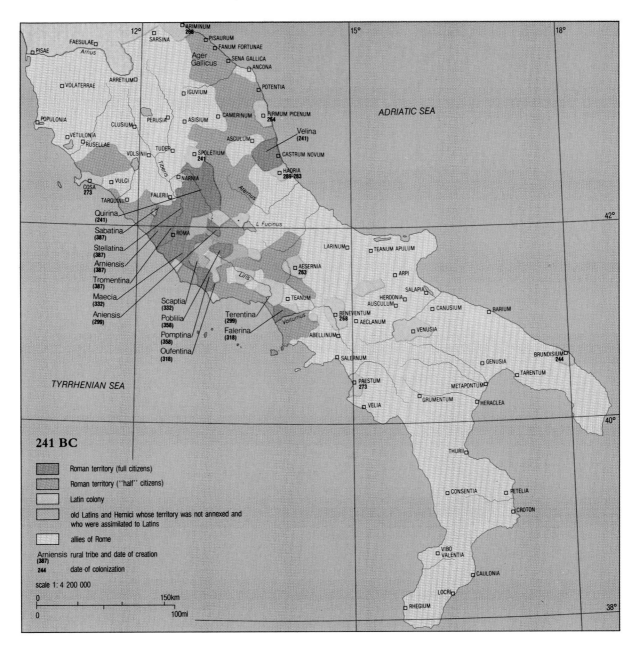

241 BC

- Roman territory (full citizens)
- Roman territory ("half" citizens)
- Latin colony
- old Latins and Hernici whose territory was not annexed and who were assimilated to Latins
- allies of Rome

Arniensis rural tribe and date of creation
(387)
244 date of colonization

scale 1: 4 200 000

0   150km

0   100mi

flexible formation called the *manipulus* (maniple, literally "handful") and adopted new weapons such as the sword and javelin. In 295 the Samnites were decisively defeated by the Roman army at Sentinum in Umbria, and in 290 they became Roman allies. Though independent in theory, they were expected to obey Rome and supply it with troops. The Sabines had been conquered earlier, and during the next few years the Etruscans and Umbrians also came under Roman control.

Only the Greek-dominated south (Magna Graecia) remained independent of Rome. After centuries of pressure from the Italic tribes of the interior, the Greek coastal cities were a declining force. After 400 the Lucanians dominated most of the Tyrrhenian coast and cities such as Neapolis (Naples) welcomed Roman protection. Tarentum, however, wished desperately to keep

its independence and called on Pyrrhus, the king of Epirus in Greece, for help. In true Hellenistic style Pyrrhus, who fancied himself as a new Alexander the Great, invaded Italy in 280 at the head of an army supported by elephants. Though he defeated the Romans at Heraclea and Ausculum, he suffered such heavy losses that in 275 he was forced to withdraw (it is from this that we get the term "Pyrrhic victory"). Tarentum, the last Greek city in Italy, fell to Rome in 272.

With the exception of Cisalpine Gaul, Rome now controlled most of the Italian peninsula, either directly or through alliances. The city itself had become wealthy on the booty of war and, with a population approaching 150,000, was one of the largest cities of the Mediterranean world. The manpower of most of Italy was at its disposal. Rome was now a power to be reckoned with.

The Rise of Rome

272 – 30 BC

The Romans were masters of the Italian peninsula by 270 BC. Over the next 250 years they extended their power over the entire Mediterranean world. The Carthaginian maritime empire, the Hellenistic east, the Iberian and Celtic peoples of western Europe all fell victim to Rome's ruthless military efficiency. The Romans claimed, and perhaps believed, that all their wars were just ones. But theirs was a wholly militaristic society.

Prayers for the expansion of Roman territory even formed part of the state religion (see pages 214–215). Under the republic, military success offered the surest route to political influence and status. External expansion was driven by the power struggles of the aristocracy in Rome itself rather than by any imperialist masterplan for world domination. Plunder and prisoners, who could be sold as slaves, provided further incentives for conquest.

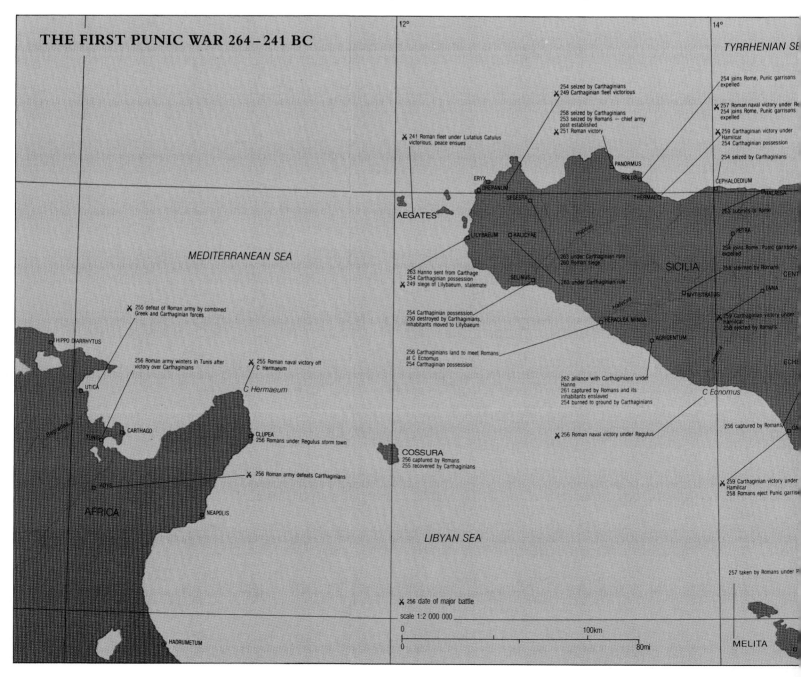

THE FIRST PUNIC WAR 264–241 BC

TYRRHENIAN SE

254 seized by Carthaginians
249 Carthaginian fleet victorious

254 joins Rome, Punic garrisons expelled

257 Roman naval victory under Re
254 joins Rome, Punic garrisons expelled

258 seized by Carthaginians
253 seized by Romans — chief army post established
251 Roman victory

259 Carthaginian victory under Hamilcar
254 Carthaginian possession

241 Roman fleet under Lutatius Catulus victorious, peace ensues

254 seized by Carthaginians

PANORMUS
SOLUS

CEPHALOEDIUM
HALAESA

ERYX
DREPANUM
SEGESTA
THERMAE

253 submits to Rome

AEGATES

PETRA

LILYBAEUM HALICYAE

254 joins Rome, Punic garrisons expelled

MEDITERRANEAN SEA

263 under Carthaginian rule
260 Roman siege

SICILIA

258 stormed by Romans

CENT

263 Hanno sent from Carthage
254 Carthaginian possession
249 siege of Lilybaeum, stalemate

SELINUS

263 under Carthaginian rule

MYTISTRATUS

ENNA

255 defeat of Roman army by combined Greek and Carthaginian forces

254 Carthaginian possession
250 destroyed by Carthaginians, inhabitants moved to Lilybaeum

HERACLEA MINOA

259 Carthaginian victory under Hamilcar
258 ejected by Romans

HIPPO DIARRHYTUS

AGRIGENTUM

256 Roman army winters in Tunis after victory over Carthaginians

255 Roman naval victory off C Hermaeum

C Hermaeum

256 Carthaginians land to meet Romans at C Ecnomus
254 Carthaginian possession

ECHE

UTICA

262 alliance with Carthaginians under Hanno
261 captured by Romans and its inhabitants enslaved
254 burned to ground by Carthaginians

C Ecnomus

CARTHAGO

CLUPEA
256 Romans under Regulus storm town

256 Roman naval victory under Regulus

256 captured by Romans

TUNIS

COSSURA
256 captured by Romans
255 recovered by Carthaginians

ADYS

256 Roman army defeats Carthaginians

259 Carthaginian victory under Hamilcar
258 Romans eject Punic garris

AFRICA

NEAPOLIS

LIBYAN SEA

257 taken by Romans under R

X 256 date of major battle

scale 1:2 000 000

0 — 100km

0 — 80mi

HADRUMETUM

MELITA

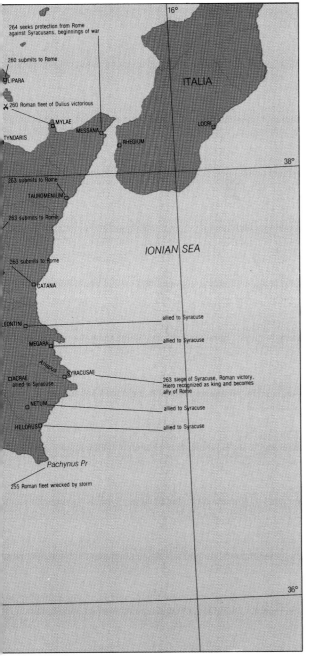

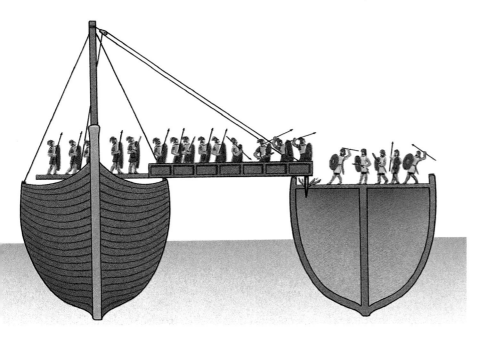

ABOVE *The Romans made few innovations in their warships, which closely followed Greek and Carthaginian designs. But Rome secured a series of early naval victories over Carthage, largely due to one Roman invention, the* corvus *(crow). This was a drawbridge that could be lowered onto the deck of an enemy ship, holding it fast. Heavily armed Roman marines then stormed across it and overwhelmed the enemy crew. The* corvus, *however, made Roman ships top-heavy and unseaworthy in bad weather, and its use was quickly abandoned.*

LEFT *A dispute over the town of Messana in Sicily was the immediate cause of the first great war between Rome and Carthage. Neither was willing to see it fall into the other's hands, since this would threaten its own security. The dispute quickly escalated into a bitter war of attrition that dragged on for more than 20 years. The Romans built a fleet to challenge Carthaginian control of the sea, and their resources ultimately proved the superior.*

THE FIRST PUNIC WAR
(264–241 BC)

In the first year of its existence (509 BC) the Roman republic signed a treaty of friendship with the Phoenician city of Carthage in North Africa. Not long independent of its mother-city Tyre, Carthage was already the dominant trading power in the western Mediterranean with an empire that included western Sicily, Sardinia, Corsica, the Balearic islands and a few colonies such as Gades (Cadiz) controlling the Pillars of Hercules (Strait of Gibraltar). In return for Carthaginian recognition of Rome's dominant position in Latium, Rome promised to respect Carthage's trading interests. Bilingual inscriptions dating to about 500 BC from the Etruscan port of Pyrgi suggest that the treaty with Rome was just one of many made by Carthage with trading partners around the Tyrrhenian Sea. The treaty was renewed in 348 and 306, and in 279 Carthage and Rome took joint action against the expansionist ambitions of Pyrrhus of Epirus. But it is clear that the growth of Roman power was causing Carthage some concern. The treaty of 348 prevented the Romans from founding colonies in Africa or Sardinia and a conflict of interests seemed increasingly likely.

A minor incident in Sicily in 264 BC led to the outbreak of the first Punic war (its name derives from Poeni, Latin for Phoenician). When the city of Messana (Messina), which was in the hands of a group of Italian mercenaries, came under attack from king Hiero of Syracuse, it appealed for help to Rome. Carthage, fearful of allowing the Romans to gain a foothold in what they regarded as their sphere of influence, joined forces with Syracuse against Rome. The subsequent war was long remembered as the costliest of all Rome's wars. The Romans enjoyed early success on land and quickly forced Hiero to change sides. They took the Carthaginian base at Agrigentum (261), but soon realized they would be unable to win complete control of Sicily while Carthage retained mastery at sea. With typical determination, the Romans built and manned a fleet of 100 large warships (quinqueremes) in only a few months. After a series of naval victories, they decided to make a direct attack on Carthage in 255, but the expedition ended in defeat. The fleet sent to evacuate the survivors was overwhelmed by a storm on its way home, and many thousands of lives were lost.

Sicily again became the focus of the war, which now became one of dogged attrition. In the end it was won because the Romans had the resources to

209

ABOVE *Hannibal (top) and Scipio (bottom) were the finest generals of the second Punic war. Despite a series of brilliant victories against Rome in Italy, Hannibal lacked the resources to achieve his strategic goals. Scipio learned from Hannibal's tactics and ultimately defeated him at the decisive battle of Zama in 202 BC. His victory earned him the title "Africanus."*

support both a large army and a large fleet, and the Carthaginians did not. In 241 the Romans destroyed the remnants of the Carthaginian fleet in a naval battle off the western tip of Sicily, thereby severing supplies to the remaining Carthaginian bases in Sicily, which were forced to surrender. Roman peace terms were surprisingly moderate: Carthage was ordered to pay a large indemnity and to withdraw from its bases in Sicily. But within a short time Carthage's unpaid mercenaries had rebelled and the Romans occupied Sardinia and Corsica as well. From 227 the administration of these new territories was made the responsibility of specially appointed magistrates – one for Sicily, one for Corsica and Sardinia. The sphere in which a magistrate exercised his authority was known as his *provincia,* or province, a term that in time came to be applied to all Rome's overseas possessions.

THE SECOND PUNIC WAR (218–202)

Reluctant to accept their defeat, in 237 the Carthaginians under Hamilcar Barca set about establishing a new overseas empire in southern Spain, where they founded a new capital, Carthago Nova (Cartagena). The Romans watched with suspicion and in 226 demanded that they confine their activities to the south of the Ebro river. Tension rose in 219 when Hannibal (247–182), the son of Hamilcar Barca, besieged the city of Saguntum, which was allied to Rome. Hannibal ignored Roman demands to withdraw and took the city, knowing that the inevitable consequence of this action would be war. Confident that their hard-won control of the sea would prevent a Carthaginian attack on Italy, the Romans planned to invade Africa. To their surprise, however, Hannibal unexpectedly marched his forces out of Spain, through Gaul and across the Alps into Italy. He realized that Carthage could not prevail in Spain against Rome's superior resources of manpower. By attacking Italy directly, he hoped to persuade Rome's Italian allies to rebel and so deprive the city of its chief advantage.

Cisalpine Gaul had only recently been incorporated into Roman Italy, following the battle of Telamon in 225. The newly conquered Gauls joined Hannibal in large numbers and with their help he won two major victories over Roman armies, at the Ticinus and Trebia rivers. The following year he advanced into Etruria and ambushed a Roman army at Lake Trasimene,

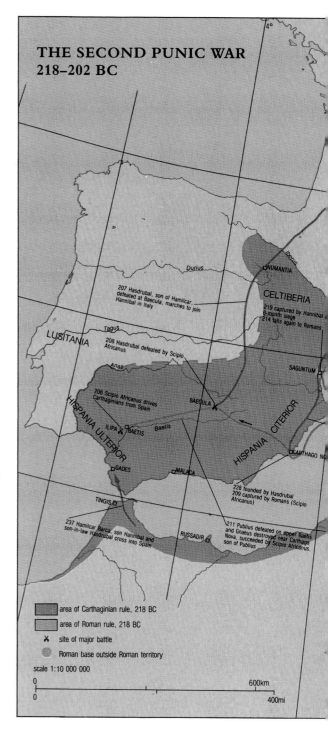

THE SECOND PUNIC WAR 218–202 BC

207 Hasdrubal, son of Hamilcar, defeated at Baecula, 6-month siege 214 falls again to Romans

CELTIBERIA

219 captured by Hannibal

LUSITANIA

Durius

NUMANTIA

Tagus

208 Hasdrubal defeated by Scipio Africanus

SAGUNTUM

Anas

206 Scipio Africanus drives Carthaginians from Spain

BAECULA

HISPANIA CITERIOR

HISPANIA ULTERIOR

ILIPA

BAETIS

Baetis

CARTHAGO NOVA

GADES

MALACA

228 founded by Hasdrubal 209 captured by Romans (Scipio Africanus)

TINGIS

211 Publius defeated on upper Baetis and Gnaeus destroyed near Carthago Nova, succeeded by Scipio Africanus son of Publius

237 Hamilcar Barca, son Hannibal and son-in-law Hasdrubal cross into Spain

RUSSADIR

- area of Carthaginian rule, 218 BC
- area of Roman rule, 218 BC
- ✗ site of major battle
- Roman base outside Roman territory

scale 1:10 000 000

0 ————— 600km

0 ————— 400mi

killing or capturing most of its 25,000 soldiers. But despite this convincing victory there was no sign of a general uprising against Rome. Hannibal decided to move to southern Italy where, he was reliably informed, discontent with Roman rule was stronger. At Cannae (216) he destroyed another Roman army in a masterly enveloping maneuver. Probably 30,000 Romans were killed. It was the worst defeat they ever suffered.

Hannibal suffered only light losses. His fortunes had never seemed brighter as some of Rome's southern Italian allies, including Capua, the second largest city in Italy, at last began to

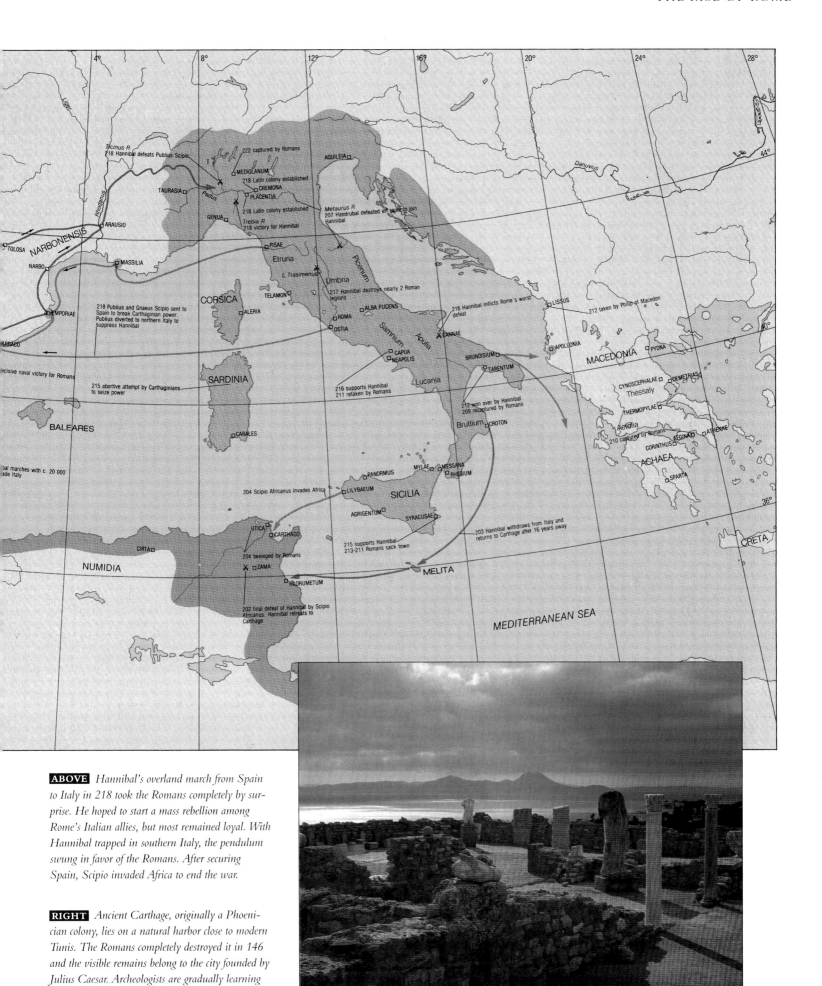

4° 8° 12° 16° 20° 24° 28°

Ticinus R
218 Hannibal defeats Publius Scipio

222 captured by Romans

AQUILEIA

Danuvius

MEDIOLANUM

218 Latin colony established
CREMONA
PLACENTIA

TAURASIA

Padus

218 Latin colony established

GENUA

Trebia R
218 victory for Hannibal

Metaurus R
207 Hasdrubal defeated en route to join
Hannibal

Rhodanus

ARAUSIO

TOLOSA

NARBONENSIS

PISAE

Etruria

Picenum

NARBO

MASSILIA

L. Trasimenus

Umbria

216 Hannibal inflicts Rome's worst
defeat

LISSUS

212 taken by Philip of Macedon

218 Publius and Gnaeus Scipio sent to
Spain to break Carthaginian power.
Publius diverted to northern Italy to
suppress Hannibal

CORSICA

TELAMON

ALERIA

217 Hannibal destroys nearly 2 Roman
legions

ALBA FUCENS

ROMA

OSTIA

Samnium

Apulia

CANNAE

APOLLONIA

MACEDONIA

PYDNA

EMPORIAE

BRUNDISIUM

CAPUA
NEAPOLIS

TARENTUM

decisive naval victory for Romans

215 abortive attempt by Carthaginians
to seize power

SARDINIA

Lucania

CYNOSCEPHALAE
Thessaly

DEMETRIAS

212 won over by Hannibal
209 recaptured by Romans

THERMOPYLAE

BALEARES

216 supports Hannibal
211 retaken by Romans

CARALES

Bruttium
CROTON

Aetolia

210 captured by Romans

CORINTHUS
AEGINA
ATHENAE

al marches with c. 20 000
de Italy

ACHAEA

SPARTA

PANORMUS

MYLAE
MESSANA
RHEGIUM

204 Scipio Africanus invades Africa

LILYBAEUM

SICILIA

AGRIGENTUM

SYRACUSAE

203 Hannibal withdraws from Italy and
returns to Carthage after 16 years away

CRETA

UTICA
CARTHAGO

CIRTA

215 supports Hannibal
213-211 Romans sack town

MELITA

204 besieged by Romans

NUMIDIA

ZAMA

HADRUMETUM

MEDITERRANEAN SEA

202 final defeat of Hannibal by Scipio
Africanus. Hannibal retreats to
Carthage.

ABOVE *Hannibal's overland march from Spain to Italy in 218 took the Romans completely by surprise. He hoped to start a mass rebellion among Rome's Italian allies, but most remained loyal. With Hannibal trapped in southern Italy, the pendulum swung in favor of the Romans. After securing Spain, Scipio invaded Africa to end the war.*

RIGHT *Ancient Carthage, originally a Phoenician colony, lies on a natural harbor close to modern Tunis. The Romans completely destroyed it in 146 and the visible remains belong to the city founded by Julius Caesar. Archeologists are gradually learning more about the culture of the Punic settlement.*

defect to him. The following year he was joined by Syracuse and Philip V of Macedon (r. 221–179). But Rome's allies in central Italy stood firm. Hannibal lacked the manpower to besiege Rome itself and was consequently in no position to force the Romans to sue for peace. The Roman general Fabius Maximus persuaded the senate not to attempt to confront him in open battle but to wear him down bit by bit by harassing his forces. Though he was not ready to admit failure, Hannibal was in fact stuck in a strategic cul-de-sac.

Notwithstanding Hannibal's invasion of Italy, the Romans had sent an expedition to Spain in 218 under Gnaeus and Publius Scipio. They won a series of victories over Hannibal's brother Hasdrubal and in 214 liberated Saguntum. Shortly after this, Roman armies laid siege to Syracuse and invaded Greece to attack Philip V of Macedon. In 211 Rome suffered a setback when both the Scipios were killed in battle in Spain. Publius Scipio (237–183), later nicknamed Africanus, the son and namesake of Publius Scipio, was sent to replace them and immediately began an aggressive offensive. He took Carthago Nova in a surprise attack in 209 and then defeated Hasdrubal at Baecula. Hasdrubal escaped and took his army overland to Italy, hoping to reinforce his brother's flagging campaign, but was defeated and killed at the Metaurus river in 207. Hannibal was now hopelessly isolated. The following year Scipio destroyed the last Carthaginian army in Spain at Ilipa and in 204 invaded North Africa. Hannibal was finally recalled to defend Carthage and succeeded in putting new heart into the Carthaginians who were on the point of agreeing to peace terms. But in a hard-fought engagement at Zama in 202 he was defeated by Scipio, in alliance with the Numidians. Carthaginian resistance was finally at an end.

Italy had suffered terribly in the war and, not surprisingly, Roman peace terms were harsh. Carthage, restricted to a small territory in its African heartland, had to pay a huge indemnity. It was barred from keeping a fleet and could not wage war without Roman permission. The Romans created two new provinces in Spain (Hispania Ulterior and Hispania Citerior) but strong resistance from the Celtiberians kept them from occupying all the territory once held by Carthage for several decades. Despite this, Rome now had no rival in the western Mediterranean. The war left a few loose ends to be tidied up in Italy. After some hard fighting, the Gauls in the north were reconquered. As a strengthening measure, many new colonies were founded there and in the south, where Hannibal had won most support. It had become difficult to persuade Romans to give up their citizenship, so the practice of founding Latin colonies was gradually abandoned in favor of colonies with full citizen rights.

THE END OF CARTHAGE

Despite the loss of its empire, Carthage continued to flourish as a commercial center and was able to pay its indemnity to Rome without difficulty. However, Rome's ally, the ambitious Numidian king Masinissa (238–149), continued to attack Carthage, which was unable to defend itself, since the Romans constantly denied it permission to make war. The Carthaginians' patience began to wear thin, and between 160 and 155 they launched retaliatory raids against Masinissa. This trivial show of independence was too much for the influential senator Cato (234–149). A veteran

RIGHT *"Latin" colonies (see page 204)* *played an important role in the defeat of Hannibal by providing secure bases for Roman forces, even in areas where the local population had gone over to the enemy. After the war, many Latin colonies were reinforced and new ones founded. But it was becoming less easy to persuade Romans to surrender their citizenship in return for land, and Latin colonies were gradually abandoned in favor of colonies of Roman citizens. Parma and Mutina (founded 183 BC) were the first of the new type of colony, Aquileia (founded 181 BC) was the last of the old. The Romans often gave their colonies hopeful names such as Placentia ("peace") and Copia ("plenty"). Many coastal garrison colonies were founded in the 190s when the fear of an invasion by Antiochos (Antiochus) III, ruler of the Seleukid (Seleucid) empire, was at its height.*

RIGHT *The grid layout of Roman colonies is reflected in the street plan of many Italian cities of colonial origin. Shown here is an aerial view of Florence, founded in the late 1st century BC.*
FAR RIGHT: Land was distributed to colonists using a system called centuriation – it was marked out in large squares called centuriae *(124 acres, 50 hectares) consisting of 100 two-*iugera *units (a* iugera *was approximately two-thirds of an acre, or 0.25 of a hectare). Traces of centuriation are clearly seen in this aerial photograph of fields in Emilia.*

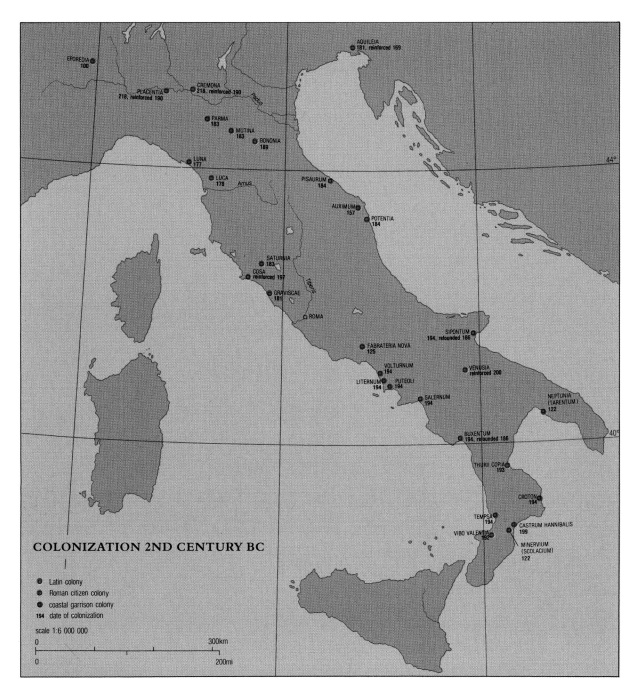

COLONIZATION 2ND CENTURY BC

EPOREDIA 100

CREMONA 218, reinforced 190
PLACENTIA 218, reinforced 190

PARMA 183
MUTINA 183
BONONIA 189

LUNA 177
LUCA 178
Arnus

AQUILEIA 181, reinforced 169

PISAURUM 184
AUXIMUM 157
POTENTIA 184

SATURNIA 183
COSA reinforced 197
GRAVISCAE 181
Tiberis
ROMA

SIPONTUM 194, refounded 186
FABRATERIA NOVA 125
VOLTURNUM 194
LITERNUM 194
PUTEOLI 194
VENUSIA reinforced 200
SALERNUM 194
BUXENTUM 194, refounded 186

NEPTUNIA (TARENTUM) 122

THURII COPIA 193
CROTON 194
TEMPSA 194
VIBO VALENTIA 192
CASTRUM HANNIBALIS 199
MINERVIUM (SCOLACIUM) 122

- Latin colony
- Roman citizen colony
- coastal garrison colony
- 194 date of colonization

scale 1:6 000 000
0 — 300km
0 — 200mi

of the war against Hannibal, he persuaded the senate, against the evidence, that Carthage was still a threat to Rome. When war broke out between Carthage and Masinissa in 149, the Romans ordered the Carthaginians to abandon their city, which they refused to do. After a three-year siege the Romans succeeded in taking Carthage, which they razed to the ground. Some 50,000 of its inhabitants were sold into slavery and its territory became the new Roman province of Africa.

ROME TURNS EAST

Rome's political interaction with the Greek world began in earnest when Pyrrhus invaded Italy in the 270s. His unexpected defeat by this relatively unknown Italian city forced the Greeks to take serious notice of Rome. By the end of the first Punic war Rome had gained control of all the Greek settlements in Italy and Sicily and in 220 it won effective control of a number of Greek cities on the east coast of the Adriatic during a war to suppress Illyrian piracy. It was this potential threat to his position in Greece that led Philip V of Macedon to join forces with Carthage in 215. The Romans reasonably enough saw Philip's action as an unwarranted stab in the back and, when Pergamon and Rhodes appealed to them for protection against Philip, seized their opportunity for revenge. After Philip's defeat at the battle of Kynoskephalai (197) Macedon was forced to

213

ROMAN RELIGION

Rome's traditional pagan religion had no systematic theology or moral teaching and the Romans borrowed their mythology freely from the Greeks and others. The Romans' chief concern was to secure the *pax deorum*, or goodwill of the gods, by ensuring that a complex calendar of archaic ceremonies was regularly and precisely observed. If a mistake was made over some detail of archaic ritual, the entire ceremony had to start again. There was no professional priesthood – the public rituals of the state gods, such as Jupiter, were carried out on behalf of the community by members of the ruling aristocracy. The private rituals of the household gods, such as Vesta (the hearth), the Penates (the store-cupboard) and the Lares (ancestral spirits), were performed by the male head of the family. No major decision was made without consulting the gods, perhaps by examining the entrails of a sacrificed animal or by watching the behavior of sacred chickens. Unusual natural events and dreams were also considered to come from the gods. Increased contacts with the Greeks led to the introduction of new cults, such as those of the healing god Aesculapius (Greek, Asklepios) and the wine god Dionysius or Bacchus

(Greek, Dionysos). As Roman power extended into the Near East and Egypt, more exotic cults followed, such as that of the Anatolian mother goddess Cybele (the *Magna Mater*, or "Great Mother.") By the 1st century BC many educated Romans, such as the writer Cicero, openly questioned the literal existence of the gods.

ABOVE *The goddess Vesta presided over the hearth, the center of any Roman household. The temple of Vesta in the Roman Forum was the symbolic family home of the Roman people. It contained a sacred hearth, tended by the six Vestal Virgins. The hearth's fire was kindled during the festival of the Vestalia on March 1st and kept alight all year long. The Romans believed that disaster would strike the state if it was allowed to go out.*

LEFT *Mithraism, an all-male cult, was introduced during the 1st century AD and was especially popular with soldiers. Like other Eastern religions, it offered an ecstatic religious experience and it had a rite of initiation. Mithras, an Iranian sun-god, killed the cosmic bull of creation, symbolizing the conquest of evil and death. From the bull's body sprang cereals and vines.*

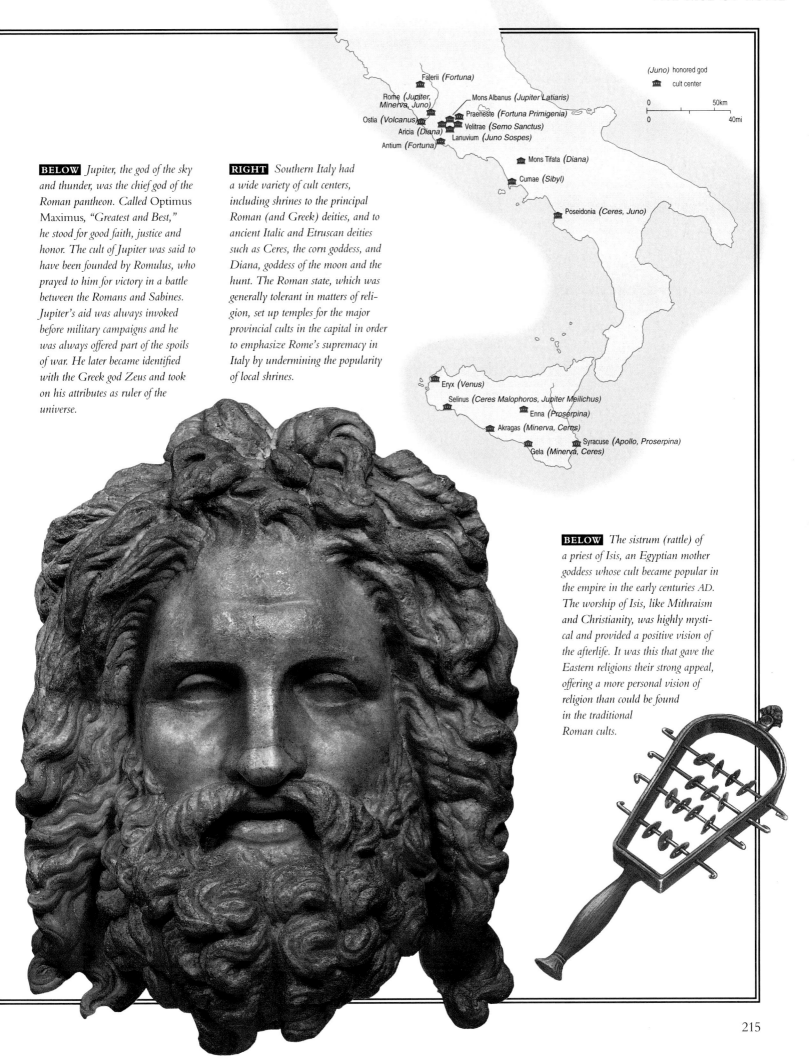

(Juno) honored god

🏛 cult center

Falerii (Fortuna)

Rome (Jupiter, Minerva, Juno)

Mons Albanus (Jupiter Latiaris)

Praeneste (Fortuna Primigenia)

Ostia (Volcanus)

Velitrae (Semo Sanctus)

Aricia (Diana)

Lanuvium (Juno Sospes)

Antium (Fortuna)

Mons Tifata (Diana)

Cumae (Sibyl)

Poseidonia (Ceres, Juno)

Eryx (Venus)

Selinus (Ceres Malophoros, Jupiter Meilichus)

Enna (Proserpina)

Akragas (Minerva, Ceres)

Syracuse (Apollo, Proserpina)

Gela (Minerva, Ceres)

BELOW Jupiter, the god of the sky and thunder, was the chief god of the Roman pantheon. Called Optimus Maximus, "Greatest and Best," he stood for good faith, justice and honor. The cult of Jupiter was said to have been founded by Romulus, who prayed to him for victory in a battle between the Romans and Sabines. Jupiter's aid was always invoked before military campaigns and he was always offered part of the spoils of war. He later became identified with the Greek god Zeus and took on his attributes as ruler of the universe.

RIGHT Southern Italy had a wide variety of cult centers, including shrines to the principal Roman (and Greek) deities, and to ancient Italic and Etruscan deities such as Ceres, the corn goddess, and Diana, goddess of the moon and the hunt. The Roman state, which was generally tolerant in matters of religion, set up temples for the major provincial cults in the capital in order to emphasize Rome's supremacy in Italy by undermining the popularity of local shrines.

BELOW The sistrum (rattle) of a priest of Isis, an Egyptian mother goddess whose cult became popular in the empire in the early centuries AD. The worship of Isis, like Mithraism and Christianity, was highly mystical and provided a positive vision of the afterlife. It was this that gave the Eastern religions their strong appeal, offering a more personal vision of religion than could be found in the traditional Roman cults.

become an ally of Rome. The Greek city states were made Roman protectorates.

In 196 Antiochos (Antiochus) III, ruler of the Seleukid (Seleucid) kingdom, occupied Thrace. Hannibal, an exile from Carthage, was among his retinue, and this was enough to persuade the Romans of his hostile intentions towards them. Antiochos foolishly provoked a war by intervening in Greece in 192. He was in no way prepared for the overwhelming Roman reaction and was quickly expelled. In 190, after he was decisively defeated at Magnesia (Anatolia), the Romans divided his Anatolian possessions between their allies Pergamon and Rhodes. They kept for themselves the indemnity payment they exacted from Antiochos, and a huge quantity of plunder.

The Romans' reluctance to annex territory after the war with Antiochos was typical of their early dealings with the Greeks. In the west it was Rome's policy to subject conquered territory to

provincial administration but in the politically sophisticated world of the Greeks, Rome at first attempted to rule indirectly through dependent local governments – essentially a system of client states. The intractable rivalries of the Greek city states rendered this more difficult than the Romans had imagined. After thwarting an attempt by Philip's son Perseus to reassert Macedonian power at Pydna (168), Roman policy altered. To demonstrate that nothing less than complete obedience would be tolerated, Macedon was divided into four separate states, the monarchy was abolished and tribute imposed. Perseus's allies, the Molossians of Epirus, were treated even more harshly: their territory was ravaged and 25,000 people were enslaved.

Continuing unrest among the Greeks forced Rome to impose harsher rule. Following a rebellion from 150 to 148, Macedon was annexed and incorporated into Rome's growing empire as the

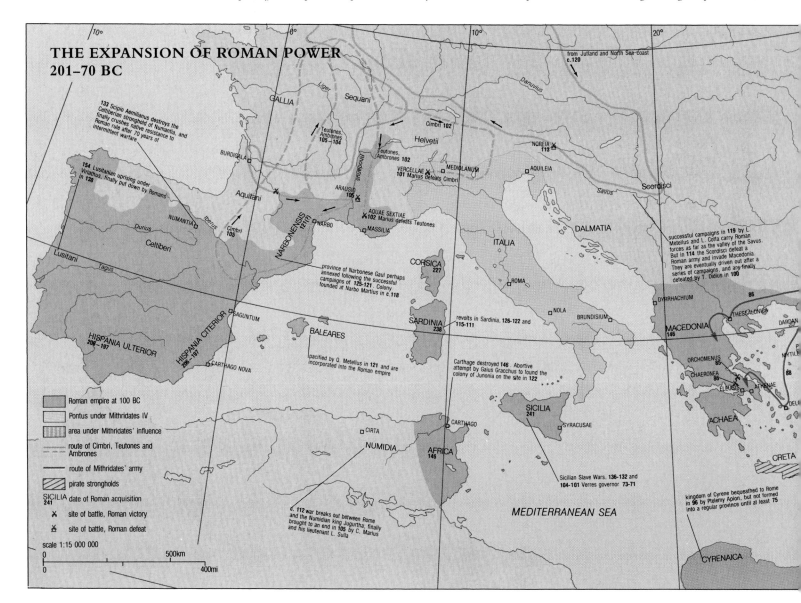

province of Macedonia. In 146 a rebellion in Achaea had also to be put down. Corinth was destroyed to provide an example for the rest of Greece, and its population massacred or sold into slavery. The whole of southern Greece was annexed as the province of Achaea. Only Sparta, whose austere militaristic traditions the Romans admired, retained a nominal independence.

THE CONSEQUENCES OF EMPIRE

The conquest of Greece greatly affected the character of Roman civilization. The mass of plunder from the wars – silver plate, fine furniture, bronze ornaments, books, statues and paintings – started a demand for all things Greek. Soon Greek craftsmen were producing works of art and other products for Roman patrons, while the influx of Greek slaves, among them musicians and cooks, transformed Roman tastes. Greek drama became popular in the late 3rd century BC – the plays of Plautus (c. 250–184), the first great Roman dramatist, were adaptations of Greek originals – and athletic games were held for the first time in Rome in 186. In 148 the first Greek-style marble temple was built in Rome (see pages 220–221).

By the mid 2nd century there was concern that familiarity among upper-class Romans with Greek culture and lifestyle was undermining the traditional Roman virtues of courage, good faith and piety. The most prominent advocate of traditional values was the writer Cato. He was not opposed to Greek influences – his own writings show how well he adapted Greek literary forms to Latin – but he believed that the taste for Greek luxury was a corrupting influence. He deliberately chose an austere lifestyle for himself and called for sumptuary laws to curb the excesses of others.

Roman society was certainly becoming more corrupt, but Cato's impassioned denunciations identified the symptoms rather than the cause. Political and economic life in Rome and Italy had been profoundly changed by Rome's rise to Mediterranean empire. Popular opposition to senatorial government virtually disappeared during the senate's successful conduct of the Punic wars, but though it was outwardly a time of unparalleled political stability and social unity, tensions were mounting beneath the surface. The Senate had always been divided into shifting factions of friends and families who united to promote particular policies and used networks of clients to vote for their favored candidates in magisterial elections. As Rome's wealth and power grew, the

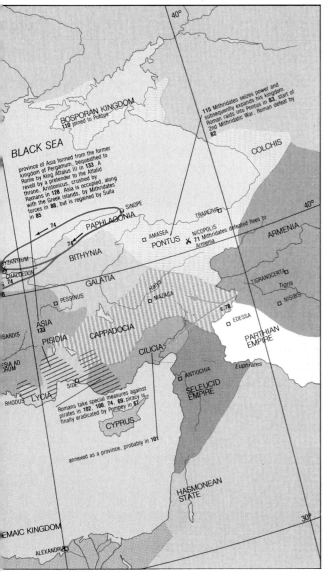

ABOVE *The city of Corinth was razed to the ground by the Romans in 146 BC to punish it for having rebelled and to set an example to the other Greek city states. Like Carthage, which was destroyed in the same year, it was refounded by Julius Caesar as a colony for veteran soldiers and poor citizens.*

LEFT *Roman expansion continued steadily for 70 years after the end of the wars with Carthage, but in the late 2nd century BC the republic was overtaken by a series of of social, political and military crises that showed the ruling senatorial order to be corrupt and incompetent. The most serious threats were posed by two migrating German tribes, the Cimbri and Teutones, who inflicted a succession of crushing defeats on Roman armies between 113 and 105, and Mithridates, the ambitious king of Pontus who almost wrested Asia and Greece from Rome's grasp in 88 BC.*

rewards of office multiplied, intensifying competition within the senatorial class. The ostentatious lifestyles of the east were adopted by ambitious aristocrats as a way of setting themselves apart from their peers and improving their chances of winning office. Bribery, corruption and the abuse of power followed.

Rome's lengthy wars produced problems of their own. Generals had originally been appointed for one year only but this practice had to be abandoned during the Punic wars. Successful generals such as Scipio Africanus could now hold office for years, allowing them to build up considerable influence. Cato saw the solidarity of the senatorial class as one of the foundations of republican government and was deeply concerned that it seemed to be threatened by the increase in competition.

CRISIS IN THE COUNTRYSIDE

Cato was the author of the earliest surviving treatise on farming, yet he appears to have been unaware of the critical state of Italian agriculture. Southern Italy in particular had been devastated during the war with Hannibal. Losses of crops and livestock alone were enough to ruin many peasant farmers, but they also had to contend with the burden of long military service. The Roman army was made up of citizen conscripts. The system had worked well when Rome's wars with its Italian neighbors were seasonal affairs, but it was quite unsuited to prolonged conflicts when large forces had to be kept in the field for years on end. Rome's military commitments hardly decreased

with the ending of the Punic wars. In the 35 years after 202 BC Rome maintained an average of 130,000 Roman citizens and Italian allies under arms. Around 13 percent of adult male citizens were on military service at any time, an incredible feat of mobilization in a pre-industrial state.

Despite military pay, the absence of menfolk from a farm for long periods all too often proved ruinous and, of course, a great many soldiers never came back. Families fell into debt and were dispossessed. Their lands were purchased by rich speculators who used war profits to build up large estates, or *latifundia*. These were worked by cheap slave labor which was in plentiful supply due to the mass enslavement of conquered peoples. The displacement of peasant freeholders from the land began to cause increasing concern, mainly because they were the chief source of recruits for the army. Once they had lost their lands, most peasants migrated to the cities, especially Rome. Here they joined the ranks of the *proletarii*, the lowest class of citizens who were not eligible for military service because they owned no property. At the same time, the active participation of Roman citizens in government was declining. The policy of creating colonies meant that Roman citizens were now scattered all over Italy and many were unable to exercise their right to vote in the assemblies. The influx of slaves also created unease. Slave revolts broke out in Sicily and Italy in 136 and were put down with difficulty.

THE GRACCHAN REFORMS

The growing discontent with the senate came to a head during the tribunate of Tiberius Gracchus (133 BC). Though tribunes had extensive powers of veto and could pass laws through the popular assembly, most were career politicians who were reluctant to challenge the senatorial order.

Not so Tiberius Gracchus (168–133), who was determined to use his powers to the full to force through land reform. The Gracchi were a leading aristocratic family so many suspected Tiberius's motives. His enemies claimed that he was cynically exploiting popular unrest to advance his own career. He argued that by seeking to protect the peasant farmer class he was safeguarding Rome's military strength.

At the heart of his reforms was the *ager publicus*, land owned by the state, much of it confiscated from rebel Italian cities at the end of the war with Hannibal. Legally,

BELOW *The crisis in the countryside exacerbated Rome's perennial difficulties of securing sufficient food supplies for its growing numbers of citizens. In 123 BC the tribune Gaius Gracchus established a subsidized corn supply for the city's poor. It was abolished during the dictatorship of Sulla (82–79), but the granting of a corn dole became a recognized way by which ambitious politicians, and later emperors, could win the backing of the Roman people. This mosaic from Ostia, Rome's commercial port through which grain imports were shipped from Sicily and North Africa, shows the distribution of a corn dole.*

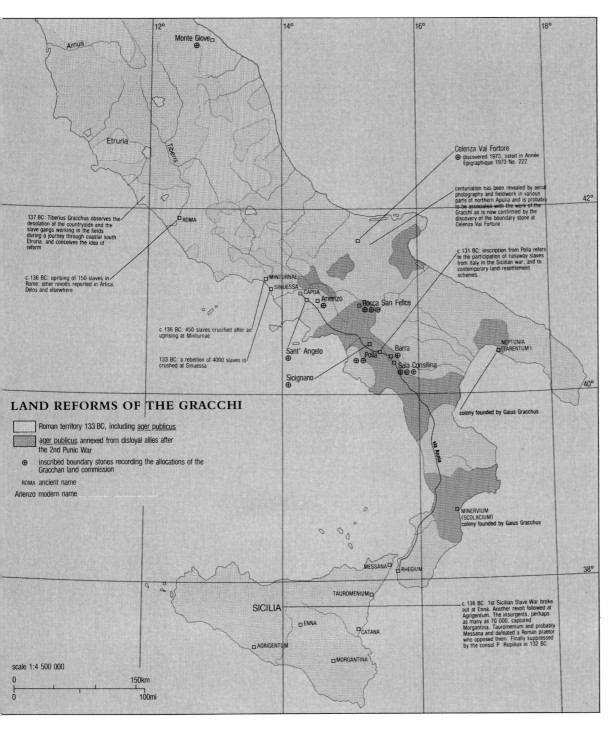

Monte Giove

Arnus

Etruria

12°

Tiberis

ROMA

14°

16°

18°

Celenza Val Fortore
⊕ discovered 1973, listed in Année
Epigraphique 1973 No. 222

centuriation has been revealed by aerial
photography and fieldwork in various
parts of northern Apulia and is probably
to be associated with the work of the
Gracchi as is now confirmed by the
discovery of the boundary stone at
Celenza Val Fortore

42°

137 BC: Tiberius Gracchus observes the
desolation of the countryside and the
slave gangs working in the fields
during a journey through coastal south
Etruria, and conceives the idea of
reform

c.136 BC: uprising of 150 slaves in
Rome; other revolts reported in Attica,
Delos and elsewhere

MINTURNAE
SINUESSA
CAPUA
Arienzo
Rocca San Felice
⊕⊕⊕

c.131 BC: inscription from Polla refers
to the participation of runaway slaves
from Italy in the Sicilian war, and to
contemporary land-resettlement
schemes

c.136 BC: 450 slaves crucified after an
uprising at Minturnae

Sant' Angelo
⊕

Polla
⊕ ⊕

Barra
Sala Consilina
⊕⊕⊕

NEPTUNIA
(TARENTUM)

133 BC: a rebellion of 4000 slaves is
crushed at Sinuessa

Sicignano
⊕

colony founded by Gaius Gracchus

40°

LAND REFORMS OF THE GRACCHI

☐ Roman territory 133 BC, including _ager publicus_

▨ _ager publicus_ annexed from disloyal allies after
the 2nd Punic War

⊕ inscribed boundary stones recording the allocations of the
Gracchan land commission

ROMA ancient name

Arienzo modern name

Via Annia

MINERVIUM
(SCOLACIUM)
colony founded by Gaius Gracchus

MESSANA
RHEGIUM

38°

SICILIA

TAUROMENIUM

ENNA

CATANA

AGRIGENTUM

MORGANTINA

c.136 BC: 1st Sicilian Slave War broke
out at Enna. Another revolt followed at
Agrigentum. The insurgents, perhaps
as many as 70 000, captured
Morgantina, Tauromenium and probably
Messana and defeated a Roman praetor
who opposed them. Finally suppressed
by the consul P. Rupilius in 132 BC

scale 1:4 500 000

0 ──────── 150km

0 ──────── 100mi

no citizen was allowed to hold more than 500
iugera (320 acres, 125 hectares) of the _ager
publicus_ but this ruling had not been enforced and many
rich landowners had acquired far more. Tiberius
proposed that all land held in excess of this limit
should be reclaimed by the state and redistributed
in small allotments to dispossessed peasants with
inalienable rights of tenure. His plan did not dis-
possess anyone of property to which they had legal
title; all the same, it aroused intense opposition
from wealthy landowners. But it had widespread
popular support, especially among the rural poor
who flocked to Rome to vote for the legislation

when it came before the popular assembly.

With the passing of the measure into law, a
land commission, consisting of Tiberius Gracchus,
his brother Gaius (c.159–121), and his father-in-
law Appius Claudius, was appointed to oversee the
redistribution of the land. Attalos III of Pergamon
had recently died and bequeathed his kingdom to
Rome. Tiberius passed a law through the popular
assembly that the royal treasure be distributed to
the recipients of land allotments to help them
stock their farms. The Senate, which traditionally
controlled public finance, became seriously
alarmed. Tiberius now put himself forward for a

REPUBLICAN ROME

The city of Rome grew spectacularly during the 400 years of the republic. Already one of the largest cities in Italy at the end of the monarchy, its population had reached 90,000 by 300 BC and was close to a million by the time of Julius Caesar at the end of the 1st century BC. Long before this the city had overflowed its circuit of defensive walls built in 378. Its growing population is a sign of the republic's increasing prosperity, much of it based on the steady flow of plunder from its conquests abroad. In 312 the city's first aqueduct, the Aqua Appia, was built by Appius Claudius to provide clean drinking water. By the time of the war with Hannibal, the poor were being crammed into multi-story tenements lacking water, toilets and cooking facilities. The population was now so large that the produce of the surrounding countryside was no longer sufficient to support it and the city was increasingly dependent on grain imports. The population changed constantly throughout this period, as less well-off citizens left to found colonies in other parts of Italy and the Mediterranean lands. Conquered peoples were brought back to Rome as slaves and in time they, or their descendants, were freed to join the citizen body.

The squalid conditions in which most of the population lived contrasted with the increasing magnificence of Rome's public buildings. The city's appearance changed rapidly in the last years of the republic, as military strongmen such as Sulla, Pompey and Julius Caesar embarked on lavish building projects to enhance their prestige and bolster their popular support. This practice continued on an ever more grandiose scale under the emperors and as a result few buildings survive from the republican period of Rome's history.

RIGHT *The circular temple in the Forum Boarium, which dates from the 2nd century BC, is the earliest surviving example of a marble temple in Rome and one of the most complete buildings to survive from the republican period. It is in the Greek style of the Hellenistic age.*

1 temple of Juno Moneta
2 Tabularium
3 Basilica Aemilia
4 temple of Jupiter Capitolinus
5 Basilica Julia
6 temples of Fortuna and Mater Matuta
7 temple of Portunus
8 temple of Hercules Victor
9 Ara Maxima
10 temple of Cybele of Magna Mater

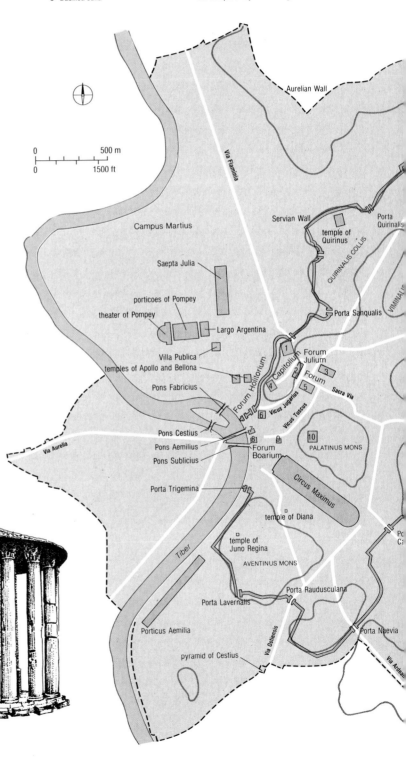

BELOW *By the late republic, Rome had spread beyond the Servian Wall, the city boundary dating from the 4th century BC. It is uncertain how far the built-up area extended at this time, but it was probably already approaching the line of the Aurelian Wall, built in the later imperial period. Rome lay at the hub of a network of roads, but its main highway was the Tiber. Food supplies shipped into the city were traded in the vast market hall of the Porticus Aemilia.*

LEFT *The embellishment of late republican Rome owed much to the power politics of the time. Rome's first Greek-style stone theater was commissioned by Pompey and dedicated by him in 55 BC. He is said to have been inspired by the beauty of the 4th-century theater of Mytilene, which was one of the largest in the Greek world. Little survives of Pompey's building but its plan can still be seen on this fragment of a marble map of Rome dating from the 3rd century AD.*

ABOVE *Stone bridges were built at several points across the Tiber. To the north of the city, the Milvian bridge (109 BC) was the crossing point for the Via Flaminia, the main road to Etruria. It was the scene of the emperor Constantine's decisive victory over his rival Maxentius in AD 312.*

RIGHT *The forum of Caesar was dedicated in 46 BC, two years before the dictator's death. It was dominated by the temple of Venus, the legendary ancestor of the Julian house. An equestrian statue of Caesar stood in the square.*

LEFT *Part of a list of consuls found at the entrance to the Forum. The two consuls were the most senior of Rome's elected government officials. The republic's forms of government were developed to suit the needs of a city state. The consulship came under increasing strain as Rome found itself at the center of a Mediterranean empire and by the time of Julius Caesar it had lost all real authority.*

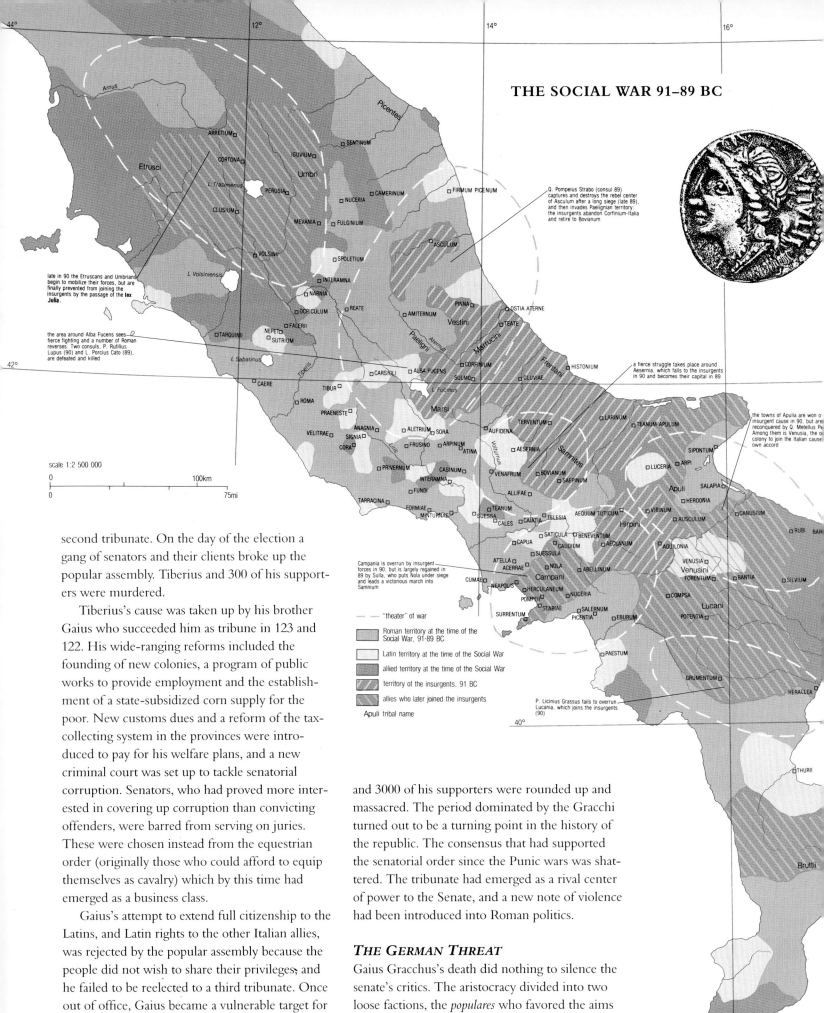

THE SOCIAL WAR 91–89 BC

late in 90 the Etruscans and Umbrians begin to mobilize their forces, but are finally prevented from joining the insurgents by the passage of the **lex Julia**.

the area around Alba Fucens sees fierce fighting and a number of Roman reverses. Two consuls, P. Rutilius Lupus (90) and L. Porcius Cato (89), are defeated and killed

Q. Pompeius Strabo (consul 89) captures and destroys the rebel center of Asculum after a long siege (late 89), and then invades Paelignian territory: the insurgents abandon Corfinium-Italia and retire to Bovianum

a fierce struggle takes place around Aesernia, which falls to the insurgents in 90 and becomes their capital in 89

the towns of Apulia are won o insurgent cause in 90, but are reconquered by Q. Metellus P Among them is Venusia, the o colony to join the Italian cause own accord

Campania is overrun by insurgent forces in 90, but is largely regained in 89 by Sulla, who puts Nola under siege and leads a victorious march into Samnium

P. Licinius Grassus fails to overrun Lucania, which joins the insurgents (90)

scale 1:2 500 000

100km

75mi

- - - "theater" of war
- Roman territory at the time of the Social War, 91–89 BC
- Latin territory at the time of the Social War
- allied territory at the time of the Social War
- territory of the insurgents, 91 BC
- allies who later joined the insurgents

Apuli tribal name

---

second tribunate. On the day of the election a gang of senators and their clients broke up the popular assembly. Tiberius and 300 of his supporters were murdered.

Tiberius's cause was taken up by his brother Gaius who succeeded him as tribune in 123 and 122. His wide-ranging reforms included the founding of new colonies, a program of public works to provide employment and the establishment of a state-subsidized corn supply for the poor. New customs dues and a reform of the tax-collecting system in the provinces were introduced to pay for his welfare plans, and a new criminal court was set up to tackle senatorial corruption. Senators, who had proved more interested in covering up corruption than convicting offenders, were barred from serving on juries. These were chosen instead from the equestrian order (originally those who could afford to equip themselves as cavalry) which by this time had emerged as a business class.

Gaius's attempt to extend full citizenship to the Latins, and Latin rights to the other Italian allies, was rejected by the popular assembly because the people did not wish to share their privileges, and he failed to be reelected to a third tribunate. Once out of office, Gaius became a vulnerable target for his enemies in the Senate. A political demonstration turned violent and on the Senate's orders he

and 3000 of his supporters were rounded up and massacred. The period dominated by the Gracchi turned out to be a turning point in the history of the republic. The consensus that had supported the senatorial order since the Punic wars was shattered. The tribunate had emerged as a rival center of power to the Senate, and a new note of violence had been introduced into Roman politics.

THE GERMAN THREAT

Gaius Gracchus's death did nothing to silence the senate's critics. The aristocracy divided into two loose factions, the *populares* who favored the aims and methods of the Gracchi, and the *optimates* who represented the senate's conservative majority.

LEFT *The Social war began in 91 BC as a result of the Romans' repeated refusal to grant citizenship to its Italian allies (socii). The main centers of revolt were in southern and central Italy. The rebels founded an independent state, Italia, with a capital at Corfinium. With one exception, the Latin colonies remained loyal to Rome, as did the Greek cities of the south. Nevertheless, the Romans were hard pressed until they conceded to the rebels' political demands, thus bringing the revolt to a rapid conclusion.*

Late in the 2nd century, when Rome faced a series of unexpected military crises, the *populares* were given fresh ammunition to attack the Senate. In 114 a Thracian tribe invaded Macedonia and defeated a Roman army. At the same time, the news that two migrating Germanic tribes, the Cimbri and Teutones, were approaching the borders of Italy caused panic in Rome. An army was rushed to intercept them, but was defeated at Noreia in 113. Italy was saved from invasion only when the tribes, for unknown reasons, decided to head for Gaul instead. It was only a temporary respite. A few years later the Germans invaded Roman territory in southern Gaul, smashing three Roman armies in quick succession. Meanwhile, another Roman army had been defeated in Africa in 110 in a war with the Numidian king Jugurtha. Public anger grew over the Senate's incompetent handling of the crisis. A tribune proposed the setting up of a court of inquiry, as a result of which several leading aristocrats were exiled.

In 108 Gaius Marius (157–86) was elected consul. An equestrian, Marius came from a minor land-owning family. He made much of his lack of noble blood during his election campaign, in which he attacked the aristocracy for their corruption and incompetence. Marius had a huge following among the plebs and the popular assembly appointed him to lead the war against Jugurtha whom he defeated in 105. The following year Marius was elected consul for a second time and given command of the war against the Cimbri and Teutones. Their temporary withdrawal gave him a breathing space to reform the Roman army. When they resumed their raids, Marius was ready for them with a first-class force. He defeated the Teutones near Massilia (Marseille) in 102 and the Cimbri at Vercellae in northern Italy the following year. Against all precedent, Marius had held the consulship throughout this period and in 100 he was elected for a fifth consecutive term.

ARMY REFORM

For his war against Jugurtha, Marius had broken with the tradition that barred those without property from military service, and recruited volunteers from the landless proletariat. He now formally ended the connection between property ownership and military service, opening the way to the creation of a standing army of career soldiers. Arms drill and weapons training, adapted from the gladiatorial schools, was introduced. The maniple of 120 men, the standard sub-unit of a legion since the 4th century, was abandoned in favor of the larger cohort of 480 men, divided into six subdivisions, called centuries, of 80 men. Each legion, which consisted of 10 cohorts, was given an eagle standard as a focus for regimental loyalty. Roman soldiers had been divided into classes according to the weapons and armor they could afford to equip themselves with. Standard equipment of oblong shield, mail coat, helmet, *pilum* (javelin) and *gladius* (a short thrusting sword) was now issued to everyone free of charge. Soldiers were made to carry emergency rations, cooking equipment and tools to build a fortified camp every night when on the march. The heavily laden men called themselves "Marius's mules."

The long-term consequences of Marius's army reforms were considerable. They gave Rome one of the most effective instruments of imperial expansion the world has ever seen. But they also created the conditions that allowed client armies to flourish, so fostering the rise of the military dictators who would ultimately destroy the republic. Since the state was not prepared to grant land or pay pensions to discharged veterans, soldiers looked to their commanders to provide for them. This dependence made it easy for power-hungry commanders to persuade their armies to back their political ambitions. Marius certainly did not foresee these consequences but they became apparent almost immediately. In 103 Marius secured the cooperation of the tribune Saturninus to obtain land grants for his veterans. The senate bitterly opposed it, and the measures were repealed after Saturninus was lynched by a mob in 100. His failure to reward his veterans discredited Marius and he was forced into exile.

THE SOCIAL WAR (91–89 BC)

As Rome's empire grew, its Italian allies began to feel less like partners and more like subjects. They shared the burdens of Rome's wars but received none of the benefits. The rejection of Gaius Gracchus's attempt to grant them greater rights had only heightened their resentment. In 91 BC the tribune Livius Drusus failed in a new attempt to enfranchise the Italian allies, with the result that a major rebellion broke out. The Social war (from *socii*, Latin for allies) was bitterly fought and the Romans won only by conceding to the rebels' demands, offering Roman citizenship to all communities that stayed loyal and to any that laid down their arms. This widening of the citizen franchise completed the romanization of Italy.

ROMAN ROADS

Rome's network of more than 55,000 miles (88,500 km) of paved roads was the most highly developed in the ancient world. The first road to be built was the 122-mile (196-km) long Via Appia, linking Rome with Capua, which was started in 312 BC during the Samnite wars. Like all the roads that came after it, the Via Appia was paved for the whole of its length and followed the straightest possible course. The road system continued to expand for the next 500 years, growing in step with the empire itself. Its main purpose was to provide the Roman army with fast routes to trouble-spots on the frontiers of the empire. The roads were well-drained and surfaced with paving slabs or cobbles so that they remained passable in every kind of weather. These surfaces were hard on the feet of both men and animals, but fully equipped legionaries on a forced march could cover up to 24 miles (39 km) in 5 hours along them. Since most roads were built and maintained by the army, construction skills formed an important part of military training. An official posting system was introduced under the empire. Post houses, where couriers could change horses, were sited every 10–15 miles (16–24 km), and official hostels every 20–30 miles (32–48 km). Good roads promoted local trade, but as road transportation was slow and expensive, most long-distance trade traveled by water.

LEFT *A surviving section of the Via Egnata, the main Roman road across Macedonia, near Kavalla in northern Greece. The road was strategically important during the civil wars of the late republic, but was replaced by more northerly routes under the empire, when the frontier was pushed north to the Danube. When the empire was divided in the 4th century AD, it became part of the main sea and land route between Italy and the eastern capital of Constantinople.*

BELOW *Roads were marked every mile (1 Roman mile equaled 1000 paces or 5000 feet/1525 m) by inscribed or painted milestones – this example, from Leptis Magna in North Africa, indicates that the road extends for 44 miles (70 km) inland. The milestones bore dedications to the current emperor and their ornateness expressed pride in Roman road-building achievements.*

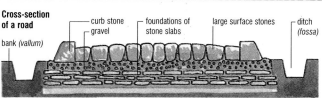

Cross-section of a road — bank (vallum) — gravel — curb stone — foundations of stone slabs — large surface stones — ditch (fossa)

LEFT *Road-building methods varied with the terrain. The aim was to create a solid, well-drained surface that could be used by troops and heavy vehicles at all times of year.*

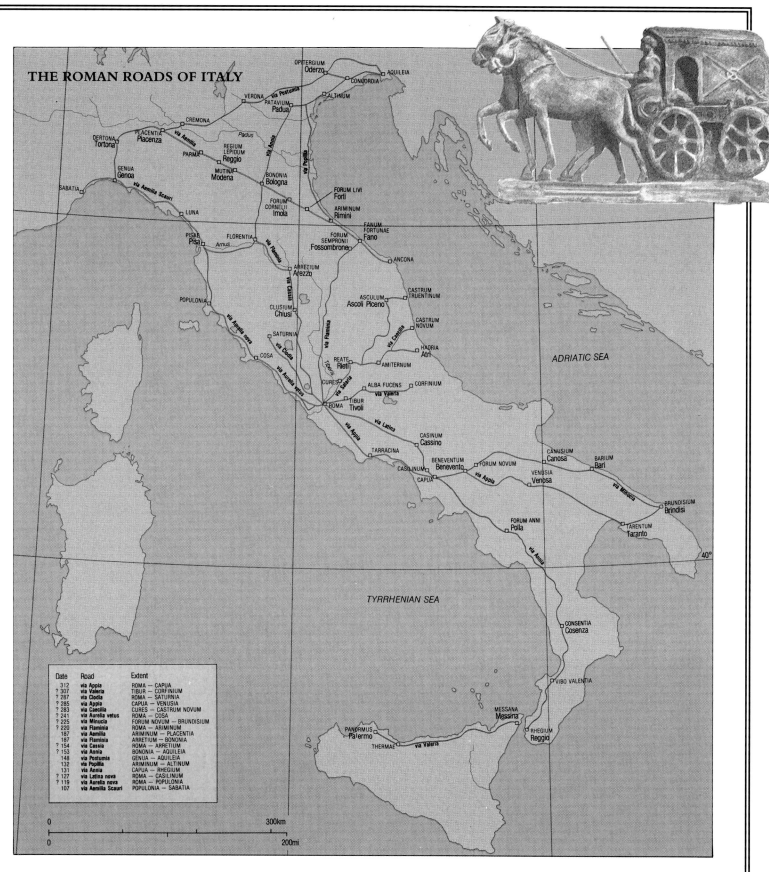

THE ROMAN ROADS OF ITALY

OPITERGIUM
Oderzo
AQUILEIA
CONCORDIA
VERONA
via Postumia
ALTINUM
PATAVIUM
Padua
CREMONA
Padus
DERTONA
Tortona
PLACENTIA
Piacenza
via Aemilia
PARMA
REGIUM
LEPIDUM
Reggio
MUTINA
Modena
BONONIA
Bologna
GENUA
Genoa
via Aemilia Scauri
SABATIA
LUNA
FORUM
CORNELII
Imola
FORUM LIVI
Forli
ARIMINUM
Rimini
FANUM
FORTUNAE
Fano
PISAE
Pisa
FLORENTIA
Arnus
via Flaminia
FORUM
SEMPRONII
Fossombrone
ANCONA
ARRETIUM
Arezzo
via Cassia
POPULONIA
CLUSIUM
Chiusi
ASCULUM
Ascoli Piceno
CASTRUM
TRUENTINUM
via Aurelia nova
via Flaminia
SATURNIA
via Clodia
CASTRUM
NOVUM
via Caecilia
HADRIA
Atri
ADRIATIC SEA
COSA
via Aurelia vetus
Tiberis
REATE
Rieti
AMITERNUM
CURES
via Salaria
ALBA FUCENS
CORFINIUM
TIBUR
Tivoli
via Valeria
ROMA
via Latina
CASINUM
Cassino
TARRACINA
BENEVENTUM
Benevento
FORUM NOVUM
CANUSIUM
Canosa
BARIUM
Bari
CASILINUM
CAPUA
via Appia
VENUSIA
Venosa
via Minucia
BRUNDISIUM
Brindisi
via Appia
FORUM ANNI
Polla
TARENTUM
Taranto
via Annia
TYRRHENIAN SEA
40°
CONSENTIA
Cosenza
VIBO VALENTIA
MESSANA
Messina
PANORMUS
Palermo
RHEGIUM
Reggio
THERMAE
via Valeria

Date	Road	Extent
312	via Appia	ROMA — CAPUA
? 307	via Valeria	TIBUR — CORFINIUM
? 287	via Clodia	ROMA — SATURNIA
? 285	via Appia	CAPUA — VENUSIA
? 283	via Caecilia	CURES — CASTRUM NOVUM
? 241	via Aurelia vetus	ROMA — COSA
? 225	via Minucia	FORUM NOVUM — BRUNDISIUM
? 220	via Flaminia	ROMA — ARIMINUM
187	via Aemilia	ARIMINUM — PLACENTIA
187	via Flaminia	ARRETIUM — BONONIA
? 154	via Cassia	ROMA — ARRETIUM
? 153	via Annia	BONONIA — AQUILEIA
148	via Postumia	GENUA — AQUILEIA
132	via Popilia	ARIMINUM — ALTINUM
131	via Annia	CAPUA — RHEGIUM
? 127	via Latina nova	ROMA — CASILINUM
? 119	via Aurelia nova	ROMA — POPULONIA
107	via Aemilia Scauri	POPULONIA — SABATIA

0 ———— 300km
0 ———— 200mi

ABOVE *The earliest roads in Italy were built by the Etruscans to link their cities. The first paved Roman roads were built during the conquest of Italy to connect Rome with the Latin colonies and speed troop movements between them. They played a crucial role in consolidating Roman control in Italy. A second major period of road building took place in the 2nd century BC, when the profits of conquest were invested in public works as a means of providing employment for the proletariat and to improve local communications.*

(Inset) Stagecoaches carried official post and government officials all over the empire. They were slow and uncomfortable, covering only 20–30 miles (32–48 km) a day.

THE DICTATORSHIP OF SULLA

Meanwhile, a new crisis had developed in the east. Mithridates VI Eupator (r. 120–63) of the Black Sea kingdom of Pontus, an energetic, imaginative and rather despotic ruler, found that the growth of Roman power in Anatolia was restricting his considerable ambitions. Emboldened by the outbreak of the Social war, he seized the independent kingdoms of Bithynia and Cappadocia in 90 BC. When the Romans ordered him to withdraw, war broke out. The small Roman forces in Anatolia were quickly routed and the Roman province of Asia (formerly the kingdom of Pergamon) fell into Mithridates' hands. The Roman administration had offered bankers, businessmen, tax farmers and slavers new opportunities for profit. These they had ruthlessly exploited, earning themselves the hatred of the local population. By styling himself a liberator, Mithridates won the support of the Greek coastal cities, and many of them willingly cooperated in a massacre of Roman citizens in 88. At the end of that year Mithridates sent a force across the Aegean Sea in response to an invitation from the Athenians to liberate Greece.

The consul Sulla (138–78), who was a veteran of Marius's wars, was appointed to lead a campaign against Mithridates. This disappointed Marius, who had hoped for the command himself. A sympathetic tribune helped secure a popular vote that dismissed Sulla and gave the command to Marius. But Sulla had the backing of his army and he marched on Rome, forcing Marius to flee. Sulla invaded Greece in 87 and succeeded in expelling Mithridates' forces a year later. He negotiated generous peace terms with Mithridates in 85, but the Greek cities that had collaborated in the rebellion against Rome were harshly treated.

Marius had taken advantage of Sulla's absence in Greece to return from exile in 86. He won over a legion to his cause, took Rome and massacred the leading *optimates*, but died shortly afterwards. When Sulla returned with a large army to Italy in 83, he counted among his supporters two young opportunists, Crassus (115–53) and Pompey (106–48). Sulla overcame fierce but disorganized opposition to take Rome in 82, leaving Pompey to mop up the final areas of resistance in Sicily and Africa. Thousands of Sulla's opponents were hunted down and killed, and their property was handed over to his supporters. Land that had been confiscated from the Italian communities that had opposed him was redistributed as allotments among 120,000 of Sulla's veteran soldiers.

Sulla now assumed the dictatorship and introduced a series of measures intended to restore stability. Most of the powers of the tribunate were abolished, the senate was enlarged by drafting new members from the equestrian order and the Senate's monopoly on jury courts restored. The number of magistrates was increased to cope with the growing administrative burden of empire and the state-subsidized grain supply withdrawn. Sulla died in 78, before the failure of his measures was apparent. His attempt to restore the authority of the senate had no general consensus to back it. Popular discontent with the Senate's self-interested failure to redress the people's complaints could not be made to go away simply by abolishing the powers of the tribunes.

ABOVE *The rivalry between Marius (top), a political outsider, and Sulla (bottom), a conservative aristocrat, caused much bloodshed. Both men distinguished themselves in successful military campaigns to defend Rome's interests abroad, but their willingness to use their armies to pursue their political ambitions at home began the final disintegration of the Roman republic.*

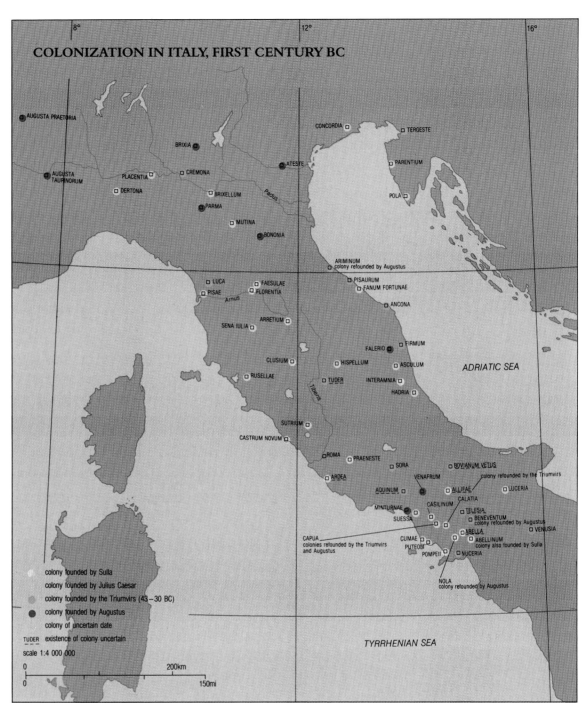

COLONIZATION IN ITALY, FIRST CENTURY BC

colony founded by Sulla
colony founded by Julius Caesar
colony founded by the Triumvirs (43–30 BC)
colony founded by Augustus
colony of uncertain date
TUDER existence of colony uncertain
scale 1:4 000 000

0   200km
0   150mi

THE RISE OF POMPEY

Sulla had shown how an ambitious general could bully his way to power with the backing of his army: others would now try to follow in his path. The first to do so was Pompey. In 70 BC he was elected to the consulship, alongside Crassus who had put down Spartacus's slave revolt the year before, though Pompey took the credit for it. Spartacus, a Thracian gladiator, had escaped in 73 and assembled a force of fugitive slaves. This had roamed southern Italy for two years until finally defeated by Crassus's army. Spartacus was killed and more than 6000 captured slaves crucified. The lines of crosses stretched from Capua to Rome.

Both Pompey and Crassus were conservatives but they restored the powers of the tribunes as a way of courting wider political support. In 67, Pompey made certain of maintaining his position at the center of Roman politics by securing a three-year command to suppress piracy in the eastern Mediterranean. It took him only three months, and he went on to conquer Mithridates' Pontic kingdom (64) and Syria (63), establishing a system of client states throughout Anatolia and Palestine. Pompey claimed his conquests increased Rome's revenue by 70 percent. He acquired so much loot that he was able to pay his veterans the equivalent of 12 and a half years' pay each.

CAMPAIGNS OF JULIUS CAESAR

Julius Caesar's campaigns spanned the entire Roman world. They were carried out for his own political advantage – his early campaigns were intended to win him prestige and wealth, his later campaigns to defeat his Roman rivals. As a general Caesar was decisive and bold, making use of rapid forced marches to catch his opponents by surprise. He wrote an account of his campaign in Gaul which was greatly admired for its simple and direct language.

ABOVE *Pompey "the Great" earned his title early in his career after defeating Sulla's enemies in Africa in 81 BC. Equally able as a general and an administrator, Pompey suppressed piracy in the Mediterranean, consolidated Roman power in the east and organized a reliable corn supply for Rome. He was at first an ally and colleague of Caesar, but his conservative instincts ultimately led him to join forces with the optimates in the senate, whereupon Caesar ruthlessly hunted him and his supporters down.*

Pompey returned to Rome in 62, demanding recognition for his settlement in the east and land for his veterans. His demands were not unreasonable, but the *optimates*, the conservative faction in Rome, were reluctant to do anything to enhance Pompey's status, and ensured that they were refused by the Senate. Their action doomed the republic. The frustrated Pompey found an ally in Gaius Julius Caesar (102–44), an ambitious member of a patrician family who had identified himself with the *populares*. After his election as consul in 59, Caesar persuaded Pompey to join with him and Crassus to push through a program of reforming legislation. Their informal pact became known as the First Triumvirate (or rule of three). Pompey's prestige, Caesar's political acumen and Crassus's wealth were such a formidable combination, they were able to ignore the Senate and work solely through the popular assemblies. Pompey's eastern settlement was finally recognized and his veterans, together with thousands of landless peasants, were granted allotments of land. Crassus's financial interests were served by a reform of the provincial tax-farming system, and

Caesar was given a military command in Gaul and Illyricum, a golden opportunity to make a reputation for himself. In 58 BC he began a six-year campaign to conquer the whole of Gaul. Crassus, now beginning to feel himself the junior partner of the triumvirate, tried to emulate Caesar's achievements by leading a campaign against the Parthians (see pages 232–233). But he was no general, and he was killed when his army was humiliatingly defeated at Carrhae in Syria in 53.

THE END OF THE REPUBLIC

The relationship between Pompey and Caesar now began to break down. Caesar's brilliantly executed campaigns in Gaul had brought him everything he could have hoped for: wealth, immense popular prestige and, most importantly, the devoted loyalty of his troops. While Caesar was campaigning in Gaul, Pompey had remained at Rome with a special responsibility to organize the city's corn supply. He faced opposition from the tribune Clodius, who had won considerable popular support by introducing a corn dole for poor citizens in 62. Rival gangs of supporters

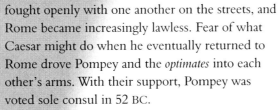

fought openly with one another on the streets, and Rome became increasingly lawless. Fear of what Caesar might do when he eventually returned to Rome drove Pompey and the *optimates* into each other's arms. With their support, Pompey was voted sole consul in 52 BC.

The senate now tried to terminate Caesar's command, but tribunes friendly to Caesar vetoed the order. Civil war between Pompey and Caesar was inevitable. Though desperate negotiations took place to try to avoid it, no compromise could be reached that would have allowed Caesar to continue his political career. At the beginning of 49 BC Caesar marched his army across the Rubicon, the small river that marked the border of his command in Gaul, and invaded Italy. It was a significant step that led irreversibly to the destruction of the republic.

Though Caesar was accompanied by only one legion, Pompey lacked a popular following. In less than two months he had been driven out of Italy. The decisiveness and speed that had marked Caesar's campaigns in Gaul were now repeated as he crushed Pompey's armies in Spain and then, before the year was out, crossed to Greece where he defeated Pompey at Pharsalus in the summer of 48 BC. Pompey fled to Egypt, where he was treacherously

murdered. When Caesar arrived shortly afterwards he was greeted with the news of his rival's death. He lingered in Alexandria where he became involved in the dynastic quarrels of the Ptolemies. Taking the side of Cleopatra, who became his mistress, he installed her and her brother Ptolemy XIV on the Egyptian throne. Further campaigns were needed in Asia Minor, Africa and Spain, where he defeated Pompey's sons at Munda in 45, before he had destroyed all opposition and made himself undisputed master of the empire.

Caesar was no Sulla – he did not follow up his triumph by persecuting his enemies. But, once in sole power, he began to show his limitations as a politician. No consensus existed to restore the republican constitution, but Caesar seems to have been without ideas for an alternative form of government. In 46 he appointed himself dictator for 10 years and then, in 44, for life. The senate was packed with his own supporters and he was personally responsible for making all appointments to the magistracies. He busied himself with an enormous range of reforming legislation. Measures were taken against debt; large numbers of poor citizens and discharged veterans were resettled in colonies in Italy and the provinces; annual pay for legionaries was almost doubled. Tax farming, which was so easily abused, was abolished in the provinces. Roman citizenship was granted to the population of Cisalpine Gaul and Latin rights extended to Provence and Sicily.

Caesar had taken to appearing in public on a gilded chair wearing the purple robe of kingship. He became the first living Roman to have his portrait shown on coins. Though he had declined the royal title, Caesar was ruling as king in all but name. His undisguised contempt for the traditions of the republic caused mounting dismay among the aristocracy, who began to fear the restoration of the monarchy. In 44 a plot to murder Caesar was hatched by a group of diehard aristocrats led by Gaius Cassius Longinus and Marcus Junius Brutus (85–42). On 15 March, the Ides of March, Caesar was publicly stabbed to death in the Senate. The conspirators were so far out of touch with popular sentiment that they fully expected their act to be greeted with celebrations. But though they proclaimed the restoration of republican liberty, all this meant to most people was a return to the corruption and disorder of the previous eighty years. Faced with the hostility of the Roman crowd, Cassius and Brutus were forced to flee and the stage was set for a new civil war.

LEFT *Caesar's undisguised contempt for republican traditions of government won him many enemies in the aristocracy. Conspirators fearful that he was planning to revive the monarchy murdered him in 44 BC. (Below) A coin issued by the conspirators in 43/2 to celebrate Caesar's murder shows daggers and the felt cap worn by freed slaves. The inscription reads EID. MAR. ("the Ides of March").*

THE FORUM

A view down the Sacra Via ("the sacred way"), Rome's oldest street, in the Forum. This complex of temples, courthouses, assembly halls and market places was the center of the city's political, business and religious life throughout most of its history. It was thronged with merchants and tradesmen, senators and orators, and the rituals of state religion were conducted in its temples. Some of its earliest monuments, such as the temple of Vesta, date from the time of the monarchy. On the right in this picture are the three surviving columns of the republican temple of Castor, later restored by Augustus. It stood close to the Curia, or senate house, begun by Sulla in 80 BC, where Caesar was struck down and murdered, and beside the Basilica Julia built by Julius Caesar in 54 and completed by Augustus.

PARTHIANS AND SASANIANS

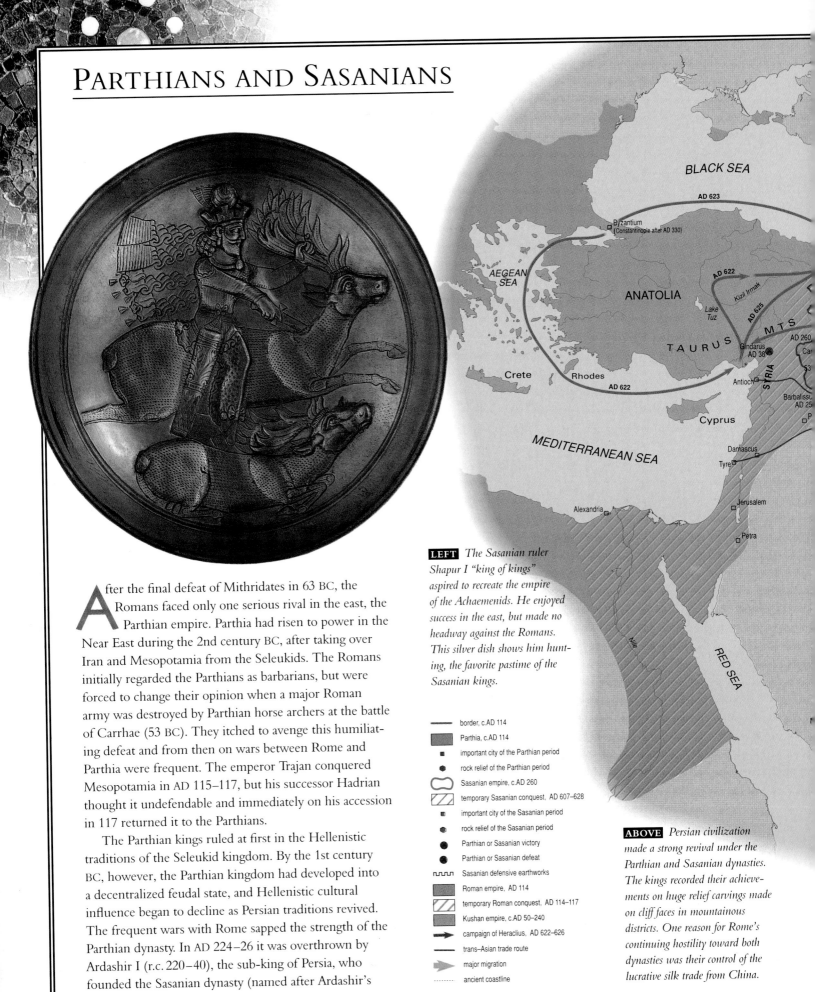

After the final defeat of Mithridates in 63 BC, the Romans faced only one serious rival in the east, the Parthian empire. Parthia had risen to power in the Near East during the 2nd century BC, after taking over Iran and Mesopotamia from the Seleukids. The Romans initially regarded the Parthians as barbarians, but were forced to change their opinion when a major Roman army was destroyed by Parthian horse archers at the battle of Carrhae (53 BC). They itched to avenge this humiliating defeat and from then on wars between Rome and Parthia were frequent. The emperor Trajan conquered Mesopotamia in AD 115–117, but his successor Hadrian thought it undefendable and immediately on his accession in 117 returned it to the Parthians.

The Parthian kings ruled at first in the Hellenistic traditions of the Seleukid kingdom. By the 1st century BC, however, the Parthian kingdom had developed into a decentralized feudal state, and Hellenistic cultural influence began to decline as Persian traditions revived. The frequent wars with Rome sapped the strength of the Parthian dynasty. In AD 224–26 it was overthrown by Ardashir I (r.c. 220–40), the sub-king of Persia, who founded the Sasanian dynasty (named after Ardashir's

LEFT *The Sasanian ruler Shapur I "king of kings" aspired to recreate the empire of the Achaemenids. He enjoyed success in the east, but made no headway against the Romans. This silver dish shows him hunting, the favorite pastime of the Sasanian kings.*

border, c.AD 114

Parthia, c.AD 114

important city of the Parthian period

rock relief of the Parthian period

Sasanian empire, c.AD 260

temporary Sasanian conquest, AD 607–628

important city of the Sasanian period

rock relief of the Sasanian period

Parthian or Sasanian victory

Parthian or Sasanian defeat

Sasanian defensive earthworks

Roman empire, AD 114

temporary Roman conquest, AD 114–117

Kushan empire, c.AD 50–240

campaign of Heraclius, AD 622–626

trans-Asian trade route

major migration

ancient coastline

ABOVE *Persian civilization made a strong revival under the Parthian and Sasanian dynasties. The kings recorded their achievements on huge relief carvings made on cliff faces in mountainous districts. One reason for Rome's continuing hostility toward both dynasties was their control of the lucrative silk trade from China.*

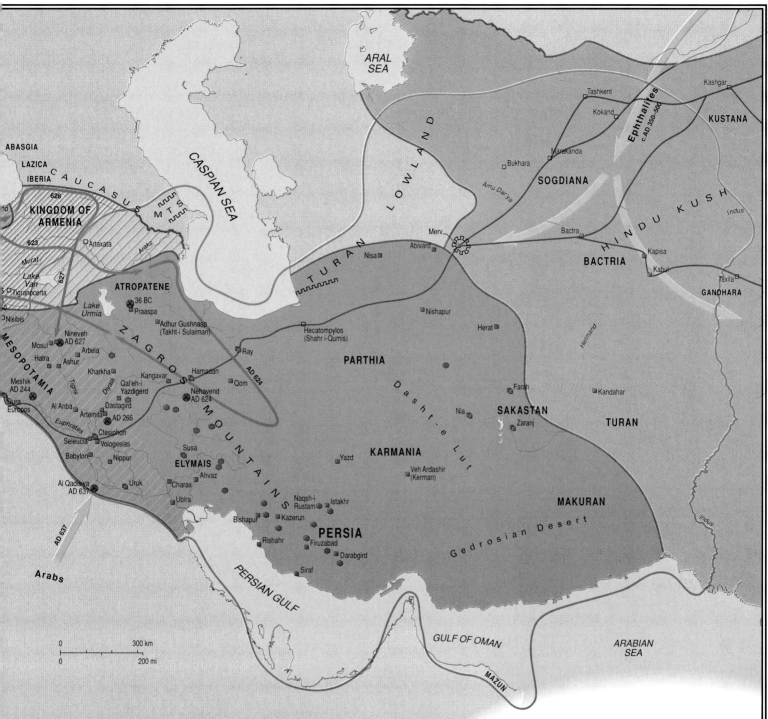

ABASGIA

LAZICA
IBERIA

KINGDOM OF ARMENIA

626
623
627

Antaxata

CAUCASUS

CASPIAN SEA

ARAL SEA

Kashgar

Tashkent

Kokand

Ephthalites
c.AD 350–500

KUSTANA

Bukhara

Marakanda

SOGDIANA

Amu Darya

HINDU KUSH

Indus

Murat

Lake Van

Tigranocerta

Nisibis

MESOPOTAMIA

Lake Urmia

ATROPATENE

36 BC
Praaspa

Adhur Gushnasp
(Takht-i Sulaiman)

TURAN LOWLAND

Nisa

Merv

Abivard

Bactra

BACTRIA

Kapisa

Kabul

Taxila

GANDHARA

Nineveh
AD 627

Mosul

Hatra

Ashur

Arbela

Kharkha

Kangavar

Hamadan

ZAGROS MOUNTAINS

Ray

Hecatompylos
(Shahr i-Qumis)

Nishapur

Herat

Helmand

Meshik
AD 244

Al Anba

Artemita

Dura Europos

Diyala

Qal'eh-i Yazdigerd

Dastagird

AD 266

AD 624

Nehavend
AD 624

Qom

PARTHIA

Dasht-e Lut

Farah

Nia

SAKASTAN

Zaranj

Kandahar

TURAN

Euphrates

Tigris

Ctesiphon

Seleucia

Vologesias

Babylon

Nippur

Susa

ELYMAIS

Ahvaz

KARMANIA

Yazd

Veh Ardashir
(Kerman)

Al Qadisiya
AD 637

Uruk

Charax

Ubira

Naqsh-i Rustam

Istakhr

Bishapur

Kazerun

MAKURAN

Gedrosian Desert

Indus

Rishahr

PERSIA

Firuzabad

Darabgird

AD 637

Arabs

Siraf

PERSIAN GULF

0   300 km
0   200 mi

GULF OF OMAN

MAZUN

ARABIAN SEA

grandfather, Sasan). The Sasanians saw themselves as the successors of the Achaemenids and aspired to recreate the empire of Darius I. Despite some spectacular victories, however, Shapur I (240–72) failed in his attempt to take Syria from the Romans. He was more successful in the east against the Kushans, conquering Sogdiana, Bactria and the Indus valley. The long-running feud between the Sasanians and the Roman empire reached its climax in the reign of Khosrau II (591–628), who launched an all-out war in 607. Syria, Palestine and Egypt were quickly conquered and a Persian army succeeded in reaching the Bosporus, but the war ended in crushing defeat at Nineveh in 627. Khosrau was assassinated and civil war

broke out. The Sasanian empire was left so weak that when the newly Islamicized Arabs poured out of the desert in 637, it quickly collapsed.

The Sasanian kingdom was highly centralized. Society was organized into a caste system of priests, soldiers, scribes and commoners. Zoroastrianism, founded in Iran in the 6th century BC and characterized by belief in a supreme being engaged in a cosmic struggle between good and evil, was established as the state religion. It is possible that this example influenced the decision to make Christianity the state religion of the Roman empire in the 4th century. The Sasanian Persian culture also had a strong formative influence on early Islamic civilization.

The Imperial Peace
44 BC – AD 284

The civil war that followed the death of Julius Caesar was far worse than the one that had brought him to power. Heading the opposition to the Senate and the self-styled liberators, Brutus and Cassius, were the consul Mark Antony (Marcus Antonius, c. 83–30 BC) and the general Lepidus (d. 13 BC). Joined soon afterwards by Caesar's ambitious 19-year old nephew and adoptive heir, Octavian (63 BC–AD 14), they formed the Second Triumvirate. More than 2000 of their opponents were purged in Rome in a reign of terror. After Brutus and Cassius were killed fighting against Octavian and Mark Antony at Philippi in

Macedonia in 42 BC, the three divided the empire among them. Octavian took Italy and the west, Mark Antony the east and a command against the Parthians. Lepidus, very much the junior partner, got Africa. He was eased out of power by Octavian a few years later and allowed to retire in peace.

Relations between Octavian and Mark Antony now deteriorated rapidly. After Mark Antony's war against the Parthians had ended in failure in 36 BC he traveled to Egypt and began a lingering affair with Cleopatra. This allowed Octavian to portray him as a decadent oriental despot, and war between them became inevitable. They met at the naval

RIGHT *Augustus zealously promoted his image by arranging to have himself portrayed in countless official statues throughout the empire. His expression was always serious, suggesting his concern for the empire, but he was shown with a serene unfurrowed brow. To the end of his life he never appeared as older than 33 years, his age when he became master of the Roman world.*

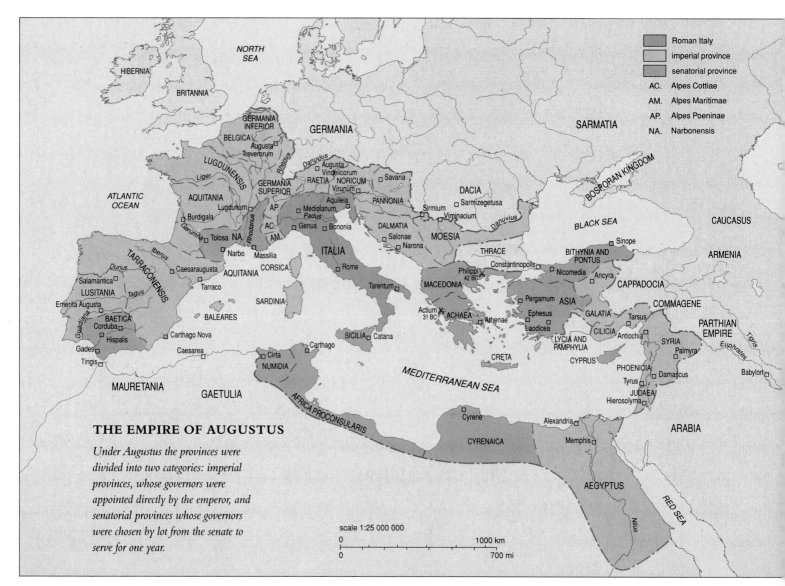

	Roman Italy
	imperial province
	senatorial province

AC. Alpes Cottiae
AM. Alpes Maritimae
AP. Alpes Poeninae
NA. Narbonensis

THE EMPIRE OF AUGUSTUS

Under Augustus the provinces were divided into two categories: imperial provinces, whose governors were appointed directly by the emperor, and senatorial provinces whose governors were chosen by lot from the senate to serve for one year.

scale 1:25 000 000

0 ——— 1000 km
0 ——— 700 mi

battle of Actium, off the Greek coast, in 31 BC. Octavian won an easy victory and Mark Antony and Cleopatra, abandoned by their troops, fled back to Egypt. When Octavian pursued them there they committed suicide rather than fall into his hands. Octavian thereupon annexed Egypt. It had remained independent of Rome until now because the Senate had been afraid to allow any general to acquire control of its enormous wealth.

THE IMPERIAL SETTLEMENT

Octavian was now undisputed master of the empire. Amid the general relief that the civil war was over, many aristocrats feared that he would become another military dictator. Octavian realized that Caesar's overt absolutism had been his undoing and immediately took steps to allay their anxieties. The size of the army had mushroomed during the civil wars. Octavian cut the number of legions from 60 to 28 and turned them into a professional long-service army, stationed mostly on the borders. An equal number of auxiliary troops, recruited from non-citizens, was also maintained. The tens of thousands of discharged veterans were resettled at his own expense.

Octavian's exercise of power was without a constitutional basis. At first he ruled as consul and submitted himself for reelection every year. In 27 BC, however, he handed the state back to the Senate and the people, thus "restoring" the republic. It was a calculated move to force the senate into finding a central constitutional role for him or face a return to civil war. Having looked into the abyss, the Senate offered Octavian the administration of the provinces of Gaul, Spain, Syria and Egypt for 10 years in addition to the consulship. Most of the legions were stationed in these provinces so the appointment effectively made him supreme commander of the army as well. He was accorded a new name, Augustus ("revered one"), by which he came to be known, and an official title *princeps* (first citizen). His successors used the title *imperator* (commander in chief), which gives us the word emperor.

In 23 BC Augustus surrendered the consulship with its administrative burdens, receiving in return proconsular powers to intervene over the heads of all the provincial governors, together with formal command of the entire army. Riots broke out when it was learned that Augustus had renounced the consulship. As assurance to the people that he had not handed power back to the Senate, he accepted the authority of tribune for life. Augustus was to receive further honors. He was created *pontifex*

POMPEII

Until its violent destruction, Pompeii was a fairly typical Italian market town of the early imperial period. The surrounding countryside was prosperous. Ash and lava flows from the nearby volcano of Vesuvius had weathered to create fertile soils ideal for cultivating vines and olives. They also provided good grazing for sheep. Local wool and cloth were exported to Rome, Gaul and Greece, and many of the town's residents had become wealthy on the trade. The townsfolk were taken by surprise when Vesuvius, believed to be extinct, erupted suddenly in AD 79. Thousands died as a rain of soft ash and pumice engulfed the town. Almost everything the ash covered was preserved: furniture, garden ornaments, wall paintings, graffiti, tools, foodstuffs and the bodies of those who did not flee in time. As a result, Pompeii offers an unrivaled picture of the lives of ordinary men and women in Roman Italy.

ABOVE *Many of Pompeii's inhabitants were wealthy and their houses were finely decorated, providing evidence of a luxurious and leisured way of life. The walls were frequently painted with colorful frescoes. Some were purely decorative, but many depicted moral or religious themes. This scene is from a remarkable sequence of life-size frescoes that were painted in about 60–50 BC. They are believed to illustrate the initiation rites of the cult of the Greek wine god Dionysos, known to the Romans as Bacchus. The cult was not approved of by the state authorities but was widely practiced in secret, especially in southern Italy.*

ABOVE *This view taken from the town's northern wall looks south along Pompeii's central paved street towards the forum.*

RIGHT *The eruption lasted three days. Many were able to flee at first, but on the second day poisonous gases and falls of fine ash asphyxiated all those that remained. When the eruption ceased the town was buried to a depth of 13 feet (4 m). Herculaneum to the west was covered under a mud and lava flow. The writer Pliny described the eruption in which his uncle, the naturalist Pliny the Elder, died after venturing too close while attempting to study it.*

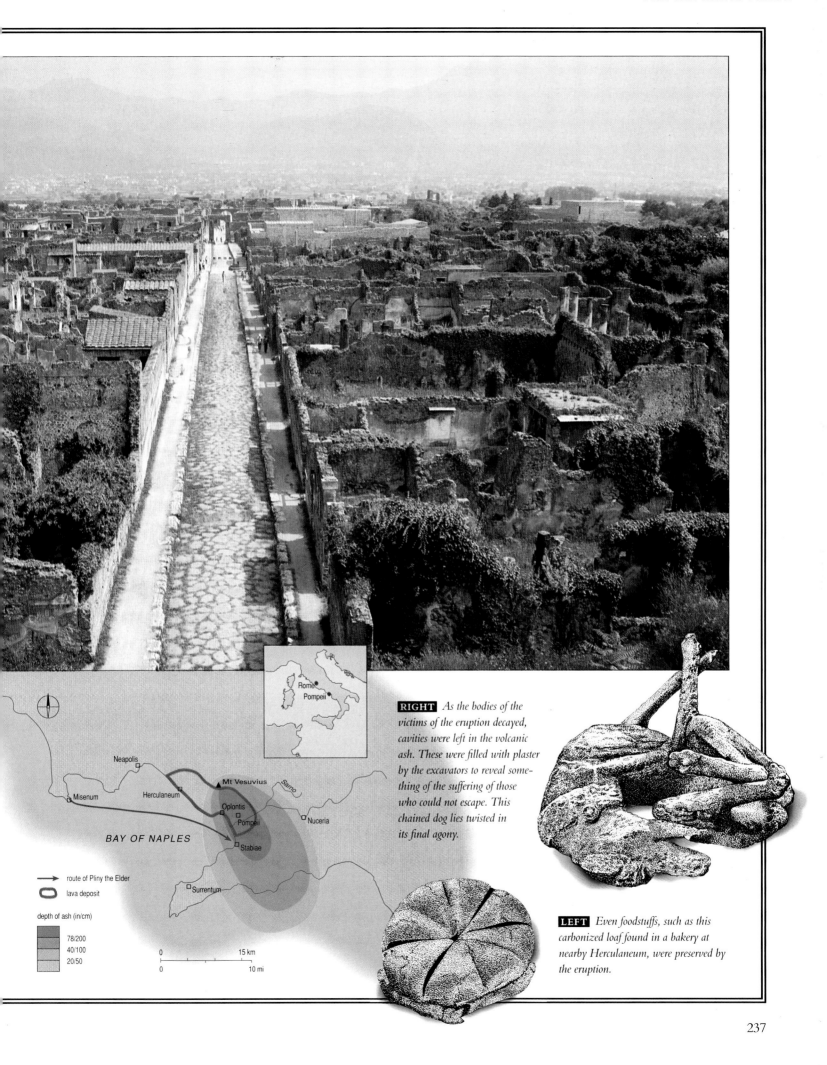

RIGHT *As the bodies of the victims of the eruption decayed, cavities were left in the volcanic ash. These were filled with plaster by the excavators to reveal something of the suffering of those who could not escape. This chained dog lies twisted in its final agony.*

Rome•
Pompeii•

Neapolis

Mt Vesuvius
Sarno

Misenum
Herculaneum
Oplontis
Pompeii•
Nuceria

BAY OF NAPLES

Stabiae

→ route of Pliny the Elder
⬭ lava deposit

Surrentum

depth of ash (in/cm)

78/200
40/100
20/50

0   15 km
0   10 mi

LEFT *Even foodstuffs, such as this carbonized loaf found in a bakery at nearby Herculaneum, were preserved by the eruption.*

maximus (chief priest) in 12 BC, and acclaimed *pater patriae* (father of the country) in 2 BC. He came to be regarded as a semi-divine figure, particularly in the east, where ruler cults had been known since the time of Alexander the Great.

Though Augustus's authority was based on what looks like an untidy collection of offices, they allowed him to exercise absolute power, while the fact that his authority had been granted to him freely by the Senate and people of Rome gave his position an acceptable constitutional foundation. He made little show of his military authority: one of his achievements was to take the army out of politics by giving the state the responsibility for resettling veterans and providing pensions. He was always careful to show respect to the senate and its traditions, consulting it on important issues. Magistrates continued to be elected but the offices became largely honorific. Provincial governors and army commanders were chosen directly by Augustus and most of his administrators were drawn from the equestrian class. The edifice of republican government still stood but the Senate had settled for a quiet life and the mere appearance of authority.

Augustus was in many ways a conservative. He introduced sumptuary laws to curb luxurious living, supported the traditional state religious cults (see pages 214–215) and encouraged marriage and family life. For writing his erotic classic *The Art of Love*, the poet Ovid (43 BC–AD 17) was banished to the Crimea on the Black Sea. However, authors who promoted the ideals of the regime, such as the poets Horace (65–8 BC) and Virgil (70–19 BC) and the historian Livy (59 BC–AD 17), were actively encouraged. Augustus embellished Rome with baths, temples, theaters, aqueducts and triumphal arches (see pages 258–259). A fire brigade and police force were organized and the people were given cash and corn doles, and entertained with free games and shows. Not surprisingly, they were enthusiastic supporters of the new order.

Outside Italy, most of the abuses that had blighted provincial administration under the republic were stamped out. Promotion of the cult of emperor gave provincials a new focus for loyalty, while the much reduced army was kept busy establishing defensible borders. The last areas of native resistance were mopped up in northwestern Spain; Galatia in Anatolia was annexed. In northern Europe, the Alpine tribes were conquered and the empire's frontier was pushed to the river Danube. Augustus tried to conquer Germany but withdrew after a humiliating defeat in AD 9. It convinced Augustus that the empire had reached its natural limits and he advised his successors not to conquer any more territories. He concentrated his efforts on creating a strong and efficient government that commanded the loyalty and respect of Roman citizens and provincials alike.

THE JULIO-CLAUDIAN EMPERORS

Augustus's powers had been granted to him for life; they could not in theory be inherited. However, the year before his death Augustus had nominated his stepson Tiberius (r. 14–37 AD) as his successor and called on the senate to accord him the same powers he enjoyed. Tiberius was an experienced administrator and a capable soldier, but he lacked confidence and had an aloof and suspicious manner that quickly alienated the Senate. Saddened by the death of his son Drusus, in AD 26 he retreated to his private villa on Capri. This left a political vacuum in Rome which was filled by plots and intrigues; rumors spread of his depraved sexual life. Tiberius was attacked most bitterly for his application of the *lex maiestatis* (a law of treason against anything that diminished the majesty of the Roman people) which he used to punish disrespect to the emperor, thus constraining freedom of speech. An accuser who obtained a successful prosecution in a case of *lex maiestatis* had the right to a share of the defendant's property. This encouraged the bringing of trumped up charges. Tiberius used the law to destroy his enemies, including members of his own family; senators used it to pursue their own feuds. An atmosphere of general terror pervaded the aristocracy in Tiberius's later years and there was general rejoicing when he died in AD 37.

Tiberius's successor, his grandnephew Gaius, better known by his nickname Caligula (r. 37–41), was welcomed at first by the Senate, but his unpredictable behavior and predisposition for violence quickly made it apparent that he was incapable of ruling. Convinced he was a god, Caligula emptied the treasury to satisfy his whims and humiliated the Senate by making his horse consul. In AD 41 he was assassinated by an officer of the praetorian guards (the imperial bodyguard). Caligula's reign exposed one of the chief shortcomings of the imperial regime: there was no constitutional means to depose a bad emperor. The Senate talked of restoring the republic but the praetorian guards forced it to recognize Caligula's uncle Claudius (r. 41–54) as the new emperor.

RIGHT *The Pont du Gard, in southern France, is one of the most famous monuments of the Roman empire. It was built during the reign of Augustus to carry fresh water supplies across the river Gard to the city of Nemausus (Nîmes). It was the Romans' mastery of the arch in large-scale construction that made possible the building of aqueducts like this (see also pages 254–255). Roman surveying was so accurate that the system feeding Nîmes, which delivered water from 15 miles (24 km) away, fell by only 58 feet (17 m) over its entire course.*

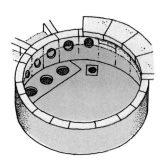

ABOVE *Water conveyed by aqueduct was delivered to the city in a* castellum divisiorum, *a basin for distributing the water. The ducts in the bottom of the basin supplied water for public drinking water fountains and other essential civic purposes: the outlets on the sides delivered water to private users. If there was a water shortage, private users would be cut off first; for the same reason, it was cheaper to have a higher outlet than a lower one.*

ROMAN GAUL

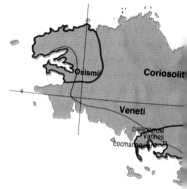

Gaul, roughly equivalent to modern-day France, the Low Countries and part of western Germany, was conquered by Julius Caesar between 58 and 51 BC. The southern province of Narbonensis was already highly urbanized but north and west of the Massif Central a Celtic tribal society prevailed. The Romans called these regions *Gallia Comata* ("long-haired Gaul"). All the amenities of Roman civilization – roads, baths, aqueducts, amphitheaters and triumphal arches – were built to support a policy of romanization. Local tribal strongholds, known in Latin as *oppida,* were made the capitals of administrative districts called *civitates*, based on the former tribal territories, and elective magistracies and Roman civic institutions were introduced. Native aristocrats who held public office were given Roman citizenship; by allowing them to assume senatorial status the emperor Claudius made it possible for them to become part of the empire's ruling elite. The Latin language and Roman religious beliefs (often assimilated with local cults) were soon adopted by the aristocracy but Celtic customs, beliefs and language long persisted among the rural peasantry. Gaul achieved its greatest importance in the 4th century AD when Augusta Treverorum (Trier) was made the seat of an imperial court.

RIGHT *Most of the population of pre-Roman Gaul were Celtic in origin. Roman Gaul was roughly divided into three economic regions. The urbanized south, where Greek colonies had been established since the 6th century BC, was character-ized by a typically Mediterranean small-scale farming economy of vines, olives and cereals. Along the Rhine was a prosperous military zone with a population of soldiers, retired veter-ans and their dependents together with various merchants, craftsmen and others attracted to the area to sell supplies to the army. The heavy fertile soils of the plains north and west of the Massif Central were well suited to the extensive cultivation of cereals for which the Rhine garrisons provided a ready market. Here the economy was organized around great estates based on villas. Cities were small and widely scattered.*

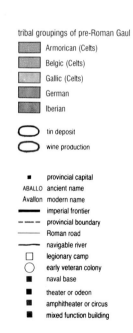

tribal groupings of pre-Roman Gaul

	Armorican (Celts)
	Belgic (Celts)
	Gallic (Celts)
	German
	Iberian

- tin deposit
- wine production

■	provincial capital
ABALLO	ancient name
Avallon	modern name
—	imperial frontier
- - -	provincial boundary
——	Roman road
——	navigable river
☐	legionary camp
○	early veteran colony
■	naval base
■	theater or odeon
■	amphitheater or circus
■	mixed function building

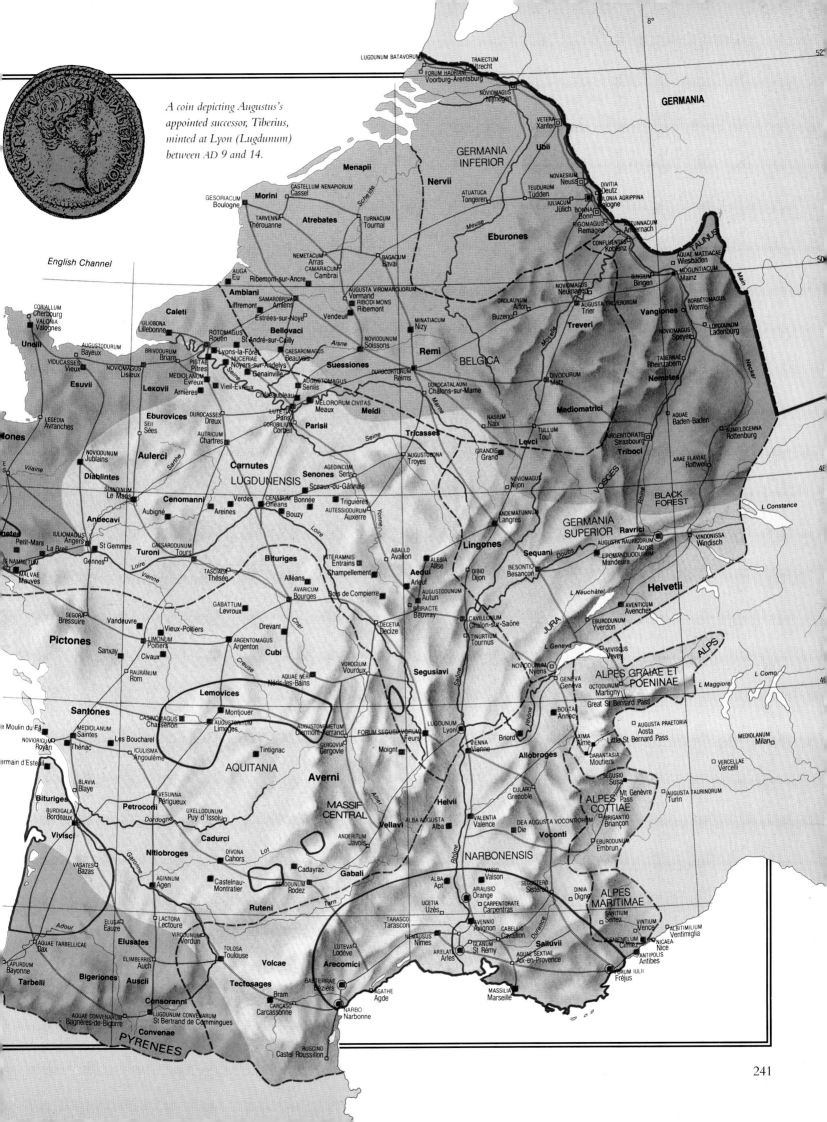

A coin depicting Augustus's appointed successor, Tiberius, minted at Lyon (Lugdunum) between AD 9 and 14.

RIGHT *Vespasian was putting down a revolt in Judaea when he was proclaimed emperor by the army in the east in AD 69. His son Titus completed the task.*

This detail from the arch of Titus, commemorating his victory in AD 70, shows booty from the temple in Jerusalem being carried in triumph through Rome.

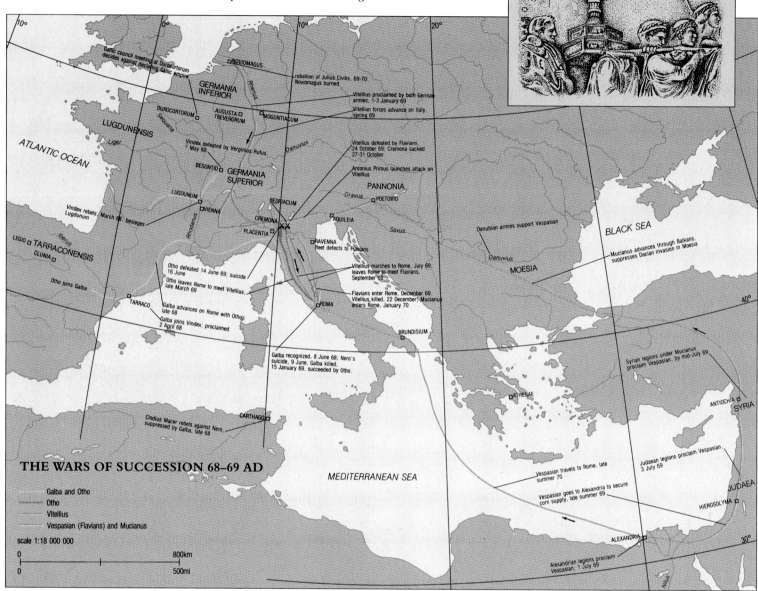

THE WARS OF SUCCESSION 68–69 AD

- Galba and Otho
- Otho
- Vitellius
- Vespasian (Flavians) and Mucianus

scale 1:18 000 000

0 — 800km
0 — 500mi

ABOVE *The civil wars in the year after Nero's death (which was known as the "year of four emperors") involved Roman armies from every part of the empire except Britain, where the forces were too isolated to play a key role in events. Vespasian was able to combine the legions of the east with those stationed on the Danubian frontier. This gave him a considerable advantage over his rival Vitellius, who had already disposed of the imperial claimants Galba and Otho, and ensured his ultimate victory.*

Claudius, disabled since childhood, was 50 years old. He had no experience of military or civil office, yet he proved to be a capable emperor. By appointing a group of freedmen as ministers of state, each responsible for a different area of administration – finance, correspondence, justice, petitions to the emperor and the imperial library – Claudius consolidated the emperor's position at the center of government. He took great interest in the provinces. Wealthy provincials were encouraged to take Roman citizenship and given the right to become senators. Claudius's position at the beginning of his reign was weak because of his lack of personal links with the army. It was largely to win popularity with the legions that Claudius

invaded Britain in AD 43. The southeast of the island was quickly conquered and Claudius hurried back to Rome to celebrate a triumph.

Claudius was not much mourned when his third wife Agrippina poisoned him in 54 to ensure the succession of Nero (r. 54–68), her 16-year-old son by an earlier marriage. For the first five years of Nero's reign effective government was in the hands of a group of able advisers, including the philosopher Seneca (c. 4 BC–c. AD 65). Agrippina tried hard to exercise a controlling influence over Nero but he had her murdered in 59. This unfilial act set the tone for the remainder of Nero's reign, which gradually descended into arbitrary tyranny. He believed he was a prodigiously talented actor

ABOVE *The fortress of Masada, at the southern end of the Dead Sea, was built by king Herod (40–4 BC). It was occupied by the Zealots during the Jewish revolt of AD 66–70 and held out under siege for more than three years after the Romans had recaptured Jerusalem. Masada's virtually impregnable position proved a severe test to the Roman siege engineers. Only after a massive ramp had been built up the surrounding cliffs were the the Roman forces able to storm the fortress. The defenders killed themselves rather than surrender.*

and insisted on entering drama competitions which he always won. In 64 a fire destroyed much of Rome. Looking for a scapegoat, Nero fixed upon the followers of a new religious cult who had already earned the unpopularity of the masses, and launched the first persecution of Christians.

Nero's downfall resulted from his neglect of the army. In 68 Vindex, the disaffected governor of the Gallic province of Lugdunensis, rebelled and persuaded Galba, the governor of Tarraconensis in Spain, to join him. As the rebellion spread through the army, the praetorian guards switched their allegiance to Galba. Nero fled from Rome and committed suicide: his death brought to an end the first dynasty of imperial Rome.

THE "YEAR OF FOUR EMPERORS"

In theory, Augustus's powers had been granted by the Senate and the Roman people, but he had achieved power only because he had the support of the army. The army now controlled the choice of new emperor: the Senate's role was merely to give formal recognition to the successful military nominee. Galba, the praetorian guard's choice, lasted less than seven months. He failed to reward the praetorians for their support so they murdered him and proclaimed another general, Otho, emperor in his place. However, the armies in the province of Germania had already proclaimed their general Vitellius emperor. After Galba's murder Vitellius marched into Italy and defeated

Otho's troops near Cremona. No sooner had he disposed of one rival than Vitellius found himself faced with another, Vespasian – then engaged in putting down a Jewish revolt in Judaea – who was proclaimed emperor by the armies in the east. Vespasian occupied Egypt where he was able to cut off Rome's corn supply, at the same time dispatching his general Mucianus to Italy with an army. The Danubian legions, under the leadership of Antoninus Primus, now declared for Vespasian as well and they too set off for Italy. Vitellius's troops remained loyal but were defeated by Primus at a second battle near Cremona. Vitellius offered to abdicate, but his troops would not let him and he was killed when Primus's forces entered Rome in December 69. Vespasian was recognized as emperor by the Senate and the armies in the west, and entered Rome early in 70.

VESPASIAN AND HIS SUCCESSORS

Vespasian (r. 69–79) had immediately to deal with two inherited rebellions, one in Gaul and the other in Judaea, a Roman protectorate since 63 BC. The first, led by a romanized German chieftain called Julius Civilis, was fairly easily suppressed by Mucianus in 70. In Judaea, however, the Romans faced the opposition of the Zealots. These Jewish religious enthusiasts had led an anti-Roman resistance movement since the time of Augustus. He had alienated devout Jews with his promotion of the imperial cult and its pagan associations, and ordered a census of the Judaean population in AD 6. Open rebellion broke out in 66 after the Roman governor executed a number of Jewish leaders involved in popular rioting against non-Jews. The small Roman garrison was quickly wiped out, and Nero dispatched Vespasian with three legions and as many auxiliaries to restore Roman rule. By 69 most of Judaea was back in Roman hands; Vespasian was preparing to besiege Jerusalem when news of Nero's death broke. Military operations were suspended while Vespasian made his bid for the imperial throne. The final suppression of the revolt was left to Vespasian's son Titus, who took Jerusalem in September 70, after a seven-month siege. The rebel cause was now hopeless but it was another four years before the last Zealot stronghold, at Masada above the Dead Sea, was finally taken.

After the upheavals of 68–69, Vespasian quickly set about restoring imperial authority and the state finances. His ten-year rule brought a measure of stability and the throne passed without incident to

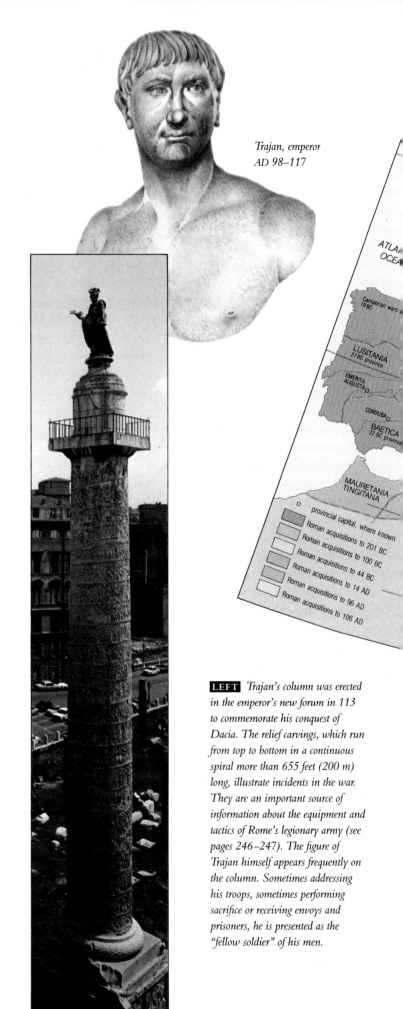

Trajan, emperor AD 98–117

LEFT *Trajan's column was erected in the emperor's new forum in 113 to commemorate his conquest of Dacia. The relief carvings, which run from top to bottom in a continuous spiral more than 655 feet (200 m) long, illustrate incidents in the war. They are an important source of information about the equipment and tactics of Rome's legionary army (see pages 246–247). The figure of Trajan himself appears frequently on the column. Sometimes addressing his troops, sometimes performing sacrifice or receiving envoys and prisoners, he is presented as the "fellow soldier" of his men.*

ATLA[...] OCEA[...]

Cantabrian wars 19 BC

LUSITANIA 27 BC province

EMERITA AUGUSTA □

CORDUBA □

BAETICA 27 BC province

MAURETANIA TINGITANA

□ provincial capital, where known
Roman acquisitions to 201 BC
Roman acquisitions to 100 BC
Roman acquisitions to 44 BC
Roman acquisitions to 14 AD
Roman acquisitions to 96 AD
Roman acquisitions to 106 AD

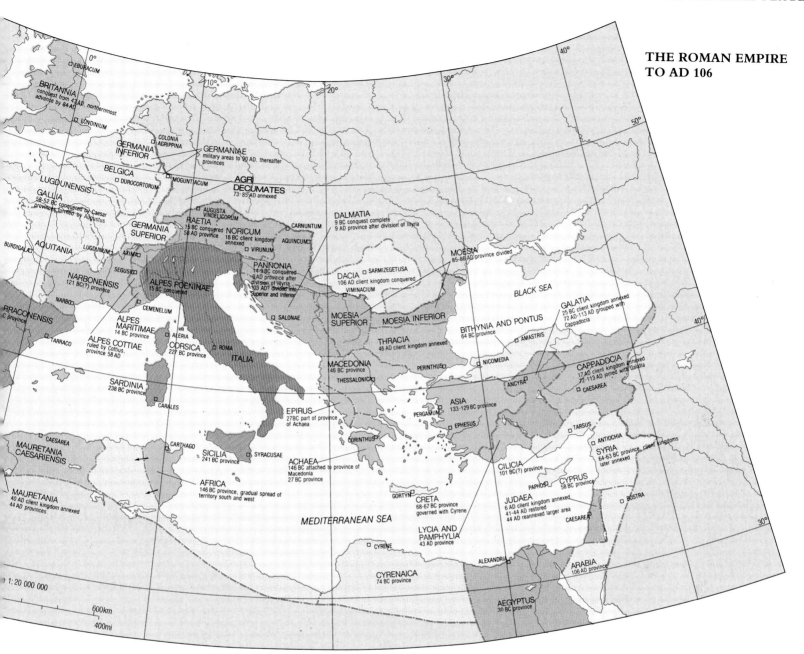

Map labels (selected, as visible):

0° 10° 20° 30° 40° 50° 40° 30°

EBURACUM
BRITANNIA
conquest from 43 AD. northernmost
advance by 84 AD
LONDINIUM
COLONIA AGRIPPINA
GERMANIA INFERIOR
BELGICA
DUROCORTORUM
MOGUNTIACUM
GERMANIAE
military areas to 90 AD. thereafter provinces
AGRI DECUMATES
73-85 AD annexed
LUGDUNENSIS
GALLIA
58-52 BC conquered by Caesar
provinces formed by Augustus
GERMANIA SUPERIOR
AUGUSTA VINDELICORUM
RAETIA
15 BC conquered
58 AD province
NORICUM
16 BC client kingdom annexed
CARNUNTUM
AQUINCUM
VIRUNUM
DALMATIA
9 BC conquest complete
9 AD province after division of Illyria
AQUITANIA
BURDIGALA
LUGDUNUM
AXIMA
PANNONIA
14-9 BC conquered
9 AD province after division of Illyria
103 AD? divided into Superior and Inferior
DACIA
106 AD client kingdom conquered
SARMIZEGETUSA
VIMINACIUM
MOESIA
85-86 AD province divided
BLACK SEA
GALATIA
25 BC client kingdom annexed
72 AD-113 AD grouped with Cappadocia
NARBONENSIS
121 BC(?) province
ALPES POENINAE
15 BC conquered
SEGUSIO
ROMA
ITALIA
MOESIA SUPERIOR
MOESIA INFERIOR
BITHYNIA AND PONTUS
64 BC province
AMASTRIS
NICOMEDIA
NARBO
RRACONENSIS
C province
TARRACO
CEMENELUM
ALPES MARITIMAE
14 BC province
ALPES COTTIAE
ruled by Cottius,
province 58 AD
ALERIA
CORSICA
227 BC province
THRACIA
46 AD client kingdom annexed
PERINTHUS
CAPPADOCIA
17 AD client kingdom annexed
72 AD-113 AD joined with Galatia
ANCYRA
CAESAREA
MACEDONIA
146 BC province
THESSALONICA
SARDINIA
238 BC province
CARALES
EPIRUS
27 BC part of province of Achaea
PERGAMUM
ASIA
133-129 BC province
EPHESUS
TARSUS
ANTIOCHIA
CAESAREA
MAURETANIA CAESARIENSIS
CARTHAGO
SICILIA
241 BC province
SYRACUSAE
ACHAEA
146 BC attached to province of Macedonia
27 BC province
CORINTHUS
CILICIA
101 BC(?) province
PAPHOS
CYPRUS
58 BC province
SYRIA
64-63 BC province, client kingdoms later annexed
BOSTRA
MAURETANIA
40 AD client kingdom annexed
44 AD provinces
AFRICA
146 BC province, gradual spread of territory south and west
GORTYN
CRETA
68-67 BC province governed with Cyrene
JUDAEA
6 AD client kingdom annexed
41-44 AD restored
44 AD reannexed larger area
CAESAREA
MEDITERRANEAN SEA
LYCIA AND PAMPHYLIA
43 AD province
CYRENE
ALEXANDRIA
ARABIA
106 AD province
1 : 20 000 000
CYRENAICA
74 BC province
AEGYPTUS
30 BC province
600km
400mi

ABOVE *Despite Augustus's advice to his successors not to conquer any new territories, the Roman empire continued to expand throughout the 1st century AD. Most new provinces were formed by annexing client kingdoms such as Cappadocia (17), Mauretania (40) and Thrace (46), but the conquest of Britain (43–84) was a major military undertaking. Trajan's early campaigns added Dacia and Arabia (106). He went on to annex Armenia (114) and Mesopotamia (115) but these were given up as being undefendable by Hadrian in 117. Dacia was the only major province to be abandoned, to the Germans, in the 3rd century.*

his sons Titus (r. 79–81) and Domitian (r. 81–96). Domitian was an energetic administrator and builder but he introduced a new reign of terror. The senatorial class lived in perpetual fear of denunciations by professional informers and judicial murder on trumped-up charges. As with Caligula and Nero before him, there was only one way out: assassination. Nerva (r. 96–98), the conspirators' chosen candidate for the succession, was accepted by a grateful Senate. Though short, his reign ushered in almost a century of unparalleled peace and prosperity for the empire. Nerva was aware that his lack of military experience gave him little appeal to the army so he adopted as his son and successor Trajan (r. 98–117), an experienced commander serving on the Rhine frontier. Nerva died of fever a few weeks later, and the empire was saved from another war of succession.

THE EMPIRE REACHES ITS LIMITS

Trajan, who was then aged about 45, had been born in the Roman colony of Italica in Spain and was the first emperor to come from the provinces. This was a sign of the widening of the Roman identity in the imperial era. A new aristocracy had emerged consisting of wealthy provincials who had prospered in imperial service. They saw themselves, and were seen by others, to be as Roman as anyone born in Rome or Italy. Trajan was a strong ruler but no tyrant; he was remembered by later generations as *optimus princeps* (the model emperor).

At home, his policies aimed to improve the welfare of the poor, support agriculture and towns, and extend the road system. The harbor at Ostia, Rome's port, was greatly improved, and a splendid new market was built in the city itself.

THE IMPERIAL ARMY

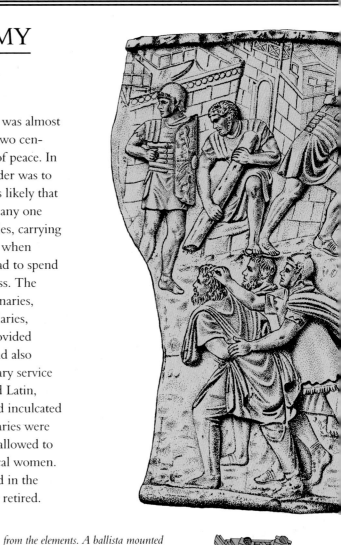

During the last years of the republic Rome was almost constantly at war. By contrast, the first two centuries of the empire saw long intervals of peace. In peacetime the first responsibility of a commander was to maintain discipline, training and morale. It was likely that half the men would be away from the camp at any one time: training, building roads, collecting supplies, carrying official mail or simply on leave. Consequently, when summoned to campaign, commanders often had to spend time bringing their men back to battle-readiness. The army contained two categories of soldier: legionaries, recruited only from Roman citizens, and auxiliaries, recruited from provincials. The latter often provided specialist troops such as cavalry and archers, and also made up the front-line border garrisons. Military service had a romanizing effect on them. They learned Latin, were introduced to the state religious cults, and inculcated in loyalty to the emperor. On discharge, auxiliaries were granted Roman citizenship. Soldiers were not allowed to marry, but many formed close liaisons with local women. They had children with them, and often settled in the neighborhood of the garrison camp when they retired.

ABOVE *The standard was a focal point for loyalty. Soldiers rallied to the standard bearer in a crisis. A legion that lost its standard was disgraced.*

BELOW *Roman troops were trained in a variety of tactical formations. Most famous was the* testudo *(tortoise), used during siege warfare to approach the walls of an enemy fortress.*

RIGHT AND BELOW *One of the most powerful pieces of Roman artillery used to attack enemy defenses was the ballista, which resembled a giant crossbow. It had two arms powered by torsion springs of twisted sinews. These gave it an effective range of about 500 yards (458 m).*
BELOW RIGHT: A light ballista being transported in a mule cart: metal cylinders protect the torsion springs

from the elements. A ballista mounted on a light carriage was sometimes used as a sort of field gun.
RIGHT: A heavy ballista for use in siege warfare. It was sometimes also mounted for defense on fortress towers.

ABOVE *Legionaries spent more time building than fighting. This scene from Trajan's column shows the construction of a camp during the Dacian wars. The men are in full armor, wearing the segmented mail cuirass introduced in the 1st century. Their shields, pikes and helmets are stacked nearby in case of attack.*

RIGHT *Auxiliary archers give covering fire for infantry soldiers who are attacking a Dacian fortress. Archers were usually recruited from the east of the empire.*

LEFT *Roman forts were built to a standard plan so that soldiers could find their way around easily. Shown here is Novaesium (Neuss) on the Rhine, a typical Roman legionary fortress accommodating around 5000 soldiers. Auxiliary forts were smaller.*

commander's house

- administration and services
- higher officers' houses
- granaries and stores
- workshops
- hospital
- cavalry barracks
- centurions' barracks
- infantry barracks

Trajan won the support of the Roman masses by making generous distributions of cash and laying on spectacular entertainments.

Since Augustus's time the empire had continued to expand steadily throughout the 1st century AD, mainly through the annexation of client states. Trajan now reverted to the aggressive expansionism of the late republic. Conquest of the kingdom of Dacia (101–106), which posed a threat to the security of the Danube frontier, was followed by that of the Nabataean Arabs (105–106) who were incorporated into the new province of Arabia. Trajan's most cherished ambition was to conquer the Parthian empire. He began by seizing the independent kingdom of Armenia in 114, which provided a base for attacks on the Parthian heartland. Two years later Trajan captured the Parthian capital of Ctesiphon on the Tigris and advanced to the Persian Gulf. He spoke wistfully of recreating the empire of Alexander the Great, but he was old and worn out and died in 117, shortly after adopting Hadrian (r. 117– 38) as his son and successor. Trajan's death marked the end of the great days of Roman expansion. Later in the 2nd century the frontier was temporarily pushed northward in Britain, and there would also be some gains in the east at the expense of the Parthians. But from now on, the empire would mostly be on the defensive.

Hadrian judged that Trajan's eastern conquests were undefendable and at the outset of his reign withdrew from all of them, except the city of Edessa. He also adopted a defensive posture in the west, building strong barriers to keep out invaders along the frontiers in Britain and Germany (see pages 268–269). Hadrian spent half of his reign traveling and probably saw more of the empire than any other emperor. An admirer of all things Greek, he spent many years in Greece and lavished new buildings on Athens.

In 132 rebellion broke out once again in Judaea. The immediate cause of the uprising was Hadrian's decision to refound Jerusalem as a Roman colony. Most insulting to Jewish feelings was his plan to build an altar to Jupiter on the site of Solomon's temple. Led by the messianic Simon "Bar Kochba" (Son of the Star), the revolt took nearly four years of savage fighting to suppress. Most of the Jewish population of Judaea were killed, enslaved or exiled. The province was renamed Syria Palaestina, Jews were barred from Jerusalem, and for a short while Judaism itself was banned.

Like Nerva and Trajan before him, Hadrian chose and adopted his successor, Antoninus Pius (r. 138–61), during his own lifetime. This system of adoption served the empire well, ensuring that each new emperor had proved his suitability for office before he actually came to power. The system was ended by Antoninus' adopted son and successor Marcus Aurelius (r. 161–80), who allowed his own patently unworthy natural son Commodus (r. 180–92) to succeed him. By this time, however, other storm clouds were gathering over the empire.

ECONOMY AND TRADE IN THE ROMAN EMPIRE

The Roman empire was effectively a vast free trade area with a single currency. Within its vast confines commerce could flourish free from the threat of piracy, war and border controls. Good roads, bridges and harbors all helped to promote trade. The empire's prosperity peaked in the 2nd century but began to slow down in the 3rd when the high cost of defending the empire led to progressive debasement of the coinage, setting off runaway inflation.

The vast majority of the population of the Roman empire were peasant farmers, freedmen or slaves. Their needs were adequately met by local producers, but there was considerable long-distance trade in basic commodities such as metals, pottery and foodstuffs, especially grain, oil and wine. The lifestyles of the small wealthy class were geared to conspicuous consumption. To satisfy their tastes, luxury products such as amber, silk, spices, aromatic resins, pigments and ivory were imported from as far afield as the Baltic, China, the East Indies and equatorial Africa. Slaves were imported from equatorial Africa and Germany. The Stoic philosopher Seneca and other moralizing Romans worried that these expensive items were a drain on the wealth of the empire, but finds of Roman metalwork and glassware, as well as coinage, in India, Malaysia, Vietnam and

LEFT *A Roman coin showing Judaea personified as a captive, with her hands tied behind her back. It was issued to celebrate the crushing of Simon Bar Kochba's revolt of 132–5.*

areas of Jewish settlement
- dense
- other

places of Jewish settlement
- ● major
- ■ other
- major Jewish cultural area
- limit of Roman empire
- important trade route

scale 1: 20 000 000
0   600
0

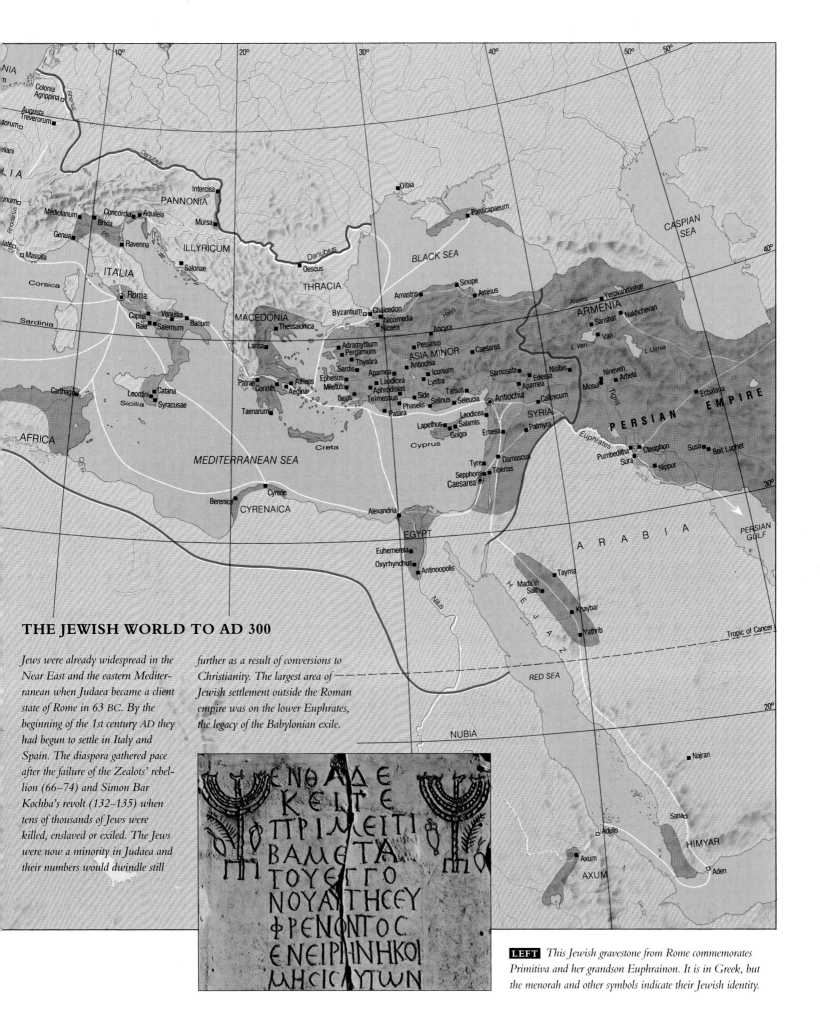

THE JEWISH WORLD TO AD 300

Jews were already widespread in the Near East and the eastern Mediterranean when Judaea became a client state of Rome in 63 BC. By the beginning of the 1st century AD they had begun to settle in Italy and Spain. The diaspora gathered pace after the failure of the Zealots' rebellion (66–74) and Simon Bar Kochba's revolt (132–135) when tens of thousands of Jews were killed, enslaved or exiled. The Jews were now a minority in Judaea and their numbers would dwindle still further as a result of conversions to Christianity. The largest area of Jewish settlement outside the Roman empire was on the lower Euphrates, the legacy of the Babylonian exile.

LEFT *This Jewish gravestone from Rome commemorates Primitiva and her grandson Euphrainon. It is in Greek, but the menorah and other symbols indicate their Jewish identity.*

249

Central Asia show that there was also a healthy demand for Roman exports.

Aside from luxury goods, the empire was essentially self-sufficient in everyday necessities and what was lacking in one region could easily be supplied by another. Most trade was generated by the empire's growing cities. Rome itself, with a population of around 1,000,000, needed to import 400,000 tons of grain annually, most of which came from Egypt, Africa and Sicily.

The army also generated a large volume of trade. More than 100,000 tons of grain were required for rations each year, while the hides of 54,000 calves were needed to provide tents for one legion alone. The requirements of the army stimulated agriculture and metalworking in the border areas, where the majority of troops were stationed, but many supplies had to be brought in from further afield. The frontier garrison towns attracted large numbers of small traders in the hope of relieving soldiers of their wages. Ironically, the increased prosperity of these areas made them more likely to become the target of cross-border raids.

The empire's system of roads (see pages 224–225) was built primarily to provide the army with fast all-weather routes, but they also promoted local trade. However, only small volumes of goods could be carried so road transportation was expensive. A fully loaded ox-cart needed six men and six boys to drive it and could make less than 10 miles (16 km) a day. To move a cartload of grain 300 miles (480 km) by road meant doubling its price. As a result, most of the empire's long-distance trade went by water, both by sea and along navigable rivers. Huge seagoing merchant ships, capable of carrying cargoes of up to 350 tons, made it cheaper to transport grain to Rome from the other side of the Mediterranean than to cart it into the city from the surrounding countryside. Recent archeological excavations have shown that grain from Egypt was even imported into Britain. The Romans chose to make their frontiers along navigable rivers since this made supplying border garrisons easier: considerable fleets were maintained on the Rhine and the Danube for this purpose.

Though trade was essential to its survival, the empire's commercial classes remained small and enjoyed neither the wealth nor the status of the landowning aristocracy. Some goods, notably pottery, were mass-produced in factories but most production was small-scale and undercapitalized, as the rich preferred to invest in land and there were no great banks to lend capital for commercial enterprises. In view of the poverty of the majority of the empire's population, it is in any case doubtful if the markets existed to support a greater amount of industrial production. This is probably one of the factors behind the surprising lack of technological innovation in the empire (see pages 254–255). The Romans were excellent engineers but, though the principles of water and wind power were well understood, they were not

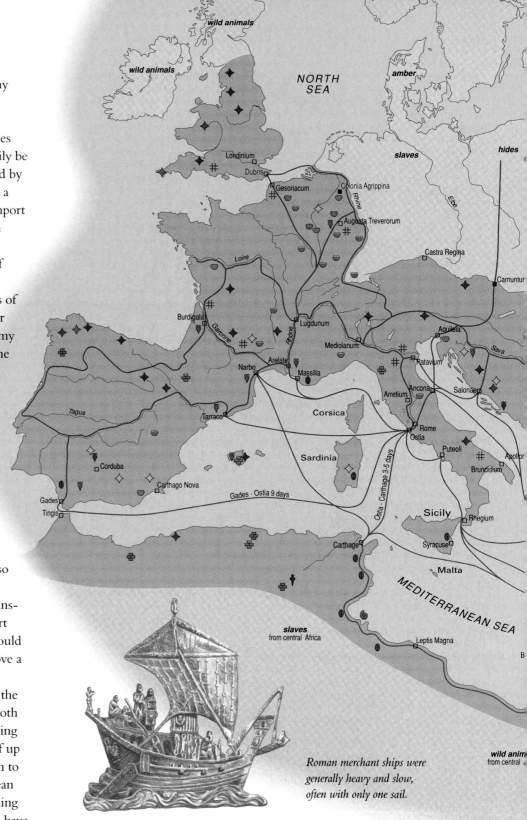

Roman merchant ships were generally heavy and slow, often with only one sail.

◆	copper
◆	gold
◆	iron
◆	lead
◇	silver
◆	tin
◑	grain
▼	olive oil
▼	wine
†	slaves

TRADE IN THE ROMAN EMPIRE

The most important trade routes of the Roman empire were the sea lanes of the Mediterranean. Hundreds of shipwrecks discovered in the Mediterranean testify to the huge volume of maritime trade in the Roman empire, as well as its risks. Most sea voyaging ceased between November and March because of the threat of winter storms. Rivers such as the Danube and the Rhine carried goods to and from the interior: the road network, virtually complete by 200, was used almost entirely for military and administrative purposes. Though Rome was the heart of the empire, the economy of Italy declined in the imperial period as a result of vigorous competition from the western provinces. Despite this, the west, in comparison to Italy and the east, remained relatively underdeveloped in economic terms.

ABOVE *Glass vessels were popular luxury items with well-off Romans, and also found customers as distant as southeast Asia. A thriving glass industry developed in the Rhineland, in part to meet the demand for Roman glass among the Germanic tribes living beyond the Rhine. Most Roman glass that has survived comes from funerary or votive offerings.*

- 🥫 brass and bronze
- ● glass
- ● pottery
- ✚ timber
- ✚ marble
- # textiles
- ● purple dye
- *slaves* imported commodity
- ■ trading post
- — trade route
- ▨ Roman empire AD200

extensively exploited. The availability of cheap slave labor may also have deterred investment in expensive machinery.

The wealth of the empire was not evenly spread. The eastern half of the empire was richer, more densely urbanized and more highly populated than the western half which, outside Italy, was relatively underdeveloped. Town life, already established for thousands of years in the east, was virtually unknown in most of the west, for example interior Spain, northern Gaul (see pages 240–241) and Britain, at the time of the Roman conquest. The Romans deliberately promoted urban living as a means of acquainting their new subjects with the Roman way of life. Dozens of new towns were founded, each of them complete with baths, forums, temples, amphitheaters and the other trappings of Roman civilization. But despite impressive economic growth in the 2nd century, most of the west remained too impoverished and underpopulated to sustain this scale of

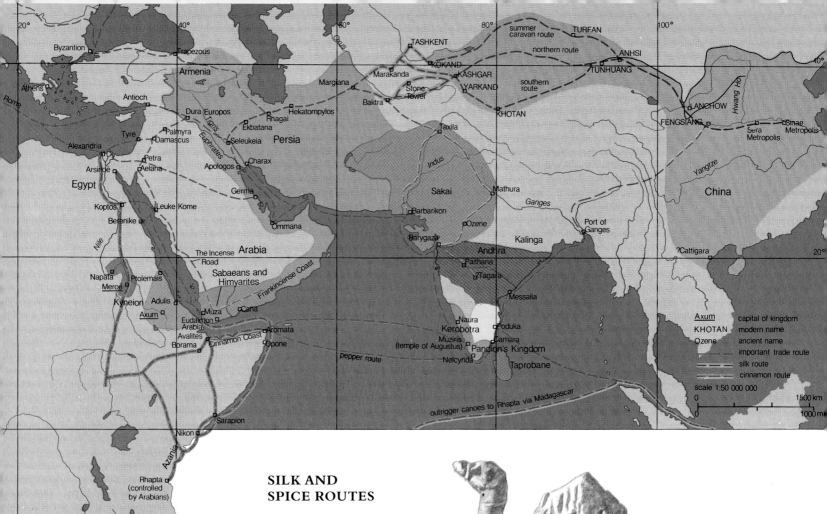

Map labels (clockwise/by region):

20° — 40° — 60° — 80° — 100°

Byzantion, Trapezous, Athens, Rome, Armenia, Antioch, Dura Europos, Tyre, Palmyra, Damascus, Rhagai, Ekbatana, Seleukeia, Persia, Hekatompylos, Margiana, Baktra, Stone Tower, Marakanda, Tashkent, Kokand, Kashgar, Yarkand, summer caravan route, Turfan, northern route, Anhsi, Tunhuang, southern route, Khotan, Lanchow, Hwang Ho, Fengsiang, Sera Metropolis, Sinae Metropolis, Yangtze, China

Alexandria, Egypt, Arsinoe, Petra, Aelana, Apologos, Charax, Gerrha, Koptos, Leuke Kome, Berenike, Ommana, Nile, The Incense Road, Arabia, Sabaeans and Himyarites, Frankincense Coast, Napata, Meroë, Ptolemais, Muza, Cana, Eudaimon Arabia, Aromata, Kyneion, Axum, Adulis, Avalites, Cinnamon Coast, Borama, Opone, Pepper route, Taxila, Sakai, Barbarikon, Barygaza, Mathura, Ganges, Ozene, Port of Ganges, Kalinga, Andhra, Paithana, Tagara, Messalia, Naura, Kerobotra, Muziris (temple of Augustus), Poduka, Camara, Nelcynda, Pandion's Kingdom, Taprobane, Cattigara, Indus, Tigris, Euphrates

Nikon, Azania, Sarapion, Rhapta (controlled by Arabians), outrigger canoes to Rhapta via Madagascar

Legend:
Axum capital of kingdom
KHOTAN modern name
Ozene ancient name
important trade route
silk route
cinnamon route
scale 1:50 000 000
0 — 1500 km
0 — 1000 mi

SILK AND SPICE ROUTES

Luxury products were imported into the Roman empire from distant places. Many of these were known to the Romans only from travelers' tales. China, the source of precious silks, was regarded as an almost mythic land of wonders – the Chinese saw the Roman empire in exactly the same light. The Romans bought cinnamon and other spices in East Africa, unaware that their true origin was in Indonesia. Direct Roman trade with the east increased greatly after seafarers from Alexandria in the 1st century AD *learned to voyage directly to India using the monsoon winds. (Above) The introduction of camels from Asia into the Sahara desert around the time of Christ led to a great increase in trade with tropical Africa.*

urbanization. Towns were comparatively undeveloped, serving as little more than administrative or military centers. This contrast between the eastern and western halves of the empire was to have a profound bearing on their economic and political fortunes during the troubled years of the late 4th and 5th centuries.

MANY PEOPLES, MANY RELIGIONS

The Roman empire united scores of different ethnic groups into a single state. Over time, Roman citizenship was extended to more and more of its inhabitants. This had the effect of helping to diminish local identities. Citizenship was eventually granted to all free inhabitants of the empire by the emperor Caracalla (r. 211–217) in 212 and by the 4th century the vast majority of the empire's citizens considered themselves in all respects to be Roman.

In republican times the main social division had been between citizens and non-citizens, with all citizens possessing equal rights. As citizenship became more widely held a new social division was opened up, with rich citizens, the *honestiores*, gradually being granted more and more legal privileges at the expense of the poor, the *humiliores*. The distinction first appears in legislation during Hadrian's reign. For example, an *honestus* who was convicted of illegally moving boundary stones (in effect, of stealing land) was sentenced to banishment, while a *humilis* convicted of the same offense received a beating and two years' hard

ATLAN OCEA

HAUT ATLAS

scale 1:20 000 000
0
600 km
400 mi

labor. However, it is clear that Hadrian's laws were only recognizing what had already been practiced for some time.

In the west, Latin gradually came to supplant local languages such as Celtic in Gaul and Punic (Phoenician) in North Africa. Distinct local dialects of Latin developed in Italy, Iberia, Dacia and Gaul. After the fall of the empire, these evolved into the Romance languages: Italian, Spanish, Portuguese, Romanian and French. The Celtic language survived in the British Isles, Basque in the Pyrenees and Libyan in much of North Africa. Latin made less headway in the eastern empire. Here it was Greek that gradually replaced local languages such as Phrygian, a language of Anatolia. However, it did not take over as completely as Latin did in the west. Demotic (late ancient Egyptian) was the everyday language of the Nile valley, and Aramaic was widely spoken in Syria and Palestine.

As the various peoples of the Roman empire worshiped thousands of different gods, religious toleration was officially practiced. The Romans recognized that many local gods possessed similar attributes to their own deities. They assumed that they were the same gods, only known by different names and assimilated them to the state cults (see pages 214–215). For example, Baal, the chief god of the Phoenicians, came to be equated with Jupiter. Roman subjects were sometimes required to make token sacrifices to the state gods as an expression of loyalty to the empire, but this pagan act was unacceptable to most Jews and Christians. Their refusal to do so seemed perverse and treasonable to the Roman authorities, who did not demand of anyone that they sincerely believed in the state gods. This attitudinal difference lay at the root both of the Jewish revolts and of the early Christian persecutions.

BELOW *The Roman empire was divided into Latin and Greek-speaking areas. Both supplanted many local languages, though there were some important survivals. Urbanization was most developed in Italy and the Greek-speaking world. There were fewer, smaller cities in the western provinces where villas had a greater role in social and economic organization. The desert restricted urbanization in the south and east of the empire. Only in Egypt, watered by the Nile, were cities densely concentrated beyond the isohyet (line) denoting 250mm annual rainfall, the limit of dry farming. There is an evident correspondence between urbanization and the area of olive-farming.*

LANGUAGES, URBANIZATION AND AGRICULTURE

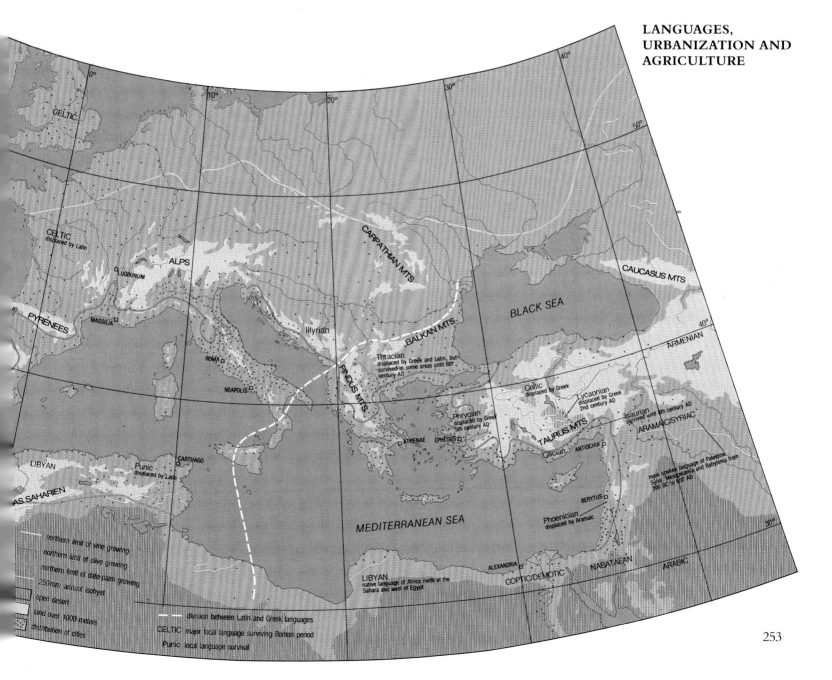

253

ROMAN TECHNOLOGY

That the Romans never developed an industrial society was not for any lack of inventiveness or enterprise: their building achievements speak for themselves in this respect. However, they were not advanced in metal-working skills. Their mechanical devices were made of wood and were ill-equipped to sustain the stresses of power-driven machinery. This partly explains why they did not extensivly exploit their understanding of wind and water power (though watermills were more common than was once assumed), but it is not the whole story. Medieval Europeans possessed no better technology yet made wide use of these power sources. Other significant factors include the availability of cheap labor, slave and free (the free poor suffered from chronic unemployment), which meant there was little incentive to develop expensive machinery. Nor did the Roman empire possess the financial institutions necessary for industrial investment. Furthermore, most people were poor. Their needs were adequately supplied by domestic or small-scale local production, while the luxury goods demanded by the small rich class could only be produced by skilled craftsmen. Unlike 18th-century Europe, the Roman empire had no middle class, and this meant there was no market for mass-produced goods to fuel industrialization.

ABOVE *A carving showing men working a* vallus *or reaping machine. It was operated by being pushed from behind; the tapered teeth cut or tore off the ears of corn and let them fall into the container. The rest of the plant was left to stand as tall stubble. So far as is known, the machine was used only on the broad, flat plains of northeastern Gaul.*

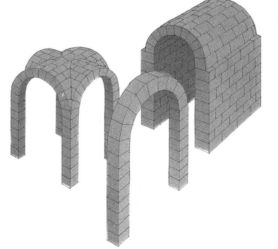

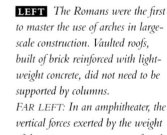

LEFT *The Romans were the first to master the use of arches in large-scale construction. Vaulted roofs, built of brick reinforced with light-weight concrete, did not need to be supported by columns.*
FAR LEFT: In an amphitheater, the vertical forces exerted by the weight of the superstructure are transferred horizontally by the keystones of the arches. A single unsupported arch will collapse beneath the pressure exerted by the keystone, but here the repeating series of arches are mutually self-supporting.

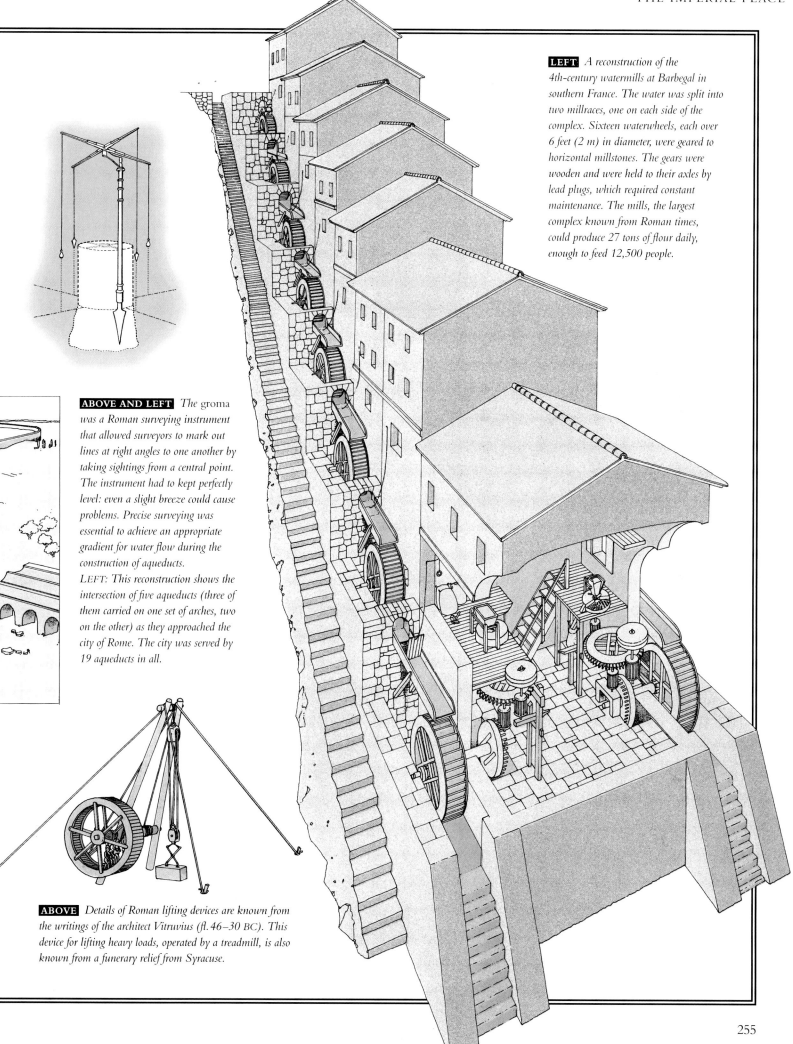

LEFT *A reconstruction of the 4th-century watermills at Barbegal in southern France. The water was split into two millraces, one on each side of the complex. Sixteen waterwheels, each over 6 feet (2 m) in diameter, were geared to horizontal millstones. The gears were wooden and were held to their axles by lead plugs, which required constant maintenance. The mills, the largest complex known from Roman times, could produce 27 tons of flour daily, enough to feed 12,500 people.*

ABOVE AND LEFT *The groma was a Roman surveying instrument that allowed surveyors to mark out lines at right angles to one another by taking sightings from a central point. The instrument had to kept perfectly level: even a slight breeze could cause problems. Precise surveying was essential to achieve an appropriate gradient for water flow during the construction of aqueducts.*
LEFT: This reconstruction shows the intersection of five aqueducts (three of them carried on one set of arches, two on the other) as they approached the city of Rome. The city was served by 19 aqueducts in all.

ABOVE *Details of Roman lifting devices are known from the writings of the architect Vitruvius (fl. 46–30 BC). This device for lifting heavy loads, operated by a treadmill, is also known from a funerary relief from Syracuse.*

THE GERMAN THREAT

After Hadrian withdrew from Trajan's eastern conquests in 117 the frontiers of the empire (see pages 268–269) remained stable for more than 100 years. The only significant change took place in the east where successful campaigning between 195 and 198 by Septimius Severus (r. 193–211) wrested northern Mesopotamia from Parthian control, this time permanently.

Along the drawn-out northern frontier, however, the Romans had been thrown onto the defensive by the Germans. Mediterranean writers had first become aware of the Germans (who had their origins in southern Scandinavia and the north German plain before 500 BC) at the end of the 2nd century BC, when they began to expand south and west at the expense of their Celtic neighbors. Two German peoples, the Cimbri and Teutones, caused panic in Rome when their migrations brought them to the borders of Italy in 113 BC, and fear of renewed Germanic invasions was the motive for Augustus's attempt to conquer Germany. By AD 6 the Romans had pacified the Germanic tribes as far east as the Elbe, but a rebellion under Arminius, a tribal leader who had previously served in the Roman army and was a Roman citizen, destroyed the Roman army of occupation at a battle in the Teutoburg forest in AD 9. No further serious attempt was made to reconquer the Germans, though frequent punitive expeditions were made against troublesome tribes.

Relations between the Germans and the Roman empire were by no means exclusively hostile, however. There was considerable cross-border trade and the Romans gave diplomatic and material support to friendly tribes. Many Germans were recruited into the Roman army. Such contacts led to dramatic changes in the social structure of the Germanic tribes in the late 2nd and early 3rd centuries AD. Power became more centralized as small tribes merged to form powerful confederations. For example on the Rhine, the Chasuarii, Chamavi, Bructeri, Tencteri and other smaller tribes emerged as the Frankish confederacy in the early 3rd century. The first signs of these changes became apparent in 167 when the

RIGHT *The Roman fondness for gladiatorial combats led to the construction of hundreds of amphitheaters. The largest was the Colosseum in Rome. Built between AD 69 and 80, it could seat 50,000 spectators. Most amphitheaters were in Italy and the west. The Greeks and other eastern provincials never developed a taste for this kind of bloodsport.*

IMPERIAL ROME

Writing of Augustus, the Roman historian Suetonius said he so embellished the city that he was justifiably able to boast: "I left Rome a city of marble, though I found it a city of bricks." All the early emperors understood the prestige that could be gained by lavish building projects and between them they transformed the appearance of Rome. After the disastrous fire of AD 64 destroyed or seriously damaged 10 of Rome's 14 administrative districts, a major rebuilding program was undertaken by Nero, including a vast new palace, the Domus Aurea (Golden House).

By the late 3rd century Rome contained 11 public baths, over 1000 pools and fountains fed by 19 aqueducts, two circuses, two amphitheaters, 36 triumphal arches and nearly 2000 palaces. A proliferation of new markets meant that the Forum was no longer Rome's commercial center, but it remained the symbolic heart of both city and the empire, continuously endowed with new temples, statues and altars. Despite the ever increasing magnificence of Rome's public face, the living conditions of the masses, by now numbering more than 1 million, remained crowded, uncomfortable and unhygienic. By the 3rd century the city's spread made it necessary to build a new outer wall.

ABOVE *Triumphal arches were one of the most important expressions of the Roman cult of victory. This one, dominating the western end of the Forum, was built in 203 to celebrate the victories of Septimius Severus over the Parthians and the Arabs.*

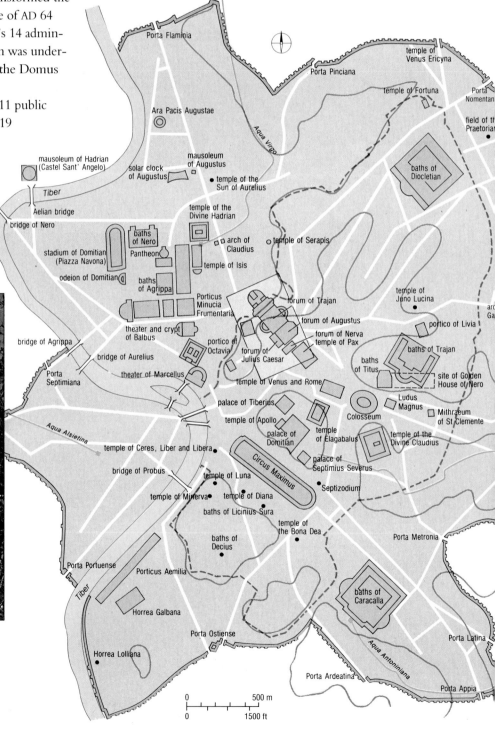

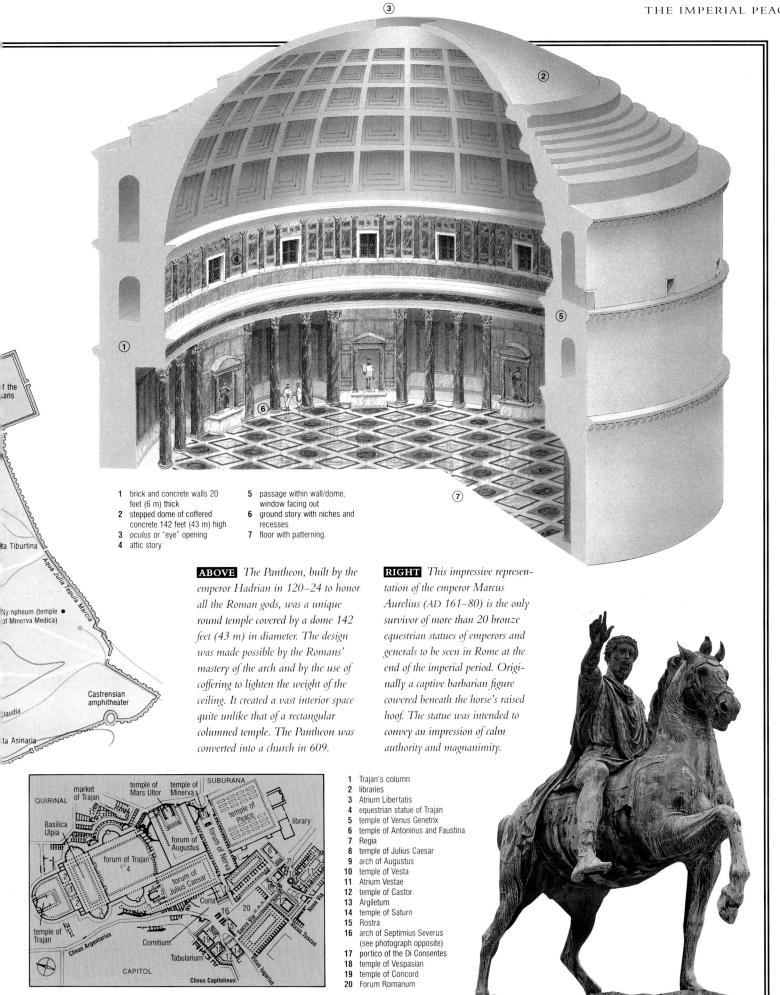

1 brick and concrete walls 20 feet (6 m) thick
2 stepped dome of coffered concrete 142 feet (43 m) high
3 *oculus* or "eye" opening
4 attic story
5 passage within wall/dome, window facing out
6 ground story with niches and recesses
7 floor with patterning.

ABOVE *The Pantheon, built by the emperor Hadrian in 120–24 to honor all the Roman gods, was a unique round temple covered by a dome 142 feet (43 m) in diameter. The design was made possible by the Romans' mastery of the arch and by the use of coffering to lighten the weight of the ceiling. It created a vast interior space quite unlike that of a rectangular columned temple. The Pantheon was converted into a church in 609.*

RIGHT *This impressive representation of the emperor Marcus Aurelius (AD 161–80) is the only survivor of more than 20 bronze equestrian statues of emperors and generals to be seen in Rome at the end of the imperial period. Originally a captive barbarian figure cowered beneath the horse's raised hoof. The statue was intended to convey an impression of calm authority and magnanimity.*

1 Trajan's column
2 libraries
3 Atrium Libertatis
4 equestrian statue of Trajan
5 temple of Venus Genetrix
6 temple of Antoninus and Faustina
7 Regia
8 temple of Julius Caesar
9 arch of Augustus
10 temple of Vesta
11 Atrium Vestae
12 temple of Castor
13 Argiletum
14 temple of Saturn
15 Rostra
16 arch of Septimius Severus (see photograph opposite)
17 portico of the Di Consentes
18 temple of Vespasian
19 temple of Concord
20 Forum Romanum

THE GERMANIC MIGRATIONS

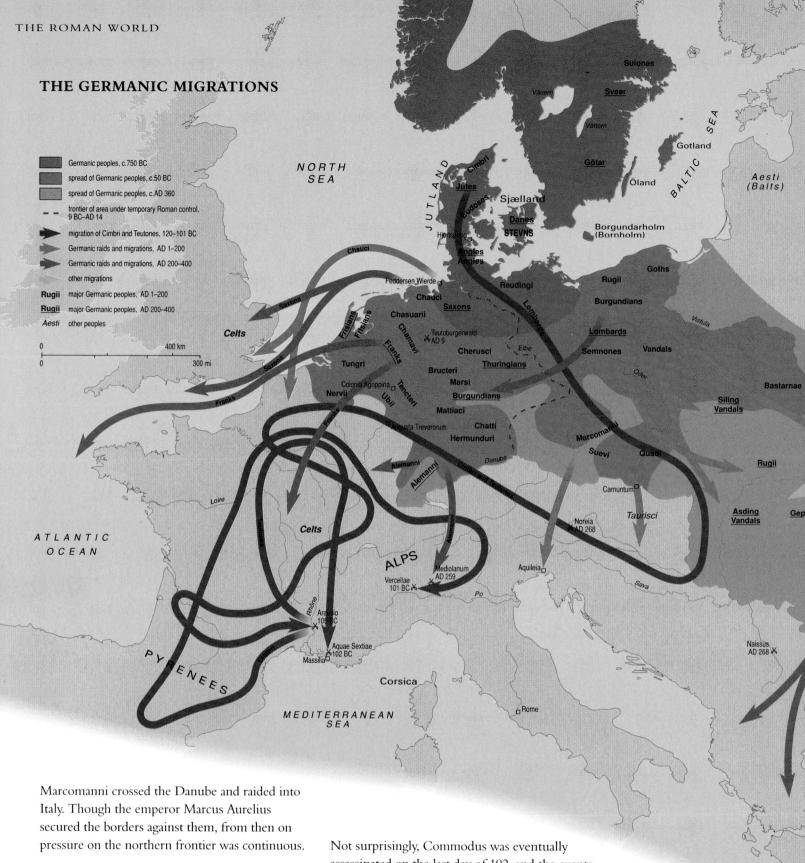

Germanic peoples, c.750 BC

spread of Germanic peoples, c.50 BC

spread of Germanic peoples, c.AD 360

frontier of area under temporary Roman control, 9 BC–AD 14

migration of Cimbri and Teutones, 120–101 BC

Germanic raids and migrations, AD 1–200

Germanic raids and migrations, AD 200–400

other migrations

Rugii major Germanic peoples, AD 1–200

Rugii major Germanic peoples, AD 200–400

Aesti other peoples

Marcomanni crossed the Danube and raided into Italy. Though the emperor Marcus Aurelius secured the borders against them, from then on pressure on the northern frontier was continuous.

THE 3RD CENTURY CRISIS

Marcus Aurelius's decision to allow his son Commodus to succeed him was a fateful one for the empire. Commodus (r. 180–192) proved to be a megalomaniac tyrant, worse even than Caligula, Nero and Domitian. Identifying himself with Hercules, he performed as a gladiator in the arena, spent freely on a debauched lifestyle and completely neglected the business of government.

Not surprisingly, Commodus was eventually assassinated on the last day of 192, and the events of his succession once again brought to the fore the fundamental underlying weakness of the imperial system.

Commodus's successor Pertinax lasted only three months. His successor Didius Julianus notoriously acquired the imperial office by bribing the praetorian guard. His reign lasted only ten weeks. He was executed by Septimius Severus (r. 193–211), a general on the Danube frontier

RIGHT *This relief of an auxiliary horseman in chain mail comes from the Roman city of Tropaeum Traiani in the remote Balkans. It was destroyed by Gothic raiders in the 3rd century and later rebuilt by Constantine.*

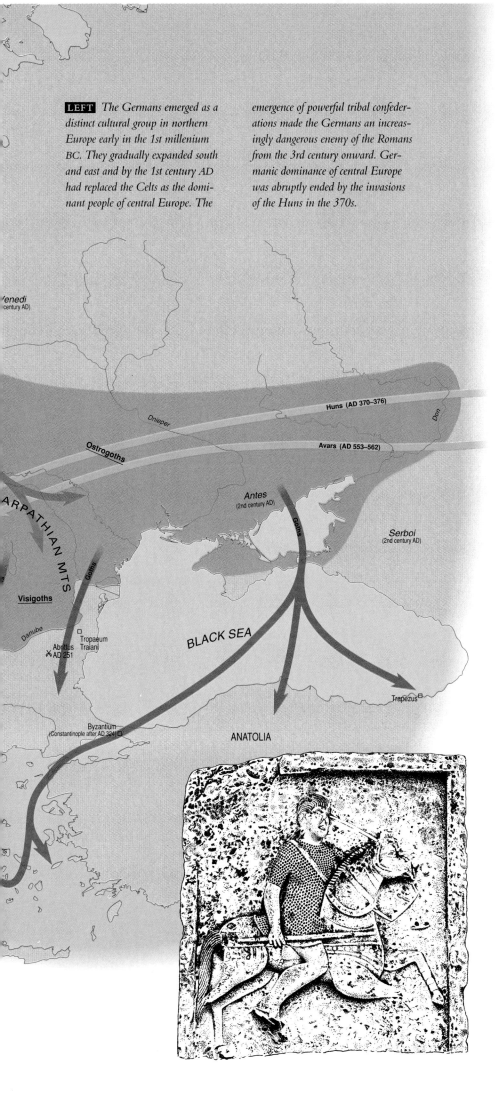

LEFT *The Germans emerged as a distinct cultural group in northern Europe early in the 1st millenium BC. They gradually expanded south and east and by the 1st century AD had replaced the Celts as the dominant people of central Europe. The emergence of powerful tribal confederations made the Germans an increasingly dangerous enemy of the Romans from the 3rd century onward. Germanic dominance of central Europe was abruptly ended by the invasions of the Huns in the 370s.*

who marched on Rome after being proclaimed emperor by his troops. Severus faced a rival in the east, Pescennius Niger, and the west, Clodius Albinus, but by 197 he was in sole command of the empire. His military successes against the Parthians (197–199) were celebrated with shows of unparalleled magnificence in Rome, and his reign seemed to promise a return to stable dynastic rule. But Severus's son Caracalla plunged the empire once again into tyranny, and he was assassinated while campaigning in the east. After his death emperors came and went in rapid succession.

Pressure by the Germanic tribes on the empire's northern frontiers became critical in the 3rd century. About this time, a new threat arose on the eastern frontier after the Parthians, discredited by their frequent defeats at Roman hands, were overthrown by the aggressive Sasanian dynasty in 226 (see pages 232–233). Though the Romans were generally successful in maintaining the borders of the empire, at least until the 260s, persistent pressure took its toll on the empire. The legions came to dominate its political life, which had destabilizing results. The emperor, ruling in conditions of almost constant warfare, had to be first and foremost a good soldier. But the legions had learned that they had the power to make and unmake emperors; consequently a poor soldier would not rule for long.

Rival candidates for power, promoted by different legions, fought each other for control of the empire while the borders were left undefended and open to invasion. For example, when Valerian (r. 253–60) withdrew troops from the Rhine to fight a usurper, the Franks immediately invaded Gaul. Even when one claimant emerged supreme for a time, he had to be ever watchful of his more successful and popular generals in case they should seize the opportunity of a new military crisis to try to snatch power. Equally, a general who felt the eye of imperial suspicion upon him often found himself forced to rebel as a means of averting the threat of a treason charge and inevitable execution.

Civil war and invasion continued without ceasing between 235 and 284. Of the 26 emperors who ruled during these years, all but one died by violence. One of the more successful, Gallienus (r. 259–68) defeated 18 usurpers in his 9-year reign, only to be murdered by his own officers. The efforts of emperors to buy the loyalty of their troops led them to debase the coinage to raise money, but this only added runaway inflation to

261

PALMYRA

almyra, the "city of the palms," was an ancient oasis settlement in the Syrian desert. It was known in the Old Testament as Tadmor and prospered from its control of the caravan route that ran from the Mediterranean to the head of the Persian Gulf to connect up with the sea route to India.

Mark Antony, attracted by Palmyra's legendary wealth, tried and failed to capture the city and it was finally incorporated into the empire as part of the province of Syria in AD 18. Its rulers continued to enjoy considerable autonomy while benefiting from the political stability and security that Roman rule brought. Palmyra's economy boomed and the city grew spectacularly. Inscriptions show that its powerful merchant families organized caravans to bring luxury products from the east to the Mediterranean world. Tariffs charged on caravans passing through the city were another important source of income and in return the local rulers policed the caravan routes from raids by nomadic Arabs. One inscription tells how one merchant "on many occasions nobly and generously assisted the merchants, caravans and fellow citizens established at Vologesias [in Parthia]" and had "defended from great danger the caravan recently arrived from there."

Palmyra achieved its greatest heights in the late 3rd century under the spirited queen Zenobia, who openly rebelled against Rome and overran most of the empire's eastern provinces. Defeated by the emperor Aurelian in 272, she was taken in triumph to Rome and allowed to spend the rest of her life in considerable luxury near Tivoli. Palmyra was heavily fortified by Diocletian and restored as a strongpoint in the empire's eastern frontier defenses, but it never fully recovered its former prosperity.

RIGHT *The great families of Palmyra, displaying their wealth even in death, were buried in impressive tower tombs containing many bodies. Sculpted tombstones, such as this one belonging to a young man of the 2nd century AD, identified the different people interred inside. The distinctive local sculptural style anticipates developments in late Roman and Byzantine art.*

BELOW *This view of Palmyra, showing the colonnaded main street leading to the agora (marketplace), theater and temple of Bel, gives an idea of the city in its prime. Palmyra's architecture was a fusion of Hellenistic Greek and Parthian styles. In the background are the trees of the oasis on which Palmyra's prosperity depended.*

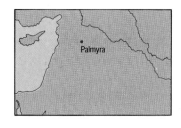

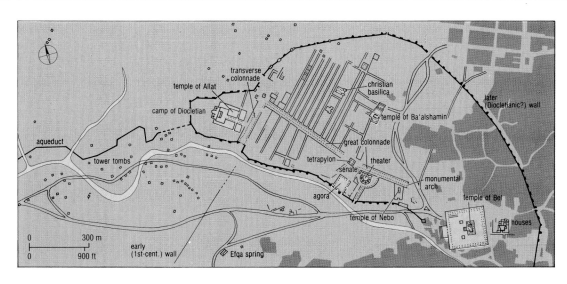

Palmyra is notable among Roman towns for its irregular layout. This may have been determined by the location of water sources during the pre-Roman history of settlement. It has been suggested that the earliest Aramean and Amorite inhabitants retained something of their nomadic lifestyle and camped informally in various parts of the site. These later developed into the different quarters of the Roman city.

the empire's woes. The growing economic crisis and the constant threat of invasion caused a decline in urban life, especially in the western empire, where a great many towns shrank to a fortified administrative core. Further economic problems were caused by population decline resulting from recurrent epidemic diseases (possibly smallpox) introduced into the empire in 165 by an army returning from campaigning in Parthia.

Not all usurpers aimed at control of the whole empire. After Valerian was captured by the Sasanians at Edessa in 260, defense of the east devolved on Odenathus, the ruler of the desert city of Palmyra (see pages 262–263). He defeated the Sasanians and then set about carving out an independent kingdom for himself in the Near East. Under his wife and successor Zenobia, the Palmyrene kingdom grew to include Egypt, Syria and much of Anatolia. In the west the usurper Postumus founded an independent Gallic empire

BELOW *Political instability, economic collapse and frequent invasions by the Germans and Sasanians brought the empire close to collapse in the mid 3rd century. The crisis reached its height in about 260 when large areas were lost to two breakaway empires, one in Gaul, the other based on Palmyra in Syria. Gallienus's military reforms restored the effectiveness of the imperial armies and the empire emerged in the 280s with most of its frontiers restored, save for some minor losses.*

THE 3RD-CENTURY INVASIONS

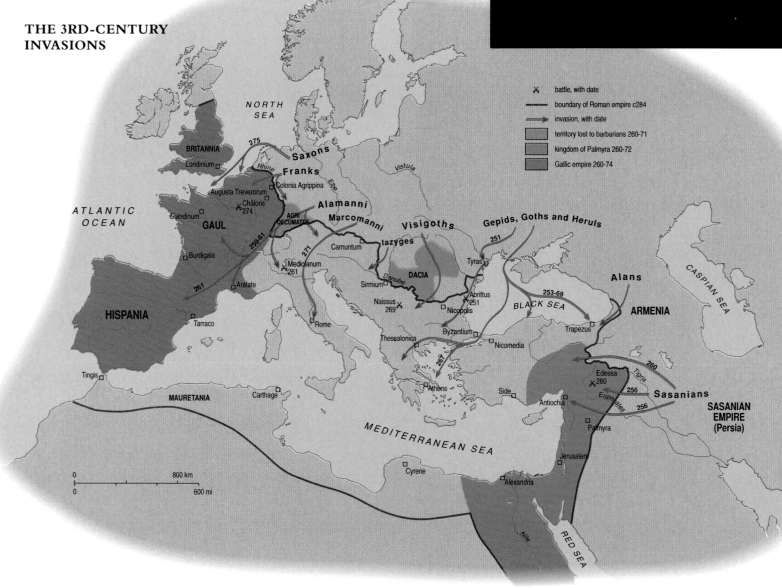

in 260, winning over the people of Gaul, Britain and Spain to his side with promises to concentrate on defending the frontiers and making no attempt to march on Rome.

REFORM OF THE ARMY

With the west lost to Postumus and the east to Odenathus, the empire's fortunes reached their lowest yet during the reign of Gallienus. Yet it was his military innovations that provided the basis for recovery. During the imperial peace of the 1st and 2nd centuries the Roman armies had become largely immobile garrisons stationed on the frontiers. The empire therefore had no in-depth defense, and when invaders broke through the frontiers, they were free to roam widely on the empire's excellent roads.

Gallienus's response was to create highly mobile field armies with a strong cavalry element that were able to operate independently of the legions, many of which were broken up into smaller and more flexible independent units. He also ended the system which reserved the highest commands to members of the aristocracy, promoting instead professional soldiers of proven talent such as Traianus Mucianus, a Thracian who had enlisted as an ordinary infantryman and rose to the rank of *dux* (general).

THE ILLYRIAN EMPERORS

These reforms did not save Gallienus but they were applied to good effect by the series of able, if short-lived, Illyrian emperors who followed him. Claudius II (r. 268–70) decisively defeated the Goths, who at this time frequently overran the Danube frontier and launched pirate raids across the Black Sea. Aurelian (r. 270–5) reclaimed the Palmyrene empire from Zenobia (272) and then reconquered the Gallic empire (274). Probus (r. 276–282) cleared Gaul of the Franks and Alamanni, and Carus (r. 282–3) sacked the Sasanian capital of Ctesiphon, avenging Rome's earlier defeats. Though these military achievements virtually restored the territorial integrity of the empire, its internal stability showed no signs of improving. After Carus was murdered, there was yet another struggle for the succession, won by Diocletian (r. 284–305). At first, Diocletian may have seemed to be just another Illyrian general, but his reign turned out to be one of the most important in Roman history. Not the least of his achievements was that he died peacefully of old age in his own bed.

BELOW *In the 3rd century the coasts of Britain and Gaul were raided by Saxon and Frankish pirates from the area of north Germany and the Netherlands today. To counter them, the Romans built the Saxon Shore forts on both sides of the Channel as bases for coastguard and naval patrols.*

ABOVE *Portchester castle (Portus Adurni) in southern England is one of the best preserved of the Saxon Shore forts. Built about 285–93, the projecting bastion towers are typical of late Roman fortifications: any attackers trying to scale the walls would be caught in crossfire from archers and catapults.*

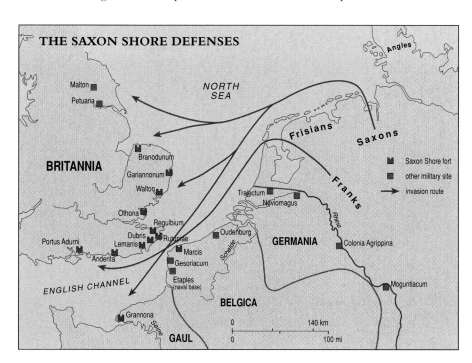

THE SAXON SHORE DEFENSES

Angles

NORTH SEA

Frisians

Saxons

Malton

Petuaria

BRITANNIA

Branodunum

Gariannonum

Walton

Trajectum

Noviomagus

Othona

Regulbium

Dubris

Rutupiae

Oudenburg

Portus Adurni

Lemanis

Anderita

Marcis

Gesoriacum

GERMANIA

Colonia Agrippina

Franks

Scheldt

Rhine

ENGLISH CHANNEL

Etaples (naval base)

Moguntiacum

BELGICA

Grannona

Seine

GAUL

■ Saxon Shore fort
■ other military site
→ invasion route

0   140 km
0   100 mi

The Christian Empire
AD 284–610

Diocletian's reign of 20 years (284–305) was the longest enjoyed by any emperor for 150 years. On coming to power he faced three major tasks: securing the frontiers of the empire, restoring the prestige and stability of the imperial office, and reviving the economy. He was only partially successful in dealing with them but the reforms he set in motion gave the empire a new lease on life. His decision to devolve part of his imperial authority to junior colleagues had the effect both of securing the defense of the frontiers (see pages 268–269), and of preventing the frontier armies from throwing up pretenders to the imperial office. Maximian, a fellow Illyrian, was given the title of Caesar before being sent west to deal with rebellions in Gaul and Britain in 286. The following year Diocletian made him co-emperor with the title of Augustus.

In 293, Diocletian appointed two more Illyrian officers, Galerius and Constantius, as Caesars. The expectation was that they would eventually succeed as the next Augusti. Under an arrangement that was known as the tetrarchy (rule of four), the empire was divided into four areas of military responsibility. Diocletian, based at Nicomedia in Asia Minor, had oversight of the east, while Galerius, at Sirmium on the Sava river in Serbia, watched over the Danube frontier. Maximian, based at Mediolanum (Milan), had responsibility for Italy, Africa and Spain, and Constantius guarded Gaul and Britain from the western capital of Augusta Treverorum (Trier).

Rome, which was too far from the frontiers to serve as a convenient residence for the emperors, ceased to be the administrative capital of the empire. Diocletian had been emperor for 20 years before visiting the city for the first time,

DIOCLETIAN'S REORGANIZATION OF THE EMPIRE

The threats facing the empire at the end of the 3rd century were so numerous that one man alone could no longer effectively direct its defense. Diocletian accordingly shared supreme power with a co-Augustus, Maximian, and with two junior colleagues, Galerius and Constantius (the tetrarchy). Diocletian introduced a far-reaching and costly program of reforms, aimed at securing the defense of the empire. To improve tax-raising efficiency throughout the empire, the number of provinces was doubled to 100, grouped into 12 dioceses under imperial deputies.

NORTH SEA

BRITANNIAE

Londinium

Augusta Treverorum

GALLIAE

Loire

VIENNENSIS

Rhône

Mediolanum

Ticinum

Arelate

HISPANIAE

Ebro

Corsica

Sardinia

Carthage

AFRICA

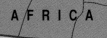

LEFT *A porphyry group of figures, usually identified as the tetrarchs. They are clasping shoulders in a show of unity. By the late 3rd century naturalism in art was being abandoned in favor of a more stylized and expressionistic style. Well suited to portraying idealized types, it was widely used for official art.*

and he completely ignored the Senate. The people of Rome, however, continued to be fed and entertained by the state and new baths and other buildings were provided.

The tetrarchy worked well. It allowed for the rapid suppression of internal rebellions and improved frontier security – both Gothic and Sasanian invasions were decisively repulsed. The arrangement was not intended to break up the empire – Diocletian by seniority and force of personality remained in overall control of imperial policy-making – but over the course of the next century it became the usual practice to have separate Augusti in the east and the west of the empire. The division of power became permanent after the death of Theodosius I (r. 379–395).

To restore respect for the imperial office, Diocletian introduced an elaborate court ritual on the Persian model. The Augusti appeared in public wearing jeweled diadems and slippers and fine robes of purple and gold. Anyone approaching the emperor was expected to prostrate themselves before him and kiss the hem of his robe. The

pretence that the emperor was simply "first citizen" was abandoned: he was now "lord and god."

Like all the 3rd-century emperors, Diocletian had achieved power through his command of the army. Once in power, however, he sought to reduce the emperor's dependence on the military by invoking the traditional Roman state cults to legitimize his authority. The gods of Rome had extended their protection to him and to his colleagues: Diocletian was the son of Jupiter, Maximian the son of Hercules. Because he had become emperor by the will of Jupiter, Diocletian did not bother to seek the Senate's confirmation of his appointment. The Senate's opinion was irrelevant. In this way Diocletian began to turn the empire into a theocratic (divinely ordained) monarchy. Christians represented a threat to the relationship between the state and the gods, and all those who refused to sacrifice to the gods were ordered to be dismissed from the army and civil service. Galerius, a militant pagan, encouraged Diocletian to outlaw Christianity in 303, and a period of brutal persecution followed.

REFORM OF THE EMPIRE

To make the empire secure, Diocletian refortified the frontiers and increased the size of the army from 300,000 to between 400,000 and 500,000 men. Many new legions were raised but they were smaller units than those that had existed under the early empire, being only about 1000 strong. The enlarged army was a severe financial burden and the empire's tax system was reformed to support it. A flexible budgeting system was introduced, allowing tax assessments to be varied annually as the need arose. The state's income was protected from the effects of inflation by arranging for many taxes to be paid in produce rather than cash.

A more efficient bureaucracy was required to administer the new system. The number of provinces was doubled to 100 and organized in groups of 12 into dioceses under a *vicarius* (deputy) who was directly responsible to the emperor. To keep a watchful eye over all the new governors and their staffs, the imperial secret service was reorganized and enlarged. As a further precaution, provincial governors were barred from holding military commands. Participation in local government had declined in the 3rd century, but service was now made compulsory and members of councils were made personally liable for collecting and delivering taxes. Price regulation was introduced to curb inflation, though it was only a

PANNONIAE
Aquileia
Siscia
Sirmium
na
Danube
BLACK SEA
Serdica
THRACIAE
ITALIA
Byzantium
MOESIAE
Heraclea
Nicomedia
Thessalonica
Cyzicus
PONTICA
Sicily
ASIANA
Tigris
Catana
Antiochia
Euphrates
Crete
Cyprus
MEDITERRANEAN SEA
Alexandria
ORIENS
Nile
RED SEA

○ capital of tetrarch
◉ principal Roman mint
— province boundary AD300
— diocese boundary AD300

dioceses under command of
　Diocletian
　Maximian
　Galerius
　Constantius

0 ——— 600 km
0 ——— 400 mi

FRONTIERS OF THE EMPIRE

The prosperity of the empire depended on its security from invasion. As outside pressure mounted, most emperors gave high priority to strengthening its frontier defenses. In Europe, the Rhine and Danube rivers provided a natural defendable frontier. Forts and watchtowers were built along their banks and there were frequent naval patrols. In areas lacking natural frontiers, such as the deserts of North Africa and the Near East, the frontier was marked by a military road called a *limes*. Forts and camps an easy day's march apart were strung out along its length. Sometimes linear barriers were built, like the earth and timber rampart that linked the headwaters of the Rhine and Danube, or Hadrian's Wall, built of stone, in northern Britain. Most Roman forces were stationed on the frontiers, which left the empire with no in-depth defense. To remedy this, the 4th-century army came to consist of two categories of troops: *limitanei*, or border garrison troops, and *comitatenses*, mobile field armies stationed behind the frontier to provide a flexible response as and where needed.

BELOW *Hadrian's Wall, built between AD 122 and 128, stretches from coast to coast for 70 miles (113 km) across northern England. For much of its length, the wall ran along the crest of an escarpment which gave a commanding view to the north. It was part of a typical* limes *system which included garrison forts, a military road and watchtowers. Impressive barrier though it was, it could not have halted a major invasion. Its purpose was to stop minor raids and to act as a base from which to watch and control the tribes living to the north.*

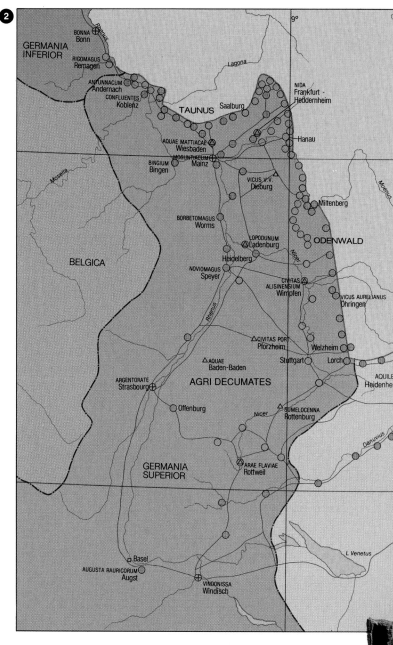

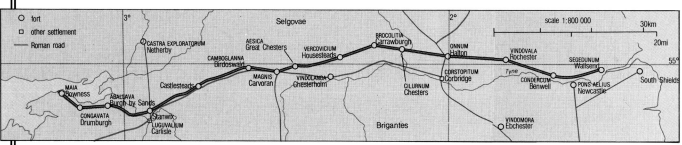

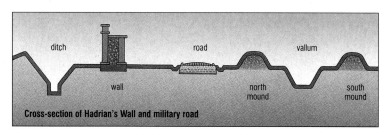

Cross-section of Hadrian's Wall and military road

RIGHT *Legionaries construct a fortress while auxiliary troops stand guard (one of the reliefs from Trajan's column). Inscriptions and slight variations in the design of watchtowers and forts show that several legions were involved in building Hadrian's Wall.*

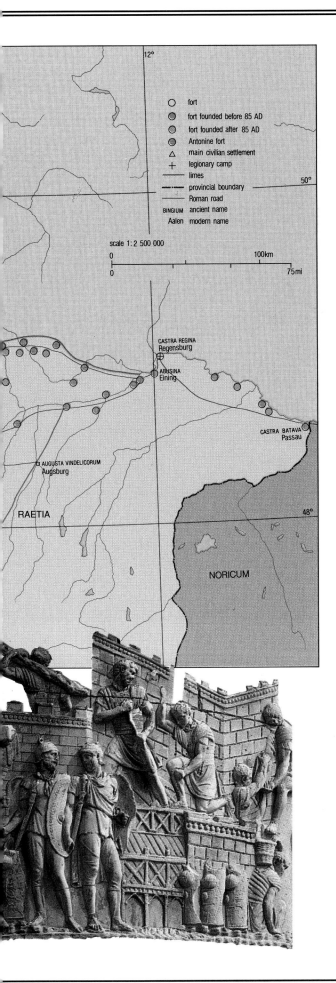

See detailed maps 1–3,
opposite and below

LEFT *In AD 73–85 the Romans
annexed the Agri Decumates to push
the frontier away from the Rhine and
Danube forward into Germany. This
shortened the Roman line of defense
quite considerably but was based on no
natural defensive feature. A 300-mile
(485-km) long limes, consisting of a
military road and earth and timber
rampart with forts and watchtowers,
was built to defend the new border. It
was abandoned in the 3rd century.*

BELOW *Early in the 4th century
Diocletian strengthened the Syrian
limes, neglected since the 3rd century,
with a military road (the* strata Dio-
cletiana*) and a chain of forts garrisoned with* limitanei *(border troops).
Their dispositions are known from
an early 5th-century document, the
Notitia Dignitatum. Frontier cities
such as Palmyra were refortified.*

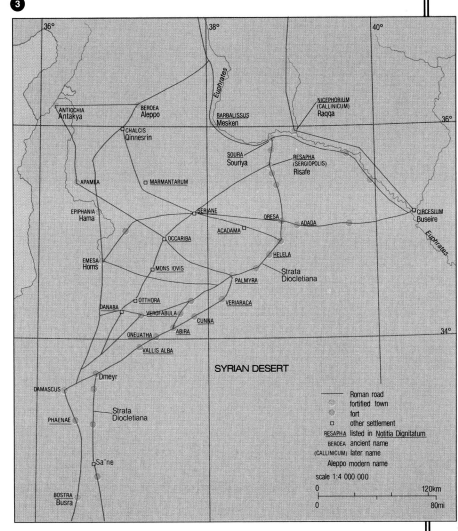

partial success as it simply drove many goods off the market. The empire's population had been in decline for some time, and to guard against labor shortages many key occupations, such as bakers and shippers, had already become hereditary obligations. Diocletian extended this to the army and the peasantry.

Diocletian's reforms were so far reaching that they amounted almost to a complete remaking of the Roman empire, turning it into a highly bureaucratic, militaristic autocracy that taxed its subjects to the hilt and attempted to regulate many aspects of their economic lives. Diocletian's association of the imperial office with divine will pointed the way – once traditional paganism had been eclipsed by Christianity – to the Roman empire's transformation into a fullblown theocratic state under emperors who claimed to rule as Christ's deputies on earth.

THE RISE OF CONSTANTINE THE GREAT

In 305 Diocletian abdicated and persuaded a reluctant Maximian to do the same. The two Caesars became the new Augusti, Galerius ruling in the east and Constantius in the west. Two relative unknowns, Maximinus and Severus, were promoted to the rank of Caesar. It was an unfortunate move since it was well known that Maxentius, the son of Maximian, and Constantine, the son of the new Augustus Constantius, harbored political ambitions. Moreover, the army had expected that the hereditary succession would be restored and so was sympathetic to their aspirations. Following the death of Constantius in Britain the next year, the troops immediately proclaimed Constantine as the new Augustus.

Galerius, meanwhile, had given the role to Severus and in 307 Maxentius, supported by his father, entered the fray on his own behalf. He captured and executed Severus before declaring himself Augustus but, to complicate matters still further, Maximian now quarreled with his son and declared himself Augustus once again. Galerius called on Diocletian to return to power: he sensibly refused but managed to persuade Maximian to abdicate. But Maximian, who could not leave politics alone, began to plot against Constantine and was forced to commit suicide in 310. Meanwhile trouble was brewing in the east, where Galerius had appointed Licinius joint Augustus to rule with him. He had refused the role to Maximinus, his Caesar, who responded by promoting himself

Augustus. By the end of 310, therefore, there were five Augusti ruling in the empire.

Galerius died in 311, shortly after calling a halt to the persecution of Christians. The following year Constantine, against the odds, defeated and killed Maxentius at the battle of the Milvian Bridge outside Rome to make himself the sole Augustus in the west. Then the death of Maximinus in 313 left Licinius as sole Augustus in the east. In the same year Diocletian had the good fortune to die peacefully in bed. For a few years an uneasy peace reigned between the two surviving Augusti, but it was clear that Constantine wanted to become sole emperor. A dispute over boundaries led to a short civil war which ended with Licinius's defeat and execution in 324.

THE SPREAD OF CHRISTIANITY

Constantine (r. 324–337) had been brought up as a pagan. In 310 he had become a devotee of Apollo after experiencing a vision of the god. He believed, however, that he owed his decisive victory at the Milvian Bridge over Maxentius to the help of the Christian God. He later recalled how he had witnessed a vision of a cross standing over the sun, accompanied by the words "Conquer with this," and he ordered the "chi rho" symbol (formed from the first two Greek letters of Christ's name) to be painted on his men's shields after being told to do so in a dream. In 313 he had issued the Edict of Milan jointly with Licinius. This extended tolerance to Christians, freeing them from the threat of persecution.

Constantine further showed his gratitude for God's help by undertaking an extensive program of church building. The greatest of his churches were the basilica of St Peter on the Vatican hill and the cathedral of St John Lateran in Rome (see pages 278–279), but other imposing churches were built at Trier in northern France (his capital in the early part of his reign), at the Holy Sepulcher in Jerusalem and above the traditional site of the nativity at Bethlehem. Constantine's mother, Helena, is said to have visited Jerusalem, where she is supposed to have discovered the cross on which Jesus was crucified.

The sincerity of Constantine's conversion has been much debated but it is far from clear what he hoped to gain if his motives were purely political. Despite Diocletian's persecutions, Christians were numerous in the Roman empire by the early 4th century, especially in the east, but they were still a minority and their penetration of the politically

SPLIT

Split, ancient Aspalathos (from the Greek name for a thorn plant that grew there), in Croatia was a suburb of the city of Salona, a former Illyrian tribal capital which, in Roman times, became the main city of Dalmatia. In the late empire Salona was an important center of Christian culture, containing many monumental Christian basilicas and carved sarcophagi. Between 475 and 480 it was the last stronghold of the deposed western emperor Julius Nepos.

After his abdication in 305 Diocletian retired to Split where he had built a seaside palace for himself. It was laid out like a military camp and was heavily fortified. Though Diocletian had withdrawn from political life, he had no illusions about the age he was living in. During the centuries that followed, the palace served as a refuge in times of trouble. In the 10th century the Byzantine emperor Constantine VII recorded that it had been occupied by refugees from Salona, abandoned because of Slavic raids. A thriving medieval town grew up in and around the palace built of stones quarried from the site. Diocletian's octagonal mausoleum was converted to a church, an ironic fate for an emperor best remembered for his persecution of Christians.

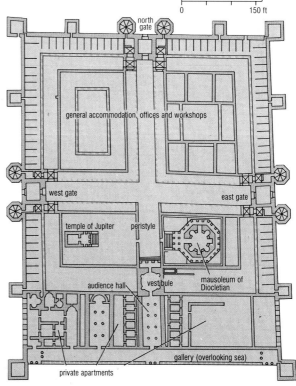

influential upper classes was slight. Without imperial patronage, they might well have remained a relatively unimportant sect. Constantine continued to employ pagan imagery on his coins and in his writings he referred simply to the "supreme deity," a phrase that could mean all things to all men. Constantine only received baptism on his deathbed, though this was not an unusual practice among Christians at that time. It may be that Constantine believed he would forfeit popular support if he were seen to be favoring Christianity exclusively, or perhaps he initially saw Christianity as just another cult to be worshiped alongside the traditional ones.

Roman emperors had always had religious duties and responsibilities. Constantine did not see his role any differently and this drew him into the greatest theological dispute of the early church. In 323 Arius, an Alexandrian priest, disputed the orthodox version of the Trinity, arguing that if Jesus was the son of God, he must be younger than God and therefore lesser than Him. God was eternal, having no beginning and no end, but Christ had a beginning and therefore was not eternal and so could not be wholly God. Fearing that God might hold him responsible if the church split, Constantine called the first general council of the church to meet at Nicaea in 325 to resolve the dispute. The orthodox view was endorsed by the council, but the Arians remained unreconciled and they regained influence under Constantine's son Constantius II (r. 337–61), who was a supporter of their views. Arianism was declared heretical in 381 by Theodosius I, after which its adherents were actively persecuted. The Christian emperors were far less tolerant of religious dissent than their polytheist pagan predecessors had been: if there was only one God, there could be only one truth.

Despite Diocletian's strengthening of the army, the empire's northern frontier remained under constant threat of invasion. Constantine's policy was in many ways similar to Gallienus's more than 50 years earlier. The army was divided into two types of troops, border garrisons called *limitanei* and mobile troops called *comitatenses*. The *limitanei* were allocated lands so that they could grow their own supplies, but they remained effective soldiers – they were not, as is often claimed, peasant militias. The *comitatenses* made up a number of field armies stationed well behind the frontiers to provide a flexible response to any invaders who broke through the border defenses. The creation of these field armies restricted the

RIGHT *Constantinople was built on the Golden Horn, an arm of the Bosporus. Surrounded by water on three sides, the site chosen for the city was strongly defendable, and it was ideally located at the center of the richest and most populous part of the Roman empire.*

BELOW *In 413 the emperor Theodosius II built the line of defensive walls that protect Constantinople's landward side. They probably represent the best investment in military architecture ever made by any state, resisting all attackers for more than 1000 years until they were finally breached by Turkish cannon in 1453. The walls gave defense in depth. First came a flooded moat and breastwork, then an outer wall 40 feet (12 m) high and lastly the main defense line, the 65-foot (20-m) high inner wall. The towers on both walls overlapped, allowing defenders on the inner wall to cover those defending the outer wall and breastwork.*

LEFT *Though an able ruler, Constantine's reputation (he is often called "the Great") was inflated after his death by Christian historians such as Eusebius (c. 260 – c. 340) who made much of his conversion to further the cause of Christianity. Constantine's portraits frequently show him as a visionary.*

CONSTANTINOPLE

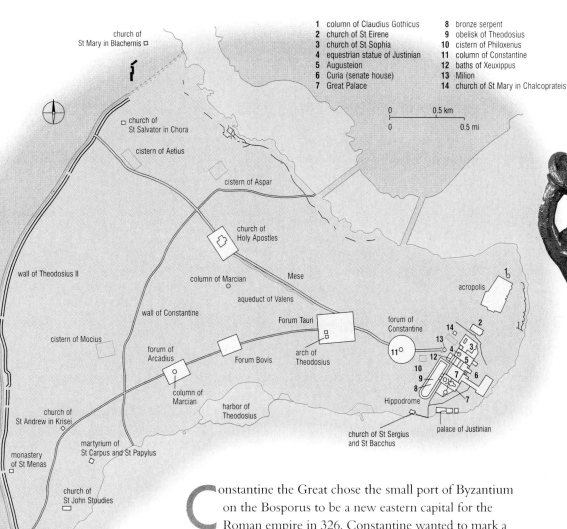

church of
St Mary in Blachernis □

1 column of Claudius Gothicus **8** bronze serpent
2 church of St Eirene **9** obelisk of Theodosius
3 church of St Sophia **10** cistern of Philoxenus
4 equestrian statue of Justinian **11** column of Constantine
5 Augusteion **12** baths of Xeuxippus
6 Curia (senate house) **13** Milion
7 Great Palace **14** church of St Mary in Chalcoprateis

church of
St Salvator in Chora

cistern of Aetius

cistern of Aspar

church of
Holy Apostles

wall of Theodosius II

column of Marcian   Mese

aqueduct of Valens

wall of Constantine

Forum Tauri

forum of
Constantine

acropolis

cistern of Mocius

forum of
Arcadius   Forum Bovis

arch of
Theodosius

column of
Marcian

church of
St Andrew in Krisei

harbor of
Theodosius

Hippodrome

monastery
of St Menas

martyrium of
St Carpus and St Papylus

church of
St John Stoudies

church of St Sergius
and St Bacchus

palace of Justinian

Golden Gate

onstantine the Great chose the small port of Byzantium
on the Bosporus to be a new eastern capital for the
Roman empire in 326. Constantine wanted to mark a
break with Rome's pagan past and from the outset his new
city, given the name of Constantinople (City of Constantine)
was planned as a Christian city. Officially inaugurated in 330,
Constantinople was modeled on the city of Rome, with
seven hills and 14 administrative districts. It was granted its
own Senate and allocated one of the empire's two consul-
ships. Financial incentives and promises of free bread for the
poor encouraged settlers to the city.

Constantinople grew with amazing speed and by the late
4th century had spread outside its original walls. At this time
the city had 11 imperial palaces, not less than 14 churches,
5 markets, 8 public and 153 private baths, 20 public and 120
private bakeries, a Hippodrome for chariot races, 322 streets
and 4388 houses, not counting the slum dwellings of the
poor. The initial building was often shoddy and there was
much rebuilding by later rulers. In contrast to Rome, which
was now in decline, Constantinople kept on expanding and
by 800 its population had risen to 1 million.

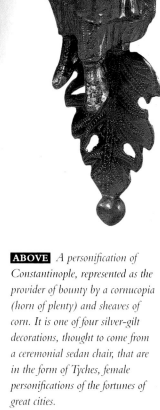

ABOVE *A personification of
Constantinople, represented as the
provider of bounty by a cornucopia
(horn of plenty) and sheaves of
corn. It is one of four silver-gilt
decorations, thought to come from
a ceremonial sedan chair, that are
in the form of Tyches, female
personifications of the fortunes of
great cities.*

EPHESUS

For the sheer scale of its remains, most of which date from the Roman period, Ephesus is one of the most impressive sites of the Eastern Mediterranean. Founded by Greek settlers about 1000 BC, the city prospered as a trading and banking center thanks to its good harbor, long since silted up. But it was most famous for the temple of Artemis which attracted pilgrims from all over the Mediterranean. Counted among the seven wonders of the world, it was a masterpiece of Hellenistic architecture, four times the size of the Parthenon. Only its foundations survive.

Ephesus came under Roman rule in 133 BC. During the reign of Augustus it became the administrative capital of the province of Asia.

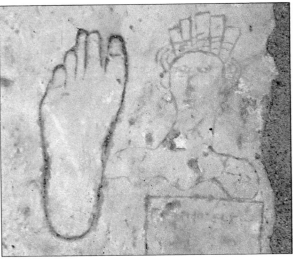

ABOVE AND LEFT *Artemis of the Ephesians, a Roman copy of the cult statue of the temple of Artemis (AD 81–96). This strange, many-breasted figure bears little resemblence to the chaste huntress of classical Greek mythology. The original Greek settlers of Ephesus may have assimilated Artemis with the popular Anatolian cult of the mother goddess Cybele. (Top left) The entrance to the temple*

of Hadrian built in AD 138. The Greek belief that the gods rewarded outstanding mortals, such as Alexander the Great, by making them into gods after their deaths persisted under Roman rule. Temples dedicated to deified emperors are common in the Greek-speaking parts of the empire. (Bottom left) A self-explanatory sign advertizing a brothel carved on a street pavement in Ephesus.

LEFT *The theater, the largest surviving structure in Ephesus, held up to 24,000 spectators. St Paul preached here when he visited Ephesus on his second missionary journey in AD 53. Running down from the theater to the silted up harbor, a bright green marsh in the middle distance, is the city's main street, the Arkadiane, built in 395–408. It was colonnaded along both sides for its entire length, making an impressive entrance to the city for anyone arriving by ship. An inscription unearthed during excavations has revealed that the Arkadiane even had street lighting.*

Ephesus prospered under Roman rule and its population reached about 250,000. When St Paul arrived in the city in AD 53 he found that a community of Christians was already established there. Ephesus went on to become the main center of Christianity in Anatolia and was the seat of the church council that condemned Nestorianism in 431. It is remembered for the legend of the Seven Sleepers which tells of seven young Christians who hid in a cave at Ephesus to escape persecution by the emperor Decius (r. 249–51). The emperor had them sealed inside the cave and they fell into a deep sleep. When they awoke 200 years later, it was to learn that Christianity had triumphed over paganism in the meantime.

The temple of Artemis was destroyed when Ephesus was sacked by Gothic pirates in 262. The city, however, staged a recovery and a magnificent colonnaded shopping street, the Arkadiane (named after the emperor Arcadius), was built there in the early 5th century, when most Roman cities in the west were declining. The subsequent silting up of the harbor led to the city's abandonment.

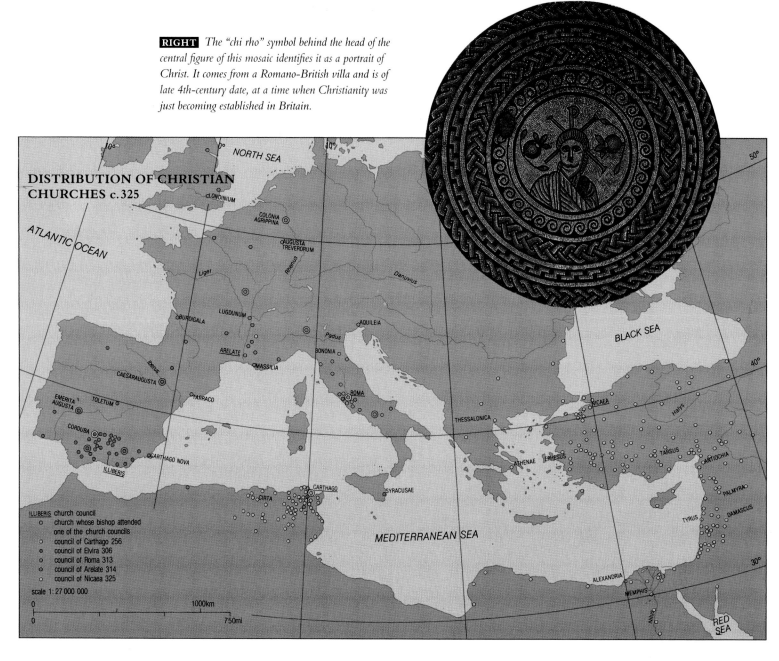

DISTRIBUTION OF CHRISTIAN CHURCHES c.325

ILLIBERIS church council
- church whose bishop attended one of the church councils
- council of Carthago 256
- council of Elvira 306
- council of Roma 313
- council of Arelate 314
- council of Nicaea 325

scale 1:27 000 000

0 _____ 1000km
0 _____ 750mi

number of troops available to man the border garrisons. In other words, the empire acquired greater in-depth defense at the expense of the frontier zones, which were consequently left yet more exposed to barbarian raiding.

One of the most important acts of Constantine's reign was the foundation of Constantinople (see page 273) as a new capital for the empire. It was to be a city without pagan associations. Constantine's decision to site it at the ancient Greek port of Byzantion on the Bosporus, the meeting point between Europe and Asia, was a stroke of genius since it possessed strong natural defenses and had excellent communications between east and west. Constantinople played an instrumental role in ensuring that the eastern half of the Roman empire survived for nearly a thousand years after the west had been overrun.

THE PAGAN REACTION

On Constantine's death the empire was divided between his three sons. By 350 the youngest, Constantius II, was left as sole emperor. In 355 he appointed Julian as Caesar in Gaul. Julian, a member of the imperial family, had been brought up as a Christian but became a secret convert to paganism while studying philosophy at Athens and Pergamon. When Constantius died in 361, Julian (r. 361–363), now in sole charge of the empire, was free to declare his true beliefs. His ambition was nothing less than the restoration of paganism. As a Neoplatonist, Julian was a pantheist but he believed that all pagan rites were divinely inspired. He affected an ascetic lifestyle and sported an unkempt philosopher's beard.

Recognizing the organizational strength of the Christian church, Julian tried to set up a pagan church with a regular priesthood. The pagan clergy were to imitate the Christians by organizing charity for the poor and encouraging wealthy pagans to contribute. Julian set an example by making food available from imperial stores. All the financial and judicial privileges that Constantine had granted the church were revoked. By withdrawing legislation against heretics Julian cynically ensured that the Christians were soon divided among themselves by all manner of theological disputes. Christians were also banned from teaching Classical literature on the grounds that a teacher should believe what he teaches. Though Julian was criticized for this even by pagans, it was a shrewd move. The pagan classics still formed an essential part of the common culture of better off Romans and the church rightly feared that Christian parents might send their children to be educated by pagans as a result.

It is impossible to say whether Julian's attempt to restore paganism might have succeeded given time. In 363 Julian led a major campaign into the heart of the Sasanian empire where he was fatally wounded during a minor skirmish, possibly by one of his own soldiers, perhaps a resentful Christian. His successor Jovian (r. 363–64), hastily chosen by the army, was a Christian, and so were all his successors. The Christianization of the empire resumed its course. The western emperor Gratian (r. 375–83) gave up the title *pontifex maximus* which the emperors had held since Augustus, withdrew financial subsidies from the pagan cults and removed the altar of Victory from the senate. Diehard pagans subsequently blamed Rome's defeats by the barbarians on this act. Finally, in 391 Theodosius I abolished pagan sacrifices, closed the temples and confiscated their estates.

CHRISTIANITY AND PAGAN CULTURE

Christianity did not develop in a cultural vacuum. The popularity of mystery cults is evidence of a widespread disillusionment with the impersonal and ritualistic worship of the traditional Roman religion. Christianity faced serious competition from the cults of Isis and Mithras, which offered believers similar assurances of salvation (see pages 214–215). The dominant pagan philosophy of the empire was Neoplatonism. Its Stoic ethics, belief in a single transcendent divinity, the immortality of the soul and free will were compatible with Christianity and had considerable influence on its development. However, doctrines such as original sin, an idea quite alien to paganism, ensured that

Christianity developed a very different moral outlook and a rather more pessimistic assessment of the human capacity for self-improvement.

Christians continued to value Classical culture. Latin-speaking Christian writers peppered their work with allusions to Virgil and Horace, Greek speakers to Homer. For many, such allusions became an end in themselves, a way of showing off to their contemporaries. Though to a modern reader these works are incredibly tedious, others such as St Augustine's *Confessions* and *The City of God* and Jerome's Latin translation of the Bible (the Vulgate) have literary and intellectual qualities that can stand comparison with the finest Classical literature. The challenge of assimilating Classical culture to Christian belief ensured that the cultural life of the late Roman empire remained vigorous and creative, despite its political decline.

State patronage of the church caused it to become a wealthy and worldly organization which could offer an attractive career for an ambitious man. Though this helped make Christianity acceptable to the Roman aristocracy, many Christians viewed these developments with misgivings and chose an ascetic way of life over wealth and comfort. Some, like St Antony (d. 365), found this in the solitary life of the hermit; others, like his contemporary Pachomius, created self-supporting communities for prayer and the simple life. Out of these would spring the monastic orders that would become so important in medieval Christianity. The Greek theologian St Basil the Great

BELOW *Julian's Mesopotamian campaign struck at the heart of the Sasanian empire. His strategic plan was to draw the main Persian army north by feigning to invade Assyria, and then advance quickly down the Euphrates to attack the Sasanian capital of Ctesiphon before Shapur II could redeploy his forces. It failed because fortified towns like Pirisabora and the garrison at Besouchis put up unexpectedly determined resistance, and the Sasanians slowed his progress by breaching river banks and canals to flood the land. By the time the Roman army reached Ctesiphon, Shapur's army was on its way back and the Romans were forced to withdraw north along the Tigris. After Julian's death in a skirmish, his successor Jovian had to make territorial concessions to Shapur in order to extricate the army.*

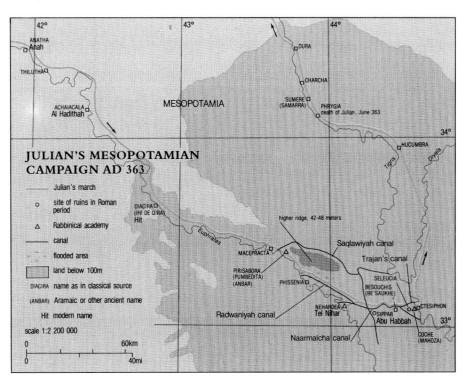

EARLY CHRISTIAN ROME

As threats to the security of the empire multiplied in the 3rd and 4th centuries, the emperors were seen more and more infrequently at Rome. Instead, the imperial court was to be found at places such as Milan or Trier, more conveniently situated for attending to the defense of the frontiers. Though Rome remained the "eternal city" to its admirers, and the symbolic heart of the empire, in practice it ceased to be its administrative capital. The absence of the emperors from Rome allowed the senatorial aristocracy to reassert its control of the city in a way not possible since the end of the republic.

After the conversion of Constantine in 312, Rome quickly emerged as a great center of Christian culture. Constantine paid for the construction of the city's first great churches. Many more followed as the wealthy transferred their patronage to the church, and gained for themselves spiritual benefits as well as enhanced prestige.

Rome was sacked twice by barbarian invaders in the 5th century and its population fell rapidly, from close to a million in 400 to only 25,000 by 550. With the decay of imperial authority, the bishops of Rome, the popes, emerged as leaders of the city. By exploiting the powerful residual prestige of Rome, the popes promoted their claims to primacy over the whole Christian church. Though their claims were not accepted in the east, the popes ensured that Rome remained the spiritual capital of western Christendom until the Reformation.

St Peter's

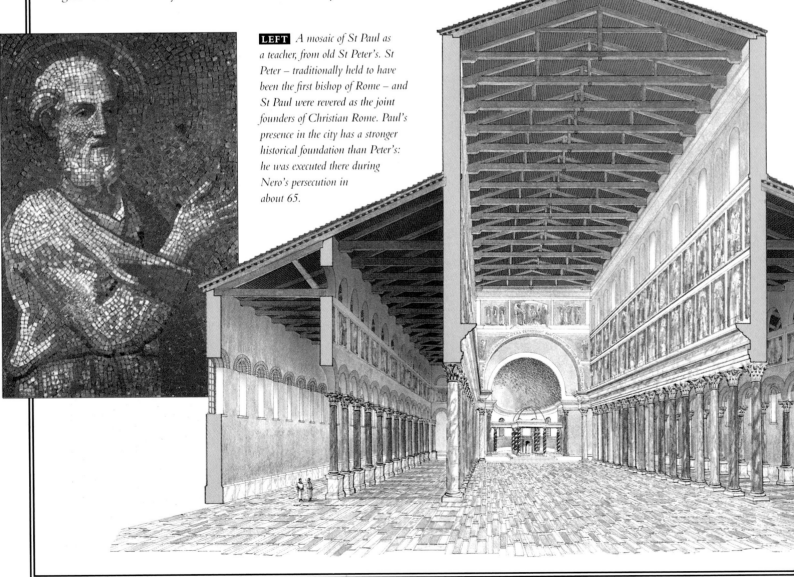

LEFT *A mosaic of St Paul as a teacher, from old St Peter's. St Peter – traditionally held to have been the first bishop of Rome – and St Paul were revered as the joint founders of Christian Rome. Paul's presence in the city has a stronger historical foundation than Peter's: he was executed there during Nero's persecution in about 65.*

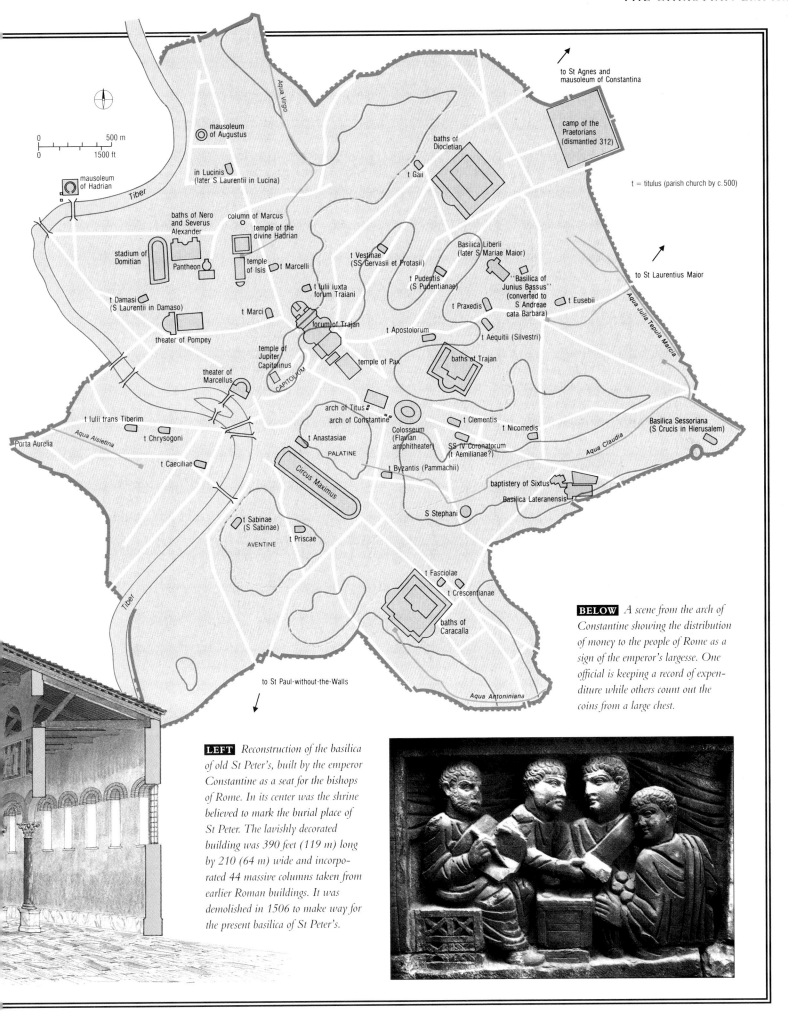

to St Agnes and
mausoleum of Constantina

camp of the
Praetorians
(dismantled 312)

t = titulus (parish church by c.500)

to St Laurentius Maior

mausoleum
of Augustus

baths of
Diocletian

Aqua Virgo

t Gaii

0   500 m
0   1500 ft

mausoleum
of Hadrian

Tiber

baths of Nero
and Severus
Alexander

column of Marcus

temple of the
divine Hadrian

Basilica Liberii
(later S Mariae Maior)

stadium of
Domitian

Pantheon

temple
of Isis

t Vestinae
(SS Gervasii et Protasii)

t Marcelli

t Pudentis
(S Pudentianae)

"Basilica of
Junius Bassus"
(converted to
S Andreae
cata Barbara)

t Eusebii

t Damasi
(S Laurentii in Damaso)

t Iulii iuxta
forum Traiani

t Marci

t Praxedis

t Aequitii (Silvestri)

theater of Pompey

forum of Trajan

t Apostolorum

temple of
Jupiter
Capitolinus

temple of Pax

baths of Trajan

Aqua Julia Tepula Marcia

CAPITOLIUM

theater of
Marcellus

in Lucinis
(later S Laurentii in Lucina)

arch of Titus

arch of Constantine

t Clementis

t Nicomedis

Basilica Sessoriana
(S Crucis in Hierusalem)

t Iulii trans Tiberim

t Chrysogoni

Aqua Aisietina

Porta Aurelia

t Anastasiae

PALATINE

Colosseum
(Flavian
amphitheater)

SS IV Coronatorum
(t Aemilianae?)

Aqua Claudia

t Caeciliae

Circus Maximus

t Byzantis (Pammachii)

baptistery of Sixtus

Basilica Lateranensis

S Stephani

Tiber

t Sabinae
(S Sabinae)

AVENTINE

t Priscae

t Fasciolae

t Crescentianae

baths of
Caracalla

to St Paul-without-the-Walls

Aqua Antoniniana

BELOW *A scene from the arch of Constantine showing the distribution of money to the people of Rome as a sign of the emperor's largesse. One official is keeping a record of expenditure while others count out the coins from a large chest.*

LEFT *Reconstruction of the basilica of old St Peter's, built by the emperor Constantine as a seat for the bishops of Rome. In its center was the shrine believed to mark the burial place of St Peter. The lavishly decorated building was 390 feet (119 m) long by 210 (64 m) wide and incorporated 44 massive columns taken from earlier Roman buildings. It was demolished in 1506 to make way for the present basilica of St Peter's.*

(330–379) drew up the first rules for monastic living, laying down a routine of prayer, mental and manual work. The rules written by St Benedict (c.480–c.547) for his monastery at Monte Cassino in central Italy established a pattern of daily living for western monasticism. The renunciation of sexuality was an important element of the ascetic life. By 400 most Christians accepted the superiority of virginity and celibacy over marriage, holding that the sole purpose of sexual activity was procreation, which should be refrained from on Sundays and church festivals. The Neoplatonists, who also regarded restraint in sexual matters a virtue, had already prepared the ground for this momentous cultural change.

THE GERMANIC INVASIONS

The fragile stability of the 4th-century empire was maintained at great cost to its citizens. High taxation was needed to pay for the large armies to defend the frontiers against the increasingly well-

organized invasions of the Germans, but the economy was declining. The *honestiores* used their privileges to avoid paying taxes so the tax burden fell most heavily on the poorer classes, driving them below subsistence level. In Gaul, peasants turned to brigandage. Soon the empire lacked the manpower to till the fields and defend the frontiers. The army came to rely on barbarian mercenaries, particularly in the west, which had a smaller population than the east. These troops proved outstandingly loyal but were a heavy financial burden.

In the 370s the Huns, Turkic nomads from central Asia, migrated into the eastern European steppes, where they came into conflict with the Germanic tribes living on the empire's northern borders. In about 372 they inflicted a crushing defeat on the Ostrogoths, throwing the other Germanic tribes into panic. The Visigoths turned to Rome for protection and were granted land for settlement in Thrace by the eastern emperor Valens, who saw them as a valuable source of

RIGHT *St Ambrose (c.340–97), bishop of Milan, was the most influential churchman of his day. Fiercely opposed to Arianism and paganism, he vigorously asserted the church's independence from the Roman state. He persuaded Gratian to surrender the imperial title of* pontifex maximus *and ordered Theodosius I to perform public penance to atone for a massacre of civilians in 390.*

BELOW *Monasticism developed in Egypt in the early 4th century and spread throughout the Levant. It was introduced into the west by Hilary of Poitiers and Eusebius of Vercelli, both exiles in the east during the reign of the Arian Constantius II (350–361). Independent traditions of monasticism emerged in Italy and the British Isles in the 6th century.*

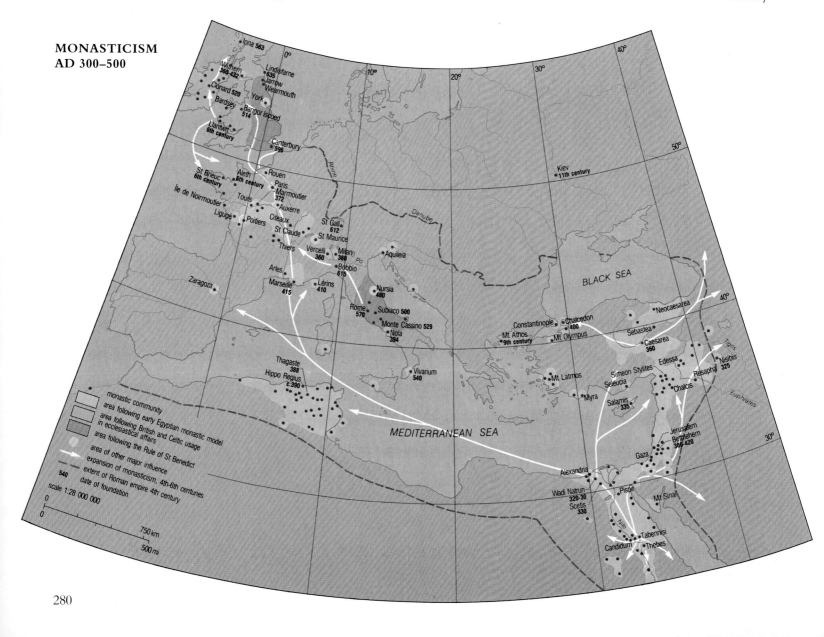

MONASTICISM AD 300–500

recruits for the army. Many groups of defeated barbarians had been successfully settled within the empire since the mid-3rd century and it seemed a reasonable enough decision under the circumstances. But the Visigoths were cheated by the officials put in charge of their settlement and they revolted in 378. Though the emperor Theodosius drew up a new agreement with the Visigoths in 382, giving them the status of federates (from *foederati*, allies), they rebelled again in 395 and under their ambitious new leader, Alaric, ravaged Greece and Dalmatia before invading Italy in 401.

Stilicho, a Roman general of German origin, succeeded in driving the Visigoths back into Dalmatia but during the hard winter of 406, a coalition of Vandals, Sueves and Alans crossed the frozen Rhine and invaded Gaul. By 409 they had swept on into Spain but they were followed into Gaul by Franks, Burgundians and Alamanni. In 407, the usurper Constantine withdrew most of Britain's garrison to oppose the legitimate western emperor Honorius (r. 395–423). Three years later Honorius gave the Britons instructions to organize their own defenses. No doubt this was intended to be a temporary measure, but the garrison never returned and Britain found itself unexpectedly independent.

Alaric rebelled again in 410. His modest demands were turned down by the Romans, so he sacked Rome. Though the capital of the western empire had moved to Ravenna on the Adriatic coast in 402, Rome remained a potent symbol, and the attack was deeply shocking. History has painted Alaric, who died soon afterwards, as a villain, but the Romans showed bad faith in their dealings with him, and he turned to violence as a last resort. His successors were more cooperative. In 425 they made an alliance with the Romans and attacked the Vandals, Sueves and Alans in Spain. They were then settled, as federates under nominal Roman sovereignty, on rich lands in western France.

The Huns, indirectly the cause of all the empire's problems, initially maintained good relations with Rome. The general Aetius used Hun mercenaries widely in the 430s to impose federate status on the Burgundians and other Germanic settlers in Gaul. However, in 441 their leader Attila turned on the empire and ravaged the Balkans before extending his rule all the way to the Rhine. In 451 he invaded Gaul but was defeated by a coalition of Romans, Visigoths, Burgundians and Franks. Attila died in 453, and a year later the power of the Huns was permanently broken by a German army at the battle of Nedao.

THE FALL OF THE WEST

In 429 a band of about 80,000 Vandals had crossed from Spain into Africa. Within ten years they had captured Carthage, Leptis Magna (see pages 284–285) and other Roman towns and set up a completely independent kingdom. North Africa was Italy's main source of grain, and this dealt the most serious blow so far against the western empire. In 455 Vandal pirates sacked Rome rather more thoroughly than Alaric had done. The assassinations in the same year of Aetius, the west's most able general, and of Valentinian III, last of the Theodosian dynasty, inflicted further damage. The Franks, Burgundians and Visigoths seized control of Gaul and Spain, and by the 470s the western empire consisted of little more than Italy.

In 475 the last legitimate western emperor, Julius Nepos, was driven out of Italy by the general Orestes, who placed his own son Romulus Augustulus on the imperial throne. The next year he was deposed by Odoacer, a barbarian general who was proclaimed king by his soldiers. Odoacer recognized the overlordship of the eastern emperor Zeno, and offered to rule Italy as imperial viceroy. The deposition of Augustulus is widely accepted as marking the end of the western Roman empire. However, Julius Nepos was still recognized as emperor in Dalmatia from 475 until his death in 480. Dalmatia then became part of Odoacer's kingdom.

A number of factors combined to bring about the the fall of the western Roman empire. The division of the empire in the 4th century had deprived the poorer, less populated and more vulnerable west of the resources of the richer east, and it was more exposed to barbarian attack than the east, which had only a short northern frontier to defend. Though the eastern emperors gave some assistance to their western colleagues, their main priority was to ensure that the east did not

ABOVE *During the 5th century, barbarian generals such as Stilicho began to exercise considerable power and influence in the western empire. An able general and an ambitious schemer, Stilicho was unjustly accused of treason and was executed in 408.*

THE FIRST WAVE OF INVASIONS

The westward migration of the Huns in the late 4th century displaced the Germanic tribes of eastern Europe and increased pressure on the empire's borders. One branch of the Goths, the Visigoths, were resettled on land in Thrace but they rebelled in 378 and 395, later advancing through Greece and Italy to sack Rome. The Rhine frontier collapsed when a coalition of Sueves, Vandals and Alans invaded Gaul and Spain in 406. In an attempt to impose a fragile control, the Romans granted the Visigoths federate status and diverted them to fight the Vandals and Sueves with promises of rich land in Gaul. The Ostrogoths were settled as federates on land within the empire.

go the same way. It was to the east's advantage that the Sasanian empire, troubled by nomadic invasions of its own and undergoing violent religious turmoil, was unable to exploit Roman weakness at this time.

The west was also politically less stable than the east. From Stilicho onwards, ambitious generals had played a dominating role in politics. The succession of short-lived emperors who succeeded Valentinian III were simply the puppets of overmighty generals such as the barbarian Ricimer. If they had outlived their political usefulness, or tried to act independently, they were murdered. The high cost of defending the empire had undermined the loyalty of its citizens so that there was little popular resistance to the invaders, who generally established themselves in their new territories with minimal disruption to most people's lives. In return for their loyalty, federate rulers were allocated the tax revenues of the areas they

were settled in. This led them to maintain the system of land ownership on which the taxes were assessed. Only in Vandal Africa was there wholesale dispossession of Roman landowners. For most, a cultured and leisured lifestyle was still possible under the new Germanic regimes. For most peasant farmers the only difference was that their taxes went to a king rather than the imperial treasury. The barbarians were inefficient tax collectors, and most people probably found themselves better off without the empire.

One of the most graphic accounts of the end of the empire comes from the *Life of St Severinus* by Eugippius, in which he describes the situation on the Danube border in Noricum (Austria) in the 470s. The few remaining garrisons of Roman troops were poorly equipped, demoralized and unpaid. One unit sent envoys to Italy to ask for their pay but they never returned so it

BELOW Attila the Hun, taking pride in the terror of his name, described himself as the "flail of God." No contemporary portraits of Attila survive, but this Renaissance medallion fits his description by a Roman envoy as a short squat man with a large head, deep set eyes, flat nose and thin beard.

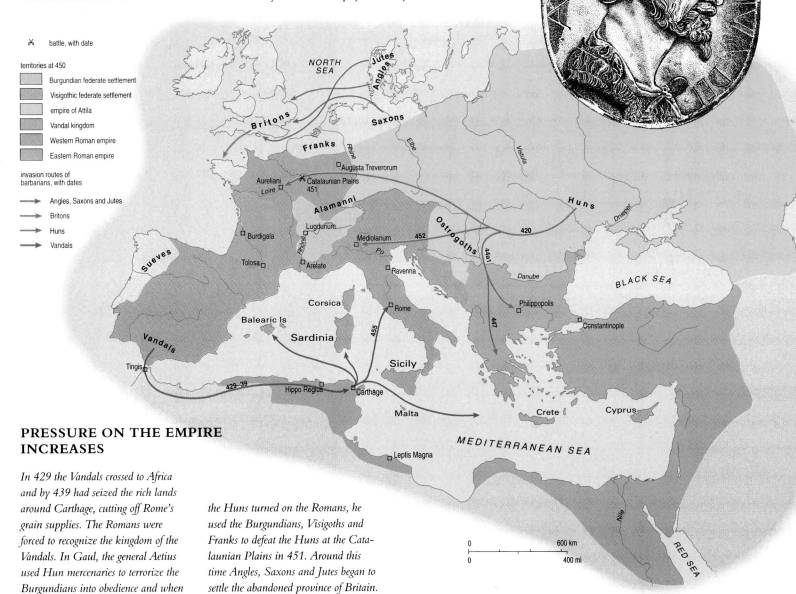

PRESSURE ON THE EMPIRE INCREASES

In 429 the Vandals crossed to Africa and by 439 had seized the rich lands around Carthage, cutting off Rome's grain supplies. The Romans were forced to recognize the kingdom of the Vandals. In Gaul, the general Aetius used Hun mercenaries to terrorize the Burgundians into obedience and when

the Huns turned on the Romans, he used the Burgundians, Visigoths and Franks to defeat the Huns at the Catalaunian Plains in 451. Around this time Angles, Saxons and Jutes began to settle the abandoned province of Britain.

LEPTIS MAGNA

A haunting reminder of Roman civilization in North Africa are the ruins of the once-great city of Leptis Magna in modern-day Libya, which fell victim to the Vandal incursions of the 5th century. The city, founded by the Carthaginians and under Roman rule since the 2nd century BC, had grown wealthy from the agricultural development of its hinterland, based on olive-growing and wheat. It was rich enough to pay an annual fine of 3 million lbs (1.3 million kg) of olive oil to Julius Caesar for having supported his rivals in the civil war. The Punic aristocracy, who continued to dominate the life of the city at that time, endowed it with many fine buildings during the reign of Augustus. Leptis' most famous native was the emperor Septimius Severus (r.193–211), who gave the city a new forum and a basilica. During the late empire, Leptis was the administrative center for the province of Tripolitania. Though it remained prosperous, there was little new building thereafter. During the 4th century, raids by desert nomads were increasingly troublesome, but it was the Vandals who finally brought about the city's decline. By the time the emperor Justinian recaptured North Africa in 533, the city was all but deserted, except for a small enclave around the harbor.

BELOW *The original Punic settlement was west of the harbor. By the 3rd century AD the Roman city extended over 1000 yards (900 m) inland. The harbor was modernized by Septimius Severus and linked to the city by a colonnaded street.*

RIGHT *Leptis Magna's beautiful theater was built in AD 1–2 through the munificence of Annobal Rufus, a Punic aristocrat who had the title of sufes, or civic magistrate. The dedication inscription is written in both Latin and Punic.*

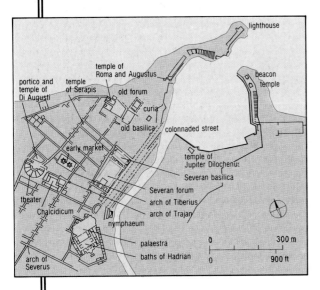

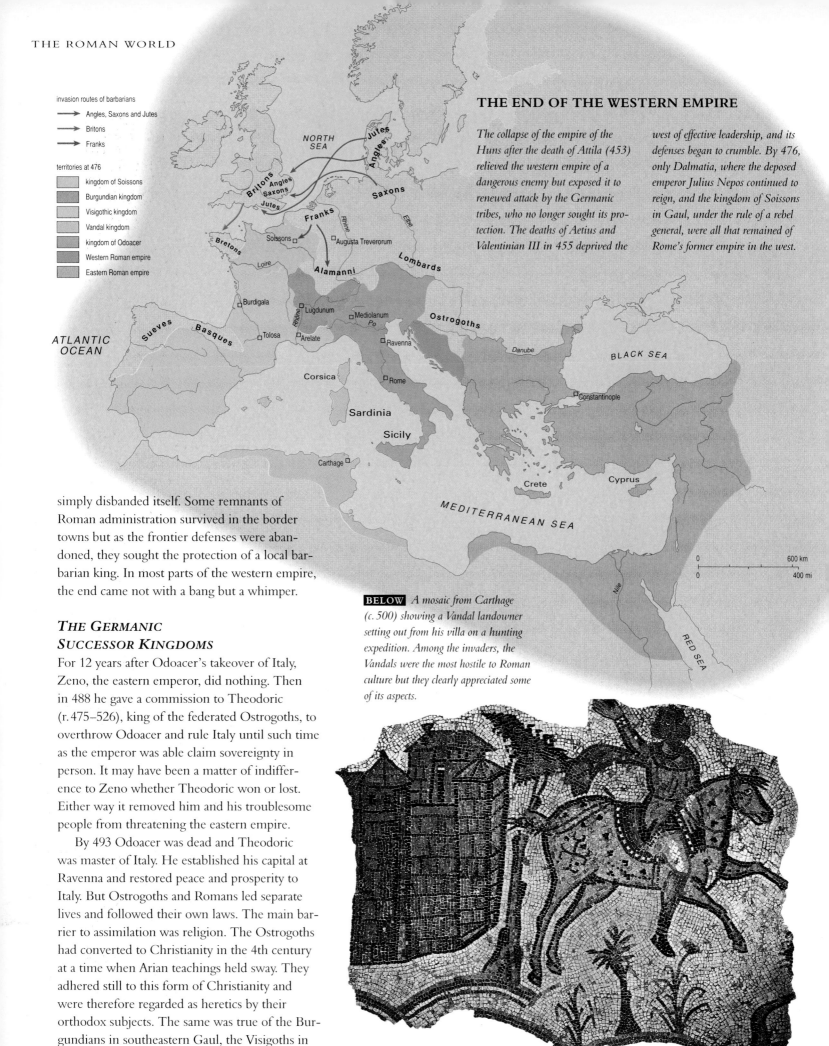

invasion routes of barbarians

→ Angles, Saxons and Jutes

→ Britons

→ Franks

territories at 476

kingdom of Soissons

Burgundian kingdom

Visigothic kingdom

Vandal kingdom

kingdom of Odoacer

Western Roman empire

Eastern Roman empire

NORTH SEA

Jutes

Angles

Saxons

Britons

Angles

Saxons

Jutes

Franks

Rhine

Elbe

Bretons

Soissons

Augusta Treverorum

Alamanni

Lombards

Burdigala

Loire

Rhône

Lugdunum

Mediolanum

Po

Ostrogoths

Danube

BLACK SEA

ATLANTIC OCEAN

Sueves

Basques

Tolosa

Arelate

Ravenna

Corsica

Rome

Constantinople

Sardinia

Sicily

Carthage

Crete

Cyprus

MEDITERRANEAN SEA

Nile

RED SEA

0   600 km

0   400 mi

THE END OF THE WESTERN EMPIRE

The collapse of the empire of the Huns after the death of Attila (453) relieved the western empire of a dangerous enemy but exposed it to renewed attack by the Germanic tribes, who no longer sought its protection. The deaths of Aetius and Valentinian III in 455 deprived the west of effective leadership, and its defenses began to crumble. By 476, only Dalmatia, where the deposed emperor Julius Nepos continued to reign, and the kingdom of Soissons in Gaul, under the rule of a rebel general, were all that remained of Rome's former empire in the west.

simply disbanded itself. Some remnants of Roman administration survived in the border towns but as the frontier defenses were abandoned, they sought the protection of a local barbarian king. In most parts of the western empire, the end came not with a bang but a whimper.

THE GERMANIC SUCCESSOR KINGDOMS

For 12 years after Odoacer's takeover of Italy, Zeno, the eastern emperor, did nothing. Then in 488 he gave a commission to Theodoric (r. 475–526), king of the federated Ostrogoths, to overthrow Odoacer and rule Italy until such time as the emperor was able claim sovereignty in person. It may have been a matter of indifference to Zeno whether Theodoric won or lost. Either way it removed him and his troublesome people from threatening the eastern empire.

By 493 Odoacer was dead and Theodoric was master of Italy. He established his capital at Ravenna and restored peace and prosperity to Italy. But Ostrogoths and Romans led separate lives and followed their own laws. The main barrier to assimilation was religion. The Ostrogoths had converted to Christianity in the 4th century at a time when Arian teachings held sway. They adhered still to this form of Christianity and were therefore regarded as heretics by their orthodox subjects. The same was true of the Burgundians in southeastern Gaul, the Visigoths in

BELOW *A mosaic from Carthage (c. 500) showing a Vandal landowner setting out from his villa on a hunting expedition. Among the invaders, the Vandals were the most hostile to Roman culture but they clearly appreciated some of its aspects.*

Spain and the Vandals in North Africa. Arianism set the barbarian rulers apart from their romanized subjects, who vastly outnumbered them. They were reluctant to give it up, despite straining relations with the eastern emperor who regarded himself as the guardian of orthodox Christianity. Only the Franks, who had converted directly to orthodox Christianity in about 500, escaped the taint of heresy, earning them the support of Constantinople and the loyalty of their Gallo-Roman subjects. As a result, by 600 the Frankish kingdom had become the strongest power in the west.

The Germanic kings had a more limited idea of the responsibilities of a ruler than the Roman emperors. Roman concepts of government survived in the church, whose organization was based on the diocesan system introduced by Diocletian, and whose legal system was based on Roman law. The church provided for the poor and the sick, it became the main provider of education, and it preserved the Latin language.

THE REIGN OF JUSTINIAN

Though it was frequently at war with Sasanian Persia, the eastern empire prospered after the fall of the west. The emperor Anastasius (r. 491–518) even managed to cut taxes and still leave his successor Justin (r. 518–527) with a full treasury. Justin was succeeded by his nephew Justinian (r. 527–65), the last great Roman emperor. Justinian saw it as a disgrace that the western provinces of the empire were occupied by barbarians, and he launched a concerted effort to recover them. In 533 he sent a force under his general Belisarius to destroy the Vandal kingdom in North Africa. Most of Justinian's courtiers predicted failure. However, the pro-Roman Ostrogothic queen of Italy, Amalasuntha, allowed Sicily to be used as a base by the invasion fleet, and the kingdom collapsed after only two battles.

Justinian used Amalasuntha's murder a year later as a pretext to invade Italy in 535. Ravenna had fallen to Belisarius by 540, but he became

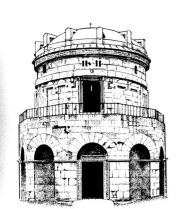

ABOVE *The mausoleum built for Theodoric, the Ostrogothic king of Italy (r. 493–526), still stands outside the walls of Ravenna, his capital. Its roof is made from a single piece of limestone 10 feet (3 m) thick, 36 feet (11 m) in diameter, and weighing 300 tons. The craftsmen who built it probably came from Syria, showing that, despite the Germanic takeover, Italy still remained part of the wider Mediterranean world*

RIGHT *The Franks were the first of the Germanic invaders to cross the Rhine in the late 4th century. They did so almost unnoticed but in 486 they disposed of the kingdom of Soissons and in 507 they drove the Visigoths out of Gaul to emerge as one of the strongest of the successor kingdoms by the early 6th century. Italy, as part of the Ostrogothic kingdom, enjoyed over a quarter of a century of peace and relative prosperity during the reign of Theodoric. At his death in 526 he exercised a protectorate over the Visigoths in Spain and had connections by marriage with the Burgundians and the Vandals in North Africa.*

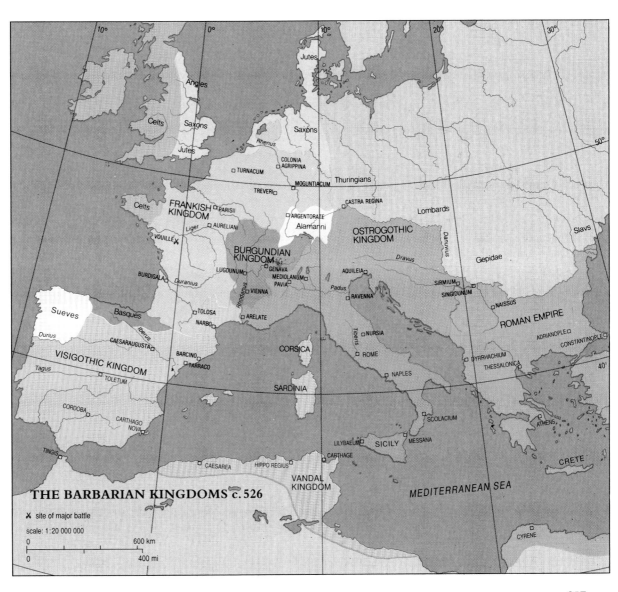

THE BARBARIAN KINGDOMS c. 526

✗ site of major battle

scale: 1:20 000 000

embroiled in a dispute with Justinian, and Ostrogothic resistance was revived by Totila (r. 541–52).
Meanwhile, war with the Sasanians diverted
Roman troops to the east. The resulting stalemate
in Italy was only broken in 552 when a new army
arrived from Constantinople led by Narses. By
554 all of Italy south of the Po was in Roman
hands, but Ostrogothic resistance continued in the
north until 562. In a separate campaign, Justinian
took advantage of a Visigothic civil war to capture
southern Spain in 554.

Justinian believed that the Roman emperor had
an equal duty to maintain religious orthodoxy in
order to secure God's favor towards the empire,
and to uphold the law. He failed to resolve divisive
theological controversies, but was responsible for
building the domed cathedral of Hagia Sophia at
Constantinople, for long the greatest church in
Christendom. The complete codification of the
Roman law, undertaken by a commission led by
Tribonian, was perhaps the finest achievement of
the Roman legal tradition. Yet because it was written in Latin, which few in the Greek-speaking east
could now understand, it had little influence.

The empire was under severe economic strain
by the end of Justinian's reign. The concentration
of forces in the west left the Balkans exposed to
raids and settlement by the Slavs, while the Sasanians made serious incursions in the east. Much
of Italy was lost again when the Lombards invaded
in 572, and southern Spain was soon retaken by
the Visigoths. But North Africa and Sicily proved
to be valuable additions to the empire's resources.

In the 560s a new wave of nomads, the Avars,
entered eastern Europe. The Romans paid them
to wipe out the remnants of the Huns but in 580
a dispute between them led to war. For ten years
the Avars raided the Balkans until the emperor
Maurice (r. 582–602) counterattacked effectively
in 592. Maurice was close to breaking Avar power
when his army mutinied in 602. He was deposed
and murdered by Phocas (r. 602–610), an incompetent despot who allowed the administrative
structure of the empire to fall apart. Slavs and
Avars overran the Balkans while the Sasanian ruler
Khosrau II (r. 591–628) seized Mesopotamia.

THE END OF THE ANCIENT WORLD

In 610 the Roman governor of Africa was
prompted by the chaotic state of the empire to
equip his son Heraclius with an army and send
him to Constantinople where he overthrew
Phocas. Heraclius (r. 610–641) spent the early

ABOVE *A detail from a mosaic
in the cathedral of St Vitale in
Ravenna shows Justinian surrounded by courtiers and church-
men; he is carrying a plate as an
offering. The mosaics of St Vitale
are among the most brilliant
achievements of late Roman art.
Seen by the shimmering light of
massed candles, the images must
have presented an awesome and
lifelike appearance.*

RIGHT *Justinian believed in his
mission to restore direct imperial
authority in the west. The Vandal
kingdom in North Africa was
easily conquered but the war
against the Ostrogothic kingdom
in Italy dragged on for another 20
years until 562. Justinian's conquests restored Roman dominance
in the Mediterranean but were
made at the cost of the Balkans
and the east which became exposed
to attack from the Slavs and Sasanians. Apart from southern Spain,
quickly lost again after Justinian's
death, no gains were made in
western Europe.*

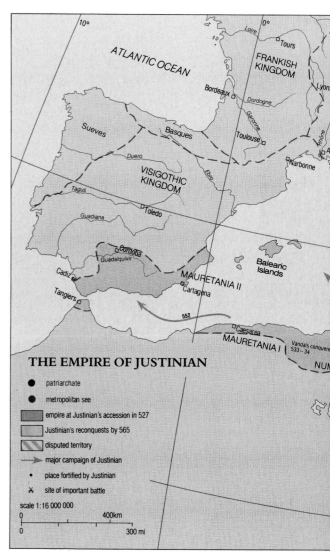

THE EMPIRE OF JUSTINIAN

● patriarchate

● metropolitan see

■ empire at Justinian's accession in 527

□ Justinian's reconquests by 565

▨ disputed territory

→ major campaign of Justinian

• place fortified by Justinian

✕ site of important battle

scale 1:16 000 000

0 — 400km

0 — 300 mi

years of his reign building a new administrative and military structure for the empire – it was obvious that the institutions of the empire of Diocletian, Constantine and Justinian could not now be revived. Greek replaced Latin in official documents. Heraclius's reforms made such a break with the past that his reign is regarded as marking the end of the eastern Roman empire and the beginning of the medieval Greek Byzantine empire (named after the old Greek name for Constantinople). However, his successors continued to regard themselves as Roman emperors until their empire was finally conquered by the Turks in 1453.

In the east the Sasanians continued to attack the empire and by 616 Syria, Palestine and Egypt had been lost. Heraclius was ready to counterattack in 622 and boldly launched a campaign directly into the heart of the Sasanian empire. In 627 the Sasanian army was destroyed at Nineveh and the empire was secure. The war weakened both empires, and they were equally unprepared for the sudden and unexpected invasions of the newly Islamicized Arabs, beginning with the capture of Damascus in 635. By 642 they had taken Syria, Palestine and Egypt from the Byzantines and completely destroyed the Sasanian empire, though much of Persian culture – particularly its artistic and literary traditions – survived to exert a formative influence on the nascent Islamic civilization. Later in the century a second wave of conquests carried Arab power across North Africa and into Spain.

With the Arab conquests the history of the ancient world comes to a final close. Byzantium and the barbarian west were already drifting apart and now the new and vigorous Islamic civilization was established as the dominant cultural and political force in the Near East and the Mediterranean. That so many of the traditions of Greco-Roman science and philosophy survived after they had been largely lost to the the Christian west is due to the Arabs, who preserved and studied their manuscripts. Without them, European scholars in the Middle Ages would not have been able to recover a knowledge of the ancient world and Classical past.

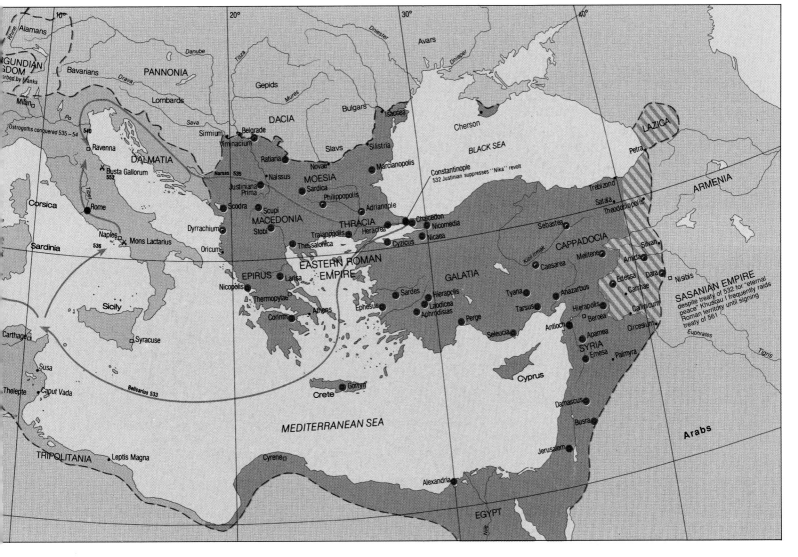

GLOSSARY

Academy A training ground for naked exercise outside Athens, with grass, trees and sacred buildings. It was made famous by Socrates, and above all by Plato, whose school of philosophy was there.

Aceramic Neolithic The early part of the NEOLITHIC period before the widespread use of pottery vessels (c. 8500–7000 BC).

Achaemenid dynasty The line of Persian kings (c. 559–330 BC) who ruled the Near East from Cyrus to Darius III.

acropolis In ancient Greece, the higher part of a town, the citadel where the palaces and temples were situated.

Agade A city in southern MESOPOTAMIA founded by Sargon (2334–2279 BC) as his capital. Its location is uncertain.

ager publicus Roman public land, administered by the state.

agora The central area of a Greek city or small town, usually a square or rectangle, with colonnades, public and sacred buildings, similar to the Roman FORUM.

Agri Decumates Territory in Germany between the upper Rhine and upper Danube comprising most of the Black Forest. Occupied by the Romans AD 69–263.

Akkad The northern part of the southern Mesopotamian plain named after the city of AGADE. See also SUMER.

Akkadian language The SEMITIC language spoken in MESOPOTAMIA from the 3rd to the 1st millennium BC. The principal known dialects were Assyrian and Babylonian.

akroterion Terracotta or marble ornament on the pinnacle or the edge of the roof of a CLASSICAL Greek building.

alluvium Silt brought down by the rivers and deposited as sediment in the floodplain.

Amarna letters An archive of diplomatic correspondence from Near Eastern rulers, written in CUNEIFORM on clay tablets, discovered during excavations of Tell el-'Amarna, the capital of the Egyptian pharaoh Akhenaten (1353–1335 BC).

amphitheater An elliptical arena surrounded by tiers of seating for staging spectator sports, such as gladiatorial combats, in the Roman world.

amphora Two-handled ("two-eared") pot for transporting oil, wine, etc. The same word is used for smaller, finer vessels of similar shape.

Anatolia The peninsula of Turkey in Asia between the Black Sea and the Gulf of Iskenderun.

Aramaic A SEMITIC language, widely spoken in the Near East before the Arab conquests and still spoken by minorities in Iran and Iraq.

Archaic The term describing the formative period of Greek civilization from the end of the Aegean dark ages (c. 750 BC) to the Persian invasions in 480 BC.

archon In Athens, a state official possessing judicial powers.

Arian heresy The teachings of the Alexandrian priest Arius (c. 230–336) who questioned the divinity of Christ.

Assyria The part of northern MESOPOTAMIA that is in present-day Iraq.

Aten The Sun disk, worshiped as the sole god in the MONOTHEISTIC religion that the pharaoh Akhenaten (1353–1335 BC) tried to impose on Egypt.

Augustus "Venerable one," the name conferred on Octavian, the first Roman emperor, by the SENATE in 27 BC and adopted as an imperial title by all subsequent emperors. Under the TETRARCHY, "Augustus" was used by the two senior imperial colleagues.

auxiliary A soldier in the Roman army who was not a Roman citizen. Auxiliaries had less favorable terms of service than legionaries, who were recruited only from Roman citizens.

awilum The so-called freemen class in Hammurabi's LAW CODE. *awilum* means "man" in AKKADIAN. See also *MUSHKENUM*, *WARDUM*.

Babylonia Southern MESOPOTAMIA.

Badarian From el-Badari, the type site of the earliest certainly identified NEOLITHIC culture of the Nile valley (c. 4500 BC).

bala A taxation and redistribution system in operation on the cities of southern MESOPOTAMIA in the time of the THIRD DYNASTY OF UR.

bark A model boat kept in a temple shrine for use by an Egyptian god when he or she went out in procession; larger barks were used on the Nile. Those at Karnak and Luxor are sizable structures.

basilica An aisled hall first used as an all-purpose public building by the Greeks and later adopted by the Romans. Also used as the pattern for most early Christian churches.

beehive tomb A dome-shaped tomb with an alley or approach and a great door used by the MYCENAEAN Greeks and other BRONZE AGE peoples.

black-figure decoration A style of Greek pottery with black figures on a tan ground (see also RED-FIGURE DECORATION).

Bronze Age The period when cutting tools were made of copper alloys, often divided into three periods: the Early Bronze Age (c. 4000–2000 BC); the Middle Bronze Age (c. 2000–1600 BC); and the Late Bronze Age (c. 1600–1200 BC). However, the chronological limits and terminology vary from region to region.

Byzantine empire The name used to describe the continuation of the Eastern Roman empire from the reign of Heraclius (610–41) until its fall to the Turks in 1453. Derived from Byzantium (Byzantion), the ancient Greek port chosen as the site for Constantinople, the empire's capital.

Caesar The family name of Gaius Julius Caesar and his adoptive son Octavian (see AUGUSTUS): used by Roman emperors as an imperial title. Under the TETRARCHY "Caesar" was the title used by the two junior imperial colleagues.

Carthage The Phoenician colony in modern Tunisia that became the major maritime power of the western Mediterranean c. 500 BC. Destroyed by the Romans in 146 BC and refounded as a Roman colony by Julius Caesar.

cataract A stretch of rapids interrupting the flow of the Nile. There are six numbered and several minor cataracts between Aswan and Khartum. The Second Cataract, the most formidable, was impassable except during the annual inundation.

cavea The semicircle of open stone benches rising in tiers that seated the audience at a Greek theater.

cella The inner room of a temple where the principal statue of the god stood.

Celts From ancient Greek *Keltoi*, a word they used to describe the barbarian peoples of central Europe.

Chalcolithic The period between the NEOLITHIC and the BRONZE AGE when stones and copper tools were in use. The dating of the period varies from region to region.

Cisalpine Gaul "Gaul-this-side-of-the-Alps," the area of northern Italy, around the Po valley, settled by the GAULS (CELTS) in the 5th century BC.

city state A state with a unified government based on one single town or city, which controlled a surrounding territory, great or small.

Classical age The period of Greek civilization from the Persian invasions (480 BC) to the death of Alexander the Great (323 BC). More generally, "classical" also describes the art and culture influenced by the Greek civilization of this period.

coffering Sunken panels in a ceiling or dome, used originally to reduce the weight of the roof but often used simply as a decorative feature.

comitatenses "Mobile troops," the field armies of the late Roman empire.

composite bow A powerful bow made of different materials, such as wood and horn, glued together. Probably developed in the Near East in the 3rd millennium BC.

concilium plebis Assembly created by the Roman citizenry in 494 BC to represent their interests and fight for their rights against the dominant PATRICIAN class.

consul The senior magistrate of the Roman republic. Two magistrates were elected annually. They shared the powers formerly exercised by the Roman kings.

Corinthian column In Greek and Roman architecture, a fluted column with an elaborately carved capital of stone foliage. Especially associated with the HELLENISTIC style.

cuneiform The script used in MESOPOTAMIA and the neighboring Near East to write on clay TABLETS. The signs were formed by pressing a rectangular-ended instrument into the damp clay to leave a wedge-shaped impression. The word is derived from *cuneus*, the Latin for wedge.

cylinder seal A cylinder engraved with a design that was rolled over a tablet of damp clay to leave a continuous impression. Used in MESOPOTAMIA and other parts of the Near East from the 4th to the 1st millennium BC.

Cynics Followers of the 4th-century BC philosopher, Diogenes of Sinope, who believed the key to happiness was self-sufficiency and independence from external responsibilities, and rejected the false, self-serving values of conventional society.

Dacia The region, roughly equivalent to modern Romania, named after its inhabitants in ancient times, the Dacians. Conquered by Trajan in AD 106 and abandoned to the Germans in 272.

deme A village or small town in Attica. The *demes* retained their basic political and social importance well into the 5th century BC.

democracy The rule of the majority. In ancient Greece, democracies were governed directly by the citizen body (which excluded groups such as women and slaves) rather than indirectly, through elected representatives, as in modern democracies.

demotic The everyday language and speech of Egyptians in the Late and Greco-Roman periods.

Diadochi Meaning successors, used of the generals who seized power in the empire of Alexander the Great after his death in 323: Ptolemy, Seleukos, Kassander, Antigonos and Lysimachos.

dictator In the Roman republic, a magistrate granted absolute powers for a period of six months only during a time of crisis. The dictatorship was the only Roman magistracy which was not elective, dictators being appointed by the CONSULS.

diocese In the later Roman empire, a group of provinces under the supervision of a *VICARIUS*.

Dorian One of the major racial/dialect groups of Greece.

Doric column In CLASSICAL architecture, a sturdy fluted column with a plain capital. The style used for the Parthenon and other temples of the 5th-century BC.

dux General or commander in the late Roman army. The word duke is derived from it.

dynasty A line of rulers, normally from a single family but sometimes from a single city or ethnic group.

einkorn An early form of wheat cultivated by Neolithic farmers in ANATOLIA and central Europe.

emmer wheat Domesticated variety of a species of wild wheat from Syria and the LEVANT. Emmer was the most common variety of wheat cultivated by the early farmers of Europe and the Near East.

en SUMERIAN word meaning high priest, ruler, lord, a title used by the rulers of early Sumerian cities, notably Uruk.

ensi SUMERIAN title used by rulers of some city states, meaning governor.

Epicureans The followers of Epicurus (c. 341–270 BC) who cultivated a philosophy of pleasure, withdrawal from the world, friendship and privacy.

Epipaleolithic The continuation of Paleolithic (Old Stone Age) cultures after the end of the last ICE AGE. It was followed by the NEOLITHIC period.

equestrian class In republican Rome, originally the class that could afford to equip itself as cavalry. By the 3rd century BC, it had lost its military function, but still remained an influential, wealthy class of landowners and businessmen below the level of the aristocracy.

Etruscans From the 8th–4th centuries BC, the dominant people of north-central Italy. Their origins are unknown.

federates From the Latin *foederati* (confederates or allies), the term is used to describe the status of barbarian peoples settled by agreement within the Roman empire from the 4th century AD.

Fertile Crescent A region of good soils stretching in an arc from the southeastern Mediterranean coast through Lebanon, Syria and southern Turkey to the foothills of Iraq's Zagros mountains near the Persian Gulf; sometimes extended to include the Nile valley. A center of early farming in the NEOLITHIC period.

forum In the Roman world, a market place or public square, usually with colonnades, temples and public buildings, equivalent to the Greek *AGORA*. The Forum Romanum was the chief public square in Rome.

Franks A confederation of the Germanic tribes of the lower Rhine that emerged in the 3rd century AD. In the 4th and 5th centuries the Franks settled in northern Gaul.

frieze A long band of relief sculpture decorating the upper stonework of a temple.

Gauls A term used by the Romans to describe the CELTIC peoples of western continental Europe, though not those of the British Isles.

geometric A style of pottery decoration with repeated geometric motifs that flourished in Greece in the 8th century BC and earlier. Also used for wall-painting and textiles.

Gilgamesh Epic An AKKADIAN poem written on 12 tablets describing the deeds of the legendary Gilgamesh ruler of Uruk and his search for immortality. It includes the story of the Flood.

gladiator A slave (or, occasionally, a volunteer) trained to fight to the death if necessary to entertain the Roman public.

Gorgon In Greek mythology, a grotesque female figure with snake hair, the sight of which might turn a man to stone.

Goths A major Germanic people of eastern Europe. In the 4th century they divided into the Visigoths ("western") and Ostrogoths ("eastern"). Both peoples subsequently settled in the Roman empire.

greaves Armor shin and knee protectors.

gun mada An annual tax paid in animals by military personnel in the regions to the north and east of the core of the empire of the THIRD DYNASTY OF UR.

Hellenistic The period of Greek civilization lasting from the death of Alexander the Great (323 BC) to the Roman annexation of Egypt (30 BC), from *Hellenos,* meaning Greek.

Hellespont The narrow sea channel dividing Europe from ANATOLIA at the northeast corner of the Mediterranean. The cities of Troy and Byzantion both owed their prosperity to their situation at this important crossroad.

helots Serfs who formed the agricultural labor force of Sparta.

hieratic The normal form of the ancient Egyptian script, mostly written on papyrus. Hieratic signs lost the pictorial character of the HIEROGLYPHIC SCRIPT and are often joined together.

hieroglyphic script A writing system in which the signs for words or syllables mostly take the form of identifiable pictures. The most important were Egyptian and Hittite hieroglyphic.

high priest In ancient Egypt, the head of the local priesthood, in particular the priesthood of Amun at Thebes.

hippeis Greek cavalry, in Athens the name of the second most wealthy class, so-called originally because they could afford to equip themselves as cavalry.

honestiores From the 2nd century AD, the upper classes (including the aristocracy, EQUESTRIANS, soldiers, civil servants and local town councillors) of the Roman empire. The class enjoyed legal privileges denied to the *HUMILIORES*.

hoplite A heavily armed and armored Greek infantry soldier.

Horus name In ancient Egypt, the first name in a king's titulary, consisting of an epithet that identifies the king as a manifestation of an aspect of Horus.

humiliores From the 2nd century AD, the lower classes of the Roman empire.

Huns A Turkic nomad people from Central Asia who dominated eastern Europe in the late 4th and early 5th centuries AD. Their empire broke up soon after the death of their greatest leader, Attila, in 453.

hunter–gatherer A term used by anthropologists to describe a mode of subsistence involving the hunting of animals, fishing and the gathering of edible wild plants.

Hyksos A people, thought to have originated in southern Palestine, who overran Lower (northern) Egypt from 1640–1532 BC.

ice age A period of global cooling leading to extensive glaciation in high latitudes, and to lower sea levels worldwide. The most recent ice age in the Earth's history lasted from around 1,000,000 years to 10,000 years ago.

Illyria The region, named after its inhabitants, the Illyrians, that was roughly equivalent to modern Albania, Bosnia and Croatia. The Illyrian language is ancestral to modern Albanian.

imperator Commander-in-chief; the title, from which the modern word emperor is derived, that was adopted by Augustus's successors.

Indo-European A word coined in the 19th century to describe an original common language from which the Indian and European languages were held to descend. It is used today of the Indo-European family of languages, though there is no certain historical foundation for their development and separation.

Ionia The central west coast of ANATOLIA and its offshore islands, colonized by the Ionian Greeks from the 11th to the 9th century BC.

Ionic column In CLASSICAL architecture, an elegant column, the capital of which is shaped like a pair of formalized ram's horns.

Iron Age The period when iron was used for tools and weapons, starting c.1400–1200 BC in the Near East. Iron did not become more widely used than bronze until the 9th century BC, and as late as the 5th century in western Europe.

Isthmus The neck of land that joins southern Greece to the mass of Europe, cut today by the Corinth canal.

iugera A Roman unit of area equivalent to two-thirds of an acre or one-fourth of a hectare.

king list A text recording the names of the MESOPOTAMIAN kings and the lengths of their reigns. The most important are the Sumerian king list, which recorded the dynasties of SUMER from mythical times to the mid 2nd millennium BC, and the Assyrian king list, which listed the rulers of ASSYRIA from before 2000 to the late 7th century.

kouros (plural kouroi) A male nude statue of a youth, of a formal ARCHAIC shape, that developed in Greece from the 7th to the 5th century BC. Its female equivalent, a *kore* (plural *korai*), was always clothed.

krater A mixing bowl for wine and water, sometimes fitted with a strainer.

kudurru An AKKADIAN term for a document recording a royal land grant. It was normally a carved stone STELE containing the details of the grant and images of the gods who guaranteed it. Some were placed in temples and others were possibly used as boundary markers.

Latin colony A colony founded during the Roman republic for poor Roman citizens. The colonists surrendered their citizenship in return for land and Latin rights, i.e. the rights enjoyed by the Latins in Rome, hence the name.

Latins A major group of Italian peoples who inhabited Latium (now Lazio) in west-central Italy. In historical times the Romans and Latins had mutual rights of intermarriage and commerce.

law codes Texts recording the judgements and appropriate penalties for various crimes, for example Hammurabi's code.

legion *(legio)* Originally the levy of Roman citizens eligible to bear arms, by 300 BC it was used to describe a division of soldiers 4000–6000 strong.

Levant The lands bordering the eastern Mediterranean from ANATOLIA to ancient Palestine.

limitanei Garrison troops in the late Roman army.

Linear A The earlier of the two BRONZE AGE Greek scripts, not yet decoded but in some way similar to LINEAR B.

Linear B The script of the MYCENAEANS in the BRONZE AGE. It has been decoded and can be read as an early form of the Greek language.

lost-wax casting A method of casting metal by using a wax model to form an intermediate clay mold. Also called *cire perdue*.

lugal The SUMERIAN word for king (literally meaning big man). The lugal may originally have been a war leader.

maniple *(manipulus)* The main sub-unit of the LEGION in mid-republican times, usually containing up to 160 men (i.e. two "centuries").

mastaba A free-standing tomb from the Early Dynastic period and Old Kingdom of Egypt. The basic form was rectangular, with a flat roof and vertical or slightly inclined walls.

mausoleum A monumental tomb. The term derives from the tomb built by Mausolus (d. 352 BC), the Persian satrap of Caria in ANATOLIA, regarded as one of the Seven Wonders of the World.

Meluhha In the 3rd and 2nd millennia BC, it seems to have referred to a country to the east of

SUMER reached by way of the Persian Gulf; most probably the Indus valley. In the 1st millennium BC, Meluhha refers to NUBIA.

menorah A seven-branched candelabrum originally used in the Temple in Jerusalem, later a symbol of Judaism.

Mesopotamia Literally "between the rivers," the name given to the fertile floodplain between the Tigris and Euphrates rivers where organized urban societies developed about 4000 BC. Mespotamian refers to the civilizations that flourished there, particularly the SUMERIAN, AKKADIAN, ASSYRIAN and BABYLONIAN.

metope In Greek architecture, a single slab of relief sculpture used in a series on the FRIEZE of a temple. The metopes were separated from each other by plainer slabs (triglyphs) with a design of vertical lines.

mina A Mesopotamian weight of about 500 g. There were normally 60 shekels to 1 mina and 60 minas to 1 TALENT.

Minoan The civilization of early Crete that flourished c. 2000–1450 BC.

Mithraism The cult of the sun god Mithras. It originated in Persia and spread to the Roman empire in the 1st century AD, where it was particularly popular among soldiers.

monotheism The belief that there is only one god.

mushkenum One of the three classes of people in Hammurabi's LAW CODE, probably a servant of the state. See also *AWILUM* and *WARDUM*.

Mycenaean The earliest civilization of mainland Greece, which flourished c. 1600–1100 BC.

Natufians Hunter–gatherers of the LEVANT who harvested wild cereals and settled in villages; by extension, that part of the EPIPALEOLITHIC period that witnessed the development of cereal grain exploitation, c. 11000–9300 BC.

necropolis A large and important burial area that was in use for a long period.

Neolithic (New Stone Age) The period of human prehistory that is characterized by the use of stone tools and the adoption of agriculture as the principal means of subsistence.

Neoplatonism Developed in the 3rd century BC, it fused Platonic, Aristotelian, STOIC and other philosophic systems. The dominant philosophy of the Roman world by the 3rd century AD.

nomarch The chief official of a NOME. In the late Old Kingdom and early Middle Kingdom of Egypt, nomarchs became local, hereditary rulers who governed their nomes more or less independently of the central authority. The kings of the 11th Dynasty began in this way. The office ceased to have political importance during the 12th Dynasty.

nome An administrative province of Egypt (from Greek *nomos*; the ancient Egyptian term was *sepat*). The nome system seems to have been elaborated in the Early Dynastic period but did not reach final form until PTOLEMAIC times.

Nubia The region on the middle Nile that is roughly equivalent to the north of modern Sudan.

obsidian A naturally occurring volcanic glass widely used for cutting tools and occasionally for vessels, mirrors and jewelry.

odeion In Greece, a concert hall like a covered theater. It always had a roof.

oligarchy Literally, "government of the few." In the Greek world, an exclusive form of government that worked to the advantage of a particular group, in contrast to a DEMOCRACY.

optimates The dominant conservative group in the Roman SENATE during the late republic.

orchestra The dancing area for the chorus in a Greek theater.

Orientalizing The style of Greek art in the early ARCHAIC period that adopted decorative and animal motifs from the Near East.

ostracism An Athenian system for taking the heat out of politics by providing for a vote of the people to decide whether an exile should take place; if so, then a second vote was held to decide who should be exiled. Potsherds (*ostraka*) were used to record the votes.

palaestra In Greece, an open-air courtyard within a colonnade, used as a wrestling school.

Panathenaic festival A state festival of Athene at Athens, publicly and lavishly celebrated with a procession, games and prizes and a huge sacrifice with the distribution of the meat.

pantheism The belief that God is identical to the material universe or the forces of nature.

Pantheon A temple built by the emperor Hadrian in Rome to honor all the gods. It was circular in shape and covered by a large dome.

papyrus Writing material made from the pith of the papyrus plant. Used first in Egypt, it later replaced clay TABLETS in the Near East when the ARAMAIC alphabet replaced the CUNEIFORM script.

Parthia Originally a SATRAPY of the ACHAEMENID empire, Parthia was later used by the Romans as the name for Persia under the Parthian dynasty (238 BC–AD 224).

patricians Roman aristocratic families who claimed descent from the original senators supposedly appointed by Romulus.

Peisistratids The dynasty of tyrants who ruled Athens from 546–510 BC.

perioikoi Literally "the dwellers around" Sparta. Unlike the HELOTS, the *perioikoi* were free but had no political rights in the Spartan state beyond local self-government.

phalanx A densely packed battle formation of HOPLITE spearmen.

pictograph A sign in a script whose picture suggests the meaning.

plebeian Any Roman citizen, rich or poor, who was not a PATRICIAN (from *plebs,* the general populace).

polytheism The belief that there is more than one god, in contrast to MONOTHEISM.

pontifex maximus The chief priest of the Roman state cults. In the imperial period the title was held by the emperors until 382, and was subsequently adopted by the popes.

populares The reformist faction in the Roman SENATE during the late republic which identified itself with the interests of the PLEBS.

praetor The Roman magistrate responsible for civil jurisdiction, second in rank to the consulship.

Praetorian guard The bodyguard of the Roman emperor.

princeps "First citizen," the title that was adopted by Augustus. The word prince is derived from it.

Proto-Neolithic Describes the transitional period between the hunting and gathering cultures of the EPIPALEOLITHIC and the farming cultures of the ACERAMIC NEOLITHIC (c. 9300–8500 BC).

provincia/**province** Roman overseas possession, under Roman administration.

Ptolemaic Refers to the Macedonian dynasty founded by Alexander the Great's general Ptolemy Soter, which ruled Egypt from 323 to 30 BC.

Punic From the Latin *Poeni* (Phoenician), the Roman name for the Carthaginians.

quaestor A Roman magistrate possessing financial responsibilities, the lowest ranking magistracy.

quinquereme A large galley, thought to be so-called because it had five oarsmen to pull each oar.

red-figure decoration A decorative style of Greek pottery with tan figures on a black ground (see also BLACK-FIGURE DECORATION).

relief Sculpture in which the design stands out from a flat surface (also called raised bas-relief).

Sabines Italian hill people living northeast of Rome, conquered by the Romans in 290 BC.

Samnites A major Italian people of the south-central Apennines, conquered by the Romans in 290 BC.

Sasanian Persian dynasty AD 224–651 that succeeded the Parthians.

satrapy A province of the Persian empire, ruled by a satrap, or governor, appointed by the king.

Saxon Shore A Roman military command area consisting of coastal fortresses on both sides of the English Channel and along the east coast of Britain. Named after the Saxons, Germanic pirates who were raiding the area.

Sea Peoples Invaders of Egypt in the 13th and 12th centuries BC. They were part of a wider movement of peoples including those responsible for the widespread destruction of settlements in the Aegean region, ANATOLIA and the LEVANT. Their precise identity and origin are disputed by scholars.

Sealand The area of marshes and lagoons at the head of the Persian Gulf. In the middle of the 2nd millennium BC the Sealand dynasty had control of much of southern MESOPOTAMIA, but little is known about its rule.

sed **festival** An Egyptian ritual of royal regeneration, almost always celebrated after 30 years of a king's reign, and thereafter at three-yearly intervals. It features prominently in the decoration of royal mortuary temples, reflecting the king's wish to rule long in the next world.

Seleukid empire The empire in Syria and the Near East founded by Seleukos Nikator, one of the generals of Alexander the Great and his principal successor in the east, and ruled by his dynasty from 321–64 BC. The Latin form of the name is Seleucus, hence it is sometimes written as the Seleucid empire.

Semitic A group of Near Eastern languages, including Akkadian, Canaanite, Amorite, Ugaritic, Phoenician, Aramaic, Hebrew and Arabic.

Senate Originally the council of the Roman kings. After the overthrow of the monarchy the Senate became the ruling body of the Roman republic.

shaft grave A burial place in a deep narrow pit, used in the early BRONZE AGE. At Mycenae there was a circle of these graves, probably marked by stone markers.

shekel A weight used throughout the Near East. Normally there were 60 shekels to the MINA.

Silk Road The overland route to China from the west.

sistrum An Egyptian musical instrument, a kind of rattle, sacred to the goddess of women, Hathor.

Slavs An important group of eastern European peoples. Though they appear in historical sources only in the 1st century AD, their origins are believed to be much older.

Sophists In Greece of the 5th century BC, itinerant teachers who gave instruction in rhetoric and other subjects for a fee.

sphinx A mythical creature with the head of a man and body of a lion.

stamp seal An engraved seal that was pressed into a damp clay surface to leave an impression.

stele A stone monument normally erected by a ruler. Stelae (plural) were often inscribed and carved with sculptured images.

stoa In Greece, a colonnade for any civil or commercial purpose, usually with rooms behind it, sometimes having two stories.

Stoics PANTHEIST followers of the 4th-century BC philosopher Zeno of Kition, who taught that happiness is to be found through submission to destiny and natural law.

Sumer The part of the plain of MESOPOTAMIA that lay to the south of Nippur. See also AKKAD.

sumptuary law Legislation intended to curb excessive expenditure or extravagant living.

tablet A flat, cushion-shaped object on which inscriptions in the CUNEIFORM script were written; normally of clay, sometimes of stone or metal.

talent A weight unit used throughout the Near East equal to 60 MINAS; ie., about 66 lbs (30 kg).

Tasian Named from Deir Tasa, a Predynastic site in Upper Egypt, the term refers to a Predynastic culture that may not be distinct from BADARIAN.

tell The Arabic term for a mound consisting of the debris of an ancient settlement. Such mounds are also called *tel* (Hebrew), *choga* or *tepe* (Persian) and *hüyük* (Turkish).

temenos The enclosure of a Greek sanctuary, the holy ground belonging to the god and governed by special rulers

tetrarchy "Rule of four," the name given by historians to the system introduced by Diocletian in which the responsibilities of government were shared by two senior emperors (AUGUSTI), each supported by a junior colleague (CAESAR).

theocracy Rule by a priesthood or monarch claiming divine authority.

thetes The Athenian lower classes, excluded from serving as HOPLITES because they owned little or no property.

Third Dynasty of Ur Royal dynasty of Ur, ruled 2112–2004 BC. The SUMERIAN traditions refer to two earlier dynasties but the 3rd Dynasty is the first that is known from contemporary documents.

tholos A round temple or building with a conical or vaulted roof.

Thrace A region of southeastern Europe in Greek and Roman times that is roughly equivalent to modern Bulgaria, European Turkey and northern Greece.

tribune The chief representatives of the Roman PLEBS, ten of whom were elected annually by the *CONCILIUM PLEBIS*.

trireme A ram-equipped galley with three banks of oars on either side, the main type of Greek warship during the period of the Persian wars.

triumvirate Joint rule by three men, the name given to the political alliances in the late Roman republic between Pompey, Crassus and Julius Caesar (the First Triumvirate), and Mark Antony, Lepidus and Octavian (the Second Triumvirate).

tyrant From *tyrannos*, a term used by the Greeks to describe a ruler whose authority was unconstitutional. The association with oppressive government came later.

uraeus The characteristic symbol of Egyptian kingship, a rearing cobra worn on the king's forehead or crown.

Vandals A Germanic people who invaded the Roman empire in 406 and ruled a kingdom based on Carthage 439–533.

vicarius Meaning "substitute," a term used in the early Roman empire for a deputy to a provincial governor. In the late empire it described an imperial deputy who supervised a group of provinces.

villa The central buildings of a Roman country estate, including a house , stores, workshops, stables, slave-quarters, farm buildings etc.

wardum A slave, and hence a servant or official of the king, in Hammurabi's LAW CODE. See also *AWILUM, MUSHKENUM*.

winged disk A sun disk with an outspread pair of wings attached. The earliest known example is from 1st Dynasty Egypt. It is associated with the god Horus and symbolizes the sun. The motif was often copied outside Egypt. In ASSYRIA it represented the sun god Shamash and perhaps Ashur. It was adopted by the ACHAEMENIDS to represent their chief god Ahuramazda.

year-name In MESOPOTAMIA dates were sometimes referred to by an event that occurred in the previous year. Lists of year-names enable the chronology of the period to be determined.

Zealots Members of a Jewish anti-Roman resistance movement of the 1st century AD.

ziggurat The anglicized form of the Akkadian ZIQQURRATU, a high mound on which a temple was situated; a MESOPOTAMIAN temple, built in successive pyramidal stages with outside staircases and a shrine on top.

LISTS OF RULERS

KINGS OF EGYPT

EARLY DYNASTIC PERIOD c.3000–2649
Narmer

1st Dynasty	2920–2770
Menes	
Djer	
Wadj	
Den	
Adjib	
Semerkhet	
Qa'a	

2nd Dynasty	2770–2649
Hetepsekhemwy	
Reneb	
Ninetjer	
Peribsen	
Khasekhemwy	

OLD KINGDOM 2649–2134

3rd Dynasty	2649–2575
Zanakht	2649–2630
Djoser	2630–2611
Sekhemkhet	2611–2603
Khaba	2603–2599
Huni	2599–2575

4th Dynasty	2575–2465
Snofru	2575–2551
Khufu (Cheops)	2551–2528
Radjedef	2528–2520
Khephren	2520–2494
Menkaure (Mycerinus)	2490–2472
Shepseskaf	2472–2467

5th Dynasty	2465–2323
Userkaf	2465–2458
Sahure	2458–2446
Kakai	2446–2426
Ini	2426–2419
Raneferef	2419–2416
Izi	2416–2392
Menkauhor	2396–2388
Izezi	2388–2356
Weri	2356–2323

6th Dynasty	2323–2150
Teti	2323–2291
Pepi I	2289–2255
Nemtyemzaf	2255–2246
Pepi II	2246–2152

7th & 8th Dynasty	2150–2134
Numerous kings, including Neferkare	

FIRST INTERMEDIATE PERIOD 2134–2040

9th & 10th Dynasty	2134–2040
Several kings called	
Khety	
Merykare	
Ity	

11th Dynasty	2134–2040
Inyotef I	2134–2118
Inyotef I	2118–2069
Inyotef III	2069–2061
Mentuhotpe II	2061–2010

MIDDLE KINGDOM 2040–1640

11th Dynasty	2040–1991
Mentuhotpe II (ruler of all Egypt from 2040)	2061–2010
Mentuhotpe III	2010–1998
Mentuhotpe IV	1998–1991

12th Dynasty	1991–1783
Amenemhet I	1991–1962
Senwosret I	1971–1926
Amenemhet II	1929–1982
Senwosret II	1987–1878
Senwosret III	1878–1841?
Amenemhet III	1844–1797
Amenemhet IV	1799–1787
Nefrusobk	1787–1783

13th Dynasty	1783–after 1640
About 70 kings, including	
Wegaf 1	1783–1779
Amenemhet V	
Harnedjheriotef	
Amenyqemau	
Sebekhotpe 1	c. 1750
Hor	
Amenemhet VII	
Sebekhotpe II	
Khendjer	
Sebekhotpe III	c. 1745
Neferhotep I	c. 1741–1730
Sebekhotpe IV	c. 1730–1720
Sebekhotpe V	c. 1720–1715
Aya	c. 1704–1690
Mentuemzaf	
Dedumose II	
Neferhotep III	

14th Dynasty
A group of minor kings probably all contemporary with the 13th or 15th Dynasty

SECOND INTERMEDIATE PERIOD 1640–1532

15th Dynasty (Hyksos)	
Salitis	
Sheshi	
Khian	
Apophis	c. 1585–1542
Khamudi	c. 1542–1532

16th Dynasty
Minor Hyksos rulers, contemporary with the 15th Dynasty

17th Dynasty	1640–1550
Numerous kings, including	
Inyotef V	c. 1640–1635
Sebekemzaf I	
Nebireyeraw	
Sebekemzaf II	
Ta'o (or Djehuti'o) I	
Ta'o (or Djehuti'o) II	
Kamose	c. 1555–1550

NEW KINGDOM 1532–1070

18th Dynasty	1550–1307
Ahmose (ruler of all Egypt from 1532)	1550–1525
Amenophis I	1525–1504
Tuthmosis I	1504–1492
Tuthmosis II	1492–1479
Tuthmosis III	1479–1425
Hatshepsut	1473–1458
Amenophis II	1427–1401
Tuthmosis IV	1401–1391
Amenophis III	1391–1353
Amenophis IV (Akhenaten)	1353–1335
Smenkhkare	1335–1333
Tutankhamun	1333–1323
Aya	1323–1319
Haremhab	1319–1307

19th Dynasty	1307–1196
Ramses I	1307–1306
Sethos I	1306–1290
Ramses II	1290–1224
Merneptah	1224–1214
Sethos II	1214–1204
Siptah	1204–1198
Twosre	1198–1196

20th Dynasty	1196–1070
Sethnakhte	1196–1194
Ramses III	1194–1163
Ramses IV	1163–1156
Ramses V	1156–1151
Ramses VI	1151–1143
Ramses VII	1143–1136
Ramses VIII	1136–1131
Ramses IX	1131–1112
Ramses X	1112–1100
Ramses XI	1100–1070

THIRD INTERMEDIATE PERIOD 1070–712

21st Dynasty	1070–945
Smendes	1070–1044
Amenemnisu	1044–1040
Psusennes I	1040–992
Amenemope	993–984
Osorkon I	984–978
Siamun	978–959
Psusennes II	959–945

22nd Dynasty	945–712
Shoshenq I	945–924
Osorkon II	924–909
Takelot I	909–?
Shoshenq II	?–883
Osorkon III	883–855
Takelot	860–835
Shoshenq III	835–783
Pami	783–773
Shoshenq V	773–735
Osorkon V	735–712

23rd Dynasty
Various contemporary lines of kings recognized in Thebes, Hermopolis, Herakleopolis and other cities; precise order is disputed

Pedubaste I	828–803
Osorkon IV	777–749
Peftjau'awybast	740–725

24th Dynasty	724–712
Tefnakhte	724–717
Bocchoris	717–712

25th Dynasty (Nubian)	770–712
Kashta	770–750
Piye	750–712

LATE PERIOD 712–332

25th Dynasty (Nubian)	712–657
Shabaqo	712–698
Shebitku	698–690
Taharqa	690–664
Tantamani	664–657

26th Dynasty	664–525
Necho I	672–664)
Psamtek I	664–610
Necho II	610–595
Psamtek II	595–589
Apries	589–570
Amasis	570–526
Psamtek III	526–525

27th Dynasty (Persian)	525–404
Cambyses	525–522
Darius I	521–486
Xerxes I	486–466
Artaxerxes	465–424
Darius II	424–404

28th Dynasty	404–399
Amyrtaios	404–399

29th Dynasty	399–380
Nepherites I	399–393
Psammuthis	393
Hakoris	393–380
Nephrites II	380

30th Dynasty	380–343
Nectanebo I	380–362
Teos	365–360
Nectanebo II	360–343

2nd Persian Period	343–332
Artaxerxes III Ochus	343–338
Arses	338–336
Darius III Codoman	335–332

GRECO-ROMAN PERIOD 332 BC–AD 395

Macedonian Dynasty	332–304
Alexander III the Great	332–323
Philip Arrhidaeus	323–316
Alexander IV	316–304

Ptolemaic Dynasty	304–30
The order and number of the kings is disputed	
Ptolemy I Soter I	304–284
Ptolemy II Philadelphus	285–246
Ptolemy III Euergetes I	246–221
Ptolemy IV Philopator	221–205
Ptolemy V Epiphanes	205–180
Ptolemy VI Philometor	180–145
Ptolemy VII Neos Philopator	145
Ptolemy VIII Euergetes II (Physkon)	170–163, 145–116

Cleopatra III & Ptolemy IX Soter II (Lathyros)	116–107
Cleopatra III & Ptolemy X Alexander I	107–88
Ptolemy IX Soter II	88–81
Cleopatra Berenice	81–80
Ptolemy XI Alexander II	80
Ptolemy XII Neos Dionysos (Auletes)	80–85, 55–51
Berenice IV	58–55
Cleopatra VII	51–30
Ptolemy XIII	51–47
Ptolemy XIV	47–44
Ptolemy XV Caesarion	44–30

Roman Emperors 30 BC–AD 395

From 30 BC, the Roman emperors ruled Egypt as a province under their personal control. In AD 395, Egypt passed to the control of the emperors in Constantinople.

MESOPOTAMIAN KINGS

KINGS OF AGADE 2334–2193 BC

Sargon	2334–2279
Rimush	2278–2270
Manishtushu	2269–2255
Narim-Sin	2254–2218
Shar-Kali-Sharri	2217–2193

THE THIRD DYNASTY OF UR 2112–2004 BC

Ur-Nammu	2112–2095
Shulgi	2094–2047
Amar-Sin	2046–2038
Shu-Sin	2037–2029
Ibbi-Sin	2028–2004

KINGS OF ASSYRIA

1813–609 BC

Shamshi-Adad I	1813–1781
Ishme-Dagan I	1780–c.1740
A succession of 45 minor kings	c.1740–1363
Ashur-uballit I	1363–1328
Enlil-nirari	1363–1328
Arik-den-ili	1317–1306
Adad-nirari I	1305–1274
Shalmaneser I	1273–1244
Tukulti-Ninurta I	1243–1207
Ashur-nadan-apli	1206–1203
Ashur-nirari III	1202–1197
Enlil-kudurri-usur	1196–1192
Ninurta-apil-Ekur	1191–1179
Ashur-dan I	1178–1133
Ashur-resh-ishi I	1132–1115
Ninurta-tukulti-Ashur	1115
Mutakkil-Nusku	1115
Tiglath-Pileser I	1114–1076
Ashared-apil-Ekur	1075–1074
Ashur-bel-kala	1073–1056
Eriba-Adad II	1055–1054
Shamshi-Adad IV	1053–1050
Ashurnasirpal I	1049–1031
Shalmaneser II	1030–1019
Ashur-nirari IV	1018–1013

Ashur-rabi II	1012–972
Ashur-resh-ishi II	971–967
Tiglath-Pileser II	966–935
Ashur-dan II	934–912
Adad-nirari II	911–891
Tukulti-Ninurta II	890–884
Ashurnasirpal II	883–859
Shalmaneser III	858–824
Shamshi-Adad V	823–811
Adad-nirari III	810–783
Shalmaneser IV	782–773
Ashur-dan III	772–755
Ashur-nirari V	754–745
Tiglath-Pileser III	744–727
Shalmaneser V	726–722
Sargon II	721–705
Sennacherib	704–681
Esarhaddon	680–669
Ashurbanipal	668–627
Ashur-etelli-ilana	c. 626–624
Sin-shar-ishkun	c. 623–612
Ashur-uballit II	611–609

KINGS OF BABYLONIA

FIRST DYNASTY OF BABYLON (AMORITE) 1894–1595 BC

Sumu-abum	1894–1881
Sumulael	1880–1845
Sabium	1844–1831
Apil-Sin	1830–1813
Sin-muballi	1812–1793
Hammurabi	1792–1750
Samsu-iluna	1749–1712
Abi-eshuh	1711–1684
Ammi-ditana	1683–1647
Ammi-saduqa	1646–1626
Samsu-ditana	1625–1595

KASSITE DYNASTY c.1570–1154 BC

Several little known kings	c.1570–1374
Kadashman-Enlil I	1374–1360
Burna-Buriash II	1359–1333
Kara-hardash	1333
Nazi-bugash	1333
Kurigalzu II	1332–1308
Nazi-maruttash	1307–1282
Kadashman-Turgu	1281–1264
Kadashman-Enlil II	1263–1255
Kudur-Enlil	1254–1246
Shagarakti-shuriash	1245–1233
A succession of five kings	1332–1216
Adad-shuma-usur	1215–1186
Melishipak	1185–1171
Marduk-apla-iddina	1170–1158
Zababa-shuma-iddina	1157
Enlil-nadin-ahi (Enlil-shuma-user)	1156–1154

SECOND DYNASTY OF ISIN c.1157–1026 BC

Marduk-kabit-ahheshu	1157–1140
Itti-Marduk-balatu	1139–1132
Ninurta-nadin-shumi	1131–1126
Nebuchadnezzar I	1125–1104

Enlil-nadin-apli	1103–1100
Marduk-nadin-ahhe	1099–1082
Marduk-shapik-zeri	1081–1069
Adad-apla-iddina	1068–1047
Marduk-ahhe-eriba	1046
Marduk-zer?	1045–1034
Nabu-shumu-libur	1033–1026

SECOND DYNASTY OF THE SEALAND c.1025–1005 BC

Three kings, names unknown

DYNASTY OF ELAM c.984–979 BC

| Mar-biti-apla-usur | 984–979 |
| Seventeen kings, dates and dynasties uncertain | c. 978–732 BC |

NINTH DYNASTY OF BABYLON 731–626 BC

Nabu-mukin-zeri	731–729
Period of Assyrian rule	728–722
Markuk-apla-iddina II	721–710
Period of Assyrian rule	709–703
Marduk-apla-iddina II	703
Bel-ibni	702–700
Ashur-nadin-shumi	699–694
Nergal-ushezib	
Mushezib-Murduk	692–689
Period of Assyrian rule	688–668
Shamash-shuma-ukin	667–648
Kandalanu	647–627

NEO-BABYLONIAN DYNASTY 625–539 BC

Nabopolassar	625–605
Nebuchadnezzar II	604–562
Amel-Murduk	561–560
Neriglissar	559–556
Labashi-Marduk	556
Nabonidus	555–539

HITTITE RULERS

OLD KINGDOM 1680–1420 BC

Labarnas I	1680–1650
Hattusilis I	1650–1620
Mursilis I	1620–1590
Several minor kings including Telepina	1525–1500

EMPIRE 1420–c.1205 BC

Tudhaliyas I	1420–1400
Hattusilis II	1400–1390
Tudhaliyas II	1390–1370
Arnuwandas I	1370–1355
Tudhaliyas III	1355–1344
Suppiluliumas I	1344–1322
Arnuwandas II	1322–1321
Musilis II	1321–1295
Nuwatallis II	1295–1271
Mursilis III	1271–1264
Hattusilis III	1264–1239
Tudhaliyas IV	1239–1209
Arnuwandas III	1209–1205
Suppululiumas II	1205–?

HEBREW KINGS

UNITED KINGDOM OF ISRAEL c.1020–928 BC

Saul	c. 1020–c. 1006
David	c. 1006–965
Solomon	c. 967–928

JUDAH 928–587 BC

Rehoboam	928–911
Asa	908–867
Jehoshaphat	908–867
Jehoram	851–843
Ahaziah	843–842
Athaliah	842–836
Joash	836–798
Uzziah	785–733
Jotham	758–743
Ahaz	743–727
Hezekiah	727–698
Manassch	698–642
Amon	642–640
Josiah	640–609
Jehoahaz	609–608
Jehoiakim	608–598
Jehoiachin	597–?560
Zedekiah	596–587

ISRAEL 928–723 BC

Jeroboam	928–907
Baasha	906–883
Omri	882–871
Ahab	873–852
Joram	851–842
Jehu	842–814
Jehoash	800–784
Jeroboam II	789–748
Menachem	747–737
Pekah	735–733
Hoshea	733–723

ACHAEMENID KINGS OF PERSIA

c. 700–303 BC

Achaemenes	
Teispes	
Ariaramnes	
Arsames	
Htstaspes	
Darius I	521–486
Xerxes I	521–486
Artaxerxes I	464–425
Xerxes II	424
Sogdianus	424
Darius II	423–405
Artaxerxes II	404–359
Artaxerxes III	358–338
Arses	337–336
Darius III	335–330

KINGDOM OF MACEDON
TEMENID DYNASTY c.640–309 BC

Perdiccas I	c. 640
Seven kings, dates of most uncertain	c. 640–413
Archelaos	413–399
Ten kings, mostly shortlived	399–356
Philip II	356–336
Alexander III (the Great)	336–323
Philip III	323–317
Alexander IV	317–309
Interregnum	309–306

DYNASTY OF KASSANDROS 305–294 BC

Kassandros	305–297
Philip IV	297
Alexander V	297–294
Antipater I (deposed, died 287)	297–294

ANTIGONID DYNASTY 294–168 BC

Demetrios I, the Poliorcetes	294–287
Pyrrhus of Epirus (deposed)	287–285
Lysimachos (king of Thrace)	285–281
Ptolemy Keraunos (son of Ptolemy I of Egypt)	281–279
Meleager (deposed)	279
Antipater II Etesias (deposed)	279
Antigonos II Gonatas	277–239
Demetrios II	239–229
Antigonos III Doson	229–221
Philip V	221–179
Perseus	181–168

SELEUKID DYNASTY
312–64 BC

Seleukos I Nikator (Satrap of Babylonia)	312–281
Antiochos I Soter	281–261
Antiochos II Theos	261–246
Seleukos II Kallinikos	246–226
Seleukos III Soter	226–223
Antiochos III the Great	223–187
Seleukos IV Philopator	187–175
Antiochos IV Epiphanes	175–163
Antiochos V Eupator	163–162
Demetrios I Soter	162–150
Alexander I Theopator Euergetes (Balas)	150–145
Antiochos VI Epiphanes Dionysos	145–142
Demetrios II Nikator (deposed)	145–139
Antiochos VII Euergetes (Sidetes)	139–129
Demetrios II (restored)	129–125
Alexander II	128–122
Cleopatra Thea (daughter of Ptolemy VI of Egypt)	125–120
Seleukos V (son of Cleopatra and Demetrios II)	125
Antiochos VIII Philometor	125–96
Antiochos IX Philopator	113–95
Seleukos VI Epiphanes Nikator	96–95
Demetrios III Philopator Soter	95–88
Antiochos X Eusebes Philopator	95–83
Antiochos XI Epiphanes Philadelphos	95
Philip I Epiphanes Philadelphos	95–83
Antiochos XII Dionysos	87–84
Philip II	69–64
Antiochos XIII Philadelphos	69–64

KINGS OF ROME
c.750–509 BC

Romulus (legendary)	
Numa Pompilius	c. 715–673
Tullus Hostilius	c. 673–642
Ancus Marcius	c. 642–617
Tarquin I	c. 616–579
Servius Tullius	c. 578–535
Tarquin II (the Proud)	c. 535–509

ROMAN EMPERORS
JULIO-CLAUDIAN DYNASTY 27 BC–AD 69

Augustus	27 BC–14 AD
Tiberius	14–37
Gaius (Caligula)	37–41
Claudius	41–54
Nero	54–68
Galba	68–69
Otho	69
Vitellius	69

FLAVIAN, NERVO-TRAJANIC AND ANTONINE DYNASTIES 69–192

Vespasian	69–79
Titus	79–81
Domitian	82–96
Nerva	96–98
Trajan (97–98 with Nerva)	97–117
Hadrian	117–138
Antoninus Pius	138–161
Marcus Aurelius (161–169 with Lucius Verus)	161–180
Commodus	180–192

SEVERAN DYNASTY 193–235

Pertinax	193
Didius Julianus	193
Septimius Severus	193–211
Caracalla (211–212 with Geta)	211–217
Macrinus	217–218
Elagabalus	218–222
Alexander Severus	222–235

PERIOD OF POLITICAL ANARCHY AND DISORDER 235–284

The many usurpers are not listed

Maximinus	235–238
Gordian I and II (in Africa)	238
Balbinus and Pupienus (in Italy)	238
Gordian III	238–244
Philip I and Philip II	244–249
Decius	249–251
Herrenius and Hostilian	251
Trebonianus Gallus Volusian	251–253
Aemilianus	253
Valerian	253–260
Saloninus	260
Gallienus (253–260 with Valerian)	253–268
Claudius II	268–270
Quintillus	270
Aurelian	270–275
Tacitus	275–276
Florian	276
Probus	276–282
Carus	282–283
Carinus and Numerian	283–284

DIVISION OF THE EMPIRE

WEST		EAST	
Diocletian (sole emperor) 284–287			
Maximian	287–305	Diocletian	284–305
Constantius	305–306	Galerius	305–311
Severus	306–307	Maximinus	309–313
Maxentius	306–312		
Constantine	306–324	Licinius Augustus	308–324
Constantine (sole emperor) 324–337			
Constantine II	337–340	Constantius II	337–361
Constans	340–350		
Magnentius (usurper)	350–353		
Julian (Caesar)	355–361	Gallus (Caesar)	355–361
Julian (sole emperor) 361–363			
Jovian (sole emperor) 363–364			
Valentinian	364–365	Valens	364–378
Gratian	375–383		
Valentinian II (Italy, Illyricum)	375–392	Theodosius	379–395
Maximus (usurper)	383–388		
Eugenius (usurper)	392–394		
Theodosius (sole emperor) 394–395			
Honorius	395–423	Arcadius	395–408
Constantius III	421	Theodosius II	408–450
Iohannes (usurper)	423–425		
Valentinian III	425–455	Marcian	450–457
Petronius Maximus	455		
Avitus	455–56		
Majorian	457–461	Leo	457–474
Libius Severus	461–465		
Anthemius	476–472		
Olybrius	472		
Glycerius	473		
Julius Nepos	473–475		
Romulus Augustulus	475–476	Zeno	474–491
		Anastasius	491–518
		Justin	518–527
		Justinian	527–565
		Justin II	565–578
		Tiberius II Constantine	578–582
		Maurice	582–602
		Phocas	602–610
		Heraclius	610–641

Acknowledgments

Abbreviations

AAA   The Ancient Art & Architecture Collection
AKG   Archiv fur Kunst und Geschichte, London
BM   Copyright British Museum, London
MH   Michael Holford
RHPL   Robert Harding Picture Library

13 Erich Lessing/AKG 14–15 MH (detail used on subsequent pages) 19tl AAA 21tr BM 22tl James Mellaart 23tl MH 25 Ashmolean Museum 27l Scala 27tr from *Warka Report* 28b Il Quadrante Edizione, Milan/Iraq Museum, Baghdad 28t Claus Hansmann/Iraq Museum, Baghdad 30b MH 30t AAA 31tr Scala 31b MH 33 Scala 35 RHPL 37 BM 38 Picturepoint 39 Michael Jenner/RHPL 41 MH 44cr John Fuller/Iraq Museum, Baghdad 44b Boutin/Explorer 45b Ashmolean Museum 45r Joan & David Oates/Iraq Museum, Baghdad 46cl Photo RMN 46cr BM 46bl Ashmolean Museum 47 MH 48–53 Photo Archive/Jürgen Liepe 54 BM 56 Rosalind Hall 56–7 Axiom/James Morris 58 MH 59 Photo Archive/Jürgen Liepe 60c Musée du Louvre, Paris/Photo: Heini Schneebeli 60r Musée du Louvre 61 MH 65 Roger Wood 66–7 MH 68 Roger Wood 71 BM 72 MH 75–77 Michael Roaf 78 Fr. Piccirillo 85 BM 86bl Barry Iverson/Time Magazine Inc. 86tr MH 86–7 Ashmolean Museum 87tr Il Quadrante Edizione 87br BM 88–9 MH 90–1 AAA 93t MH 93c AAA 95tl Staatliche Museen, Berlin (Vorderasiatisches Museum) 95tr Erich Lessing/AKG 96 Michael Roaf 97 RHPL 100–1 Erich Lessing/AKG 102 Zefa Pictures 103cr & br Michael Roaf 104 MH 105l Giraudon 106–7 BM (detail used on subsequent pages) 109 Hirmer Fotoarchiv/National Museum, Athens 110–11 Ekdotike Athenon/Heraklion Museum 111tr Hirmer Fotoarchiv 111b D.A. Harissiadis 112 Ekdotike Athenon/National Museum, Athens 114t Ashmolean Museum 114c National Museum, Athens/RHPL 115tl & r Ekdotike Athenon/National Museum, Athens 116–17 Ekdotike Athenon 118–19 Deutsches Archäologisches Institut, Athens 122–23 Scala 123 Andromeda Archives 124 RHPL 125 Ekdotike Athenon 127 Sonia Halliday 128 Edwin Smith 129 Hirmer Fotoarchiv 131 Ekdotike Athenon/National Museum, Athens 132–33 Ekdotike Athenon/Agora Museum, Athens 134l Wadsworth Atheneum, Hartford, Conn./J. Pierpont Morgan Collection 134r BM 135l J. Henderson Bequest/BM 135c Giraudon/Archaeological Museum, Chatillon sur Seine 136r MH 136–37 Ekdotike Athenon/National Museum, Athens 137tr Metropolitan Museum of Art, New York 138 MH 139 C.M. Dixon 140–41 Ekdotike Athenon 147tl BM 148 Victoria & Albert Museum 150b Ekdotike Athenon/BM 150–51 Ekdotike Athenon/National Archaeological Museum, Athens 152l Hirmer Fotoarchiv/Delphi Museum 152r A.A.M. Van der Heyden 152–53 Spectrum Colour Library 155 Scala 158l & r MH 158–59 Antikensammlung, Munich 159r Caecilia H. Moessner/Staatliche Antikenmuseum, Munich 159b reproduced with the permission of the Master and Fellows of Corpus Christi College and of the Fitzwilliam Museum, Cambridge. Copyright, Fitzwilliam Museum, Cambridge 160 MH 161 BM 162 Ekdotike Athenon/National Museum, Athens 164–65 Zefa Pictures 168–69 RHPL 170–71 Ekdotike Athenon 173–75 Spyros Tsardavoglou 177 MH 178–79 Scala 181–83 Ashmolean Museum 189t & bl Délégation Archéologique Française en Afghanistan 190–91 Palestrina Museo Nazionale/Photo: Mauro Pucciarelli 192–93 Scala (detail used on subsequent pages) 196t Scala 197tl Ashmolean Museum 197tr Scala 197b Fotocielo 199 Scala 203c Mauro Pucciarelli 204l Scala 204r Giraudon 211 Sonia Halliday 212–13 Air Ministry, Rome 214b MH 214t Werner Forman Archive 215 Scala 217 Dave Longley/Mick Sharp 221t Mauro Pucciarelli 221r Mario Gerardi 224c Sonia Halliday 224br Michael Vickers 229l Deutsches Archäologisches Institut, Rome 230–31 Erich Lessing/AKG 232 BM 234 John G. Ross/RHPL 236 Scala 236–37 Mauro Pucciarelli 239 MH 240 Rheinisches Landesmuseum 243 Zefa Pictures 244 Mario Gerardi 249 Leonard von Matt 251 BM 256–67 Didier Barrault/RHPL 258 Mario Gerardi 259br Ronald Sheridan/AAA 262–63 Sonia Halliday 264–65 Ronald Sheridan/AAA 268–69 L. & R. Adkins 271 T. Latona/Zefa Pictures 272 Erich Lessing/AKG 272–73 Sonia Halliday 273 BM 274cl Michael Dixon 274bl Sonia Halliday 274r Scala 274–75 Sonia Halliday 276 Royal Commission on Historical Monuments 278 Scala 279 Deutsches Archäologisches Institut, Rome 281 Scala 284–85 RHPL 286 MH

Every effort has been made to trace copyright holders of the pictures used in this book. Anyone having claims to ownership not identified above is invited to contact Andromeda Limited.

Illustrations on the following pages are by John Fuller:
18bl, 18bc, 20, 27tc, 27cr, 28-29, 50, 52, 55, 58, 61, 62, 63, 76, 81, 83, 88, 93, 95tl, 98, 99, 103tr, 109, 111, 112, 115, 118, 125tl, 125tr, 125bl, 128bl, 129br, 132, 135tr, 135br, 151, 153bc, 156, 163tr, 163br, 166, 167, 186, 187, 189, 195, 199, 200bl, 200c, 200-201, 201tc, 201tr, 206, 219, 220bc, 221c, 221bc, 222, 223, 229bc, 237, 242, 246tl, 246br, 246-247, 247br, 248, 254cl, 262, 271tr, 283, 287.

Further Reading

GENERAL

J. Boardman, J. Griffin, O. Murray (eds), *The Oxford History of the Classical World* (Oxford, 1986)
C. Freeman, *Egypt, Greece and Rome* (Oxford, 1996)
B. D. Smith, *The Emergence of Agriculture* (New York, 1995)

THE ANCIENT NEAR EAST

J. M. Cook, *The Persian Empire* (London, 1983)
H. Crawford, *Sumer and the Sumerians* (Cambridge, 1991)
N. Kramer, *The Sumerians* (Chicago, 1963)
Kuhrt, A. *The Ancient Near East 3000–300 BC* (2 vols, London, 1995)
J. Oates, *Babylon* (London, 1979)
C. Redman, *The Rise of Civilization: From Early Farmers to Urban Society in the Ancient Near East* (San Francisco, 1978)
M. Roaf, *Cultural Atlas of Mesopotamia and the Ancient Near East* (Oxford and New York, 1990)
H. W. F. Saggs, *The Might that was Assyria* (London, 1984)
H. W. F. Saggs, *The Greatness that was Babylon* (London, 1962)

EGYPT

C. Aldred, *The Egyptians* (London, 1984)
J. Baines and J. Málek, *Atlas of Ancient Egypt* (Oxford and New York, 1984)
N. Grimal, *A History of Ancient Egypt* (Oxford, 1992)
B. Kemp, *Ancient Egypt* (London and New York, 1989)

GREECE

J. Boardman, *The Greeks Overseas* (Harmondsworth, 3rd edn, 1980)
J. K. Davies, *Democracy and Classical Greece* (London, 1978)
W. G. Forrest, *A History of Sparta 950–192 BC* (London, 1968)

S. Hood, *The Minoans* (London, 1973)
H. D. F. Kitto, *The Greeks* (Harmondsworth, 1951)
R. Lane Fox, *Alexander the Great* (London, 1973)
P. Levi, *Atlas of the Greek World* (Oxford and New York, 1985)
R. Meiggs, *The Athenian Empire* (Oxford, 1972)
O. Murray, *Early Greece* (London, 2nd edn, 1993)
Lord W. Taylour, *The Mycenaeans* (London, 2nd edn, 1990)
F. W. Wallbank, *The Hellenistic World* (London, 1992)

ROME

P. Brown, *The World of Late Antiquity* (London, 1971)
A. Cameron, *The Later Roman Empire* (London, 1993)
T. J. Cornell, *The Beginnings of Rome* (London and New York, 1995)
T. Cornell and J. Matthews, *Atlas of the Roman World* (Oxford and New York, 1982)
M. Crawford, *The Roman Republic* (London, 1978)
J. F. Drinkwater and A. Drummond (eds), *The World of the Romans* (New York and London, 1993)
A. H. M. Jones, *The Decline of the Ancient World* (London, 1966)
F. Millar, *The Roman Empire and its Neighbours* (London, 2nd edn, 1981)
H. H. Scullard, *From the Gracchi to Nero: A History of Rome 133 BC–AD 68* (London, 5th edn, 1982)

Quotations from the Mari letters pp. 38, 41 are from S. Dalley, *Two Old Babylonian Cities* (London and New York, 1984). Quotations from the laws of Hammurabi, pp. 39–40, from H. W. F. Saggs, *The Greatness that was Babylon.* Quotation of Solon's poetry p. 132, from O. Murray, *Early Greece.*

INDEX

Page numbers in *italics* refer to illustrations or their captions

A

Abisare, king of Larsa 37
Abu Simbel, temples 62, *62*
Abusir, pyramid *64*
accounting systems *46*
  Ubaid 21
Aceramic period 16, *18*, *45*
Achaea (Greece) 184, 217
  Achaean league 183–84
  Achaeans (mentioned by Homer) 118
Achaemenes, founder of Persian dynasty 92
Achaemenid empire 92, 96–7, 100–1, *100*, 102, *103*, 145
Achilles, legendary Greek hero 124, *134*, 175
Acropolis (Athens) 131, 133, 138, *138*, *140*, 156
acropolis 120
Actium (Greece), sea battle 234
Adad-nirari II, Assyrian king 83
administration
  Assyrian 88
  Egyptian 50, *61*
  Mesopotamian states 41
  Persian empire *99*, 100–1
  Roman 216, 267, 278
  3rd Dynasty of Ur 34
  see also civil service, government
Aegean Sea
  Bronze Age 108–19
  dialects of *119*
  Greek dark age 118–19, *119*
Aegospotami (Thrace), battle 161
Aeneas, legendary founder of Rome 195
Aeolis (Anatolia) *116*
Aeschylus, Greek dramatist 148, 161, *166*
Aesculapius *see* Asklepios
Aetius, Roman general 281, 282, *283*, 286
Aetolian league 183–84
Afghanistan 24, 76, 96, 182
afterlife, beliefs in 52, 53, *54*, 64, *215*, 274
Africa *211*, 213, 226, 234, 250, 283
  East *148*, *252*
  Egypt 55, *55*, *148*
  North 284, 288
  tropical 55
Agade, dynasty and empire *28*, *29*, 32–3, 38
Agamemnon, Mycenaean king 108, *113*, 114
Agesilaos, Spartan king 168
Agis IV, Spartan king 184
agriculture *see* farming
Agrigentum (Sicily) 198, 209
  see also Akragas
Agrippina, mother of Nero 242
Ahmose I, Egyptian king 54
Ahuni, Aramaean ruler 84
Aischylos *see* Aeschylus
Akhenaten, Egyptian pharaoh 58, 59, 60, *60*, 73
Akhetaten (el-'Amarna) 58, 59,

60, *60*, *61*
  letters 59, *61*
Akkad (Mesopotamia) 28, 29, *29*, 32, 33, *33*, *36*
  language 28
  writing 46
Akko, Egyptian vassal state 59
Akragas (Sicily) *154*
Akrotiri (Thera) *108*, 113
Akshak (Iraq) 29
Al Mina (Syria) 120
Alalah (Syria) *46*, 72, *72*, 76
Alalia (Corsica), sea battle 123
Alamanni 265, 281
Alans 281, *282*
Alaric, Visigothic leader 281
Albinus, Clodius, claimant Roman emperor 261
Alcibiades, Athenian statesman 166, 167
Aleppo *see* Yamhad
Alexander the Great, king of Macedon 101, 167, 168, 172, *173*, *177*, 180, *181*
  accession 175–6
  captures Babylon 94, 180
  conquers Egypt 63, 180; and Asia 180–82
  death of *95*, 181, 182
  founds colonies *180*, 182
  invades Persian empire 176–77, *176*, *180*
  plunders Persepolis 102
  successor kingdoms *184*, *191*
Alexandria (Egypt) 138, 180, 181, *181*, 188, 229, *252*
Alkaios, Greek lyric poet *159*
Alkibiades *see* Alcibiades
Alkmaionid family 133, 156
alphabet *80*
  Aramaic 83, 100
  Greek 124
  Phoenician 124
  see also writing
Amalasuntha, Ostrogothic queen 287
Amar-Sin, 3rd Dynasty king of Ur 30
Amarna letters 59, *58*, *61*, 73
Amenhotep *see* Amenophis
Amenophis III, Egyptian pharaoh 55, *56*, 59, 73
Amenophis IV *see* Akhenaten
Ammonites 78, 88
Amorites 34, 38, 41
Amphipolis (Thrace) 173
amphitheater *254*, *256*, 258
Amun, Egyptian sun-god 56, 57, *57*, 58, 62, *63*, *71*
Amurru, Egyptian province *58*, 59
An, sky god 26
Anastasius, Roman emperor 287
Anatolia 40, 72, *74*, 83, 168, 183, 186, 227
  Celtic invasions 183
  early center of farming 16; and metalworking *21*
  source of obsidian 19
  trade 38
  tribal peoples 72
Andronikos of Kyrrhos, astronomer *139*
Angles *283*

Anshan (Zagros mountains) 32
Antigone (Sophocles) *161*
Antigonos Doson, king of Macedon 184
Antigonos Gonatos, king of Macedon 183, 184, *184*
Antiochos I, Seleukid king 184, 185
Antiochos III, Seleukid king 184, 185, 186, 188, *212*, 216
Antiochos IV, Seleukid king 186, 188
Antipater, governor of Macedon 183
Antonius, Marcus *see* Mark Antony
Anubis, Egyptian god *71*
Aphrodite, Greek goddess *125*
Aplahanda, ruler of Carchemish 38
Apollo, Greek god 113, *125*, *127*, *150*, 152, *152*, *153*, 270
Apollonius of Perge, Greek astronomer 191
Apu, Egyptian province *58*, 59
aqueducts 220, *255*, 258
Aquileia (Italy) *212*
Arabia, Roman province 245, 248
Arabs 91, 233, 248, *258*, 262, 289
Aramaeans 76, 78, *80*, 82, 83
Aramaic *80*, *82*, 83, 100, 253
Ararat, Mount 90
Aratama I, Mittanian king 73
Aratos, leader of Achaean league 184
Arcadian league 170
Archaic Greece 124, 131
  art 134–35, *134*, *135*, *152*
Archaic Rome 200, *200*, *201*
Archelaos, Macedonian king 172
arches *254*, *258*
Archimedes, Greek mathematician 190
Ardashir I, Sasanian king 232
Argishti I, Urartian king 85
Argos (Greece) 115, 126, 130, *130*, 143, 149, 154, 156, *157*, 160
Arianism 272, *280*, 286, 287
Aristagoras, tyrant of Miletos 143
Aristarchos of Samos, Greek mathematician 190
Aristophanes, Greek dramatist 166
Aristotle, Greek philosopher 130, 138, 166, *166*, 167, *167*, 168, 175
armor 105, *146*, *147*, *204*, *261*
army 68, 88, 104, 123
  Macedonian 172
  Persian 145
  Spartan 157, 170, 184
  see also hoplites, Roman army, soldiers, warfare
Arpad, Assyrian vassal state 89
Arsaces I, Parthian king 185
art 22, *60*

Archaic Greek 134–35, *134*, *135*, *152*
  Hellenistic 190, *191*
  Minoan *109*, *111*, 112
  Mycenaean *112*, *115*
  Spartan 131
  Sumerian 27
  see also frescoes, friezes, mosaic, painting, sculpture
Art of Love, The (Ovid) 238
Artaxerxes I, king of Persia 101, 102
Artaxerxes II, king of Persia 101, 168, 169, 170, 175, *176*
Artaxerxes III, king of Persia *180*
Artemis, Greek goddess 113, *125*, 274, *274*, 275
Arvad, Phoenician port 82, 84
Aryans 37
Ashkelon, Palestinian state 59
Ashur (Mesopotamia) 38, 39, 76, 78, 83, 89
  god 76
  see also Assyria
Ashur-dan II, Assyrian king *82*, 83
Ashur-sharrat, Assyrian king 89
Ashur-uballit I, Assyrian king 73
Ashurbanipal, Assyrian king 89, 90, 91, *91*, 92
Ashurnasirpal II, Assyrian king *82*, 84, 86, *87*, 93
Asklepios, Greek god of healing 150, *150*
Assyria 38, 39, 40, 59, 72, 74, 76, 77, *80*
  administrative reforms of Tiglath-pileser 88
  empire of Tiglath-pileser and successors 85, 88–91
  end of empire *90*, 92
  expansion, 13th century BC 73, 74, 78
  invades Egypt 90, 91
  overrun by nomads 76
  relations with Babylonia 75, 84–5
  revival, 10th century 83, 84
  Shalmaneser III's campaigns *82*, 85
  treatment of defeated peoples 84
  warfare *105*
  writing 46
Astarte, Near Eastern goddess 27, *125*
astrology *93*
astronomy 190–91
Astyages, king of the Medes 96
Aswan Dam (Egypt) 62
Aten, Egyptian sun disk 58, 59, 60
  Great Temple of 60, *61*
Athene, Greek goddess of wisdom 113, *123*, *125*, *139*, 156
Athens 126, 130, 138, *138*, *139*, *140*, 156, *168*, *184*
  Athenian league 169, *169*, 173
  constitutions 132, 154
  cultural achievements 138, 161, *166*

democracy 133–34, 154–56
  "Long Walls" 138. *168*
  Peisistratid tyranny *130*, 132–3, 138
  Peloponnesian war 157, *157*, 167
  Periclean Athens 138, 156, *156*, 161
  rebuilt by Hadrian 138, 248
  rise of 131–32
  rivalry with Sparta 151, 154
  sacked 118, 138, 148
  social classes 132
  Solon's reforms 132
  see also Acropolis, Parthenon, theater
athletics *see* sport
Athos, Mount *145*
Atreus, treasury of (Mycenae) 115
Atropatene, Persian satrapy 183, 186
Attalos, Macedonian general 175, 176
Attalos I, king of Pergamon *182*, 183, *183*, 185
Attalos III, king of Pergamon 219
Attica (Greece) 119, 120, 132, 133, 138, 160
Attila the Hun 281, *283*, *286*
Augusta Treverorum (Trier) 240, *240*, 270, 278
Augustulus, Romulus, last Roman emperor in west 282
Augustus, first Roman emperor 234, 235, *235*, 238, *238*, *245*, 256, 258, 274, 284
Aurelian, Roman emperor 262, 265
Aurelius, Marcus, Roman emperor 191, 248, *259*, 260
Ausculum (Italy), battle 207
Avaris (Egypt) 53, 112
Avars 288, *288*
Ay Khanoum (Afghanistan) 188, 189, *189*
Aya, Egyptian high-priest 59

B

Baal, Phoenician god 253
Babylon *36*, 38–9, 40, 42, 59, 88, *90*, 94, *94*, *95*
  captured by Alexander the Great 94, 180
  falls to Cyrus the Great 92
  Hanging Gardens 94, *94*
  rebuilt by Nebuchadnessar 92
  sacked by Assyrians 91, 94; and by Hittites 41, 72, 75
  ziggurat 42, 94
  1st Dynasty 37
  2nd Dynasty 76
Babylonia 76, 78, *80*, *82*, 83, 84–5, 86, 88, *90*, 91
  Kassite rulers of 75–6
  neo-Babylonian empire 92, 96
Babylonian language 75
  Map of the World *93*
  writing 46
Bacchus, Roman god of wine 214, *236*

Bactra/Bactria 100, 181, 185, 186, 188, 190
Baecula (Spain), battle 212
Balawat, gates of 82
Bar-rakib, king of Sam'al 88
barbarians *see under individual peoples*
Barbegal (France) 255
barley 16, 19
Beirut (Lebanon) 81
Belisarius, Roman general 287
Bel-shar-usur (Belshazzar), Babylonian ruler 92, 95
Besouchis (Iraq) 277
Bethlehem 270
Bible, The 32, 59, 92, 94, 95
  translation 277
  see also Old Testament
Bythinia, Persian satrapy 183, 226
Black Sea 80, 123, 148
Boeotia (Greece)170
Boeotian league 169, 170, 173
Boghazkoy (Turkey) *see* Hattusas
brass 90
Brennus, Celtic leader 183
bricks 18, 18, 95, 100
Britain 123, 148, 182, 242, 245, 248, 250, 265, 266, 281, 283
  Christianity established 276
  raided by Franks and Saxons 265
bronze 24, 85, 93, 131
  casting 45
  see also sculpture, bronze, weapons
Bronze Age 82
  Aegean 108–19
  Italy 195
Brutus, Marcus Junius, Roman politician 229, 234
Buddhism 188
Buhen (Nubia) 51
building techniques
  pyramids 65
  Roman 254
  use of mudbrick 18
bull
  in Minoan culture 110, 111, 112, 113
  in Mithraic worship 214
Burgundians 281, 282, 283, 286, 287
burials
  Bronze Age Italy 195
  Chatal Huyuk 23
  Egyptian 64
  Jericho 19
  Mycenaean 114, 114, 115, 117
  Roman 200, 200
  Ubaid 21
  Ur 28
  see also tombs
Byblos, Phoenician port 80, 82, 84
Byzantion/Byzantium, Greek trading city , 173, 273, 276

C

Caesar, Julius, Roman dictator 188, 220, 227, 228, 229, 240, 284
  campaigns 228
  murder of 229, 234
  reforms of 229

refounds Carthage 211; Corinth 217
Calah *see* Kalhu
Caligula, Roman emperor 238
Cambyses, Persian king 63, 97
camels 252
Canaan/Canaanites 58, 59, 74, 76, 78, 80, 80
Cannae (Italy), battle 210
Cappadocia, Persian satrapy, later kingdom 226, 245
Capua (Italy) 210
Caracalla, Roman emperor 252, 261
Carchemish (Anatolia) 76, 83, 92
Caria, Persian satrapy 177
Carrhae (Anatolia), battle 228, 232
Carthage (North Africa) 82, 123, 184, 202, 282, 283, 286
  destroyed by Rome 211, 212–13
  see also Punic war, first and second
Carthago Nova (Spain) 210, 212
Carus, Roman emperor 265
Castor, temple of (Rome) 231
Catalaunian Plains (France), battle 283
"Catalog of Ships," Homer's 113, 117
cattle 17, 19
Cato, Roman senator 212, 217, 218
Celts 182, 183, 184, 203, 204, 240, 253, 256
  see also Gauls
Ceres, corn goddess 215
Chaironeia (Greece), battle 172, 173, 175
Chaldeans 76, 82, 82, 83, 85, 88
Chandragupta Maurya, Gangetic ruler 183, 188
Chatal Huyuk (Anatolia) 19, 21, 22–3, 23
China 252
chi rho symbol 270, 276
Christianity 63, 233, 249, 270, 271, 273, 277, 286
  Constantine converted to 270, 272, 272, 273
  at Ephesus 275
  in Rome 278, 278, 279
  spread of 270, 272, 276, 276
  see also monasticism
Christians 253, 267, 280
  persecuted 243, 253, 267, 270, 278
church councils 272, 275, 276
Cicero, Marcus Tullius, Roman writer 214
Cimbri 217, 223, 256
Cimmerians 90
Cimon *see* Kimon
Cisalpine Gaul 207, 210, 229
cities
  first 24, 24
  see also towns
City of God, The (Saint Augustine) 277
city states
  Greek 101, 120–41, 166, 170, 216
  Italian 194, 196
  Mesopotamian 24–47

Phoenician 82
city walls 28, 117
civil service
  Egyptian 50
  Ur, 3rd Dynasty of 34
  see also administration, government
Civilis, Julius, German chieftain 244
Claudius, Appius, Roman senator 219, 220
Claudius, Roman emperor 238, 240, 242
Claudius II, Roman emperor 265
Cleopatra, Egyptian regent 174
Cleopatra VII, queen of Egypt 188, 229, 234
cleruchies 151, 156
Clodius, Roman tribune 228
Clouds, The (Aristophanes) 166
Cnidos (Anatolia), sea battle 169
coinage 96, 126, 151, 188
coins 80, 181, 219, 223, 229, 241, 248
Colosseum (Rome) 256
comedy 163, 166
Commodus, Roman emperor 248, 260
comitia centuriata 198, 199
concilium plebis 202
Confessions (St Augustine) 277
Constantine, Roman emperor 221, 270, 272, 272, 273, 277, 279, 289
Constantine VII, Roman emperor 271
Constantinople 272, 273, 273, 276, 288
Constantius, tetrarch 266, 270
Constantius II, Roman emperor 272, 276, 280
copper 24, 36, 82, 118
  smelting 19, 21, 45
  see also weapons, copper
Corcyrans 160
Corfinium (Italy) 223
Corinth (Greece) 126, 126, 127, 130, 156, 157, 157, 160, 170, 184, 217
  destroyed by Romans 126, 185, 217, 217
Corinthian league 175, 176, 183
Corinthian war 168
corn dole 218, 226, 228
Corsica 123, 210
corvus 209
Crassus, Roman tribune 226, 227, 228
Cremona (Italy), battles 244
Crete 109, 119
  Minoan 108, 109
  Mycenaean 117
Croesus, king of Lydia 96, 97
Ctesiphon, Parthian capital 248, 277
Cumae (Italy) 122
Cunaxa (Persia), battle 101, 168, 176
Cybele, Anatolian mother-goddess 189, 191, 214, 274
Cycladic islands 117, 152
Cyprus 82, 117, 121, 135, 151, 183
Cyrus the Great, Achaemenid king of Persia 81, 92, 96

conquests 96, 142
death of 97
Cyrus the Younger, satrap of Sardis 168, 176

D

Dacia 245, 245, 247, 248
Dahshur (Egypt) 66
Damascus (Syria) 84, 89, 289
Danube, river 238, 248, 250, 251, 260, 265, 268, 283
Darius I (the Great), Achaemenid king of Persia 95, 100, 102, 103, 172
  campaigns 97, 100, 142, 143, 145
  empire 98–9, 233
Darius II, Achaemenid king of Persia 101, 168
Darius III, Achaemenid king of Persia 177, 177, 180
dark age
  Aegean118–19, 119, 121
  Near East 41, 76, 120
Datis, Persian commander 143, 144, 145
David, Hebrew king 78, 78, 79, 80
debt-bondage, early Rome 202
Decelea (Greece) 161
Decius, Roman emperor 275
Delian league 151, 156, 157, 160, 161
Delos (Cyclades) 151
Delphi (Greece) 152, 152, 153, 173, 183
  oracle of 96, 133, 145, 152, 153
Demeter, Greek corn goddess 125, 191
Demetrias (Thessaly) 186
Demetrios, king of Macedon 183
democracy, in Athens 133–4, 167
Demosthenes, Athenian statesman 173, 175, 183
Demotic Egyptian 253
Dendara (Egypt) 63, 70
Der (Iraq) 89
Diadochi, wars of the 182–83, 184
Diana, Roman moon goddess 215
Diocletian, Roman emperor 262, 265, 266, 269, 271, 272, 287, 289
  death of 270
  reforms 266, 266, 267, 270
  retirement 270, 271
Diodotos, Bactrian king 185
Dionysios (tyrant of Syracuse) 168
Dionysius *see* Dionysos
Dionysos, Greek god of wine 133, 152, 158, 162, 191, 214, 236
  festival 161, 162, 166
Diyala river (Iraq) 76
Djoser, Egyptian king 52, 64
Dodona (Greece), theater at 164
Domitian, Roman emperor 245
Dorians 115, 116, 119, 121, 123, 124, 127
Drakon, Athenian lawgiver 132

drama 133, 161, 161, 162, 162, 166, 217
Drusus, Livius, Roman tribune 223
Dumuzi, legendary king of Uruk 26
Dur-Kurigalzu (Iraq), ziggurat 77, 88
Dur-Sharrukin (Iraq), ziggurat 43, 91

E

Eannatum, king of Lagash 29
Early Dynastic period
  Egypt 48, 49–50
  Mesopotamia 24, 28–9, 30
ebony 118
Edessa (Anatolia) 248, 264
Edfu (Egypt) 70
Edict of Milan 270
Edom/Edomites 78, 88
Egypt 48–71, 89, 151, 183
  administration 50
  Assyrian invasions 90, 91
  conquered by Alexander the Great 63, 177, 180
  Early Dynastic period 48, 49–50
  First Intermediate period 53, 56
  Hittite wars 59, 69, 74
  Hyksos invasions 53, 53, 54
  Jews in 188
  Late Period 63, 68, 70
  in Levant 53, 53, 54, 55, 58, 59, 73, 74, 78, 80, 92
  Middle Kingdom 53, 54, 66, 68
  monasticism in 280
  New Kingdom 54–5, 56, 62, 78
  Nile, river 48, 48, 49, 50, 52
  Nubian kings 62, 63, 63, 91
  Old Kingdom, 50–3, 51, 65, 66, 68
  Persian rule 63, 101
  Predynastic period 48, 49
  Ptolemaic kings 186, 187 188, 191
  pyramids 42, 52, 53, 54, 64, 64, 65, 66
  relations with Kassites 76
  religion 51, 57, 58, 59, 70, 71
  Romans in 187, 188, 234, 244
  Second Intermediate period 53
  technology 54
  theocratic kingship 50, 53
  Third Intermediate period 56, 62, 63
  tombs 50, 51, 52
  trade 24, 48, 55, 55, 56, 250
  warfare 68, 69, 74
  weapons 69
  writing 49, 50
  3rd Dynasty 50
  4th Dynasty 50
  5th Dynasty 52
  11th Dynasty 52, 56
  12th Dynasty 48, 53, 56, 66
  13th Dynasty 53
  17th Dynasty 53
  18th Dynasty 56, 72
  19th Dynasty 59
  20th Dynasty 56
  see also names of individual kings and pharaohs

einkorn 16, 19
Ekallatum, fortress (Iraq) 38
El-'Amarna *see* Akhetaten
el-Kharga oasis (Egypt) 49
Elam/Elamites 29, *33*, 34, 37, 75, 76, *76*, 89, *90*, 91, 92
electrum 31
elephants 183, 186, *188*, 207
Eleusis (Greece) 138
Elgin, Lord, British diplomat *140*
Elis (Greece) *157*, 160, 170
emmer wheat 16, 19
Enheduanna, Sumerian priestess 32
Epaminondas, Theban general 170, 172
Ephesus (Anatolia) 274–75, *275*
Ephiltes, Athenian politician 155
Epicureans 191
Epicurus, Greek philosopher *167*
Epidauros (Greece) *150*
Eratosthenes, Greek astronomer 190
Eretria (Euboea) 143
Eridu (Iraq) 20–1, 24, 42, *44*
Esarhaddon, Assyrian king *90*, 91
Eshnunna (Iraq) 38, 39
Etemenanki ziggurat (Babylon) 94
Etruria (Italy) 196, 210
Etruscans 123, *148*, 194, 196, *196*, *197*, *202*, 204, 207
language 194, 196
Etruscan league 196
Euboea 119, 122, 157
Euclid, Greek mathematician 190
Eugippius, late Roman historian 283
Eumenes, governor of Pergamon 185
eunuchs 88
Euphrates, river 20, *24*, 30, *84*
Euripedes, Greek mathematician 166, 172
Eusebius, Christian historian *272*
Evans, Sir Arthur, excavator of Knossos 108, 110, *110*
Exekias, Athenian vase painter *158*

F

Faiyum (Egypt) 48, *71*
farming 19, 22, 36
    Anatolia 16
    birth of *16–7*
    Crete 109
    domestication of animals 17, 19
    domestication of crops 18, 19
    Indus valley civilization 36
    Italy 218
    Nile 48, *48*
    olive 253
    Roman empire 250
    wild cereals 16, *17*
    wild goats 16, *17*
    wild sheep 16, *17*
    wild cattle *17*
    see also names of individual crops
flax 19

Florence (Italy) 212
Fertile Crescent 16, *17*, 19
food surpluses 24, *27*
Forum (Rome) 200, *214*, *231*, 258
Forum Boarium (Rome) *201*, 220
Frankish confederation 256
Franks 261, 265, *265*, 281, 282, *283*, 287, *287*
frescoes *108*, *110*, *236*, *240*
frontiers, Roman empire 238, 248, 250, 256, 260, 261, 267, 268, *268*, 269, 276, *282*, 286

G

Gades (Cadiz, Spain) 82, 210
Galatia (Anatolia) 238
Galba, Roman emperor 243
Galerius, Roman emperor 266, 267, 270
Gallienus, Roman emperor 261, *264*, 265, 272
Gaugamela (Persia), battle *177*, 180
Gaul 123, *203*, 228, *228*, 251, 261, 265, *265*, 280, *286*
    Germanic invasions *265*, 281, 282, *282*, 287
    rebels against Rome 244, 266
    Roman province 240, *240*, *241*
Gauls *203*, 210, 212
    see also Celts
Gaza 62, 76, 88, 89, 180
Ge, Greek earth-mother goddess *153*
geometry 190
Germans *223*, 256, 260, *264*, 281, *282*
    invasions 280–81, *282*, *283*, *286*
    migrations 260, *261*, *264*, 265
    successor kingdoms 286–87, *287*
    see also individual peoples and tribes
Germany 248, *269*
Gilgamesh, Sumerian epic hero 26
Giza (Egypt) 52, *66*
Girsu (Iraq) 29, *33*, *36*
glass *45*, 118, *135*, *251*
glazed brick *95*, *100*
goats 19
gold 24, *86*, *139*
    casting *45*
    mines 142, 151, *152*, 173
gods 267, 275
    Egyptian *71*
    Greek 125
    Roman 214, *215*, *255*
    see also individual names of gods, and religion
goddesses *23*, *108*, *111*, *112*, *125*, *215*, *274*
    see also individual names of goddesses
Gordion (Turkey), Phrygian capital 90
Gorgon, mythological creature *135*, *150*
Gortyn (Crete) *124*
Goths *261*, 265, 267
government
    Athenian 131, 133–34, *139*
    Egyptian 50

Hellenistic 190
    Mycenaean 117
    Roman 198, 199, 202–3, 216, 218, 238, 242, 260, 267, 287
    tyrannies 126, *127*
    see also administration, civil service *and* democracy
Gracchus, Gaius, Roman politician 219, 222
Gracchus, Tiberius, Roman politician 218, *218*, 222
grain *154*, *218*, 248, 250, 282
    see also names of individual grains
Gratian, Roman emperor 277, *280*
Greece and Greek world 119
    Archaic 124, 131, *134*, 135
    architecture *160*
    army 145
    citizenship 170
    city states 101, 120–41, *166*, 170
    Classical age 142–71
    colonies 120, 121, *121*, 122, 123, 126
    culture 124, 126, *136*, *154*
    dark age 118, 119, *119*, 124
    exploration and travel *148–9*
    Hellenistic age 172–91
    language 113, 119, *119*, 124, 182, 253, *253*
    law 124, *124*
    Mycenaean 113, *113*, 117
    philosophers 166–68
    poets *166–67*
    population growth 120, *121*
    pottery 126, 132, *134*, 158
    religion 125, *150*, 152, 161
    Roman conquest of 216, 217
    soldiers 146, *147; and see* hoplites
    sport 136, *136*, *137*
    theater 140, 153, 162, *162*, *163*
    trade *80*, 120, 123, *126*, *148*, *154*
    Visigoths in 281
    wars with Persia 100, 101, 142–51, *144*
    writing 124
    see also individual city states, and Dorians, Ionians, Macedon
groma 255
Gudea, ruler of Lagash *33*
Gungunum, ruler of Larsa 37

H

Hades *150*, 174
Hadrian, Roman emperor 138, 232, *245*, 248, 252, 253, 256, 274
Hadrian's Wall 268, *268*
Halab *see* Yamhad
Halaf culture 19, *21*
Haldi, Urartian war god 85, 90
Halikarnassos (Anatolia) 177
Hama, Assyrian vassal state 89
Hamadan (Iran) 96, 100
Hamazi (Zagros mountains) 29
Hammurabi, king of Babylon 34, 38, 41, 72, 75, 94
    conquests 38, 39
    law code 39–40
Hanging Gardens of Babylon 94, *94*
Hannibal, Carthaginian general

210, *210*, *211*, 212, *212*, 216
Hanno, Phoenician sailor *148*
Harappa (Pakistan) *34*, 36, 37
Haremhab, Egyptian general *55*, *56*, 59
Harran (Turkey) 92
Hasdrubal, Carthaginian general 212
Hassuna culture 19, 20
Hathor, Egyptian goddess *56*, 70, *71*
Hatti, Hittite weather god 75
Hattusas (Boghazkoy, Turkey), Hittite capital 72, 73, 74, *75*, 76, 96
Hattusilis I, Hittite king 72
Hattusilis II, Hittite king 74
Hebrews/Hebrew kingdoms 59, 76, 78–81
    see also Jews
Hector, legendary Trojan hero 124
Heiro, king of Syracuse 209
Helena, mother of Constantine 270
Heliopolis (Egypt) 71
Hellenistic Age 172–91
    civilization 190–91
Hera, Greek mother goddess *123*, *124*, *128*
Heraclea (Italy), battle 207
Heracleitus, Greek philosopher *166*
Heracles (Roman, Hercules) legendary hero 175, *189*, 260, 267
Heraclius, first Byzantine emperor 288, 289
Herakleitos *see* Heracleitus
Herakles *see* Heracles
Herculaneum (Italy) *236*, *237*
Herihor, Egyptian general 62
Hermes, Greek messenger god 125, *125*
Herod, king of Judaea 243
Herodes Atticus, public benefactor of Athens *140*
Herodotus, Greek historian 48, 96, *99*, 142, 143, *148*, 166
Herophilos of Chalkedon, Greek physician *150*
Hesiod, Greek poet 148
Hipparchus, Athenian tyrant 133
Hippias, Athenian tyrant 133, 143
Hippocrates, Greek physician 150
Hiram, king of Tyre 82
History of the Peloponnesian War (Thucydides) 160
Hittites/Hittite empire 40–1, 55, *55*, 59, 69, 72, 73–4, *74*, 75, 83
Homer, Archaic Greek poet 114, 118, 133, *148*, 277
    Iliad 108, *113*, 117, *118* 119, 124
Honorius, Roman emperor 281
hoplites 124, 126, 127, 144, 146, *147*, 155, 172, *176*
Horace (Quintus Horatius Flaccus), Roman poet 238, 277
horse 54, 68, 76, 90, *261*
    races *136*
Horus, Egyptian sky god 48,

50, *56*, 70, 71
Hostilius, Tullus, king of Rome 198
Huns 280, 281, *282*, *283*, 288
hunter–gatherers 16, 19
hunting *23*, *54*, *232*
Hurrians 40, 72, 76
Hyksos 53, *53*, 54, 55, 68

I

Ibbi-Sin, king of Ur 34, 37
ice age 16, *17*
Idrimi, king of Alalah 72
Iliad (Homer) 108, *113*, 117, *118* 119, 124
Ilipa (Spain), battle 212
Illyria/Illyrians 172, 184, 265, 270
Imhotep, Egyptian civil servant 52
Inanna, Sumerian love goddess 26, *27*, 125
India 188, *252*
Indus valley 34, 36, 96, 97, 181, 183, 188
    civilization 34–7, *34*, *35*
Ionia/Ionians 119, 121, 123, 124, 138, 142, 149, 151
Ipsos (Turkey), battle 183, *184*, *188*
Ireland *182*
iron *45*, 85, 105, *116*, 119
Iron Age 82, *195*, 200
irrigation 44
    Ay Khanoum 189
    canals 20, *44*, 86
    Chatal Huyuk 22
    Indus valley civilization 36
    Mesopotamia 19, 20, *21*
Ishbi-Erra, ruler of Isin 34, 37, 38
Ishme-Dagan, king of Ashur 38
Ishpuini I, Urartian king 85
Ishtar, Akkadian goddess *27*, 86, *91*
Isin (Iraq) 34, *36*, 37, 38, 76
Isis, Egyptian goddess, object of mystery cult *71*, 188, 191, *215*, 277
Islam 233, 289
Israel 80, 84, 88
Issos (Anatolia), battle 177
Isthmian games 136, *137*
Italia, rebel state *223*
Italic people 194
Italy 117, 121, 204
    early 194
    farming 218
    languages *194*
    Ostrogothic kingdom *287*, *288*
    Roman conquest and colonization of 194–201, *205*, 206–7, *206–7*
Itjtawy (Egypt) 56, *66*
ivory *86*, *87*, *111*, 118, *139*, *173*, *201*

J

Jebusites 80
Jemdet Nasr period, Mesopotamia 24
Jericho (Jordan) 18, *18–19*, 19
Jerusalem 59, 62, 78, 80, 186, *242*, 243, 244, 248

Holy Sepulcher 270
jewelry 28, 118
  gold *86*
Jews 244, *249*
  Assyrian deportations 92
  in Babylon 81
  in Egypt 81, 188
  religion 253
  revolts against Rome *243*,
  244, 248, 253
  Roman deportations 248, *249*
Jovian, Roman emperor 277,
  277
Judaea, Roman province (later
  kingdom) *242*, 244, 248, *249*
Judah, Hebrew kingdom 80,
  88, 92
Judas Maccabaeus, Jewish
  leader 186
Jugurtha, king of Numidia 223
Julian, Roman emperor 276,
  277
Julianus, Didius, Roman
  emperor 260
Jupiter, chief god of Romans
  201, 214, *215*, 248, 253, 267
Justin, Roman emperor 287
Justinian, Roman emperor *139*,
  284, 287–88, *288*, 289
Jutes *283*

K

Ka'aper, Egyptian priest *51*
Kalhu (Tell Nimrud, Iraq) *46*,
  84, 86, *86–7*, *88*, *93*, 104
Kallias, treaty of 151
Kallikrates, Athenian architect
  138
Karnak, temple (Thebes) 56,
  56, *57*, 62, 74
Kas (Anatolia), shipwreck 118
Kashta, Nubian king 62
Kaskas 72, 73, 76
Kassandros, Macedonian king
  183
Kassites 41, 75
  kudurrus *76*
  rulers of Babylon 74, 75–6,
  76
Kea (Cyclades)112
Khania (Crete) *108*, 112
Khendjer, Egyptian king 53
Khephren, Egyptian king 52,
  66
Khnum, Egyptian creator god
  71
Khosrau II, Sasanian king 233,
  288
Khufu, Egyptian king 52, *66*
Kimon, Athenian leader 138,
  151, 154, 156
King's Peace (Persian–Greek
  treaty) 169, 170
Kinyps (Libya), Spartan colony
  123
Kish, Mesopotamian kingdom
  29, *46*
Kition (Cyprus) 82
Klearchos, Greek philosopher
  189
Kleisthenes, Athenian lawgiver
  133, 134, 154
Kleomenes III, Spartan king
  184
Knossos (Crete) 108, *108*,
  109, 110, *110*, *111*, 112,
  113

Konon, Athenian general *168*,
  169
Koroneia (Greece), battle
Kot Diji (Indus valley) 36
Kurigalzu II, Babylonian king
  76
Kush, Upper Nubian kingdom
  53, 55
Kylon, Athenian leader 131
Kynoskephalai (Thessaly),
  battle *184*, 185, 213
Kynouria (Greece) 130
Kypselids 126. *158*
Kypselos, tyrant of Corinth
  126, *126*
Kythera (island), 112

L

Lachish, Egyptian vassal state
  59, *104*, *105*
Laconia (Greece) 127, *130*, 154
Lagash, city state 29, 32, 33, *33*,
  104
*Lamentation over the Destruction
  of Ur, The* 34
land reforms, Gracchan 218,
  219, *219*, 222
languages
  Akkadian 28
  Aramaic *80*, *82*, 83, 100, 253
  Celtic 183, 253
  Etruscan 194, 196
  Greek 113, 119, *119*, 124,
  182, 253, *253*
  of Italy *194*
  Latin *194*, 253, *253*, 277, 287
  of Roman empire 253, *253*
  Sumerian 28, 32, 75
  Urartian 85
lapis lazuli 76, *114*
Lares, ancestral deities 214
Larsa, city state *36*, 37, 38, 40
Latial culture *199*
Latin language *194*, 253, *253*,
  277, 287
Latin league *198*
Latin rebellion *204*
Latin war 204
Latium *194*, 195, 198, *198*, *202*,
  204
Laurion (Greece) *142*, 145
laws and law codes
  Archaic Greek 124, *124*
  Athenian 132
  Hammurabi 39–40
  Macedonian 176
  Roman 202, *203*, 238, 253,
  287
  Ur, 3rd Dynasty of 34
Layard, Austen Henry,
  excavator of Kalhu 86, *87*
lead smelting 19
Lefkandi (Euboea) *116*, 118
legion/legionaries 185, 223, 261
  247
Leonidas, Spartan king *144*,
  148
Lepidus, Roman general 234
Leptis Magna (Libya) 282, 284,
  284
Lesbos *116*, *159*
Leuktra (Greece), battle 170
Levant 48, 59
  Assyrian rule 84
  Egyptian influence 53, *53*, 55
  58
  farming 19

migrations 76
  Mittani influence 72
Libya 62, 109, 284
  language 253
Licinius, Roman emperor 270
Life of St Severinus (Eugippius)
  283
Livy (Titus Livius), Roman
  historian 194, 198, 200, 238
Longinus, Gaius Cassius
  (Cassius), Roman politican
  229, 234
Lucanians 122, *204*, 207
Lugalzagesi, king of Umma 32
Luxor (Egypt) *56*, 57
Lycurgus *see* Lykourgos
Lydia 96, 142, 177
Lykourgos, Spartan lawgiver
  130
Lysandros, Spartan general 168
Lysimachos, Diadochi ruler of
  Thrace 183, *184*
Lysistrata (Aristophanes) 166

M

Macedon 101, 143, *169*, 172,
  172, 183, 213, 216
  conquers Greece 173, 175,
  176
  Philip II *172*, 173
  relations with Rome 213,
  216–17
  royal tombs 174, *174*, *175*
  wars of the Diadochi
  183–185, *184*
  see also Alexander the Great
Macedonia, Roman province
  185, 217, 223
Magnesia (Thessaly), battle
  184, 186, 216
Mallia (Crete) *108*, 112
Manishtushu, king of Agade 32
Mannea, attacked by Assyria 90
Mantinea (Greece) *157*, 160,
  170
Map of the World, Babylonian
  93
Marathon (Greece), battle 100,
  143–45
Marcius, Ancus, legendary king
  of Rome 198
Marcomanni 260
Mardonios, Persian general
  143, 145, *145*, 148, 149
Marduk, Babylonian god 42,
  92, 94, *94*, 96
Marduk-apla-iddina II,
  Babylonian king 89
Marduk-zakir-shumi,
  Babylonian king 85
Mari, Mesopotamian city state
  29, 38, 41, *95*
Marius, Gaius, Roman general
  and consul 223, 226, *226*
Mark Antony, Roman triumvir
  234
Masada, Jewish fortress *243*,
  244
Massalia (Marseille) 123, 223
Massinissa, Numidian king
  212, 213
mastabas 50, *64*, *66*
mathematics 93, *93*, 124, 190
Maurice, Roman emperor 288
Maxentius, Roman Augustus
  221, 270
Maximian, Roman Augustus

266, 267, 270
Maximinus, Roman Augustus
  270
Maximus, Fabius, Roman
  general 212
Medes 83, 88, *90*, 92, 96
medicine *93*, 150, *150*
Mediolanum (Milan) 266, 278,
  280
Meditations (Marcus Aurelius)
  191
Mediterranean Sea
  trade 120, *251*, 262
Megara (Greece) 126, 131, 156,
  160, 170
Megiddo, Palestinian state 59
Mehrgarh (Baluchistan) 34
Melos (Cyclades) 112
Meluhha (probable Indus
  valley) 34
Memnon of Rhodes, Greek
  mercenary 176
Memphis (Egypt) 50, *66*, *71*,
  100, 180
Menander, Greek dramatist
  166
Menander, Bactrian king 188
Mentuhotpe, Egyptian king 53
Menua, Urartian king 85
Mesilim, king of Kish 29
Meskalamdug, king of Ur *31*
Mesopotamia 19–21, 24, 40,
  41, 44, 97, *245*
  Early Dynastic period 28–29,
  32
  irrigation 19, 20, *21*
  mathematics 93
  technology 44, *45*
  trade 24, 34, 36
  *see also individual city states and
  kingdoms, and especially* Akkad,
  Ashur, Assyria, Babylon,
  Sumer, Ur, Uruk
Messana (Sicily) 209, *209*
Messenia (Greece) 127, 130,
  130, 154, 156, *157*, 170
metalworking 21, *21*, 85, *85*
Methone (Macedon), battle
  173, 174
Midas, Phrygian king 90
migrations
  Aryans 37
  Celts *182*, *203*, 204, 256
  Dorians *116*, 119
  Germans 223, 256, 260, *260*,
  261, *264*, *265*, 280–81, *282*,
  283
  Hittites 72
  Huns 280, *282*
  Ionians *116*, 119
  Palestinians 53
  Persians 92
  Phrygians 76
  Sea Peoples 62, 76, *116*, 118
Miletos (Anatolia) 117, 126,
  143, 177
Milindapanho (Buddhist
  text)188
Miltiades, Athenian general
  144
Milvian Bridge (Rome), battle
  221, 270
Minerva, Roman goddess of
  wisdom *201*
Minoan civilization *108*, 109,
  112–13
  arts *109*, *111*, 112
  colonies 112

frescoes *108*
  religion *111*, 113
  trade 112
Minos, legendary king of Crete
  109, *110*, *111*, 112, 113
Mithradates I, Parthian king
  186
Mithraism *214*, *277*
Mithridates VI, king of Pontus
  217, 226, 227, 232
Mittani, Near Eastern empire
  55, *55*, 59, 72–3
Moab/Moabites 78, *78*, 88
Mohenjo–Daro (Pakistan) *34*,
  36, 37
monasticism 277, 280, *280*
Montu, Theban god 57, *57*
Mucianus, Roman general 244
Mucianus Traianus, Roman
  general 265
mudbricks 18
mummification 70, *71*
Munda (Spain), battle 229
Mursilis, Hittite king 41, 72
Musasir (Iraq) 85, 90
Mushki, Anatolian tribal
  people 76
Mut, Theban god 57, *57*
Muwatallis II, Hittite king 59,
  74
Mycenae (Greece) 108,
  109,113, 114–15, *114*, *115*,
  118
Mycenaean Greece *108*, 110,
  113, 114, *114*, 115, 117–18
  art *112*, *115*
  kingdoms *113*
  trade *108*, *114* 117, 118
Mykale (Anatolia) sea battle
  149
Mytilene (Lesbos) 126

N

Nabataea, Arab kingdom 190
Nabonidus, Babylonian king
  92, 96, 97
Nabopolassar, Babylonian king
  92, 94
Nabu-mukin-zeri, Babylonian
  king 88
Nabu-Nasir, Babylonian king
  88
Nagasena, Buddhist monk 188
Nanna, Sumerian moon god
  30, *31*, 32
Napata (Nubia) *55*, 62, *63*
Naqada culture *48*
Naram–Sin, king of Agade *28*,
  32–3
Narmer, Egyptian king *48*, 49,
  50
Narses, Roman general 288
Natufians 16, 18
Naukratis (Egypt), 123
naval warfare 126, *157*, 188,
  234
Naxos (Cyclades) 130, 143,
  151, 170
  sphinx *153*
Neapolis (Naples) 207
Nebuchadnezzer I, Babylonian
  king 76, 80, 92, 94
Nebuchadnezzer II,
  Babylonian king *94*, *95*
Necho II, Egyptian pharaoh
  92, 148
Nedao, battle 281

Nefertiti, Egyptian queen *60*, *61*
Neolithic period 16–23
Neoplatonism 277, 280
Nepos, Julius, Roman emperor 271, 282, *286*
Nero, Roman emperor 242–43, 244, 245, 258, *278*
Nerva, Roman emperor 245
"Nestor, Cup of" *115*
Nestorianism 275
Nicaea (Anatolia) 272
Nicomedia (Anatolia) 266
Niger, Pescennius, claimant Roman emperor 261
Nile, river 48, *48*, 49, 50, 52, *63*
Nineveh *28*, 39, 76, 78, 83, *89*, 92, *104*
  Sasanian army defeated 233, 289
  Sennacherib's capital 91, *91*
Nippur (Iraq) 32, 42
nomads 78, *78*, 83, 120, 186, 188, 284
Noreia (Italy), battle 223
Novaesium (Neuss) *247*
Nubia *48*, 56, *62*, *187*, 188
  Egyptian influence *51*, *52*, 62
  Lower 53, 55
  Upper 62
Nubian dynasty (Egypt) 62, 63, *63*, 91

O

obsidian 19, 22
Octavian *see* Augustus
Odenathus, king of Palmyra 264
Odoacer, king of Italy 282, 286
Odyssey (Homer) *118*, 119
Oedipus the King (Sophokles) 161
Old Babylonian period 37
Old Testament 81, 262
  see also Bible, The
olive 109, 253, 284
Olympias, mother of Alexander the Great 175
Olympic games 124, 128, 136, *136*, *137*
Olympos, Mount 125
Olynthos (Macedonia) 173
Oresteia (Sophokles) 161
Orestes, Roman general 282
Osiris, Egyptian god 71
Ostia (Italy)*198*, *218*, 245
ostracism 134, 154, 155, 160
Ostrogoths 280, *282*, 286, 287, 288, *288*
Otho, Roman emperor 243, 244
Ovid (Publius Ovidius Naso), Roman poet 238
Oxus, river *189*

P

Pachomius, monk 277
Paestum (Italy) 122, *122*, *123*, 204
paganism
  restored by Julian 276–277
painting 166, 204
  Akhetaten *61*
  frescoes *108*, *110*, 236, *240*
  frieze *56*, *152*, *158*

Lucanians 122, *204*
Greek vase *136*, 158, *158*, *159*, *161*
  wall *23*, 166, 174, *197*
Palatine hill (Rome) 200, *200*
Palestine 62, 63, 91, 183, 227, 289
  conquered by Pompey 227
  Egyptian expansion into 55, 92, *187*, 188
  migration from 53, *53*
Paleolithic period 16
Palestrina (Italy) *199*
Palmyra 262, *262*, *263*, 264, *264*, *269*
Panathenaic games *137*
Pantheon (Rome) *259*
Paphlagonia, Persian satrapy 183
Parmenion, Macedonian general 181
Parrattarna, Mittanian king 72
Parthenon (Athens) 133, *139*, *140*, 156, *160*, 161
Parthia 185, 186, 190, 232
  wars with Rome 228, 232, *232*, 248, 258,
Pasargadae (Iran), Persian capital 96, 100
Pataliputra (India) 188
Pausanias, Spartan general *144*, 149
Peiraeus (Greece) 131, 138, *168*
Peisistradids *130*, 132–3, 138
Peisistratos, Athenian tyrant 161, 162
Pella, Macedonian capital 172
Peleset *see* Philistines
Peloponnesian war 101, 156–57, *157*, 160–61, 167, 168
Penates, Roman household god 214
Pentelikon, Mount (Greece) 133
Perdiccas I, Macedonian king 172
Perdiccas, Macedonian regent 182
Pergamon (Anatolia) *183*, 185, 186, 190, *191*, 213, 216
Pericles, Athenian statesman 138, 156, *156*, 160, 161
Persepolis (Iran), Achaemenid capital *99*, 100, 102, *103*, 180
Perseus, son of Philip of Macedon 185, 216
Persian empire 83, 142, *143*
  administration 100–101
  conquered by Alexander the Great 176–77, *176*
  conquers Egypt 63
  of Cyrus the Great 96–97. *96*
  of Darius 97–100, *99*
  wars against Greeks 97, 100, 142, 143–51, *143*, *144*, 149, *169*
  see also Persepolis, Parthia, Sasanians
Pertinax, Roman emperor 260
Petra (Jordan) 190
Phaistos (Crete) *108*, 112
phalanx 146, 147, *185*
pharaohs 55, 68, 76
  see also individual names
Pharsalus (Greece), battle 229
Pheidon, tyrant of Argos 126

Phidias, Athenian sculptor *129*, *139*, 156
Philip II, king of Macedon 101, 170, 172, *172*, 173, *173*
  tomb 174, *174*, *175*
Philip V, king of Macedon 184, 212, 213
Philippi (Macedon), battle 234
Philistines 62, 76, 78, 80
philosophy, Greek 191
  see also individual philosophers
Philotas, Macedonian general 181
Phocas, Roman emperor 288
Phoenicia/Phoenicians 76, *82*, 92, 124
  conquered by Alexander the Great 177, 180
  conquered by Assyria 80
  colonies 81–82, 123
  trade *80–1*, 81, 82, 87, *116*
Phrygia/Phrygians 76, 83, 90, 177
  language 253
Pi-Ri'amseses (Egypt) 62
Pictor, Q. Fabius, Roman historian 194
pigs 19
Pindar, Greek poet *166*
Pisistratus *see* Peisistratos
Pius, Antonius, Roman emperor 248
Piye, Nubian king of Egypt 63, *63*
Plataea (Greece), battle 100, 144, *144*, 149
Plato, Greek philosopher 130, 138, 166, 167, *167*, 168
Plautus, Roman dramatist 217
Pliny the Elder, Roman naturalist 236
Pliny the Younger, Roman writer 236
plow 20, 44
Polybius, Greek historian *202*
Pompeii (Italy) *177*, 227, 236, *236*, 237
Pompey (Gnaeus Pompeius Magnus) Roman soldier and triumvir 220, *221*, 226, 227–28, *228*, 229
Pompilius, Numa, legendary king of Rome 198
Pont du Gard (France) *238*
Pontus, Asian kingdom 217, 226
Porchester castle (Britain) *265*
Poseidon, Greek god of the sea 113, *125*
Poseidonia *see* Paestum
Postumus, Gallic usurper 264
Potidaea (Greece), attacked by Athens 160
pottery
  decoration 158, *158*, *159*
  early 16,19, 21, *21*
  trade *21*, 44, 118, 123, 248
  vases *134*, 136, *137*, 158, *158*, *159*
Praeneste (Italy) *191*, *202*, 227
praetorian guard 238, 243
priestesses *31*, 32, 111
priests 28
  Ashur 76
  Egyptian *51*, 57
  see also Theban high-priests
Primus, Antonius, Roman general 244

Probus, Roman emperor 265
Protagoras of Abdera, Greek philosopher 166
provocatio, *203*
Psammetichus, Egyptian pharaoh 91
Ptah, Egyptian god 70
Pteria (Hattusas) *75*, 96
Ptolemy Keraunos, Macedonian king 183
Ptolemy I, king of Egypt 183, *183*
Ptolemy II, king of Egypt 184, *187*
Ptolemy IV Philopater, king of Egypt 188
Ptolemy V, king of Egypt 186, 188
Ptolemy XIV, king of Egypt 229
Punic war, first 209–10, *209*, 213
Punic war, second 184, *184*, 210–12, *210*
Pydna (Macedon), battle 185, 216
Pylos (Greece) *116*, 117, 118, 119
pyramids 42, 52, 53, 54, 64, *64*, *65*, 66
  Abusir *64*
  building methods *65*
  Giza 50, 52, *66*
  Saqqara 52
  step pyramid *64–5*
Pyrgi, Etruscan port 209
Pyrrhus, king of Epirus *206*, 207, 209, 213

Q

Qadesh (Syria), battle 55, 59, *69*, 74
Qargar (Syria), battle 84
quinquereme 209

R

Ra, Egyptian sun god 50, 52, 58, 64, 70, 71
Ramses II, Egyptian pharaoh 55, 59, 62, *62*
  campaigns 59, *69*, 74
Ramses III, Egyptian pharaoh 62
Ramses XI, Egyptian pharaoh 62
Raphia (Rafa, Israel), battle 185
Ravenna (Italy) 281, 286, 287, *287*, 288
Regillus, Lake (Italy), battle 203
Rehoboam, Hebrew king 80
religion 24, 28, 58, 286
  afterlife, beliefs in 52, 53, *54*, 64, *215*, 274
  Babylonian 92
  cults *189*, 191, *214*, *215*, 236, 274, 277
  Egyptian 50, 51, 53, 58, 59, 60,70, 71
  Greek 125, *150*, 152, 161
  Hittite 75
  Minoan *110*, *111*, 113
  Mycenaean 113
  Roman 208, 214, *214*, *215*, 253
  Sasanian 233

see also Christianity, gods, goddesses, Jews
Republic, The (Plato) 167
Rhine, river *240*, 250, *251*, 256, 268, 281, *282*, 287
Rhodes 112, 119, *135*, 186, 213, 216
Ricimer, general 283
Rim-Sin, king of Larsa 38
Rim-Sin II, king of Larsa 40
Rimush, king of Agade 32
roads
  building methods 224
  military 268, *268*, 269
  Persian empire 100
  Roman *221*, 224, *224*, *225*, 250, *251*
3rd Dynasty of Ur 34
Roman army 198, 218, *219*, 224, 235, 238, *245*, 246, *246*, *247*, 256
  demoralization of 283
  forts and fortifications *247*, *265*, 268, *268*, 269
  reformed by Diocletian 267; by Gallienus 264, 265, 272; by Marius 223
  reliance on mercenaries 280
  political power of 238, 242, 243, 244
  praetorian guard 238, 243
  under Constantine 272
  weapons 207, 223, 246, 247
  see also frontiers *and* legion/legionaries
Roman state
  and Carthage 82, 184, *202*, 211, 212–13; *see also* Punic wars
  Christianity, spread of 270, 271, 273, 276, *276*, 277, 280, *280*
  citizenship 170, 198, *203*, *206*, 222, 223, 240, 246, 252
  civil wars 226, 229, 234, 242, *242*
  colonies 203, 204, *204*, 212, *212*, 220, 227
  constitution 199, 202–203, 238
  conquest of Italy 204, 206–207
  consuls 199, *221*
  corruption 218
  destruction of Corinth 185, 217, *217*
  diocesan system 287
  early history of 194–297
  economy 248, 250–52, *261*, 267
  and Egypt *187*, 188, 229, 234
  empire 234–65, *245*, 266–89, *286*
  expansion outside Italy 184–85, 186, 187, 191, 208–17, 223, 226, 227, *228*, 238, *244*, 245, 248
  factions 222, 223, 226, 228
  frontiers 238, 248, 250, 256, 260, 261, 267, 268, *268*, 269, 276, *282*, 286
  Gaul 240, *240*, 241
  and Germans 223, 256, 261, *264*, *265*, 280–83
  Gracchan reforms 218, 219, *219*, 222
  and Greece 185, 186, *186*, 213, 216–17, *217*, 226

and Jews 242, *243*, 244–45, 248, *248*, 249
Illyrian emperors 265, 270
imperial cult 238
invasions 261, *264*, *265*, 280–83, *282*
law 202, *203*, 238, 253, 287
languages 253, *253*
and Macedon 213, 216–17
magistracies 199, 202; *see also* consuls, tribunes
monarchy 198, 202, *203*
patricians 199, 202
plebeians 199, 202–03, 223
plebiscites 202
population decline 264, 270
provincial government 210, 216, *235*, 238, 267, 287
Punic wars 209–213, *209*, *210*, *211*
religion 208, 214, *214*, *215*, 233, 253
republic 198–99, 200, 202, *202*, *217*, *226*, 228–29
roads *221*, 224, *224*, *225*, 250, *251*
romanization 240, 246
Senate 198, 199, *208*, 217, 219, 222, 235, 238, 243
social divisions 252
Social war 222, 223, *223*, 226
and Spain 212, 238, 251, 265
trade 200, 248, 250–52, *251*, 262
technology 250–51, 254, *254*, *255*
tetrarchy 267
towns 251, 252, *253*, 264
tribunes 202, 226, 227, 229
Triumvirate, First 228
Triumvirate, Second 234
villas *240*
voting *219*
warfare 126, 185, 206–7, 223, *246*, 247
Rome, city of 138, 217, 245, 266
  Archaic 200, *200*, *201*
  Christian 278, *278*, *279*
  Forum 200, 214, *231*, 258
  imperial 258, *258*, *259*
  origins 195, 198
  population 220, 250, 278
  republican 220, *220*, 221
  sacked 278, 281, 282, *282*
  walls 200, *203*, *220*, 221, 258
  water supply 220, *255*
Romulus 195, 198, 199, 200, *200*, *215*
Royal Cemetery, Ur 28, 30, *30*, *31*
Rusa I, Urartian king 90

S

Sabines 195, 198, 204
Sacred War 173
Saguntum (Spain) 210
Sahure, Egyptian king *64*
St Ambrose *280*
St Antony 277
St Augustine 277
St Basil the Great 277, 280
St Benedict 280
St Paul 275, *275*, 278
St Peter 278, *279*
St Peter's (Rome) 270, 278, *278*, *279*

Sakas, nomadic people 97
Salamis (Greece) sea battle 100, *144*, 148
Salona (Dalmatia) 271
Sam'al, Assyrian vassal state 88
Samaria, Assyrian vassal state 89
Samarran culture 19–20
Samnites 206, 224
Samos 130
Samsu-iluna, Babylonian king 40, 75
Sappho, Greek poetess *159*
Saqqara (Egypt) *42*, *51*, 52, *64*
Sardinia *80*, 82, 210
Sardis (Anatolia) 96, 100, 142, 143, 145, 148, 185
Sarduri I, Urartian king 85
Sarduri II, Urartian king 88
Sargon I, king of Agade 28, *29*, 32
Sargon II, Assyrian king 88, 89, 90, *90*, 91
Sasanians 232–33, *232*, 261, 264, *264*, 267, 277, *277*, 283, 288, 289
Saturninus, Roman tribune 223
Saul, Hebrew king 78
Saushtatar, Mittanian king 72
Saxons 265, *283*
Schliemann, Heinrich, excavator of Troy and Mycenae 108, 109, *115*
science
  Greek 168
  Hellenistic 188, 190
  Near East 93, *93*
  see also astrology, mathematics, medicine
Scipio, Gnaeus 212
Scipio, Publius (Africanus), Roman soldier *210*, 211, *212*, 218
Scipio, Publius, the Elder 212
sculptures
  Archaic Greek135
  bronze *36*, *82*, 85 *85*, *93*, *125*, *131*, *134*, *135*, *136*, *195*, *197*, *200*, *204*, 259
  busts *34*, *60*, *61*, *118*, *271*
  clay *44*, *45*, *112*
  figurines *23*, *26*, *87*, *111*, *163*
  gold *30*, *139*
  heads *28*, *125*, *173*
  iron 85
  ivory *86*, *139*, *173*, *201*
  Parthenon *160*
  Persepolis *103*
  relief *86*, *89*, *91*, *100*, *103*, *104*, *150*, *245*, *268*
  wood *51*, *53*, *69*
  see also statues
Scythians 97, 100, 142, *148*
Sea Peoples 62, 76, *116*, 118
sea voyaging *44*, *82*,112, 123, 148, 250, *250*
Sealand Dynasty 30
seals
  cylinder *28*, 104
  stamp 19, *23*, *35*
Seleucus *see* Seleukos
Seleukid kingdom 185–86, *191*, 216, 232
Seleukos, founder of Seleukid dynasty 183, *188*
Sellasia (Greece) 184
Semna (Nubia) *52*

Senate, Roman 198, 199, 208, 217, 219, 222, 235, 238, 243
Seneca, Lucius Annaeus, Roman philosopher 242, 248
Sennacherib, Assyrian king 63, 91, *91*, *93*, 94
Sentinum (Italy), battle 207
Senwosret I, Egyptian pharaoh 53
Senwosret III, Egyptian pharaoh *52*, 53
Seqenenre II, Egyptian pharaoh 54
Serapis, Greco-Egyptian god 181, 188
Servius Tullius, king of Rome 198, 200
Seth, Egyptian god *71*
Sethos I, Egyptian pharaoh 59
Sevan, Lake (Armenia) *84*, 85
Severus, Septimus, Roman emperor 256, *258*, 260, 261, 270, 284, *284*
Shabaka, Nubian king 63
Shalmaneser I, Assyrian king 74
Shalmaneser III, Assyrian king *82*, 84, 85
Shalmaneser V, Assyrian king 89
Shamshi-Adad I, king of Ashur 38, 41, *42*, 73
Shamash-shum-ukin, king of Babylon 89, 91
Shapur I, Sasanian king 233
Shapur II, Sasanian king 277
Shar-Kalli-Shari, king of Agade 33
Sharrum-kin *see* Sargon I
sheep 19, 109
Shoshenq I, Egyptian pharaoh 62, 80
Shoshenq III, Egyptian pharaoh 62
Shubat-Enlil (Syria) 38
Shulgi, 3rd Dynasty king of Ur 30, *30*, 34
Sicily *80*, 82, 117, 121, 123, 226, 250, 288
  Punic war, first 209, 210
Sidon, Phoenician city 59, 81
siege warfare 104, 170, *246*
Sikyon (Greece) 126, 130
silk 252
silver 24, 199
  casting *45*
  mines *142*, 145, *152*, 161
Simmurru, Assyrian vassal state, 89
Simon "Bar Kochba," Jewish leader 248, *249*
Simonides, Greek poet 148
Sin, Babylonian moon god 92
Siwa (Libya) *177*, 181
slaves 28, 55, *55*, 105, 117, 134, *142*, 208, 251
  revolts 218, 227
Slavs 288, *288*
Smirmium (Serbia) 266
Snofru, pyramid of *66*
Sobek, Egyptian god *71*
Social War, 222, 223, *223*, 226
Socrates, Greek philosopher 138, 166, *166*, 167, *167*
Sogdiana, Persian province 181
Sokrates *see* Socrates
soldiers
  Egyptian 69

Greek 146, *147; and see also* hoplites
  Near Eastern *104*, 105, *105*
  Roman 246, *246*, *247; and see also* Roman army
  see also warfare
Solomon, Hebrew king 79, 80
  temple 62, 80, 248
Solon, Athenian lawgiver 132
Sophocles, Athenian dramatist 161
Spain
  Arab invasion 289
  Germanic invasions 281, 282, *282*
  Ionian colonies 123
  Phoenician colonies 82
  Punic wars 210, *211*, 212
  Romans in 212, 238, 251, 265
Sparta 127, 130, 131, *131*, 143, 145, 169, 170
  admired by Romans 131, 216
  army 157, 170, 184
  art 131, *134*, *135*
  attitudes to women 130, 135
  constitution 127, 130
  education 130
  Peloponnesian war 157, *157*, 168
  period of domination 168–69, *169*
  Persian wars 100, 144, *144*, 145, 149
  reduced to minor power 184
  rivalry with Athens *129*, 151, 154, *169*
  warfare 130, *147*
Spartacus, slave leader 227
Sphakteria (Greece), battle *129*, *157*
spice 252
Split (Croatia) 270, 271, *271*
sport
  in Greek world 136, *136*, *137*
  Isthmian games 136, *137*
  Olympic games 124, 128, 136, *136*, *137*
  Panathenaic games *137*
  in Rome 217
Standard of Ur *31*
statues *204*
  Asklepios (Epidauros) *150*
  Aurelius, Marcus (Rome) *259*
  Alexander the Great *177*
  Athene (Parthenon) *139*
  Augustus, emperor *235*
  "Dying Gaul, The" *182*
  Victory of Paionios (Olympia) *129*
  Winged bull (Kalhu) *87*
Stilicho, Roman general *282*, 283
Stoicism 191, 248, 277
Stone Ages *see* Neolithic *and* Paleolithic periods
Suetonius, Roman historian 258
Sueves 281, *282*
Sulla, Roman dictator *218*, 220, 226, *226*, 227, *227*, 231
Sumer (Mesopotamia) 26, 28, 29, *29*, 32, 33, *33*, *36*, 38
Sumerian civilization 20, 27, 28, 93
  decline 37–8
  language 28, 32, 75
Sumerian King List 24, 25, 29, 33

Sumuel, king of Larsa 37
Suppiluliumas I, Hittite king 73, 74, 75
Susa, Elamite capital 34, *43*, *46*, 76, 76, 92, 100, *100*, 104, 180
  palaces *100*, *105*
Sybaris (Italy) 122
Symmachy, Hellenic league 184
Syracuse (Sicily) 121, *157*, 160, 161, 212
Syria 84, 88, 227, 262, 289

T

Tabal (Anatolia) 91
tablets
  clay 34, *46*, *58*, *93*, *94*, 113
  cuneiform *28*, 29, 74
Taima (Arabian desert) 92
Takelot II, Egyptian pharaoh 62
Tanagra (Greece), battle 157
Tarentum (Sicily) 127, 198, 207
Tarquin I, legendary king of Rome 198, 200
Tarquin II, legendary king of Rome 198
Tarquinia (Italy) *195*
Tashtepe (Iran) 85
Tatius, Titus, Sabine leader 195
Taweret, Egyptian goddess 70
taxes *33*, 34, 48, 112, 222, 267
Taxila (Pakistan) 188
technology 54
  Near East 44, *44–5*
  Roman 250–51, 254, *254*, *255*
Tefnakhte of Sais, Egyptian ruler 63
Telamon (Italy), battle 204, 210
Tell al-Rimah (Iraq) *43*, *45*
Tell al-Sultan *see* Jericho
Tell el-Dab'a *see* Avaris
Tell el-Fakhariyeh (Turkey) *see* Washukanni
Tell Nimrud *see* Kalhu
temples 24, 28, 39, 42, 70, 277
  Abu Simbel *62*
  Akhetaten (El-'Amarna) 60, *61*
  Akragas (Concord) *154*
  Alexandria (Serapeum) 181
  Athens (Wingless Victory) *138*, *140; and see* Parthenon
  Babylon (Esagila) *94*
  Delphi (Apollo) *153*
  Dendara (Hathor) 63
  Ephesus (Artemis) 274, *274*, 275
  Hattusas (Hatti; Yazilikaya) *75*
  Jerusalem, Solomon's 62, 80
  Karnak (Amun) 56, *56*, *57*, 62
  Luxor (Amun) *56*, 57
  Nippur (Enlil) 42
  Olympia (Zeus) *128*
  Paestum 122, *123*
  Palmyra (Bel) *262*
  Parthenon (Athene) 133, *139*, *140*, 156, *160*, 161
  Pergamon (Zeus)190
  Praeneste (Fortune Primigenia) 227
  Rome (Castor) *231*; (Jupiter) 201; (Vesta) *214*, 231; (Forum Boarium) 220
  tower *84*, 85
  Ur (Nanna) *31*, 42

Uruk (An and Eanna) 26, *26*, 27, 42
see also ziggurats
Ten Thousand, March of the 101, 168, *176*
tetrarchy 267
Teutones 217, 223, 256
Thasos (Greek island), rebels against Athens 151, 157
theaters *163*
  Athens 140, *162*
  Delphi *153*
  Dodona *164*
  Leptis Magna *284*
  Rome *221*
  Sparta *131*
Theban dynasty 53, *53*
Thebes (Egypt) 53, 56–7, *56*, 62, 63, *63*, 74
  high-priests 56, 62, *63*
  temples 56, *71*
Thebes (Greece) 157, 169–70, *169*, 172, 173
Themistocles, Athenian statesman 145, 148, 151
theocratic kingship
  Egypt 50, 53
  Romans 267
Theodoric, king of Ostrogoths 286, *287*
Theodosius I, Roman emperor 128, 267, 272, 277, *280*, 281
Theodosius II, Roman emperor *272*
Thera (Cyclades) 112, 113
Thermopylai (Greece) 148, 183, 186
Theseus, legendary Greek hero 113
Thespis, Greek poet 162
Thessaly 101, 173
Thoth, Egyptian god of wisdom 71
Thrace 40, *145*, 183, *245*
  annexed by Antiochos III 186, 216; by Philip of Macedon 101, 173
  invaded by Darius I 97, 142, 143
  overrun by Celts *184*; and by Visigoths 280, *282*
Thucydides, Greek historian 160
Thutmose, Egyptian sculptor 61
Tiber, river 198, *200*, *221*
  bridges *221*
Tiberius, Roman emperor 238, *241*
Tibur (Tivoli, Italy) 198, *202*
Tiglath-pileser I, Assyrian king 76, 78
Tiglath-pileser III, Assyrian king 85, 88, *88*, 90, *90*
Tigranes I, Armenian king 186
Tigris, river 20, *24*
Til-Tuba, battle *89*
tin 24, 118, 123
Tingis (Tangier) 82
Tiryns (Greece) 117, 118
Titus, Roman emperor *242*, 244, 245
tombs 64
  Egyptian 50, *51*, 52
  Etruscan *195*, 196, *197*
  Latin *199*
  Macedonian 174, *174*, *175*
  Mycenaean *112*, 117

Palmyra *262*
Ur 30, *31*
see also burial
tools
  bone *18*
  metal 24, *45*
  plow 20, 44
  stone *18*, *19*
  wood *18*
see also technology
Totila, Ostrogothic king of Italy 288
Tower of Babel 42, 77
Tower of the Winds (Athens) *139*
towns 24, *253*
  first 19, 20
  Roman 251, 252, *253*, 264
  see also cities
trade 19, 21, *21*, 24, 34, 36, 38, 123
  Carthaginians 123
  copper 24, 36, 82, 118
  ebony 118
  Egyptian *48*, 55, *55*, 56, 76
  glass 118, *251*
  gold 24
  grain *154*, 248, 250
  Greek *80*, 120, *121*, 123, *126*, *148*, *154*
  Indus valley civilization 34, 36
  ivory 118
  jewelry 118
  Kassites 76
  Meluhha 34
  Minoan 112
  Mycenaean *108*, *114*, 117, 118
  obsidian 22
  ostrich eggs 118
  Palmyra 262
  Phoenicians *80–1*, 81, 87, *116*
  pottery *21*, *44*, 118, 123, 248
  precious stones 24
  Roman 200, 224, 248, 250–52, *251*, *252*, 262
  routes 49, 123, 250, 252
  salt 19
  silk *252*
  silver 24
  spice *252*
  stone 19
  terebrinth resin 118
  timber 24
  tin 24, 118, 123
  weapons 118
  wine 248
tragedies *see* drama
Trajan, Roman emperor 63, *232*, *244*, 245, 248
  column *245*, *268*
Trasimene, Lake (Italy) 210
tribunes 202, 226, 227, 229
Trier *see* Augusta Treverorum
trireme 126, *145*, 148, 151, 155, 176, 188
Triumvirate, First 228
Triumvirate, Second 234
Trojan horse 118
Trojan War 114, 118, *118*
Troy, ancient city 108, *113*, 118, *118*, *176*
Tudhaliya I, Hittite king 72
Tukulti-ninurta II, Assyrian king 83
Tulis (Thrace) 183
Tunisia 82

Tushpa (Turkey) *84*, 85, 88
Tushratta, Mittanian king 73
Tutankhamun, Egyptian pharaoh 55, *56*, 59, sarcophagus *59*
Tutenkhaten *see* Tutankhamun
Tuthmosis I, Egyptian king 55, *55*, 72, 74
Tuthmosis IV, Egyptian king 73
Tutkulti-Ninurta I, Assyrian king 74
Twelve Tables, Archaic Roman law 202
tyrants 126–7, *126*, 130, 132–33, 143
Tyre, Phoenician city 59, 81, 177
Tyrtaeus, Spartan poet 131

U

Ubaid culture 20, 21, *21*, 44
Ugarit (Syria) 76, 82
Untashnapirisha, Elamite king 76
Ur 21, 28, 29, 30, *30*, *31*, 32, 37
  sacked 34
  ziggurat *30*, *31*, *42*
  3rd Dynasty 27, 30, *31*, 33–4, *33*, 36, 37, *94*
Ur-Nammu, king of Ur 30, *30*, 33, 34, 42, *42*
Urartu *84*,85, 88, *89*, 90
Urmia, Lake (Iran) *84*, 85, 90
Uruk 21, 24, 26, *26*, 27, 28, 29,32, 42, 46
  seals *28*, 104
Uruk period 21, 24, 26, 28
Urukagina, king of Lagash 29
Urzababa, king of Agade 32
Utuhegal, king of Uruk 33, *33*

V

Valentian III, Roman emperor 282, 283, *286*
Valerian, Roman emperor 261, 264
Valley of the Kings (Thebes) *56*, 57, *59*
Valley of the Queens (Thebes) 57
Van, Lake (Turkey) 85, *85*, 90
Valens, Roman emperor 280
Vandals 281, 282, *282*, 283, *283*, 284, 286, *286*, *287*, *287*, *288*
Vapheio (Greece) 112
vases 27, *134*, 136, *137*, 158, *158*, *159*
Veii (Etruria), besieged by Rome 204
Vercellae (Italy) 223
Vergina (Macedon), royal burial place *173*, 174
Vespasian, Roman emperor *242*, 244–45
Vesta, Roman goddess 214, *214*, *231*
Vestal Virgins *214*
Vesuvius, Mount (Italy) 236
Via Appia 224
Via Egnata 224
Villanova culture 194, *195*
Vindex, governor of Lugdunensis 243
Virgil (Publius Vergilius Maro), Roman poet 238, 277

Visigoths 280, 281, 282, *282*, *283*, 286, *287*, 288
Vitellius, Roman emperor 243, 244
Vitruvius, Roman architect 255
Vulture Stele 104

W

Warad-Sin, king of Larsa 36
warfare 54, 68, *69*,
  armor 105, *146*, *147*, *261*
  Assyrian 83
  Diadochi, wars of the 182–83, *184*
  Egyptian 68, *69*
  elephants *188*
  forts and fortifications 170, *170*, *247*, *265*, 268, *268*, *269*, *271*
  Greek wars with Persia 101, 124, 125, 142–51, *144*
  hoplites 124, 126, 127, 144, *146*, *147*, 155, 172, *176*
  naval 126, *157*, 188, 209, *209*, 234
  Near East 104–5, *104*, *105*
  Peloponnesian war 101, 157, *157*, 167, 168
  phalanx 146, *147*, 185
  prisoners 105, *105*
  Punic war, first 209–10, *209*, 213
  Punic war, second 184, *184*, 210–12, *210*
  Roman 126, 185, 206–7, 223, *246*, *247*
  siege 104, 170, *246*
  Sparta 130
  tactics 104–5, *105*, *146*, *147*, 170, 172, *246*
  Trojan War 114, 118, *118*
  warships *209*
  see also army, soldiers, Roman army, weapons
Warka vase 27
warships *209*
Washukanni, Mittanian capital 72, 73
watermill 255
water supply 38, 39, 86, *238*
  Nineveh *91*
  Rome 220
  see also aqueducts
watermill 254, *255*
weapons
  axes 104
  ballista *246*
  bow 54, 68, *69*, 105
  bronze 28, 68, 104, *105*, *114*
  copper 104
  iron 105, 119
  Egyptian 54, 68, *69*
  Greek 146, *147*, 172
  Mycenaean 117
  Near East 104–105, 207, 223
  Roman 207, 223, *246*, *247*
  siege weapons 104, 173, *246*
  war chariots *45*, 54, 68, 76, 82, 105, 117
Wenamun, Egyptian temple servant and traveler 62
wheat 19, 109, 284
  see also farming
wheel *45*
wind power 44, 254
women 130, *134*, 135, *159*
writing 26, 29, 46, *46*

Akkadian 46
alphabet *80*, 124, 194
Babylonian 46
cuneiform 28, 29, 46, *58*, 74, *80*, 100
Egyptian 49, 50, *51*, 80
Greek 124
Indus valley civilization *35*
Linear A 112, 113
Linear B *111*, 113, *116*, 124
origins 46, *46*
pictographic 24, 26, 36, 46
uses of 46

X

Xenophon, Athenian commander 101
Xerxes, Persian king 102, 172
  campaigns 97, 100, 101, 130, 145, *145*, 148

Y

Yamhad (Aleppo) 38, 72, *72*
Yasmah-Addu, king of Mari 38, 41
Year of the Four Emperors *242*, 243

Z

Zagros mountains (Iran) 16, 19, *21*, 29, 34, 75, 180
Zama (North Africa), battle 212
Zanakht, Egyptian king 50
Zawi Chemi Shanidar (Iran) 16
Zealots *243*, 244, 249
Zeno, Greek philosopher 166, *167*, *282*, 286
Zenobia, queen of Palmyra 262, 264, 265
Zeus, supreme god of Greeks 113, 124, 125, *125*, 128, *150*, *189*, *215*
  temples 128, *129*, 138
Zeus Ammon, oracle of 177, 181
ziggurats 42, *42–3*, 86
  Babylon 42, 94
  Dur-Kurigalzu 77
  Dur-Sharrukin *43*
  Eridu 21
  Saqqara *42*
  Susa *43*
  Tell al-Rimah *43*
  Ur *30*, *31*, *42*
Zimri-Lim, ruler of Larsa 38, 41
zodiac, signs of *93*
Zoroastrianism 233